Hysteria Beyond Freud

Hysteria
Beyond Freud

Sander L. Gilman
Helen King
Roy Porter
G. S. Rousseau
Elaine Showalter

UNIVERSITY OF CALIFORNIA PRESS
Berkeley   Los Angeles   London

University of California Press
Berkeley and Los Angeles, California
University of California Press
London, England
Copyright © 1993 by
The Regents of the University of California

Library of Congress Cataloging-in-Publication Data

Hysteria beyond Freud / Sander Gilman . . . [et al.].
    p.   cm.
    Includes bibliographical references and index.
    ISBN 0-520-08064-5 (alk. paper)
    1. Hysteria—History. 2. Hysteria—Social aspects—History.
 I. Gilman, Sander L.
 RC532.H88 1993   92–30932
 616.85'24'009—dc20   CIP

Printed in the United States of America

1 2 3 4 5 6 7 8 9

The paper used in this publication meets the minimum requirements
of American National Standard for Information Sciences—Permanence
of Paper for Printed Library Materials, ANSI Z39.48–1984 ∞

CONTENTS

v

INTRODUCTION
The Destinies of Hysteria

Hysteria, it is often said, has disappeared this century, its problems solved by Freud, or its investigation discredited by the antics of Charcot. And accompanying its alleged disappearance there has been a declining interest in its history among most historians. Yet hysteria was extraordinarily prominent in nineteenth-century medicine and culture.[1] It posed in direct and personal form the key questions of gender and mind/body relations, and, as Henri Ellenberger has shown in his *Discovery of the Unconscious,* it formed the springboard for the discovery of the unconscious in psychoanalysis.[2]

In this light, it is odd that only two full-length scholarly surveys of its history have been published within the last half century: Ilza Veith's *Hysteria: The History of a Disease* (Chicago: University of Chicago Press, 1965), and Etienne Trillat's *Histoire de l'Hysterie* (Paris: Seghers, 1986). There have been, of course, other approaches, for example, in the work of practicing doctors, amateur historians, and psychoanalytic theorists.[3] Yet these two books have had a curious lack of influence. In the late 1960s, broad cultural and contextual approaches had not yet been developed within medical history, and there was little sense of the wider implications of Veith's newly published and widely praised history. Veith wrote as an internalist medical historian who construed the history of hysteria in its realist dimension only, without casting an eye on its forms of representation or its broad social and cultural subtleties of class, gender politics, and ideology.[4]

Trillat too took an internalist approach, meticulously consulting the history of a medical condition without considering the cultural, contextual, or discursive resonances that have come to preoccupy humanists and historians in the last decade. In any case, because it was published in France, never translated into English, and not widely publicized, *Histoire de l'Hysterie* had little impact on the anglophone academic community.

Over the last decade, scholarship has, of course, been changing—enormously. Medical history has moved from a positivist to a critical phase and has begun to shift from the scientific history of disease to the cultural history of diseases and the study of illness as metaphor.[5] The history of therapeutics now takes more account of the complex dynamics of doctor/patient relationships.[6] The mind/body problem is no longer regarded as a technical or logical problem, focusing on canonical texts, for historians of philosophy or philosophers of mind to study. One could claim without exaggeration that in our time the social construction of *both* mind and body have come into their own.[7] And above all, feminist scholarship has lavished great attention upon demystifying the gender and social control encoded in women's diseases, especially the hysteria diagnosis, in the age of Freud.[8] No less important, the role played by language and discourse in the analysis of virtually all medical conditions, ancient and modern, has been magisterially enlarged and problematized, and recent discourse theory has taught historians of all territories, medical and nonmedical, that the social history of language cannot be overlooked when tracing the rise and fall of medical conditions: plague, gout, dropsy, consumption, cholera, influenza, as well as the more psychosomatic conditions.[9]

More specifically, the face of hysteria has itself altered, at least implicitly, in light of the work of such psycholinguists and psychoanalysts as Jacques Lacan, Hélène Cixous, and Julia Kristeva.[10] Each has provided insight into the language-gender dimensions of contemporary hysteria and its semiotic groundings. In their work, word and image, doctor and patient, speaker and listener, have gathered new identities. Kristeva has argued with particular force that medical appearances can never be considered entirely apart from their linguistic moorings, any more than from their gender-based dimensions. And as a decade of new interdisciplinary research has marched forward during the 1980s, the interface of literature and medicine has become one of the most frequently played-upon themes in scholarship on both sides of the Atlantic.[11]

This broad movement has also intensified exploration of the semiotic and linguistic dimensions of recent, or at least relatively modern, hysteria. But even if the medical diagnosis of hysteria has languished, for reasons this book attempts to explore as an ancillary theme, the *condition* of hysteria as a state of mind has been revived through the intersections of these newly developing fields of inquiry. "Hysteria as a state of mind" especially describes thinkers of all types, not just patients, who concern themselves with the intersections of bodies and texts, and with medical conditions and discursive practices. Hysteria has thus been fragmented: everyone now seems to own a piece of it. Its grip is not confined to one field; its monopoly not limited to medicine. No longer, and perhaps never again, will it be the narrow province of medical doctors or a handful of medical historians.

Hence the time seemed ripe for a reexamination and reassessment, not merely to chronicle hysteria's fragmentation or to narrate the fraught and tangled interplay between Charcot and Augustine, Freud and Dora, but to describe the entire career of the disease entity, or at least the problematic label and curious category: its long-term rise and alleged fall, its invention, construction, development, ascendency, obsolescence, and now relatively sudden disappearance.[12]

It seemed to us particularly germane as these transformations occurred in the 1980s to demonstrate that Freud was not the *beginning* of anything new in the history and conception of the condition but rather the *end* of a long wave. Though we are in no sense whatever compiling a complete history of hysteria, we wanted to extend our gaze to cover European civilization over three thousand years, while simultaneously concluding our narrative with the launching of psychoanalysis from the base of *medical* hysteria as it was construed in the late nineteenth century. The Viennese founder of psychoanalysis was not the kingpin of a new province of *hysteria*—however the condition or the category was defined—but the thinker best able to marshal the resources of an already rich kingdom that had seen itself rise and fall many times in the past.[13] In the popular imagination hysteria begins and virtually ends with Freud, his antecedents and sequels accorded relatively minor consequence; much cultural history is conceptualized and written out as if all psychiatric thought before the 1890s consisted of footnotes leading up to the work of the one—and only one—great transformer, Sigmund Freud.[14] Professional historians of science and medicine often link hysteria to a "mechanical revolution" and "nervous revolution" that transformed the face of modern science, but even they remain uncertain how the scientific revolution impinged upon the development of hysteria.[15]

We believe this corrective should be launched as a *historical* discussion as well as a case study in the relations of realism and representation to this baffling human condition. We are sensitive to the differences between so-called "real hysterics," who still present themselves as patients in clinics and waiting rooms, and the wide repertoire of metaphors that has attached to the condition over the centuries, just as other metaphors have attached to consumption, cancer, and now AIDS. Our treatment weaves the real and the representative, especially when we launch into far-ranging discussions of the social history of hysteria. We want to replace existing notions with more accurate, less mythologized, and less heroic ones about Sigmund Freud.

Although this book is a five-hander, it has been our aim from the start to produce not a collection of disparate essays but a consecutive and coherent synoptic interpretation, tracing the story forward from antiquity into the present century. The five of us hold different ideological viewpoints and come from different disciplines and nationalities; allegiance to the various theoretical bents of our disciplines prompts us to differ from one another more than we agree. But we are also bound by the shared views that, first, now is the time to reconsider hysteria; second, our differences will bring a type of balance to the evolving discourses (by which we mean all types of writing by hysterics and their doctors, as well as writings by nonmedical figures) of hysteria that will stand the reader—the imagined, ideal reader of this book—in good stead. Finally, we are united by our common interest in the linguistic and semiotic aspects of medicine at large, and by the internal contradictions, silences, and gaps we find in this remarkable discourse of hysteria.[16]

We saw both historical and critical elements as essential to the book. In our conceptualization there had to be copiously documented sections on the historical development of hysteria: one dealing with the ancient world, a second located in the period from the European discovery of the ancient medical texts in approximately the fourteenth century (when Hippocrates and Galen were being translated into Latin and read anew) to the end of the Enlightenment (construed as "the long eighteenth century"). Whatever small overlap might exist on the boundaries of these first two parts (around the fourteenth and fifteenth centuries), both sections were necessary for our revisionism and for thorough analysis of the development of hysteria over eighteen hundred years.

But after chronological surveys guiding the reader from the Athenian world to the high European Enlightenment, *Hysteria Beyond Freud* intentionally veers into another mode. From this point forward there was no need to chart and plot hysteria as the first two historical sections do. Instead, we required discussions of three seminal but by no means exhaustive topics. All of us realize that we have been coaxing out the representations of hysteria, rhetorically searching for its metaphors and metonymies, visually following its iconographic relations and imagery—all this out of a belief in the significance of the cultural representations of illness within society. This is not to say that we discard realist medical analysis, empirical cause and effect, the patient in therapy, diagnosis and cure, much less the genuine neurochemical and technological advances that diminish human suffering and increase longevity. But the five of us are nevertheless persuaded that realism and representation, ideology and gender, have been held too far apart in the discussions about human bodies and their so-called pathological states; we are also united in the belief that medical material adds a valuable dimension to the understanding of the creation of social categories in all these different epochs.[17] The boundary between the historical first section (King and Rousseau) and the thematic second one (Porter, Showalter, Gilman) marks the turning point in the book's architecture.

One condition of this shift is the new version of historicism King and Rousseau wish to impose. This is not the new, upper-case Historicism—if there is *one* such version—but a more contextualized and, in Helen King's case, more scrupulous philological examination measured against the reigning cultural trends of the ancient world.[18] King examines the early history of hysteria in antiquity, more precisely explaining why Classical hysteria is in reality but a mare's nest, a spurious entity invented by later physicians in the Middle Ages and Renaissance and legitimated after the event by medical historians.[19] This view overthrows Veith's and will no doubt disturb medical historians who consider the older views gospel. But King also demonstrates why the *category* is so doubtful and supports her argument with the verbal and historical documentation of a classicist with her particular joint training and expertise in ancient history and anthropology. After King's revisionism it may well be that studies of Hippocrates will never again be the same. Certainly no one will ever again be able to reiterate the now discredited notion that Hippocrates is the father, the discoverer, the inventor of a Western hysteria that has endured with constancy over the course of many centuries.

George Rousseau explores the legitimation of these later doctors and medical historians and—crucially—the implications of this dire legitimating for Renaissance and Enlightenment culture. Rousseau's task is to chart the fate of hysteria as the body's anatomical model gradually moves away from a one- to two-sex model, and as Cartesian and Newtonian science sweeps through Europe.[20] In this sense he, too, necessarily imposes the mold of realism on his revisionary historical task. But as Western culture was transformed in the seventeenth and eighteenth centuries under the weight of science, secularism, and economic and political reform, as the cults of certainty, progress, and optimism gradually replaced those of uncertainty, pessimism, even gloom-and-doom, hysteria found itself at the center of a debate about melancholy and the nerves, and about gender, sex, and the fabric of human culture far exceeding its own local, anatomic, and medical domain. And in this sense it was hysteria construed as a *category*—almost a philosophical category—rather than as a medical diagnosis or set of therapies.[21] But as certain tenets of Enlightenment culture gained strength, especially the reliance on reason, observation, logic, predictability, secularism, and the waning of a faith in superstition and magic, hysteria continued to find itself reinvigorated and regenerated.[22] A self-renewing discourse, it was capable of transforming itself both as diagnosed disease, medical category, and—linguistically—as a critique of male-female relations. Rousseau shows that hysteria's uniqueness lies specifically in these acts of transformation, especially under the teachings of Dr. Thomas Sydenham, the so-called "English Hippocrates" and medical associate of John Locke, the doctor-philosopher. Sydenham, according to Rousseau, is the unacknowledged hero of hysteria: the first doctor to see beyond its ironclad gender boundaries, the first to apply the illness to men, the first to gaze into its psychogenic origins. Sydenham alone made the unique transformative power of hysteria his first principle: on this fundamental belief he built everything else in his theoretical medical scheme.[23]

Despite the similarity of historical approaches taken by King and Rousseau, a counterpoint exists between their chapters, and then again between these chapters and the rest of *Hysteria Beyond Freud*. Yet for our discussion of hysteria *after* 1800 it seemed best to make thematic divisions along clearly defined lines. After traversing the nineteenth-century border, it was no longer necessary to provide a full "history of hysteria" except to glance at areas that had been underdeveloped or misconstrued. For this period extending from approximately 1800 to the overlaps of Charcot and Freud, mountains of writing have, of course, already accumulated. The physiological aspects of hysteria circa 1800 had been developed by all sorts of medical commentators in the period and during the next two generations of doctors (i.e., between 1780 and 1840).[24] Georges Didi-Huberman, a contemporary medical historian in France, discussed its diagnosis and appearance in the light of visual images and artistic representations;[25] Wolfgang Lederer, its sexual implications in *Gynophobia ou la Peur des Femmes*.[26] And a veritable host of scholars dealing with Charcot and Breuer had written about nineteenth-century hysteria. But the philosophical, epistemological, ethical, and even more crucial literary, social, and pictorial traditions had not been well-studied. Nor had hysteria been construed as a "discourse," or as overlapping discourses, in the brilliant way that critics such as Hayden White and other hermeneutical theorists have looked at historical pasts, as partaking of the same attributes as all other discourses: rhetoric, metaphor, voice, speaker, speech act, and the implied power relations vis-à-vis race, gender, and sex established within the discourse.[27] Furthermore, these previous students of hysteria had not understood what more culturally oriented scholars began to see in the 1980s: that the developing meta-critique of hysteria had inscribed all sorts of power relations as well as developed a subcritique of gender arrangements that often masqueraded as a pure, objective, realistic, and scientifically validated discourse of hysteria.[28] These are developments still awaiting due amplification. They are among the ones we seek to revise and amplify here.

Toward this specific goal Elaine Showalter, author of *The Female Malady* (1987) and recently of *Sexual Anarchy* (1991), examines hysteria over the last two centuries as an expression of the inscription of gender relations within medical discourse. Throughout its history, hysteria has been primarily constructed as a female malady, but it has also been a disorder of men. Applying feminist methods and insights to the symptoms and studies of male hysteria, Showalter shows that issues of gender are as significant in masculine experience as in the history of women. Not only the treatment, but also the historiography of hysteria, has been influenced by the traditional gender roles assigned to the therapist and the hysteric. When feminists occupy the roles of doctor, psychoanalyst, or historian, the narratives of hysteria change.[29]

If medical discourse has assumed a whole set of gender relations in the last two centuries, the discourse of hysteria has been the chief site of debate over matters related to sex and gender relations. This localization within hysteria is the theme of Roy Porter's chapter. It is a point that seems accessible but is knottier and more elusive than it at first appears. It is not at all surprising that the old Cartesian mind/body dualism should have endured as long as it has, nor that mind and body should have played such a magisterial role, as Rousseau shows, in the commentary on Enlightenment revelations (and, as often, obfuscations) on hysteria.[30]

But Porter proceeds further than this point: he shows how the old mind/body questions became attached to the self-definition of medicine itself as a sphere of exclusive cognitive expertise. At the beginning of the period that forms the backdrop of his thematic study—approximately 1800—medicine still hovered in self-conscious doubt as a domain of knowledge. At the beginning of the period, doctors and the paramedical world had begun to professionalize and gather in institutional and organizational ways that would continue throughout the nineteenth century; a century later, medicine's claims were bolder. Medicine now claimed to be more a rational *science* than an inexact art: shorn of its older magical and irrational tendencies, it was now the sister subject of philosophy, science of the cognitive. Yet in medicine this application had to be grounded within a specific discourse that was already controversial. Where to locate the site of hysteria in a safe medical discourse in which there was neither fierce debate nor professional divergence? In manias, for example, or gout (now moribund after three centuries of tireless writing and speculation)? Better to place it in an already *controversial* zone, as Porter shows us in his chapter, and let hysteria be fought about within the already bloody battlefields of Regency and Victorian philosophical discussions of mind and body.[31]

From the complex relation of clinical medicine and philosophy, an ancillary question presents itself: the matter of speculative thought in relation to realism, and medicine in relation to representation.[32] If medicine had become cognitive by the nineteenth century, it could claim to be *exclusively* so because its models of representation were then so monolithically realistic. Set the chronological dials earlier, to 1840 or 1860, for example, and one glimpses an England or France in which the medical doctors are virtually *certain* that medicine is a rapidly advancing science in which much more was known to them than had ever been available in the history of mankind, and that soon even more would be discovered. A science as positivistic and progressive as mid-nineteenth-century medicine worried little about the representational—metaphoric, imagistic, artistic—versions of its wisdom. Yet paradoxically and almost as a counterpoint to this certainty about the knowledge of all (even in theories of hysteria) was the concomitant sense that medicine still had an arduous road to hoe before it would be a rigorous science like mathematics, physics, or astronomy. Most of those who viewed medicine as an *art* were usually willing to concede a large portion of ambiguity to the medical situation, medical predicament, the scenario, case history, *toute la chose medicale* in the hysteria diagnosis. More specifically for our purposes, if hysteria had significant representational dimensions, how had it been pictured in art? In what sets and constellations of images? And how had its victims become figures in drawings and other media?

This is the question Sander Gilman pursues in his illustrated chapter. Given his previous work on the iconography of disease,[33] it is not surprising that he has set hysteria in a wide context, viewing its sufferers as one instance among many of the stigmatization of the pathological. Beginning with the late eighteenth century, many types had been stigmatized—not merely hysterics, but diverse "lunatics" over the broad spectrum of race, religion, and gender. Sodomites as well as hermaphrodites; the mad as well as the moody; Jews as well as blacks; and many other social pariahs as well—all were differentiated and eventually stigmatized. Stigma, indeed, was an ingrained habit of the hegemonic thought of the nineteenth century, a region of the imagination well understood by thinkers as diverse as Vico, Kierkegaard, and Nietzsche.[34] But the stimatizing of the hysteric was something else: more pronounced if also more elusive. The label *hysteric* became a key encodement of difference and danger, not just in respect to nubile girls or frustrated widows, but in the larger evaluation of cultural, national, and racial characteristics at a time when nationalism was on the ascendency.

Thus the eclectic representations of hysteria, as explored in this book, look inward to a developing micro history—of doctor/patient pairings in the clinical setting, playing their games of power, control, and liberation—while simultaneously looking outward, treating hysteria as a language for assimilating yet pathologizing the unknown, the unacceptable, the uncontrollable. The hysteria diagnosis has long been the frail and unsuccessful attempt to frame the fearful symmetry of one of the most potent tigers of the mind. Yet the beast, so to speak, is even larger than this. Once it becomes clear to what degree the pathology of the unknown became encoded in the hysteria diagnosis it also becomes evident that the category hysteria must never be far from the historian's imagination. Otherwise, *all* human relations, not merely the pairings mentioned, take on attributes of "hysterical discourse," in one medium or another.

The reader will notice a multitude of lacunae in this book—omissions of more types than one. For example, it will be observed that no professional psychoanalyst has been included among the authors, and that psychoanalysis and approaches fundamentally psychoanalytical are not included. The omission is by design: whereas none of us has any particular aversion to psychoanalysis as a therapy or method, our collective strategy was to provide a historical and representational approach that led up to, *not followed from,* Freud.[35] We attempted to gaze at our various forms of representation with the eyes of historians of psychology or psychiatry rather than as scholars living in the aftermath of the Freudian revolution, and even less as scholars persuaded of the claims of psychoanalysis itself.

We have also said relatively little about religion and religious experi-

ence. There can be no doubt of its importance in the medieval world
and beyond. But no matter how central religion was during the early
period, this is not a book about the interface of religion and medicine,
or of hysteria and possession, subjects that no doubt merit more attention than they have received but which cannot be fully treated here. The
theme of possession—whether or not leading to hysterical symptoms—
has itself been the subject of recent scholarship, as Rousseau notes, none
of which we hoped to include in any detail in our eclectic approach. Possession is such a large canvas to survey that to focus on it would have
fatally diverted us from the real focus of this book.

Our eclecticism may also be faulted for omission of any thorough, or
systematic, treatment of the recent fortunes of hysteria in the work of
Lacan, Kristeva, and other deconstructionists and poststructuralists. The
reply is that here, too, as in the case of Freud, we have tried to see things
primarily from a *pre*-Lacanian point of view. We are sensitive to Lacan's
concept of the Other and to the work of the Lacanian analysts at l'Ecole
de la Cause Freudienne. But surely a pre-Kristeva angle of vision will
not exonerate us, any more than it will please our critics to know that
we have not tried to deconstruct hysteria.[36] References to these figures
do appear in our text as early as Rousseau's chapter, which explores a
theory of "female numbness" in relation to hysteria partly derived from
the works of the French writer Marguerite Duras. But Elaine Showalter's
chapter makes better use of these figures, even if they do not play a central role in her conception of what is to be privileged about hysteria.

A thorough illumination of the linguistic representations of hysteria
by other scholars would enrich our discussions. Although this book devotes itself to the history and representations of hysteria, it has not un-
earthed the hidden metaphors of hysteria. A whole book could have
been written, and we hope it will be, merely on these metaphors of control, pathologization, stigmatization, castigation. An example drawn
from the field of metaphors of incorporation is Dorothy Kilgour's *From
Communion to Cannibalism: Metaphors of Incorporation.*[37] Hysteria has given
rise to metaphors worthy of study in their own right, in much the way
that Susan Sontag has identified those in the domain of illness and
AIDS. We hope others will build on our work and trace the evolution
of these languages of hysteria.

The bibliography of hysteria is by now a developed province in itself.
The previous histories never provided their readers with a proper bibliographical essay or the equivalent, delineating the enormous amount
of writing devoted to this subject. Indeed, so much has accumulated that
it would require an expert and systematic bibliographer to perform the
task. Only Mark Micale has undertaken any of this work, and his writing

on the subject is exemplary and in the bibliographical area second to none.[38] Micale has studied *male* hysteria in particular and demonstrated its trajectory from the Greeks to the present. Whether or not we acknowledge it explicitly in the following chapters, all five of us have profited from his studies and from his presentation at the Wellcome Institute in 1990 (see paragraph that concludes this introduction).

This then is not a full-scale history of hysteria, proceeding in linear time, each chapter surveying a period or historical unit. Nor is it an attempt to rewrite Veith under contemporary circumstances where the new ideologies and critical methodologies prevail, nor will it survive a strict and rigid post-Foucaldian application. The age of Foucault has passed, and with it the sense that mere representation apart from historical contexts is sufficient; in its wake a new commitment has arisen to historical rigor and accountable epistemological threshold.[39] This is especially true in such fields as the history of psychiatry and in discussions of the discourses on madness, wherein scholars can be radically "historical" without writing proper "histories of madness." All five of us are admittedly the children of Foucault in ways extending beyond our ability to verbalize them, especially insofar as we concur that in our contemporary world, power, authority, and marginalization are mirrored in the overlaps of hysteria, madness, and psychoanalysis. And we were also fortunate, as we pondered ancient and modern hysteria, to profit by the fruits of Foucault's labors in his multivolumed histories of sexuality. But we write here neither as converted Foucaldians nor as primarily historical revisionists intent upon correcting a fallible record. If our first two chapters appear to do just that, the reason—as we have already indicated—arises out of our belief that something fundamental in the historical *tradition* had to be corrected before we could proceed to our thematic analyses.

Many books could be and will be written about hysteria. We believe our groupings are richer for some of the reasons given above. No readers, or potential authors of such books, can close the covers of this book without questioning the disappearance of hysteria after so many centuries, or without being persuaded by our central theme: that Freud inherited a tradition surrounding hysteria. Freud came to hysteria at the end of a three-thousand-year-old lineage: he was not its progenitor—a truth more easily stated than applied and a historical fact often forgotten.

Early versions of these essays were presented at a conference held at the Wellcome Institute for the History of Medicine in London in April 1990. We are grateful to the Wellcome Trustees for making funds available for this meeting, and to Steve Emberton and Frieda Houser for the smooth running of this fruitful occasion. George Rousseau is grateful to Leila Brownfield and Linda Benefield for their kindness in accomplishing various of the tasks associated with the production of a book of this size. We owe particular thanks to William Schupbach and David Brady of the Wellcome Institute for their efforts in obtaining and organizing the many illustrations so necessary to Sander Gilman's chapter. We are equally grateful to our editor at the University of California Press, Elizabeth Knoll, for her encouragement throughout this project.

G. S. Rousseau
Roy Porter

NOTES

1. See Jan Goldstein, *Console and Classify: The French Psychiatric Profession in the Nineteenth Century* (Cambridge: Cambridge University Press, 1988).

2. See H. Ellenberger, *The Discovery of the Unconscious: The History and Evolution of Dynamic Psychiatry* (New York: Basic Books, 1962); Ellenberger was, not ironically, one of the principal reviewers of Veith's book (see n. 3).

3. These are the two mentioned, and there have been no histories of hysteria since 1900. The last one in French before Trillat's was G. Abricossoff's *L'hysterie aux 17 et 18 siècles* (Paris: G. Steinhill, 1897). Of interest here is Trillat's brief but valuable discussion of the methodological issues involved in writing the traditional history of hysteria; see E. Trillat, "Trois itinéraires a travers l'histoire de l'hysterie," *Historie des Sciences Médicales* 21 (1987): 27–31.

4. An idea of the disciplinary milieu among medical historians in which Veith wrote is gained by consulting Edwin Clarke, ed., *Modern Methods in the History of Medicine* (London: Athlone, 1971), who wrote before the ideologies of class, race, and gender held any sway in the history of medicine—his plea was for a balance between medical training and knowledge of history, but it was a nominalistic, realistic history of persons, places, and things in which gender and sex, class and race, language and representation, played a small role. Another contemporary approach not very different from Veith's is found in I. Macalpine and Richard Hunter, *George III and the Mad Business* (New York: Pantheon Books, 1969), which sheds further light on the discipline of the history of medicine at the time and the epistemological problems involved in the perception of writing the history of madness during the 1960s. For the historiography of medicine, itself a scant discourse in the last half century, and as it would have appeared in the mindset of scholars like Veith and others of her generation, see R. H. Shyrock, "The Historian Looks at Medicine," *Bulletin of the History of Medicine* 5 (1937): 887–894; G. Rosen, "A Theory of Medical Historiography," ibid., 8 (1940): 655–665; idem, "Levels of Integration in Medical Historiography," *Journal of the His-*

tory of Medicine 4 (1949): 460–467; George Mora, *Psychiatry and Its History: Methodological Problems in Research* (Springfield, Mass.: C. C. Thomas, 1970), works that represent a portion of the methodological atmosphere in which Veith wrote.

5. For medicine and metaphor see Susan Sontag, *Illness as Metaphor* (New York: Random House, 1979); C. M. Anderson, *Richard Selzer and the Rhetoric of Surgery* (Carbondale: Southern Illinois University Press, 1989); P. Radestsky, *The Invisible Invaders: The Story of the Emerging Age of Viruses* (New York: Little, Brown

6. The newer approaches had been anticipated in the 1960s by E. L. Entralgo in *Doctor and Patient* (London: Weidenfeld & Nicholson, 1969); but see also C. Webster, "Medicine as Social History: Changing Ideas on Doctors and Patients in the Age of Shakespeare," in *A Celebration of Medical History,* ed. L. Stevenson (Baltimore: Johns Hopkins University Press, 1982); Roy and Dorothy Porter, *Patient's Progress: Doctors and Doctoring in Eighteenth Century England* (Oxford: Polity Press, 1989); Roy and Dorothy Porter, *In Sickness and in Health: The British Experience, 1650–1850* (London: Fourth Estate, 1988); Roy Porter, *Health for Sale: Quackery in England, 1660–1850* (Manchester: Manchester University Press, 1989).

7. For the broad historical approach, see G. S. Rousseau, ed., *The Languages of Psyche: Mind and Body in Enlightenment Thought* (Berkeley, Los Angeles, Oxford: University of California Press, 1990).

8. The most thorough historical background remains Goldstein's *Console and Classify,* but another good place to start, within the realm of theory, is the diverse discourse of post-Lacanian feminist theory as found in E. Grosz, *Jacques Lacan: A Feminist Introduction* (New York: Routledge, Chapman & Hall, 1990); E. Pagels, *Adam, Eve and the Serpent* (New York: Vintage Books, 1989); C. J. Adams, *The Sexual Politics of Meat* (Oxford: Polity Press, 1990), themselves immensely diverse and astute and linked only by their concern for the female plight in the world of poststructuralism and postmodernism. An important statement of the epistemological problems involved is found in *In Dora's Case: Freud—Hysteria—Feminism,* ed. C. K. Bernheimer and Claire Kahane (New York: Columbia University Press, 1985). For iconography and hysteria, see H. Speert, *Iconographia Gyniatrica: A Pictorial History of Gynecology and Obstetrics* (New York: Macmillan, 1973); for feminism and Freud, D. Silverman, *Art Nouveau in Fin-de-Siècle France: Politics, Psychology, and Style* (Berkeley, Los Angeles, Oxford: University of California Press, 1989). An approach to some of these problems grounded in Romantic literature is found in D. L. Hoeveler, *Romantic Androgyny: The Woman Within* (University Park, Pa.: Penn State University Press, 1990).

9. For language and social history as they impinge on the discourses of hysteria and on various theories of medicine, see G. S. Rousseau, "Towards a Semiotics of the Nerve: The Social History of Language in a New Key," in *Language, Self, and Society: A Social History of Language,* ed. Peter Burke and Roy Porter (Oxford: Polity Press, 1991), 213–275; Rousseau, "Literature and Medicine: The State of the Field," *Isis* 52 (1981): 406–424.

10. Illuminating for bringing together many of the ideas of these theorists

is E. Grosz, *Sexual Subversions: Three French Feminists* (Sydney, Boston: Allen & Unwin, 1989).

11. As evidenced in the wide attention given to this juncture in contemporary psychoanalytic literature and in the contemporary journal *Literature and Medicine* as well as in such books (chronologically arranged and a mere sampling) as J. B. Lyons, *James Joyce and Medicine* (Dublin: Dolmen Press, 1973); R. Antonioli, *Rabelais et la medecine* (Geneva: Dros, 1976); E. Peschel, *Medicine and Literature* (New York: Neale Watson Academic Publications, 1980); S. S. Lanser, "Feminist Criticism, 'The Yellow Wallpaper,' and the Politics of Color in America," *Feminist Studies* 15 (1989): 415–441; T. Caramagno, *Virginia Woolf* (Berkeley, Los Angeles, Oxford: University of California Press, 1991), a study of her depression and mental maladies; R. Lutz, *Neurasthenia* (New York: 1991). For more popular statements about the real and representational affinities of the two realms, see I. McGilchrist, "Disease and the Novel, 1880–1960," *TLS,* January 17, 1986: 61, and Leon Edel, "Disease and the Novel," *TLS,* May 30, 1986: 591, contributions to a debate on the subject.

12. However significant the Darwinian metaphors of rise and fall, evolution and flow, are in this context, they are less vital than the social construction of hysteria. Indeed, the debate between social constructionists and realists or essentialists has reached epic proportions, as group after group decodes the strengths of each method, some coming down on the side of the one, some on the other, and some (such as John Boswell, the Yale historian of homosexuality in early modern civilization) for a blending of the two. But the politics of representation also pose crucial questions: do we choose our representations because they are power-influenced and thereby capable of enhancing our own positions (as Michel Foucault argued) or because they are in some abstract ontological sense true (as in the ongoing current debates in the newly developing field of literature and science)? The antagonisms of realism and social constructionism have emerged as a field in itself, posing new problems for the decade of multiculturalism, and not without genuine implications for the construction of the category hysteria. For anticipations of the debate in both medicine and philosophy, see P. Wright and A. Treacher, eds., *The Problem of Medical Knowledge: Examining the Social Construction of Medicine* (Edinburgh: Edinburgh University Press, 1982); O. Moscucci, *The Science of Woman: Gynecology and Gender in England 1800–1929* (Cambridge: Cambridge University Press, 1990); C. E. Russett, *Sexual Science: The Victorian Construction of Womanhood* (Cambridge, Mass.: Harvard University Press, 1989); I. Paperno, *Chernyshevsky and the Age of Realism: A Study in the Semiotics of Behavior* (Stanford, Calif.: Stanford University Press, 1989); J. Leplin, ed., *Scientific Realism* (Berkeley, Los Angeles, London: University of California Press, 1984); D. F. Greenberg, *The Construction of Homosexuality* (Chicago: University of Chicago Press, 1989).

13. An essential task of this book, for example, is the charting of these gains and losses in some detail during the centuries that form the basis of modern European culture from the Renaissance to the end of the Enlightenment, vital

epochs whose medicine, and certainly whose hysteria, have been discussed much less than they deserve.

14. One corrective to this historically false view is found in the important work of Jan Goldstein; see especially her *Console and Classify.*

15. The "mechanical revolution" has profited from three decades of superior scholarship, but the study of the "nervous revolution" continues to lie in a more primitive state within the history of science and medicine. It has been the subject of recent scholarship among neurochemists, neurophysiologists, medical historians, and historians of science; for a comprehensive statement of the problem see G. S. Rousseau, "Cultural History in a New Key: Towards a Semiotics of the Nerve," in *Interpretation in Cultural History,* ed. Joan Pittock and Andrew Wear (London: Macmillan, 1991), 25–81; J. Mullan, "Hypochondria and Hysteria: Sensibility and the Physicians," 25 (1984): 141–177; within the history of ideas, M. Kallich, *The Association of Ideas and Critical Theory in Eighteenth Century England* (The Hague: Mouton, 1970); M. H. Abrams, *The Mirror and the Lamp: Romantic Theory and the Critical Tradition* (Ithaca, N.Y.: Cornell University Press, 1953); for the Victorians, J. Oppenheim, *"Shattered Nerves": Doctors, Patients, and Depression in Victorian England* (Oxford: Oxford University Press, 1991).

16. These consistencies and contradictions, and their particular cultural and historical appearances, form one of the central themes of this book. They constitute a further reason that we do not claim to write here primarily as "historians of medicine" but as students of the intersection of discourse and culture. For aspects of this intersection see S. Benstock, *Textualizing the Feminine: On the Limits of Genre* (Norman: University of Oklahoma Press, 1991); and Timothy Reiss, *The Discourse of Modernism* (Ithaca, N.Y.: Cornell University Press, 1982).

17. For an example of what the abstract point means for the practicing historian, see Londa Schiebinger, *The Mind Has No Sex? Women in the Origins of Modern Science* (Cambridge: Harvard University Press, 1989).

18. Another example proceeding in this careful philological manner for the Middle Ages is the work of Caroline Bynum in *Holy Feast and Holy Fast: The Religious Significance of Food to Medieval Women* (Berkeley, Los Angeles, London: University of California Press, 1987); idem, *Gender and Religion: On the Complexity of Symbols* (Boston: Beacon Press, 1986).

19. For these later inventions see Simon Bennett, M.D., *Mind and Madness in Ancient Greece* (Ithaca, N.Y.: Cornell University Press, 1978); L. F. Calmeil, *De la folie considérée sous le point de vue pathologique, philosophique, historique et judiciare* (Paris: Baillière, 1845); an anonymous work attributed to "a society of physicians in London" and published as "Medical Observations and Inquiries," *Critical Review,* June 1757: 540–541, 544–545; L. M. Danforth, *Firewalking and Religious Healing: The Anastenaria of Greece and the American Firewalking Movement* (Princeton, N.J.: Princeton University Press, 1990).

20. For the two-body model see Laqueur, *Making Sex*; for Newtonianism and medicine, see three books by L. King: *The Medical World of the Eighteenth Century* (Chicago: University of Chicago Press, 1958); *The Road to Medical Enlightenment,*

1660–1695 (London: Macdonald, 1970); *The Philosophy of Medicine: The Early Eighteenth Century* (Cambridge, Mass.: Harvard University Press, 1978), esp. pp. 152–181. For the philosophical issues involved in sexuality in general and their relation to historicism and social construction, see A. I. Davidson, "Sex and the Emergence of Sexuality," *Critical Inquiry* 11 (1987): 17–48.

21. For the eighteenth-century debate on female gender in relation to functioning society see: P. Hoffmann, *La femme dans la pensée des Lumières* (Paris: Ophrys, 1977); D. Spender, ed., *Feminist Theorists: Three Centuries of Key Women Thinkers* (New York: Pantheon Books, 1983); B. Hill, *Women, Work and Sexual Politics in 18th-Century England* 1990); L. Schiebinger, *The Mind Has No Sex? Women in the Origins of Modern Science* (Cambridge, Mass.: Harvard University Press, 1989); Moscucci, *Science of Woman*; B. S. Anderson et al., *A History of Their Own: Women in Europe from Prehistory to the Present* (New York: Harper & Row, 1988).

22. Valid as the reinvigoration was, there is no mention of hysteria in some of the classic interpretations of the period, for example in P. Gay's *The Enlightenment: An Interpretation*, 2 vols. (New York: Alfred A. Knopf, 1966–69), which devotes much space to medicine. The canvas painted by Gay and other synthetic historians of the Enlightenment provides a further reason for our revisionist treatment.

23. Although there is no such subgenre as the historiography of Sydenham studies, it is clear that over a century ago Sydenham's significance for hysteria was intuited but not demonstrated; see J. Brown, M.D., *Horae Subsecivae: Locke and Sydenham and Other Papers* (Edinburgh: David Douglas, 1890).

24. An early anticipation of this approach within the British tradition is found in Alexander Thomson, *An Enquiry into the Nature, Causes, and Method of Cure, of Nervous Disorders* (London, 1781); an example of the commonly found physiological dissertation in France is H. Girard, *Considerations physiologiques et pathologiques sur les affections nerveuses, dites hysteriques* (Paris, 1841).

25. See G. Didi-Huberman, *Invention de l'Hysterie: Charcot et l'Iconographie Photographique* (Paris: Macula, 1982); useful as this work is, it lacks the sweep and erudition of Sander Gilman's chapter concluding this book.

26. Paris: Hachette, 1970; trans. in 1968 as *The Fear of Women* (New York: Grune & Stratton, 1968).

27. See White's influential essay "The Forms of Wildness: Archaeology of an Idea—Noble Savage as Fetish," in *The Wild Man Within: An Image in Western Thought from the Renaissance to Romanticism*, ed. E. Dudley and M. E. Novak (Pittsburgh, Pa.: University of Pittsburgh Press, 1972), 3–38.

28. An important exception is Jan Goldstein's work, especially as found in "The Hysteria Diagnosis and the Politics of Anticlericalism in Late Nineteenth-Century France," *Journal of Modern History* 54 (1982): 209–239, and her *Console and Classify*; T. Laqueur's "Orgasm, Generation and the Politics of Reproductive Biology," *Representations* 14 (1986): 1–14. The matter is further substantiated bibliographically in the thorough researches of M. Micale, referred to in many of the chapters of this book.

29. Others who helped retrieve these lost voices include: Patricia Fedikew, "Marguerite Duras: Feminine Field of Hysteria," *Enclitic* 6 (1982): 78–86; Bernheimer and Kahane, eds., *In Dora's Case*; Terry Castle, "Learned Ladies," *TLS*, December 14–20, 1990: 1345–1346.

30. These traditions of learning are brought together in Rousseau, ed., *Languages of Psyche*.

31. Porter's discussion should be complemented with the important writings on nineteenth-century hysteria of Mark Micale.

32. Some of the theoretical cruxes have been addressed in the controversies surrounding Richard Rorty and his influential book *Philosophy and the Mirror of Nature* (Princeton, N.J.: Princeton University Press, 1980), and others such as G. Levine, ed., *One Culture: Essays in Science and Literature* (Madison: University of Wisconsin Press, 1987); the problem of metaphor in both the realist and representative domains by M. B. Hesse, *Models and Analogies in Science* (Notre Dame: University of Indiana Press, 1966); *The Structure of Scientific Inference* (Berkeley, Los Angeles, London: University of California Press, 1974); idem, "Habermas, Foucault, and Metaphor in Science," *Proceedings of the Von Leer Institute of the Hebrew University of Jerusalem* (1992, Jerusalem). But see also an important statement by Hayden White, "Historical Emplotments and the Problem of Truth," presented to the Conference on the Holocaust, University of California, Los Angeles, 1990; and for the role of representation as a presiding category in contemporary sensibility, J. F. Lyotard, *The Postmodern Condition: A Report on Knowledge* (Minneapolis: University of Minnesota Press, 1984).

33. See S. Gilman, *Seeing the Insane* (New York: John Wiley & Sons, 1982); *Difference and Pathology: Stereotypes of Sexuality, Race, and Madness* (Ithaca, N.Y.: Cornell University Press, 1985); *Disease and Representation: Images of Illness from Madness to Aids* (Ithaca, N.Y.: Cornell University Press, 1988), as well as many articles and reviews.

34. One can imagine Hans Mayer listening to the list of these pariahs and reconsidering his omission of hysterics from his brilliant study of the representation of the outsider; see his *Outsiders: A Study in Life and Letters* (Cambridge, Mass.: MIT Press, 1984).

35. If William McGrath's evidence is correct about the politics of hysteria, we may have enhanced the validity of our work by this exclusion rather than harmed it; see W. J. McGrath, *Freud's Discovery of Psychoanalysis: The Politics of Hysteria* (Ithaca, N.Y.: Cornell University Press, 1986).

36. For another form of deconstruction, see McGrath, *Freud's Discovery*.

37. Princeton, N.J.: Princeton University Press, 1990.

38. See Mark S. Micale, "Hysteria and Its Historiography: A Review of Past and Present Writings," *History of Science* 27 (September, December, 1989): 223–262; 319–351; idem, "Hysteria and Its Historiography: The Future Perspective," *History of Psychiatry* 1 (March, 1990): 33–124; idem, "Charcot and the Idea of Hysteria in the Male: Gender, Mental Science, and Medical Diagnosis in Late Nineteenth-Century France," *Medical History* 34 (1990): 363–411; and idem, "Hysteria Male/Hysteria Female: Reflections on Comparative Gender Construc-

tion in Nineteenth-Century France and Britain" in *Science and Sensibility: Gender and Scientific Enquiry, 1780–1945,* ed. Marina Benjamin, (Oxford, Basil Blackwell, 1991), 200–239.

39. As evidence we again suggest that the reader consult Goldstein's *Console and Classify* for evidence of what the post-Foucaldian methodology does in practice.

PART I

Historical

ONE

Once upon a Text

Hysteria from Hippocrates

Helen King

LABELS AND ORIGINS: A NAME WITHOUT A DISEASE?

In the beginning was Hippocrates, the Father of Medicine, who freed the emerging science from the chains of superstition, introduced empirical observation and the bedside manner, and both identified and named "hysteria." So runs the established wisdom on the Hippocratic origins of both medical science in general and of the diagnosis of hysteria in particular. Yet recent work on Hippocratic medicine has called into question much of this tradition. Once it was an acceptable scholarly pursuit to debate the inclusion of particular treatises in the canon of "The Genuine Works of Hippocrates": now it is widely accepted that not a single text of the Hippocratic corpus can be attributed with any certainty to the Father of Medicine.[1] In place of a canon of "Genuine Works," we have a diverse set of multi-author texts. Once the Hippocratic doctor was seen as a model of medical etiquette and morality: now he can be restored to his own historical and cultural context, where he becomes only one of the numerous brands of healer competing for clients in the ancient world, unafraid to improve his chances of employment by the use of tactics questionable by later standards.[2] With the improved visibility made possible by the new Hippocratic studies, the time has surely come to reexamine the texts so confidently labeled by the nineteenth-century Dr. Robb as "Hippocrates on Hysteria"[3] and to review the relationship between the text of the Hippocratic corpus, its interpreters over time, and the discussions of hysteria.

Since the Hippocratic texts are so often quoted—and misquoted—in

3

contemporary debates on the status of the diagnosis hysteria, such a study will not only contribute to the growing body of work on Hippocratic medicine and its place in ancient society but also inevitably feed into these debates. Eliot Slater, questioning the value of the diagnosis in our own times, has argued that "the justification for accepting 'hysteria' as a syndrome is based entirely on tradition and lacks evidential support."[4] This tradition goes back to the alleged origin of the diagnosis of hysteria in the Hippocratic corpus, and it is only by reclaiming the relevant texts from their use in the tradition that we can understand and question the diagnosis in later centuries. If a fresh reading of the ancient texts shows that their use by the tradition is unwarranted, this will have important implications for the history of hysteria in general.

Recent work on hysteria in the Hippocratic corpus by medical historians, psychologists, and physicians is, almost without exception, based on the history of hysteria published in 1965 by Ilza Veith. On the name itself she wrote,

> In the Egyptian papyri the disturbances resulting from the movement of the womb were described, but had not yet been given a specific appellation. This step was taken in the Hippocratic writings where the connection of the uterus (*hystera*) with the disease resulting from its disturbance is first expressed by the term "hysteria." It appears in the thirty-fifth aphorism, which reads: "When a woman suffers from hysteria . . . "[5]

Since the publication of Veith's book, these points have achieved canonical status. For example, R. A. Woodruff states that "the name, hysteria, has been in use since the time of Hippocrates"; P. B. Bart and D. H. Scully refer back to "the time of Hippocrates, who coined the name"; and S. B. Guze cites Veith as his only source for the "information" that "disorders diagnosed as hysteria have been encountered for about 2,500 years" and furthermore that, "as everyone knows, the term *hysteria* originated in Greek antiquity."[6] These apparently confident assertions cover not only the origin of the word "hysteria," but also the very essence of ancient Greek gynecology. R. Satow, a psychotherapist and sociologist, asserts that "'hysteria' has been a label used for a potpourri of female ailments and non-ailments alike since antiquity. . . . The Greeks and Romans called almost all female complaints hysteria and believed the cause of all these female maladies to be a wandering uterus. . . . In various Hippocratic texts the term hysteria is applied to a large variety of female complaints."[7]

What "everyone knows" is, however, not necessarily true. The earth is not flat, although once "everyone knew" that it was. Even leaving aside the attempt to use Egyptian evidence, which has already been widely questioned,[8] Veith's claims for Greek medicine are seriously flawed. As only one recent writer on hysteria, E. Trillat,[9] has recognized, the "various Hippocratic texts" applying the term "hysteria" to many different complaints simply do not exist; moreover, to suggest that Hippocratic gynecology is about calling almost everything "hysteria" is a gross oversimplification. A total revision of our understanding of the tradition is thus long overdue.

Let us return to the text claimed by Veith as the inaugural moment of hysteria, "the thirty-fifth aphorism." It is a significant choice, since the *Aphorisms* is one of the most widely translated and best-known works of the Hippocratic corpus, believed for many centuries to have been written by Hippocrates himself as a distillation of the wisdom of a lifetime's clinical experience, and thus taken to be one of the most genuine works.[10] Immediately, however, we encounter a difficulty; there *is* no "thirty-fifth aphorism." A. Rousselle[11] has criticized Veith for reading back contemporary ideas into antiquity, but the problem is greater than this would suggest; Veith puts too great a trust in poor secondary sources. What she is referring to here is, in fact, *Aphorisms* 5.35 (L 4.544), which does not use the term "hysteria" at all; instead, using the plural form *hysterika*, it begins *Gynaiki hypo hysterikōn enochloumenei*, and it may be translated as: "In a woman suffering from *hysterika*, or having a difficult labor, a sneeze is a good thing."

What are these *hysterika*, and what is so good about a sneeze? Such questions plunge us directly into the heart of the hysteria debate. It is tempting to translate *hysterika* as "hysterics," but an apparently familiar word does not necessarily convey the meaning we would most naturally expect. Galen of Pergamum noted the difficulties of translating this aphorism (K 17b.824–825). *Hysterika*, he wrote in his commentary on the *Aphorisms*, could refer to all diseases of the womb[12] or to only a particular condition called *hysterikē pnix* (best translated "suffocation of the womb"), described by a number of post-Hippocratic writers and which will be discussed at length below, or to problems with the afterbirth, also known as *ta hystera*. He favors setting the aphorism in the context of *hysterikē pnix*, for the following reasons. First, *hysterika* cannot refer to the afterbirth, because *hystera* and *hysterika* are not the same word. Second, it cannot refer to all diseases of the womb, because Hippocrates says that it is helped by sneezing. Clearly, not all diseases of the womb are helped by sneezing and, since Hippocrates cannot be wrong, Galen concludes that the passage must refer to *hysterikē pnix*.

There is, however, no reason why we must follow Galen's line of argument since, despite his objections, there is nothing to prevent translating the phrase as "When a woman suffers from diseases of the womb." The argument that not all such diseases are helped by sneezing does not necessarily apply to pre-Galenic medicine. A sneeze expels various kinds of matter that may cause disorders, and thus has value in many situations; in a specifically gynecological context, substances such as mustard, black or white hellebore, and castoreum were widely recommended in the ancient world to promote menstruation or the expulsion of the afterbirth.[13] Since retained menses were thought to be the cause of many female disorders, the expulsive value of a sneeze could often be beneficial.

It is in a passage of Pliny the Elder, written a century before Galen, that the sternutatory powers of mustard appear in the narrower context of "suffocation of the womb." Mixed with vinegar, mustard was thought to rouse women suffering from an epileptic fit or "vulvarum conversione suffocatas,"[14] translated in the Loeb edition as "fainting with prolapsus" but more literally meaning "suffocated by the turning of their wombs." This may suggest another value of the sneeze, which was seen as being of particular importance in "suffocation." Many ancient writers discuss the difficulty of knowing whether a sufferer from the condition they call "suffocation of the womb" is, in fact, alive or dead. Pliny himself gives the case of a woman who lay as if dead for seven days with "conversio vulvae," turning of the womb.[15] In such cases, it was necessary to test for life by holding a feather or a piece of wool at the nostrils. A sneeze was welcomed as evidence of the presence of life.

Sneezing, due to its expulsive powers, can thus be "a good thing" for many disorders affecting women, but by the first century A.D., when Pliny was writing, it had come to be seen as particularly valuable in "suffocation of the womb" because it could recall to life a patient lying as if dead. It is thus possible that it had the first meaning in *Aphorisms*, but that this had been overlaid with the second by the time of Pliny. Galen, writing a hundred years or so after Pliny, put together the broad context of the *Aphorisms* passage and the more specific context of Pliny; the example thus makes us aware of the possible changing interpretations of a text over time.

Regardless of how we choose to translate the passage, it should above all be noted that this is not what Veith called "a specific appellation": a disease label. Veith admits that the form *hysterikos*, "from the womb," "connected with the womb," or, when applied to a woman, "liable to disorders of the womb," is "more frequently used,"[16] but she does not acknowledge that it is in fact used exclusively, and moreover that the *Aphorisms* example is only a further case of this general type.

It is not difficult to find the source for this particular misconception on the part of Veith. The idea that it is in the Hippocratic corpus that hysteria is not only described but also given its name can be traced back beyond her to the Emile Littré edition of 1839–61, the gynecological volumes of which—numbered 7 and 8—appeared in 1851–53. For the present purpose, a study of these must concentrate on the additional French material supplied by Littré. This appears in two forms. First, for many of the Hippocratic texts he provides section headings for each chapter; these have no analogue in the Greek manuscripts. This applies to the three volumes of the *Gynaikeia*, known in English as *Diseases of Women*,[17] where several passages are headed "Hystérie." Second, additional material appears in the translation itself, where Littré uses the medical categories of his own time. The misplaced confidence of the title used by Robb in his article "Hippocrates on Hysteria"[18] is based on translating Littré into English while simultaneously incorporating distinctions made only in the headings.[19] As Rousselle has recently suggested, these owe far more to nineteenth-century debates and theory than to the Hippocratic texts they are supposed to summarize.[20] Just as Adams aimed to make the Hippocratic texts that he selected as "The Genuine Works of Hippocrates" intelligible to "any well-educated member of the [medical] profession at the present day,"[21] so Littré "read Hippocrates in his own image and in the image of the medicine of his time,"[22] with the explicit intention of using Hippocratic wisdom to improve the medical practice of his own day. "Until the nineteenth century, medicine nourished itself on Hippocrates—or at least on that which it believed it could find in Hippocrates."[23]

The section headings written by Littré go further than merely labeling certain sections "Hystérie." In addition to this, Littré distinguishes between imagined movement of the womb, which he classifies as hysteria, and real movement, which he describes as displacement. He thus makes such comments as, "This section appears to be a confusion of imaginary with real movements of the womb"; "This appears to be some displacement of the womb rather than hysteria"; and "The fact remains that there is confusion between imaginary and real displacements."[24] He believes that the Hippocratic texts do not make sufficiently clear the distinction he seeks, in contrast to Veith, who—again, wrongly—claims that "the Hippocratic physician was aware of the importance of a careful differentiation between hysterical symptoms and those of organic disease."[25] The writers of these ancient texts make no such distinction. They describe what is, for them, a real and organic condition: the movement of the womb (*hystera*) to other parts of the body. Since it is Littré, rather than any Hippocratic physician, who is interested in the distinction, it may be suspected that Veith is basing her remarks on the Littrean section headings rather than on the Greek text.

The origin and process of transmission of the error in translation should now be plain. Littré read the Hippocratic corpus in the context of the mid-nineteenth century, in which hysteria was a recognized condition of debated etiology; he expected to find hysteria in the text, duly found it, and drew it out in the headings he wrote for the various sections. Robb translated into English the passages headed by Littré as "Hysteria," and subsequent readers of the Hippocratic corpus have accepted the categories imposed by Littré on his material. Taking only the *Aphorisms* passage, Littré translates "Chez une femme attaquée d'hystérie . . ." while Francis Adams gives "Sneezing occurring in a woman with hysterics," and J. Chadwick and W. N. Mann have "When a woman is afflicted with hysteria." In giving "When a woman suffers from hysteria . . ." Veith is following the widely available Loeb translation.[26]

Thus the diagnosis of hysteria is one made not by the ancient authors of the texts, but rather by the nineteenth-century translator of the Hippocratic corpus. At this point it would be possible to argue that this is of only minor importance; granted, the tradition is wrong to claim that the Greeks invented the name and thus the diagnostic category of hysteria, but if the Hippocratic texts nonetheless contain the first clinical descriptions of hysteria, should we much concern ourselves with the origin of the name? As a result it becomes necessary at this point to begin to consider what we are to understand by "hysteria." When a translator reads the diagnosis into a text, this would seem to suggest the belief that there is a fixed entity called hysteria, constant over time and place, so that we can say with Charcot that "L'hystérie a toujours existé, en tous lieux et en tous temps,"[27] and with D. W. Abse that "in fact, east and west, hysteria continues unabated in various guises."[28] If we believe this, it will be of relatively little significance that the *name* "hysteria" is not Hippocratic. A concept may exist even if it is not named; as G. Lewis points out, the ancient Hebrews had no word for what the Romans were to call *lex talio,* the law of retribution in kind, but they did say "An eye for an eye and a tooth for a tooth."[29] Further general questions about hysteria will also need to be addressed. Is it a disease like any other, and thus a fit subject for medical study and treatment? Is it a disease at all?[30]

If hysteria is constant, found throughout history, worldwide, we can begin to talk about whether or not Hippocratic medicine recognized it, regardless of whether the Hippocratics named it, just as we can talk about whether tuberculosis, epilepsy, and gonorrhea were recognized. Furthermore, if it is historically constant, a body of text of the length of the Hippocratic medical corpus should, statistically, contain some cases of it. Any decision that it is constant therefore prejudges the question of whether or not it existed in Hippocratic times: by definition, it must have done, and our task is only to find the sections in the texts which provide a more or less accurate match with our chosen clinical picture. This task, however, is complicated by the belief that hysteria, like chlorosis, is a disorder that apparently disappeared in our own century; as Trillat says, "L'hystérie est morte, c'est entendu."[31] This could lead us to apply more stringent criteria to the Hippocratic texts, to conclude that hysteria was not present in classical Greece, and thus to revise our views on the significance of its apparent disappearance from the medical scene.

There are however two main obstacles standing in the way of a decision to treat hysteria as a historical constant. The first is that, unlike tuberculosis, epilepsy, and gonorrhea, hysteria is in no way a clearly defined disease entity for which most medical practitioners in our society would draw up the same list of symptoms; the second, that an integral part of the definition of hysteria often consists in its supposed ability to mimic symptoms of other diseases.

Contemporary medical writers on hysteria fall into two main groups. One group accepts that hysteria is "a valid, independent syndrome"[32] and, in applying this label, makes use of the Perley-Guze criteria, which list over fifty symptoms in ten areas; exhibiting twenty-five symptoms in nine out of ten areas qualifies as hysteria, in the absence of any other diagnosis.[33] One area is entirely concerned with menstrual difficulties;[34] since menstrual suppression is by far the most common symptom in Hippocratic gynecology—for reasons that relate to the belief that amenorrhea indicates the presence of a dangerous reservoir of unshed blood[35]—it should not be surprising that retrospective diagnosis of hysteria in the Hippocratic texts is common. The second group's position is conveniently summarized by Slater's (1965) lecture "Diagnosis of 'hysteria.'"[36] The single quotation marks around "hysteria" say it all. Slater picks up the Perley-Guze point that the label hysteria is applied "in the absence of any other diagnosis" and concludes that the diagnosis merely indicates the "absence of relevant physical findings"; it is "a disguise for ignorance and a fertile source of clinical error . . . not only a delusion but also a snare" and "a way of avoiding a confrontation with our own ignorance."[37] Edward Shorter suggests that diagnoses such as hysteria have often covered an undetected uterine infection.[38] C. D. Marsden, too, points out that a high percentage of patients diagnosed as having hysteria turn out to have an underlying organic disease and concludes that "there can be little doubt that the term 'hysterical' is often applied as a diagnosis to something that the physician does not understand."[39]

Slater therefore argues that "the justification for accepting 'hysteria' as a syndrome is based entirely on tradition and lacks evidential support."[40] F. Walshe's response to Slater, significantly using the same title but omitting the quotation marks around the word "hysteria," defends "the concept of hysteria as a nosological entity in its own right."[41] The debate in medical circles continues, and Slater's contribution is discussed at length in Alec Roy's (1982) collection of essays, *Hysteria.*[42] R. Mayou gives a fair summary of the medical situation when he writes that there is at present "no agreement about diagnostic criteria" for hysteria.[43]

The second difficulty encountered in regarding hysteria as something constant is that, if anything *is* a widely accepted part of the definition, it is the suggestion that it can mimic the symptoms of *any* other disease.[44] In this case, how can hysteria itself be a disease, and what is to prevent it from taking such radically different forms in different epochs as to be almost unrecognizable as the same condition? The corollary is also true; as Shorter puts it, "every organic disease imaginable . . . has at one time or another been classified as hysteria."[45] Does a condition with such indistinct and shifting borders exist in any meaningful sense? As Trillat puts it, hysteria is "une maladie qui n'en est pas une, tout en l'étant . . ."[46]

Nineteenth-century medical literature suggests that hysteria can manifest itself in a highly dramatic form; in the ideal type of Charcot's "grande hystérie," violent muscular contractions culminating in the arched posture (*arc-en-cercle*), paralysis, loss of voice, retention of urine, anesthesia, and blindness. In a recent study of admissions for hysteria to the Edinburgh Royal Infirmary in the late eighteenth century, however, G. B. Risse found that only a minority of alleged victims had fits of this kind; most women sufferers had loss of appetite or other digestive problems, menstrual difficulties, and fainting spells, symptoms suggestive of many organic diagnoses.[47] Yet one relatively constant feature of the diagnosis of hysteria in modern times is that it implies that the physical symptoms so labeled, whether dramatic or not, have no recognized organic cause. It should now be clear why hysteria has been described as "that most unsatisfactory of psychiatric syndromes."[48]

Marsden's recent discussion shows the widest possible extent of the definition of "hysteria." "Physicians use the term to describe the symptom (conversion disorder or disassociation state), the illness (somatization disorder or Briquet's syndrome), the personality (histrionic), a form of anxiety (phobic anxiety after Freud), an epidemic outbreak (mass hysteria) and irritating patients (if female they are hysterical; if male they

are psychopaths)."[49] The irritation felt by doctors toward hysteria patients is eloquently expressed in the words of a doctor writing in 1908,
a time when the contracture or "drawing up" of a limb was a common
symptom: "As Vance cut off the plaster cast from a 14-year-old girl
whose leg had 'drawn up' a year previously, she cried, 'It is going to draw
up; it is going to draw up,' at which Vance said severely, 'If it does draw
up, I will break your d____d little neck.'"[50]

Other contemporary writers argue for a restriction of the definition
of hysteria, excluding the syndrome and the personality type and using
hysteria only for a universal human reaction, comparable to anxiety or
depression.[51] Shorter's suggestions may be helpful here, insofar as they
permit a degree of universality, while incorporating variation among
cultures. He accepts that "'hysteria,' it appears, is a real psychiatric disease, in addition to being an epithet with which men have stigmatized
women across the ages." However, he goes on, "the presentation of 'hysterical' symptoms tends to be molded by the surrounding culture" to
a greater degree than that of, for example, the symptoms of schizo-
phrenia. A major question to ask therefore concerns the social construction of the disease: Why is it that, from a wide repertoire of the possible,
"certain symptoms are selected in certain epochs"?[52] I will return to this
important question, in relation to the Hippocratic texts.

DEFINITIONS: THE TEXTUAL TRADITION

Thus the questions raised by hysteria are not only legion but often
directly contradictory. Is hysteria another word for ignorance, or the
perfectly adaptable mimic? Is it a dramatic performance or a minor
gynecological disturbance? Is it caused by the womb or has it no organic
cause? Is it a wide-ranging category, a "non-verbal language,"[53] or something universal but very specific? Beneath these questions lies the major
one for anyone trying to write about the history of hysteria: that is,
what definition should be used for the purposes of the present work?
J. M. N. Boss takes what may appear to be an attractive option when
tackling this problem; he writes, "In this paper the word 'hysteric' is used
in the manner of the period of the writings referred to."[54] As I have
already shown, however, in the ancient period the word "hysteria" is not
used at all; *hysterikos,* "hysteric," is used, but with the very specific meanings "coming from the womb"/"suffering due to the womb." One way
around this problem would be to restrict the present study to those sections of the corpus traditionally seen as descriptions of hysteria; for
example, those so labeled by Littré. As I have already shown, the diffi-

culty here is that Littré imposes his own distinction between "real" and "imaginary" movements of the womb, a distinction alien to the ancient Greek writers. An alternative would be to study all sections of the corpus in which the womb is described as moving to another part of the body, but this only reiterates the point that later writers use hysteria for symptoms with no organic cause, whereas the Hippocratics regard womb movement as something entirely organic.

The difficulties of deciding what constitutes hysteria for the purposes of a historical study are by no means unique; indeed, they are directly comparable to those encountered by J. Gabbay in his discussion of the disease concept "asthma." Gabbay asks how far we "can rely on present-day knowledge of asthma to analyse historically the social nature of medical knowledge"[55] and concludes that we cannot assume that all writers in the past who used the term were referring to the same thing. With hysteria, of course, the problems are greater, because our sources are not even using a common name. Gabbay raises the question whether a diachronic study of a disease concept investigates a constant natural entity, or a vast range of different concepts,[56] and shows how this question all too easily leads the historian to the stage of "historical paralysis."[57] Like Medusa's head, the question, What exactly are we studying? turns the onlooker to stone.

Although it has this malign power, the question must at least be addressed, even in a negative way. To clarify: in the present work I am discussing neither all texts in which the writers name the condition they describe hysteria, nor all texts mentioning a particular combination of symptoms that I choose to label hysteria. Instead, I have chosen here to concentrate on a set of early texts conventionally linked by subsequent writers: a finite series of texts, each drawing on an increasingly fixed group of those written by earlier writers, yet each simultaneously—to some extent—incorporating the ideas of its own age. I am thus studying hysteria from the perspective of a developing tradition of reading the Hippocratic corpus, a textual tradition that culminates in Littré. In order to illuminate the growth of this tradition, I will also draw on texts produced outside it in order to provide the necessary context for its origin and development.

Before turning to a more detailed study of the Hippocratic texts conventionally used as evidence for hysteria in ancient Greece, it is worth considering what implications the use of the label "hysteria" may have, for Littré and other writers.

The Greek adjective *hysterikos* means "from the womb"; as such, it is a purely physical description of cause, showing the part of the body from which other symptoms emanate. In a woman, as another Hippocratic text puts it, "the womb is the origin of all diseases,"[58] so it would be fair to say that, in Hippocratic gynecology, all diseases are hysterical. But this word cannot have the same nuances for us as for an ancient author.

Littré uses hysteria in a rather different way. In his *Dictionnaire de la langue française* (1863–77) he defines hysteria as follows: "Hystérie: maladie nerveuse qui se manifeste par accès et qui est characterisée par des convulsions, la sensation d'une boule qui remont de la matrice dans la gorge et la suffocation" (Hysteria: nervous disorder that manifests itself in the form of a fit and is characterized by convulsions, by the sensation of a ball rising from the womb into the throat, and by suffocation). To understand Littré's position, we must first understand the debate within which he is situating himself. Boss has traced the etiology of hysteria up to the seventeenth century.[59] He argues that, before about 1600, the "hysteric affection" was, as the name implies, attributed to the womb. In the early seventeenth century hysteria was linked not only to the male condition known as hypochondria, in which the spleen was thought to give off vapors, but also to melancholy, found in both sexes. Robert Burton saw hypochondria and hysteria as forms of melancholy; Sydenham believed that both sexes could suffer from hysteria, but that in women it was the most common condition next to fever.[60] Thus there was a shift in "the limits of hysteria, as it united with hypochondria and annexed parts of melancholy's crumbling empire."[61] At the same time the cause of hysteria came to be seen as being the brain, or the whole person. In the eighteenth century, hysteria was increasingly classified as a neurosis; the excess blood naturally present in the female body led to increased nervous irritability, especially under the influence of too much meat, coffee, or tea and insufficient exercise.[62] At this time, "According to the conventional medical wisdom, hysteria was a chronic, quintessentially feminine, disease resulting from the peculiar constitution and physiology of women."[63] The only certain way to make sure one's fragile nerves were not further weakened was to conform to the "prevailing social and biological notions of womanhood."[64]

By the mid-nineteenth century, when Littré was writing, some doctors believed that the cause of hysteria was a physical disorder of the womb; others did not.[65] For most writers of this period, however they may have envisaged the mechanism of its production, hysteria nevertheless "was rooted in the very nature of being female."[66] Pierre Briquet rejected the idea that the womb was responsible, preferring the explanation of a "neurosis of the brain" in someone of the "hysterical type"; in other words, the hysterical personality was a necessary part of the development of the disorder.[67]

In some historical periods the implications of the label hysteria are thus that the disease originates in the womb, while in others the implications are very different, hinting that there is no organic origin for the symptoms. Littré's dictionary makes his own position clear; he follows writers such as B. C. Brodie, who in a lecture published in 1837 wrote that "hysteria . . . belongs not to the uterus, but to the nervous system."[68]

HIPPOCRATIC HYSTERIA:
THE WOMB AND ITS DESTINATIONS

For the Hippocratic writers, however, the texts that have been used in the construction of hysteria described something resulting from a firmly organic cause, the movement of the womb. It is to the role of the womb that we must now turn. The Hippocratic texts suggest that movement of the womb is caused by menstrual suppression, exhaustion, insufficient food, sexual abstinence, and dryness or lightness of the womb, and that it can be cured by marriage and/or pregnancy, scent therapy, irritant pessaries, and various herbal concoctions administered by mouth, by nose, or direct to the vulva.

Since the womb is believed capable of movement around much of the body, these texts attribute a wide range of symptoms to womb movement. In searching for Hippocratic hysteria, we could therefore narrow down the field by identifying some combination of symptoms which so closely resembles the picture of hysteria in later historical periods that the problem of the absence of a disease label might be dismissed. The question raised by this approach is, of course, which historical period's image of hysteria we should take as our ideal type against which the Hippocratic texts are to be measured—*hysterikē pnix* in the early Roman Empire? or the hysteria of the mid-nineteenth century? Another, more productive, way of approaching the problem is to start from the opposite end, asking which sections of the Hippocratic corpus have traditionally been used as evidence that hysteria was found in classical Greece. Robb's "Hippocrates on Hysteria"[69] translates the *Aphorisms* passage and five chapters of the gynecological treatises: *Nature of Woman,* chapter 87; *Diseases of Women* book 1, chapter 7, and book 2, chapters 123–125. He also gives brief summaries of *Diseases of Women* book 2, chapters 126–127.

It is significant that these chapters are among the very small group of Hippocratic texts used in recent discussions of hysteria, the other major chapter most commonly brought into the debate being *Diseases of Women* 1.32.[70] Robb also cites the appendix to *Regimen in Acute Diseases,* which distinguishes between *pnix*—a breathing difficulty usually translated as "suffocation"—caused by the womb and that caused by spasm or convulsions: if the patient feels pressure from the fingers, it is from the womb; if not, it is a convulsion.[71] However, close study of the above passages from *Diseases of Women* and *Nature of Woman*, so often the only examples of Hippocratic hysteria given in contemporary discussions, reveals that they have in common only a reference to the womb moving to another part of the body, and the symptom of *pnix*. The affinity between these is not, however, constant. For example, the womb may move in the absence of *pnix*, as in *Diseases of Women* 2.127 (L 8.272–274); this section is headed "Hystérie" by Littré. It is also worth noting that such features of nineteenth- and twentieth-century hysteria as grinding the teeth, loss of voice, cold extremities, and limb pains or paralysis do feature in the Hippocratic texts, often in the company of movement of the womb and suffocation, but may be found in the absence of either or both and may be attributed to a named organic cause; for example, in *Diseases of Women* 2.110 (L 8.234–238) they arise from a red flux.

The difficulties of finding a passage in the Hippocratic texts to serve as a paradigm for Hippocratic hysteria are increased when we look at Littré's classifications and at the texts themselves. Thus, of the six texts used by Robb,[72] only four are in fact headed "Hystérie" by Littré: one chapter from *Nature of Woman*, 87 (L 7.408), and three from *Diseases of Women*, 2.123–125 (L 8.266–270). Not only do they give largely different combinations of symptoms and prescribe different remedies, but in none of them does even the adjective *hysterikos*, "from the womb," appear.

This last point is of particular interest. Since the noun is not used in this period, it is entirely irrelevant for M. R. Lefkowitz, in a discussion of fourth-century medicine, to claim that "the term hysteria means 'wombiness'."[73] Maybe it does; but since it is not used, this is of little importance. One also searches for it in vain in the later gynecological writers of antiquity, such as Soranus and Aretaeus of Cappadocia, in whose work there does exist a condition thought to originate in the womb and to cause symptoms of suffocation, tooth grinding, loss of voice, and so on, but which is called not hysteria but *hysterikē pnix*, "suffocation caused by the womb." The classic description of the symptoms that came to be collected under this label is Soranus's *Gynecology* 3.26–29; section 2.11 of Aretaeus is also headed "On *hysterikē pnix*" (CMG vol. 2, pp.32–34) but, unlike Soranus, he lists the remedies in a separate section, 6.10, "Treatment of *hysterikē pnix*" (CMG vol. 2, pp.139–141).[74]

The theories of Aretaeus and Soranus will be discussed in detail below. However, it is worth discussing why neither the category of hysteria nor that of *hysterikē pnix* has a place in Hippocratic medicine. Not only does *pnix* exist as a symptom in the Hippocratic gynecological texts, and *hysterikos* as an adjective, but one of the sections used by Robb and many others—*Diseases of Women* 1.7 (L 8.32)—even introduces the description with "If *pnix* suddenly occurs." Nevertheless, in these texts the two are not explicitly brought together. Why should this be so?

One of the reasons why neither hysteria nor *hysterikē pnix* is a Hippocratic category is simply that Hippocratic gynecology does not work by fitting collections of symptoms into preexisting categories. We can learn a great deal from studying the ways in which the Hippocratic writers choose to describe and to name disease. In many cases, ancient gynecology distinguishes and separates different combinations of symptoms according to cause and treatment, rather than subsuming many symptoms under a single disease label that "covers over all the clinical detail";[75] it emphasizes description of symptoms rather than diagnosis.[76] Any attempt to impose the diagnosis of hysteria on the Hippocratic texts may therefore risk distorting their approach to illness.

Indeed, looking at the Hippocratic corpus in general, not all Hippocratic texts name the diseases they describe. V. Di Benedetto distinguishes four ways of presenting a disease in these texts: as "another disorder," as "if" or "when" followed by one or more symptoms, as "if" or "when" followed by the name of a disease, or by giving the name of the disorder at the very beginning of the section. He suggests that these different ways of presenting disease reflect a culture in which the relationship between doctor and disease is defined in more than one way. The "if symptom x, therapy y" form is the most ancient, found also in Assyrian and Babylonian medicine, but in Hippocratic medicine it is slightly modified because the patient and the disease are separated and the possibility admitted that different patients may suffer in slightly different ways from what is nevertheless the same disease. Turning this last point on its head, the Hippocratic writers thus have the notion of a disease as something unitary which, due not only to the differences between patients in age, sex, temperament, and coloring, but also to variations in climate and season, may nevertheless manifest itself in a variety of ways. One disease: different symptoms, according to other factors affecting its presentation.[77]

When the Hippocratic texts give a specific name to a disorder, it may be taken from the affected part; from the way in which the disorder presents itself; from the specific sensation caused; or from something that happens in the course of the disease.[78] Although there is no name given to the disorder, or disorders, in the texts usually seen as "Hippocratic hysteria," their opening words are relevant here. These fall into two categories. Some start by describing the movement of the womb: "When the womb turns to the head" in *Diseases of Women* 2.123 (L 8.266). Others start with the symptoms of *pnix*, suffocation: the opening of *Diseases of Women* 1.32 (L 8.76) translates as "If *pnix* suddenly seizes a pregnant woman." The later name hysteria comes from the part believed to be affected: the womb. However, in the Hippocratic texts being considered here, the focus is either on the part that causes the symptoms or on the symptom that seems to have a central position: *pnix*. I will shortly return to the specific significance of this sensation in classical medicine.

The texts traditionally used as examples of hysteria in the Hippocratic corpus exhibit several features that make it difficult to merge them into one picture. I now propose to discuss those most commonly used by later commentators in order of their appearance in the gynecological treatises, and to set them within the context of the imagery associated with "woman" in ancient Greece.

The first description of interest is the second chapter of *Diseases of Women* book 1 (L 8.14–22), a discussion of menstrual suppression in a childless woman. Menstrual suppression is of central importance in Hippocratic gynecology,[79] due to a physiology of the female outlined in the previous chapter, *Diseases of Women* 1.1 (L 8.10–14). Regular menstrual bleeding is seen as essential to female health—after maturity, outside pregnancy, and before the "drying out" of the menopause—because of the quality of female flesh. In women who have given birth, the body is "broken down" and its internal channels opened by childbirth and the lochia. A woman who has not given birth will suffer more pain if the flow of her menstrual blood is obstructed; because her body is more resistant, firmer, and more "thickly-packed," there is less open space into which the blood can travel. The writer of this chapter goes on to say that a woman's flesh is softer and of a looser texture than that of a man, and draws an analogy between female flesh and sheepskin, and between male flesh and a rug. If a fleece and a rug of equal weight are placed over water or in a damp place for two days and nights, the fleece will be found to have become much heavier than the rug. This is because sheepskin has a greater capacity to absorb water: a capacity shared with female flesh.[80]

Aristotle's characterization of woman as "a deformed male" and "a mutilated male" is well known, as is its persistence in Western culture.[81] However, Aristotle's biology may be seen as only one manifestation of the classical Greek belief that women are both fundamentally different from, and inferior to, men. In the seventh century B.C., the poet Hesiod expressed this belief in chronological terms; women, the *genos gynaikōn* or "race of women," were created later than men. Before Zeus sent the first woman and mother of the "race," Pandora, as one stage in the sequence of gift and counter-gift between gods and men, men lived like the gods. The arrival of Pandora and her daughters creates the need for sexual reproduction and agricultural labor, since women are voracious consumers of all that a man can produce.[82] In the *Timaeus*, Plato too presents women as a late addition to the human race; in the second generation of humanity, men who acted in a cowardly or unjust way in the first are reborn as women.[83]

Defining the female in terms of the male is one way of expressing difference; chronology is another. Other images of male/female relations express it in other ways but show similar persistence: the agricultural metaphor, in which man ploughs the field that is woman and sows the seed in her passive body, or the war/childbirth opposition, in which man sheds the blood of others to defend the city in war, while woman bleeds from her own body and replenishes the city's stock of men.[84] By locating female difference at the level of the flesh, Hippocratic medicine incorporates the ideas of fundamental difference, sexuality, and bloodshed into its image of woman.

The direct consequence of the difference between the flesh of the two sexes is that women absorb more fluid from the digestive process, needing menstruation to remove the excess from their bodies. As a result, in the Hippocratic texts women are often described as "wetter" than men. Women are loose-textured and soft to the touch, thus by their very nature retaining moisture, and this retention is even presented as the explanation for women having breasts.[85] A further factor mentioned in *Diseases of Women* 1.1 is their way of life. A man does more strenuous and tiring work, which dries out any excess moisture he may have accumulated; women live sedentary lives, leaving menstruation as the only way of purging them of the excess fluid building up in their bodies.

It is in the context of these beliefs about the female body that *Diseases of Women* 1.2 should be read. In certain circumstances, even in the wet body of a woman, the womb may be deprived of sufficient moisture. The childless woman, due to the lack of spaces in her body in which moisture can be stored, is at particular risk, above all if she abstains from the "moistening" activity of sexual intercourse. In such a woman, the "dry and light" womb may suddenly "turn around"[86] and move up in search of moisture. Menstruation stops, and if it does not occur for three months there will be *pnix* from time to time, intermittent fever, shivering, and pain in the limbs. If there is no bleeding by the fourth month, these symptoms will worsen and will be joined by those of thick urine, a swollen abdomen, grinding the teeth, loss of appetite, and difficulty in sleeping. In the fifth month all symptoms will be worse; if the condition persists into the sixth month with no menstrual loss, it will have become incurable, and the woman will suffer the additional symptoms of vomiting phlegm, extreme thirst, discomfort if touched, gurgling sounds from the blood in the womb which is unable to come out, loss of voice or difficulty in making herself understood, and irregular breathing. Finally the abdomen, legs, and feet will swell: death is imminent.

The disorder described in *Diseases of Women* 1.7 is similar, although it does not follow this month-by-month pattern, but the explanation for the symptoms is different, since the central point seems to be that they depend on the location to which the dry womb moves. The affected group is described as women not having intercourse, but older rather than younger women because their wombs are lighter in weight. Elsewhere in these texts it is explained that the younger the woman, the more blood there is present in her body.[87] If a woman's vessels are emptier than usual and she is more tired, the womb, dried out by fatigue, turns around and "throws itself" on the liver because this organ is full of moisture. This causes sudden *pnix,* by interrupting the route of the breath through the belly. During this *pnix,* the whites of the eyes are turned up, the woman is cold, and her complexion is livid; she grinds her teeth and has excess saliva, like a sufferer from Heracles' disease, another name for the condition that the Hippocratics usually called the sacred disease and which we would probably call epilepsy. Sometimes phlegm will run down from the head, causing the womb to leave the liver and return to its proper place, and the *pnix* will stop because the womb is now full of fluid and heavy. If the womb stays on the liver or in the area of the hypochondria for a long time, however, the sufferer will be choked; if it moves to the mouth of the bladder, it will cause strangury; or it may go to the limbs or side.

Diseases of Women 1.32 (L 8.76) gives an almost identical etiology for *pnix* and a very similar picture of symptoms, but it concerns the condition in a pregnant woman. Not only fatigue but also insufficient food can cause the womb to move; the womb itself is described as being overheated as well as dry. As in 1.7, phlegm—described as cold—may run down from the head and cause the womb to return to its proper position; if the womb does not return quickly, there is danger to the fetus.

The alleged hysteria texts in *Diseases of Women* 2.123ff. are much shorter than those so far discussed and give little information on the women most likely to be affected or on the mechanisms by which the symptoms are produced. Instead, they start by naming the location to which the womb has moved (without saying why it has traveled there), then give a short list of "signs," and finally outline the treatment. *Diseases of Women* 2.123 (L 8.266) opens: "When the womb moves to the head and the *pnix* stops there, the head is heavy." The signs are that the patient says she has pain in the channels in the nose and under the eyes: there is lethargy and foaming at the mouth. The first treatment is to wash her with warm water; if this does not work, cold water or cooled boiled laurel or myrtle water should be put on the head, and the head anointed with rose oil. Sweet smelling fumigations should be applied below, foul smelling substances to the nostrils; she should eat cabbage and drink cabbage water.

Diseases of Women 2.124 (L 8.266–268) has an identical format and concerns movement to the heart; *Diseases of Women* 2.125 (L 8.268–270) and 2.126 (L 8.270–272) concern movement to the hypochondria, for which drinks of castoreum and fleabane[88] are among the recommended remedies. As is usual in these texts, a range of different substances is given, perhaps in order to aid the doctor in catering for a range of abilities to pay, or to allow for seasonal difficulties in obtaining the substances. In general, in addition to pessaries, washing, bandages around the body to keep the womb in place,[89] oiling, and drinks, these texts make much use of fumigation, a frequent remedy for gynecological conditions.

The most detailed description of fumigation occurs in a text that is not traditionally used by later writers on hysteria: *Diseases of Women* 2.133 (L 8.284–286). This covers a forty-day program of pessaries and fumigations for a condition in which the womb moves to the hip joint, the mouth of the womb is closed and tilted, and the menstrual blood, unable to leave by its usual route, moves instead to the breasts. It is worth translating in full not only because of the details of the fumigation process, recommended to return the womb to its place and open it so that the menstrual blood can come out—part of the treatment for hysterical suffocation for many centuries—but also because it is only one of many chapters that could be used to show the existence of womb movement texts, the details of which the hysteria tradition chooses to ignore. Contributing to its neglect by the hysteria tradition is the fact that Littré diagnoses it not as hysteria but as "Obliquité latérale devenant chronique" leading to menstrual suppression, swollen breasts, and, eventually, breast cancer.

The description of fumigation reads as follows.

First give a fumigation to the womb. Take an earthenware pot with two-sixths capacity, put on it a dish, and fit them together so that no air can get in. Then pierce the bottom of the dish and make a hole. Put in the hole a reed, about a cubit long. The reed must be properly inserted in the dish so that no vapor escapes. When you have prepared this, place the dish on the pot and plaster it round with clay. When you have done these things, dig a hole in the ground, two feet deep, large enough to make room for the pot. Then burn firewood, until you have made the hole red-hot. When it is red-hot, take out the wood and the biggest and hottest pieces of charcoal, but leave the ashes and embers in the hole. When the pot is heated up and vapor rises, if the vapor is very hot, hold back; if not, she is to sit on the end of the reed, and pass it into the mouth [of the womb], then fumigate. If it cools, throw on red-hot charcoal, taking care that the fumigation is not too fiery. If, by adding the charcoal, the fumigation becomes more fiery than it should be, take away the charcoal. One should construct the fumigation in fine, still weather, so she is not cold: she should be covered with garments. In the pot you should put dry garlic, and pour in water so that it rises two digits above, and soak it well, and pour in seal oil too. Heat this. The fumigation must go on for a long time. After the fumigation, if she is able, she should wash her whole body as she pleases, the lower back and below the navel in particular. Give for dinner barley cake or wheat bread, and boiled garlic. On the next day, if she is weak from the fumigation, intermit that day: if not, go back to the fumigation. While she is being fumigated, if she is able to examine it, order her to touch the mouth [of the womb]. The fumigation itself inflates the womb, makes it more upright and opens it. It is because it is like this, and can do such things, that you should use a fumigation.[90]

On the constituents of this fumigation, it is noteworthy that elsewhere in this treatise seal oil is described as the best substance to use in a fumigation for movement of the womb to the hypochondria.[91] Garlic, like castoreum and fleabane, features because of its strong smell. In descriptions of therapy for womb movement, the olfactory qualities of substances often account for their use. The pattern is usually that fragrant substances are applied to the vulva, in order to attract the womb back, while foul-smelling substances are placed under the nostrils to drive the womb away from the upper parts of the body.[92] In addition—and in apparent contradiction—fragrant oils may be rubbed on the head and strong-smelling substances drunk, often in wine.

Littré's diagnosis apart, there seems little reason why the womb movement described in 2.133 should have been omitted from the construction of the hysteria tradition. That section demonstrates the prevalence of the combination of womb movement and menstrual suppression throughout *Diseases of Women*. Returning to the alleged hysteria texts, *Diseases of Women* 2.127 (L 8.272) is another description of movement of the womb to the liver, which defines the affected group in a way different from that of the writer of 1.7. Where 1.7 saw the most likely sufferer as an older woman not having intercourse, 2.127 suggests movement to the liver is more common in older unmarried women and young widows, especially the childless and the sterile, because these women lack the beneficial purging of childbirth and the lochia. Here the argument is more reminiscent of 1.2. Section 2.128 (L 8.276) discusses movement to the hypochondria, for which a fumigation followed by intercourse is recommended, and 2.129 (L 8.276) covers movement to the ribs, which can cause a cough, pain in the side, and what feels like a ball in the side. Section 2.130 (L 8.278) concerns movement to the hips or flanks, and 2.131 (L 8.278) movement to the middle of the waist, in which the drawing up of the limbs is mentioned as a symptom.

A further set of texts concerning womb movement may be found at 2.200ff.; two significant points for the later history of hysteria occur in 2.201 (L 8.384), where it is recommended that the patient's groin and inner thighs should be rubbed with aromatics to cure movement of the womb to the diaphragm, and 2.203 (L 8.388), where we read, "When the womb causes *pnix*, light a lamp and snuff it out under the nostrils" and, later in the same chapter, "Take a lamp, throw on it a little oil, light it, and when it is extinguished hold it near the nostrils." The first therapy is used in a famous passage of Galen, which will be discussed below: the second, also found in one of the texts used in the hysteria tradition, *Nature of Woman* 87 (L 7.408),[93] occurs in many later discussions of hysteria.

It can be seen that the Hippocratic texts do indeed work by describing symptoms rather than giving a single disease name to these chapters, and that where they group symptoms and therapies together they do so according to the part of the body to which the womb is believed to have moved. Of these therapies, the recommendation of marriage/pregnancy occurs only in the discussion of womb movement to the hypochondria in *Diseases of Women* 2.128 (L. 8.276), which ends by saying that, after fumigation, the patient should sleep with her husband: "release from this disease, when she is pregnant." Nevertheless, it is this treatment for womb movement that has received most attention in the secondary literature, above all in the work of the psychoanalyst and classicist Bennett Simon, in his *Mind and Madness in Ancient Greece*. This includes a chapter titled "Hysteria and Social Issues," which opens with the familiar error:

"Hysteria, the disease of the 'wandering uterus,' was given its name by the Greeks."[94] Simon's overall approach to hysteria combines that of I. M. Lewis's study of spirit possession, trance, and shamanism, which presents the possessed state as an indirect mode of protest used by powerless and peripheral sectors of society,[95] with a Freudian model. According to what Simon calls a "psychodynamic understanding of hysteria," "a hysterical symptom, for a Greek woman, permitted a safe expression of certain unmet needs," as a result of which expression the doctor would intervene on the woman's behalf as the "wished-for good father."[96] To summarize the "culturally sanctioned dumb show"[97] that Simon envisages, an unmarried or widowed woman is supposed to feel sexually frustrated and to express this frustration by hysteria: the doctor then legitimates her wish by announcing that the cure consists in letting her have what she wants, since it is precisely marriage and childbirth that will make her healthy again.

This approach is inadequate because it shows little understanding of the institutional position of women, the ideal of marriage as universal, the ideal age at first marriage of fourteen for girls, and so on.[98] It also fails to come to terms with the fact that, in most of the texts labeled "Hystérie" by Littré, the marital status of the sufferer is not given[99] or she is explicitly described as married.[100] In his discussion Simon cites only one Hippocratic passage, *Diseases of Women* 2.151 (L 8.326), in which the woman patient is said to suffer in the same way as those who are struck with the sacred disease. In another passage on this last disease, Simon reveals that, like Veith, he has not studied the Greek text of the Hippocratic corpus in sufficient detail. After a brief discussion of the "madness of Heracles," which "was considered by some to be a case of epilepsy,"[101] Simon states, "To my knowledge, the Hippocratic corpus contains no mention of the mythical characters who went mad and were portrayed so vividly on the Athenian stage and in vase painting." However, as I have mentioned above, in *Diseases of Women* 1.7 (L 8.32) the writer states that women with the condition he describes resemble sufferers from "Heracles' disease"; *hypo tēs hērakleiēs nousou,* which Littré translates "aux épileptiques." The characters of myth, who had influenced the folk names of diseases, are thus present even in the Hippocratic corpus.

It is, furthermore, inappropriate to describe hysteria as a "safe expression" of a woman's needs when loss of voice, grinding the teeth, and "movement of the womb to the liver," far from being a safe way of attracting attention, may be the signal for the Hippocratic doctor to tie bandages around the patient's waist, place foul-smelling substances under her nose, insert beetle pessaries, inject hot oil into the womb, or shower her with cold water. As examination of the texts has already shown, and contrary to what Simon implies, marriage and childbirth are rarely the prescribed remedies for this combination of symptoms,[102] and it is also unusual for the remedy to consist of something that could be seen as a form of indirect sexual gratification; for example, fragrant ointments to be rubbed on the vulva[103] or the vaginal insertion of objects specifically described as resembling the male sexual organ.[104] Finally, it is inappropriate to use Simon's "psychodynamic model" when in Hippocratic medicine there is no line drawn between psychological and organic illness.[105]

A similar approach to that of Simon is taken by Rousselle, who states that "Greek women had no legal right to make any decision regarding their own marriage: they could not ask a man to marry them, or even decide that they wanted to be married or to accept an offer of marriage, so it is perhaps not surprising that their impotent anger should take the form of a disease in which their womb was literally suffocating them."[106] D. Gourevitch traces the disappearance of "the hysterical virgin from medical literature" between the Hippocratics and the medicine of the Roman Empire; she attributes this disappearance to institutional change since, if the age at first marriage falls even further, fewer girls will remain to become hysterical.[107]

However, such approaches are rooted in our own society's views on what is normal for a woman, on the nature of hysteria, and on the relationship between medicine and sexuality. Yet for the writers of the Hippocratic texts—and probably for the patients they treat—intercourse and pregnancy rightly belong to the domain of the pharmacopoeia, due to their dramatic and beneficial physical effects. Not only does intercourse moisten the womb, thus discouraging it from moving elsewhere in the body to seek moisture, but it also agitates the body and thus facilitates the passage of blood within it. Furthermore, childbirth breaks down the flesh throughout the body and, by making extra spaces within which excess blood can rest, reduces the pain caused by the movement of blood between parts of the body. It causes complete purgation (*katharsis*) of excess blood and may thus cure many women whose problems originate in menstruation. Since all disorders of women ultimately result from their soft and spongy flesh and excess blood, all disorders of women may be cured by intercourse and/or childbirth, to which marriage and pregnancy are the necessary precursors. There is thus nothing special about the prescription of these in cases of movement of the womb.

Hippocratic medicine thus gives a pharmacological interpretation to what we may be tempted to see as the social processes of marriage and motherhood. We should, of course, never forget that the Greek word for mature woman, *gynē*, also means "wife." Womb movement, however, calls up a battery of other therapies, many of which—like the fumigation described above—make use of foul- and sweet-smelling substances. These therapies lie behind the assertion frequently made in later writers—but not in such authors as Soranus and Galen—that the Hippocratic womb was thought to be an independent living being, fleeing from foul smells but moving to seek out more pleasant odors. We must now decide whether any such belief is necessarily implied by the use of scent therapy.

Such therapy relies on the idea of connections existing between parts of the body, and in particular in the gynecological texts on the presence of a *hodos* or "way" from the nostrils and mouth to the vagina.[108] This is never anatomically described but is implicit in many therapies used. For example, a test to determine whether a woman can conceive involves putting a clove of garlic or another strongly scented substance at one end of the *hodos* and discovering whether the scent reaches the opposite end. If so, there is no obstruction present, and the woman can conceive.[109] Disorders of the womb can also be treated by using the *hodos*. A summary of treatments of the womb in *Diseases of Women* 2.137 mentions the top and the bottom of this tube as appropriate sites for the administration of medication.[110] If the womb has moved upward, foul-smelling substances are held at the nose, pleasant-smelling substances to the vulva, so that the womb is simultaneously repelled from above and attracted down to its correct place.[111] If the womb moves down, or starts to come out of the body through the vulva, foul smells are placed there and sweet smells at the nostrils to draw it up again.[112] There is no explicit discussion of the mechanism by which such therapy is supposed to work.

PLATO AND ARETAEUS: THE WILD WOMB?

It is significant for later medicine that these descriptions of scent therapy also contain no suggestion that the womb is animate; that is, that it is a living being with a desire for sweet smells and a revulsion for foul smells. This brings us to a further important passage, Plato's *Timaeus* 91a–d, a description of the womb as animal, which has been highly influential in the history of hysteria. The womb is seen by Timaeus of Locri as a living creature desiring union, which, if it remains unfruitful (*akarpos*) beyond its proper season, travels around the body blocking passages, obstructing breathing, and causing diseases. C. M. Turbayne says "Plato's account follows that of Hippocrates who, in his *Sicknesses of Women,* coined the word 'hysteria' and ascribed hysteria to the wandering womb." [113] As one would expect, Veith is cited in a footnote. [114] Furthermore, this link between womb and animal is taken by F. Kudlien to be the assumption behind the "well known ancient concept" of uterine suffocation. [115]

Plato lived from about 428 to 347 B.C. and was thus writing at the same time as the authors of *Diseases of Women,* or a few years after. Is it therefore valid to merge his theories with theirs and conclude that the Hippocratic scent therapy necessarily implies the belief that the womb is animate, "a living thing inside another living thing," as the second-century A.D. medical writer Aretaeus later wrote? [116] The difficulty with this approach is that there are clear differences between the gynecology of *Timaeus* and that of the Hippocratic corpus, and there is ample evidence that the idea of the womb being—or being like—an animal was disputed even in antiquity. Its best-known expression, apart from the passage in *Timaeus,* is in Aretaeus, who states that movement of the womb mostly affects younger women, whose way of life and judgment are "somewhat wandering" so that their womb is "roving" (*rhembodēs*). Older women have a "more stable" way of life, judgment, and womb. This in itself varies from the Hippocratic theories, which tend to link movement of the womb with *older* women, whose wombs are lighter. [117] It is in this section too that Aretaeus describes the womb as *hokoion ti zōon en zōōi,* usually translated as "like some animal inside an animal" but which could be less emotively rendered "like a living thing inside another living thing."

It has been suggested that the words of Aretaeus are based on a recollection of having read *Timaeus* at school: [118] as may be seen from the work of Soranus, also writing in the second-century A.D., this was certainly a very outdated idea in second-century medicine. Soranus explicitly rejects the claim of "some people" that the womb is an animal, although he admits that in some ways it behaves as if it were, for example, in responding to cooling and loosening drugs. He reinterprets the success of therapy involving sweet- or foul-smelling substances to attract or repel the womb, saying that these work not because the womb is like a wild animal emerging to seek pleasant scents and fleeing from foul ones, but because the scents cause relaxation or constriction. [119] Galen, writing shortly after Soranus, discusses and rejects what he regards not as Hippocrates' but as Plato's theory of the womb as a living creature in *On the Affected Parts* 6.5. After quoting from *Timaeus* he writes, "These were Plato's words. But some [physicians] added that, when the uterus during its irregular movement through the body touches the diaphragm, it interferes with the respiratory [movements]. Others deny that the uterus wanders around like an animal. When it is dried up by the suppression of menstrual flow, it extends quickly to the viscera, being anxious to attract moisture. But when it makes contact with the diaphragm during its ascent, it suppresses the respiration of the organism."[120]

It is thus clear from Soranus and Galen that, at least by the second century A.D., medical opinion was split on whether womb movement necessarily entailed assigning the status of "living thing" or "wild animal" to the womb. It may further be questioned whether Plato's account— or, perhaps, the Locrian's account, since it is by no means certain that the passage represents Plato's own views[121]—is in any way following the Hippocratic *Diseases of Women,* as Turbayne argues. In general, *Timaeus* shows a strong humoral theory of disease in which the four humors are linked to the four elements: earth, air, fire, and water. The use of humoral theory in the *Diseases of Women* is minimal, perhaps because the female body is so heavily dominated by blood.

The description of the womb and of conception in *Timaeus* should be read in the context provided by the preceding sections on the human body, which show that analogies in which certain parts of the body are compared to living creatures are common in *Timaeus.* That part of the soul which is concerned with bodily desires is tied up in the body "like a wild creature";[122] a disease is described as being like a *zōon,* in that it has a natural span of life.[123] At the start of the second generation of mankind, all those who have proved cowardly or unjust in the first become women; it is at this point that the gods put into *all* human beings a *zōon* that desires sexual union. In males, the penis has a disobedient and self-willed nature, "like a *zōon*" and, like the savage part of the soul, it does not obey reason, the *logos.*[124] When the womb is described, all that is different is that it is no longer put beside the *zōon* in a simile, but appears in a metaphoric relationship; not "like a living thing," but "a living thing desiring to bear children."[125] In both cases what is significant is that the organ moves independently of the will, in an uncontrolled way. Since Plato/Timaeus has already mixed apparently nonfigurative uses of *zōon* (the gods put a living creature in all humans) with obvious similes (the penis is like a *zōon*), it would be unwise to make too much of the way in which the womb is described. It should also be noted that animal analogies are used elsewhere for the organs. Not only woman is thought to have a *zōon* inside her, since Plato himself likens the penis to an animal, and in Aristotle it is the heart that is like an animal, this in turn being likened to the genitals in a further analogy.[126]

In men, the *zōon empsychon* that makes the penis behave "like an ani-

mal" is in the seed, which comes from the spinal marrow.[127] The theory
of the origin of the semen is consistent with Hippocratic anatomy, which
traces its path up the spinal cord, behind the ears and to the head.[128]
In the description of the corresponding part in woman, the womb,
there are however some obvious differences from Hippocratic theories.
Timaeus says that in coitus minute invisible and shapeless *zōa* are sown
in the womb, where they will grow to maturity. Apart from the very general sowing analogy, this does not correspond to anything in the corpus;
indeed, in the Hippocratic *Generation* 6 and 8, both male and female contribute seed, the sex of the child being determined by the strongest
seed.[129]

Aretaeus's analogy is thus not characteristic of the medicine of his
time but, on the contrary, stands out as an anachronism: Plato's (or
Timaeus's) medicine, while sharing some anatomical features with Hippocratic theories, demonstrates many individual points. Galen and Soranus mention the belief that the womb is not just *like* an animal, but
is an animal, yet Galen ascribes this only to Plato. From the list of treatments of which he disapproves, Soranus apparently thinks that the use
of scents in therapy tends to imply the belief that the womb is an animal.
However, the central role of scent therapy in disorders of the womb in
the Hippocratic texts does not mean that the Hippocratic writers would
inevitably have regarded the womb as an independent animate part of
the body; as Soranus's own explanation of why scent therapy works
shows, it would be possible to use this technique within an entirely different conceptual framework, openly rejecting the animate womb theory.

I would also question whether we would be so ready to read into Hippocratic medicine ideas of the womb as an animal, were it not for the
influence of the imagery of *Timaeus* on Aretaeus and on other writers
to the extent that Galen finds it necessary to refute the theory. Our own
medical theories play a part in this: because it is self-evident to us that
the womb not only is not a living creature, but also cannot move around
the body, any suggestion that it does so move is startling, demands explanation, and may be given more weight than it deserves.

STIFLING AND SUFFOCATION:
THE DEVELOPMENT OF THE TEXTUAL TRADITION

In my discussion of the ways in which the Hippocratics classify disease,
I have emphasized that the disease label hysteria, far from being applied
in these texts for the first time, is a much later invention. The developing
hysteria tradition uses only a selection of the Hippocratic texts on womb

movement; within this selection, it ignores the disagreement on such matters as the most susceptible category of woman, and the variation in symptoms according to the part of the body that the womb reaches in its quest for moisture. It also takes and merges distinctive images and therapies from these texts, regardless of their relative importance in Hippocratic medicine.

In the texts used to support this developing tradition, the symptom that stands out, and that is indeed sometimes used to introduce the Hippocratic disease description, is *pnix,* usually translated as suffocation. It is now necessary to consider the significance of this symptom in some detail. If we are to take seriously Shorter's suggestions that "the presentation of 'hysterical' symptoms tends to be molded by the surrounding culture" and that we should therefore be asking why "certain symptoms are selected in certain epochs,"[130] we need to reject our fascination with womb movement—which was, after all, seen as unproblematic by classical Greek writers—and instead explore the implications of *pnix* in the very specific context of classical Greek medicine.

In his recent history of hysteria, Trillat poses a very pertinent question: is it the womb or the woman who suffocates in these texts?[131] He suggests that this is not clear from the Hippocratic texts; however, unlike the Littré translation, the Greek text is often relatively straightforward on this issue, due partly to the convention by which Hippocratic writers often used plural terms for the womb. This enables us to see that, although in some cases it is the woman who suffers from the *pnix,*[132] it is generally the *womb* that is "stifled"; for example, "When the womb (sing.) stifles"; "If the womb (plural) arrives at the heart and stifles (plural)."[133] I am proposing the translation "stifles" rather than "suffocates" for reasons that will shortly become clear.

In order to grasp the implications of *pnix,* the stifled womb that in turn stifles the woman, it is necessary to return to the question of what the Hippocratic writers—and the culture within which they practiced—understood to be the nature of woman. "Not only was the cause of hysteria rooted in the very nature of being female, but also in the belief that that nature was prone to disorder": thus W. Mitchinson, in a recent article on nineteenth-century Canadian medicine.[134] This interest in nature takes on a different coloring in the key hysteria text of the early seventeenth century, Edward Jorden on "the suffocation of the mother," which was written to show that this disorder should not be "imputed to the Divell" but rather has "its true naturall causes."[135]

In Jorden's sense, nature is also fundamental to the Hippocratic texts. One of the achievements of Hippocratic medicine which it is commonplace to admire is its movement away from explaining disease as *divine* in origin—the result of displeasing a deity, as in the opening of the *Iliad,* or of failing to fulfill a ritual obligation—in favor of *natural* explanations.[136] The Hippocratic text usually quoted in this context is *On the Sacred Disease,* in which the alarming symptoms of epilepsy are shown to have a natural explanation, making it no more and no less sacred than any other disease. In the Hippocratic *Diseases of Women* 2.151[137] an explicit comparison is drawn between a group of symptoms classified by Littré as hysteria and the sacred disease. It would be wrong to conclude from this that medical writers in the ancient world had correctly understood the similarity between the mechanisms by which these two disorders, as we define them, are produced; what is important is the suggestion that there is a natural explanation not only for the symptoms produced by womb movement but also for that movement itself.[138]

For the history of medicine, it does not matter that the "natural" explanations given—the movement of the womb around the body, the constitution of the female—are ones in which we do not believe; what is important is that nature, not the gods, is thought to be responsible. There is however a further aspect of the production of the symptoms which explains why they naturally affect only women; women, by nature, have wombs, and "the womb"—implying both "not the gods" and "no other part of the body"—"is the origin of all diseases" according to the Hippocratic text *Places in Man.*[139] Menstruation is, as the second-century A.D. writer Soranus puts it, "the first function" of the womb,[140] and the writer of the Hippocratic text *Nature of the Child* describes as "simply a fact of her original constitution" the naturally wetter and more spongy flesh of the female which makes a woman produce excess blood.[141] This blood moves to the womb every month prior to leaving the body in that flow that is, among other names, called *hē physis,* "nature,"[142] or *ta kata physin,* "the natural things."[143]

For the Hippocratic writers, then, menstruation and nature are synonyms; all diseases of women come from the womb and thus from the nature of female flesh, the wet and spongy texture of which causes the accumulation of large amounts of blood, making menstruation necessary to female health. As *Generation* 4 puts it, "if the menses do not flow, the bodies of women become sick."[144]

The symptom of *pnix* arises from the nature of woman. There is some disagreement in the ancient medical writers as to whether women are by nature hot or cold. For Aristotle, whose ideas on this point were historically more influential than those of the Hippocratics, women are cold, too cold to concoct blood into semen.[145] Difficulties arise with this position because, in humoral pathology, blood is hot and wet. If women have more blood than men, surely they should be hotter than men? In the debate given by Plutarch in *Moralia*,[146] a doctor takes up precisely this position in order to argue that women are the hotter sex; this is also the argument used to prove women's hot natures by "Parmenides and others," according to Aristotle,[147] and a related argument appears in the Hippocratic *Diseases of Women* 1.1,[148] which says that "the woman has hotter blood, and because of this she is hotter than the man."

It is however possible to argue that women are cold, despite their excess blood. Other speakers in the Plutarch passage claim that menstrual blood is not normal, "hot" blood, but a cold and corrupt form. The Hippocratic writer of *Regimen* 1.34 does not go this far; he accepts that menstrual blood is hot but argues that, since they purge the hot every month, women end up being cold![149]

There is also a third option; the womb, due to the way in which its role in conception and gestation is imagined, can be classed as hot, whether or not the menstrual blood or the woman herself is considered cold. Aristotle, for whom women are cold, can thus retain the traditional analogy by which the womb is compared to an oven.[150] This analogy appears in a wide range of types of source material. By committing necrophilia, the tyrant Periander of Corinth was—in the words of the historian Herodotus—"putting his loaves into a cold oven."[151] In the *Dream Book* of Artemidorus, an important source for ancient imagery, a hearth (*hestia*) and a baking-oven (*klibanos*) can represent women, because they receive things that produce life. Dreaming of seeing fire in a hearth means that your wife will become pregnant.[152] In the Hippocratic texts *Generation* and *Nature of the Child* there are several occasions in which the womb is described in terms of the heat it generates, in one of which the embryo is compared to bread baking in an oven. Intercourse heats the blood and thus produces heat in the whole body, and the development of the seed in the womb is due to its being in "a warm environment."[153] Whether women are classified as hot or cold, they have within them an oven to heat the seed.

How should this influence our understanding of *pnix*? The sensations of suffocation and stifling are not necessarily identical. Suffocation implies an obstacle preventing breathing; in this it resembles strangulation but, whereas the former suggests to us something over the mouth and nose, the latter suggests something around the neck. Stifling additionally implies heat, which is why it is to be preferred as a translation of *pnix*. Overlap is of course possible, since pressure around the neck or over the mouth may also cause a feeling of heat. Greek words related to *pnix*, such as *pnigos* and *pnigmos,* mean stifling heat, while a *pnigeus* is an oven. Support for the importance of heat in *pnix* in the period of the Hippocratic texts may be gained from Aristophanes' play *Frogs,* in which the god Dionysus asks the hero Heracles for a way to Hades which is neither too hot nor too cold. Heracles suggests "by rope and stool"—that is, to hang oneself. Dionysus replies, "No, that's stifling."[154] Heracles goes on to suggest hemlock, which is rejected as "too cold." The use of a hot/cold opposition again associates *pnix* with heat.

It is thus because the Hippocratic writers have absorbed the traditional and powerful image of womb as oven that they associate its movement with the production of excess heat. This suggests a further aspect of the common recommendation of pregnancy as the best cure for many disorders of the womb; if nothing is cooking in a woman's oven, its heat will overwhelm her in some way unless something is done to use up that heat. The underlying image of womb as oven in these texts could account for other symptoms. Women with *pnix* feel cold at their extremities, perhaps because all their body heat moves toward the womb.

In the cultural context of Hippocratic medicine, *pnix* thus implies something more than "difficulty in breathing." It points us to something fundamental to that culture's image of the female, as an oven in which the seed is cooked. The supposed movement of that oven to other parts of the body in search of moisture to dampen down the fire can therefore be seen as causing heat in the affected part; the womb itself is stifled, and this can be transmitted to the woman sufferer. Being a woman, for the Greeks of this period, means having an oven inside you; an oven that is a natural—and socially acceptable—target when a physical cause is sought for dramatic somatic manifestations.[155]

I have already demonstrated the variations within the Hippocratic corpus on such questions as the heat or coolness of the woman and the most likely category to suffer from womb movement. There is one Hippocratic passage in which *pnix* is explicitly linked to physical obstruction of breath. This is *Diseases of Women* 1.7, in which the womb, dried out by fatigue, moves to the liver because this organ is full of moisture. The result is sudden *pnix,* due to what is described as the interruption of the route of the breath through the belly. It is this etiology, rather than the general image of woman, or womb, as hot, which is taken up by later writers seeking to account for *pnix.* However, due to their general beliefs about the role of breath, heat still plays a part in such theories.

In later classical medicine *pnix* apparently becomes simply obstruction of respiration; however, nothing in the history of medicine is really simple. The implications of the shift in terminology require further exploration of the conceptual universe of these writers, since respiration itself does not have the meaning we would most naturally assume.

The difficulty of using words such as respiration, veins, arteries, and pulse is that we regularly employ them within an anatomy and physiology completely different from those of ancient writers. Furthermore, theories of breathing, nutrition, and blood movement were themselves changed many times before William Harvey, and not necessarily as part of a linear process of experiment and discovery. To translate the Hippocratic *phlebs* (channel) as "vein" is to imply it is different from another sort of channel that is an "artery." The distinction between arteries and veins was probably first made by Praxagoras of Cos in the late fourth century B.C., not in the context of an emerging theory of the circulation of the blood around the body, but instead because he believed blood and pneuma traveled through different systems.[156]

Respiration is an excellent example of these difficulties, which also allows us to look at the presentation of hysteria in one of the immediately post-Hippocratic writers most relevant for the hysteria tradition: the fourth-century B.C. philosopher Heracleides of Pontus (ca. 390–310 B.C.). Although we may use respiration to mean breathing in general, behind the word inevitably lies our knowledge of the process by which oxygen is taken in and carbon dioxide given out. If we translate the title of a treatise by Galen, *De usu respirationis,* as "On the use of respiration," it may be difficult for us to appreciate the implications of the term within the science of the second century A.D. and before. A theory once widely held however is that of skin-breathing, discussed from before the time of Hippocrates to that of Galen. In the mid-fifth century B.C., the philosopher Empedocles proposed that all living things breathe through the pores of their skin.[157] Plato preserves a version of skin-breathing that also accounts for the movement of blood in the body; air enters through the skin to replace that exhaled through the nose and mouth, while also entering through the nose and mouth to replace that exhaled through the skin. The resulting movement, rather than the heart, is thought to be responsible for sending blood to those parts of the body requiring its nutriment.[158] When Galen uses words for respiration, he includes within it skin-breathing.

Aristotle suggests that the function of respiration is to cool the innate heat generated in the body by food; Galen goes further, arguing that breathing occurs "for the sake of the innate heat" and, elsewhere, that "the use of breathing is the conservation of the innate heat."[159] By this he means that breathing regulates the innate heat either by fanning it or by cooling it.

Skin-breathing and innate heat play an important role in Galen's theory of "hysterical suffocation," especially in relation to a story that becomes part of the hysteria tradition: the apparently dead woman whose revival is described in a lost work by Heracleides of Pontus. In his discussion of the most severe form of hysterical suffocation in *On the Affected Parts* 6.5 Galen refers to this story as follows:

> For [Heracleides] says that that woman who had neither breath nor pulse could only be distinguished from a corpse in one way: that is, that she had a little warmth around the middle part of her body.[160]

After Heracleides, Galen says, doctors developed tests for the presence of life: wool held at the nose, or a vessel of water on the navel. In the later tradition a deep concern remains over the ability of hysteria to mimic death—particularly since one of the symptoms is supposed to be the absence of any pulse—and stories are told of women mistaken for dead who revive on the edge of the grave.[161] Although *Apnous* is lost, the story of the woman is repeated in several other writers of antiquity. The closest to Galen in both wording and time is Diogenes Laertius, a writer of the third century A.D., who states that the woman's body was *apnoun kai asphykton*, "without breath or pulse," for thirty days. As well as this last detail, Diogenes Laertius adds further information about the circumstances, and this is duplicated in other writers.[162] The story told by Heracleides apparently concerns Empedocles, who told his friend Pausanias how he had realized the woman was not dead from observing the innate heat. Clearly she was able to breathe through her skin, and eventually recovered, much to the amazement of the onlookers who attributed this to a miracle performed by Empedocles.

This story was very popular in the sixteenth century; one medical writer of that period who used it was Pieter van Foreest. Instead of following Diogenes Laertius, who said that the woman was without breath or pulse for thirty days, he uses the version given prior to Galen, by Pliny in the first century A.D.[163] This sets the story within a discussion of souls that leave the body and return to it, which is in turn followed by accounts of people who recovered from apparent death. Pliny writes, "This topic is the subject of a book by Heracleides, well known in Greece, about a woman who was seven days without breath but was called back to life." Van Foreest repeats the "seven days" as well as Pliny's remark that "the female sex seems particularly liable to this disease, since it is subject to turning of the womb."[164] In his *scholia* on this section, van Foreest follows Galen's theory on the innate heat, which is also used to account for the coldness of the extremities. He then states that learned authorities all agree that patients with this condition should not be buried until the *third* day.[165] Why should he give the third, rather than using seven or thirty? Perhaps the solution is to be found in the use of the story in early Christian writing. Origen (ca. A.D. 185–ca. A.D. 254) refers unbelievers to it in the context of Christ's resurrection from the dead: although Origen does not say how long the woman in the story in Heracleides lay dead, the figure of three days may come from this analogy.[166]

Galen was thus not the only ancient writer to associate the story with a condition of the womb; however, where Pliny merely says that women are more likely to suffer in this way because their wombs move, Galen gives a full etiology accepting the theories of innate heat and skin-breathing.

GALEN AND HIS INFLUENCE:
WINNERS AND LOSERS IN THE TEXTUAL TRADITION

Thus far, this chapter has covered the Hippocratic origins of the hysteria tradition in detail, while also mentioning the distinctive contributions of a small group of other writers: notably Plato and the second-century A.D. medical writers Aretaeus, Soranus, and Galen. It is however important to consider the question of the significant period between the fifth/fourth century B.C., when the Hippocratic texts used here were being written, and the second century A.D. This is not an easy question to address. For the period immediately after the Hippocratics, literary medical sources are sparse. Works cited in later writers have not survived; we often read the extant fragments through the hostile eyes of an opponent, so that it is difficult not only to trace and date significant changes, but even to know what exactly was written.

Heracleides of Pontus (390–310 B.C.), whose lost work *Apnous*—mentioned by Pliny, Galen, and Diogenes Laertius among others—has already been discussed, is the only fourth-century writer other than Plato who is incorporated into the hysteria tradition. Other writers of the period are briefly introduced to the tradition, only to be rejected. Thus, for example, Soranus describes and criticizes the therapy used for hysterical *pnix* by Diocles of Carystos, who also worked in the fourth century B.C.; he "pinches the nostrils, but opens the mouth and applies a sternutative; moreover, with the hand he presses the uterus toward the lower parts by pressing upon the hypochondriac region; and applies warm fomentations to the legs."[167]

In the third century B.C. important advances in anatomy were made in association with the medical school of Alexandria; the work of Herophilus of Chalcedon in particular is said to have included dissection of animal and human subjects, neither of which was practiced by the Hippocratics. For the history of hysteria, even more important than the fact that Herophilus is credited with being the first to identify the Fallopian tubes and ovaries is the attribution to him of the first description of the ligaments (which he called membranes) anchoring the womb in the abdominal cavity, a discovery which, in a positivist science, would have proved false the theory that the womb is capable of movement around the body.[168]

No discussion by Herophilus of suffocation caused by the womb survives. His follower Mantias, who lived from around 165 to 90 B.C., wrote on pharmacology, and one of the two surviving fragments of his work with a gynecological theme concerns hysterical suffocation. This fragment too is transmitted in the work of Soranus, who tells us that Mantias recommended playing flutes and drums when an attack was imminent, and giving castoreum and bitumen with wine when an attack was over. It is interesting that the discovery of the "membranes" does not appear to have significantly changed the therapy.[169]

A further source for the period from the third to the first centuries B.C. consists of the surviving papyrus fragments from Greco-Roman Egypt, giving recipes, some of which may be identified as originating in the Hippocratic corpus. One very ancient collection of recipes, largely based on *Diseases of Women* and dating to the third or second century B.C., mentions "suffocation from the womb" but recommends dried otters' kidneys in sweet wine—the only time this recipe occurs in Greek literature.[170] A further recipe is given for a cough after the suffocation. Another papyrus dated to around 260–230 B.C. is too fragmentary for any reconstruction of the recipe, but it concerns a "hysterical woman" (*gynē hysterikē*); in the following line it is possible to read the word *pnigmos*.[171] A papyrus from the early first century B.C. is even less legible, but the editor's reconstruction includes the words *hysterikai* and *hysterikais*.[172] Papyri therefore show that Hippocratic recipes and variations on them continued to circulate in the ancient world; taken with the fragment of Mantias, they give further support to the proposal that the disease category *hysterikē pnix* existed as a diagnosis in the second century B.C.

The next significant literary source comes from the Roman world: Celsus, writing in the early first century A.D. Book 4 of his work is arranged according to the parts of the body, and includes a chapter on diseases of the womb.[173] This begins with a description of an unnamed but violent (*vehemens*) illness that comes from the womb, an organ Celsus regarded as second only to the stomach in its influence on the rest of the body. The condition he describes takes away the breath, so that the woman falls down as if she had epilepsy; however, unlike in epilepsy, the eyes are not "turned," there is no frothing at the mouth, and the sinews are not stretched. Instead, the patient sleeps. Some women suffer from this throughout their lives. Celsus does not investigate the etiology of the condition, but he gives recommendations for treatment: venesection, cupping-glasses, an extinguished lamp wick or other strong-smelling material held to the nostrils, cold water poured over the patient, hot wet poultices, and massage of the hips and knees. To prevent further attacks he recommends that the woman should abstain from wine for a year, be massaged regularly, and put mustard on her lower abdomen daily so that the skin reddens. He adds some suggestions for emollients, drinks (including castoreum), purges, and fumigations.

Some of this material is familiar; the cold water, lamp wick, and castoreum, for example, are no different from the Hippocratic recommendations, nor is the concern to distinguish the condition from epilepsy. Other suggestions are new; in particular, venesection, although used in the Hippocratic corpus, has not previously been discussed in association with this condition. As P. Brain has recently shown, although Galen gives the impression that venesection was a common therapy in the Hippocratic texts, it is in fact found only about seventy times in the entire corpus, and *Diseases of Women* contributes only one example.[174] In Soranus it is recommended for hysterical suffocation, while for Galen it is the remedy of choice for menstrual suppression.[175]

In the second century A.D. three medical descriptions of hysterical suffocation were produced, of differing importance to the growth of the hysteria tradition. By far the most influential in subsequent centuries was the work of Galen of Pergamum, although his triumph was not complete until after the eleventh century A.D., when the translation of Arabic texts into Latin returned Galenic theory to the West. Until that time, although Arabic physicians were heavily influenced by Galenism, the many short gynecological treatises produced in the West were largely based on Soranus's *Gynecology*. However, this work was also disseminated in the East, through the Byzantine encyclopedists who used Soranus for their gynecological summaries. Its subsequent fortunes have been influenced by the fact that, although writers such as the sixth-century Aetius used it extensively, it survives in just one manuscript: the late fifteenth-century Paris BN gr. 2153 (Paris, Bibliothèque National, Greek manuscript number 2153), only discovered and identified by Dietz in 1830. The second-century writer most heavily influenced by Hippocratic sources was however neither Galen nor Soranus, but Aretaeus of Cappadocia, who had considerably less impact than either of the others on the later history of hysteria. Neither Soranus nor Aretaeus was translated into Arabic; nor, however, were the Hippocratic *Diseases of Women* and *Nature of Woman,* so that the Arabic descriptions of uterine suffocation derive from the Galenic version and its later interpreters: Oribasius, Aetius of Amida, and Paul of Aegina. The triumph of Hippocrates over Galen was delayed until the availability of printed Latin editions of the Hippocratic texts in the late sixteenth century.[176] I now propose to look in turn at the texts of Aretaeus, Soranus, and Galen, establishing their contribution to the tradition, before turning to their use in late antiquity and beyond.

As has been discussed above, the description of *hysterikē pnix* in Aretaeus's *Of the Causes and Symptoms of Acute Diseases* is today best known for its description of the womb as being "like an animal inside an animal," less emotively rendered as "like one living thing inside another." Like the Hippocratic writers, Aretaeus not only believes that the womb can move within the body but also advocates scent therapy, in which foul odors such as pitch, burned hair, an extinguished lamp, or castoreum are applied to the nose and fragrant substances rubbed into the external genitalia; unlike them, however, he knows of the membranes anchoring the womb in place.[177] To us, the children of the "scientific method," these points may seem contradictory, but Aretaeus manages to combine them.

He describes the womb—"the seat of womanhood itself"—as being "all but alive," moving of its own volition upward to the thorax, or to left or right within the lower abdomen. It is when it moves upward and remains there for a long time, pressing violently on the intestines, that the patient experiences *pnix,* described as being like epilepsy[178] without the spasms. Pressure is put on the liver, diaphragm, lungs, and heart, causing loss of breath and voice, while the carotid arteries are squeezed as a result of "sympathy" with the heart, causing a heavy head, loss of sensation, and deep sleep. Aretaeus then mentions a similar condition, characterized by *pnix* and loss of voice, which does not arise from the womb; the two differ in that only in cases arising in the womb will scent therapy help, and only in these cases do the limbs move.

When the womb moves up the body there will be "hesitation in doing her tasks, exhaustion, loss of control of the knees, dizziness, and her limbs are weakened; headache, heaviness of the head; and the woman feels pain in the channels at either side of her nose."[179] The pulse will be weak and irregular, the breathing imperceptible, and death follows suddenly; it is difficult to believe that it has occurred, since the patient has such a lifelike appearance. Recovery, too, happens suddenly; the womb rises up very easily, and just as easily returns to its place. Here Aretaeus uses another image, as vivid as that of the "living thing inside another living thing": the womb sails high in the water like a tree trunk floating, but it is pulled back by its membranes, of which those joining the neck of the womb to the loins are particularly capable of distending and contracting in a way that is likened to the sails of a ship.[180] The condition is more likely to affect young women, since their way of life and understanding are "wandering," less firmly based.

Aretaeus thus combines womb movement with anchoring membranes, while continuing the exploration of a number of key themes in the hysteria tradition; for example, the difficulty in telling whether a sufferer from this condition is dead or alive, and the resemblance to epilepsy. Although much of the therapeutic material is Hippocratic, in particular the use of scent therapy, fumigation, and sneezing,[181] he follows Celsus rather than the Hippocratics in recommending venesection from the ankle, while adding that one should pull out hairs from the patient in order to rouse her.[182] He introduces the idea of "sympathy" in order to explain how the highest parts of the body can be affected by the womb; although the membranes prevent it from traveling that far, the womb can nevertheless exert an influence on these parts.

The survival of such Hippocratic ideas in the late antique and medieval worlds will be discussed later. However, as I have already mentioned, the main influence on late antiquity came from Soranus, the Hippocratics being read largely through the eyes of Galen until the mid-sixteenth century and beyond.[183] Sections of Soranus's work were translated from Greek into Latin by Caelius Aurelianus in the fifth century, and—more important in terms of his later influence—by Muscio in the sixth century, thus making his ideas available in the Latin-speaking West. As for the Greek East, Soranus was the main source for the gynecological sections of the encyclopedias of Aetius of Amida in the mid-sixth century and Paul of Aegina in the seventh century, becoming in the East "la bible de la gynécologie et de l'obstétrique jusqu'à la Renaissance."[184] What did Soranus contribute to the textual reservoir drawn on by the hysteria tradition?

The ideas of Soranus, in contrast to those of Aretaeus, are set in the context of the theories of the "methodist" medical sect. This arose in the first century A.D. in response to the dogmatist and empiricist positions. The fundamental difference between the latter two sects lay in their beliefs concerning the best way of acquiring knowledge. Where the dogmatists, despite some differences of opinion, agreed on the use of observation, dissection, and experiments in order to speculate on the "hidden causes" of diseases, the empiricists believed that no form of research could ever lead to an understanding of nature, and thus that the only route to knowledge was through the accumulated experience of past cases, which the practitioner could combine with his own experience in order to choose the correct therapy. Where the dogmatist was interested in causes, the empiricist looked for cures.

Methodism, in contrast to these sects, was based on a strict division of causes of symptoms into three conditions of the body: *status laxus,* in which the body or affected part is lax and wet, leading for example to a flux; *status strictus,* a constricted and dry state, of which amenorrhea was seen as a case in point; and *status mixtus,* a combination in which some parts of the body are constricted and others lax. Treatment characteristically began with a three-day fast, then built up the patient through diet and exercise, before moving on to aggressive treatments such as vomiting, shaking, or sneezing.[185]

While Soranus is never a slave to the "method,"[186] it is methodist theory that leads him to reject some commonplaces of Hippocratic medicine. For example, there is no place in the method for Hippocratic ideas of the superiority of right over left. Nor does Soranus accept the theory that the female body is qualitatively different from the male in terms of the porosity of its flesh; women are the same as men, except that they have some different organs, but even these organs are made of the same substance and subject to the same conditions. As a result of this reasoning, there is no place in Soranus's gynecology for the Hippocratic theory that menstruation is essential to female health as a means of purging the excess blood that naturally accumulates due to the wet and spongy consistency of female flesh. On the contrary, Soranus goes so far as to say that menstruation is bad for a woman's health, except insofar as it is necessary to conception. Intercourse is harmful, and permanent virginity is best for both men and women. Pregnancy, thought by earlier writers to relieve certain gynecological disorders, is in fact bad for women; it leads to exhaustion and premature old age.

Soranus also rejects the Hippocratic idea that the womb moves to other parts of the body. The womb cannot move; although he rejects dissection in principle, he quotes Herophilus of Chalcedon's research as proof that it is held in place by membranes.[187] Soranus nevertheless accepts that there is a condition in which the major symptom is *pnix,* but he attributes it to inflammation of the membranes around the womb causing a *status strictus.*[188] In particular he rejects any idea that the womb is an animal; it "does not issue forth like a wild animal from the lair, delighted by fragrant odors and fleeing bad odors,"[189] and he attributes this misunderstanding to its ability to respond to certain agents by stricture or relaxation. In treating the condition, he completely rejects the usual list of substances employed in scent therapy (they cause torpor and upset the stomach), together with sneezing (too violent) and intercourse; sexual intercourse cannot cure disease, since it has such bad effects on even a healthy body. Venesection is acceptable, however, after the patient has been warmed and rubbed with olive oil in order to relax her. The condition exists in both an acute and a chronic form, and treatment should take account of this.[190]

While the gynecological theories of Soranus continued to circulate widely in both East and West through their use by the encyclopedists, the dominant influence on medicine as a whole in the Greek East was not Soranus but Galen. Where suffocation of the womb is concerned, Galen's descriptions eclipsed those of Soranus; writing as late as 1937, P. Diepgen describes Galen's picture of the hysterical attack as still being recognizable.[191]

In his treatise *On the Affected Parts*, Galen himself calls the condition either *hysterikē pnix* or *apnoia hysterikē*, "absence of breath caused by the womb." Aretaeus had managed to combine the anchoring membranes with movement of the womb, while Soranus rejected womb movement and attributed the symptoms to inflammation of the membranes; Galen's new etiology was, however, to prove the most influential in the history of hysteria. He accepts that the womb is indeed the origin of the condition, but in place of movement to another part of the body, or inflammation, he blames retention of substances within the womb. The disorder manifests itself in a number of different forms—sometimes through lying motionless with an almost imperceptible pulse, sometimes through weakness while the patient remains conscious, and sometimes through contracture of the limbs.[192]

A much-quoted section of *On the Affected Parts* reads: "I myself have seen many *hysterikai* women, as they call themselves and as the *iatrinai* call them."[193] *Iatrinai*, literally "female healers," may also be translated as midwives. *Hysterikai* is usually translated as "hysterical" but, in view of what has already been said about ancient medical terminology, it would be more accurately translated as "suffering from the womb." In a recent article, Trillat attaches great significance to this passage. As has already been mentioned, Trillat recognizes that the word *hysteria* never appears in the Hippocratic corpus; however, on the basis of this passage of Galen, he asserts that it is in Galen's work "qu'apparait le mot d'hystérie," albeit in adjectival form.[194] Of course, this is not particularly significant since, as I have already shown, the adjective *hysterikos* also appears in the Hippocratic corpus. However, Trillat goes on to use the Galenic passage as the basis for his statement, "Hippocrate adopte la théorie populaire et rejette le nom. Galien rejette la théorie mais adopte le nom" (Hippocrates adopts the popular theory and rejects the name. Galen rejects the theory but adopts the name).

This raises many questions. There is little evidence for the theory of the wandering womb in classical Greek "popular thought" apart from Plato's *Timaeus,* and Plato is hardly the Greek equivalent of the man on the Clapham omnibus. In the Roman Empire of Galen, there may be better grounds for believing that women described themselves as *hysterica.* A relevant passage from outside the medical corpus is Martial, *Epigrams* 11.71, where Leda tells her aged husband she is *hysterica* as a device to make him summon young doctors to carry out what was then thought to be the standard treatment, sexual intercourse. Moreover, can we accept that it is Galen who "adopte le nom"? We have already seen that the evidence of papyri from the third and second centuries B.C., taken with the fragment of Mantias preserved in Soranus, suggests on the contrary that the category *hysterikē pnix* existed at least four hundred years before Galen. Indeed, elsewhere Galen distances himself not only from the word *hysterikos*—referring to "the so-called hysterical symptoms"—but also from *pnix,* saying that *apnoia,* absence of breath, is a more appropriate term.[195]

The passage from Martial is also of interest in that Galen too—unlike Soranus—regards sexual intercourse as beneficial for sufferers, and in his new etiology of the condition this therapy, mentioned in the Hippocratic corpus but only as one of many recommendations for suffocation caused by the womb, is given a central role. He considers that those most vulnerable to the disorder are "widows, and particularly those who previously menstruated regularly, had been pregnant and were eager to have intercourse, but were now deprived of all this."[196] This passage is interesting, not only because it omits the childless, seen as particularly susceptible in several Hippocratic texts, but also because it points Galen toward the cause of the problem. He does not accept the Hippocratic etiology of womb movement in search of moisture, since dissection proves that it cannot occur; the womb may *seem* to move, but "it does not move from one place to another like a wandering animal, but is pulled up by the tension" of the membranes holding it in place.[197]

Why do these membranes become tense? He suggests that it is because they are filled with menstrual blood, unable to move into the womb either because of its thickness or because the orifices through which the blood passes into the womb are closed. Thus one cause of the condition is menstrual retention. This is not however the origin of the most severe form of *hysterikē pnix*. Galen believes that women too contribute "seed"; this is not an entirely new idea, since some Hippocratic writers believed in its existence. For Galen, female seed does not elevate the female to an equal position with the male, since it is naturally inferior to male seed.[198] Seed too can be retained in the womb, where it presents far more of a threat to health than retained menses.[199] Galen goes on to compare the effect of such retained substances to that of the bite or sting of a poisonous creature; small amounts cause dramatic and possibly fatal symptoms.[200] Retained seed can rot, causing noxious humors to affect the rest of the body through "sympathy"; for Galen, as for Aretaeus, this is how the breathing can be affected without the womb moving to put physical pressure on the diaphragm. It is an infinitely malleable concept that can claim Hippocratic credentials: *On Joints* (57) describes the "brotherly connections" that exist between parts of the body, permitting, among other things, the wanderings of the womb.[201] Thus, where the Hippocratics attributed different groups of symptoms to the different organs to which the womb could move, Galen suggests that the basic cause is retained matter, different symptoms owing most to the nature of this matter; for example, black bile leads to despondency.[202]

Monica Green has pointed out that it is of particular interest that, despite his rejection of the belief that the womb is a wandering animal, Galen nevertheless manages to retain the use of the full scent therapy. *On the Method of Healing, to Glaucon* includes a brief reference to its use in treating a "rising" womb, while in another treatise Galen lists substances—including castoreum and burned hair—to be placed at the nose of a woman with this condition.[203] In a passage from *On the Affected Parts* taken up by the hysteria tradition, Galen describes the case of a woman who had been a widow for a long time and who was told by a midwife that her symptoms were due to her womb being "drawn up." The woman applied to her external genitalia "the customary remedies" (details of which are not given here) for this condition and passed a quantity of thick seed; the suggestion appears to be that rubbing in the traditional scented ointments causes orgasm, and thus releases the retained matter.[204] For Galen, both menstrual blood and seed must be evacuated, otherwise they will become toxic and poison the body; scent therapy continues, but its rationale changes.

The third century A.D. is, in many ways, a hiatus in the development of the hysteria tradition. One source that should be considered here is a papyrus from Greco-Roman Egypt, which has been dated to the third

or possibly the fourth century A.D. In a collection of magical spells, one
is included to be used in cases of "the rising up of the womb." It calls
upon the womb to "return again to your seat, and that you do not turn
into the right part of the ribs, or into the left part of the ribs, and that
you do not gnaw into the heart like a dog, but remain indeed in your
own intended and proper place."[205] This fascinating source shows that
the idea of a mobile and animate womb continued to flourish in the context of popular belief; the reference to it gnawing "like a dog" should
perhaps be read in the context of Greco-Roman ideas concerning the
insatiable sexual appetites of dogs—and women—together with the connection between *kuōn*, meaning dog, and *kuein*, meaning to be pregnant.
In this spell we are not very far from the womb of Plato's *Timaeus*, running through the body when its desire to conceive is thwarted.[206]

In the late fourth century A.D., a further literary source is of interest
because it makes explicit the identification of the Greek *hysterikē pnix* and
the Latin *suffocatio*. This is the *Book of Medicines* of Marcellus Empiricus,
which gives remedies for the disorder in a section on acute and chronic
conditions of the head. It identifies only two symptoms—severe head
pains and suffocation—which, if originating in the womb, "the Greeks
call *hysterikē pnix.*" The condition is considered comparable to epilepsy,
frenzy, and dizziness, except in its organ of origin.[207]

FURTHER CONTRIBUTIONS TO THE TRADITION

The Greek East

Returning to the set of connected texts which makes up the hysteria
tradition, the Byzantine empire preserved many medical ideas of antiquity through the work of encyclopedists such as Oribasius, Aetius, and
Paul of Aegina.[208] Such writers, often dismissed as "the medical re-
frigerators of antiquity" working in "une époque de stagnation," were
nevertheless more than compilers whose labors have preserved for us
the work of earlier writers; "not dumb copyists," they selected and
paraphrased, added and cut material, according to the specific needs of
their audience.[209] Although they may add little new to our picture, they
are of interest because they combine the elements of Soranus's and
Galen's accounts in different ways. Thus, for example, it will be seen that
both Aetius and Paul use Soranus, but—like Galen—bring back the scent
therapy that he had rejected. Both use Galen's ideas of retained matter
that must be expelled, while Aetius repeats the story of the widow. It is
also in the work of these encyclopedists that certain remedies for the
condition become standardized, while it is through them that many of
the ideas of earlier writers reached Islamic medicine.

In the upper echelons of the Byzantine world, knowledge of classical literature was regarded as the mark of an educated man. Medical education too was largely textual, traditional, and classical. We know of very few teaching centers in the fifth to seventh centuries A.D.; those students who neither came from a medical family nor were apprenticed to a physician were obliged to rely largely on texts for their instruction in both theory and practice.[210]

Alexandria again became an important medical center from the late fourth century A.D.; the medical student there would read about eleven Hippocratic treatises—including the Hippocratic *Aphorisms* and *Diseases of Women*—and fifteen or sixteen texts from the Galenic corpus. The Hippocratic texts were, however, read through a "Galenic filter."[211] Alexandria is associated with the seventh-century encyclopedist Paul of Aegina, whose work was itself based to a large extent on the fourth-century, seventy-volume work of Oribasius. It is easy to underestimate the work of Oribasius, Paul, and their successors. N. G. Wilson summarizes: "Very little can be said of any positive achievement of Alexandrian medicine. Paul admits openly in his introduction that he contributes practically no original material of his own." However, he goes on to point out that Paul's work circulated widely,[212] and it is important to see which parts of the hysteria tradition were strengthened by the choices made by such writers.

Oribasius's compilation, derived from the work of Galen, Soranus, and a number of lost works, was itself summarized in two editions of nine and four books respectively. His description of the anatomy of the womb and other female sexual organs, explicitly taken from Soranus, survives in the seventy-volume version of his work.[213] For his discussion of *hysterikē pnix*, which survives in the nine-volume *Synopsis*, Oribasius uses the lost work of Philumenos of Alexandria,[214] which recommends bandaging the extremities, rubbing the lower limbs, and scent therapy; foul odors at the nostrils, and sweet oils injected into the womb. Shouting at the patient and provoking sneezing are also acceptable, with bleeding once she is conscious. Castoreum is also highly recommended; even on its own, it may produce a cure. In an earlier chapter Oribasius gives further remedies for *pnix*, including the by now familiar list of foul-smelling substances, namely bitumen, castoreum, gum resin, pitch, cedar resin, extinguished lamp wicks, burned hair, rue, asafetida, onion, and garlic.[215] This closely resembles the list of substances Soranus criticized earlier writers for using; and, of course, Soranus also disagreed with the use of loud noises to rouse the patient. Thus, despite following Soranus's anatomy of the womb, Oribasius takes his remedies from the traditions Soranus despised.

The capital of the Byzantine empire, Constantinople, was another medical center. Oribasius worked there in the fourth century, and it was later to be associated with Aetius of Amida—whose sixteen-volume compilation, made in the sixth century, was based on Oribasius and others—and with Alexander of Tralles, whose twelve-volume *Therapeutica* was probably written a few decades after Aetius.[216] The work of Oribasius, Aetius, and Paul was later transmitted through the collection of medical knowledge compiled by Theophanes Nonnos in the tenth century. Nonnos worked as part of a deliberate program to stimulate learning, initiated by the emperor Constantine Porphyrogenitus, who was concerned with encouraging education and himself wrote several books and poems.[217]

Aetius based his description of *hysterikē pnix* on Galen's *On the Affected Parts*, merging this with the Philumenos material preserved by Oribasius.[218] He accepts that the womb, which only *seems* to move, causes the condition, the higher organs being affected through "sympathy." Using the Galenic model of the body, he describes how spasms reach the heart via the arteries, the brain through the spinal marrow, and the liver through the veins.[219] As a means of discovering whether or not the patient lives, he repeats a test given in Galen, by which either a woolen thread was placed at the nostrils, or a bowl of water on the navel.[220] However, even if no movement occurred in the wool or the water, he warned—again, following Galen—that it was possible that life remained. He sees the disorder as seasonal; it happens mostly in winter and autumn, especially in young women who use drugs to prevent conception.[221] This appears to be a special concern of Aetius, although it recalls Plato's image of the womb deprived of the offspring it desires, running wild through the body. For Aetius, as for Galen, the cause of the symptoms is the decay in the womb of seed or other material, which cools: the coldness is then passed on to the brain and heart.[222] He cuts out the story from Heracleides, but repeats—indeed, claims as his own eyewitness account[223]—Galen's story of the widow who felt "pain and pleasure at the same time" before expelling the corrupt seed; here, however, a little more detail is given by Aetius, so that we are explicitly told that the remedies used consisted in sweet ointments rubbed into the genitalia, something that is recommended again later in this passage.[224] Like Philumenos and Oribasius, Aetius recommends shouting at the patient and repeats word for word the advice of Philumenos-Oribasius that "castoreum alone often cures."[225] The status of scent therapy is reinforced, even increased.

The description of *hysterikē pnix* given by Paul of Aegina[226] in the seventh century follows Aetius closely, but states that the womb itself "rises up"[227] to affect by sympathy the carotid arteries, heart, and membranes. The patient loses her senses and her power of speech, the limbs being "drawn together." The cause—as in Galen—is the womb being full of seed or of some other substance that becomes rotten.[228] Most sufferers die suddenly during the spasms; the pulse becomes frequent and irregular, and asphyxia then follows. Breathing, at first faint, is cut off. The condition is most prevalent in winter and autumn, and most affects the lascivious, and—in almost the exact words of Aetius—those who use drugs to prevent conception.[229] During the attack the extremities should be bandaged and the patient rubbed all over. Foul-smelling substances— including stale urine—should be placed at the nostrils, and cupping and anal suppositories used. Sweet-smelling substances should be employed in order to draw the womb back to its proper place. To rouse the patient, one should shout at her roughly and induce sneezing with castoreum, soapwort, and pepper.[230] Like Soranus and Oribasius, Paul separates treatment for the fits, or *paroxysmoi,* from treatment for the whole body; the latter begins with venesection[231] and goes on to purging, exercise, and baths.

Although the tendency in the East was toward the compilation of encyclopedias, one independent Greek text, probably from the sixth century, survives in a ninth-century manuscript. This is the *Book of Metrodora,* a practical treatise in many ways reminiscent of Hippocratic medicine. It includes some remedies for *hysterikē pnix,* which make use of the traditional foul- and sweet-smelling substances, namely castoreum, rue with honey, and pig's dung with rose water.[232]

Thus in Byzantine medicine a composite picture of *hysterikē pnix* was built up, incorporating the Galenic belief in retained substances poisoning the body, Soranus's anchoring membranes, Hippocratic scent therapy, venesection as in Celsus, and a belief in the value of sneezing, derived from the Hippocratic *Aphorisms* and Galen's commentary on them, which will be discussed in detail below. Although the main authorities, Soranus and Galen, had vigorously denied that the womb could move, this idea came close to being reinstated by Paul of Aegina. Aetius preserved the Galenic tests to determine whether the patient still lived, while writers with otherwise divergent views agreed on the therapeutic value of castoreum.

The Latin West

In the West, meanwhile, the picture was in some ways very different. Although the *Aphorisms* circulated widely, few of the works of classical medicine survived, especially after knowledge of Greek declined during the fifth and sixth centuries. Although in northern Italy some Byzantine commentaries and encyclopedias were adapted into Latin during the sixth century—among them, the work of Oribasius—most "new" medical texts were short works based on Soranus.[233] The late fourth- or early fifth-century[234] Latin version of Soranus by Caelius Aurelianus survived into the Middle Ages, while the fifth- or sixth-century version by Muscio circulated more widely. Muscio plays down Soranus's attack on the idea that the womb moves around the body, going so far as to add to Soranus's introduction to the condition a new phrase claiming that the womb rises up toward the chest.[235] Thus the versions of Soranus that circulated in the West included womb movement from an early date.

Several of the texts produced in the West originated in Africa, among them the works of Caelius Aurelianus and Muscio. Predating these is the late fourth century *Euporiston* of Theodorus Priscianus, a pupil of Vindicianus, whose own *Gynaecia* was a text on parts of the body and their development in the womb. Originally written in Greek, the *Euporiston* was translated by Theodorus Priscianus himself into Latin.[236] This version contains a section entitled *De praefocatione matricis*, which follows the constriction/relaxation approach of Soranus, omits womb movement, but includes scent therapy. In A.D. 447 another African writer, Cassius Felix, took a different approach, publishing an encyclopedia allegedly based on Greek medical writers of the logical, or dogmatic, sect, but in fact owing much to Soranus as translated by Caelius Aurelianus; this contains a very Hippocratic description of hysterical suffocation, incorporating womb movement as well as scent therapy.[237]

Other Latin texts of this period survive and are probably more representative than the African works of medicine in the West after the fall of Rome. A dialogue allegedly between Soranus and a midwife, apparently designed as a midwives' catechism, is preserved in a ninth-century manuscript but may date to the sixth century; this is the *Liber ad Soteris*.[238] Another short text from this period is the *Gynaecia* by pseudo-Cleopatra.[239] It mentions a condition called *suppressiones vulvae*, the main symptom of which is difficulty in speaking and which thus may be identified with *hysterikē pnix*; however, womb movement is not mentioned, nor is scent therapy advised.

The ancient Hippocratic theories were not, however, entirely lost to the West. Between the fifth and seventh centuries A.D. many Hippocratic texts were translated into Latin at Ravenna, among them *Aphorisms* and *Diseases of Women* (1.1, 1.7–38, and extracts from 2).[240] Several texts on womb movement and suffocation are included in such translations.[241]

Also translated was Galen's *On the Method of Healing, to Glaucon*, with its reference to scent therapy for a moving womb; the Ravenna commentator considers that, by using scent therapy, Galen is apparently endorsing the wandering womb theory.[242]

It is, however, as misleading to regard the work of the scholars of Ravenna only as translation as to dismiss the Byzantine writers as mere compilers. It is important to understand the purposes for which they used these texts, since these in turn influenced the translation. These purposes fall under two headings: practice and instruction. Hippocratic medicine was seen above all as being of immediate relevance for medical practice; the Ravenna texts are thus not academic editions, but manuals. As a result the more theoretical or speculative Hippocratic texts were neglected, while those selected for translation were adapted according to the different moral and historical context within which they were now to be used.[243] The second, closely related aspect—instruction—led to the recasting of some texts in new formats in which extracts were set out in question-and-answer form, as dialogues like the *Liber ad Soteris*, as calendars, as visual representations, or as letters. The letter format, direct and personal, was very popular, an example being the *Epistula ad Maecenatem*, the *Letter to Maecenas*. Also known as the *De natura generis humani*, this comprises extracts from the Hippocratic *Diseases of Women* (1) and from Vindicianus. The *Epistula ad Maecenatem* is found in the ninth-century manuscripts Paris BN Lat. 7027 and Paris BN Lat. 11219, and in these manuscripts it includes two passages of *Diseases of Women* used in the hysteria tradition: 1.7, on movement of the womb to the liver, and 1.32, on movement of the womb in a pregnant woman.[244] The late eighth century/early ninth century manuscript Leningrad Lat. F.v.VI.3 is a handbook including Latin translations of sections from *Diseases of Women*, one of which is our 2.127, a further description of the movement of the womb to the liver. In the recipes given for cures, substitutions are made in the pharmacopoeia according to what was available in the period.[245]

The Arab World

Another route of transmission of Hippocratic ideas to the West was through the Arab world. The most obvious contact between medical systems took place after the Arabs took Alexandria in A.D. 642, possibly while Paul of Aegina was there; the medical school at Alexandria continued to exist until around A.D. 719, probably still using Greek as its language of instruction.[246] The great age of translation began in the ninth century; Greek manuscripts were taken as booty in conquest, and those translating them into Arabic—sometimes through the medium of Syriac—enjoyed royal patronage. From this time onward, versions of Hippocratic texts, based on several manuscripts, were produced; the most famous early translator was Ḥunain ibn Isḥāq al-ʿIbadi—known to the West as Johannitius—the Christian son of a druggist, who was also responsible for translating works by Galen, Oribasius, and Paul of Aegina. Ḥunain also listed all the works of Galen that had been translated into Arabic or Syriac by about A.D. 800; these included such key works in the hysteria tradition as *On the Affected Parts*, *On Difficulty in Breathing*, and the commentary on the *Aphorisms*, from which the Hippocratic *Aphorisms* themselves were excerpted and then transmitted separately.[247] There thus exists a striking contrast between East and West in the ninth century; as R. J. Durling puts it, "Whereas European knowledge of Galen was limited to a few Galenic works, and those either unimportant or clearly spurious, Arabic translations of almost all his writings were made." Something similar occurs with regard to much of the Hippocratic corpus; in contrast to the Latin West, where emphasis was placed on translating those texts of immediate practical value, the Arabic translators did not neglect the more theoretical and speculative treatises, so that the "Arabic Hippocrates" is more complete than the "Latin Hippocrates."[248] This does not, however, apply to Hippocratic gynecology; neither *Diseases of Women* nor *Nature of Woman* was translated into Arabic, although two Byzantine commentaries on *Diseases of Women* 1.1–11 were in circulation in the Arab world before the eleventh century, together with Byzantine medical encyclopedias.[249]

The main means by which Greco-Roman ideas were transmitted was through the compilation of new encyclopedic works. The *Firdaws al hikma* (Paradise of Wisdom) of ʿAli ibn Rabbān aṭ-Ṭabarī (810–861) was completed in 850 and includes approximately 120 quotations from the Hippocratic corpus, and a large amount of Galenic material, together with extracts from other Greek and Islamic writers such as Aristotle and Ḥunain.[250] Aṭ-Ṭabarī believes that the essential wetness of woman leads to menstrual loss; retained moisture sinks to the lowest part of the body and then comes out, "just as in a tree the excess moisture comes out as gum."[251] In his section on uterine disorders, he includes suffocation of the womb. He writes, "Sometimes, through damming-up of menstrual blood and lack of sexual intercourse, vapours develop." He explains that the retained blood becomes thick, and produces vapors that then affect the whole body, causing such symptoms as painful breathing, palpitations, head pain, and suffocation of the womb.

A further discussion of suffocation occurs in the context of womb movement. The womb can lean to one side, but sometimes it actually rises up until it reaches the diaphragm, causing suffocation. "Then the woman loses consciousness, with the result that her breath is stopped. Then one puts a bit of wool under her nostrils in order to see whether she is alive or dead." The cause here is not menstrual blood, but accumulated seed; if there is an "excess, lack or absence" of intercourse, seed will accumulate in the womb, rot, and become poisonous and thick. The womb then moves to the diaphragm and the woman suffocates.[252]

Thus womb movement was readily combined with a Galenic etiology of retained seed or menses, but to this mixture aṭ-Ṭabarī added the explanatory device of vapors. Where Greco-Roman writers employed the concept of sympathy to account for the effects of the womb on other parts of the body, writers in the Arab world also used vapors; as we shall see, this development entered the western hysteria tradition when texts were translated from Arabic to Latin from the eleventh century onward.

The next writer from the Arab world who should be considered here is Muḥammad ibn-Zakariyya' ar-Rāzī (Rhazes), whose Kitāb al-Ḥāwī, a twenty-four-volume collection of excerpts from Greek, Arabic, and Indian writers known in Latin as the Continens, was written around A.D. 900.[253] Also translated into Latin was his Kitāb al-Mansori, which includes a chapter on uterine suffocation. Here Rhazes gives a basically Galenic account of the condition, including retained menses and seed, the patient falling down as though dead, and scent therapy; he includes the recommendation that a midwife should rub the mouth of the womb with a well-oiled finger. He does not say that the womb moves, although he describes a sensation "as if something is pulled up."[254]

The work of ʿAlī ibn-al-ʿAbbas al-Majūsī, known in Europe as Haly Abbas, was produced in the tenth century A.D. It too combines Hippocratic etiologies with a predominantly Galenic approach, often read through the eyes of Paul/Aetius; but al-Majūsī plays down the membranes anchoring the womb, claiming instead that the womb can move around the body. He includes both sympathy and vapors. He explains that suffocation of the womb is a very dangerous condition because sympathy leads to the vital organs, the brain and heart, being affected. If a woman does not have intercourse, a large quantity of seed will collect and will "stifle and extinguish the innate heat." Retained menstrual blood has similar effects.[255]

In a separate section on treatment, he retains the Hippocratic scent therapy, but explains its success partly in terms of vapors. Bad smells administered to the nose rise to the brain, "warming, dissolving and diluting the cold vapors," but also driving the womb back down.[256] For al-Majūsī, the womb is "more or less an independent living being," yearning for conception, annoyed by bad smells and leaning toward pleasant smells. Plato's description of the womb as an animal desiring conception was known to the Arab world through Galen.[257] Al-Majūsī also recommends sexual intercourse as a cure, especially for virgins, whose strong desire for sex and thick menstrual blood predisposes them to the condition.[258] In the absence of this, he repeats the Galenic therapy of instructing a midwife to rub sweet-smelling oils on the mouth of the womb, and states explicitly that this has the same effect as intercourse, in warming and thinning the seed, so that it can drain away and the woman can "find peace."[259]

Also working in the tenth century was Ibn al-Jazzār, whose main work was the *Kitab Zād al-Musāfir* in seven books. This was a particularly important source for medieval European medicine; it was translated into Latin, Greek, and Hebrew, and is known in Latin as the *Viaticum*.[260] Book 6, chapter 11, describes suffocation of the womb; the condition begins with loss of appetite and the chilling of the body, which is attributed to corruption of retained seed, particularly in widows and young girls of marriageable age. From the seed a *fumus*—a smoke, or vapor—rises to the diaphragm, because the diaphragm and womb are connected; then, since further connections exist between the diaphragm and the throat and vocal chords, suffocation ensues. Similar problems may result from retained menses, and scent therapy and the application of fragrant oils to the mouth of the womb are recommended. Repeated here is a version of the story given in Galen of the woman who lay as dead but was known to be alive by the presence of innate heat; here, however, Galen rather than Empedocles becomes its hero![261]

Finally, Ibn Sīnā (Avicenna), born in A.D. 980, included discussions of hysterical suffocation in his *Qānūn* (the *Canon*); translated into Latin by Gerard of Cremona in twelfth-century Toledo, this influential text was printed thirty-six times in the fifteenth and sixteenth centuries.[262] He devotes four successive chapters to the condition, its signs and cures, and the preferred regimen for sufferers. He bases his description on Galen as interpreted by Aetius, favoring sympathy (*communitas*) over vapors, and including the test for life with a piece of wool and the story of the widow; cures include phlebotomy and the rubbing of scented oil into the vulva, while the regimen includes the use of foul-smelling substances at the nose and sweet scents at the vagina.[263]

Thus it can be seen that the distinctively Hippocratic features of womb movement, scent therapy, and the therapeutic value of sexual intercourse survived even in the directly contradictory environments of

Galenic theory and Islamic culture. Despite the rejection of the moving womb by both Soranus and Galen, it soon returned to the fore in the explanations of hysterical suffocation given by writers and compilers in both East and West. In the Arabic world, Soranus's *Gynecology* may not have been translated, so his attack on the theory of the mobile womb may have remained unknown;[264] as for Galen, although he explicitly rejects Plato's womb-as-animal theory in *On the Affected Parts*, he implicitly accepts it in *To Glaucon*, thus leaving the matter open for future commentators. Such elements of the hysteria tradition as the wool test for life and the story of the widow and the midwife, retained by the Byzantine encyclopedists, continue to survive in Arabic medicine; the story of the woman raised from apparent death by Empedocles is found in Ibn al-Jazzār but plays a minor role, perhaps because the short reference to it in Galen is insufficient for its reconstruction.

In terms of the most likely victims for the condition, it is of interest that Galen's preference for widows is ignored; virgins become a prime target. This is not a return to Hippocratic etiology since, as I have argued above, the Hippocratic hysteria texts rarely give a particular target population for womb movement; furthermore, when a particular group is specified, this tends to be the childless in general (since their flesh is not "broken down"), older women not having intercourse, or young widows. The Hippocratic text that may be at the root of this interest in virgins is one that was available in the Arab world, since it is cited twice by Rhazes: the *Diseases of Young Girls*.[265] This is a short and vivid description of a condition that arises not from womb movement, but instead from retention of menstrual, or possibly menarcheal, blood. The target population consists of *parthenoi*—meaning young girls, unmarried women, and/or virgins—who are "ripe for marriage" but remain unmarried. Their blood is described as being plentiful due to "food and the growth of the body." If "the orifice of exit" is closed, the blood that has moved to the womb ready to leave the body will travel instead to the heart and diaphragm, causing visions, loss of reason, and a desire to commit suicide by hanging. The author states that he orders girls with this condition to marry as quickly as possible; if they become pregnant, they will be cured. I would suggest that this text, retrospectively diagnosed as hysteria by several writers during this century, lies behind al-Majūsī's interest in the thick blood of a virgin and in intercourse as a cure, as well as explaining Ibn al-Jazzār's target population of girls of marriageable age.[266]

Finally, in these writers, a new explanatory device is used to account for the effects of the womb on other parts of the body: vapors. Yet the concept of sympathy continues to exist, sometimes—as in Ibn al-Jazzār—involving very precise connections between particular organs of the body.

THE MEETING OF THREE WORLDS

Returning to western Europe, most of Galenic medicine had been lost with the decline, from the late fourth century onward, in knowledge of the Greek language.[267] Soranus dominated gynecology in general; his writings, perceived as shorter and more practical than those of Galen, were preserved in abridged Latin versions that reinstated the womb movement he had so vehemently rejected. Hippocratic medicine fared worse, although *Aphorisms* continued to circulate after its translation into Latin in the sixth century; the Ravenna translations also included some of the sections of *Diseases of Women* describing womb movement. Some Galenic treatises, too, were translated at Ravenna; however, whereas 129 works of Galen were translated into Arabic, only 4 existed in Latin before the eleventh century. One of these was the practical work *On the Method of Healing, to Glaucon* but, as has been discussed above, this can be read as a further reinstatement of the wandering womb. The third volume of Paul of Aegina's encyclopedia, which includes his largely Galenic description of *hysterikē pnix* plus details of scent therapy, was translated into Latin, but probably only in the tenth century.[268]

The emphasis in the West lay firmly on the instructional and practical aspects of ancient medicine; thus the traditional therapies for hysterical suffocation were transmitted when discussions of its causation were not. The category of suffocation of the womb appears in several anonymous collections of texts from the eighth to the twelfth centuries. I have already mentioned Leningrad Lat. F.v.VI.3, a Latin manuscript dating from the eighth or ninth century which contains several short texts on gynecology, all of which show some resemblances to the second book of the Hippocratic *Diseases of Women*.[269] Of these, *De causis feminarum* gives practical advice on what to do "si vulva suffocantur" (if the womb is suffocated), giving the Greek name for the condition as "styrecersis": is this a garbled form of *hysterikē pnix* or *hysterika*? The patient should be given burned and pulverized stag's horn in wine or, if she has a fever, in hot water.[270] Another text in this collection, the *De muliebria causa*, claims that "uribasius"—Oribasius, the only authority named in these texts—recommends one drachma of agaric for suffocation of the womb.[271] This is repeated in a section of the following text, the *Liber de muliebria*, which later gives a more complex recipe for suffocation of the womb, in which the patient is choked at the neck, so that it is turned back to the chest.[272]

It was in the eleventh and twelfth centuries that Galenic treatises were returned to the West, through the translations from Arabic into Latin made by Constantine the African in the late eleventh century at Salerno and Monte Cassino; a few Galenic treatises were translated directly from Greek into Latin in the twelfth and thirteenth centuries, and these translations are usually of higher quality.[273] The effect of Constantine on the history of medicine cannot, however, be overemphasized; his arrival in Italy with a cargo of books of Arabic medicine, which he translated into Latin at Monte Cassino, transformed the "theoretical impoverishment" into which medical knowledge in the West had fallen. For our purposes here, what is most significant is that his translations included Galen's commentary on the Hippocratic *Aphorisms,* and works of al-Majūsī and Ibn al-Jazzār.[274] Constantine translated much of the *Kamil* of al-Majūsī as the *Liber Pantegni*; this work was translated again in the early twelfth century by Stephen of Pisa as the *Liber Regius* and was printed in 1492 and 1523. The *Kitāb Zād al-Musāfir* of Ibn al-Jazzār was translated in an abbreviated form as the *Viaticum,* while Constantine's *Expositio Aforismi* is a translation from the Arabic of Galen's commentary on the Hippocratic *Aphorisms.*[275]

What effect do these texts have on the hysteria tradition in the West? We have already seen the wide range of variations that can occur on the theme of womb movement. In the Hippocratic texts a dry, hot, and light womb rises in search of moisture; Soranus believes that the anchoring membranes prevent any movement, while for Aretaeus, although the womb moves it is pulled back by its membranes, thus affecting the higher parts of the body only through sympathy. In Galen the problem is a womb filled with retained seed or menses, rotting to produce coldness. In Arabic medicine a Hippocratic mobile womb becomes a mobile womb with Galenic contents, and vapors as well as sympathy explain its effects on the higher parts. In the Latin West the focus on Soranus had been combined with acceptance of womb movement; while some extracts from Hippocratic gynecology circulated, Galenic theory was lost until the eleventh century.

The return of Galenic medicine from the Arabic world led to yet another variation on this theme of womb movement and its mechanisms. It was in the twelfth century at Salerno in southern Italy that the texts of the Hippocratic corpus, Soranus, and Galen finally came together after their varied travels through the Latin West, the Greek East, and the Islamic world.[276] The result was not a critical comparison of these traditions, but instead the decline of Soranus and the rise of the Galenic medical system of humoral balance and imbalance. One of the "masters" of the school of Salerno in the twelfth century was Johannes Platearius. In his description of suffocation of the womb, in the late twelfth-century encyclopedia and textbook *De aegritudinum curatione,* he combined Galen and Paul of Aegina with Ibn al-Jazzār's claim that the symptoms were caused by vapors rising from the corrupt seed, menses, or other retained humor. However, Platearius went a step farther than this, suggesting that it was not the vapors, but the womb filled with vapors, that rose in the body to put pressure on the organs of breathing.

Green has argued that, since the Latin translations of al-Majūsī's *Kamil* omitted the later section in which he describes scent therapy in terms of the womb as an animal annoyed by foul smells and seeking pleasant scents, this particular merger of the mobile womb with Galenic theory may come, not from Islamic medicine, but from the survival of the idea in popular thought in the West.[277] Other features of Platearius's description are more familiar, showing the overall dominance of the Galenic material found in the newly available Arabic sources; he recommends the Galenic tests of the woolen thread at the nose of the patient, or a glass flask full of water placed on her chest, and among his suggested cures one finds sneezing provoked with castoreum or pepper, and the use of foul scents at the nose and sweet scents at the vulva. However, here too Green points out that non-Galenic ideas surface; although Galen never specifically advised marriage as a cure, Platearius recommends it if the cause is retained seed. Again, al-Majūsī did explicitly prescribe sexual intercourse as a cure; but, again, this was omitted from the Latin translation of his work.[278] It seems that the survival of Hippocratic theories—the wandering womb from *Diseases of Women* and the therapeutic value of intercourse from sections of that treatise and from *Diseases of Young Girls*—should not be underestimated.

Another writer associated with Salerno in the twelfth century is the female physician Trota, whose name is associated with a number of treatises of this period which are found in nearly a hundred manuscripts from the thirteenth to fifteenth centuries.[279] Suffocation of the womb is mentioned in both the more empirical *Ut de curis,* which refers to it occurring in young girls with epilepsy, and the more theoretical and Galenic *Cum auctor.*[280] The *Cum auctor* version owes much to Ibn al-Jazzār, although it does not specify conclusively whether suffocation results from vapors, or the womb itself, rising up inside the body. Scent therapy is recommended, and the story of the woman who lay as if dead but was known to be alive through the presence of the innate heat, is transmitted through the *Cum auctor;* as in Ibn al-Jazzār, Galen becomes its hero.[281]

The influence of Galenic theory grew with the translation of other important Arabic texts into Latin; in particular, Ibn Sīnā's *Qānūn*. The work of Soranus became "virtually obsolete by the thirteenth century";[282] the gynecological works of the Hippocratic corpus languished in the wings until the sixteenth century. However, one Hippocratic text remained in the center stage: the *Aphorisms,* including the section on gynecology with the text with which this chapter began, the alleged origin for the label/diagnosis *hysteria,* 5.35: "In a woman suffering from *hysterika,* or having a difficult labor, a sneeze is a good thing."

Aphorisms circulated in both the Latin West and the Arabic world; in the latter, from before A.D. 800, it was coupled with the commentary of Galen, *In Hippocratis Aphorismi.* This commentary, probably written in A.D. 175, was restored to the West when Constantinus Africanus translated it from Arabic into Latin in the eleventh century. In terms of its printed editions in the Renaissance, it was the third most popular Galenic treatise after *Ars medica* and *De differentiis febrium.*[283] The central position of the *Aphorisms* from the eleventh century onward results not only from its perennial popularity as a series of practical tips,[284] but also from its inclusion in the *Articella,* a group of medical writings "used for centuries at Salerno and elsewhere as a textbook for introductory courses in medicine."[285] The central text of the group is Ḥunain ibn Isḥāq's *Isagoge,* in Constantine's translation from the Arabic; in addition to the *Aphorisms,* the nucleus also contains Galen's *Tegni* (the *Ars parva*), the Hippocratic *Prognostics,* Theophilus on urines, and Philaretus on pulses.

I have argued that the opening words of *Aphorisms* 5.35 can best be translated "In a woman suffering from *hysterika,*" where *hysterika* means disorders of the womb. But this translation depends on reading the text without the Galenic commentary that instead pushes for a very specific translation, *hysterikē pnix.* By looking at changes in the Latin translation of this aphorism, it is possible not only to trace its gradual incorporation into the hysteria tradition, but also to provide a test case for the period in which the humanists began to carry out philological work on the Galenic and Hippocratic texts. When were these texts read as the object of serious study? It is the brief *Aphorisms,* not the lengthy Galenic commentary, which occupied a central place in the medical curricula of the Renaissance. Despite its impressive printing history, I would argue that Galen's commentary was little read before the sixteenth century.

The earliest Latin translations of *Aphorisms,* found in manuscripts dating from the eighth to the twelfth centuries A.D., can be traced back to fifth/sixth-century Ravenna.[286] Such Latin translations are very literal, the writers apparently having an equally weak grasp of both Greek and medicine. The translation reads "Mulieri de matrice laboranti aut difficulter generanti, sternutatio superveniens, optimum" (In a woman troubled by the womb or giving birth with difficulty, a sneeze coming on unexpectedly is best).[287] At this period, then, the aphorism was not associated with hysteria or suffocation of the womb.

The *Articella* uses a different Latin translation of the *Aphorisms*, possibly produced in the eleventh century, and linked to the name of Constantinus Africanus. It is not known whether this was made from a Greek manuscript of *Aphorisms*, or by merely extracting the aphorisms from a copy of Galen's commentary. Whatever its source, it gives for 5.35, "Mulieri que a matrice molestat aut difficulter generanti: sternutatio superveniens bonum." It thus differs little from the Ravenna translation; a sneeze becomes "good" instead of "the best thing," and the womb continues to "distress" or "trouble" the woman. Fifteenth-century printed editions of the *Articella* retain slight variations on this translation, which remains the most commonly used well into the sixteenth century.[288] Some editions give two translations, setting this so-called *versio antiqua* beside the *traductio nova* of Theodorus Gaza. The new translation runs, "Mulieri quam vitia uteri infestant, aut que difficulter parit, si sternutamentum supervenit, bono est." The opening words, "In a woman in whom disorders attack the womb," again keep this aphorism within a very general gynecological context. Another variation in printed editions of the *Articella* is to print both translations together with a rearrangement of the *Aphorisms* by the part of the body discussed, on *a capite ad calcem* lines; thus the edition of 1519 gives this aphorism under "Concerning sneezing" and "Concerning the female generative organs."[289]

A further development in the printed versions of the *Articella* is that, where the manuscript versions gave only the Hippocratic text of the *Aphorisms*, the printed editions from 1476 give Galen's commentary beside it. Galen is thus "given a privileged status compared with other commentators."[290] However, an important question remains: Did anyone read the lengthy commentary, which sets it firmly in the context of *hysterikē pnix*, as opposed to uterine disorders in general? Galen considers that *apnoia*, or absence of breath, is more accurate than "suffocation," seeing a spontaneous sneeze both as a "sign" (*sēmeion*) that the patient has revived, and as a "cause" (*aition*) of recovery, since in itself it revives the patient.[291] However, despite Galen's conclusion that *hysterika* is equivalent to *hysterikē pnix*, the connection with the translation of the Hippocratic aphorism is not made. Neither the terminology of suffocation nor that of hysteria appears in the Latin of the *Aphorisms*; instead, the woman is said to be "troubled by the womb" or to have "disorders attack the womb." Reading the long discussion of the meaning of *hysterika* in Galen's commentary should lead to a change in the translation of the aphorism, away from this general terminology and toward that of hysterical suffocation, but no such change is made at this time.

It is in the fifteenth century that the first signs of close study of Galen's commentary and its implications for the translation of the aphorism appear, in the work of Ugo Benzi (1376–1439). Benzi wrote commentaries on the *Canon* of Avicenna, the *Tegni* of Galen, and the Hippocratic *Aphorisms*, omitting books 3 and 7; this last was probably first published in 1413 or 1414 while he was lecturing on medicine in Parma, but it was later revised. Like his contemporaries, of course, he still based his translations not on the Greek, but on "the medieval Latin versions from the Arabic." Although he follows the *versio antiqua* translation, he improves the Latin, discusses the views of Galen and Avicenna on uterine suffocation—in particular, on whether it is the womb or merely vapors that rise up the body—and also glosses the aphorism as follows: "Sternutatio superveniens mulieri suffocationem matricis patienti aut difficulter parienti est bonum" (A sneeze spontaneously occurring in a woman suffering from suffocation of the womb or a difficult labor is a good thing).[292]

The translation of Theodorus Gaza is used by Lorenzo Laurenziani (ca. 1450–1502),[293] while Niccolò Leoniceno (1428–1524) gives both this and the *verso antiqua* beside his own translation, which begins with another variation on the theme of general uterine disorders, "Mulieri qua uterinis molestant."[294]

The connection between text and commentary is made conclusively only in the 1540s, when the *Aphorisms* are first the object of detailed philological interest. The availability of printed Greek and Latin editions of the Galenic and Hippocratic works from the 1520s onward had no immediate impact but, after twenty years, comparison of the text both with the Greek manuscripts of *Aphorisms* and with Galen's commentaries is made, and the aphorism becomes explicitly "hysterical."

Antonio Brasavola's annotated edition of the *Aphorisms* and its Galenic commentary was printed in 1541 at Basel. It discusses not only Galen's commentary but also the use of *hysterika* in Marcellus's commentary on Dioscorides, Philotheus, and Paul of Aegina. Brasavola (1500–1555) reasserts the identity of *hysterika* as *hysterikē pnix*, but still he does not take the step of adjusting the translation of *Aphorisms* 5.35, instead giving a variation on Leoniceno's translation, which reads: "Mulieri, quae uterinis molestatur, aut difficulter parit, superveniens sternutatio, bonum."[295]

The earliest translation I have found in which the terminology of the suffocation of the womb is directly applied to *Aphorisms* 5.35 is that of Leonhart Fuchs (1501–1566). Printed in 1545, this gives "Mulieri quae ab uteri strangulationibus infestatur, aut quae difficulter partum edit, sternutamentum superveniens, bonum." Here, for the first time, the translation itself becomes "hysterical"; "in a woman who is attacked by uterine suffocation," a translation justified by Fuchs on the grounds that Galen and Philotheus explain that *hysterika* equals suffocation here. He goes on to demonstrate that the basis of his translation is the comparison of Greek manuscripts, discussing whether a word in Galen's text should read *lunga* or *pniga*.[296]

The edition of Guillaume Plancy (1514–ca. 1568) takes the process a stage further. In this publication of 1552 the Latin reads "Mulieri hystericae, aut difficulter parienti, sternutamentum superveniens, bonum." A note justifies the translation by a reference to Galen's *On the Affected Parts* 6.5.[297] The connection has been made, not only between aphorism and commentary, but between the Galen of the commentary and the Galen of *On the Affected Parts*.

Once the aphorism has reentered the hysteria tradition, it is—with a few exceptions—there to stay. Claude Champier (fl. 1556) also mentions "vulvae strangulatus," while Jacques Houllier (ca. 1510–1562) follows Plancy's translation.[298] In keeping with his general interest in a return to the Greek classics in order to end error in medicine, Houllier also recalls Hippocratic ideas, giving a further type of suffocation due to a dry womb seeking moisture, for which a sneeze is less beneficial than baths.[299]

Thus, once the aphorism is read—rather than merely printed—in the context of Galen's commentary, it ceases to be understood as a reference to disorders of the womb in general, and comes to be absorbed into the hysteria tradition, that set of connected texts repeated by successive commentators on suffocation of the womb.

Glancing at its fortunes in vernacular editions, the English translation of the *Aphorisms* of 1610 by "S. H." gives "Sneezing hapning to a woman grieved with suffocation of the wombe, or having a painfull and difficult deliverance is good."[300] This is also found in a seventeenth-century manuscript in the British Library, Sloane 2811.[301] A commonplace book of the seventeenth century includes a Latin translation of the *Aphorisms,* giving "Mulieri hysterica, aut difficulter parienti sternutamentium superveniens bonum"—a variant of Plancy—and an English translation, reading "Sneezing happening to a woman seized with suffocation of the womb: or that hath a difficult deliverance: is good."[302] The comment on this aphorism is that sneezing shakes off noxious humors and restores the natural heat that was almost extinguished. In the same book appears a work entitled "Select Aphorisms concerning the operation of medicaments according to the place." This contains a section (pp. 121ᵛ–122ʳ) on "Hystericalls" which describes how the womb is drawn to aromatics and repelled by their contraries. It discusses how this mechanism works, and roundly rejects the belief of "some sotts" that the womb possesses "the sense of smelling." Even in the seventeenth century scent therapy is defended, but this does not mean that the womb is regarded as an animal.

If the old discussion of the implications of scent therapy for the status of the womb as, in the words of Aretaeus, "a living thing inside another living thing" is still itself alive and well in the seventeenth century, has the hysteria tradition made any progress over the two thousand or so years of its existence? I would argue that some change has, by this time, occurred. The tendency before the sixteenth century was toward an accumulation of descriptions, explanations, and remedies. Some features—such as scent therapy at both ends of the body, the use of an extinguished lamp wick to rouse a patient, and the application of aromatic oils to the sexual organs—went back to Hippocratic medicine, as transmitted by Galen. Others, although derived from the Hippocratics, were transformed by Galen's reinterpretation; for example, Hippocratic *pnix* concerns a hot womb seeking moisture to douse its fire, yet after Galen it becomes "obstruction of respiration," and the womb is seen as being filled with cold and corrupt substances rather than being hot and light. Other features remained in the tradition despite all that could be said to condemn them, most notably, the wandering womb, in coexistence with apparently contradictory features such as anchoring membranes.

TRADITION OR TRUTH?

By the mid-sixteenth century, the hysteria tradition was complete: the translation into Latin of texts from the Arabic and Greek made available virtually the full range of authors discussed above. Every commentator on suffocation of the womb knew which ancient authorities to consult for a description. Since these ancient authorities had themselves known and used the work of many of their predecessors, it is not surprising that the result was often merely further repetition. Latin and Middle English treatises from the thirteenth to fifteenth centuries tend to be heavily dependent on the Arabic writers' versions of Galen, and retain the features of scent therapy, provoking a sneeze as a cure (as opposed to welcoming a spontaneous sneeze), venesection, and therapeutic intercourse.[303] However, in the mid-sixteenth century something new does occur: the stated desire to compare authorities, not only with each other, but with reality.

As an example of this we may take the work of Pieter van Foreest (1522–1597), *Observationum et curationum medicinalium*, Book 28 of which concerns women's diseases.[304] As the title suggests, rather than simply repeating the authorities, he also presents cases that he himself has seen. Observations 25–34 concern suffocation of the womb, covering cases due to retained seed or menses in widows, in pregnant and other women, and of varying severity. Rhazes, Ibn Sīnā, and Galen are cited; Galen is particularly favored and, although he is a supporter of the Hippocratic revival, van Foreest accepts Galen's attack on the Hippocratic theory that the womb dries out and seeks moisture.[305] He notes that the ancients believed the womb itself traveled the body, whereas "more recent writers" believe it is vapors that rise. The motif of the woman who uses hysteria to manipulate men is reintroduced, echoing Martial's epigram on women who announce they are *hysterica* in order to have intercourse with a young doctor; van Foreest states that some women simulate hysterical suffocation by imagining sexual intercourse, and he cites the "notorious poem" mocking this.[306]

His use of his own observations is first suggested when, after repeating Galen's statement that the symptoms from retained seed are worse than those from retained menses, he adds, "And this is true."[307] Even Galen must be tested against experience. Observation 27 repeats the story of the woman who lay as if dead, based on Pliny, and gives the standard tests for life, adding that a sneeze is more reliable than the wool or water tests. Observation 28 includes Galen's story of the widow who was cured after passing some thick seed. In Observation 30, on hysterical suffocation in pregnancy, he gives two cases he himself has seen, one dated to October 1589, while in Observation 31 he describes the case of a woman called Eva Teylingia, who was married in 1561 and was known to his wife. She was unsuccessfully treated by several named doctors for suffocation, and "on the third day I myself was called." Van Foreest's therapy—based on foul-smelling substances placed in the navel—was successful. In Observation 33 he gives the case of a girl of twenty, treated in September 1579, and in Observation 34 he gives a case dated March 1566.

Such works as this were used by Edward Jorden in his treatise of 1603, *A Briefe Discourse of a Disease Called the Suffocation of the Mother*.[308] What is most striking about this work, in which he sets out to show "in a vulgar tongue" that symptoms "which in the common opinion are imputed to the Divell" are in fact due to the suffocation of the womb, is not the use of authorities such as Hippocrates, Galen, Pliny, and Ibn Sīnā, but his citation of recent cases seen and reported by men such as van Foreest, Amatus Lusitanus, and Andreas Vesalius.

Is this, then, the triumph of experience over tradition? It is not. As T. Laqueur puts it, "Experience, in short, is reported and remembered so as to be congruent with dominant paradigms."[309] Many elements of the hysteria tradition have an extraordinary vitality as paradigms, continuing to be repeated well into the nineteenth century. To take one example, Jorden himself repeats the story of the woman who lay as if dead but was known to be alive by the presence of the innate heat; he uses the version given by Pliny.[310] This story has inordinate staying power, turning up many times in seventeenth-century literature; for example, Guillaume de Baillou (1538–1616) claims that many women are being buried alive because it is wrongly assumed that the absence of a pulse indicates death.[311] In the nineteenth century, Thomas Laycock's *Treatise on the Nervous Diseases of Women* has a section on "Apparent Death" citing Diogenes Laertius's version of the same story, here diagnosed by Laycock as hysteria. As a general rule, Laycock recommends delaying burial in such cases until there are signs of decomposition.[312] He refers readers to Leigh Hunt's play *A Legend of Florence*, first performed in 1840, the year of publication of Laycock's own work. In this play, the moral and married Ginevra, receiving letters from a nobleman who declares his love for her, has a fainting spell and is mistakenly buried—fortunately, in an open vault. She wakes up but has difficulty persuading the people of Florence that she is not a ghost:

> I am Ginevra—buried, but not dead,
> And have got forth and none will let me in.
> (act 4, scene 4)

This highly popular piece of drama, seen by Queen Victoria a number of times and regarded as Leigh Hunt's greatest dramatic success, was in turn based on Shelley's "Ginevra," published in 1821.[313] In Shelley's version, Ginevra marries a man she does not love and, on her wedding night, falls into a trance that drifts into death itself, in order to keep faith with her disappointed lover.

> They found Ginevra dead: if it be death
> To lie without motion or pulse or breath,
> With waxen cheeks, and limbs cold, stiff, and white,
> And open eyes . . .
> (lines 145–148)

Shelley's words echo Diogenes Laertius's third-century A.D. account of the woman "without breath or pulse" but preserved, according to Galen, by her innate heat. Such powerful motifs as apparent death weave in and out of the medical accounts of suffocation of the womb and of later hysteria. Do such elements survive simply because they make such good stories? Or is the persistence of certain parts of the tradition evidence for the *accuracy* of that tradition, and thus for the accuracy of the diagnosis of hysteria?

Throughout this chapter I have emphasized how medicine worked as a series of texts. Medical education, particularly where it concerned women's bodies, was based on the text in the Byzantine, Islamic, and medieval worlds; even after publication of Vesalius's *De humani corporis fabrica* in 1543, "anatomy and surgery continued to be taught from books rather than from experiment and observation."[314] Specifically, in the texts of the Hippocratic corpus, neither the diagnosis of *hysterikē pnix* nor of hysteria is made. The womb moves, causing a range of symptoms according to its eventual destination. At an unknown date, possibly—from the medical papyri—in the second century B.C., a disease category of suffocation of the womb is created by the merger of a number of discrete Hippocratic texts giving symptoms, causes, and therapies. Galen challenges the label, but keeps the concept and develops a different explanation based not on womb movement so much as retained blood and seed. In the early Roman Empire, further stories are added to the disease picture, surviving in the different cultural climates of the Latin West, Greek East, and Arabic world. Particularly resistant to change are two of the original Hippocratic components, womb movement and scent therapy: so too is the need to give the concept antiquity by tracing it back in its entirety to the father of medicine.

I would suggest that what we hear in such texts as those discussed here is not the insistent voice of a fixed disease entity calling across the centuries, but rather what Mary Wack has called "the rustle of parchments in dialogue."[315] Indeed, it is rarely even a true dialogue. Deaf to pleas from anatomy and experience, the texts continue to tell one another the traditional stories. The language may shift—the womb travels, vapors rise, sympathy transmits symptoms through the body—but the message remains the same: women are sick, and men write their bodies. Nineteenth-century hysteria, a parasite in search of a history, grafts itself by name and lineage onto the centuries-old tradition of suffocation of the womb, thus making Hippocrates its adopted father. It is time that father disowned his hybrid child.

ACKNOWLEDGMENTS

Sections of this chapter have been presented to the Pybus Club (Newcastle, 1985), the Classical Association Triennial Meeting (Oxford, 1988), a conference organized by the Wellcome Institute for the History of Medicine (London, 1990), and the Liverpool Medical History Society/ Society for the History of Science (Liverpool, 1991). I am grateful to all who made suggestions as to its improvement on these occasions, but above all to the careful and generous scholarship of Monica H. Green and Mark Micale.

NOTES

A Note on Ancient Texts

Many of the ancient writers cited here—for example, Hesiod, Martial, and Plato—are easily accessible in translation. Where no particular edition is specified, the Loeb Classical Library version may be used. This gives the ancient text with an English translation on the facing page.

The medical writers are less readily available to the general reader. In particular, few of the relevant works of the Hippocratic corpus have been translated into English. In the interests of consistency, all texts from the Hippocratic corpus are cited from the standard Greek edition with French translation of E. Littré, *Oeuvres complètes d'Hippocrate*, 10 vols. (Paris: Baillière, 1839–61), abbreviated L. References are given in the form L volume.page number; for example, L 8.34. The specific locations, in the Littré edition, of the texts used, with the abbreviations used in the notes, are as follows:

Airs, Waters, Places, L 2.12–93
Aphorisms, L 4.458–609
Coan Prognoses, L 5.588–733
Diseases of Women, L 8.10–463 = *DW*
Diseases of Young Girls, L 8.466–471
Epidemics 2, L 3.24–149; 6, L 5.266–357 = *Ep.*
Generation, L 7.470–484 = *Gen.*
Glands, L 8.556–575
Nature of the Child, L 7.486–538 = *NC*
On Joints, L 4.78–339
On the Sacred Disease, L 6.352–397
Prorrhetics 1, L 5.510–577

Nature of Man, L 6.32–69
Nature of Woman, L 7.312–431 = *NW*
Places in Man, L 6.276–349
Regimen, L 6.466–637
Regimen in Acute Diseases, Appendix, L 2.394–529 = *Acut. Sp.*
Superfetation, L 8.476–509

Generation and *Nature of the Child* are available in an excellent English translation by I. M. Lonie, *The Hippocratic Treatises "On Generation," "On the Nature of the Child," "Diseases IV"* (Berlin: De Gruyter, 1981). Ann Hanson is preparing an edition and English translation of *Diseases of Women* for the Corpus Medicorum Graecorum series.

The following abbreviations are used for the works of Artistotle:

GA = *Generation of Animals*
HA = *History of Animals*
PA = *Parts of Animals*
MA = *Movement of Animals*

The text referred to in the notes as "Ps-Aristotle, *On Sterility*" is found in the Loeb Classical Library as the tenth book of *History of Animals*. Its authenticity as a work of Aristotle has long been doubted, although it is possible that it was an early work. It may date to the third century B.C. Ps-Aristotle, *Problems* is something very different, a collection of questions and answers—on matters ranging from why the old have white hair to why man sneezes more than any other animal—brought together perhaps as late as the fifth century A.D. and, with other works wrongly ascribed to Aristotle such as the *Masterpiece*, highly popular in the early modern era.

Several medical writers of antiquity are cited in the editions of the Corpus Medicorum Graecorum (hereafter CMG) and the Corpus Medicorum Latinorum (hereafter CML). They are referred to in the form CMG volume number, page.line (e.g., CMG vol. 2, p.34.7).

For the works of Galen, the standard edition remains that of C. G. Kuhn, *Claudii Galeni Opera omnia*, 20 vols. (Hildeheim: Olms, 1964–5 [reprint of the version of 1821–1833]). References to Galen are given in the form K volume.page (e.g., K 14.176).

1. The dates traditionally assigned to Hippocrates are ca. 460–ca. 370 B.C. Despite a tradition, developed several centuries after his death, claiming to give his biography and family tree, little is known of his life and work. The texts associated with his name—the Hippocratic corpus—cover a period far longer than a lifetime, show wide variations in style and content, and in many cases are "multi-author concoctions": see G. E. R. Lloyd, *The Revolutions of Wisdom* (Berkeley, Los Angeles, London: University of California Press, 1987), 132. On the manuscript tradition and assembly of the various treatises into a "Hippocratic corpus," possibly as late as the tenth century A.D., see in general J. Irigoin, "Tradition manuscrite et histoire du texte: Quelques problèmes relatifs à la Collection Hippocratique," *Revue d'histoire des textes* 3 (1973): 1–13, with F. Pfaff, "Die Ueberlieferung des Corpus Hippocraticum in der nachalexandrinischen Zeit," *Wiener Studien* 50 (1932): 67–82. On the papyri so far found which give fragments of Hippocratic texts, see M.-H. Marganne, *Inventaire analytique des papyrus grecs de médecine* (Geneva: Centre de recherches d'histoire et de philologie de la IVe section, Ecole pratique des Hautes Etudes 3, 12, 1981), updated by A. E. Hanson, "Papyri of Medical Content," *Yale Classical Studies* 28 (1985): 25–47. "Genuine Works" comes from the title of Francis Adams's *The Genuine Works of Hippocrates* (London: Sydenham Society, 1849). Although the search for at least one section of the Hippocratic corpus that can securely be attributed to Hippocrates—the so-called "Hippocratic question," on which see G. E. R. Lloyd, "The Hippocratic Question," *Classical Quarterly* 25 (1975): 171–192—is no longer the main aim of Hippocratic studies, it still exerts a powerful fascination. Thus, for example, even W. D. Smith, whose discussion in *The Hippocratic Tradition* (Ithaca, N.Y.: Cornell University Press, 1979) challenges the dominant paradigm in order to expose the development from the third century B.C. onward of the myth of the life and works of Hippocrates, tries to prove that *Regimen* is a "genuine work." Shortly after the publication of Smith's *Hippocratic Tradition,* Mansfeld produced an article arguing the case for another text of the Hippocratic corpus, *Airs, Waters, Places*—making use of precisely the same evidence as Smith drew on in defense of *Regimen.* See J. Mansfeld, "Plato and the Method of Hippocrates," *Greek, Roman and Byzantine Studies* 21 (1980): 341–362.

2. In 1922 Charles Singer described (imagined?) Hippocrates as "Learned, observant, humane . . . orderly and calm . . . grave, thoughtful and reticent, pure of mind and master of his passions"; see his *Greek Biology and Greek Medicine* (Oxford: Clarendon Press, 1922). The social position of the Hippocratic doctor is best handled by Lloyd in *Magic, Reason and Experience* (Cambridge: Cambridge University Press, 1979); *Science, Folklore and Ideology* (Cambridge: Cambridge University Press, 1983); and *Revolutions of Wisdom.* Competition was an important social value in the Greek world, seen as a normal part of human activity; see the poet Hesiod, *Works and Days* 11–20, where "potter vies with potter." This description of preclassical society could be used to suggest that the Hippocratic doctor (Greek *iatros*) would normally be in competition not only with mages,

purifiers, begging priests, and quacks (literally "deceivers"): for this list see the Hippocratic text *On the Sacred Disease* 1 (L 6.354–356).

3. Dr. Robb, "Hippocrates on Hysteria," *Johns Hopkins Hospital Bulletin* 3 (1892): 78–79.

4. E. Slater, "Diagnosis of 'Hysteria,'" *British Medical Journal* (1965): 1395–1399; quotation is taken from p. 1396.

5. I. Veith, *Hysteria: The History of a Disease* (Chicago: University of Chicago Press, 1965), 10. For an appreciation of Veith's considerable contribution to the history of medicine, see Showalter (chap. 4, this volume) and M. Micale, "Hysteria and Its Historiography: A Review of Past and Present Writings (1)," *History of Science* 27 (1989): 223–261, here pp. 227–228.

6. R. A. Woodruff, D. W. Goodwin, and S. B. Guze, "Hysteria (Briquet's Syndrome)" (1974), in *Hysteria*, ed. A. Roy (Chichester: John Wiley, 1982), 117–129 (quotation, p. 118); P. B. Bart and D. H. Scully, "The Politics of Hysteria: The Case of the Wandering Womb," in *Gender and Disordered Behavior: Sex Differences in Psychopathology*, ed. E. S. Gomberg and V. Frank (New York: Brunner/Mazel), 354–380 (quotation, p. 354); S. B. Guze, "The Diagnosis of Hysteria: What Are We Trying to Do?" *American Journal of Psychiatry* 124 (1967): 491–498 (quotations, pp. 491, 493); see also J. Sauri, "La concepcion Hipocratica de la histeria," *Actas Luso-Espanolas de Neurologia Psiquitria y Ciencias Afinas* 1 [4] (1973): 539–546, esp. p. 539. Veith's control of the Greek material is questioned by H. Merskey, "Hysteria: The History of a Disease: Ilza Veith," *British Journal of Psychiatry* 147 (1985): 576–579.

7. R. Satow, "Where Has All the Hysteria Gone?" *Psychoanalytic Review* 66 (1979/80): 463–477 (quotation, pp. 463–464).

8. Sauri, "Concepcion Hipocratica de la histeria," 539–546, following Veith, attributes the belief in a migratory womb to the ancient Egyptians, who were supposed to have exerted a particularly strong influence on the "Cnidian" texts of the Hippocratic corpus; see esp. pp. 540 and 542. The traditional classification of the corpus into "Cnidian" and "Coan," with its suggestion that the Cnidian texts represent an earlier, prerational strand in opposition to the rational medicine of the school of Cos with which Hippocrates was associated, is increasingly seen as an unnecessary complication in the study of Greek medicine. See further R. Joly, *Le niveau de la science hippocratique: Contribution à la psychologie de l'histoire des sciences* (Paris: Eds Belles Lettres, 1966); I. M. Lonie, "Cos versus Cnidus and the Historians," *History of Science* 16 (1978): 42–75, 77–92; A. Thivel, *Cnide et Cos? Essai sur les doctrines médicales dans la collection hippocratique* (Paris: Eds Belles Lettres, 1981). G. R. Wesley, *A History of Hysteria* (Lanham, Md.: University Press of America, 1980), 1–8 (which gives Hippocrates "credit for coining this term [hysteria]" but alleges an Egyptian origin for the clinical description; however, by attributing the words of Plato, *Timaeus* 91c, to the Egyptian Papyrus Ebers he shoots himself in the foot). Lloyd, *Science, Folklore and Ideology*, 65

n. 21 and 84 n. 100, does not, however, accept the implied link between Egyptian and Greek theories of the wandering womb. See further on this point Hanson, "Papyri of Medical Content," 25–47, and the discussion of the relevant papyri in H. Merskey and P. Potter, "The Womb Lay Still in Ancient Egypt," *British Journal of Psychiatry* 154 (1989): 751–753, which concludes that "the wandering womb did not come from Egypt."

9. E. Trillat, *Histoire de l'hystérie* (Paris: Eds Seghers, 1986); see esp. p. 14.

10. Adams, *Genuine Works of Hippocrates*, 50–54; B. Chance, "On Hippocrates and the Aphorisms," *Annals of Medical History* 2 (1930): 31–46. For criticism, see Smith, *Hippocratic Tradition*, esp. p. 238. On the importance of the *Aphorisms* in the late antique tradition and in the Middle Ages, see I. Müller-Rohlfsen, *Die Lateinische Ravennatische Übersetzung der hippokratischen Aphorismen aus dem 5./6. Jahrhundert n. chr.*, Geistes- und socialwissenschaftliche Dissertation 55, Hartmut Lüdke, Hamburg, 1980, p. xviii; A. Beccaria, "Sulle tracce di un antico canone latino di Ippocrate e di Galeno II. Gli Aforismi di Ippocrate nella versione e nei commenti del primo medioevo," *Italia Medioevale e Umanistica* 4 (1961), 1–75; P. Kibre, "Hippocrates Latinus: Repertorium of Hippocratic Writings in the Latin Middle Ages: II," *Traditio* 32 (1976), 257–292.

11. A. Rousselle, "Images médicales du corps. Observation féminine et idéologie masculine: Le corps de la femme d'après les médecins grecs," *Annales E.S.C.* 35 (1980): 1089–1115, esp. p. 1115 n. 27.

12. Indeed, it is used in this way by the second-century A.D. writer Aretaeus of Cappadocia, who entitles chapter 11 of his *On the Causes and Symptoms of Chronic Diseases*, book 4, "Concerning *Hysterika*" (CMG vol. 2, 79–82). A separate chapter in his work on acute diseases, 2.11, deals with *hysterikē pnix* (CMG vol. 2, pp.32–35).

13. Pliny's *Natural History* gives many examples of these uses: for mustard (Pliny, *Natural History* 20.87.237), black or white hellebore (25.31.53), and castoreum (beaver-oil, 32.13.28). And cf. the Hippocratic *Aphorisms* 5.49 (L 6.550). After intercourse, sneezing could cause miscarriage (Pliny, *Natural History* 7.6.42).

14. Pliny, *Natural History* 20.87.238. Note that "conversion" in this context has none of the later, post-Freudian implications of "hysterical conversion," simply meaning a physical turning. Beaver-oil is also used by Pliny as a fumigation or pessary for women suffering "from their wombs" (*Natural History* 32.13.28). In other words, the substances promoting sneezing can expel from above or from below, and from either location can succeed in returning wombs to their correct position.

15. Pliny, *Natural History* 7.52.175; see below page 34 for the use of this case in the literature of hysteria.

16. Veith, *Hysteria*, 10. In Aristotle, *On the Generation of Animals* 776a11, we are told that woman is the only *hysterikon* animal; the Loeb translation gives

"alone of all animals women are liable to uterine affections," A. L. Peck, *Aristotle: Generation of Animals* (London: Heinemann, 1942), 467. Cf. the Hippocratic texts *Prorrhetics* 1.119 (L 5.550) and *Coan Prognoses* 343 (L 5.658) and 543 (L 5.708).

17. *Gynaikeia* is a word of some complexity, and hence difficult to translate into one English word; literally "women's things," it can mean not only "diseases of women" but also "menstruation," "lochia," "external female genitalia," and "cures for women's diseases." For examples, see *Diseases of Women* 1.20 (L 8.58); 1.74 (L 8.156); *Nature of Woman* 67 (L 7.402); *Epidemics* 2.1.8 (L 3.88); 6.8.32 (L 5.356); *Coan Prognoses* 511 (L 5.702); 516 (L 5.704); Ps-Aristotle *On Sterility* 634b12.

18. Robb, "Hippocrates on Hysteria," 78–79.

19. Cf. Trillat, *Histoire de l'hystérie*, 14.

20. Rousselle, "Images médicales du corps," 1090.

21. Adams, *Genuine Works of Hippocrates*, v.

22. Smith, *Hippocratic Tradition*, 31.

23. M.-P. Duminil, "La recherche hippocratique aujourd'hui," *History and Philosophy of the Life Sciences* 2 (1979): 153–181, esp. p. 154 (my translation).

24. L 8.275, on Hippocrates's *Diseases of Women* 2.128 [hereafter *DW*]; 8.327, on *DW* 2.150; 8.309, on *DW* 2.137.

25. Veith, *Hysteria*, 13.

26. Adams, *Genuine Works of Hippocrates*; J. Chadwick and W. N. Mann, *The Medical Works of Hippocrates* (Oxford: Basil Blackwell, 1950), 166; W. H. S. Jones, *Hippocrates* IV (Loeb Classical Library, London: Heinemann, and Cambridge: Harvard University Press, 1931), 167.

27. Cited in Trillat, *Histoire de l'hystérie*, 272.

28. D. W. Abse, *Hysteria and Related Mental Disorders*, 2d ed. (Bristol: Wright, 1987), 91.

29. G. Lewis, *Day of Shining Red* (Cambridge: Cambridge University Press, 1980), 71–72.

30. Trillat, *Histoire de l'hystérie*, 10.

31. Ibid., 274.

32. R. A. Woodruff, "Hysteria: An Evaluation of Objective Diagnostic Criteria by the Study of Women with Chronic Medical Illnesses," *British Journal of Psychiatry* 114 (1967): 1115–1119, esp. p. 1119.

33. Guze, "Diagnosis of Hysteria," 494–495.

34. See also Woodruff, Goodwin, and Guze, "Hysteria (Briquet's Syndrome)," in *Hysteria*, ed. Roy, 122–123.

35. H. King, "Sacrificial Blood: The Role of the Amnion in Ancient Gynecology," *Helios* 13.2 (1987): 117–126 (=*Rescuing Creusa*, ed. M. B. Skinner [Lubbock: Texas Tech University Press, 1987]).

36. Slater, "Diagnosis of 'Hysteria,'" 1395–1399.

37. Ibid., 1399; E. Slater, "What Is Hysteria?" in *Hysteria*, ed. Roy, 40. See also H. Merskey, "The Importance of Hysteria," *British Journal of Psychiatry* 149

(1986): 23–28: "Whenever we are at the margin of our ability to decide on a diagnosis, hysteria is a diagnostic possibility" (p. 24).

38. E. Shorter, "Les désordres psychosomatiques sont-ils 'hystériques'? Notes pour une recherche historique," *Cahiers internationaux de Sociologie* 76 (1984): 201–224, esp. p. 208.

39. C. D. Marsden, "Hysteria—A Neurologist's View," *Psychological Medicine* 16 (1986): 277–288, esp. pp. 282–283. For a general discussion of retrospective diagnosis and its perils, see Micale, "Hysteria and Its Historiography," 43–46.

40. Slater, "Diagnosis of 'Hysteria,'" 1396.

41. F. Walshe, "Diagnosis of Hysteria," *British Medical Journal* (1965): 1451–1454, esp. 1452.

42. Roy, *Hysteria*.

43. R. Mayou, "The Social Setting of Hysteria," *British Journal of Psychiatry* 127 (1975): 466–469, here p. 466.

44. J. Wright, "Hysteria and Mechanical Man," *Journal of the History of Ideas* 41 (1980): 233–247, esp. p. 233; W. Mitchinson, "Hysteria and Insanity in Women—A Nineteenth-Century Perspective," *Journal of Canadian Studies* 21 (1986): 87–105, here p. 92.

45. E. Shorter, "Paralysis—The Rise and Fall of a 'Hysterical' Symptom," *Journal of Social History* 19 (1986): 549–582, here p. 551.

46. Trillat, *Histoire de l'hystérie*, 54.

47. Risse, "Hysteria at the Edinburgh Infirmary: The Construction and Treatment of a Disease, 1770–1800," *Medical History* 32 (1988): 1–22.

48. Mayou, "Social Setting of Hysteria," 466.

49. Marsden, "Hysteria—A Neurologist's View," 279.

50. Quoted in Shorter, "Paralysis," 578 n. 51.

51. Mayou, "Social Setting of Hysteria," 466–468; Shorter, "Désordres psychosomatiques sont-ils 'hystériques'?" 205; Shorter, "Paralysis," 550–551; see also Abse, *Hysteria and Related Mental Disorders*, 23–25.

52. Shorter, "Paralysis," 574 and 549; see Shorter, "Désordres psychosomatiques sont-ils 'hystériques'?" 202.

53. D. C. Taylor, "Hysteria, Play-acting and Courage," *British Journal of Psychiatry* 149 (1986): 37–41, defines hysteria as "the laying claim to sickness for which there is no objective evidence" and thus that hysteria is "a commonplace reaction" (p. 40). The "non-verbal language" suggestion is made by E. M. R. Critchley and H. E. Cantor, "Charcot's Hysteria Renaissant," *British Medical Journal* 289 (1984): 1785–1788, here p. 1788.

54. J. M. N. Boss, "The Seventeenth-Century Transformation of the Hysteric Affection, and Sydenham's Baconian Medicine," *Psychological Medicine* 9 (1979): 221–234, here p. 221.

55. J. Gabbay, "Asthma Attacked? Tactics for the Reconstruction of a Disease Concept," in *The Problem of Medical Knowledge: Examining the Social Construction of Medicine*, ed. P. Wright and A. Treacher (Edinburgh: Edinburgh University Press, 1982), 23–48, quotation p. 29.

56. Gabbay, "Asthma Attacked?" in *Problem of Medical Knowledge*, Wright and Treacher, 33.

57. Ibid., 42.

58. The Hippocratic *Places in Man* 47 (L 6.344).

59. Boss, "Seventeenth-Century Transformation," 221–234.

60. W. Mitchinson, "Hysteria and Insanity in Women," 89.

61. Boss, "Seventeenth-Century Transformation," 232.

62. Risse, "Hysteria at the Edinburgh Infirmary," 2–4.

63. Ibid., 17.

64. Ibid., 16.

65. Cf. H. Landouzy, *Traité complet de l'hystérie* (Paris and London: Baillière, 1846), with Littré; Landouzy accepts the curative powers of marriage but asks an important question that follows from the Hippocratic recommendation: "Peut-on épouser avec sécurité une hystérique?" (p. 303). See also H. Merskey, *The Analysis of Hysteria* (London: Baillière Tindall, 1979), 12 ff.; H. Ey, "History and Analysis of the Concept" (1964), in *Hysteria*, ed. Roy, 3–19.

66. Mitchinson, "Hysteria and Insanity in Women," 90.

67. F. M. Mai and H. Merskey, "Briquet's Concept of Hysteria: An Historical Perspective," *Canadian Journal of Psychiatry* 26 (1981): 57–63.

68. B. C. Brodie, *Lectures Illustrative of Certain Local Nervous Affections* (London: Longman, 1837), 46.

69. Robb, "Hippocrates on Hysteria," 78–79.

70. Ibid., 79. Sauri, "Concepcion Hipocratica de la histeria," 539–546, uses *DW* 1.7 and 2.123–125; J. Palis, E. Rossopoulos, and L. C. Triarhou, "The Hippocratic Concept of Hysteria: A Translation of the Original Texts," *Integrative Psychiatry* 3 (1985): 226–228, translate *NW* 3 (L 7.314–316), 73 (L 7.404), 75 (L 7.404), and 87, with *DW* 2.123–125, while Veith, *Hysteria*, p. 10 n. 1, is "primarily based" on *DW* 1.7, 1.32, and 2.123–127.

71. *Acut. Sp.* 35 (L 2.522). This is an interesting distinction; classical Greek uterine *pnix*, which so many writers want to identify as "hysteria," is distinguished by normal sensations, yet "hysteria" in later historical periods is supposed to involve "local loss of sensation." See Wright, "Hysteria and Mechanical Man," 233.

72. Robb, "Hippocrates on Hysteria," 78–79.

73. M. R. Lefkowitz, *Heroines and Hysterics* (London: Duckworth, 1981), 13.

74. The entry of the word "hysteria" into European language is surprisingly late. The French *hystérie* appears in dictionaries in 1731, and "hysteria" itself in 1801. One conclusion that could be drawn from this is that, because of the very recent origin of "hysteria," the medical profession has sought to give it some respectability by projecting it back into Hippocratic medicine.

75. G. Lewis, "A View of Sickness in New Guinea," in *Social Anthropology and Medicine*, ed. J. B. Loudon (London: ASA Monograph 13, Academic Press, 1976), 88.

76. L. Bourgey, *Observation et expérience chez les médecins de la collection hippocratique* (Paris: J. Vrin, 1953), 149–152.

77. V. Di Benedetto, *Il medico e la malattia: La scienza di Ippocrate* (Turin: Einaudi Paperbacks 172, 1986), 18–21, 89–91, 4.

78. Ibid., 21–23. Lloyd, in *Revolutions of Wisdom*, 203–206, points out that the terminology of classical Greek medicine is characterized by "a certain conceptual vagueness"; ordinary Greek is preferred to technical terms.

79. C. M. T. Clologe, *Essai sur l'histoire de la gynécologie dans l'antiquité grecque jusqu' à la collection Hippocratique* (Bordeaux: Arnaud, 1905), 63: "Les anciens s'étaient beaucoup occupés de la menstruation."

80. *DW* 1.1 (L. 8.10–12); Greek *ischyros, stereos, pyknos*. See W. A. Heidel, *Hippocratic Medicine: Its Spirit and Method* (New York: Columbia University Press, 1941), 91; P. Manuli, "Donne mascoline, femmine sterili, vergini perpetue: La ginecologia greca tra Ippocrate e Sorano," in *Madre Materia*, by S. Campese, P. Manuli, and G. Sissa (Turin: Boringhieri, 1983), 147–192, here p. 188. See A. E. Hanson, "Anatomical Assumptions in Hippocrates *Diseases of Women* 1.1," paper delivered at the APA, 1981, and R. Parker, *Miasma* (Oxford: Clarendon Press, 1982), 230, on the sheepskin analogy; the latter points out that the powers of absorption of the fleece account for its use in rituals of purification. In *Superfetation* 34 (L 8.506), sheepskin is used in therapy. A young girl who does not menstruate alternates among hunger, thirst, fever, and vomiting excess fluid. The remedy, warm lambskins placed on her abdomen, may be intended to draw out the excess fluid which should have come out as menstrual blood.

81. Aristotle, *GA* 728a17 ff. and 737a; S. R. L. Clark, *Aristotle's Man* (Oxford: Clarendon Press, 1975); M. C. Horowitz, "Aristotle and Woman," *Journal of the History of Biology* 9 (1976): 183–213; L. Dean-Jones, "Menstrual Bleeding According to the Hippocratics and Aristotle," *Transactions of the American Philological Association* 119 (1989): 177–192.

82. Hesiod, *Works and Days*, 45–105 and 373–375; idem, *Theogony*, 594–602; N. Loraux, "Sur la race des femmes et quelques-unes de ses tribus," *Arethusa* 11 (1978): 43–87.

83. Plato, *Timaeus* 90e–91a.

84. P. DuBois, *Sowing the Body: Psychoanalysis and Ancient Representations of Women* (Chicago: University of Chicago Press, 1988); N. Loraux, "Le lit, la guerre," *L'Homme* 21 (1981): 37–67; King, "Sacrificial Blood," 117–126 (= Rescuing Creusa, Skinner).

85. E.g., *Airs, Waters, Places* 10 (L 2.44 and 2.50); *Nature of the Child* 15 (L 7.494); *Glands* 16 (L 8.572).

86. In Greek, *strephontai hai metrai*, close to the Latin *converto*.

87. Younger women have the most blood, due to "the growth of the body and the diet." *Diseases of Young Girls* (L 8.466); confirmed in *DW* 2.111 (L 8.238–240).

88. Castoreum and fleabane (*konyza*) appear together on many occasions; e.g., *DW* 2.128 (L 8.274); 2.200 (L 8.382); 2.201 (L 8.384).

89. Bandages around the body occur in 2.127 (L 8.272) and 2.129 (L. 8.278).

90. A translation of this text was given in my Ph.D. thesis, *From Parthenos to Gynē: The Dynamics of Category*, University of London, 1985. I am taking the Greek *stomachos* here to mean "mouth of the womb" rather than "mouth," although it can have many anatomical meanings and occurs in 2.203 (L 8.388) with the meaning "mouth." This is clearly not a "paint by numbers" format: if the reader tries to carry out the instructions in the order given, the jar will be sealed before the garlic and seal oil go in. Similar warnings about the possibility of exhaustion in the patient occur at *DW* 2.181 (L 8.364), 3.230 (L 8.442), and 3.241 (L 8.454). The vegetable substances used in scent therapy are discussed in S. Byl's "L'odeur végétale dans la thérapeutique gynécologique du Corpus hippocratique," *Revue Belge de Philologie et d'Histoire* 67 (1989): 53–64.

91. *DW* 2.126 (L 8.272); cf. 2.203 (L 8.390).

92. E.g., *DW* 2.131 (L 8.278), where the substances to be used are not specified.

93. *NW* 87 (L 7.408) reads, "In suffocation caused by movement [of the womb], light up the wick of a lamp then snuff it out, holding it under the nostrils so that she draws in the smoke. Then soak myrrh in perfume, dip wool in [so it is thoroughly impregnated] and insert. Also give her a drink of resin dissolved in oil."

94. B. Simon, *Mind and Madness in Ancient Greece* (Ithaca, N.Y.: Cornell University Press, 1978), 238.

95. I. M. Lewis, *Ecstatic Religion* (Harmondsworth, Middlesex: Penguin, 1971), and Mayou, "Social Setting of Hysteria," 467.

96. Simon, *Mind and Madness in Ancient Greece*, 242, 251.

97. Ibid., 243.

98. Fourteen is the ideal age of menarche in medical writers (D. W. Amundsen and C. J. Diers, "The Age of Menarche in Classical Greece and Rome," *Human Biology* 41 [1969]: 125–132); for age at marriage, see W. K. Lacey, *The Family in Classical Greece* (London: Thames & Hudson, 1968), 162, and M. L. West, *Hesiod: The Works and Days* (Oxford: Oxford University Press, 1978), 327.

99. *DW* 2.126 (L 8.270–272); *DW* 2.130 (L 8.326); *DW* 2.203 (L 8.386–392).

100. *DW* 2.128 (L 8.274); *DW* 2.129 (L 8.276); *DW* 2.131 (L 8.278–280).

101. Ps-Aristotle, *Problems* 30; Simon, *Mind and Madness in Ancient Greece*, 222.

102. Marriage and childbirth are recommended therapies in many Hippocratic texts outside the hysteria tradition; e.g., *DW* 1.37 (L 8.92), 2.115 (L 8.250), 2.119 (L 8.260), 2.128 (L 8.276), 2.133 (L 8.302), *Gen.* 4 (L 7.476).

103. *DW* 2.150 (L 8.326), 2.201 (L 8.384).

104. *DW* 3.222 (L 8.430).

105. Di Benedetto, *Il medico e la malattia*, 4.

106. A. Rousselle, *Porneia: On Desire and the Body in Antiquity* (Oxford: Basil Blackwell, 1968), 69.

107. D. Gourevitch, *Le mal d'être femme: La femme et la médecine dans la Rome antique* (Paris: Eds Belles Lettres, 1984), 119.

108. Hanson, "Anatomical Assumptions in Hippocrates"; Manuli, "Donne mascoline, femmine sterili" in *Madre Materia*, by Campese, Manuli, and Sissa, 157.

109. E.g., *DW* 2.146 (L 8.322), 3.214 (L 8.414–416), 3.219 (L 8.424), 3.230 (L 8.440); *Superfetation* 25 (L 8.488–490); *NW* 96 (L 7.412–414); *Aphorisms* 5.59 (L 4.554).

110. L 8.310: Greek *anō/katō*.

111. *DW* 2.123 (L 8.266), 2.154 (L 8.330), a description of a "wild" womb, translated by Littré as "irritated"; 2.201 (L 8.384), a discussion of *pnix*. See Byl, "L'odeur végétale," 56–58.

112. *DW* 2.125 (L 8.268), 2.137 (L 8.310), 2.143 (L 8.316), 2.145 (L 8.320).

113. C. M. Turbayne, "Plato's 'Fantastic' Appendix: The Procreation Model of the *Timaeus*," *Paideia*, special issue, 1976: 125–140, quotation from p. 132.

114. Ibid., 140 n. 11.

115. F. Kudlien, "Early Greek Primitive Medicine," *Clio Medica* 3 (1968): 305–336, quotations from p. 330. See also S. Byl and A. F. De Ranter, "L'étiologie de la stérilité féminine dans le Corpus hippocratique," 303–322, in *La maladie et les maladies dans la Collection hippocratique* (Actes du VIᵉ Colloque hippocratique), ed. P. Potter, G. Maloney, and J. Desautels (Quebec: Eds du Sphinx, 1990), 321.

116. Aretaeus, 2.11 (CMG vol.2, pp.32.28–33.1); the relevant passage reads "and the sum of the matter is that the womb in the female is *hokoion ti zōon en zōōi*."

117. *DW* 1.7 (L 8.32).

118. Ann Hanson, pers. comm.; F. Adams, *The Medical Works of Paulus Aegineta*, vol. I (London: Welsh, 1834), 458, suggests that the *Timaeus* passage "ought perhaps not to be taken in too literal a sense, considering that philosopher's well-known propensity to mystification."

119. Soranus of Ephesus, *Gynecology* 3.29 (CMG vol. 4, p.113.3–6); O. Temkin, *Soranus' Gynecology* (Baltimore: Johns Hopkins University Press, 1956), translates, "For the uterus does not issue forth like a wild animal from the lair, delighted by fragrant odors and fleeing bad odors: rather it is drawn together because of the stricture caused by the inflammation." "Wild animal" is the Greek *thērion*, in contrast to Aretaeus's more neutral *zōon*, "living thing."

120. Based on R. E. Siegel, *Galen on the Affected Parts* (Basel and New York: S. Karger, 1976), 187, translating *On the Affected Parts* 6.5(K 8.425–426), the Latin version of which reads: "Haec dicente Platone, quidam addiderunt, uterum, quum ita per corpus errans ad septum transversum pervenerit, respirationem interturbare. Alii errare ipsum veluti animal non dicunt, sed ubi suppressa sunt menstrua, exiccatum ac humectari cupientem ad viscera usque ascendere; quum vero ascendendo nonnunquam septum transversum contingat, idcirco animal respiratione privari."

121. D. F. Krell, "Female Parts in *Timaeus*," *Arion* 2 (1975): 400–421, esp. p. 404.

122. Plato, *Timaeus* 70e: Greek *hōs thremma agrion*.

123. Ibid., 89b–c.

124. Ibid., 71a; 91a–b.

125. Not *hoion zōon*, but *zōon epithymētikon enon tēs paidopoiias* (91c).

126. Aristotle, *PA* 666a 20–23 and 666b 16–17; *MA* 703b 21–26; see S. Byl, *Recherches sur les grands traités biologiques d'Aristotle: Sources écrites et préjugés* (Brussels: Palais des Académies, 1980), 124.

127. Plato, *Timaeus* 73c ff.

128. *Gen.* (L 7.473–474); *Nature of Man* 11 (L 6.58).

129. L 7.478–480.

130. Shorter, "Paralysis," 574 and 549.

131. Trillat, *Histoire de l'hystérie*, 16.

132. E.g., *DW* 1.2 (L 8.32), use of *hē gynē*, "the woman."

133. *Pnigei, DW* 2.201 (L 8.384); *DW* 2.124 (L 8.266).

134. Mitchinson, "Hysteria and Insanity in Women," 91.

135. E. Jorden, *A Briefe Discourse of a Disease Called the Suffocation of the Mother* (London: J. Windet, 1603).

136. See Trillat, *Histoire de l'hystérie*, 7.

137. L 8.326.

138. See Trillat, *Histoire de l'hystérie*, 33; Abse, *Hysteria and Related Mental Disorders*, 2.

139. *Places in Man* 47 (L 6.344); cf. "the cause of numberless diseases," L 9.396.

140. *Prōton ergon*, Soranus, *Gynecology* 3.6.

141. *Nature of the Child* 15 (L 7.494), the translation given is that of I. M. Lonie, *The Hippocratic Treatises "On Generation," "On the Nature of the Child," "Diseases IV"* (Berlin: De Gruyter, 1981), 8; the original Greek literally means "her original nature."

142. *Ep.* 7.123 (L 5.468).

143. *Ep.* 6.8.32 (L 5.356); *DW* 3.230 (L 8.444).

144. L 7.476.

145. Aristotle, *PA* 650a 8ff.; *GA* 775a 14–20; Horowitz, "Aristotle and Woman," 183–213.

146. Plutarch, *Moralia* 650a–651e.

147. Aristotle, *PA* 648a 28–30; *GA* 765b 19.

148. L 8.12–14.

149. L 6.512.

150. Greek *kaminos*; Aristotle, *GA* 764a 12–20.

151. Herodotus, 5.92.

152. Artemidorus, *Oneirocritica: The Interpretation of Dreams*, trans. R. J. White (Park Ridge, N.J.: Noyes Press, 1975), 2.10.

153. *Gen.* 4 (L 7.474–476); *NC* 12 (L 7.486)—Greek *en thermōi eousa*, trans. Lonie, *Hippocratic Treatises*, 6—*NC* 30 (L 7.536).

154. Greek *paue, pnigeran legeis* (line 122).

155. The use of similar imagery does not end in the classical Greek period. Around A.D. 1565, Teresa of Avila suffered symptoms that, in the nineteenth century, were retrospectively diagnosed as hysteria. These included contractive spasms, sweating and chills, as well as feeling "like a person who has a rope around his neck, is being strangled and trying to breathe" (C. M. Bache, "A Reappraisal of Teresa of Avila's Supposed Hysteria," *Journal of Religion and Health* 24 (1985): 300–315, esp. pp. 310 and 305).

156. M.-P. Duminil, "Recherche hippocratique aujourd'hui," 156; D. J. Furley and J. S. Wilkie, *Galen on Respiration and the Arteries* (Princeton, N.J.: Princeton University Press, 1984), 22. A similar difficulty exists between the Latin *conceptio*, meaning retention of the male seed, and our "conception," meaning the fertilization of the ovum by the sperm; see the Budé edition of Soranus (ed. P. Burguière, D. Gourevitch, and Y. Malinas, 1988), p. xcv.

157. Empedocles in H. Diels and W. Kranz, *Die Fragmente der Vorsokratiker* I (Berlin: Weidmannsche, 1951), fragment 31 B100; Furley and Wilkie, *Galen on Respiration*, 3–5.

158. Plato, *Timaeus* 76b1–e9, discussed by Furley and Wilkie, *Galen on Respiration*, 7–8.

159. On Aristotle, see above, n. 150; the quotations are from Galen, *On the Usefulness of Breathing*, chap. 3 (K 4.492 and 4.508), using the Furley and Wilkie edition, *Galen on Respiration*, 109 and 131.

160. Galen, *On the Affected Parts* (K 8.415).

161. See discussion in M. D. Grmek, "Les *Indicia mortis* dans la médecine gréco-romaine," in *La mort, les morts et l'au-delà dans le monde greco-romaine*, ed. F. Hinard (Caen: Centre des Publications de l'Université, 1987), 129–144, and A. Debru, "La suffocation hystérique chez Galien et Aetius: Réécriture et emprunt de 'je,'" in *Tradizione e ecdotica dei testi medici tardoantichi e bizantini* (Atti del Convegno Internazionale Anacapre 29–31 ottobre 1990), ed. A. Garzya (Napoli: M. D'Auria, 1992), 79–89.

162. Diogenes Laertius, *Lives of the Philosophers* 8.61. The remaining fragments of *Apnous* or *Peri tēs apnou* (On the absence of breath, also known as On the causes of disease) are given in the edition of the fragments of Heracleides edited by F. Wehrli, *Die Schule des Aristoteles: Heft VII, Herakleides Pontikos* (Basel: Schwabe, 1953). On Empedocles as a "showman" among early cosmogonists, see Lloyd, *Revolutions of Wisdom*, 101.

163. Pliny, *Natural History* 7.52.175; Latin *exanimis*, "without breath," can also mean "without life." The *editio princeps* of Pliny was published in 1469, but abridgments and extracts circulated throughout the Middle Ages: see M. Chibnall, "Pliny's *Natural History* and the Middle Ages" in *Silver Latin II*, ed. T. A. Dorey (London: Routledge & Kegan Paul, 1975), 57–78; book 7 was certainly in circulation from the early ninth century A.D.; see L. D. Reynolds, ed., *Texts and Transmission: A Survey of the Latin Classics* (Oxford: Clarendon Press, 1983), 307–316.

164. Literally *conversio volvae*. The Budé edition of Pliny gives a "medical" translation, "la rétroversion," while the Loeb uses the rather vague "distortion."

165. Pieter van Foreest (1522–1597), *Observationum et curationum medicinalium, liber vigesimus-octavus, de mulierum morbis* (Leyden: Plantin, 1599), Obs. 27, 167–168; the story is also given by Nicolas de la Roche (fl.1542) in *De morbis mulierum curandis* (Paris: V. Gaultherot, 1542), 65^(r–v).

166. Origen, *Against Celsus* 2.16, 402: Heracleides frag. 78 Wehrli.

167. Soranus, *Gynecology* 3.4.29 (CMG 4.112.18–23); trans. O. Temkin, 153.

168. J. Longrigg, "Superlative Achievement and Comparative Neglect: Alexandrian Medical Science and Modern Historical Research," *History of Science* 19 (1981): 155–200; P. Potter, "Herophilus of Chalcedon: An Assessment of His Place in the History of Anatomy," *Bulletin of the History of Medicine* 50 (1976): 45–60; H. von Staden, *Herophilus: The Art of Medicine in Early Alexandria* (Cambridge: Cambridge University Press, 1989).

169. Mantias frag. 11: Soranus, *Gynecology* 3.4.29 (CMG IV p.112.22–23); von Staden, *Herophilus*, 517–518. On the effects of these discoveries on medical writing, see D. Gourevitch, "Situation de Soranos dans la médecine antique," in *Soranos d'Ephèse: Maladies des femmes 1.1*, Budé ed. (Paris: Eds Belles Lettres, 1988), xxxiv–xxxv.

170. Marganne, *Inventaire analytique des papyrus grecs*, no. 155, pp. 283–286; P. Ryl. 3.531 (= PACK² 2418). On the huge therapeutic repertory of Hippocratic gynecology, see Di Benedetto, *Il medico e la malattia*, 17. It is possible that the remedies that occur only once in the medical corpus simply represent the attempt of a healer to think of something entirely new in order to impress the patient. See the descriptions of the competitive social context of early medicine in G. E. R. Lloyd's *Magic, Reason and Experience* (Cambridge: Cambridge University Press, 1979), *Science, Folklore and Ideology* (Cambridge: Cambridge University Press, 1983), and *Revolutions of Wisdom*, 68–69 and 96 on the importance of innovation in Hippocratic medicine, and 103–104 on rivalry.

171. Marganne no. 93, pp. 168–169; P. Hibeh 2.191 (= PACK² 2348).

172. Marganne, *Inventoire analytique des papyrus grecs*, no. 8, pp. 16–17; B K T 3.33–34 (= PACK² 2394).

173. Latin *vulva*; Celsus 4.27, CML vol. 1, pp. 180–181.

174. DW 1.77 (L 8.172), in which blood is let at the ankle in order to ease a long and difficult labor; P. Brain, *Galen on Bloodletting* (Cambridge: Cambridge University Press, 1986), 113–114.

175. Soranus, *Gynecology* 3.28.4 (CMG vol. 4, p.111.8); Galen, *On Venesection against the Erasistrateans in Rome* (K 11.201; Brain, *Galen on Bloodletting*, 45); it is recommended that this be done at the ankle, to encourage the flow of blood away from the womb (*On Treatment by Venesection*, K 11.283, 11.302–303; Brain, *Galen on Bloodletting*, 93).

176. See in general M. H. Green, *The Transmission of Ancient Theories of Female*

Physiology and Disease through the Early Middle Ages, Ph.D. dissertation, Princeton University, 1985, with M. Ullmann, *Islamic Medicine* (Edinburgh: Edinburgh University Press, 1978), 11–15, and the discussion of the rediscovery of Hippocratism in V. Nutton, "Hippocrates in the Renaissance," in *Die hippokratischen Epidemien*, ed. G. Baader and R. Winau, *Sudhoffs Archiv* Beiheft 27 (Stuttgart, 1990), 420–439.

177. On the content of Aretaeus see O. Temkin, "History of Hippocratism in Late Antiquity: The Third Century and the Latin West," in *The Double Face of Janus and Other Essays in the History of Medicine*, by O. Temkin (Baltimore: Johns Hopkins University Press, 1977), 167–177, esp. p. 170. Aretaeus uses the word *hymenes* for these membranes; see 2.11.5 (CMG vol. 2, p.33.29), 4.11.9 (CMG vol. 2, p.81.28), and 6.10.1 (CMG vol. 2, p.139.27). Scent therapy is discussed in a separate section on remedies for hysterical suffocation, at 6.10.3 (CMG vol. 2, p.140.17–19). It is worth noting here that the discussion of Aretaeus in Veith's *Hysteria*, 22–23, wrongly asserts that he gives a "brief reference to male hysteria." In fact, although he mentions an unnamed condition, described as having some symptoms in common with suffocation of the womb, and affecting both sexes, in his discussion of satyriasis in 2.12.4 he explicitly denies that suffocation of the womb can affect men, since men do not have wombs (CMG vol. 2, p.35.11–12).

178. In his discussion of epilepsy itself, Aretaeus includes the symptom of "*pnix* as if strangled"; see 1.5.6 (CMG vol. 2, p.4.27).

179. 2.11.4 (CMG vol. 2, p.33.15–17); I translate *phlebes* as "channels."

180. "High-sailing" is *akroploos*, 2.11.5 (CMG vol. 2, p.33.29); the membranes around the womb are "like the sails of a ship" in 4.11.9 (CMG vol. 2, p.81.31) and 6.10.1 (CMG vol. 2, p.140.3–4).

181. Aretaeus goes beyond *Aphorisms* 5.35, and says that sneezing, when accompanied by pressure on the nostrils, can make the womb return to its place; 6.10.5 (CMG vol. 2, p.141.7–9).

182. Venesection occurs at 6.10.3 (CMG vol. 2, p.140.14) and 6.10.6 (CMG vol. 2, p.141.14–15) where the removal of hairs is also discussed.

183. Smith, *Hippocratic Tradition*.

184. Gourevitch, "Situation de Soranos," in *Soranos d'Éphèse*, Budé ed., xxxi. On the establishment of the text of Soranus, see P. Burguière, "Histoire du texte," in *Soranos d'Éphèse*, Budé ed., xlvii–lxv. On Caelius Aurelianus, see M. F. Drabkin and I. E. Drabkin, *Caelius Aurelianus: Gynaecia fragments of a Latin version of Soranus's Gynaecia from a thirteenth-century manuscript* (Baltimore: Johns Hopkins University Press, 1951), and J. Pigeaud, "Pro Caelio Aureliano," Mémoires du Centre Jean Palerne 3: Médecins et Médecine dans l'Antiquité (Université de Saint-Etienne, 1982), 105–117.

185. In general see P. Manuli, "Elogia della castità: La *Ginecologia* di Sorano," *Memoria* 3 (1982): 39–49; Gourevitch, "Situation de Soranos," in *Soranos d'Éphèse*,

Budé ed., vii–xlvi; p. xiii discusses the correct terms for the three conditions of the body. On the difficulty in reading our main source for the "sects," see O. Temkin, "Celsus' 'On Medicine' and the Ancient Medical Sects," *Bulletin of the History of Medicine* 3 (1935): 249–264; W. D. Smith, "Notes on Ancient Medical Historiography," *Bulletin of the History of Medicine* 63 (1989): 73–109; Lloyd, *Revolutions of Wisdom*, 158–171. See also M. Frede, "The Method of the So-called Methodical School of Medicine," in *Science and Speculation*, ed. J. Barnes, J. Brunschwig, M. Burnyeat, and M. Schofield (Cambridge: Cambridge University Press, 1982), 1–23.

186. Gourevitch, "Situation de Soranos," in *Soranos d'Éphèse*, Budé ed., xlv.

187. O. Temkin, *Soranus' Gynecology* (Baltimore: Johns Hopkins University Press, 1956), 9; Green, *Ancient Theories of Female Physiology and Disease*, 34; Lloyd, *Revolutions of Wisdom* (Berkeley and Los Angeles: University of California Press, 1987), 164–165.

188. Soranus, *Gynecology* 3.29.5 (CMG vol. 4, p.113.5–6).

189. Ibid. (CMG vol. 4, p.113.3–5), trans. Temkin, 153.

190. Ibid., 3.28.4 (CMG vol. 4, p.111.8); the acute and chronic forms are distinguished at 3.28.1 (CMG vol. 4, p.110.22).

191. P. Diepgen, *Die Frauenheilkunde der Alten Welt: Handbuch der Gynäkologie XII*, 1 (Munich: Bergmann, 1937), 233. On the identity of the short treatise *De gynaeciis liber, hoc est de passionibus mulierum*, attributed to Galen and including references to hysterical suffocation, together with scent therapy, see M. H. Green, "The *De Genecia* Attributed to Constantine the African," *Speculum* 62 (1987): 299–323, esp. p. 30 n. 9. There also exists an Arabic commentary on *Diseases of Women* 1.1–11, which is attributed to Galen; Green, *Ancient Theories of Female Physiology and Disease*, 118–119 n. 5, argues that this attribution merits further investigation, since Galen wrote that he planned a commentary on this text.

192. Galen, *On the Affected Parts* 6.5 (K 8.414–437).

193. *On the Affected Parts* 6.5 (K 8.414). See T. C. Allbutt, *Greek Medicine in Rome* (London: Macmillan, 1921), 344.

194. E. Trillat, "Trois itinéraires à travers l'histoire de l'hystérie," *Histoire des Sciences médicales* 21 (1987): 27–31, esp. p. 28.

195. *On the Affected Parts* 6.5 (K 8.424), use of *tōn hysterikōn legomenōn symptōmatōn*; see also the commentary on *Aphorism* 5.35, K17B.824.

196. *On the Affected Parts* 6.5 (K 8.417); the English translation given here is that of Siegel, which is not always to be trusted: p. 184.

197. K 8.426 and K 8.430, trans. Siegel, p. 189. Galen himself wrote a treatise called "On the Anatomy of the Uterus," which, like *On the Affected Parts*, was translated into Arabic; see M. Ullmann, *Die Medizin im Islam* (Leiden: Brill, 1970), 35–68.

198. See in particular the Hippocratic text *Generation*: Lonie, *Hippocratic Treatises*, esp. pp. 1–5. For the writer of these texts, female seed is weak and thin,

male strong and thick. On Soranus and the context of his work see Gourevitch, "Situation de Soranos," in *Soranos d'Éphèse*, Budé ed., xix.

199. *On the Affected Parts* 6.5 (K 8.420, 424, and 432–433).

200. *On the Affected Parts* 6.5 (K 8.421–424).

201. *Sympaschei*, K 8.424; *adelphixia*, *On joints* 57 (L 4.246); in the sixteenth century, the Latin *communitas* is the preferred term.

202. Further discussion of the mechanism by which these symptoms are produced may be found in *On the Method of Healing, to Glaucon* 1.15 (C. Daremberg, *Oeuvres anatomiques, physiologiques, et médicales de Galien* [Paris: Baillière, 1854–6], Vol. II, p. 735), where the seed becomes wet and cold, chilling the body.

203. Green, *Ancient Theories of Female Physiology and Disease*, 50–52. Scent therapy too is described in *On the Method of Healing, to Glaucon* 1.15 (Daremberg, *Oeuvres anatomiques*, Vol. II, p. 735), and also in *On Compound Medicines according to Site* 9.10 (K 13.320).

204. *On the Affected Parts* 6.5 (K 8.420); cf. *DW* 2.201 (L 8.384) on rubbing aromatics into the groin and inner thighs.

205. *PGM* VII 260–272; K. Preisendanz and A. Henrichs, *Papyri Graecae Magicae*[2] (Stuttgart: Teubner, 1974). The translation is that of J. Scarborough, in *The Greek Magical Papyri in Translation*, by H. D. Betz (Chicago: University of Chicago Press, 1986), 123–124.

206. Pandora is created with a *kyneos noos*, the mind of a bitch (Hesiod *Works and Days* 67). On the sexuality of the dog, see for example Aristotle, *HA* 540a 24 and 574b 27. *Kuōn*, dog, can mean the genitals of either sex.

207. Marcellus Empiricus, fl. A.D. 395; see *De medicamentis liber*, chap. 1.25 (CML vol. 5, pp.60.35–61.3). The *editio princeps* of Cornarius was printed in 1536; p. 32 has a note in the margin by this passage saying *suffocatio de vulva* (J. Cornarius, *De medicamentis empiricis, physicis, ac rationabilibus liber* [Basel: Froben, 1536]).

208. On encyclopedism, see P. Lemerle, *Byzantine Humanism: The First Phase*, Australian Association for Byzantine Studies, Byzantina Australiensa 3, Canberra 1986, chap. 10; medical treatises receive only a brief mention on p. 341.

209. See M. Meyerhof and D. Joannides, *La Gynécologie et l'Obstétrique chez Avicenne (Ibn Sina) et leurs rapports avec celles des Grecs* (Cairo: R. Schindler, 1938), 6. A reassessment of the period is given by V. Nutton, "From Galen to Alexander, Aspects of Medicine and Medical Practice in Late Antiquity," in *Dumbarton Oaks Papers* 38 (1984), 1–14 (= V. Nutton, *From Democedes to Harvey* [London: Variorum Reprints, 1988], chap. 10, 2–3).

210. J. Kollesch, *Untersuchungen zu den pseudogalenischen Definitiones Medicae* (Berlin: Akademie-Verlag, 1973), 14; J. Duffy, "Byzantine Medicine in the Sixth and Seventh Centuries: Aspects of Teaching and Practice," in *Dumbarton Oaks Papers* 38, ed. Scarborough, 21–27.

211. J. Duffy, "Byzantine Medicine in the Sixth and Seventh Centuries: As-

pects of Teaching and Practice," in *Dumbarton Oaks Papers* 38, ed. Scarborough, 21–27; here 21–22.

212. N. G. Wilson, *Scholars of Byzantium* (London: Duckworth, 1983), 48, and see also 85–86.

213. Oribasius, *Collectiones medicae* 24.31 (CMG vol. 6.2,1, pp.41–46).

214. Oribasius, *Synopsis* 9.45 (CMG vol. 6.3, p.305.10–28), trans. C. Daremberg, in *Oeuvres d'Oribase*, ed. U. Bussemaker and C. Daremberg, 6 vols. (Paris: Impr. Nationale, 1851–1876), vol. 6, pp. 539–540. Philumenos of Alexandria was the author of a work on gynecology, and another on venomous animals and remedies for their stings and bites (see Allbutt, *Greek Medicine in Rome*). The latter is available as CMG vol. 10.1.1. Philumenos uses the same remedies for certain poisons as for *hysterikē pnix* (pp. 14.19 and 22), thus echoing Galen's view that retained seed and menses acted like a poison on the body. About Philumenos himself little is known; even his date is variously given as the first century A.D., ca. A.D. 180, or the third century A.D. He does not explicitly use Galen—which lends support to the earliest date—but the above reference to *hysterikē pnix* may imply knowledge of Galen's theories.

215. Oribasius, *Synopsis* 9.41 (CMG vol. 6.3, p.301).

216. G. Baader, "Early Medieval Latin Adaptations of Byzantine Medicine in Western Europe," in *Dumbarton Oaks Papers* 38, ed. Scarborough, 251–259, esp. p. 252; Wilson, *Scholars of Byzantium*, 57–58; Duffy, "Byzantine Medicine," in *Dumbarton Oaks Papers* 38, ed. Scarborough, 21–27, esp. 25–27.

217. Wilson, *Scholars of Byzantium*, 142–143.

218. 16.68; while the completion of the CMG Aetius is awaited, Book 16 appears only in the unsatisfactory edition of S. Zervos, *Aetii sermo sextidecimus et ultimus* (Leipzig: Mangkos, 1901), of which see pp. 95 ff.; Soranus is cited on p. 97.26. An English translation is available in J. V. Ricci, *Aetios of Amida: The Gynecology and Obstetrics of the Sixth Century A.D.* (Philadelphia: Blakiston, 1950), where the relevant sections may be found on pp. 70–76. See also A. Garzya, "Problèmes relatifs à l'édition des livres IX–XVI du Tétrabiblon d'Aétios d'Amida," *Revue des Etudes Anciennes* 86 (1984): 245–257.

219. Zervos, *Aetii sermo*, p.96.1–3.

220. Galen, *On the Affected Parts* 6.5 (K 8.415).

221. Zervos, *Aetii sermo*, p.97.14. See further J. M. Riddle, *Contraception and Abortion from the Ancient World to the Renaissance* (Cambridge, Mass. and London: Harvard University Press, 1992), 92–97. Riddle argues that Aetius "displayed a knowledge of contraceptives and abortifacients greater than anyone else in antiquity, except Soranus and Dioscorides" (92).

222. Ibid., p.97.26–28.

223. Ibid., p.98.1. Debru argues that the use of the first person in other people's stories is characteristic of this genre; see Debru, "La suffocation hystérique." Note that this readiness to turn a general story into a personal experi-

ence is evident even in the writings of one person; Nutton shows that the stories Galen had read or heard thirty years before were transformed into his own eye-witness accounts in his later writings. See V. Nutton, "Style and Context in the *Method of Healing,*" in *Galen's Method of Healing,* ed. F. Kudlien and R. J. Durling (Leiden: Brill, 1991), 1–25; see pp. 12–13.

224. Zervos, *Aetii sermo,* p.98.1–8; p.99.18–22.

225. Ibid., p.100.7; p.101.1–3 (= Oribasius, *Synopsis* 9.45.6).

226. 3.71 (CMG vol. 9.1, p.288.8–289.21). This is translated into English in Adams, *The Medical Works of Paulus Aegineta,* 345–346.

227. CMG vol. 9.1, p.288.8; Greek *anadrome.*

228. CMG vol. 9.1, p.288.19–20.

229. CMG vol. 9.1, p.288.24–27; cf. Zervos, *Aetii sermo,* p.97.12–14.

230. CMG vol. 9.1, p.289.6–8; Zervos, *Aetii sermo,* p.99.8–10 gives the same three substances.

231. CMG vol. 9.1, p.289.16; cf. Soranus, *Gynecology* 3.28.1 (CMG vol. 4, p.110.22).

232. G. Del Guerra, *Il libro di Metrodora* (Milan: Ceschina, 1953), 41, and "La medicina bizantina e il codice medico-ginecologica di Metrodora," *Scientia Veterum* 118 (1968): 67–94:89.

233. Green, *Ancient Theories of Female Physiology and Disease,* 135 and 174–175 nn. 5 and 6.

234. Baader, "Early Medieval Latin Adaptations of Byzantine Medicine," in *Dumbarton Oaks Papers* 38 (1984): 251–252.

235. Muscio should be consulted in the V. Rose edition of *Sorani Gynaeciorum vetus translatio Latina* (Leipzig: Teubner, 1882), 4.26–29 (pp. 58–61); compare with M. F. Drabkin and I. E. Drabkin, *Caelius Aurelianus.* The added phrase is *ascendente sursum ad pectus matrice,* and it occurs at Rose p.58.9–10 and Drabkin p.76.367–368.

236. V. Rose, *Theodori Prisciani Euporiston Libri III* (Leipzig: Teubner, 1894), 228–230. On Theodorus Priscianus, see O. Temkin, "History of Hippocratism in Late Antiquity: The Third Century and the Latin West," in *Double Face of Janus,* by Temkin, 174.

237. V. Rose, *Cassii Felicis De Medicina ex Graecis Logicae Sectae Auctoribus Liber Translatus* (Leipzig: Teubner, 1879), chap. 77, pp. 187–189. See Temkin, "History of Hippocratism," in *Double Face of Janus,* by Temkin, 228; and Green, *Ancient Theories of Female Physiology and Disease,* 167.

238. Rose, *Sorani Gynaeciorum,* 131–139; Baader, "Early Medieval Latin Adaptations of Byzantine Medicine," in *Dumbarton Oaks Papers* 38, ed. Scarborough, 251.

239. Green, *Ancient Theories of Female Physiology and Disease,* 153.

240. For criticism of the view that Hippocratic writings were unknown in the West before the fifteenth century, see P. Kibre, "Hippocratic Writings in the

Middle Ages," *Bulletin of the History of Medicine* 18 (1945): 371–412, and "Hippocrates Latinus," *Traditio* 36 (1980): 347–372, esp. p. 347 n. 1. Green, *Ancient Theories of Female Physiology and Disease*, 142, 146–147; Latin manuscripts such as the early ninth-century Paris BN 11219, which contains *DW* 1.7–38, can be traced to Ravenna. On Ravenna, see Müller-Rohlfsen, *Die Lateinische Ravennatische.*

241. See further I. Mazzini and G. Flammini, *De conceptu* (Bologna: Patron Editore, 1983); M. E. Vazquez Bujan, *El de mulierum affectibus del corpus Hippocraticum: Estudio y edición crítica de la antigua traducción latina* (Compostela: Universidad de Santiago, 1986); Irigoin, "Tradition manuscrite," 1–13.

242. For a translation of this commentary, see N. Palmieri, "Un antico commento a Galeno della scuola medica di Ravenna," *Physis* 23 (1981): 197–296, esp. 288–289, discussed in Green, *Ancient Theories of Female Physiology and Disease,* 151–153.

243. Green, *"De genecia* Attributed to Constantine," 311; I. Mazzini, "Ippocrate latino dei secolo V–VI: tecnica di traduzione," in *I Testi di Medicina Latini Antichi: Problemi Filologici e Storici,* I. Mazzini and F. Fusco, Atti del I Convegno Internazionale, Università di Macerata, Bretschneider, 1985, 383–387, esp. p. 385.

244. Beccaria, "Antico canone latino di Ippocrate," 36 and 38–39; Kibre, "Hippocrates Latinus," 280–282; J. Agrimi, "L'*Hippocrates Latinus* nella tradizione manoscritta e nella cultura altomedievali," in *I Testi di Medicina Latini Antichi,* Mazzini and Fusco, 391–392. On the relationship between the *Epistula ad Maecenatem* and Vindicianus, see M. E. Vazquez Bujan, "Vindiciano y el tratado *De natura generis humani,*" *Dynamis* 2 (1982): 25–56.

245. P. Diepgen, "Reste antiker Gynäkologie im frühen Mittelalter," *Quellen und Studien zur Geschichte der Naturwissenschaften* 3 (1933): 226–242, esp. 228–229; G. Walter, "Peri Gynaikeion A of the Corpus Hippocraticum in a Latin Translation," *Bulletin of the Institute of the History of Medicine* 3 (1935): 599–606.

246. M. Ullmann, *Islamic Medicine* (Edinburgh: Edinburgh University Press, 1978), 8. The terms *Arabic medicine* and *Islamic medicine* are misleading; many of those whose work is considered here were not Muslims or were not of Arab origin. The reader should take warning. Veith, *Hysteria,* 94–97, pays little attention to the Arab world, saying merely that "the three leading Muslim physicians [Ibn Sina, Rhazes and Haly Abbas] did not write much about hysteria." The difficulty in studying the fortunes of the hysteria tradition in the Arab world is the paucity of texts available in European languages; however, since many of these works were translated into Latin, it is at least possible for the scholar without Arabic to make some preliminary comments.

247. Irigoin, "Tradition manuscrite," 1–13; D. Lippi and S. Arieti, "La ricezione del *Corpus hippocraticum* nell'Islam," in *I Testi di Medicina Latini Antichi,* Mazzini and Fusco, 399–402; Meyerhof and Joannides, *Gynécologie et l'Obstétrique*

chez Avicenne, 6; Ullmann, *Islamic Medicine*, 11; M. Meyerhof, "New Light on Hunain Ibn Ishaq and His Period," *Isis* 8 (1926): 685–724.

248. R. J. Durling, "A Chronological Census of Renaissance Editions and Translations of Galen," *Journal of the Warburg and Courtauld Institutes* 24 (1961): 230–305, esp. p. 232. See also Lippi and Arieti, "Ricezione del *Corpus hippocraticum*," in *I Testi di Medicina Latini Antichi*, by Mazzini and Fusco, 401.

249. M. Ullmann, "Zwei spätantike Kommentare zu der hippokratischen Schrift 'De morbis muliebribus'," *Medizinhistorisches Journal* 12 (1977): 245–262; Green, "*De genecia* Attributed to Constantine," 303 n. 15, 305 n.22; Ullmann, *Islamic Medicine*, 11–12.

250. On aṭ-Ṭabarī, see M. Meyerhof, "Ali at-Tabari's 'Paradise of Wisdom,' One of the Oldest Arabic Compendiums of Medicine," *Isis* 16 (1931): 6–54, esp. 13–15; E. G. Browne, *Arabic Medicine* (Cambridge: Cambridge University Press, 1921), 37–40.

251. *Firdaws* 2.1, chap. 16; A. Siggel, "Gynäkologie, Embryologie und Frauenhygiene aus dem 'Paradies der Weisheit Über die Medizin' des Abu Hana ʿAli b. Sahl Rabban at-Tabari nach der Ausgabe von Dr. Zubair as-Siddiqi, 1928," *Quellen und Studien zur Geschichte der Naturwissenschaften und der Medizin* 8 (1941): 216–272, esp. p. 242.

252. *Firdaws* 4.9, chap. 17; Siggel, "Gynäkologie, Embryologie," 244–245.

253. Ullmann, *Islamic Medicine*, 43.

254. Chap. 87, De praefocatione matricis; I am using the edition of 1534, *Rhasis Philosophi Tractatus nonus ad regem Almansorem, de curatione morborum particularium* (Paris: Simon de Colines, 1534).

255. *Kamil* I 9.39; A. A. Gewargis, *Gynäkologisches aus dem Kamil as-Sina'a at-Tibbiya des ʿAli ibn al-ʿAbbas al-Magusi*, Inaugural dissertation, Friedrich-Alexander-Universität, Erlangen-Nürnberg, 1980, 43. On al-Majūsī, see Browne, *Arabic Medicine*, (1921), 53–57, and Meyerhof and Joannides, *Gynécologie et l'Obstétrique chez Avicenne*, 7.

256. *Kamil* II 8.12; Gewargis, *Gynäkologisches*, 76.

257. Gewargis, *Gynäkologisches*, 18; see further, U. Weisser, *Zeugung, Vererbung und Pränatale Entwicklung in der Medizin des arabisch-islamischen Mittelalters* (Erlangen: Lülung, 1983), 146–147, and U. Weisser, "Das Corpus Hippocraticum in der arabischen Medizin," in *Die hippokratischen Epidemien*, ed. G. Baader and R. Winau, *Sudhoffs Archiv* Beiheft 27 (1990): 377–408.

258. Gewargis, *Gynäkologisches*, 44 and 80, picking up Aetius (Zervos p. 97.13) on the susceptibility of the young to suffocation. See also Green, *Ancient Theories of Female Physiology and Disease*, 114, and ʿArib ibn Saʿid, *Le Livre de la Génération du Foetus et le Traitement des Femmes enceintes et des Nouveau-nés*, edited and translated by H. Jahier and N. Abdelkader (Algiers: Librairie Ferraris, 1956).

259. Gewargis, *Gynäkologisches*, 77.

260. On Ibn al-Jazzār, see J. Schönfeld, "Die Zahnheilkunde im 'Kitab Zad

al-musafir' des al-Gazzar," *Sudhoffs Archiv* 58 (1974): 380–403; R. Jazi, "Millénaire d'Ibn al-Jazzar, pharmacien maghrébin, médecin des pauvres et des déshérités," *Revue d'Histoire de la Pharmacie* 33 (1986): 5–12, 108–120; idem, "Aphrodisiaqu es et médicaments de la reproduction chez Ibn al-Jazzar, médecin et pharmacien maghrébin du xe siècle," *Revue d'Histoire de la Pharmacie* 34 (1987): 155–170, 243–259; M. W. Dols, *Medieval Islamic Medicine: Ibn Ridwan's Treatise 'On the Prevention of Bodily Ills in Egypt'* (Berkeley, Los Angeles, London: University of California Press, 1973), 67–69.

261. Here I am using the Latin translation of the *Viaticum* given in *Opera Ysaac* (Lyons: B. Trot & J. de Platea, 1515), an abbreviated form of the Arabic text; the *Viaticum* version of this chapter is conveniently given by Green in *Ancient Theories of Female Physiology and Disease*, 249.

262. Ullmann, *Islamic Medicine*, 46; on Avicenna in the West, see N. Siraisi, *Avicenna in Renaissance Italy: The Canon and Medical Teaching in Italian Universities after 1500* (Princeton, N.J.: Princeton University Press, 1987).

263. *Qānūn* III 21.4.16–19. I am using the ed. *Libri in re medica omnes* (2 vols.), 942–943 (Venice: Valgrisi, 1564). Meyerhof and Joannides, *Gynécologie et l'Obstétrique chez Avicenne*, p. 66, argue that rubbing aromatic oil into the mouth of the womb to imitate copulation, as recommended by Avicenna, is absent from Greek medicine—yet it is present not only in Galen but also in the Hippocratic corpus.

264. Green, *Ancient Theories of Female Physiology and Disease*, 75–76 and 119–120, nn. 9–10.

265. *Diseases of Young Girls*, also known as *On Virgins*, L 8.466–470; Ullmann, *Die Medizin im Islam*, 32.

266. Diagnoses of hysteria in E. T. Withington, "The Asclepiadae and the Priests of Asclepius," in *Studies in the History and Method of Science*, ed. C. Singer, vol. 2 (Oxford: Clarendon Press, 1921), 192–205, esp. p. 200; Diepgen, *Die Frauenheilkunde der Alten Welt*, 194; W. D. Smith, "So-called Possession in Pre-Christian Greece," *Transactions and Proceedings of the American Philological Association* 96 (1965): 403–426, esp. p. 406; B. Simon, *Mind and Madness in Ancient Greece*, 243; Lefkowitz, *Heroines and Hysterics*, 14; Manuli, "Donne mascoline, femmine sterili," in *Madre Materia*, Campese, Manuli, and Sissa (Turin: Boringhieri, 1983), 147–192, esp. p. 161. For discussion of the text and its probable context of menarche, see H. King, "Bound to Bleed: Artemis and Greek Women," in *Images of Women in Antiquity*, ed. A. Cameron and A. Kuhrt (London: Croom Helm, 1983), 109–127; H. King, *From Parthenos to Gynē: The Dynamics of Category*, Ph.D. thesis, University of London, 1985, 175–182.

267. Green, *Ancient Theories of Female Physiology and Disease*, 132–133.

268. J. L. Heiberg, *Pauli Aeginetae libri tertii interpretatio Latina antiqua* (Leipzig: Teubner, 1912), xiii, cited by Green, *Ancient Theories of Female Physiology and Disease*, 184, n. 82.

269. F. P. Egert, *Gynäkologische Fragmente aus dem frühen Mittelalter nach einer Petersburger Handschrift aus dem VII–IX Jahrhundert* (Berlin: Ebering, 1936).

270. Ibid., I 26.

271. Ibid., II 16; see discussion on p. 54.

272. Ibid., III 23.

273. H. Schipperges, "Die Assimilation der arabischen Medizin durch das lateinische Mittelalter," *Sudhoffs Archiv* Beiheft 3 (Wiesbaden, 1964); Green, "*De genecia* Attributed to Constantine," 299–323; G. Baader, "Early Medieval Latin Adaptations of Byzantine Medicine," in *Dumbarton Oaks Papers* 38 (1984), 259; Durling, "Renaissance Editions and Translations of Galen," 233; on Constantinus Africanus, see P. O. Kristeller, "The School of Salerno: Its Development and Its Contribution to the History of Learning," *Bulletin of the History of Medicine* 17 (1945): 138–194.

274. Green, "Constantinus Africanus and the Conflict between Religion and Science," in *The Human Embryo: Aristotle and the Arabic and European Traditions,* ed. G. R. Dunstan (Exeter: University of Exeter Press, 1990), 47–69, esp. pp. 49 and 62 n. 7.

275. Ullmann, *Islamic Medicine,* 53–54; Green, *Ancient Theories of Female Physiology and Disease,* 220.

276. Green, *Ancient Theories of Female Physiology and Disease,* 234. On the school of Salerno, see Kristeller, "School of Salerno," 138–194; G. Baader, "Die Schule von Salerno," *Medizinhistorisches Journal* 13 (1978): 124–145.

277. S. de Renzi, *Collectio Salernitana* II (Naples: Filiatre-Sebezio, 1853), 338–339; Green, *Ancient Theories of Female Physiology and Disease,* 263–266, and Monica Green, pers. comm. 16.11.91.

278. Green, *Ancient Theories of Female Physiology and Disease,* 267–268.

279. Ibid., 303 nn. 49 and 50, 306 n. 68, 310 n. 90; S. M. Stuard, "Dame Trot," *Signs* 1 (1975): 537–542; J. F. Benton, "Trotula, Women's Problems, and the Professionalization of Medicine in the Middle Ages," *Bulletin of the History of Medicine* 59 (1985): 30–53. Monica Green is currently editing the Trotula manuscripts.

280. Green, *Ancient Theories of Female Physiology and Disease,* 274–275.

281. Ibid., 285 and n. 91; the text is also given in n. 91.

282. Ibid., 316.

283. On its date see D. W. Peterson, "Observations on the Chronology of the Galenic Corpus," *Bulletin of the History of Medicine* 51 (1977): 484–495; on Renaissance editions, see Durling, "Renaissance Editions and Translations of Galen," 243.

284. Kibre, "Hippocratic Writings in the Middle Ages," 380; but see Nutton, "Hippocrates in the Renaissance," in *Hippokratischen Epidemien,* by Baader and Winau: p. 437 points out that the Paracelsian Petrus Antonius Severinus rejected the *Aphorisms* as part of his recasting of Hippocrates in a Paracelsian mold.

285. P. O. Kristeller, "Bartholomaeus, Musandinus and Maurus of Salerno and Other Early Commentators of the 'Articella,' with a Tentative List of Texts

and Manuscripts," *Italia Medioevale e Umanistica* 19 (1976): 57–87, esp. pp. 59 and 65.

286. A. Beccaria, "Sulle tracce di un antico canone latino di Ippocrate e di Galeno II: Gli Aforismi di Ippocrate nella versione e nei commenti del primo medioevo," *Italia Medioevale e Umanistica* 4 (1961): 1–75, esp. p. 23.

287. Müller-Rohlfsen, *Die Lateinische Ravennatische*, xviii–xix and 72.

288. I am using the first edition of 1476, published by N. Petri at Padua. On the *Articella*, see Kibre, "Hippocratic Writings in the Middle Ages," 382–384; Baader, "Early Medieval Latin Adaptations of Byzantine Medicine," in *Dumbarton Oaks Papers* 38, ed. Scarborough, 259; Nutton, "Hippocrates in the Renaissance," in *Hippokratischen Epidemien*, ed. Baader and Winau, 420–439; Kristeller, "Other Early Commentators of the 'Articella,'" 57–87; on the translation of *Aphorisms* used, see pp. 66–67.

289. De sternutatione, p. xliiii^r; De membris generationis in femellis, p. xlviii^r.

290. See Nutton, "Hippocrates in the Renaissance," in *Hippokratischen Epidemien*, ed. Baader and Winau: pp. 425–426 discuss how the "unity between Galen and Hippocrates was reinforced by the power of print."

291. Galen, *In Hippocratis Aphorismi*, K 17B.824.

292. The 1493 edition does not give the aphorisms themselves in full: see Ugo Benzi, *Senensis super aphorismos Hypo. et super commentus Gal. eius interpretis* (Ferrara: Laurentium de Valentia et Andrea de Castro Novo, 1493). For the full version, see *Expositio Ugonis Senensis super aphorismos Hypocratis et super commentum Galieni* (Venice: B. Locatellus, 1498), p. 125^r. See D. P. Lockwood, *Ugo Benzi: Medieval Philosopher and Physician 1376–1439* (Chicago: University of Chicago Press, 1951), 35–36 and 217–219. Benzi tidies up the translation, giving the correct form, *molestatur*, in place of the *molestat* or *molestant* of other versions.

293. Lorenzo Laurenziani, *In Sententias Hippocratis praefatio* (Florence: Antonius Miscominus), 1494.

294. Niccolò Leoniceno, *Commentum Nicoli super aphorismos* (Bononie: Benedictum Hectoris, 1522).

295. Antonio Musa Brasavola, *In octo libros aphorismorum Hippocratis et Galeni, Commentaria et Annotationes* (Basel: Froben, 1541), 828. On Brasavola, see Nutton, "Medicine, Diplomacy and Finance: The Prefaces to a Hippocratic Commentary of 1541," in *New Perspectives on Renaissance Thought: Essays in the History of Science, Education and Philosophy in Memory of Charles B. Schmitt*, eds. J. Henry and S. Hutton (London: Duckworth, 1990), 230–243.

296. Leonhart Fuchs, *In Hippocratis Coi septem Aphorismorum libris commentaria* (Paris: Roigny, 1545), 412–413; the discussion of *lunga* versus *pniga* is on pp. 414–415.

297. Guillaume Plancy, *Galen in Aphorismi Hippocratis commentarius* (Lyons: Roville, 1552), 340.

298. Claude Champier, *Aphorismi ex nova Claudii Campensii interpretatione*

(Lyons: C. Ravot, 1579), 120; Jacques Houllier, *In Aphorismos Hippocratis commentarii septem* (Paris: Jacques de Puys, 1582), 284–285.

299. I. M. Lonie, "The 'Paris Hippocratics': Teaching and Research in Paris in the Second Half of the Sixteenth Century," in *The Medical Renaissance of the Sixteenth Century,* ed. A. Wear and R. K. French (Cambridge: Cambridge University Press, 1985), 155–174, esp. pp. 158–160.

300. *The Whole Aphorismes of Great Hippocrates* (trans. S. H.) (London: H. L. for Richard Redmer, 1610), 93.

301. B. L. Sloane ms. 2811, p. 23.

302. B. L. Sloane ms. 2117, p. 23^v and p. 281^r.

303. See for example the thirteenth-century work of Walter Agilon in P. Diepgen, *Gualteri Agilonis, Summa medicinalis: Nach den Münchener Cod. lat. Nr 325 und 13124 erstmalig ediert mit einer vergleichenden Betrachtung älterer medizinischer Kompendien des Mittelalters* (Leipzig: Johann Ambrosius Barth, 1911), chap. 42 of which, on suffocation of the womb, is heavily dependent on Ibn Sina, and includes a version of the woman who lay as if dead, in which Galen becomes the hero-narrator (p. 149). Also from the thirteenth century is the *De naturis rerum* of Thomas of Brabant; chap. 59 on the womb discusses suffocation. See C. Ferckel, *Die Gynäkologie des Thomas von Brabant: Ein Beitrag zur Kenntnis der mittelalterlichen Gynäkologie und ihrer Quellen* (Munich: Carl Kühn, 1912). The *De proprietatibus rerum* of Bartholomeus Anglicus (d. 1260) also includes suffocation in a general chapter on the womb, in Book 5 chap. 49 (Strasbourg: G. Husner, 1485); so does the thirteenth-century work of Joannes Actuarius, *Methodi Medendi libri sex,* in Book 4 chap. 8 (Venice: Gualterio Scoto, 1554). The material is thus copied from text to text, becoming increasingly familiar—an essential section in any work claiming the status of encyclopedia. For its appearance in a more specialized work, see also the fifteenth-century Middle English text given by M.-R. Hallaert, *The 'Sekenesse of wymmen': A Middle English Treatise on Diseases in Women,* Scripta 8 (Brussels: OMIREL, UFSAL, 1982), in which lines 375–482 describe "suffocation of the mother" (i.e., of the womb).

304. Pieter van Foreest, *Observationum et curationum medicinalium, liber vigesimusoctavus, de mulierum morbis* (Leyden: Plantin, 1599).

305. Ibid., 154–155.

306. Ibid., 167: Hysterica vitulo se simulat esse marito.

307. Ibid., 167: Et hoc est verum.

308. Jorden, *A Briefe Discourse of a Disease Called the Suffocation of the Mother.*

309. T. Laqueur, *Making Sex: Body and Gender from the Greeks to Freud* (Cambridge, Mass., and London: Harvard University Press, 1990), 99; for a more optimistic view of the relationship between science and experience in this period see D. Jacquart and C. Thomasset, *Sexuality and Medicine in the Middle Ages* (Cambridge: Polity Press in association with Oxford: Basil Blackwell, 1988), 46.

310. Jorden, *Disease Called the Suffocation of the Mother,* 10^v.

311. Guillaume de Baillou, *De virginum et mulierum morbis* (Paris: J. Quesnel, 1643), 206.

312. Thomas Laycock, *A Treatise on the Nervous Diseases of Women* (London: Longman, 1840), 317–318; based on Daniel Le Clerc, *Histoire de la Médecine,* p. 85 of the edition of 1702.

313. Leigh Hunt, *A Legend of Florence* (London: Edward Moxon, 1840).

314. Durling, "Renaissance Editions and Translations of Galen," 245; Gewargis, *Gynäkologisches,* 6.

315. M. F. Wack, *Lovesickness in the Middle Ages: The Viaticum and Its Commentaries* (Philadelphia: University of Pennsylvania Press, 1990), 292 n. 6.

TWO

"A Strange Pathology"

Hysteria in the Early Modern World, 1500–1800

G. S. Rousseau

Some will allow no Diseases to be new, others will think that many old ones are ceased; and that such which are esteemed new, will have but their time: However, the Mercy of God hath scattered the great Heap of Diseases, and not loaded any one Country with all: some may be new in one Country which have been old in another. New Discoveries of the Earth discover new Diseases . . . and if Asia, Africa, and America should bring in their List, Pandoras [sic] Box would swell, and there must be a strange Pathology.
—SIR THOMAS BROWNE, "A Letter to a Friend, Upon Occasion of the Death of his Intimate Friend"

It will always be a mistake . . . to treat past philosophies in a decontextualized way, viewing them simply as addressed to a canonical set of distinctively philosophical themes. Even the most abstract intellectual systems cannot be regarded simply as bodies of propositions; they must also be treated as utterances, the rhetorical aims and purposes of which we need to recover if we are to understand them properly. Moreover, once we commit ourselves to recontextualizing the great scientific and philosophical systems of the past in this way, we must guard above all against the tendency to reconstruct their intellectual context with anachronistic narrowness.
—QUENTIN SKINNER, *New York Review of Books*

I

Even in the earliest historical periods in the murky ages between 1300 and 1600, old man Proteus offers a steadfast clue to understanding the evolution of hysteria. In its progression from the Greeks to the medieval world, hysteria—as Helen King suggests—was transformed many times, such that by 1400 it was understood as something different from the conceptions given it by Hippocrates and Soranus. Vast cultural shifts—religious, socioeconomic, and political—as well as the growth of medical theory in the Renaissance, prompt hysteria to continue its prior altera-

tions and constructions after approximately 1500; so that by the period
of the French and American revolutions it assumed a different set of
representations altogether.

These historical transformations and representations—especially
their protean ability to sustain the existence of a condition called hysteria
without a stable set of causes and effects or, more glaringly, a category
identifiable by commonly agreed upon characteristics—constitute the
substance of this chapter. Throughout I will be attempting to explain
how a category—hysteria—evidently without a fixed content can endure
throughout the course of history.[1] Furthermore, among all medical conditions hysteria formed the strongest critique of the traditional medical
model up to the advent of psychiatry and psychoanalysis. Before approximately 1800 its discourses were compiled by doctors who were
themselves often terrified of their hysterical patients, as is evident in the
early *Malleus Maleficarum*. Hysteria is a unique phenomenon in the entire repertoire of Western medicine because it exposes the traditional
binary components of the medical model—mind/body, pathology/nor-
malcy, health/sickness, doctor/patient—as no other condition ever has.

My purpose here is dual: to show what hysteria was thought to be, as
well as trace its representations. Within this goal I have a set of alternatives: whether to focus on what doctors chose to make of hysteria, or to
gaze at its representations by those who were not doctors. Inevitably I
work here sporadically as a historian of science and medicine whose eye
is never far from the medical alternatives doctors chose to take, while
inquiring into the representations of hysteria made by those who were
not doctors. This is the "as is" (history) and the "as it could have been"
(representations) of hysteria, strewn with a broad range of metaphors
and language that attached to the condition.

But even in a historical and representational treatment like this one,
it is easy to forget that for the modern era the history of hysteria extends
over a period of four centuries (1400–1800), and because this somewhat
synchronic view enables us to chart the flow of hysteria in its recorded
versions, we possess certain advantages over both the doctors and the
patients who were entrapped in their particular moment. This angle of
vision is, of course, double-edged: we are also entrapped by our moment, and many voices of hysteria must have been lost over the centuries. Nevertheless, modern methods of research permit access to a
wide body of knowledge about this condition not available before.[2] Furthermore, some disjointed concepts pertinent to hysteria's transformations must be considered: in our time, when the revolt against Freud
has been so vehement, it is important to remember that he launched

his psychoanalysis exclusively on the basis of his studies of hysterical women. As a consequence, hysteria in our century has assumed a more important role in psychiatry than have other categories.[3] Although the diagnosis of hysteria in both women and men has virtually disappeared in our time, in practice its symptoms have been transformed into the medically sanctioned "conversion syndrome" and then (mysteriously and perplexingly) have gone underground.[4] It is easy to forget that the ancient threat of an invasive and irrepressible female sexuality, a patent menace in epochs studied in this chapter, is in the lay imagination to-day far from having been removed in our own time.[5] Indeed, the social oppression of women throughout history has only recently—since the eighteenth century—been acknowledged in any organized way, and this restraint bears serious implications for hysteria. Finally—and it will seem extraneous in this discussion about a complex but nevertheless presumed-medical category—because so much of hysteria in the period 1500–1800 is embedded in discursive practices, much more sensitive attention must be paid to language if we hope to disentangle hysteria's transformations.

We are thus presented with something of a paradox. On the one hand, hysteria appears to be a category without content; on the other, hysteria has an amorphous content incapable of being controlled by a clear category. The history of hysteria (*pace* Dr. Ilza Veith, the already-mentioned Freudian medical historian who amassed a great deal of information about hysteria) is therefore only a part of the story I tell here. Its representations count as much. No matter how complete any history, its discursive facet can only hope to be one part, its total realism requiring a larger canvas than historical narrative. The challenge I face is that I aim to "fill up" both categories (the medical category and its broader nonmedical representations) at the same time—a double task. But both require amplification, even when conjoined as they are here. Moreover, the medical category itself is so inadequate for the early period (1500–1800) that I often rebel against its constraints. The history of hysteria is as much the "his-story" of male fear—in this case literally his-story—as the history of Dr. King's *hysterikē pnix* or any other wandering wombs. It is also the history of linguistic embodiments, rhetorics, and emplotments, many of which remain to be decoded and interpreted here.[6]

Two truths then seem to emerge with rather startling disparity: first, that Dr. Thomas Sydenham, acclaimed as the "English Hippocrates," rather than Charcot or Freud, is the unacknowledged hero of hysteria (his entrance to my story is necessarily delayed until a later section as my organization is essentially chronological); second, that language,

rather than medicine (either theory or therapy), is the medium best able
to express and relieve hysteria's contemporary agony. (The same conclusion can be drawn concerning other conditions, such as depression, but
conventional hysteria or twentieth-century conversion syndrome is different in that its somatic involvement is much greater.) This is the conjunction of language and the body: hysteria's radical subjectivity. And as
I shall suggest below, hysteria is also the most subjective of all the classifications of disease. These are bold assertions, and no one at this time
wants to promote a history of medicine based on heroes and heroines.
But writing—perhaps self-expression through any of the arts, rather
than treatment with drugs or psychotherapy—alleviates the modern hysteric's pain and numbness best.[7] To validate this claim we will prove that
there remains no better medical therapy for contemporary hysteria, certainly no more effective remedy when hysteria is, as in Sydenham's version of the 1680s, presented as a "disease of civilization" rather than as
organic lesions caused by psychogenic factors.[8] If we ask what the three
hundred years between 1500 and 1800 can teach us about hysteria, the
answer can be found by looking at two factors: gender-based pain and
social conditions, neither of which falls within accepted categories of
modern medicine. It is consequently no small wonder that to its observers hysteria has continued to be one of the most elusive of all maladies;[9] less so—as I suggest—to writers, poets, or artists, who have often
adopted a gaze that differs from the traditional medical one. If we assign
to hysteria a broad repertoire of gender-based pains caused by social
conditions, we have the beginnings of a definition that pleases few medical theorists. We provide a set of contents incapable of being bound together by any logically constructed and demonstrably coherent category,[10] and so our contents will be unsatisfactory to philosophers.

   Moreover, of all the diseases classified in this early modern period,
hysteria has been the medical condition most likely to generate private
languages and discourses—languages that capture the cries and whis-
pers of unspeakable agonies, most of which do not remain as single narratives because patients never recorded them. This was as true in the
sixteenth and seventeenth centuries as it is of the twentieth. Hysteria's
expressions of physical and emotional numbness and of chronic pain
were captured in a personal, often disjointed, medium, most striking in
its intrinsic subjectivity. Subjectivity, above all, has been the teleology of
the annals of hysteria in Western civilization.[11]

   More specifically, mourning and melancholia, especially the grief and
ecstasy associated with hysteria, are the shadow-categories that have
haunted modern theories of subjectivity and representation since Freud.
But even Freud intuited the history of this development in his inau-

gural linking of *Hamlet* and *Oedipus Rex* in his discovery of the Oedipus complex, in which Hamlet came to represent the figure that proves (and ruefully denies) the Oedipal rule, as much as literary criticism has taken *Hamlet* as its exemplary defective (hence modern) tragedy. And modern theorists (including Jacques Lacan, Walter Benjamin, and Nicolas Abraham) have repeatedly returned to Hamlet's disordered grief as touchstones for their insight into subjectivity and representation. From these positions it is only a short step to the feminist, psychoanalytic, and deconstructive attempts to articulate a supplementary position before, within, or beyond the interpretative paradigms practiced in Freud's (and Oedipus's) name. In our time, these have embraced—in brief—the literary, psychoanalytic, and deconstructive symptoms of hysteria: in Hamlet's famous phrase, the "forms, moods, shapes of grief." [12]

But if mourning and melancholia have haunted modern categories of subjectivity and representation, language alone has recognized the silences beyond itself (i.e., beyond verbal language and discourse) to which the (usually female) hysteric has had to ascend if her desire, not always limited to the sexual realm, was to be acknowledged. The point is admittedly elusive, even if concretized in a tangible history of medicine. Historically speaking, hysteria has been the condition beyond others that wedded the body to body language, especially to gestures, motions, gaits, nonverbal utterances. As such, it never reflected—certainly not in the Renaissance or Enlightenment—a simple ontology of the mind or of mind functioning together with body, but rather captured the chronic numbness and ineffable despair usually incapable of being grasped in the subtleties of written language. [13]

Ever since the Cartesian revolution of the seventeenth century and perhaps even before then, the *philosophical* concept of body had been of little use to theories of hysteria—viewed, as we shall see, as a metaphysical medical category—nor have mind and body, in conjunction, offered solutions to unravel the riddle of hysteria. Perhaps the difficulty arises from the suppressed desire of those who have presented themselves with hysterical symptoms. Language *and* desire; more precisely, desire *in* language; Julia Kristeva's yoking of these loaded words and their difficult concepts proved more useful, especially for the unspeakable realms of pain that she believes transcend language: the metalinguistic spaces. [14] Language and desire may ultimately be the only categories through which the hysteric can arrive at self-understanding: language used in the act of self-analysis and offering balm to heal the hysteric. The traditional remedies discussed later in this book have usually produced little improvement.

Michel Foucault speculated in his history of madness about the "hysterization of women's bodies" through which the pejorative image of the "nervous woman" had been constituted.[15] Such negative imaging was necessary in patriarchal cultures that confined power solely in the males to ensure civic cohesion. But Foucault's analysis would have been richer, and certainly more complete, if he had included the "hysterization of women's language," especially as it had been muted with the passage of time. For hysteria has been the condition paradoxically both constituted by and consistently misinterpreted by medical observation; the condition that neither the mere presence of the physician (whether appearing as savior or soothsayer) nor the persistence of his therapy can control. Sequences of despair, pain, numbness, and conversion syndrome ulti-mately could not be cured by makeshift remedies or the herbal con-coctions of the Renaissance and Enlightenment apothecaries. Today, instead of examining the fabric of the society perpetuating this chronic physical and mental pain,[16] we deny (perhaps imprudently) that hysteria exists. We drug patients until the pain is obliterated, the despair forgot-ten; until physicians can claim that questions such as "where has all the hysteria gone?" cease to exist as valid medical concerns.

II

I have suggested that a broad overview such as this cannot be narrated without remembering that we today are subject to all the tensions and confusions of contemporary culture.[17] Our versions of modernism nec-essarily differ from those of other readers, but a narrative of the evolu-tion of thought about hysteria without interjections and self-conscious reflections, sans broad contexts and even problematic digressions, will not proceed much further than Veith's narrowly conceived diachronic history. This may seem small justification, but it actually advances the understanding of hysteria. In this context it makes sense to inquire eclec-tically into the cultural transformations that affected hysteria as the world moved from the Middle Ages to the Renaissance, and from there to the period of the seventeenth century, when so many of the salient features of Enlightenment hysteria were established. The relation of hysteria to witchcraft is also germane here. Set the chronological dials to the tenth or eleventh century, and few witches are to be found in Europe. By the fourteenth and fifteenth centuries they roam the continent, having over-taken it.[18] To which specific conditions is their proliferation to be attrib-uted? And, more significantly, were these witches female hysterics in disguise? The question is hard to answer authoritatively, but it assumes (rightly I think) that hysteria has a content that can be misinterpreted or disguised. Even more crucial to the culture of the Renaissance, it was hysteria more than any other phenomenon that played a major role, as I maintain below, in the demystification of witchcraft.

Despite the variety of explanations for the historical rise of witchcraft, none is satisfactory, and given that the matter is central to the evolution of hysteria and its growth in the Renaissance, it merits discussion here. So many explanations have been tendered, with so many agendas underlying them and in so many historical contexts ranging from political history to the role of women in early European society, that no one theory has prevailed.[19] Nor, on balance, does one explanation seem more reasonable than another. The account offered by Jules Michelet, the great French social historian of the nineteenth century, may therefore be as valid as the alternatives, although Michelet recounted it as myth rather than fact, and his narrative suggests a playful naughtiness as well.[20] Michelet claimed that during one of the interminable medieval crusades, women, who had been left alone on their farms, out of boredom began to converse with the animals and plants, the trees and birds, even the clouds and the moon.[21] Apparently no one objected to this behavior. But eventually the men returned and found their women talking to the creatures of nature, to the trees and the wind. It was then, Michelet says, that men, finding this babbling intolerable, invented witchcraft. From the start, witchcraft was—he suggests in the parable—a male idea, even a male invention. To silence the women, the men burned them and branded them witches.

This explanation for the genesis of witchcraft seemed as reasonable to Michelet as any other version. But for Marguerite Duras, the contemporary French writer who retells Michelet's myth fable in several of her short stories and uses it as a leitmotif, it becomes a potent myth that captured the essence of the masculine suppression of female desire and female discourse. Whether in its Micheletian or Durasean version (or in some other form), the fable suggests a direct line from the late Middle Ages to fin-de-siècle Vienna; from the women who once knew how to speak freely to the wind and the clouds to those now—like Duras, Kristeva, and other feminists—whose crusade in our century seeks to retrieve the female speech (Kristeva's utterances of *jouissance*) that once was theirs.[22] Considering the degree to which phallocratic and patriarchal discourse continue to be major concerns of our contemporary intellectual dialogue, as Elaine Showalter shows in chapter 4, the historical discourse of hysteria cannot be conceptualized or reconstructed as a specialized province of medical history. Hysteria, even in its early medical versions among the ancient Greeks, represented more than a set of medical diagnoses and pharmaceutical therapies. From the start it was emplotted in discourses that extended beyond the medical domain and opened to a vision embracing a wider culture and broader civilization than the medical one could ever imagine. It was the public language embodying the female's plight. And it was for good reason then, as we shall see, that Sydenham observed that hysteria was, and always had been, "a disease of civilization," a seemingly mysterious pronouncement requiring broad contextualization before we can understand what he meant.

The salient historical point is that modern hysteria or conversion syndrome, as distinct from ancient *hysterikē pnix*, first rises to prominence as an explicit diagnostic category within the development of demonology. This is why the relation between content and category, already mentioned, is so crucial for an understanding of hysteria's development before Freud, and why its anomalous mixture of gender and social conditions (especially religion) makes it a unique malady throughout the realm of medicine. By the time of Chaucer and Boccaccio, Christianity had affirmed a cosmology that viewed creation as embodied with spiritual powers, both angelic and demonic. Christ's disciples and their followers over the centuries had been locked in an apocalyptic struggle against the armies of the night, as every English epic from Spenser to Milton and Blake had acknowledged. Satan could possess the human soul, turning victims into demoniacs, and individuals—especially witches—could enter into compacts with the devil. From the late fifteenth century, in a movement peaking in the seventeenth, authorities, ecclesiastical and secular alike, comandeered the courts to stop the epidemic spread of witchcraft, and concomitantly clamp down on the rise of hysteria it was engendering.[23] It was then impossible to distinguish between individual and mass hysteria, or even to know if the two categories existed. The wrath of the rabble, the crowd, the mob, was not understood as it would be in the eighteenth century. Besides, mass hysteria is a nineteenth-century invention that exists nowhere in the vocabulary or intellectual purview of the periods surveyed here, even if its effects were often felt.[24]

Though some witches were self-confessed, most were identified through public accusations. To sustain the charge of witchcraft, certain standard behavioral and physical identifications (especially the *stigmata diaboli*) normally had to be proven. Given that witchcraft was held to be a mortal offense everywhere in the realms of Christianity, it was crucial that such tests be judicially convincing. Meticulous courtroom procedures were developed throughout Europe to winnow true demoniacs and witches from those erroneously or falsely accused—those whose prima facie manifestations of possession were due to other causes—to illness, accident, suggestion, or even fraud. Expert witnesses were heard, especially physicians; often these were the same physicians who were compiling medical definitions of hysteria.[25]

The doctors by 1400 had generated no single theory or even multiple theories of hysteria.[26] They continued to ponder the links among sexual physiology, pleasure, and love, but they were uncertain of the proper emphasis to be given to any of these, let alone the roles of cause and effect. Mary Wack's conclusion about women and lovesickness in the Middle Ages and early Renaissance is surely correct. "In any case," she writes, "it is clear that a certain branch of medical writers on lovesickness began to consider it a disease linked to the sexual organs and their humors."[27] Hysteria had not yet become the exclusive medical category it would be in the early decades of the seventeenth century. There is no reason to assume that in the legal domain doctors entertained greater doubts about the existence of diabolism than did other experts: indeed, physicians' testimony was often accusatory and ended in executions. But familiarity with the vagaries of the human organism, especially when sick, fevered, or maniacal through the ravages of natural disasters such as floods, storms, earthquakes, and so on, and the opportunity to vie with the clergy for authority over the human body, often led doctors to insist that supposed signs of possession—tics, convulsions, anesthesias, swoonings, hypnotic trances—were the work of illness rather than Satanism.[28]

Substitute "nervous" or "neurotic" for "demonically possessed," and a remarkable parallel between this early modern world and our own develops.[29] That is, the physicians then were asked to distinguish between real and false witches based on certain anatomical conditions; our doctors, at least since Freud altered the face of hysteria through his psychoanalytic reforms, distinguish between genuine conversion syndrome and somatic derangement caused by neurotic or psychotic agency. The first variety (conversion syndrome) entails so-called genuine hysteria, the latter no hysteria at all. Yet such demarcation clarifies the entire point of conversion syndrome. And here, precisely at this impasse between the two, our feminists have contributed a perspective that cannot be ignored despite their patent lack of medical expertise. Indeed, it may be that the feminists' psychological distance from this professional medical world, where so much *other than* scientific cause and effect is at stake, has permitted their deep insight into this matter.

The feminists have demonstrated that Marguerite Duras's writings, for example, thrive on notions of the *transformation* of hysteria—especially the intuition that hysteria in our century is alive and widespread, though often invisible to the gazer who cannot read its signs, but it is transformed, like Proteus, in its signals and modern dress.[30] Although Duras has not pursued the social consequences of her argument (she is, after all, no sociologist), it would not be hard to do so. For if the medieval hysteric's geographical locale was the farm on which she toiled and conversed with family and neighbors; if the Georgian woman's world was the Ranelagh and Vauxhall Gardens where she paraded, and the town and country houses where she sought pleasure;[31] if the Victorian woman's interior purview was the dark bedroom in which she pretended to see nothing at night, certainly not her husband's naked body and aroused sexual organs; then today these locales have *not disappeared* but have been transformed into other social locations: the health club, the bedroom with its paraphernalia of biofeedback machines, the therapists' waiting rooms, the pain clinics, even the beauty salons and ever-proliferating malls.[32] Paradoxically, it seems today that these are the locales of *health* and therefore of pleasure and happiness. Yet it may be, upon closer observation, that they are merely the places where modern hysteria—what our vocabulary calls stress—has learned to disguise itself *as health.*

The method used in the detection of witches in the early period also bears such close parallels to methods of the last two centuries that they cannot be overlooked, not merely because of their similarities but also because they provide clues to the nature of hysteria itself. Here it is interesting to note that the signs and symptoms of hysteria have remained constant over many centuries. From the late Middle Ages to the Salem witch-hunting trials in New England (and even later), the same methods to detect witches were used to detect other medical conditions.[33] In the early period, women were pricked with sharp needles to locate the devil's claw: that insensitive patch of skin was considered the infallible sign of witchcraft. Five centuries later—in the late nineteenth century—the great medical clinicians like Dr. Pierre Janet in Paris were *still* declaring that medical practice had gone no further: "In our clinics," Janet proclaimed, "we are somewhat like the woman who sought for *witches.* We blindfold the subject, we turn his head away [notice that the pronoun has changed its gender], rub his skin with our nail, prick it suddenly with a hidden pin, watch his answers or starts of pain; the picture has not changed."[34]

Numbness—an unfeeling patch of skin—was still the sign of possession and witchcraft five centuries later. The concept of numbness altered its versions during the Enlightenment, as we will see, but it remained a constant test at the peripheries of the early and late period (Renaissance and modern), and there is even evidence that the condition existed in the middle period (Enlightenment), despite the absence of the word *numb* from the hysterical patient's vocabulary. A century after the appearance of the nineteenth-century narratives about women like Charlotte Perkins, who as a hysteric became *permanently numb*, Duras continues to write stories about the literal physical numbness of contemporary women, and our finest feminist critics continue to proclaim that hysteria, although officially diagnosed by the physicians as having disappeared, is still *with us*. The evidence lies in some of the titles of their recent work: Alice Jardine, *Gynesis: Configurations of Woman and Modernity*; Roberta Satow, "Where Has All the Hysteria Gone?"; Dianne Hunter, "Hysteria, Psychoanalysis, and Feminism: The Case of Anna O"; Patricia Fedikew, "Marguerite Duras: Feminine Field of Hysteria."[35]

The questions raised by this development may appear less than scholarly but must be put nevertheless. Why all this writing about hysteria if hysteria has disappeared? How can numbness have been the *semiotic of hysteria* as long ago as the sixteenth century, disappeared for centuries, and reappeared in the last century? Stated otherwise, what has been the middle zone of hysteria—its high Enlightenment versions? Has it returned, so to speak, in the modern witch's (i.e., today's hysteric) numb patch of skin?[36] What is the *pathology* of hysteria if numbness has continued (admittedly with major lapses in the Enlightenment) to be its major sign—the basis of its semiology—over seven or eight centuries? And how does Helen King's Hippocratic story relate to this lingering malaise? Even holy women and saints of the early period—the Margery Kempes and Saint Theresas—had presented themselves with signs that were interpreted as hysterical by those who examined them, further evidence of the many physical shapes and forms that numbness could take in its religious guises.[37] Here it is wise to remember that King left us with hysteria as a condition capable of afflicting *women only*. Seven centuries later, Victorian women remained its main victims despite abundant new research conducted in the century from 1750 to 1850 demonstrating that male hysterics also abounded then. And in our time one has to look very far indeed to find a male correlative of the feminist position that hysteria still abounds but has gone underground.[38]

The explanation for the persistence of hysteria throughout history lies in the concept of imitation. However, because imitation thrives on complex notions of representation (an elusive concept to begin with), this matter of the "content" of hysteria is incapable of swift and simple presentation.[39] Representation is further complicated by the mysterious-sounding notion, propounded by Sydenham, that *"hysteria imitates culture"*; a discovery that makes him, rather than later physicians often associated with hysteria, the unacknowledged hero of that illness before Freud and Charcot.[40] Sydenham was the first to proclaim that hysteria imitated other diseases, and he maintained—by implication—that hysteria was *itself* somehow an imitation of civilization: an idea as well as a linguistic construction that we shall need to explore if we are to grasp the evolution of hysteria in the early modern period. But how can an organic derangement, a bodily disorder, even a medical disease (if hysteria can be classified in this fashion in comparison to other organic diseases) imitate a society, a civilization, a culture? What can be meant by such a notion of imitation?

Sydenham observed that the crucial hysterical symptom was always produced by tensions and stresses within the culture surrounding the patient or victim. That is, the symptoms themselves (the conversion symptoms the patient presented) proved to be constant over time (involuntary swoonings, faints, fits, twitchings, nervous tics, eating and sleeping disorders), and the symptoms clearly differed from a more general "numbness." But the *cultural* tensions producing these symptoms varied enormously. Sydenham was not a cultural historian—he was a radical empiricist more than anything, an observer—but he realized that the human conditions varied greatly from one period to another.[41] In this context, because of him the concept of hysteria held by physicians over the previous two hundred years was transformed. For him the symptom leading to the condition of hysteria "imitated" the culture in which it (the symptom) had been produced.

It was not simply chance that the precise aspect of civilization producing the symptom should have been identified by Sydenham and applied by his followers in *nervous* categories and *nervous* language. Tension, stress, and the large constellation of concepts aligned to these words—all derive from a revolution in thinking about the body which occurred in the late seventeenth century.[42] In amalgamating an old medical condition (hysteria) with new cultural beliefs and practices (especially the body's mechanico-nervous organization), Sydenham was not merely displaying that he was an original thinker but was himself enveloped in the science and society of his era.[43] That much is patently clear. But it has been much less evident that the new footing on which he placed hysteria owed as much to the scientific milieu of his day—a post-Cartesian radical dualism that called attention anew to the nerves—as it did to any concept of imitation and representation, whether construed in medical or nonmedical terms.[44] Furthermore, my own intrusion of Sydenham—

introducing him into the narrative long before his chronological appearance justifies itself—is essential if his achievement as the major transformer of Enlightenment hysteria is to be understood. If we construe
hysteria in this imitative way rather than viewing it narrowly as an neu-
ropsychological puzzle, we begin to glean why women have been de-
monized for so long and why women continue to express their own
brand of contemporary numbness in the twentieth century. For the condition that arises by the production of symptoms that imitate the stresses
inherent in a civilization requires social—even sociological—as well as
medical analysis. Even further, the gaze must be extended to mentalities
other than the exclusively medical, such as that of Julia Kristeva, the
physician who writes about language and desire, and about language
itself imitating the raging desire of women.

III

These leaps from witches in the Renaissance to Dr. Sydenham, switching
from Sydenham to Kristeva and Duras, are not as disjointed and dis-
connected as they may appear, for only by possessing some sense of the
synchronic hysteria does the richness of its diachronic development
emerge.[45] This synchronicity amounts to the convergence of all theories
of hysteria, past and present, as if one beheld them simultaneously in
the mind. The chronological view is, naturally, less confusing. Even for
a condition as perplexing as hysteria, the diachronic or chronological
view suggests focus and precision even when there is none; it gives the
illusion of a well-wrought argument when there are only a myriad of
theories and dozens of fractured images of the hysteric. Three hundred
years after Sydenham wrote his dissertation on hysteria,[46] Duras presented hysteria as *imitation* in terms of a female numbness; Sydenham—
in contrast—generated his theory of *hysteria as imitation* without any sense
that he was the first "doctor" to have happened upon this insight. He
merely observed from the hundreds of cases he treated that this was the
truth. Sydenham and Duras may seem odd partners with no commonal-
ity; in the realms of hysteria, however, they share much territory.
Duras's novels and poems capture the persistent anesthesia of modern women living on the verge of nervous breakdowns as a result of
their socioeconomic, marital, and sexual duress. Sydenham's notion is
that pathological conditions of the female nervous system produce the
hysterical symptoms with which the patient presents herself, but—like
Duras—he believes the symptoms arise from social conditions that en-
slave not only women but also, as we will see, men. Duras's numb pain,

like the witch's claw, is the basis of three of her works: the short prose/poem *The Malady of Death, La Douleur,* and *The Ravishing of Lol Stein,* a story about two women (Lol Stein and Tatiana Karl), both of whom have settled for loveless marriages. Sydenham's women are not usually chronicled in this detail; few of his case histories survive apart from his medical notes.[47] Duras's women are characterized by a numbing pain that has few somatic symptoms, except the sense that they are suffocating and (according to her female protagonists) the indescribable sensation characterized by the words *void* and *death-in-life*.[48] Duras strives to describe the mental agony produced by the unrelenting, numbing pain. Unlike Sydenham's hysterics and those of Charcot, for her victims, no physical cause of their disturbances can be found. Duras's hysterics suffer nevertheless, sunk into their private hells, where they exist on the edge of total despair.

Duras's view opposes that of Ilza Veith, the medical historian who saw hysteria as an elusive medical disease whose code had never been cracked. Veith and Duras are contemporaries, Europeans of the same generation who lived through the Nazi holocaust and a revolution in the professionalization of women. Even so, Veith never explained why it was so important to crack the code in the first place. The medical historians of her generation, whose mind-sets were formed in the aftermath of the Freudian revolution in psychoanalysis, took it upon faith that hysteria was the most elusive, and therefore challenging, psychosomatic illness.[49] In her noble attempt Veith summoned as her protagonists the major doctors in history: Hippocrates and Sydenham, Thomas Willis and Franz Anton Mesmer, the celebrated Charcot and Freud, on grounds that they had moved closer to its psychogenic etiology. But Veith left many questions unanswered and took a narrow, almost parochial, view. She never explored the role of women in society, their traditional, phallocratic image as creatures with an insatiable and voracious erotic appetite, nor did she probe the implications of Plato's view (*Timaeus* 91c), expanded by Aretaeus, that the womb was an animal capable of wreaking destruction,[50] as it was exemplified in Euripides's *Hippolytus,* where it rages over Phaedra's body like an animal in heat. In this play, it seems never to have occurred to the stubborn patriarch, King Theseus, to relieve Phaedra's agony and (as Duras would claim) numbness, any more than it would have occurred to the Renaissance biologists to relieve the hysterical symptoms of their female patients by acknowledging the social stresses and the thwarted sexuality that produced this condition in the first place. Throughout these early periods women were regularly placed on trial by men for witchcraft, regularly perceived as fallen Eves and despised for their seductive propensities; repression of their sexuality by authoritative men (in medicine, theology, the law) became the visible, public sign of an allegedly raging womb: a private gynecological disorder the men themselves claimed never to understand fully.[51]

These differing opinions hardly complete the picture of hysteria but they do serve to bring out significant aspects of the medical condition and its social contexts that have usually not been addressed in the now dormant annals of European hysteria. For the history of hysteria has been so bogged down in the technical anatomy of uterine debility that its larger pathology and its cultural resonances have been overlooked.[52] The Greeks did not employ a vocabulary of female numbness, any more than the horror-struck observers recoiling from Renaissance witches suspected numbness in the witch's claw, but a long-range view of hysteria demonstrates a continuity of its symptoms down through the ages despite its protean ability to transform itself. No matter what its medicalization has been, hysteria, at least until the early nineteenth century, has been so inextricably entwined with the lot of women that the two can hardly be separated. Unquenchable sexual appetite was long thought to lie at the very root of the malady, especially by theologians and moralists in early Christian times.[53] And the noteworthy aspect of this voracious female desire in both its pagan and Christian forms is that besides being inherently contagious it was conceptualized as *morally dangerous* (to the individual, family unit, state, world community). Other women, observing its effects, would imitate it and develop their own versions. This voraciousness instilled male fear (engendering a type of male hysteria); the other dimension—contagion—was construed as a virulent form of miasma which patriarchy has always opposed, whether it be the patriarchy of the Athenian city-states or Nazi Germany, Stuart England, or the Fourth Republic of France.

But what is the *source* of this raging female appetite? Is it in fact ultimately *theological?* Was it due to an innate lewdness *within* the female anatomy or psyche arising out of the labia over which women had no control, and which was living proof of a postlapsarian world whose irrepressible, erotic appetite was the scar women bore for the sin of the edenic apple? Or was the perception of this female appetite something else? Something culturally ordained? Something socially constructed? These are the types of questions uniformly avoided in the discussion about hysteria, revealing one reason why its reconsideration "before Freud" has been so long overdue. Only in our poststructuralist time, and in full view of the feminist avalanche of scholarship and dialogue, has the approximation of an answer begun to emerge. But—with a polite riposte to the narrowly Freudian Veith—conventional explanations about sexual repression, depression, grief, virginity, and widowhood have been insufficient to fit the historical facts of the last twenty centuries. Hysteria may indeed be, as Alan Krohn has suggested, "the elusive disease";[54] it has also been the transformative, protean condition par excellence.

I V

If this approach has validity, then hysteria will *always* be present in society unless some miracle occurs—it can never disappear altogether, because its essentially protean nature compels it "to *imitate*" other diseases.[55] According to this line of reasoning, the unwritten history of hysteria—the history that lies beyond the narrow medical gaze—is not Veith's chronological summary of medical theories narrowly conceived, but rather a *social* history of hysteria placed in large cultural contexts that do not mute the gleanings of literary and artistic voices. This broad record, if appended to the medical one, is more revealing than the narrow "medical gaze" because hysteria itself is a reflection of the cultures it imitates.[56] The matter to be dealt with in an approach such as this book hopes to promote thus raises the nature of the *problem of hysteria itself.* And hysteria the category, rather than the set of patients presenting symptoms over many centuries, becomes par excellence the barometer responding, through its finely tuned antennas, to the perpetual stresses of gender and sexuality. As such, it is also a barometer of the cultural stresses weighing on sexual relations and gender formations. The forms of the barometric responses in the Renaissance and Enlightenment constitute much of the contents that follow. (In this view the panic and presenting symptoms of the AIDS patient who internalizes his sickness and moral condition deserve the classification hysteria, although it is rarely given in our time and cannot, of course, apply to all AIDS patients.) Moreover, hysteria will *always* elicit controversy among so-called "internalist historians" as well as among positivistic doctors who remain unconcerned with its cultural dimensions[57]—those who merely want to diagnose its symptoms and prescribe medications for its abatement, versus those observers, like Sydenham and Duras, who locate it in larger cultural contexts. The controversial dimension penetrates to every aspect of hysteria's "internalist history," and must not imply any criticism, for example, of Helen King's methodology. The point rather encompasses the difference between textual traditions of hysteria that persist over the centuries, and socially constructed categories that necessarily keep fashioning hysteria anew. The material I cover suggests that hysteria continued to be redefined in the early modern world according to the terms of changing cultural dynamics, while always serving the interests of its somatizers and diagnosticians. Viewed sociologically, *mass hysteria* is not a category apart from personal, individual hysteria, but is rather another version of the same protean, imitative stress brought out into the light of public groups, private agony having gone public.[58]

V

This approach, then, entails a social reconstruction of hysteria. In it, the hegemony of Hippocrates and his wandering womb, as we have seen in the previous chapter, is diminished and limited; it is to be read as another imaginative, if erudite, patriarchal voice in what will become during the Renaissance and Enlightenment a litany of voices making pronouncements grounded in imagination and observation but ignoring their cultural contexts. Male voices, such as those of Hippocrates and others discussed by Helen King who came later, cannot be omitted from the evolution of hysteria, but they must be located in larger contexts if hysteria is ever to transcend its local, internalist histories. Hippocrates could not have written as he did had he been female (Hippocrata), any more than a female Plato would have viewed the womb as an animal: voracious, predatory, appetitive, unstable, forever reducing the female into a frail and unstable creature. These views are those of men with little firsthand knowledge of this part of the female anatomy.[59] Once the Renaissance and Enlightenment are considered, it becomes evident that considerations other than those of paganism and Christianity must be brought to light if hysteria is to be fully explained. We must understand the relation of hysteria to inspired personal vision, to shamanism, and in extremely cold climates to so-called Arctic hysteria, said to be the natural habitat of shamanism, a subject deemed of the first importance to comparative anthropologists in the early part of this century.[60]

Gradually it becomes clear that few topics in this narrative are as important as the conception of women held throughout the course of history. The views of antiquity were not uniform, of course, but they seem to be so in contrast to the chaos of the early modern period, especially in the transition from medieval culture to the Renaissance. By the Elizabethan period, roughly 1600, it is no longer possible to invoke any major view of women, despite our postmodern temptation to do so.[61] Women have already acquired a "history" that permits them to be seen from different perspectives, each view claiming to be equally valid. It is even said that this new diversity is one certain proof of female frailty, a trait made especially resonant by the Shakespearean line: "Frailty, thy name is woman!"

This view of woman as the quintessence of frailty is the one the Renaissance grapples with. Woman, whether viewed in theological or medical contexts, whether by the ancient scholiasts or the derivative Aristotelian biologists and philosophers, whether concretized as weak virgin, bride of Christ, or as deranged Ophelia (another hysteric of course), continues to be conceptualized as part *animal*, part *witch*; part *pleasuregiver*, part *wreaker of destruction* to avenge her own irrationality—anything but as strong, rational creature resembling *homo mensicus*, this view coexisting while men of the Renaissance debate the heresies of Gallilean astronomy and the subtleties of Cartesian physiology.[62]

For these reasons, and others not provided here for lack of space, it serves no purpose to compile further narrow internal histories of hysteria classified according to various chronological periods or taxonomic schemes. Old man Proteus has been too sly for that. Although a route such as the mind/body relation appears on the surface to hold out infinite promise for theories of hysteria in the late Renaissance, it is also limited. The notion that mind/body dualism can crack the code, so to speak, of the "elusive neurosis" is doomed to failure, if anything resembling a complete explanation of how the patient proceeded from initial symptom to eventual physiological dysfunction is expected. Ultimately Descartes is a *minor* figure in our story, major though dualism is for hysteria in the epoch of its most formative transformation (as we shall see). Cartesianism did not change hysteria's destiny other than to erect a new, and long insurmountable, roadblock in the form of mental torment versus physical pain. But hysteria's definition had been troubled before the advent of the great dualist and would continue to be long after his demise and the decline of his philosophy in Europe.[63]

Before Descartes's famous discovery of the pineal gland, the human amalgam of mind and body was thought to have made man unique among living creatures. *Cartesian hysteria*—if one can posit such a medical configuration—must be turned inside out to be seen for what it really is, or to ponder how it could have been conceptualized by its seventeenth-century viewers. Cartesian discussions of hysteria that got bogged down in mind *and* body, mind *or* body, as virtually all did, ultimately contributed little to the therapy or recovery of its victims, and, even worse, revealed nothing about its etiology. It was not Descartes or any other radical dualist who penetrated deeply into the nature of the disorder, but a practicing physician who, however dualistic his own intellectual formation had been, was not especially Cartesian in his approach to medicine. This physician, moreover, laid more emphasis on experience and observation than on theory and philosophy, and for all his obeisance to the major scientific and philosophical currents of his time, recognized that in some profound way hysteria was culturally conditioned.[64] This physician was Thomas Sydenham, and it is important that he should be viewed both diachronically and synchronically: located within his time as his place and time are historically approached, and also viewed synchronically and backward, as if the entire history of hysteria converged at the point where Sydenham's theory of hysteria sits poised directly in the center.

VI

An approach to hysteria which is at once broadly historical, cultural, and contextual but also recognizes the central importance of discourse and rhetorical encoding to this narrative continuum requires a high threshold of cultural explanation and a discussion of the role of realism and representation in the explication of the malady. The discourses of hysteria cannot be viewed as neutral texts generated independently of the considerations of gender, ideology, politics, religion, nationalism, and professional authority, as if (when considered in clusters by centuries or periods) they were so many neutral corpuses or bodies (here, too, the metaphors). It is sinful enough to consider hysteria in Western society only—a white European's version.[65] To interpret these Western discourses on their own terms, without standing apart from their own systems and gazing at the role played by these narratives in the power structures in which they were generated, commits a crime that violates the first principles of the new enriched history. Produced under specific conditions at particular historical junctures, these narratives naturally reflect their moment as well as does any other writing, and it is therefore naive to imagine that the intricacies of realism and representation besetting other genres (especially prose genres) should disappear here. On the contrary, those dimensions of representation are all the more stringent here in view of the imitative nature of the condition of hysteria, and the temptation to rewrite the history of hysteria as a set of commentaries on a finite number of physicians—as Veith did—should be resisted. Sydenham's genius was the intuitive leap that recognized that culture and imitation—society and representation—could have the direst medical consequences for a malady that had bewildered doctors for centuries. He may not have been a sophisticated critic of language or its representations; nevertheless, he gazed deeply into the copula of disease and representation as each had been generated by the culture.

Concomitantly, if Sydenham's theory of hysteria as *imitation* has scientific and medical validity, the most thorough student of hysteria, the one capable of explaining the most about the labyrinths of its historical evolution, will be the cultural historian who inquires into the gender-based origins of female suffering with an eye always vigilant to hysteria's discourses. It is not only that the history of medicine is incomplete; even cultural history is inadequate to the challenge of hysteria if discourse and representation are omitted. We may well inquire why this should be when so many other maladies have remained the exclusive territory of the medical gaze. Yet even these less perplexing illnesses have been poorly represented by their chroniclers. Despite the intuitive literary analyses of Susan Sontag in *Illness as Metaphor,* as yet there are no satisfactory cultural accounts of, for example, consumption, cancer, or even such seemingly monolithic medical conditions as the almost risible gout.[66]

The diseases of the plague—bubonic fever, cholera, typhoid fever, influenza—have fared better than the above maladies in their narrative representations because it has been impossible to imagine and then represent them narratively apart from the historical conditions in which they arose. They are, of course, social diseases precisely *because* of their communicability, and their essential nature as "communicable conditions" mandates viewing them in social contexts. Even the novice historian sees that the first great European wave of bubonic plague cannot be considered apart from fourteenth-century socioeconomic conditions; that the advent of cholera in the Indian subcontinent cannot be narrated without focusing on empire and colonialism. But those maladies less apparently intrinsic to particular cultures have not fared so well.[67] Loosely speaking, there has been a sense, strengthened by Susan Sontag, that each era has somehow produced and then mythologized a particular malady: the Enlightenment had its gout (was there ever a disease more indigenous to a culture?); the Romantics, consumption (well captured in the Keatsian aesthetic implied by the famous line, "Ah, what ails thee knight, alone and palely loitering?"); the decadents and aesthetes, tuberculosis; our own twentieth century, cancer and AIDS.[68] However, although there is something in the notion, it remains loose: a figment of the historical imagination, a mere chimera; a metaphoric and analogous reading of medical history; a description of disease in relation to culture no one would want to construe literally.

The geography of hysteria lends itself to no such facile sets of interpretations. Occurring neither under conditions of contagion (like plague) nor as the product of a culture's elusive mythology (we must never forget that the hysteric's pain is somatic, bodily, not imaginary), the hysteric's pain is *real* (the problem of realism again). Yet hysteria has been *less* tied to its cultural dimensions than any of these medical conditions, this despite Sydenham's notion that it always *imitated* that culture. Until the last two centuries, hysteria was the female malady par excellence, and when our best modern female critics reiterate that women writers must be hysterical, that they have no choice in the matter, they bring together the key signposts of the malady when viewed historically: feminism, the body, culture, and discourses. Thus an authority no less insightful than Kristeva has pronounced that "women's writing is the discourse of the hysteric"; Juliet Mitchell has added that in our time—and perhaps she would extend the claim to include all time—"the woman novelist must be an hysteric, for hysteria is simultaneously what a woman can do to be feminine and refuse femininity, within practical discourses."[69]

Therefore, as we approach the next historical period after King's, we extend our gaze into the realm of the Renaissance and Enlightenment woman. How did her status differ from that of the medieval woman? Was her hysteria therefore different? We inquire into the new stresses creating numbness and panic and ask, Why was Renaissance woman thought to be so influenced by the moon and so possessed of the devil? We can readily see that the pathological symptoms of her hysteria would imitate the symptoms of other conditions: the fits and faints, as well as the tremors, tics, coughs, hiccups, grimaces, gnashing of teeth, pulling of hair, bashing of head, and all the other aberrations occasioned by the five senses. Other conditions may have produced the last of these symptoms, yet what caused the numbness and panic in the first place, and how did they get represented?[70]

The feminist historians have demonstrated in a vast and important body of new scholarship that Renaissance women were experiencing profound stress and frustration; that as women were promised and therefore expected more, they found themselves actually receiving less in an increasingly complex society within an often confusing religious milieu.[71] Woman's role was still seen as entirely domestic: centered on her household, often her farm, perpetually surrounded by her children, viewed as odd if she took time out for anything other than devotions and even more peculiar if her time was used for writing or painting or secular subjects. It was all too easy to denounce her as overly sexed, and label or stigmatize her behavior as deviant by pointing to the somatic signs noted by her male doctors: apothecaries as well as physicians and surgeons.[72]

In the Renaissance and again in the nineteenth century, these somatic dysfunctions were often called "stigmata" by physicians searching for the "stigma" of hysteria. The line from the fourteenth century to the nineteenth is almost continuous in this sense. Stigma was eventually altered to symptom in the semiology of clinical analysis—in the seventeenth century—and this may be why so many medical lectures appeared in the nineteenth century (like that of the French neurologist, Pierre Janet) entitled "the major symptoms of hysteria."[73]

But hysteria had also been construed as the first cousin, so to speak, of medieval love sickness, a condition about which doctors of all types, theological as well as medical, had pronounced for centuries.[74] During the Middle Ages love sickness was said to afflict *both* women and men, although women were said to have the much greater propensity for affliction. Among women, retained seed that became corrupted and poisonous was construed as the direct cause; this construction continued in the time of Johannes Weyer and Edward Jorden. Once love sickness was linked to female sexual organs by the sixteenth century, it was all too easy for medical doctors to construe it as a pathological condition of women only. The genderization of many of these conditions in the Renaissance—hysteria, love sickness, but not melancholy, which was often viewed as male—has never been told in any detail.[75] Nevertheless, gradually over three or four centuries, the European doctors accomplished this feat of genderization for reasons that have been described as "patriarchal" by feminist historians but whose precise details elude even the best of this group of researchers. The result was a genderizing of love sickness that made it the favorite malady of diseased female genital physiology, usually said to lead directly to the *furor uterinus* with which doctors such as Jorden and Robert Burton will become obsessed.

The larger sexual and cultural dimensions of love sickness were as implicit in the Middle Ages as they would be through the eighteenth century, especially in the moral stigma attached to purging of the female seed from the vagina lest it wreak havoc. Both purging and retention were harmful to the woman once she had undergone puberty; sexual intercourse, in marriage, was the only acceptable option to her. In a Western anatomical model that had women ejaculating internally, there was no healthy space for a retained seed. Female orgasm was essential to the process of conception because the orgasm released the female seed, just as sexual intercourse was required if this seed were to combine with the male seed. Female seed constantly retained, whether through lack of sexual intercourse or excessive female masturbation, contained the source of anatomical imbalance and led to derangement. The only circumstances under which the *male* seed had to be purged were religious or moral, as when pubescent boys were encouraged to masturbate to diminish their sexual aggressivity, or when adult men were advised to do so while their wives were pregnant. There was no place for such male purging in the anatomical or medical sphere.

The codes pertaining to purging of seed and arousal to ejaculation were grounded in beliefs about the differences in male and female anatomy. As Mary Wack has commented, "the arousal was often achieved by a woman who manipulated the [female] patient manually,"[76] and there was no equivalent among males of purging the seed from anywhere in the scrotum. The object was, of course, to arouse the woman to orgasm so that she ejaculated the retained putrifying seed. But such a highly charged practice could hardly have been expected to flourish in Christian lands, where the church vehemently objected to it and where medical doctors dared not state what they really believed about its medical efficacy for fear of ecclesiastical retaliation. Wack is no doubt correct in noticing that some of the medieval doctors—her excellent example is the fourteenth-century Bona Fortuna's *Treatise on the Viaticum*—did not write entirely in elisions but actually recommended masturbation by an *obstetrix*, and some even described the manual techniques to be used.[77] Still, the discourse on sexuality from the fourteenth to the seventeenth century was not so liberal as to permit female masturbatory practices for the purgation of seed to flourish.[78] More direly for the lot of women, female sexuality was checked and impeded in other ways than the recoil shown among male doctors when faced with the prospect of describing on paper an allegedly curative female masturbation therapy. But female morbidity was not limited then to the sexual organs. It also extended to the soul, which would soon also be genderized and pathologized in the form of possession and diabolic ecstasy. The common metaphor in all these applications was morbidity: whether of the sexual organs, the whole body, the eternal soul, or merely the passions of the mind. The trope of the pathological was reinvigorated as it had never been in ancient discourse.[79]

What was said about *men*? Their love suffering was rarely, if ever, linked to pathology of the sexual organs. Even Jacques Ferrand, the already mentioned author of the most widely read treatise on love sickness (1623), and Felix Platter (Platterus) are silent on this matter in their medical works on the subject, and Foucault, who understood the genderization of the sexual organs all too well, is less explicit than his inquisitive readers like.[80] The explanation given to the few cases recorded is almost entirely psychological. Men were said to be amorous and suffer unrequited love just as women do, but the combination of work and responsibility compelled them to drown their unrequited love in anger. Anger was their primordial passion: everything in history confirmed it. In fact, all known history could be interpreted, it was said, as responses to this male anger, which had been alternately unbridled and restrained: wars, peace, aggression, fear of annihilation, the lot.[81] Besides, men were too busy in the workplace and arenas of politics to have the leisure—the argument went—for erotic reverie. Burton reflects this progression all too clearly in the psychological portions of *The Anatomy of Melancholy*. For men, a cycle was thus set up of erotic infatuation, unrequited love, love sickness, anger, and, finally, melancholy. Hysteria was preempted: nowhere did the sexual organs enter into the sequence, nor was there space for priapic phalluses or morbidly wandering scrotums. The key for men, as theorists of melancholy such as Burton understood all too well, was repressed *anger*. Their erotic disappointment centered on anger well suppressed and culturally validated, always predictably resulting in melancholy. Women were permitted no such amplitude. The role of anger was hardly considered a possibility for their erotic ills. Fear and terror consumed them, as did the nocturnal visions and spectorial world of incubi and succubi so common among those suffering from the hallucinations of love sickness and hysteria.[82] But a *female* love sickness predicated mainly on psychological causes was unknown before Weyer and Jorden. Like the larger and more prevalent hysteria, love sickness continued to be conceptualized by the male physicians as something anatomical, physiological, humoral, pathological—an irreducibly *feminine* medical condition. No wonder that love sickness thrived, reaching something of a national epidemic in Western Europe by the time Ferrand published his medical classic work on "erotic melancholy" in 1623 and Shakespeare began to write plays.

Already by the sixteenth century Johannes Weyer (Weir), the Dutch physician, pronounced that hysteria was a *bodily* disease like all other medical conditions and must be semiologically construed (i.e., through signs and symptoms).[83] A half century later, in 1603, Edward Jorden, the author of an influential work in the Galenic humoralist tradition titled *A Briefe Discourse of a Disease Called the Suffocation of the Mother*, claimed that the *diabolic* could be translated into the *natural*—that hysteria could have natural causes. This step was significant because it pointed the way for the largely male-authored medical discourses on hysteria that followed for three centuries, but it was less innovative than it may seem on the surface. Helen King provided some reasons in chapter 1, especially in discussing the doctrine of "vapors," but there are other reasons as well.

Veith summarized the works of these figures, especially Weyer, Ambroise Paré (the French physician), and Jorden, and has commented on their importance as successors to the *Malleus Maleficarum* (1494), the so-called "Witches Hammer," which she sums up as "the most extraordinary document to emanate from the witch mania."[84] No reason exists to doubt her conclusion that "a careful study of this fantastic document reveals beyond doubt that many, if not most, of the witches as well as a great number of their victims described therein were simply hysterics who had suffered from partial anesthesia, mutism, blindness, and convulsions, and, above all, from a variety of sexual delusions."[85] She has been persuasive in explaining the medicalization of hysteria in the light of its cultural and narrative dimensions. Veith also points out that Weyer took unpopular positions on hysteria. Having little theological or political ambition, he could pursue clinical observation with relatively little regard for the reception his views would receive. But it must also be noted that while Weyer was a shrewd observer, he made few theoretical advances when compared to Hippocrates and Harvey, Feuchtersleben and Freud, who were able to take more leaps than he did. Veith analyzes the story of the young hysteric, discussed in Weyer, said to vomit ribbons that she claimed had been inserted daily into her stomach by the devil. After praising Weyer for detecting the fraudulent nature of the account, Veith states: "Weyer was a superb observer, and though a skeptic, he was credulous."[86] Veith's appraisal captures Weyer's double bind: on the one hand, he was doubtful of these supernatural explanations and resisted them; on the other, he remained a creature of his time, unable to extricate himself from notions of possession in hysterical cases. For his ambivalence, Weyer had to withstand the attacks of authoritative contemporaries such as Jean Bodin, the prestigious philosopher and economic thinker attached to the court of Henry III, who championed the theory of demonic possession in hysteria.[87]

In establishing hysteria as a natural disease rather than a theological condition of the soul, it must be noted that Weyer and Jorden performed similar functions, but that Weyer saw more deeply into the female condition. He exonerated hysterics from the charge of diabolism and pronounced them innocent of witchcraft; he broke away from the regimens of physical and mental cruelty advanced by the *Malleus Maleficarum* (tortures of many types);[88] and he sympathized with the predicament of women and compassionated with their violent dreams and phantoms, treating them as victims and patients rather than as malingerers and accomplices. Not enough is known about Weyer's life to ground these views securely in larger biographical contexts; still, whatever the particulars of that Dutch life of the sixteenth century, Weyer can be viewed as a type of Renaissance Philippe Pinel or J.-E.-D. Esquirol who, rather than wishing to see these mentally ill women tried and punished, pitied them and commiserated with their misery.[89] Within the context of hysteria, Weyer was foremost a humanitarian who paved the way, however small, to improve the lot of these disturbed women. Even so, he had few, if any, clues into the nature of the phenomenon itself, much less into its natural history in the way that the eighteenth-century physicians were to construct these "case histories": the causes of these natural (i.e., conversion) symptoms; what these women have in common; and why these symptoms appear preeminently in women.

Weyer's humanitarianism is incontestable: his writing abounds in it as it does in close observation of hysterical symptoms. But detection is not tantamount to insight, and the process of medicalization, while admirable for its empiricism and humanitarianism, cannot be compared with the deep vision of the sort Thomas Sydenham demonstrated.

Weyer's contemporaries, however, fared no better. Timothy Bright, for example, an English physician trained in medicine at Trinity College, Cambridge, chased melancholy rather than hysteria, the two conditions then being closely allied. Bright's approach was partly physiological, partly psychological, mainly concerned—as the title of his treatise on melancholy says—with discovering the "reasons of the strange effects it [melancholie] worketh in our minds and bodies."[90] Even so, Bright's main approach led him to explore "nourishmentes," or the transformation of food into "the melancholicke humour." As he says: "Whether good nourishmente breede melancholie by fault of the bodie turning it into melancholie, & whether such humour is founde in nourishmentes, or rather is made of them" (title of chap. 3). There was in the humoralist Bright no sense of demonic possession—melancholy was also medicalized in Bright's treatment—nor was there reference to a gender-based condition; rather Bright attributed the cause to an all-powerful soul wreaking havoc on the body's bile through these nourishments.

By contrast Jorden, a humoralist born two generations after Weyer, developed a uterine pathology exclusively based on the wandering womb and the bodily production of vapors. Jorden was summoned with three other doctors to testify in the case of Elizabeth Jackson, arraigned on a charge of bewitching the fourteen-year-old Mary Glover.[91] This young girl began to suffer from "fittes . . . so fearfull, that all that were about her, supoosed that she would dye." She grew speechless and occasionally blind; her left side was anesthetized and paralyzed. These were the classic symptoms, recognized before Jorden compiled his narrative, but was their source sorcery or illness? Magic or disease? Glover was diagnosed and then treated by leading doctors from the Royal College in London. When she failed to respond to their therapies, usually herbal concoctions and other chemical preparations, they pronounced, all too predictably, that something in the case was "beyond naturall" in her symptoms. Jorden demurred, finding for disease. When Justice Anderson—a notorious hammer of witches—overrode his evidence, Jorden felt compelled to defend his theory that Glover's symptoms constituted a disease (insensibility, choking sensations, difficulty in eating, convulsions, epileptic and periodical fits: conditions, he insisted, physicians alone were qualified to determine).

This defense became the substance of the already mentioned *Briefe Discourse*. Jorden named Glover's condition the "suffocation of the mother" (i.e., matrix or womb), more simply called the "mother," preferring this usage to the older medical term "hysterica passio."[92] In seventeenth-century parlance these phrases became interchangeable with "hysteria," or its more common adjectival form, "hysterical." All referred back, medically and etymologically, to the womb, anatomy and language converging on the same part of the body that had been the source of hysteria from its inception. For Jorden, such conditions (not to be confused with symptoms) as the esophagian ball, respiratory and digestive blockages, panicky feelings of suffocation and constrictions, all pointed clearly to a uterine pathology. One can readily imagine how this approach shocked ecclesiastical authorities. Even Jorden's medical colleagues revolted against the theory of a uterine pathology as the sole source for the genesis of a medical condition. Harvey had not yet made his discoveries about the heart and the circulation of the blood; another generation would have to pass before Descartes infused anatomy and physiology with radical mechanism and materialism. Jorden's expectations about the reception of his medicalization of hysteria are unknown, but if he thought his radical medicalization would meet with receptive arms he was mistaken. In a religiously crazed world in which Galileo had recently been tried and others before him beheaded for heresy, it was not easy to claim that uterine debility was the *single* and *sole* cause of disturbances thought for so long to be the work of the devil.[93]

Jorden recognized that his views in *Briefe Discourse* would be controversial, if not heretical, although his fundamental notion about disease itself, especially the idea that illness is always cured by its contrary (hot by cold, dry by wet, and so forth), was thoroughly traditional and commonplace. As he wrote in *Briefe Discourse*: "Diseases are cured by their contraries . . . and the more exact the contrarietie is; the more proper is the remedy: as when they are equall in degree or in power."[94] To establish his case for uterine debility as the major cause of hysteria, he drew heavily upon ancient authority, especially the Hippocratic and Galenic ideas with which he was familiar. Jorden did not subscribe to the notion, mentioned above as held by Plato and perhaps popular in ancient folk belief, of the womb as an "animal within the animal,"[95] perhaps the somatic prototype of Freud's free-floating unconscious, the "mind within the mind." Instead he aired the idea, found in Hippocrates and discussed by Plato, of the *wandering* womb—the extraordinary belief that the uterus, when deprived of the health-giving moisture derived from sexual intercourse, would rise up into the hypochondrium (located between the stomach and the chest) in a quest for nourishment. Such predictable wandering, he believed, provoked painful sensations of oppression, constriction, and choking, sometimes leading to vomiting, forced breathing, and spasms.[96]

It was a fanciful geography of hysteria, based only in part on Hippocratic tradition, medical reading, and a certain amount of erudition in the later classics, but there was more supposition than observation in its construction, even in those premicroscopic days when anatomy was not what it would be after the seventeenth-century microscopists and nineteenth-century cell theorists performed their experiments. Although Jorden did not intend it, his hypothesis of the wandering womb further fueled the fiction of female inadequacy, in which women were salvaged and restored by male complementarity—further because it had been circulated since ancient times and was now reinvigorated by Jorden. Nowhere is his fable more transparent than in the positive value placed on the healthful vaginal moisture that allegedly secured the womb and held it in place. But this fluid was provided only by the presence of the male seed—otherwise the cavity remained hollow and dry.[97] The anatomy of this dry and unsafe condition had, as we have seen, been discussed throughout the Middle Ages. Consequently, all uterine mania and pathology derived from this unhinging and subsequent "wandering" of the womb. As long as it remained secure, so Jorden's theory went, the female retained her healthful balance: no amount of personal anguish or grief (Jorden's "affections of the mind") could dislodge her equilibrium, for hysteria was entirely a matter of the derangement of her vaginal cavity, and for precisely this reason Jorden and his contemporaries believed hysteria could never be a male disease. Although meat and drink, the humoralist Jorden believed, were "the Mother of most diseases, whatsoever the Father bee, for the constitution of the humours of our bodies is according to that which feedes us,"[98] the cause of this illness was a life-threatening dryness in the vaginal cavity. The health of the female, therefore, depended primarily on retaining a balanced vaginal moisture, best provided by male seed through sexual intercourse.

It was an extraordinary theory laden with mythic qualities, not least the notions of solitary wanderings and life-threatening peregrinations. What better way to portray female frailty than by using the organs of reproduction themselves—a notion the poets and playwrights of the time will repeat, metaphorize, and mythologize. Jorden's language, especially his vivid and dramatic images of solitary female journeys and his constant analogies of the role of gender in these dramatic wanderings (as in the mother and father of disease), confirms the degree to which his fiction of the "suffocation of the Mother" is gender-based.[99] Constructed on the rock of female anatomic inadequacy (i.e., compared to the male), it suggests the idea that nature and perhaps even the deity had intended from the beginning to program, as it were, the female species for hysteria. Throughout the early modern period, Western medicine, especially medical theory rather than its applied therapies, was based on hypotheses generated in a dense jungle of verbiage, including abundant neologisms, which later proved to be more proximate to the fictions of the poets than to those of radical empiricists. Jorden's theory of the pathological "mother" was itself a metonymy loaded with cultural significance at the turn of the seventeenth century.[100]

Furthermore, Jorden claimed that all uterine irregularities—menstrual blockage, amenorrhea, the retention of putrescent "seed," and assorted other "obstructions"—generated "vapours" that wafted through the body, inducing physical disorders in the extremities, the abdomen, and even the brain.[101] For this there was no empirical evidence; even the alleged "vapours" would later prove to be imaginary. The vapors were said to wreak bodily havoc and induce pathological states that were facilitated by the symbiotic interactivity of the entire organic system. A power of "sympathy," Jorden reasoned, linked the womb to the rest of the body: to the head (then thought to be the seat not of the brain—that came later in the seventeenth century—but of the imagination);[102] to the senses (which determined feelings); and finally to the "animal soul" that governed motion, thereby producing twitches, paroxysms, palsies, convulsive dancing, stretching, yawning, and other terrifying behaviors. Many accidents could trigger the condition, Jorden admitted, since "the perturbations of the minde are oftentimes to blame for this and many other diseases."[103]

Veith, noting Jorden's inclusion of such "perturbations of the minde"

and his advocacy of therapeutic comfort, counsel, and support, extols
the Elizabethan doctor for anticipating the conception of hysteria as a
psychological malady.[104] She commends him as well for "extraordinary
perceptiveness" in recommending pharmacological prescriptions for
hysteria, while claiming at the same time, and seemingly contradictorily,
that "he was the first to advise anything resembling psychotherapy for
hysteria." Some of Jorden's prescriptions were traditional herbs and natural medicines that seem inappropriate today but were common at the
time. The originality of Jorden's analysis of hysteria lay in his grasp
of the power of the mind over the body. For that reason he urged
the physician to confirm the patient's fantasies, even when the doctor
knows better. For example, Jorden recounted the successful treatment
of the Countess of Mantua, who believed her acute lingering melancholy
and hysteria resulted from her having been betwitched. Her physicians
placed nails, needles, and feathers "into her close stoole when she tooke
physicke, making her believe they came out of her bodie."[105] Jorden also
demonstrates his familiarity with Galen's remarks on hysteria. Recount-
ing the case history of a male patient who believed he was impotent, Jorden reports that his physician prescribed "a foolish medicine out of
Cleopatra, made with a crowes gall and oyle . . . whereupon he recovered
his strength."[106] Jorden lists many superstitious remedies that he believed could be effective because of the great power of the mind over
the body. Jorden epitomized it this way: "According to
the saying of *Avicen*, that the confidence of the patient in the meanes
used is oftentimes more available to cure diseases than all other remedies whatsoever."[107] The confidence patients placed in these and other
remedies—prayers, offerings, exotic rituals—enabled Jorden to feel
confident in his own prescriptions.

Jorden's modernity was incontrovertible when compared to his contemporaries. Nevertheless, his remedies did not entail an essentially
psychological approach. The main thing in his treatment was to "let the
bodies bee kept upright, straight laced, and the belly & throat held
downe with ones hand . . . apply evil smells to their nostrils, and sweet
smells beneath . . . tie their legs hard with a garter for revulsion sake."[108]
In an anticipation of psychotherapy, he advised appeasing inflamed
passions by "good counsell and perswasions: hatred and malice by religious instructions, feare by incouragements, love by inducing hatred, or
by permitting them to enjoy their desires."[109] Although Veith would like
to establish Jorden's therapies as precursors to the modern treatments
of hysteria, her interpretation is misleading and, what is more, overlooks
its rather pedestrian medical traditionalism. Jorden's recognition of the
role played by consciousness in the genesis of disease was neither new

nor properly psychogenic, as Veith claims. The *Briefe Discourse* was conventionally couched within the framework of the then current humoral medicine in its perception that all manners of disorders arose from a concurrence of certain physical complaints with the passions and senses. In this capacity there is nothing "psychogenic" about the theory of the "wandering womb" or the "suffocation of the Mother." Moreover, it is anachronistic to claim, as Veith does, that a staunch Galenic humoralist such as Jorden could have wished to advance either an exclusively *somatic,* or an essentially *psychological,* account of the "Mother": his concern was rather to establish a *natural* theory, based upon the integrated operations of the entire organism, so that "the unlearned and rash conceits of divers [persons who proportion] the bounds of nature unto their own capacities . . . might be thereby brought to better understanding and moderation." Not that he would, of course, preclude supernatural agency in principle:[110]

> I doe not deny but that God doth in these days worke extraordinarily, for the deliverance of his children, and for other endes best knowne unto himself; and that among other, there may be both possessions by the Devil, and obsessions and witchcraft, &c. and dispossession also through the Prayers and supplications of his servants, which is the onlely meanes left unto us for our reliefe in that case. But such examples being verie rare now adayes, I would in the feare of God advise men to be very circumspect in pronouncing of a possession: both because the impostures be many, and the effects of naturall diseases be strange to such as have not looked thoroughly into them.

Aiming to prove to the vulgar, "who are apt to make every thing a supernaturall work which they do not understand," that Mary Glover's "passio hysterica" was a mundane disorder, Jorden explained that each of the tell-tale symptoms of witchcraft could easily be proven by the expert physician to be *naturally* caused. This position differs from the one Shakespeare was to take in *King Lear* (see section VII). Shakespeare is less monolithically consistent than Jorden about fraud and natural genesis. "Consider a little," Jorden invited readers, "the signes which some doe shew of a supernaturall power in these examples":

> One of their signes is insensibilitie, when they doe not feele, being pricked with a pin, or burnt with fire, &c. Is this so strange a spectacle, when in the Palsie, the falling sicknesse, Apoplexis, and diverse other diseases, it is dayly observed? And in these fits of the Mother it is so ordinarie as I never read any Author writing of this disease who doth not make mention thereof.[111]

What Jorden proved in relation to anesthesias was applied to other symptoms, in addition to pointing out the connection between mind and body in hysteria:

> There also you shall find convulsions, contractions, distortions, and such like to be ordinarie Symptoms in this disease. Another signe of a supernaturall power they make to be the due & orderly returning of the fits, when they keepe their just day and houre, which we call periods or circuits. This accident as it is common to diverse other chronicall diseases, as headaches, gowtes, Epilepsies, Tertians, Quartans &c. so it is often observed in this disease of the mother as is sufficiently proved in the 2nd Chapter. Another argument of theirs is the offence in eating, or drinking, as if the Divell ment to choake them therewith. But this Symptom is also ordinarie in uterin affects, as I shew in the sixt Chapter: and I have at this time a patient troubled in like manner. Another reason of theirs is, the coming of the fits upon the presence of some certaine person. The like I doe shew in the same Chapter, and the reasons of it, from the stirring of the affections of the mind.[112]

The passage continues to emphasize that mind and body, working together, play a major role in hysteria. Like other passages, this one offers an abundance of signs, especially in the reference to the "affections of the mind," that Jorden primarily aimed to translate the "diabolical" into the natural, working within a familiar explanatory scheme that saw no reason to polarize or select between the organic and the mental. In this process he was simply an educated man of his times. When evaluating Jorden and Weyer, we can say that both physicians "medicalized" hysteria but, from our perspective, neither recognized the role played by the patient's cultural environment, especially as related to the lot of women. Both doctors were persuaded that hysteria arose from bodily ailments and somatically grounded emotional distresses; women were anatomically more pliant and imaginative than men and thus more suspectible to the condition, a disease of the reproductive organs. Yet neither considered the domestic and social stresses with which these female patients were unable to cope. Neither considered the kinship between the hysteric's "affections of the mind" and her emotions stirred in relation to the socioeconomic factors involved: a women's domestic situation, sexual status (and the double standard vis-à-vis that sexuality), her legal and economic misery, her persistent disappointments, the lack of hope in a hard life rarely abated by anything except death. It may be expecting too much for doctors of the sixteenth century to be social scientists, but it can also be said, on balance, that neither doctor seems to have had a glimmer of insight into hysteria *in relation to* class structure and social stratification, of which there was then an abundance, even in their agrarian European and English civilization.

According to the views of Weyer and Jorden and the many other Renaissance physicians who wrote about hysteria (i.e., the Swiss Aureolus Paracelsus, the French Paré, and Laurent Joubert, the chancellor of the University of Montpellier, among dozens of names now forgotten or unmentioned here),[113] the female patient (to the degree that she was medicalized and removed from her mythic and diabolic status) was an integrated, organic hierarchy: a symbiosis of soma and psyche to be viewed apart from the social and economic reality in which she functioned. The Renaissance humanists had viewed her more totally: as a creature with a past and present history, with a future determined as much by cultural as biological forces. The great humanists—the Petrarchs, Erasmuses, and Mores—lived before Jorden, and those to whom Weyer's theories were available seem not to have incorporated the medicalization of hysteria into their system of thought. For the Renaissance humanists, the condition of hysteria still lingered in the twilight of a supernatural and diabolic world: a zone all the more perplexing to them inasmuch as medicine, as the Rabelais scholar Georges Lote has noted, was "*the* science of the sixteenth century, exercising great influence and inspiring confidence."[114]

In addition, ideas about hysteria were then fermenting in a religious and intellectual milieu in which medicine was rapidly being revolutionized anyway. Learned and imaginative thinkers such as Rabelais, who had also been medically trained at Montpellier, probably absorbed more than we think about this process of medicalization.[115] Rabelais himself comments ironically in *Gargantua and Pantagruel* (through the mouthpiece of the witty Dr. Rondibilis) on the womb as an "animal," parodying the Platonic tradition discussed above.[116] But not even Rabelais, Mikhail Bakhtin has suggested in *Rabelais and His World,* with all his (Rabelais's) sophisticated medico-anatomical training, linked hysteria to the sociocultural position of women. The Dr. Rondibilis who wants to purvey his point about only women having a womb, and a womb that it is moreover just "an animal," is far more concerned with the gulf that lies between realism and literary representation than with any socioeconomic bases of female hysteria. (Rabelais and Shakespeare later classified women according to their virtue and modesty, their courage and beauty, but neither saw the correlation between health and wealth.) Rich women, whether virgins or widows, were given no dispensation when sunk in the depths of hysteria's abyss. There is no sense anywhere in Weyer and Jorden, for example, that the melancholy of the affluent differs from that of other groups. Class-based hysteria enters the discussion later, at the end of the eighteenth century, as the symptoms of the affluent are said by doctors such as the Scottish Cheyne and James M. Adair and the French Joseph Lieutaud, to arise from different causes.[117] In the period from approximately 1450 to 1700, the only distinction is bodily sign; as long as the sign is evident, all else proves irrelevant: so imbued with certainty is the semiology of the hysteric. By 1600 or 1650 medicalization became widely assimilated, as evidenced in the thought of a physician such as Thomas Fienus, especially the notion that hysterics are no longer witches to be detected, tried, and burned at the stake.[118] In our twentieth-century, post-Freudian sense of female numbness viewed through the discourses of hysteria composed by Kristeva and Duras, this medicalization of hysteria caused a regression in woman's lot rather than advancement and brought little understanding of the plight of women that had lain at the heart of the condition in the first place. Once medicalized, hysteria became the deviant sport of Renaissance and Enlightenment doctors who justified any therapy in the name of calming female fits and faints. Viewed from the perspective of muting the more genuine causes in woman's lot, it was a short step from Dr. Jorden's therapies of foul smells, tight garters, and "crow's gall and oyle" to the clitoridectomies and ovariectomies of the nineteenth century. Women would have to wait for male physicians to liberate them—wait even after Freud and his colleagues arrived in Vienna.

VII

The conjunction of hysteria and modernity thus arises at the moment of its medicalization at the turn of the seventeenth century. Once hysteria became medicalized, its theory was not significantly revised except for the alteration of its somatic locations. Many decades were to pass before a majority of doctors became persuaded about the naturalness (as distinct from the demonization) of the condition. Here and there, as we shall see, there were some major discoveries of insight, for example Sydenham's, but the new hypothesis always leaned upon, and reflected, the prevailing medical theory of the day, hysteria being always a remarkably elusive disease.[119] The larger matter about hysteria in the seventeenth century essentially entails the repetition of its medical diagnoses. After Weyer's and Jorden's medicalization, there was no significant insight into its nature until the advent of Willis and Sydenham. During that period (ca. 1600–1660), the voices of the nonmedically trained prove to offer as much insight as those of physicians and other caretakers. If we want to understand seventeenth-century hysteria, we do well to consult the social history of women of all classes: a record revealing as much as the medical treatises that commonly crib from one another without having engaged in empirical research or brought forth anything new to the main argument.[120]

The personal records of hysteric patients in that period—the non-medical voices we want to hear—are virtually nonexistent.[121] It is not that the historian-archaeologist of hysteria has forgotten to listen to them but rather that the doctors in the seventeenth century did not record what their female patients said or did in any detail. For example, Richard Napier, an early Stuart parson-physician, compiled in a career spanning many decades casebooks of hysterical patients, but even here *his* voice speaks more forcefully than the patient's.[122] Napier, as Michael MacDonald has demonstrated, habitually explained hysteria and all manner of melancholy states as proceeding from particular concatenations of bodily ailments and emotional distresses. Nor had Napier broken entirely free of the old supernaturalism or magic, occasionally linking hysteria to possession despite his clear awareness of its medicalization. By way of remedy, he prescribed "physick"—usually herbal purgatives, together with supportive advice and prayers. Missing from his compilations are comprehension of, or compassion for, the domestic travails of his female patients—the social conditions alluded to above. Class and rank figure nowhere. He discovered hysteria everywhere in the female world: all diagnosis and therapy originate, he believed, in the pathological body (the wandering womb) and in emotional grief (usually loss and depression); never was the distress seen as socially or economically determined.

Napier found no examples of hysteria among malingerers. Indeed, those pretending to be ill, to be hysterical, to escape poverty and duty by faking fits and starts are remarkably absent from the early seventeenth-century world: its medicine as well as its imaginative literature and art.[123] The degree to which Napier anticipated the modern view is extraordinary. Compare Napier on malingerers to Dr. Alan Krohn, for example:

> It should be stressed that hysterics are not faking, playing games, or simply seeking attention. . . . The hysteric is neither a malingerer nor a psychopath in that the sorts of parts he plays, feelings he experiences, and actions he undertakes have predominantly unconscious roots—he is usually not aware of trying to fool or deceive. When the hysteric uses cultural myths or lives out a cultural stereotype, he is usually not making a conscious choice of identity.

Moreover, in Napier's world there were two almost conflicting intellectual tendencies destined to keep women in biological chains: on the one hand, a persistent demonization of her as part witch, part animal, with a "wicked womb" (not so different from the one flaunted in Germaine Greer's *The Female Eunuch*[124]); on the other, a more humane view derived from the recent medicalization of her most emblematic disease (i.e., hysteria), which served to demystify her gender status.

The theological and religious consequences of these views were significant: even there, medicalization played a significant although clearly more osmotic role.[125] Nevertheless, throughout the seventeenth century, women remained slaves, so to speak, of their biology, a fate similar to that which they experienced in antiquity; more time was needed to erase their image as voracious wombs paradoxically embodied in decrepit witches or insatiable pleasure-givers.[126] Furthermore, the seventeenth-century conception connected the "spell" created by the older demonic frenzy to the "spell" of the menses, or *menarche,* rampaging furiously through the female body, causing violent paroxysm and anatomic upheaval. So long as woman was biologically mythologized, there was no hope of grounding her hysteria—her anxiety and panic, her twitches and epileptic convulsions—in a *social* fabric where she could be viewed as a rational being. The radical medicalization of hysteria, culminating in the eighteenth century, was well on its way by the time Jorden and his medical colleagues had died. By then, the representations of the female body had, as it were, been turned inside out; charted as ugly in anatomical drawings as well as idealized as beautiful on canvases and in literary texts, and within this paradoxical relationship covertly placed within the "ugly-beautiful" tradition in which the late Renaissance basked. But male fear of demonic female sexuality would not be quelled so quickly. Perhaps a word such as *hystero-phobia* should be coined to describe the male response to female sexuality in the period between the world of Harvey the anatomist and that of the radical Enlightenment physiologists, between the 1620s and the 1690s.[127] In any case we will see that this male fear was no irrelevant obstacle on the road to the radical medicalization of hysteria.

These developments are clearly mirrored in thinkers as diverse as Shakespeare and Robert Burton, the scholar-author of the 1621 *Anatomy of Melancholy.* Burton, who had read Weyer, Jorden, and many other sources on hysteria, believed that fits of the "Mother" could be occasioned equally by body disease and by inordinate passions, appetites, and fancy, and similarly advised a dual package of pills and precepts. Burton gazed deeply into the class filiations of both melancholy and hysteria, believing that "hired servants" and "handmaidens"—no matter what their age—were rarely afflicted. The "coarser" the woman, the less likelihood of her presenting with hysteria. Shakespeare, who may not have heard of either Weyer or Jorden, nevertheless responded acutely to "the Mother" as one of the important ideas of his time, metaphorizing it and even building it into the fabric of several of his plays. His sources are complex and deeply interfuse with the ideological dimensions of hysteria in the late sixteenth century and its troubled relation to magic and witchcraft. For example, there is no doubt that Shakespeare was familiar with Samuel Harsnett's antipapist pamphlet *A Declaration of Egregious Popishe [sic] Impostures . . . Under the Pretence of Casting Out Devils* (1603). Harsnett, a churchman with a checkered past by the time he wrote the *Declaration* early in life, had served on various commissions to inspect those who claimed to exorcise devils. He had heard vivid accounts of possessed women. From the time he was a student at Cambridge, he pondered the boundaries between fraudulent witchcraft and natural possession, especially in cases in which female hysteria was claimed to have manifested itself as a natural disease. His *Declaration* spoke loudly to his generation, especially to Shakespeare, who took the names of the spirits mentioned by Edgar in *King Lear* from it. Harsnett also recounts in the *Declaration* the case of a man afflicted with *hysterica passio*, a term he uses interchangeably with "the Mother," and he writes as if the case were an anomaly. But other Elizabethans had also commented on "the Mother," under different circumstances and in contexts other than political or medical ones, and had written about it both as natural illness and natural metaphor for female sexuality. A decade or so later the poet Drayton invoked "the Mother" as a simile for "a raging river" in his well-known *Poly-Olbion* (1612–1622)—no doubt a poetic trope for unbridled female sexuality—as well as considered it a genuine female malady:

As when we haplie see a sicklie woman fall
Into a fit of that which wee the Mother call,
When from the grieved wombe shee feeles the paine arise,
Breakes into grievous sighes, with intermixed cries,
Bereaved of her sense; and strugling still with those
That gainst her rising paine their utmost strength oppose,
Starts, tosses, tumbles, strikes, turnes, touses, spurnes and spraules,
Casting with furious lims her holders to the walles;
But that the horrid pangs torments the grieved so,
One well might muse from whence this suddaine strength should grow.[128]

Thus by the turn of the seventeenth century the confluence of several streams of thought vis-à-vis hysteria had, so to speak, coagulated. M. E. Addyman considers Shakespeare's assimilation of the doctrine of hysteria to be sufficiently important to have warranted a book-length study.[129] "It seemed to me," she claims, "that, while *hysterica passio* formed a potent symbol in *Lear* and offered a detailed vocabulary for certain effects, its role was limited; but of Leontes [in *The Winter's Tale*] one could say that he was a hysteric, and the elucidating of that comment would reveal much of interest about the nature of the play."[130] For Addyman, hysteria and its natural progression to insanity constitute the essence of Lear's disintegration. After Lear's mode of being and basis for authority have been irrevocably shaken, he inquires: "Who is it that can tell me who I am?" (I. iv. 250). When he no longer knows himself, he exclaims to the fool, "O fool, I shall go mad!" (II. iv. 289). After expressing his anguish over his rejection by his daughters and the sight of his servant in Regan's stocks, Lear cries out:

> O, how this mother swells up toward my heart!
> Hysterica passio, down, thou climbing sorrow,
> Thy element's below!
> (II. iv. 55–57)

Addyman's observation, which has eluded many Shakespeareans, is that Lear conceptualizes the horror of the disenfranchisement he is soon to experience in the very terms of—indeed in the very language of—the newly medicalized condition. "Some new world," she writes, "some terrible knowledge which will not accommodate existing patterns of speech and habit, is about to be brought into being, and it is experienced in its first inner stirrings as 'this mother,' as '*hysterica passio*.'"[131] Why, we wonder, was hysteria, among all the various medical conditions then, perceived as capable of such drastic transformations, especially if figures as diverse as Shakespeare and Burton responded so forcefully to it?

The different uses of hysteria made by Shakespeare in *Lear* and *The Winter's Tale* do not diminish his creative response—on the contrary, they heighten it. A form of knowledge for the great tragic protagonist (Lear) becomes the basis for character and destiny in the later romantic one (Leontes). Hysteria signified to Shakespeare not simply a medical malady—for him it became more than a newly discovered disease recently emancipated from its demonic bondage. The transition from demonic profile to medical malady was indeed in the thick process of transition during the Elizabethan period. As Addyman observes, "Lear's *hysterica passio* is a form of knowledge: it is the mode and limitation of his awakening to the world which exists beyond his will"; for Leontes it represents more than anything "his maladjustment" itself, the essence of his dis-ease.[132] It would be literal-minded, perhaps even obtuse, to inquire how Shakespeare conceived of a *male* hysteric in an era when the doctors had observed few.[133] Narrative, especially great imaginative literature such as Shakespeare's plays, or (conversely) popular narrative, such as pamphlets and tracts, has always provided science and medicine with some of its best ideas; narrative brilliantly leaps to hypotheses doctors would not, perhaps could not, intellectually and imaginatively dare to make.[134] The doctors saw the "mother" as feminine, but in the popular imagination it was something (however mysteriously) that could afflict men. It is unknown how Elizabethan medical authorities responded to Shakespeare's use of the term *hysterica passio,* and it may be that his usage in the plays was ignored. Still, the question about male hysteria in the Renaissance must be put in a medical context before it takes on significant meaning, and even more specifically must be addressed in relation to the category of hysteria raised at the beginning of this chapter.

Perhaps the point about Leontes, and presumably the larger point about hysteria in the Renaissance that Addyman wishes to make, is that Leontes's hysteria signifies the amalgam of disease and confusion—indeed, a diseased confusion—in which his child, adult, and sexual self coexist; it is not a narrowly conceived and almost clinical hysteria that Shakespeare embodies through the figure of Leontes (as it might have been in Jorden's treatment), but a metaphoric and symbolic hysteria. Similarly Robert Burton enlarged the domain of melancholy and brought it to the very foreground of his agenda, making it, as Devon Hodges has suggested, the basis for an anatomy and ontology of the cosmos.[135] But if Burton's *Anatomy of Melancholy* demonstrates an almost uncontrollable impulse to dissect every form of knowledge as a symptom of the cultural transformation of his time, his larger signifier—melancholy—is hewn out of the stone of an even larger transformer: this category—melancholia and hysteria—reflecting the cultural shifts that to Burton virtually defy explanation. As in the plays, where hysteria—the *hysterica passio*—represents both the states of knowledge themselves and the psychological frames of mind of two of Shakespeare's most interesting figures, Burton uses the category hysteria to connect forms of knowledge that have been undergoing monumental conceptual shifts in his lifetime. Both responses, Burtonian and Shakespearean, demonstrate the magisterial significance of hysteria for the late Renaissance world: a meaning it could never have acquired had it not been for the medicalization of the one malady with secular and cultural overtones.[136]

The question to be pondered then is *why medicalization took the radical turn it did when it did,* and throughout this chapter I have been suggesting that among the reasons (it was not the only reason) was the altering status of women in the period from roughly 1600 to 1700 as social, economic, political, and even biological creatures. In brief, I am suggesting that doctors radically medicalize disease and become more positivistic in their approach to illness in times of unusual stress placed on one or both of the sexes.[137] This principle may seem an arbitrary correlation between disease and gender. Eventually historical sociologists will bear it out, and a great deal of research into the history of the body, the sociology of medicine, and the history of gender will be required before we can understand how the principle developed in its crucial period in early modern Europe.[138]

In the discipline of anatomy, then a rapidly changing body of knowledge, as well as in medical research and empirical speculation more generally, the view of women was being revised. Throughout much of the seventeenth century, medical research promulgated the traditional view of the female reproductive apparatus as an inferior, imperfect, almost inverted equivalent of the male.[139] The notion that women were essentially and fundamentally *different*—radically other and strange—had not yet taken hold; they continued to be viewed as males manqué. It had long been known that female orgasm was unnecessary for conception and that menstruation occurred independent of erotic excitation, but these relationships had not yet been put into contexts that could change the old patriarchal views and create an independent biological niche for women. As Thomas Laqueur has emphasized, seventeenth-century medical theory commonly endorsed the classical view of the female reproductive system as inherently deficient, even deformed, a pathological inversion of the normative male.[140] Menarche and puberty were cosmically ordained to upset body functioning, producing physical irregularities and pain that spawned further behavioral disruptions. Pregnancy and childbirth entailed seasons of sickness, sometimes leading to postpartum insanity. Menopausal women became moody and predatory. All such disturbances were clearly caused by a single aberration—by the seventeenth century the term *womb* was used metaphorically as well as literally. Men had no such ordained anatomy, no such predictable vulnerability, no such biological destiny.

Gender, however, was not the only factor governing the category then occupied by hysteria. Most physicians combined their learning in anatomy and physiology to religious, astrological, and astronomical beliefs in the diagnosis and treatment of these uterine syndromes. By the 1640s, a small library of medical literature conjoining these realms, natural and supernatural, had developed and was regularly producing books composed for an audience of doctors and their patients. John Sadler's *The*

Sicke Womans Private Looking-Glasse, wherein Methodically are handled all uterine affects, or diseases arising from the wombe; enabling Women to informe the Physician about the cause of their griefe is a fine specimen of the genre, and also interesting for its metaphors of hysteria and versions of linguistic representation.[141] Sadler, a licensed physician, practiced humoral medicine in Norwich and specialized in female diseases. The fifteen chapters of his book aim to explain how virtually all female health and reproduction is governed by the health of the uterus and its motions: the rising, falling, and stasis of the womb washed into health by regular discharges and frequent pregnancy. Even so, Sadler devotes a whole chapter (13) to the question "whether devils can engender Monsters [of birth]," and despite his negative conclusion the fact remains that he was willing to spend so much time answering it. Sadler nowhere invokes the word "hysteria," but his references to the "weeping of the Wombe" (chap. 4), the "suffocation of the mother" (chap. 6), and "the hystericall passions" (p. 62) make evident that hysteria constitutes, of course, his true subject matter. His approach, common in the time, is semiotic: he searches for proximate "causes" and "signs" in an attempt to provide "prognosticks" and "cures," these necessary four components providing the physician with knowledge of the real state of the patient's womb. Once in possession of this knowledge, he prescribes from a wide variety of herbal remedies considered in conjunction with "the planet's influence" on the patient, as his astrological epigraph attests. His approach emphasizes that hysterical diseases arise primarily from the "suppression" or "overflowing" of the "menses"—from unnatural discharges— and this is why he starts his book with a discussion of unhealthy menstrual discharges, the single most common cause of hysteria.

"How many incurable diseases," inquired William Harvey, the famous discoverer of the circulation of the blood, "are brought about by unhealthy menstrual discharges?"[142] The question was rhetorical, replicated dozens of times by Harvey's medical brethren. Like his peers, Harvey regarded women as slaves to their biology; the idea had already been generated in the great literature of the Renaissance, especially by Shakespeare and the dramatists. Gross female appetites, the "furor of the uterus" that was by now being called *furor uterinus* by the doctors,[143] drove the entire sex, governing their words and deeds on earth, even necessitating a cosmic theology at whose center was an Edenic myth laying all culpability on Eve for mankind's irrevocable sin.[144] No matter what women did with their biology, in the Christian myth they were destined to sin as a consequence of it. In matters anatomic and physiologic, there was—so to speak—no free will. This specific topic the late

Renaissance theologians debated almost *ad nauseam*.[145] The church admonished its parishioners as well as serious students, as it had been cautioning for centuries, against the sins of the womb in less vivid anatomies, but secular opposition claimed that the retention of seed was equally, if also biologically, harmful. Jane Sharp, a male "quack doctor" in England who assumed a female pseudonym, advised lusty maidens to marry (and have sexual intercourse) or face the dire consequences of hysteria.[146] Harvey, the anatomist, provided the empirical secular raison d'être: without gratification, overheated wombs would spark "mental aberrations, the delirium, the melancholy, the paroxysms of frenzy, as if the affected person were under the dominion of spells," this final phase revealing how a semantic sleight of hand could perpetuate witchcraft insinuations in secular contexts. In summary, male hegemonic culture was still affirming that women, especially in their rudimentary biologic sense, were not very different from men. But they were more mysterious, as the Romantic poets, especially Wordsworth, would continue to claim: mystery—the mystery of their dreams and desire rather than of their anatomies—is what distinguished them. Whether as witches or hysterics, whether in their normal state or pathologically demented as hysterics sometimes were, their imaginations were deemed to be of another order from men's. Yet the very notion of "women as mysterious" was a male construct. Oddly, it remains a fundamental concept of twentieth-century sexual theory, as when Jacques Lacan cryptically pronounces that

> it can happen that women are too soulful in love, that is to say, that they soul for the soul. What on earth could this be other than the soul for which they soul in their partner, who is none the less *homo* right up to the hilt, from which they cannot escape? This can only bring them to the ultimate point . . . (ultimate not used gratuitously here) of hysteria, as it is called in Greek, or of acting the man, as I call it.

Historically speaking, not until the post-Cartesian world of the Enlightenment, and even later, did the notion of a resolute female difference mandating respect for its inalterability take a firm hold.

Harvey, forever the Aristotelian zoologist, explicitly drew the parallel between bitches in heat and hysterical women. In these pronouncements picturing the insatiable, ferocious, animal-like womb, he was closer to Plato and Euripides than he realized. A leader among those decrying the retention of seed, he warned that women who "continue too long unwedded, are seized with serious symptoms—hysterics, furor uterinus,

&c. or fall into a cachectic state, and distemperatures of various kinds."[147] For "all animals, indeed, grow savage when in heat, and unless they are suffered to enjoy one another, become changed in disposition." Thus hysterical women direly needed *medical* attention, for "to such a height does the malady reach in some, that they are believed to be poisoned, or moonstruck, or possessed by a devil."

What, then, was to be done? Harvey advised prophylactic measures, above all "the influence of good nurture," with its power to "tranquilize the inordinate passions of the mind."[148] But if this view represented a continuation and further medicalization of the effects of Jorden's "passions of the mind," it also embedded a theory of sex whose double standard is apparent from our perspective. Harvey's advising of pro-phylactic repression was, of course, restricted to women. In his own mind there was no contradiction because the raging womb—the *furor uterinus*—by definition reflected a female state of affairs. How else could it be? He did not see, nor did his medical brethren suspect, that men, like "all animals" also "grow savage when in heat." Or if he did see, men were exempt from the need for repression by virtue of a more protective anatomic apparatus that had been ordained, it seemed, by Nature. Here then was gender formation at the hands of the scientific elite of the day—the Harveys and his like—in tacit league to invoke biology to en-grave the theory.[149] The sexual repression of males and its deleterious consequences would not be understood until the nineteenth century, as we shall see in chapters 3 and 4, by Roy Porter and Elaine Showalter. Eventually it became evident, as they demonstrate, that repression itself was counterproductive, rendering the already hysterical only more hys-terical. Nevertheless, seventeenth-century formulations, by construing hysteria according to the Greek model as primarily a gynecological dis-order, activated the disease concept emplotted within a discourse of gen-der stigmatization. This is why hysteria the category and hysteria the medical discourse lie so proximate to the discourses of gender in this period of early modern history. Women were on trial, and male doctors sat on the right hand of the already male judges.

This might seem a clear invitation for the historian of hysteria to chuck medical theory altogether and instead invoke social history. After all, sickness did not always excuse the hysterical: in Shakespeare's and Harvey's time, hysteria was suspected to be the stigmata of vice, the wages of intemperance, even though no one put forth a lucid or persua-sive theory explaining how this could be so. Two centuries later—in the mid-eighteenth and early nineteenth centuries—thinkers as diverse

as Adam Smith and Samuel Johnson, Jane Austen and Harriet Martineau, reported that the sick are commonly judged to be narcissistic
egoists, extravagantly demanding of other people's time, patience, and
resources.[150] And who can forget the gloomy fate of the self-indulgent
Emma Bovary, repaid in both life and death for her mortal sins? How
then did hysteric sickness become the just reward of a defective personal
morality and deformed female sexual apparatus? And what were the social or cultural determinants of this *other* conversion syndrome?

As *men* were largely exempt from the anatomic stigmata, their own
morality was not held accountable. If the hysterical female became somatically ill through lack of self-control or personal discipline, it had
to be explained why control and discipline were intrinsically different from that expected of the male. In other words, why was the raging
erotic appetite of women different from its male counterpart?[151] These
questions were not answered in the seventeenth century—in many cases,
not even raised. Furthermore, if we set the chronological dials to approximately 1600 or 1650, we observe little, if any, discussion of the social components. If sexual intercourse was the adjudged best remedy for
hysteria, and marriage the guarantor for intercourse, is it not significant
that in this period marriageable women greatly outnumbered eligible
men?[152] If marriage was closed to a certain segment of the female population, can it be that women concocted hysterical symptoms as an alibi
to enhance their prospects for marriage? There were, it would seem, few
better ways to ward off the often fatal "womb disease" than the acquisi-
tion of a marriage partner. Also, in that time (male) physicians were increasingly prescribing intercourse through marriage as a prescription to
avoid hysteria.[153] Such prescription was no doubt abetted by the very
slow and incremental secularization of countries like England and other
northern Protestant lands (the secularization was slower in the Catholic
countries). But—we must ask—did the doctors perhaps have another
agenda in recommending intercourse as the best remedy? And can hysteria have been a successful method for the otherwise erotically lost
woman, so to speak, to mediate her anxiety and internal guilt? These
are modern concepts, to be sure, but not without universal application,
even in the period of early modern Europe. Finally, we must examine
the roles played by class. These cannot be omitted either, for as early as
the time of Boccaccio and Rabelais leisured ladies are said to be the most
prone to erotic melancholy and hysteria; even if there is as yet no theory
of class in relation to these illnesses, the idle and rich, the affluent and
bored, remain the best candidates for affliction.

VIII

This gender asymmetry differentiated males entirely. They suffered crises and anxieties too, as both the medical and imaginative literature (plays, poetry) of the day demonstrate, but much less so in the romantic and erotic sphere. As the seventeenth century unfolded they were increasingly conceptualized and represented as public creatures: open, straightforward, rational, communicative, educated; working and functioning in public, in the broad light of day where their best virtues could be seen; and, as we have already suggested, mediating their romantic disappointments—which many obviously had—in the anger said to be almost preternatural to the male condition from time immemorial.[154]

The imaginative literature of the seventeenth century—especially its plays and poetry—make it apparent that the gender gulf widened as the century progressed. Perhaps this is why marriage itself was transformed from a realistic, almost literalist, view to the more idealized one found in the Miltonic theogony. Difference of every kind was introduced into the speculative discourse of gender, buttressed often by medical and empirical observation, but also by religious and moral observations that discriminated among the kinds of friendship suitable to each sex. In Milton's epic, the sexes are already so far apart, so anatomically and biologically differentiated, that idealized female mystique and well-grounded male rationality become the twin pillars on which the great poet can construct his Christian myth.[155] As the gender differences widened, the sexes found themselves increasingly categorized into stereotypes irreducibly female or male. No one cause can be assigned to these new arrangements, but their effects are miraculously captured in Jacobean and Restoration drama, especially in the roles of the rake, fop, madman, cuckold, unfaithful husband, as well as—on the other side—the virgin, widow, coquette, dreamer, foolish old duchess. Within these groupings and categorizations, appropriate diseases attached to each character type, as virgins and widows frequently found themselves cast as hysterics while clerics and students were depicted as melancholics.[156] There was no deviation. When generalizing in this fashion, over large periods of time (half centuries rather than decades), it is tempting to grasp for the obvious trend without differentiating the subtleties. Nevertheless, if one compares the archetypal conceptions of women and men from roughly 1600 to 1700, large, even monumental, differences abound.[157] If the rake is taken as a representative example in 1600 and then 1700, his transformed social identity makes the point, especially within the contexts of the developing libertinism predicated on gender and sexuality.[158] In the world of Ben Jonson and John Donne, for example, he is a marginal figure in the panoply of social types: libertine, wanton, promiscuous, pictured as ravingly heterosexual; by the time he reaches his maturity in the English Restoration, especially on the stage, he displays a newly acquired bisexual identity and stands in extreme contrast to those who promote the ideals of romantic marriage and the newly domesticated family.[159] As Randolph Trumbach has written, "somewhere in this transition from one sexual system to another—from a system of two genders of male and female, to a system of three genders of man, woman, and sodomite—was . . . the growth of equality between men and women that was part of the modern European culture that was emerging in northwestern Europe around 1700 in all the structures of life."[160] This equality probably signaled a transition from one anthropological sexual system to another; it did not diminish the gender differentiation on which so many theories of hysteria were then built.

Besides, the genuine underlying reasons for gender differentiation were as patently social and political as they were biological and anatomic. Political turmoil and eventual restoration of the rightful monarch, at least in England, resulted in a new sense of the nation, and with this fervid nationalism came new commerce, new professions, new military might, new wealth, and most apparent to the man or woman in the street, new urban sprawl. When Charles II returned from France in 1660, the greater London area had only about three hundred thousand people; by 1700, it had swelled to a city of six hundred seventy-five thousand, and by 1800, almost a million. With this growth a new set of social and professional relations developed and caused greater gender stress. Prostitution, female and male, arose as a profession for the first time in England, as did new and sometimes dangerous sexual liaisons between persons of different and same sexes.[161] Crime, violence, squalor, and suffering caused by poverty all reached new levels, as the Newtons and Lockes at the close of the seventeenth century were creating their intellectual revolution. Socially speaking, the world of 1700 was a vastly different place from the England of the Elizabethans just a hundred years earlier, and nowhere was the difference more palpable than in the relation of the sexes.[162]

Under the strain of the new stress, hysteria became—for the first time in Western civilization—a *male* disease. Not surprisingly, it was a consequential moment for the history of both hysteria and gender. From this Restoration world two more radical breakthroughs in the theory of hysteria will emerge, both by Sydenham: the first, that hysteria can "imitate any disease," and the second, the notion that it is "the commonest of all diseases." [163] The question we must pursue is why the same generation—not merely the same physician—gives rise to both ideas, and we go a long way toward finding the answer if we isolate the new social roles of males in the Restoration. In both the Elizabethan and Restoration imagination, hysteria and melancholy were intrinsically linked. Throughout the seventeenth century they increasingly overlapped, especially when female patients were diagnosed as afflicted with the one as well as the other.[164] The medical theory of both periods reveals an unusual coexistence extending beyond overlap and reciprocity; it often demonstrates confusion and chaos centered on the issues of gender (is hysteria a *female* malady and melancholy a *male*?) and sex (does uterine anatomy predispose *women* to hysteria while *male* grief afflicts the intercostal cavity, causing melancholy and hypochondria?).[165]

By the later period (the Restoration) men are being portrayed in a way altogether different than three generations earlier. The Restoration stage presented, of course, a theater experience very different from its Tudor-Stuart antecedent. More limited to the upper crust in its audience, it also controlled their responses more, and in this sense it can be compared with Richard Foreman's contemporary "Ontological-Hysteric Theatre," which attempts to exploit the hysterical syndrome by dramatizing naturalistic triangles of persons enmeshed in alienating situations. And the Restoration stage presented a more limited repertoire of characters—especially male rakes, fops, wits, wit-would-be's, as well as squires, gentlemen, statesmen, soldiers—often consumed in erotic adventures while drawn to the very brink of the old Burtonian melancholy by unrelenting male competition. At the same time this national stage remained coherent in its class structure and a faithful index of the collective erotic fantasy of the age, holding up the *male* victims of a predatory female eros forever in disguise. Why didn't the medical doctors recognize that in this dramatic representation lay one of the secrets of hysteria?—that it is as much a male as female condition, and therefore in no small degree socially rather than biologically constituted, as by now (i.e., after 1660) it was widely accepted that men did not have the defective female anatomic (i.e., reproductive) apparatus that had been the nemesis of women for centuries. This is the quintessence of the matter and gives us pause in the twentieth century as we wonder why this gender difference had not always been obvious. Not until the 1680s did these ideas and ideologies coalesce in the written discourses of the "English Hippocrates"—so-called for his genius in clinical observation and faithful recording of what he observed in his patients—Dr. Thomas Sydenham (1624–1689).

IX

Although well educated and possessing a first-class scientific mind, Sydenham seems an unlikely candidate for the imaginative leaps attributed to him. The son of landed gentry in Dorset in the West Country, he had been educated at Oxford, where he became acquainted with many of the prominent early members of the Royal Society. But the English Civil War soon drove him from Oxford's colleges to the battlefield, where he gained—in the words of his biographer—"his first introduction to manhood." [166] As a young soldier he acquired some of the practical attitudes that would benefit him as a mature doctor. Later, in the 1670s, he built an urban medical practice in England second only to that of Thomas Willis, the famous "nerve doctor," in the prestige and political eminence of its patients. It is important that Sydenham's practice was located in London and that most of his patients were what we would call city dwellers, for in that era before the dawn of psychiatry and psychotherapy, the illustrious urban physician, such as Sydenham, could expect half the complaints of his patients to be nervous (their term) or psychological (our term). [167]

Because Sydenham had suffered from the gout since his twenties, his own poor health required him to use his medical knowledge in the most practical way. [168] It wasn't sufficient to be speculative and theoretical about medicine and its therapies when the doctor himself was a patient. Professionally, Sydenham's practice dealt with the diagnosis and treatment of regular, individual patients of stature, wealth, and fashion. He did not seek out the rich—they came to him. [169] His compassion for the ill was such that he may have been the most sought-after physician in the realm. In brief, medicine was his life. When the brilliant young John Locke came to London with his new medical degree from Oxford, it was in Sydenham's clinic that he most hoped to begin his practice, and he did. [170] Sydenham's reputation as an effective medical therapist had reached such a pinnacle by the 1680s that only the wealthy and powerful could afford his services, although he regularly ministered to the poor as well. In such patient-doctor encounters, demonological accusations were never taken seriously (these being more attractive to the lower classes than to his suave patients), thereby leaving the field open for new explorations of such mysterious afflictions as hysteria.

Sydenham, no medical historian or avid reader of medical classics, worked principally by observation. He believed that experimentation was successful only when several physicians made an identical diagnosis; otherwise, he concluded, the experiment was not even scientific. So much did he derive from his reading in Bacon, his medical education at Oxford, and his own intuition. By the time he gathered his thoughts about hysteria in the early 1680s he had read much Bacon (who did not pronounce on hysteria)—Sydenham's idol along with Cervantes—and had independently confirmed the earlier observations of Charles Lepois (the Italian physician also known as Carlo Piso, 1563–1633) that hysteria was *not* entirely an anatomic condition and, as a result, that males were just as susceptible as females.[171] Lepois had rebelled against the earlier theorists of hysteria, and his comments demonstrated to what degree he disagreed with the medical establishment:

> We believe we are correct in concluding that all the hysterical symptoms . . . have been attributed to the uterus, the stomach and other internal organs for the wrong reason. All [these symptoms] come from the head. It is this part which is affected not by sympathy but idiopathically and produces motions which make themselves felt throughout the entire body.[172]

"The hysterical symptoms are almost all common to both men and women," Lepois wrote in the 1620s.[173] But if Lepois looked to the brain, in the head, Sydenham felt no such constraint to search anatomically at all. Instead, he seemed to have been partially liberated from the pressure to specify a unique somatic seat for the disease. He wrote little and measured his words.[174] What he wrote he penned laconically and empirically, without cynicism or malice toward his patients, addressing himself only to what he believed truly counted: clinical reality.

Veith has summarized the biographical and medical circumstances under which Sydenham wrote the *Epistolary Dissertation*. No reason exists to recount them here, for there is little to add, except to observe Sydenham's reason for accepting Dr. William Cole's invitation to set down on paper his thoughts "concerning the so-called hysterical diseases."[175] Cole, a noted physician, had a large practice of his own in which he treated his own hysterical patients.[176] Considering Sydenham one of the greatest living physicians, he asked the venerated doctor why hysteria had proved so elusive. Sydenham's answer in the *Epistolary Dissertation* was brief; coming from Sydenham it must have astonished many of his medical brethren. Whether through compassion or insight, he admitted how difficult hysteria was to cure. He empathetically reflected

that the pain suffered by hysterical patients was more severe than that
in patients with other illnesses. He was the first in the medical establishment (after Lepois, mentioned above) to break from the uterine etiology; the first to degenderize hysteria by removing its erotic stigma
altogether; the first also to claim that no single organ was responsible
but a combination of "mental emotions" and "bodily derangements"
working through the nerves and the then all-important animal spirits.
In this last matter he differed radically from Lepois, who had thought
the brain the somatic seat of hysteria.[177]

In brief then, Sydenham arrived at radical conclusions:

1. He claimed that hysteria afflicted both men and women.
2. He considered hysteria the most common of all diseases.
3. He viewed hysteria as a function of civilization, that is, the richer
   and more civilized and influential the patient, the more likely he
   or she was to be afflicted.

A few years earlier, Willis had also concluded independently of
Lepois that hysteria might be applicable to men, given its lodging—according to Willis—in the nervous stock, spanning the brain and the spinal cord.[178] He derived this attitude from his theory of sympathy, which
led him to reject inherited Hippocratic versions of hysteria. Willis's main
argument was with the notion of a "wandering womb" as anatomically
"suffocating" the rest of the body as it supposedly rampaged and choked
other organs and deprived them of their rightful space. He also held
objections to this view based on the normal and pathological dry-moist
conditions in the body. Hysteria was an important concern to Willis from
the beginning of his medical career. He challenged Nathaniel Highmore's etiology from "bad blood" in a huge treatise written in Latin and
entitled *Affectionum quae dicuntur & hypochondriacae pathologia* ... (1672),
all as part of a larger campaign to give the brain a much greater role in
the genesis of illness and to convert many conditions into diseases of the
nervous system. The specific route for our condition, he believed, was
that the uterus "radiated" (his word) hysteria through an infinity of
neural pathways extending into every organ and tissue of the human
corpus. Willis applied his notions of corporal sympathy to hysteria and
then extended this route of nervous transmission to other female conditions, including chronic "head ache" (of the intense variety suffered
by his contemporary, the brilliant and rich Lady Conway), coma, som-
nolency, epilepsy, vertigo, apoplexy, and generalized paroxysm (i.e.,
numbness), among many others. These and other conditions were owing, Willis thought, to *nervous* disorders he often termed "paralysis of

the nerves."[179] But why omit men, Willis asked, unless the anatomy and physiology of the genders differ? However, Willis chose not to investigate the possibility, concentrating instead on his medical practice and treating the large number of female hysterics in his waiting rooms with a wide repertoire of drugs. The first of the great "nerve doctors" who flourished during the pan-European Enlightenment, Willis anticipated our current medical practice of prescribing drug-based therapies. Indeed, he would be at home today in our neuropsychiatric institutes where pharmacology reigns supreme and patients are drugged for almost every form of depression, anxiety, and pain.

However, Sydenham gazed more deeply into hysteria than Willis: if Willis discovered hysteria through theory, Sydenham came to it from practice. Like his predecessor, Sydenham intuitively demystified hysteria by rendering it an authentic medical affliction, neither diabolical nor fanciful but rational, empirical, mechanical, even mathematical, and, most crucially, calling it "an affliction of the mind" or, in our parlance, a psychological malady.[180] The advancement in his thinking was part of a larger Restoration anatomic movement that had demystified the reproductive organs of the female body.[181] Sydenham's psychologizing of hysteria was crucial. Yet he probed further than Willis: he stressed hysteria's *imitative* function—an altogether new idea—and noticed its protean potential to convert the original psychological distress into somatic reality. As Foucault intimates in his own work on hysteria in chapter 5 of *Madness and Civilization*, Sydenham was also more compassionate than Willis and penetrated further into the wasted lives of his female patients. Whether women merely elicited from Sydenham more compassion than men is unknown, and nothing in his writing offers a clue, but he was less suspicious than most of his medical colleagues that women's hysterical complaints were faked. By virtue of the silences in his *Dissertation*—revealing silences given his already Spartan style and avoidance of rhetoric—he apparently ruled out the possibility that these physical symptoms originated in the patient's attempt to deceive his or her physician, or, furthermore, that hysteria was an imaginary illness. In his view pain itself was a felt emotion, as real as fear, love, grief, and hate; he refused to contemplate the possibility that a woman presenting with demonstrable somatic pain was imagining or fabricating her anger or fear.[182]

In matters of gender application, Sydenham claimed that the radical mood swings of women—spasms, swoonings, epilepsies, convulsions, sudden fits—were also known among men, especially, as he wrote, "among such male subjects as lead a sedentary or studious life, and grow pale over their books and papers."[183] Caprice, in both women and men, was the norm: violent laughter suddenly altered to profuse weeping, each succeeding the other in fits and starts. Nothing in the behavior of either gender, Sydenham thought, was grounded in reason, nor could actions be explained. Emotional instability was the hysteric's hallmark. But who were these "studious" types? Certainly not the farmers or rustics of eighteenth-century England or France, but the upper and leisured classes, many of whom had attached themselves to colleges, churches, and government posts. Implicit rather than explicit in Sydenham's male hysteria was a built-in class notion. The fact that "women are more subject than men," as Sydenham comments, has nothing to do with general anatomical differences or with female reproductive anatomy. Sydenham believed rather that the proclivity was an expression of the *whole person*, arising from a convergence of the mind and nerves mediated through the "animal spirits." These were subtle distinctions, especially the specific locations of anatomic difference. If hysteria was more prevalent and severe among women than men, it was because their anatomic nervous constitutions were weaker. These were important steps and linkages, especially the new significance attached to the mysterious animal spirits,[184] and the relatively new idea that the bodily strength of the nervous constitution was gender bound and gender determined.[185] By 1670 or 1680, not enough research on the nerves had been performed to justify such conclusions; what had been learned was speculative and theoretical; what is most interesting about Sydenham's position was that while he took a giant leap in the psychologizing of hysteria, he also laid out an agenda for "the weak and nervous feminine constitution" that would play a magisterial role in European hysteria for more than two centuries. The latter theory is, ideologically at least, a more controversial accomplishment and must be addressed now.[186]

This analytic interpretation of Sydenham's three-part contribution is not meant to diminish it in any way. Surely Veith is right to praise him as "the great clinician" of hysteria and hail him for psychologizing it. Yet Veith has analyzed hysteria narrowly, considered apart from its philosophical, social, and ideological contexts—an opposite approach to that of Quentin Skinner (quoted in the epigraph to this chapter); Sydenham himself, narrowing his focus to the weak and nervous feminine constitution, further genderized the perplexing malady, as Freud would later do in fin-de-siècle Vienna. Even so, the term *nervous constitution* was no rhetorical flourish or linguistic elision for Sydenham, no metaphor or analogy to describe something sensed but improperly understood. To Sydenham and his colleagues it denoted the quintessence of the body's mechanical operations: the amalgam of its superlative, integrative network.[187] It was metaphoric, of course, to the degree that all language is, but in terms of representation the description was believed to be identical with the body's most essential anatomical network. The nervous system was, in short, the body's greatest miracle, without which neither sensation nor cognition could exist. Therefore, it is inappropriate to use the approaches of literary criticism to assume the concept represented merely a metonymy or metaphor for Willis, Sydenham, or the other anatomists and physicians in the aftermath of Descartes who began to make the nerves the basis of the new medical science.[188]

Sydenham believed that "of all chronic diseases hysteria—unless I err—is the commonest."[189] By common he meant not simply prevalent then and in the past and presumably in Western and non-Western cultures, but constantly on the increase, and *spreading,* especially among the rich and the influential.[190] Although Sydenham had treated cases of poor women, beggars, and vagrants who presented hysterical symptoms, he considered them exceptions. The "common" cases to which he refers existed among the leisured and idle: He wrote, "There is rarely one who is wholly free from them [hysterical complaints]—and females, it must be remembered, form one half of the adults of the world."[191] He does not elaborate on this remark. Although he has much to say in the *Dissertation* about the proximate and direct causes, as well as the pathogenesis of hysteria, he does not explore one of his most brilliant insights about the social pervasiveness of hysteria. He sees hysteria as "the most common of all diseases" because afflictions of the mind now (i.e., in the seventeenth century) have assumed an importance they did not have previously. To generalize the matter to a principle: as life for the leisured and influential becomes more complex, society's maladies also alter. A hundred years ago, according to Sydenham's reasoning, hysteria may have been less prevalent, but by the end of the seventeenth century, in the complex urban milieu previously described, hysteria is on the rise and will continue to increase so long as the social milieu (its economic conditions, political institutions, class arrangements, etc.) grows increasingly complex. The observation entails no philosophy of history or philosophy of medicine, to be sure, but does demonstrate a profound insight into the relation of culture and disease.[192]

Sydenham saw all this *before* the nineteenth-century growth of hysteria; indeed, he claims to have witnessed an explosion—an epidemic— during the English Restoration. Prophetic of things to come, he intuited that hysteria had persisted throughout the ages among *both* genders, although it had gone largely undiagnosed; within this context, he glimpsed the havoc wreaked on human lives by rapid socioeconomic

change and the new lack of personal repression. The libertinism and
hedonism of the Restoration were unparalleled in previous generations.
If Sydenham could somehow have been reborn into Freud's Vienna, he
would neither have denied nor been amazed by hysteria's new prominence. He who had recognized that hysteria "is the commonest of all
diseases" would not have been surprised by its explosion under the
strain of even further gender arrangements in a nineteenth-century
world in which interconnecting, almost organic, complexity created new
stresses; where male individualism and selfhood were being threatened
as they had not been before; and where women demanded rights (especially the vote) more vigorously than ever before. If the female nervous
constitution was perceived to be weaker than the male in the English
Restoration, it was deemed to be even weaker around 1900.[193] This last
matter—the historical development of the so-called weak feminine constitution—forms an integral part of the story of hysteria in the aftermath
of Sydenham. Nothing in its nineteenth-century formulations can be understood without glimpsing how the genders became further differentiated according to this nervous system.

But Sydenham also detected something even more extraordinary
about hysteria: its protean ability to transform itself and its symptoms.
He wrote in 1681: "The frequency of hysteria is no less remarkable than
the multiformity of the shapes which it puts on. Few of the maladies
of miserable mortality are not imitated by it."[194] It is an extraordinary
insight. This suspected ability "to imitate" is what rendered hysteria,
Sydenham thought, *unique among maladies*. No one had detected this
remarkable and elusive capability before. It is as if Sydenham were asking, What is hysteria if it possesses this power of transformation? It is
not surprising that "whatever part of the body it attacks, it will create
the proper symptom of that part. Hence, without skill and sagacity the
physician will be deceived; so as to refer the symptoms to some essential
disease of the part in question, and not to the effects of hysteria."[195] Hysteria in Sydenham's construal was thus a singular malady. As in the recent profiles of such conditions as cancer or AIDS, the natural history
of hysteria was such that it always brought with it another "history" personal to each patient:

> Hence, as often as females consult me concerning such, or such bodily ail-
> ments as are difficult to be determined by the usual role for diagnosis, I
> never fail to carefully inquire whether they are not worse sufferers when
> trouble, low-spirits, or any mental perturbation takes hold of them. If so,
> I put down the symptoms for hysteria.[196]

Our contemporary diagnostic practices may not differ so drastically as we think. Yet Sydenham's hysteria was a sickness born of emotional agitation and physical enfeeblement, one arising, for example, when "mental emotions" were superadded to "bodily derangements," such as "long fasting and over-free evacuations (whether from bleeding, purging, or emetics) which have been too much for the system to bear up against." And—more germane to protean transformation—its symptoms had been so extraordinarily protean because, rather as with volcanic eruptions, the disorder broke out in whichever bodily system was currently weakest.[197] Long before Freud then, Sydenham was the first thinker to consider hysteria a disease of *civilization,* unlike most other maladies. Construing hysteria as "a farrago of disorderly and irregular phenomena," he saw the unreliability of much previous medical theory about the condition and commented: "If we except those who lead a hard and hardy life, then no persons are exempt from its tentacles." For him, hysteria was not a single disease but a broad range of medical conditions: a hodgepodge—a "farrago"—of changing symptoms, the premier emblem of the class of diseases, or conditions, that defied predictability: anomalous, *sui generis,* exempted from the regularity of all other diseases.

X

The succession of medical theory in the Restoration and eighteenth century was therefore relatively clear. In the progression from Willis and Sydenham to Cheyne and Bernard Mandeville—the satirist of *The Fable of the Bees*—and their successors later in the eighteenth century, it was Sydenham who took the largest strides. Willis made free use of the hysteria diagnosis in managing sick women, saw hysteria as a somatic disturbance, treated patients with drug-based therapeutics, and considered the probability that men could be afflicted too. Inasmuch as women of all ages and ranks could suffer from it, he prudently dismissed the notion of Dr. Nathaniel Highmore, his contemporary, that hysteria was due to bad blood.[198] He doubted that it was owing to any specific uterine pathology and identified the central nervous system, spanning the brain and the spinal cord, as the true site. Being "chiefly and primarily convulsive," he argued, "hysteria flared on the brain, and the nervous stock being affected."[199] The animal spirits were specially vulnerable: "The Passions commonly called Hysterical . . . arise most often [when] . . . the animal spirits, possessing the beginning of the Nerves within the head, are infected with some Taint." So he, like Sydenham, concluded that hysteria could not, technically speaking, be solely a female complaint; he offered the weaker nervous constitution as the reason why women were worse afflicted.[200] The obvious conclusion, although both Willis and Sydenham were too cautious to proffer it, was that men with clear symptoms of hysteria were effeminate.[201]

These schematizations shifted the ground to the nervous system as the key through which to understand and interpret hysteria as a category as well as human illness, and the paradigmatic shift is important for Enlightenment medicine.[202] But if hysteria, as both Sydenham and Willis claimed, was the Proteus of maladies—the elusive medical condition par excellence—then we should expect the medical theory of the period to view the nervous system as the key to practically *all* illness, not merely hysteria.

This it did. The best theory of the day did not, naturally, endow the nerves with the key to every disease, but once the mechanical philosophy had completed its work and the paradigmatic shift was absorbed (roughly by 1700), there were few if any diseases without nervous implications. Eventually this monolithic attribution would be seen for the foreshadowing of modern nervousness that it is. At the time, it was viewed as the only respectable medical course possible. Dealing with affluent clienteles, the highly influential Italian physician Georgio Baglivi and satirist Bernard Mandeville carved out comparable concepts of hysteria to encompass the protean ailments of the polite, whose sensibilities to pain were as extensive as their vocabularies, and who may have been adroit at manipulating the protective potential of sickness. Mandeville, a brilliant writer of prose, was sensitive to the languages of hysteria, especially their jumbled vocabularies and dense metaphors. He had commented profusely on the metaphoric kingdoms of "the animal spirits"— commenting pejoratively most of the time and demonstrating how little he believed that medical writers had followed the pious credos of the Royal Society espousing *nullius in verba,* loosely "nothing in the word." In his dialogic *Treatise of the Hypochondriack and Hysterick Passions,* Mandeville makes a character proclaim: "You Gentlemen of Learning make use of very comprehensive Expressions; the Word *Hysterick* must be of a prodigious Latitude, to signify so many different Evils," suggesting that a type of "madness" would arise from nomenclature itself, a form of illness every bit as real as the genuine "hysteric's affliction."

Drawing upon his extensive clinical experience, Baglivi demonstrated how patients commonly presented symptom clusters resistant to rigid disease categories, though responsive to the personal tact and guile of the physician.[203] Mandeville, for his part a profound social commentator as well as a sought-after medical practitioner, made much of the fashionable life-style pressures disposing women to hysteria while their husbands sank into hypochondriasis.[204] Was there a *determinant* anatomico-physiological etiology for the disorder? Mandeville, like Sydenham, deflected the question, concentrating instead upon those behavioral facets—languor, low spirits, mood swings, depression, anxiety—integral to the presentation of the self in everyday sickness. Mandeville's substantial contribution to the theory of hysteria was revisionary more than anything else. He ridiculed the elaborate speculative models of mechanico-corporeal machinery floated by Willis, especially the idea that erratic mood shifts were literally due to "explosions" in the animal spirits, and derogated the highly analogical language Willis used to capture the iatromathematical motion of these nervous eruptions. Mandeville was less troubled by Willis's theory of *sympathy* than with his version of *idiopathy*: the idea that the "explosion" could convey its neuroanatomic effects throughout the body by sympathy. Idiopathy and "detonation" were Mandeville's unrelenting gripe, especially the unpredictable onset of the "detonations," not a theory of medical sympathy that had historically antedated Willis nor neurophysiological disagreement about the manner of conveyance through the nervous pathways. Furthermore, the metaphoric dangers of "detonation in the human body" struck the satiric Mandeville as comic, even hilarious. Anatomic detonations, nervous explosions, sudden eruptions: what reason did nature have for infusing the human microcosm called "the body" with these sudden "detonations," especially if they could "explode" at any moment and throw the organism into a paroxysm of hysterical illness?[205]

Subsequent theorists of hysteria took up Mandeville's caveat, favoring the sympathetic transmission over the idiopathic. But by now—the eighteenth century—the neural transmission of hysteria had almost completely replaced the "bloody" and uterine, "explosions" or not. The old dualistic categories of spirit and body, rational and physical dimensions, were replaced by a more or less integral "nervous system" (however poorly defined and ill understood) transmitting all manner of "nervous disorders," of which hysteria was indubitably the supreme. As the discourse on hysteria made its way through the world of the Enlightenment, at least three of its most cherished beliefs were quashed. Set the dials roughly to the first quarter of the eighteenth century and hysteria is now a rampantly spreading malady that clearly afflicts *both* genders, women primarily because of their *weaker nervous systems,* and while stress and daily routine are crucial in its genesis, nothing is more important than *the state of the nerves* and *the animal spirits* that govern them.

When Baglivi wrote in *The Practice of Physick, reduc'd to the ancient Way of Observations, containing a just Parallel between the Wisdom of the Ancients and the Hypothesis's of Modern Physicians* (1704) that "Women are more subject than Men to Diseases arising from the Passions of the Mind, and more violently affected with them, by Reason of the Timorousness and Weakness of their Sex," he meant weakness in the *nerves*. Baglivi was widely read throughout Europe, from north to south, from the avant-garde medical schools of Holland to those in Spain and Salerno. His theory of "Diseases arising from the Passions of the Mind" as diseases of gender took hold almost instantly. This eighteenth-century view represented a narrow conception of a disease that had puzzled doctors for long, even if men and women then invested in the ideologies of the animal spirits in ways now almost irretrievable. It was a narrow conception, and it demonstrates that the paradigmatic shift from a uterine to a nervous model for hysteria was the most significant shift the conception of hysteria experienced since its medicalization in the sixteenth century and until its genuine psychogenic formulation in the nineteenth.

XI

I hope I have explain'd the Nature and Causes of Nervous Distempers *(which have hitherto been reckon'd* Witchcraft, Enchantment, Sorcery *and* Possession, *and have been the constant Resource of Ignorance) from Principles easy, natural and intelligible, deduc'd from the best and soundest* Natural Philosophy.
—GEORGE CHEYNE, *The English Malady*

The paradigmatic shift is, of course, self-evident to the careful reader of these discourses, especially as former "hysterical" complaints now become monolithically "nervous." Sydenham died in 1689, almost at the moment that Newton's *Principia* (1687) was being interpreted and Locke's *Essay Concerning Human Understanding* (1690) printed, works providing evidence that paradigmatic shifts were then taking place in other fields as well as in medical theory.[206] Within a generation, to be hysterical was to be *nervous*: the two became synonymous, the latter eventually a shorthand, a metonymy, almost a code word, for the broad class of hysterical and hypochondriacal illnesses. Another feature of the theory of hysteria (not merely the fact of its existence as a medical condition) affords a clue to this transformation into nervous illnesses: the sense that nervous disease *permeates* society. This pervasiveness had never been a primary dimension of the older theories of hysteria.[207] For generations, at least since the time of Weyer and Jorden, it had been thought that hysteria was present and could be found in segments here and there but that it was not omnipresent or pervasive in European society. Now, in the generation between the death of Sydenham and the succession of the Hanoverians (1689–1714), the pervasiveness of nervous disease became as entrenched as the mechanical revolution in science more widely.[208] Was it for that reason, perhaps, that a large number of cases began to surface in the eighteenth century in comparison to previous periods? Even more puzzling, why should diagnoses of hysteria suddenly reach such epidemic proportions? Were there the cases to support the diagnoses, or were doctors on some type of crusade to hystericize (i.e., neuralize) medical illness and encourage the perception that disease was now fundamentally nervous?

The answers must be sought in the discourses themselves as well as in the views of women then and in social transformations then occurring. Today, we tend to think of the nineteenth century as the golden age of hysterical women in part because—we think—the eighteenth century refused to problematize the female sex[209]—that is, to see women in all their biologic and social complexity. Yet authoritative social history reveals the opposite: for example, Sydenham's remarkable social construction of women and their chief disease. The degree to which an epoch problematizes women varies of course; it is perfectly true that *all* epochs problematize their women; nevertheless, in the period of the Enlightenment it was high. Throughout the Restoration and eighteenth century, at least in the British Isles and France, even the healthy woman was still seen as a walking womb. Several dozen rebels—the Bluestockings, the Aphra Behns and Charlotte Charkes, the Lady Mary Wortley Montagus and Madame de Staël's, and other sophisticates in the leading courts and capital cities of Europe—challenged this characterization, but they and their cohorts were unable to put a significant dent in the armor of that social world.[210]

For some, spleen and vapors, often used interchangeably, were still proofs of demonic possession rather than somatic ailment; this is not surprising since witches were still being tried in the early eighteenth century (until the 1730s), even if not so vigorously as they had been previously.[211] But for most, "the vapors" was the colloquial cousin of hysteria, as Dr. John Purcell, a self-professed "nerve doctor," insisted.[212] Dr. John Radcliffe, for whom Oxford's Radcliffe camera is named, was dismissed from Queen Anne's service after telling Her Majesty that she suffered only from the vapors, thereby implying that hers was an imaginary and doubtful malady. This was nothing Her Majesty wished to hear; the Queen wanted a diagnosis indicating *real illness* that could be treated with acceptable therapy, not some imaginary delusion, like "the vapors," for which her character could be impugned and to which no attention would be paid.[213] We glimpse a different view in the poet Pope's treatment of Belinda when she descends into "The Cave of Spleen" in canto 4 of the famous mock-epic poem *The Rape of the Lock* (1714). Belinda's sudden hysterical seizure embodies the older connotation of the medical doctors, and becomes the sign of the unstable postpubescent and nubile nymph burdened with her essential uterine stigmata:[214]

> Safe past the *Gnome* thro' this fantastic Band,
> A branch of healing *Spleenwort* in his hand.
> Then thus address the Pow'r—Hail wayward Queen
> Who rule the Sex from Fifty to Fifteen,
> Parent of Vapours and of Female Wit,
> Who give th' *Hysteric* or *Poetic Fit*,
> On various Tempers act by various ways,
> Make some take Physick, others scribble Plays.
>   (lines 55–60)[215]

The poetry succeeds brilliantly here because of a sustained ambivalence between real and imaginary delusion: "*Hysteric*" and "*Poetic*" fits: that never-never land capturing genuine dementia versus imagined, even feigned, vapors. Pope thereby enables Belinda to enjoy a status unavailable in actual life had she been the historical, precocious, upper-class Arabella Fermor suffering from medically diagnosed hysteria.[216] Unlike Belinda, real patients craved diagnoses that did not brand them as possessed or deluded by imaginary or pretended illnesses. They wanted to be told by their physicians and apothecaries that they were suffering from genuine nervous afflictions that had attacked specific parts of their nervous systems for which there existed pharmacological remedies and other tonic nostrums.[217] Alternatively, in medical theory as distinct from the diagnostic and therapeutic spheres, nothing persuaded doctors and patients alike so well as numbers and mathematics. So long as the physician could quantify the malfunction of the diseased animal spirits and apply arithmetic and even Newtonian fluxions to the motions (i.e., the contractions and expansions) of the nervous system, both diagnosis and therapy seemed possible. Specialized "nerve doctors" were well served by iatromechanical training. For the rest, quantification and numbers had proceeded so far in the mechanical imagination of the day that nothing therapeutic succeeded so well as pills and potions designed to normalize the mechanical motions of the animal spirits within the nerves that had caused the hysteria in the first place. The path ahead for the theory of hysteria lay then in its iatromechanical applications, i.e., its mathematical charting.[218] The followers of Sydenham, especially Baglivi and Mandeville, and of their counterparts Archibald Pitcairne (a Scot who became an important professor of medicine in Leyden and Edinburgh) and Herman Boerhaave in Holland,[219] avowed a medical Newtonianism aspiring to establish the laws—static, dynamic, hydraulic—governing the mechanics of the organism and preferably couching their findings in these mathematical expressions. Anatomical attention to the body's solids would provide, they contended, surer foundations for medical laws than the traditional Galenic preoccupation with the humors and fluctuations of the fluids. Dr. George Cheyne in particular had nothing but scorn for talk of humors and those "fugitive fictions," the animal spirits.[220] Mechanist physicians, treading lightly in Willis's footsteps, pointed to the experimentally demonstrable role of the nervous system—a sensory skeleton variously imagined as comprising nerves, fibers and spirits, strings, pipes, or cords—in mediating between brain and body, anatomy and activity. As I have described elsewhere, Cheyne and his medical peers in Enlightenment England launched an aggressively somaticizing drive to modernize medicine in a Newtonian mode. "Physic," Cheyne advised his brethren, must aspire to the condition of physics. The possibility of diseases, especially hysteria, springing primarily from the mind was discounted—no longer, in the main, because such disorders would be deemed diabolically insinuated, but because they would thereby be rendered empirically unintelligible. For the theory of hysteria this represented an invigorating somaticizing that totally undid Sydenham's *cultural* unraveling.[221]

The Newtonian mechanics of cause and effect meant that no reflex, no disturbance of consciousness, no sensation or motor response, was to be admitted without presuming some prior organic disturbance communicated via the senses and the nerves. "Every change of the Mind," pronounced the enthusiastic Newtonian Dr. Nicholas Robinson in 1729, "indicates a change in the Bodily Organs,"[222] a view Cheyne endorsed in *The English Malady* by adumbrating its workings in the intimate interplay between the digestive organs and healthy nerves' tonicity:

> I never saw a person labour under severe, obstinate, and strong nervous complaints, but I always found at last, the stomach, guts, liver, spleen, mesentery [i.e., thick membranes enfolding internal organs], or some of

the great and necessary organs or glands of the belly were obstructed, knotted, schirrous, spoiled or perhaps all these together.[223]

Cheyne subsumed hysteria—which in his fashionable medical practice covered a multitude of symptoms ranging "from Yawning and Stretching up to a mortal Fit of Apoplexy"—under the umbrella of nervous diseases, its being due to "a Relaxation and the Want of a sufficient Force and Elasticity in the Solids in general and the *Nerves* in particular."[224] Cheyne's "nerves" thereby endorsed the Sydenham/Willis exoneration of the womb, relocating the distemper as the neighbor of the spleen and vapors, and closely situated next to melancholy. Time elapsed, however, before the educated public caught up with Cheyne's reforms, and even someone as knowledgeable of Cheyne's theory of hysteria as the novelist Samuel Richardson, Cheyne's great friend, conflated his version of hysteria with the vapors and spleen. In Richardson's last novel, *Sir Charles Grandison* (1753), the willowy heroine Clementina endures the three stages of "vapours" Cheyne described in *The English Malady*, proceeding from fits, fainting, lethargy, or restlessness to hallucinations, loss of memory, and despondency (Cheyne recommended bleeding and blistering at this stage), with a final decline toward consumption. To cure her, Sir Charles follows Cheyne, prescribing diet and medicine, exercise, diversion, and rest, and the story is considerably affected when Clementina's parents adopt unquestioningly Dr. Robert James's further recommendation that "in Virgins arrived at Maturity, and rendered mad by Love, Marriage is the most efficacious Remedy."[225]

In the perceptions and practice of early Georgian medicine, these nervous complaints constituted a block of relatively nonspecific ailments and behavioral disorders. One need merely think of the letters and diaries of the period to see what resonance spleen and vapors emitted.[226] They are even more frequently referred to in the poetry and drama of the period, where virtually no author is exempt. From the mad hack's attacks of spleen in Jonathan Swift's *Tale of a Tub* to Clarissa Harlowe's persistent bouts with vapors in the Richardson novel of that name, the nervous ailment exists as mundane reality as well as cliché and complex trope.[227] Gender proves no discriminating factor, as men and women alike, and in almost equal numbers, fall prey to its sudden attacks. But diagnosed inaccurately, the same symptoms could denote lunacy, insanity, dementia: the same madness Swift's hack clearly suffers from in the Rabelaisian *Tale of a Tub*.[228] To our way of thinking, the broad category melancholy would not seem to fit under this conception of hysteria. Yet it then did, one evidence of which is the consistent interchange of the two words in even the most technical medical literature. Furthermore, the line between melancholy and madness was delicate and thus greatly feared. Melancholy, madness, hysteria, hypochondria, dementia, spleen, vapors, nerves: by 1720 or 1730 all were jumbled and confused with one another as they had never been before. Anne Finch, the Countess of Winchelsea and a poet much admired by Pope and Wordsworth, turned this confusion about the status of hysteria to her advantage in *The Spleen: A Pindarique Ode by a Lady* (1709). This is her most ambitious work: a phantasmagoria about life, death, and the nocturnal reverie world—all conceived and executed by pondering reality through the gaze of the splenetic poet.[229]

The leading "nerve doctors"—the Mandevilles and Cheynes and their group of lesser epigoni—grounded these hysterical symptoms entirely in somatic origins: to make certain through tact and expertise that patients understood that virtually all hysterical complaints were worlds apart from gross lunacy. Thus Dr. Purcell, mentioned earlier as a fashionable nerve doctor, claimed that "the vapours"—a condition colloquially synonymous with hysteria—consisted entirely of an organic obstruction located "in the Stomach and Guts; whereof the Grumbling of the one and the Heaviness and uneasiness of the other generally preceding the Paroxysm, are no small Proofs."[230] Noting that one of Hippocrates's noblest contributions to medicine lay in recognizing that epilepsy was not a divine affliction ("the sacred disease") but entirely natural, Purcell insisted that the vapors (what the French would call the "petit mal") were akin to epilepsy (the "grand mal"); indeed that "an epilepsie, is Vapours arriv'd to a more violent degree."

What had become of Sydenham's revolutionary insights—the social conditions, daily stresses, nocturnal excesses, wasting away of women in a patriarchal world, all of which he had believed were important in the genesis of hysteria? Where was the view that the new Enlightenment codes of politeness and refinement, and the encroachment of unwanted foreign customs on civilized English and French life (coffee, tea, chocolate, snuff, etc.) played a part in creating these hysterical complaints? In England and later in Western Europe they had gone underground, subservient to, or overwhelmed by, a scientific milieu bristling with vigorous Newtonianism.[231] It is not easy to imagine that a wave of Newtonianism diverted the nerve doctors to such a preponderant degree despite theories such as Robinson's (note 231); nevertheless, the fact is that it did. Mental illness in our time has been construed so completely within the light of socioeconomic determinants, when it is not considered a genetic or hormonal disorder requiring chemical correction, that we find it hard to imagine an approach to hysteria so monolithically iatromathe-matical as the Newtonian one of Cheyne's world. Yet for a generation at least, extending well beyond the second quarter of the eighteenth cen-tury, personal and social stress were discounted as uninteresting to the theories of hysteria, while the limelight fell on the application of the new "mathematical medicine" to existing cases.

Indeed, inquiry into the etiology of hysteria as a valid form of ex-ploration regressed: all cases were deemed to result from deviant phys-iologies of the nervous system that could be understood only by New-tonian or other mechanical analyses. As the century evolved, it became clear that lunacy, insanity, and madness represented the great fears— the *grand peur*—of these early Georgians, not the chronic hysteria that doctors like Mandeville and Cheyne claimed they could *always* cure now that it was somaticized and released from its previous diabolical moor-ings. Lunacy was feared as the great hangman because even the best of the Newtonian doctors had no clue to its genesis and cure.[232] In cases of hysteria there was at least hope for the patient. Its onset, as the doctors assuaged their patients, had not even been mi'lady's or his lordship's fault. Madness, on the other hand, represented an unequivocal failing in the popular imagination: a fatal lapse of the soul, a disjunction of mind and body; the stigma *ne plus ultra*; in the brave new world of the Enlightenment it was a final, irrevocable state, usually ending in incar-ceration. It was not until late in the century that a new class of humane physicians—the Batties, Monros, Chiarugis, Crichtons, Pinels—demon-strated the same humanitarian attitude to madness that the Willises, Sy-denhams, and Cheynes had for hysteria and other nervous disorders.[233]

Medical science thus led early Enlightenment physicians to make a great play of the organic rootings of problematic disorders. But so too did bedside diplomacy. Confronted with indeterminate ailments, Cheyne, for example, pondered the problem of negotiating diagnoses acceptable to doctor and patient alike. In his remarkable autobiography and tantalizingly ambiguous self "case history," he claimed to empathize with these victims because he himself suffered from such disorders.[234] Physicians were commonly put on the spot by "nervous cases," he noted, because such conditions were easily dismissed by the "vulgar" as marks of "peevishness," or, when ladies were afflicted, of "fantasticalness" or "coquetry."[235] But his own somaticizing categories were pure music to his patients' ears, for they craved diagnoses that rendered their hyster-ical disorders *real.* The uninformed might suppose that hysteria, the spleen, and all that class of disorders were "nothing but the effect of Fancy, and a delusive Imagination": such a charge was ill-founded,

Cheyne assured them, because "the consequent Sufferings are without doubt real and unfeigned."[236] Even so, finding *le mot juste* required tact. "Often when I have been consulted in a Case," Cheyne mused, "and found it to be what is commonly call'd Nervous, I have been in the utmost Difficulty, when desir'd to define or name the Distemper."[237] His reason was the predictable desire not to offend, "for fear of affronting them or fixing a Reproach on a Family or Person." For, "if I said it was Vapours, hysterick or Hypochondriacal Disorders, they thought I call'd them Mad or Fantastical."

What precisely was the sociology and linguistics of this annotated disgust? Did the patients disown their hysteria and the similar maladies because they reflected a perverse life-style? Some moral or religious failing? Or was it that somehow centuries of uterine stigma could not be wiped away so quickly, not even by the reforms of Willis and Sydenham? Throughout his prolific medical writings, commenting on the recoil of his patients in the face of a diagnosis of nerves or spleen, even when he gave the complaints a somatic basis, Cheyne recognized the degree to which he would have to educate them. Sir Richard Blackmore, another fashionable "nerve doctor," experienced similar difficulties, to the point of admitting that his hysterical patients were often viewed as freaks suffering from "an imaginary and fantastick sickness of the Brain."[238] The freaks thus became "Objects of Derision and Contempt," and naturally were "unwilling to own a Disease that will expose them to Dishonour and Reproach."

While Enlightenment doctors ignored what we would call the sociology of hysteria, they did accept the lack of gender distinctions. Blackmore was as mechanical and Newtonian a physician as one could find in the early eighteenth century, certainly as "mechanical" as Robinson, his colleague, but he lost no opportunity to show that hysterical symptoms in women were identical to those in hypochondriacal men. Ridiculing uterine theories of hysteria as so much anatomical jibberish, Blackmore concluded, as Cheyne did, that "the Symptoms that disturb the Operations of the Mind and Imagination in hysterick Women"—by which he meant "Fluctuations of Judgment, and swift Turns in forming and reversing of Opinions and Resolutions, Inconstancy, Timidity, Absence of Mind, want of self-determining power, Inattention, Incogitancy, Diffidence, Suspicion, and an Aptness to take well-meant Things amiss"—"are the same with those in Hypochondriacal Men."[239] The condition, he maintained, was common to both sexes, and the many names given to it—melancholy, spleen, vapors, hysteria, nerves, among dozens of others—all amounted to the same thing: a genuine malady with somatic pathology requiring a new understanding between doctor and patient. The sensitive physician demonstrated his expertise by ridiculing theories that these nervous complaints were the result of a diseased womb, and he recommended identical therapy for hysteric male and female patients.

To gain acceptance for the term *hysteric* and its symptoms, these physicians proposed to yoke them with more common organic illnesses, investing them with labels and copper-bottomed organic connotations, for example, by speaking of "hysterick colic" or "hysterick gout." The tendency persisted for sixty or seventy years at least. Thus one woman Cheyne treated had a "hysterick lowness," another "frequent hysterick fits"; eventually the word *hysteric* was so flattened and became so neutral in its connotations as to mean almost nothing at all. The physician thereby spared himself the accusation of merely trading in words— which he was consciously doing anyway in view of the number of conditions that had come under the umbrella of "nervous"—and imputations of shamming also were avoided. Robinson, already mentioned, insisted that such nervous disorders were not "imaginary Whims and Fancies, but real Affections of the Mind, arising from the real, mechanical Affections of Matter and Motion."[240] His reason was that "neither the Fancy, nor Imagination, nor even Reason itself . . . can feign . . . a Disease that has no Foundation in Nature," a position that hurls down the gauntlet to Sigmund Freud.[241] Organic agencies, such as stone, tumor, fistula, and so on, thus had to initiate the chain of reactions, no matter what the conversion process entailed: "The affected Nerves . . . must strike the Imagination with the Sense of Pain, before the Mind can conceive the Idea of Pain in that Part." Here then was the all-important role of the nerves in sensation, as well as all human pleasure and pain.

Cheyne, Blackmore, Robinson, and their contemporaries did not seek to deny the contribution of consciousness to the genesis of nervous disease nor reduce mind to body (Baglivi, so influential in southern Europe, went the other way, reducing all body to mind—a mind whose passions had been shaped exclusively by the state of the nerves). But their aspirations as "scientific" doctors treating "enlightened" patients (usually the elite of the population) disposed them to insist upon the priority of physical stimuli as part of their two-pronged strategy to win the confidence of their patients and the esteem of their medical peers. They relied on their academic-medical credentials to enforce this approach as being both objective and true. Credentials were, after all, one of the main factors in determining authority, popularity, and fashionability.[242] The most sought-after doctors in London and Edinburgh,

Oxford and Cambridge, as well as at the spas and in the major cities of other countries, had been decorated, so to speak, for their academic achievements. If this approach rendered the species man—in a world increasingly explained by new theories about the sciences of man— *l'homme machine*, its philosophical materialism also had beneficial effects. Thus the establishment of nervous conditions as valid medical diseases helped to secure the credit of medicine itself in an era of rampant quacks and proliferating mountebanks, when doubts about its validity as a science were at an all-time high.[243]

More locally, within the realm of medical theory, this state of affairs amounted to a neurological approach to hysteria, which Veith has claimed was "sterile" in a "controversial century."[244] Oddly, it was the dominance of this neurological approach to hysteria and the triumph of the nerve doctors with their patients (physicians such as Cheyne) that led Veith to this disastrous conclusion. Countering her judgment, we might note (without adopting any Victorian or Darwinian notions about the evolution of medicine or medical conditions) that late twentieth-century medicine has vindicated the neurological approach and returned to it the primacy of neurobiology.[245] This may prove nothing in itself but at least demonstrates the longevity of the neurological approach. Furthermore, the Enlightenment nerve doctors were immensely sympathetic to their patients. Even in an age, such as ours, when hysteria has become so politically and academically charged, this fact within the history of hysteria cannot be lightly dismissed. In the case histories detailed in the final section of *The English Malady*, Cheyne drew attention to the real woes of sufferers burdened with misery, depression, *taedium vitae*, ennui, hysteria, and melancholy—not least, to his own nervous misery.[246] His patients, unlike Sydenham's, shared one common thread: they uniformly came from the ranks of the rich and the famous.

XII

Hysteria thus came of age in the openness of the Enlightenment, more specifically in the sunlight of the Newtonian Enlightenment. Virtually no important doctor in the first half of the eighteenth century placed the root of hysteria in the uterus, and this fact tells us as much about the patients of the epoch as its mostly male physicians. The modernization proved anatomically liberating, while also helping to discredit the theory based on the misogynistic sexual stigma of the voracious womb.[247] The new emplacement of hysteria in the world of Cheyne and his "nerve doctor" colleagues moreover skirted vulgar reductionism. Its unmistak-

able language of the nerves—amounting to the heart of its linguistic discourse—pointed toward the mutual interplay of consciousness and body
through the brain and the (often) still perplexing animal spirits as the
primary nervous medium.[248]

This new linguistic footing, which had been developing since the days
of Willis and Mandeville, had profound cultural and gender-based implications: cultural because society itself was growing "nervous" in ways
no one had anticipated, and gender-based as a consequence of this new
nervous model of mankind mandating a weaker nervous constitution for
women than men. The desexualization of hysteria was, of course, one
part of a movement during the Enlightenment that demystified the
entire body.[249] This process included the reproductive organs and the
newly privileged mind over matter, as in Hume's examples and (especially under the weight of Linnaean taxonomy) the rule of species over
gender. With demystification also came the shedding of much of the
shame of hysteria. Its sufferers at mid-century were now seen as the victims of an interestingly delicate nervous system buckling under the pressures of civilization, typically the thorn in the flesh of elites moving in
flashy, fast-lane society.[250] This was the essence of Cheyne's message in
his best-selling book, *The English Malady*.

But the cultural reasons for this "delicate nervous constitution" were
to remain hidden and elusive for some time. Its personal effects, especially for patients, were described ad infinitem; the other effects, the
larger images of those living an affluent life, could be seen in the new
image the emerging Georgians held of themselves. At home, in the bedroom, this might entail paralysis, fear of the dark, as well as dread of
the incubus and succubus, as evidenced by sleepwalking and amnesia.[251]
(If the weekly and monthly magazines can be considered reliable, amnesia was more common than we might think.) These were the standard
images of the somnambulant melancholic or insomniac hysteric in the
caricatures of the time, as the accompanying plate demonstrates. More
locally still, within the context of a now desexualized female hysteria,
the suggestion was that coquetry verged on hysteria.[252] To the vulgar,
as Pope had suggested in *The Rape of the Lock*, hysteria might signify
nothing more than coquetry itself. But these examples, medical and
literary, signified something more deeply ingrained in the world of the
Georgians than has been thought: namely, the nervous self-fashioning
of Augustan society.

Stephen Greenblatt and others among the New Historicists have written about such self-fashioning in the Renaissance.[253] Yet the latter period
of the Enlightenment is even more revealing of the great personal ten-

"Madwoman in Terror," ca. 1775, Mezzotint by W. Dickinson, after a painting by Robert Edge Pine. Engraving in the Wellcome Institute in London. The portrait illuminates the early female iconography of hysteria, in this instance a mad young woman of perhaps twenty or so whose wild hair is strung with straw, and whose eyeballs flash with terror and fear. A bandana is wrapped around her head; in fury she has torn the garment from her breast, which now lies bare. A feathery or animal garment clings loosely around her, and she is chained and roped, evidence that she poses a threat to others and is dangerous to herself. Window high up in the left corner makes clear that this is a cell for lunatics where she has been incarcerated.

sions it raised between the sexes in a milieu of increasing desexualization in which women continued to enjoy greater freedom and equality than they had before. The Augustan wits—the Addisons and Swifts, virtually all the Scriblerians—encouraged us to believe that logic, wit and intelligence—all part of the realm of the mind—were the sine qua nons of polite society then. But the tension between men and women revolved around more than matching wits, competing intellects, wit and wit-would-be, even in a "republic of letters" governed by an obsessive commitment to refinement and politeness, manners and etiquette. In addition, and most important, there was the unrelenting search for personal identity and self-fulfillment. This need is what the novel and drama of the period capture par excellence, and nothing reflects the mood of the epoch better than its great imaginative literature.[254]

All these cults of sensibility—as I have called them elsewhere[255]—demanded rising standards of behavioral achievement and necessarily called attention to their opposites: the realms of pathology and abnormality. This is why the medicine of the day, especially its theory based on bodily signs and symptoms, the semiology and pathology of illness, cannot be dismissed as so much esoterica.[256] We have devoted two generations of study to the literary language of the Georgians; their ideas of body would well repay half that attention. The Lady Marys and Duchess of Portlands were hardly norms capable of emulation, yet in their bodily motions were codified the brilliant new urbanity of the age. Their sophisticated postures swirled round in rarefied atmospheres of courtliness and polite town society, abiding by a code of language and gesture in which the body was always required to be disciplined and drilled, coy and controlled; always mannered, as we see everywhere from the roles of dancing masters, acting teachers, tutors, governesses, and gymnasts of the age.[257] Even so, new inner sensibilities had to find expression through refined and often subtly veiled bodily codes: one's bearing around the tea table, in the salon, at the assembly and pump-room, in town and country, at home and abroad, paradoxically revealing yet concealing at the same time, in actions, gestures, and movements that spoke louder than words.[258]

This was the source of tension now superimposed on the gender pressures spawned in the Restoration under the weight of urban sprawl and new sociopolitical arrangements. In England at least, the gender rearrangements of the Restoration were elevated to exponential highs in the ages of Anne and the Georges. Isn't this a principal reason why the drama from Etherege and Congreve to Gay and Goldsmith assumes its particular trajectory vis-à-vis the sexes and gender arrangements?

Urban sprawl, new forms of consumer consumption, gender rearrangements, interpersonal tensions, crime and violence, class mobility, the transfer of money and goods into a process of unprecedented consumption: the phrases appear to describe our vexed world. This was, however, the eighteenth century, consuming itself in newly found nationalism and wealth and basking in its accompanying leisure time, especially in food and drink.[259] The lingua franca of such expression-repression-expression lay in the refined codes of nervousness: a new body language, ultraflexible, nuanced yet thoroughly poised within ambivalence. The essence of the code lay in these bodily gestures of recognition—whether blushing or weeping, fainting or swooning—which could act as sorting-out devices in times of doubt, certainly when love and marriage were involved. The comic drama from approximately 1730 onward demonstrates what heightened requirements the code placed on actors who tried to reflect it; our lack of recognition of the code itself results, in part, from the rarity with which any of these plays is now performed. Words were also tokens of recognition for the sensible and sensitive: sorting-out devices too. Under duress and at great expense, the language (of gestures *and* words) could be learned, but even among the rich and great, the smart and chic, it was acquired at the cost of great personal risk and self-doubt.

Risk lay everywhere in the new social arrangements represented—almost mimetically—in the proliferating idioms of nervous sensibility. The sheer number of the idioms then available has prevented us from seeing deeply (and some might say darkly) into the risks involved. Upon occasion we have even denied that the idioms existed. Readers today may well wonder: What cults of nervous sensibility? And why *nervous*?[260] Want of *nerve*, for example, betrayed a clear effeminacy, unacceptable in all classes from the highest rakes and fops to the lowest laborers. Paradoxically, want of *nerves*, exposed a rustic dullness, a latent tedium, a resulting boredom odious to the British for all sorts of reasons and feared among the highest ranking of both genders. Yet florid, volatile nervousness—in both men and women—betrayed excess and confusion: symptoms that could result in hysterical crisis. And hysteria, no matter what appellation it was given and no matter how culturally positive in the popular semiotics of that world, was a refuge of last resort. It was the cry of the person (usually female) unable to cope with the sharp cultural dislocations and social norms that had occurred in such a relatively short time. Within this taxonomy of disease, then, hysteria was the final limit beyond which no condition was more baffling, none capable of producing stranger somatic consequences. The semiotics of the nerves, leading to understanding of hysteria, is therefore a way of knowing, and thereby decoding, the infirmity of excess, in much the same way that Foucault's hysteria is an understanding derived through comprehension of the female's inner spaces. And it was through this semiotics of the nerves that Foucault made the grandest claim of all: "It was in these diseases of the nerves and in those hysterias [of the period 1680–1780], which would soon provoke its irony, that psychiatry took its origin."[261]

The quest was rather for a golden mean filtered by decorum—the same variegated decorum extolled by the age. But decorum had its snares too; it was easier to conceptualize or verbalize than to put into practice, as weepy heroine upon heroine lamented, usually to her detriment, in the fictions of the age. The snare was the retention of one's individuality within this bodily and verbal control. In practice, the act resembled treading on a tightrope, the walker forever balancing over the abyss. This was the beginning of a way of life—as Cheyne above all others in his age seems to have recognized—where the participants lived on the edge and in the fast lane. Richard Sennett, the American sociologist, has located the origins of modern individualism within this fast-paced eighteenth-century culture.[262] More precisely, we might counterargue, individualism was created out of nervous tension and ambivalence over the self: the accommodation between the hyper-visible, narcissistic individual and a society that had craved it (i.e., the individualism), while at the same time demanding conformity to the civilizing process. This was the self-fashioning of the urbane Augustans, the codes on which the sexual politics of the new hysteria of the eighteenth century depended, and it would not have come about without the prior hypostases of the great nerve doctors—the Sydenhams and Willises, the Mandevilles and Cheynes—which resulted in the nervous codes that elevated sensibility to a new pinnacle.[263]

Here then was a different route to the golden age of hysteria, a different dualism than the old Cartesian saw about mind and body. This Georgian self was less a divided Cartesian self—the now unisex woman or man riveted by conventional mind and body—than a creature part public, part private, often hidden behind a mask (sometimes a literal vizard) that curtailed self-expression as well as permitted it to flourish. Here, in this passionate sexual ambivalence, was the heart (one might as well claim the stomach and liver for the visceral effect it had on lives then) of the cults of nervous sensibility. It imbued Augustan and Georgian culture; eventually it made inroads in Holland, France, Italy, all Europe. And it left its mark on the best philosophers: the Voltaires and Hallers and Humes without whom an eighteenth-century "Enlightenment" is unthinkable.[264] It energized the Diderots and Sternes, the Casanovas and Rousseaus, as well as the fictional Clarissas and Evelinas, the Tristram Shandys and other noted "gentlemen"—and gentlewomen—of feeling. How then could nervous sensibility have been born without a medical agenda that demystified the body and a subsequent Newtonian revolution that concretized its best hypotheses?[265]

In the intellectual domain, this nervous tension surfaced as a Sphinxian riddle of psyche-soma affinities, and spurred, in part, the literally hundreds of works on mind and body we have heard about for so long.[266] But in more familiar corners—at home and in church, in the theater and public garden, everywhere in polite society—it also appeared in subtle ways: in bodily motion, gait, affectation, gesture, even in the simple blush or tear, and in the most private thought that now could be read by another. Nervous tension was thus domesticated for the first time in modern history. Viewed from another perspective, it was also being mechanized for the first time, as manners themselves coagulated into an abstract code-language of mechanical philosophy: on the surface a loose application of Newtonian mechanics to the body's gait and gestures, but an application nevertheless.[267]

The self-fashioning of nerves was thus significantly expanded: from mechanical philosophy it was medicalized, familiarized, domesticated, and eventually transformed into the métier of polite self-fashioning and even world-fashioning, in the sense that its code was eventually adopted as a universal *sine qua non* for those aspiring to succeed in the beau monde. The consequences for human sexuality and social intercourse were incalculable because passion and the imagination were implicated to such an extraordinary degree, as were the links between hysteria and the imagination. As soon as the imagination was aroused or disturbed, even in the most imperceptible way, somatic change was indicated. Of this sequence, the physicians had been certain from the mid-eighteenth century, if not earlier. "It appears almost incredible," Peter Shaw, His Majesty George II's Physician Extraordinary and the English champion of chemical applications in medicine, wrote in *The Reflector: Representing Human Affairs, As They Are: and may be improved* (1750, number 228), "what great Effects the Imagination has upon Patients." Later on the point was reiterated by William Heberden, another noted clinician in the tradition of Boerhaave whose life spanned nearly the whole of the eighteenth century and of whom Samuel Johnson said that he was "*ultimus Romanorum,* the last of our great physicians." Heberden was as much a product of this "nerve culture" as anyone else. After years of clinical experience he found that the indication of hysteria usually began "with some uneasiness of the stomach or bowels."[268] He listed the symptoms: "Hypochondriac men and hysteric women suffer accidities, wind, choking, leading to giddiness, confusion, stupidity, inattention, forgetfulness, and irresolution." The symptoms were diverse, perhaps too diverse; a powerful and wild imagination lay at their base. But when Heberden pronounced on the root cause of hysteria, he could only say that the condition was fundamentally *nervous,* that is, fundamentally real or nonimaginary; in his words, "for I doubt not their arising from as real a cause as any other distemper."[269]

Such nervous self-fashioning lay at the base of the social cults and linguistic idioms of Enlightenment sensibility, and were as influential as any other force in generating the theory of hysteria that we see reflected in the writings of the nerve doctors and their students.[270] The process would not be reversible. The doctors did not impose their vision of society on their culture; it was life with its tensions that drew even the doctors into its orbit and caused their theories utterly to reflect this new society.

Just as important, nerves in the new culture precluded moral blame, because there could be no censure in a social, almost *Zeitgeist,* disease. Enlightenment swoons and their subsequent numbness in both women and men came from the act of buckling under the pressures of civilization, especially for the elite who moved within the fast lane of society. The new violence and the threat of its omnipresence enhanced the panic, as John Gay and the early novelists observed. Amelia's strange disorder is described by Captain Booth in Fielding's *Amelia* in terms that make clear the price she has paid for living in the new fast lane. Booth knows not what to call her "disease," but eventually lands on "the hysterics," which seems as accurate to him as any other appellations. Fielding's case history is not very different from the one Jane Austen will narrate with laser precision in *Sense and Sensibility*; its Marianne Dashwood, with her swoons and sighs, is another "hysteric" whose case has not yet been discussed in the detail it deserves, meticulously recounted as it is in that novel from the first onset of fits and starts to the patient's near demise and eventual recovery. In all these cases, real and imagined, panic stemmed not merely from male violence but from a new type of female as well, and society's fears were substantiated almost daily by the culprits and vagabonds apprehended and brought into the courts of law.[271] Life in the fast lane then, at least for the new urban rich, entailed high living, conspicuous consumption, reckless spending, more travel than previously (especially to the developing seaside resorts), late nights, and new gender arrangements, all combining to set off the beau monde from the other ranks of society. Neurological chaos in the body merely mirrored the social disorder of the time. Though the comparison may not have struck the average aristocrat, these forms of disorder never stood apart, nor did the hysteria of its women and men.

But did a delicate nervous organization predispose one to the buckling under, or did the buckling under alter the body's nervous organization? The question is hard but cannot be overlooked or swept away. The approach to the answers taken by the nerve doctors was not, as Veith has suggested, sterile; they recognized the psychogenic burdens of their patients and the role played by mind and imagination, even though the doctors grounded virtually all their diseases in nervous structures. This monolithic attribution remains the difficult aspect of their "hysteria diagnosis" for us. Even so, the doctors often failed (almost always) to see the sociological roots of numbness and its radical enmeshment in language and its representations.[272]

This is a revelatory indication of the degree to which the new nervous culture of the eighteenth century had made inroads into the philosophy, psychology, and medicine of the time. In brief, Cheyne and his colleagues scientized hysteria by radically neuralizing it. They did not invalidate consciousness in human life or reduce mind to body. Theirs was rather a crusade against duplicitous disease, campaigned for in the sunny light and quasi-blind optimism of high Enlightenment science. Not even hysteria could hide from them or prove elusive. If the Enlightenment nerve doctors came back today—*Cheyne recidivus*—they could not agree with our contemporary Dr. Alan Krohn about hysteria as "the elusive neurosis." To them, hysteria was fundamentally knowable: a neurology of solids, an iatromathematics of forces, a neural web of nerves, spirits, and fibers.

XIII

By the mid-eighteenth century, nerves seem to have run wild; the resulting hysteria was chronic among all those living in the fast lane and endemic, for different reasons, among the nation at large. Some women knew they had it, others did not: the inconsistency was less a defect of medical theory than the extreme fluidity of the diagnosis. For hysteria was not poured into a rigid mold by either the doctors or their patients. The diagnosis was usually made to fit the sufferer: a nonreductive expression of disorder. Linguistically speaking, hysteria profited from a new and very malleable vocabulary of the nerves as flexible and adjustable to the particular situation as the patient's symptoms themselves. In formal writing, by mid-century this vocabulary had been expressed in new nervous discourses: of poets, novelists, critics, didactic writers, in narratives of all sorts. An aesthetic of "nervous style" began to emerge, endorsed by male writers, found suspect by female, which was unabashed in calling itself, after its patriarchal affinities, masculine, strong, taut—anything but feminine or epicene. And if style was then genderized to this degree, why should medicine not have been, especially the maladia summa hysteria—the genderized condition par excellence? Cheyne, above all, exploited this protean nervous idiom and procrustean vocabulary in his best-seller *The English Malady,* the real reason for its instant success. So too did his followers and disciples.

One of these, representative of these disciples in several ways, was Dr. James Makittrick Adair. Like Cheyne and William Cullen, Adair was also a Scot who had been deeply influenced by the Scottish Enlightenment. But Adair was also a Cheyne follower who saw what benefits could accrue to his career by worshiping, so to speak, within the "Temple of the English Malady." Adair had been taught in Edinburgh by Robert Whytt, the "philosophic doctor" who related "nervous sensibility" to every aspect of modern life, and he never forgot the great medical precept of his teacher, which resounded in the lecture theaters Adair attended: "The shapes of *Proteus,* or the colours of the *chameleon,* are not more numerous and inconstant, than the variations of the hypochondriac and hysteric diseases."

But it was Cheyne's thought that lay in the deepest regions of Adair's imagination throughout his professional medical career.[273] Always acknowledging his teacher's famous essay of 1764–65 on nervous diseases (Whytt's *Observations on the nature, causes, and cure of those disorders which have been commonly called nervous, hypochondriac, or hysteric, to which are prefixed some remarks on the sympathy of the nerves*), Adair served up explanations his readers wanted to hear about hysteria. He also provided them with a natural history of nerves in the linguistic and cultural domain:

> Upwards of thirty years ago, a treatise on nervous diseases was published by my quondam learned and ingenious preceptor DR. WHYTT, professor of physick, at Edinburgh. Before the publication of this book, people of fashion had not the least idea that they had nerves; but a fashionable apothecary of my acquaintance, having cast his eye over the book, and having been often puzzled by the enquiries of his patients concerning the nature and causes of their complaints, derived from thence a hint, by which he readily cut the gordian knot—"Madam, you are nervous"; the solution was quite satisfactory, the term [nervous] became quite fashionable, and spleen, vapours, and hyp, were forgotten.[274]

It is an extraordinary explanation, showing the continuity of eighteenth-century nervous self-fashioning. It not only casts light on the aftermath of Cheyne's career following his death in 1743 and on Whytt's much-discussed treatise of 1764 but resonates with class filiation. Adair saw how shrewd his medical brethren had been to classify as "nervous" those behavioral disorders free of determinate organic lesions: that is, vapors, spleen, hysteria, hypochondria, melancholy, and the dozens of subcategories spawned from these. Adair also recognized that naming and labeling played a large role in the hysteric's conceptualization. The Gordian knot was unraveled when words were deciphered. Likewise, in the previous generation, when Dr. Nicholas Robinson published a "Newtonian dissertation on hysteria" and wrote that every maiden had become so nervous that coining new words to describe its minute grades was necessary, he knew whereof he spoke. He himself compiled a whole vocabulary of remarkable neologisms that had been coined in his time: hypp, hyppos, hyppocons, markambles, moonpalls, strong fiacs, hockogrogles—all jocularly describing hysteria's grades of severity. Still, it was the great male poet, the dwarf of Twickenham, who used the vernacular of nerves to describe the living consequences of male hysteria. As he lay dying at fifty-five, Alexander Pope claimed to those gathered around him that he "had never been hyppish in his life." There was no need to gloss the phrase. Presumably all knew what he meant.

The very sturdy and nonhysterical Lady Mary, already mentioned, may have considered the "little poet of Twickenham" to be, like his fierce enemy Lord Hervey, a member of the "third sex." But even Lady Mary would have had to admit that Pope was essentially "male." How came it to pass that Pope, whose "long Disease, my Life" had paved the way for him to become more intimate with medical literature than he would otherwise have been, assumed male hysteria to be in the normal course of affairs?[275] One can demonstrate, as I have tried, that as far back as the Elizabethan era, and probably earlier, males were assumed to be natural targets for "the mother," this despite their obviously not having the requisite anatomical apparatus. The progress of medical theory in the aftermath of Sydenham and outside the Cheyne-Adair circle also needs to be consulted if we are to understand how male hysteria shaped up in the eighteenth century.

For the fact is that virtually every serious medical author who wrote about hysteria after Sydenham's death in 1689, even the skeptics among the medical fraternity, included *men* among their lists of those *naturally* afflicted: in England, for example, these authors included some of the best-known doctors of the age, including Nathaniel Highmore, Richard Blackmore, Bernard Mandeville (the physician-satirist), John Purcell, and Nicholas Robinson; in Scotland, Thomas Cupples, Lawrence Fraser, William Turner, and nearly the whole of the Edinburgh medical school; in Holland, the "Eurocentric" Boerhaave and his far-flung students, including Jan Esgers, C. van de Haghen, Lucas van Stevenick, as can be gleaned from dozens of medical dissertations written on hysteria at Leiden and Utrecht; in Denmark, Johannes Tode; in Switzerland and Bohemia, a certain number; in France, Jean Astruc, Nicholas Dellehe, J. C. Dupont, Pierre Pomme, and even the so-called father of psychiatry and transformer of therapies for the suffering insane, the great Philippe Pinel;[276] in Germany, Gustavus Becker, C. G. Burghart, Georg Clasius, C. G. Gross, J. F. Isenflamm, Johann Christoph Stock; in Italy, A. Fracassini, P. Virard, G. V. Zeviani. These names suggest little if anything now, but in their time these figures constituted something of an international gallery of medical stars.[277]

The treatment of *males* among the hysterically afflicted, and especially males of the upper classes, was a veritable industry in the eighteenth century. Whether the doctors were persuaded that males were clinically afflicted in the same way as women (*sans* "the mother" and the rest of the female reproductive apparatus) we may never know, and Mark Micale's biographical researches do not extend far enough back to offer a clue.[278] Yet the medical literature from Sydenham forward speaks for itself and is unequivocal on the matter. Moreover, there seems to have been no major opponent to Sydenham's view about male hysteria to challenge his theory in the long course of the eighteenth century, neither in England nor elsewhere. Once the notion of *male hysteria* took root as a clinically observed phenomenon, which it had not done a hundred years earlier, its existence appears to have been guaranteed. The huge annals of eighteenth-century medical literature corroborate this position, and examples citing Sydenham as their fount are replete in the record. It is more difficult, however, to discover examples roughly contemporary with Sydenham, perhaps suggesting to what degree the notion of male hysteria had been absorbed into the medical imagination.[279]

For example, consider the curious but still far from clear relationship between Thomas Guidott and John Maplet. Both were English physicians practicing in the Restoration and early eighteenth century in and around Bath. Guidott owed his entire Bath practice to Maplet, who helped him acquire it. After Guidott lost his practice in Bath through imprudence, libel, and squandering, he moved to London, remained loyal to his former patron, and continued to diagnose and treat his

(Maplet's) ailments until the end of his life.[280] This would seem to be a case of professional patronage larded over with friendship, but it also had its profound medical side useful in these explorations of male hysteria. What survives are Guidott's accounts (not Maplet's), and considering Guidott's colorful character, his record may not be entirely reliable or complete. But it does provide enough information to comprehend what it was about Maplet's "male hysteria" that so attracted and excited Guidott, who wrote many years after Maplet's death:

> [He] was of a tender, brittle Constitution, inclining to Feminine, clear Skin'd, and of a very fair Complexion, and though very temperate . . . yet inclinable to *Hysterical* Distempers, chiefly Gouts and Catarrhs, which would oftentimes confuse his Body, but not his Mind [mind and body construed as separate entities], which was then more at Liberty to expatiate, and give some Invitation to his Poetick Genius . . . to descant on the Tormentor, and transmit his Sorrow into a Scene of Mirth.[281]

Multiple aspects of this analysis give us pause: Guidott's strange linking of hysteria to gout and catarrh and in other writings his subclassification of "hysterical gout"; his post-Cartesian version of the mind/body split; the assumption that creativity and hysteria ("Poetick Genius" and "the Tormentor") are cousins; above all, the presumption that in educated and intelligent males like Maplet "hysterical mania" is merely the outward sign (again a semiotics of the malady) of an almost "Feminine" nervous "Constitution." Here, in nervous anatomy and "Tender Constitution," lies the origin of temperamental sensitivity in men. Later, Guidott discusses Maplet's delicate nerves, metaphorically isolating them as "suspects" in this quasi-criminal hysterical disorder.[282] "Suspects" in both the positive and pejorative dimension: positive in that they virtually breed sensitivity and creativity; negative in their pathological predisposing toward the condition. All this is what we would expect after unraveling and decoding the complex medical theory of the time.

Much less expected is Guidott's leap to friendship. He claims to be "attracted" to the nervous, brittle, delicate, tender, frail, white-skinned Maplet—not attracted sexually, certainly, nor primarily as a consequence of Maplet's professional generosity, although one would presumably be interested in the arm and leg of patronage, but attracted intellectually and humanly. Guidott's life is not sufficiently understood to hazard any guesses about his sexuality, but his case history of Maplet suggests the existence by approximately 1700 of a new Sydenhamian paradigm about *male hysteria* that yokes anatomy, physiology, and psychology to culture, gender formation, and society.[283]

What better evidence could there be of *gender* basis in this account? Maplet is the "tender, nervous, brittle" male who has become afflicted and requires diagnosing and treating by Guidott; he is also the soft, creative, nervous male predisposed to hysteria and friendship. Guidott's language does not yet reveal the developed jungle of nerves and fibers that will flourish in Cheyne and Richardson, and later even more metaphorically and densely in the fictions of Sterne and the Scottish doctors. But it remains one of the earliest and most interesting accounts of *male* hysteria in English, certainly a prototype of sorts. Guidott himself was somewhat "poetically inspired," though he is not known to have been "hysterical." He had composed poetry at Oxford and wrote poetic satire when he quarreled with the London physicians.[284] And he had matured in a world overrun with male enthusiasts of all sorts—the broad spectrum that permeates the great satires of the age, such as Swift's *Tale of a Tub*. Guidott's London, like that of Sydenham, his contemporary, displayed ranting enthusiasts on every corner, often said by the "doctors" to be male hysterics let loose on the Town. Though their numbers increased and decreased according to the luck of the time, decade by decade, their presence was commonly explained, as Swift had suggested in the *Tale,* in the language of the vapors and spleen, nerves and fibers, all their raving and madness attributable to "hysterical affections."

This was a motif—the connection between religious inspiration and *male* hysteria—that would extend throughout the course of the eighteenth century. As newly inspired sects became more visible, so too the varieties of their *male* hysterics, and in almost every case where documentation survives there lingers the implication of a "hysterical affection" of one or another variety. If epilepsies and convulsions were the signs of secular distraction, they also afflicted men crazed in groups by their religious enthusiasm; Philippe Hecquet, a French physician of the ancien régime, claimed in *Le naturalisme des convulsions dans les maladies de l'épidémie convulsionnaire* (1733) that convulsions among the mob were anatomically experienced no differently than among individuals.[285] Charles Revillon, another French physician, supported this view in *Recherches sur la cause des affections hypochrondriaques* (Paris: Hérissant, 1786), explaining that sudden and unexpected catastrophic events trigger hysteria in the "mob's body" exactly as they do in the individual body. Historically there were—to browse through the century cursorily—the strolling French prophets, or Camizards, in the first two decades; the new alchemists and preachers of the mid-century; the melancholic visionary poets (the Grays, Smarts, Collinses, Cowpers), all of whom suffered some type of religious melancholy and were either incarcerated in their colleges, like Gray, or in madhouses); to say nothing of the non-religious sects and the spate ranging from Hogarth's comic varieties to Dame Edith Sitwell's gallery of rogues.[286] Male hysteria coursed down through the century. Whole books could be written about it, deriving much of their information from the pages of popular reviews like the *Gentleman's Magazine*, one of the most widely circulated outlets of the Enlightenment, British or non-British. For example, the November issue of 1734 recounts a story embellished by the twist of cross dressing. Both the husband and wife have been "hysterically affected," she more acutely than he. More familiar than she with the medical profession, the husband persuades a friend to impersonate a physician, who treats his hysterical wife by prescribing "the simple life." The wife is duped, follows her therapy, and recovers. More common cases reveal afflicted males, prescribed to by bona fide doctors, who do *not* recover quickly.

By 1775, Hugh Farmer, the dissenting minister who was the friend of Dr. Philip Doddridge and enemy of Joseph Priestley, persuaded his publishers that there was sufficient interest in contemporary male hysteria to resuscitate it in the oldest extant texts. Farmer did so himself in *An Essay on the [male] Demoniacs of the New Testament*, a work aimed to show how ancient the lineage of inspiration was.[287] Farmer, like Christopher Smart and William Cowper, had himself been afflicted with a variety of religious melancholies that left him as debilitated as many chronic male hysterics. As a dissenting minister with a parish to look after and duties to attend to, Farmer was utterly uninterested in male license and liberty and, like Smart and Cowper, had maintained a queasy fear of women, especially older, sisterly women who forever rescued him and looked after him. The mindsets of all these figures lie far from the medical theory I discussed earlier, but not so far as to escape its effects. As I continue to suggest here, culture is a large mosaic whose individual pieces do fit together if the historian can only relate them. The English lyric poets, those of the ilk of William Collins and Smart, who were diagnosed male hysterics and melancholics, glimpsed the solipsism of their condition. All they discovered was an omniscient God whose powers of insight they could worship and emulate through their own visionary capabilities.[288] More broadly though, the greater the *resistance* to hysteria among men (in that century there was a surfeit of resistance), the more it revealed about their male sexuality in an era growing increasingly patriarchal and fastidious about its sexual mores. All these conditions and individual cases, far-flung and disparate as they are, some more anecdotal than others, presaged the scenario for male hysterics in the nineteenth century.

Still, the preeminent matter of gender in cases more or less hysterical hardly vanished in the second half of the eighteenth century. Granting that both sexes could become afflicted, perhaps in equal degree, profound questions about hysteria's anatomical prefigurements lingered. This is not surprising after centuries in which the feminine gender base had been strengthened by *men* exorcising hysterical *women* in need of help. No one to my knowledge has ever attempted to compile a list of eighteenth-century cases by gender.[289] If it were tried, even on a limited basis, it would be evident that women were *said* to have become afflicted in far greater numbers. The trend is even reflected in the lamp of imaginative literature. One and only one clearly delineated hysterical figure, for example, appears in Fielding's mock-epic novel *Tom Jones*: the young Nancy Miller, steeped in love sickness. Given the care with which Fielding is known to have constructed his symmetrical work of heroic proportions, the fact is not insignificant and can be demonstrated with similar results for other writers of the epoch. In Tobias Smollett there are many more: even the male hysteric Launcelot Greaves, a modern British version of Don Quixote, whose "nerves" become damaged from his circulation in a crime-ridden, dangerous environment. Smollett was morbidly fascinated with crime in an almost sociological way. He eventually concluded that it had perpetrated the most heinous attack against the society of his day and formed the bedrock on which chronic diseases like hysteria flourished.[290]

Provided that medical and nonmedical discourses are gazed at in tandem, and without undue concern for validity in evidence, it becomes apparent that for most of the eighteenth century the nerves, not gender, were the burning issue for hysteria; that is, the nerves in their variegated anatomical, physiological, vivisectional, linguistic, ideologic, and even political senses. In the first published treatise on nymphomania, M. D. T. Bienville's curious work of 1775, there is no distinction whatever in regard to gender, no sense that the irritation or excitation of the genital area specifically is the cause of his new nymphomania.[291] "Nymphomania," Bienville wrote, arises from "diseased imagination" taking root on the nervous stock, and it could afflict men as readily as women. Perhaps this occurred, in Bienville's view, because both genders had the potential for a "diseased imagination." It is an odd position to maintain, considering that his mind was formed in a world in which the close connection between sex and hysteria was taken for granted. Cases of "erotomania," a fierce and heightened form of erotic melancholy caused by love sickness, were regularly chronicled in the newspapers of the day. Erasmus Darwin, the poet and scientist, had mentioned one severe case

(James Hackman's shooting of Martha Ray), but others were also written up. In all of them, the nervous system had flared out of control as the result of passion. The nerves were the zone Bienville was trying to penetrate in his discourse; the healthy or unhealthy state of the nerves, as well as the anatomic condition of the genital area (morbid, tonic, flaccid, put to use or not, aroused), the determinants. Bienville, a French mechanist about whom surprisingly little is known, ultimately wanted little truck with an underlying mental malady.

Turn the page, so to speak, to more literary annals, and hysteria blends in with other conditions from which its commentators barely differentiate it. Hysteria, hypochondria, melancholy—all are nervous maladies of one grade or another. Sterne's eternally melancholic Tristram may have been, in just this sense, the greatest and most self-reflective male hypochondriac of all the fictional characters of the century. He calls his confessional book "a treatise writ against the spleen," and knows, as his opening paragraph makes plain, that his animal spirits and nervous fibers have been irrevocably mutilated, rendering him a type of male hysteric. This is why he (like so many male patients in the next century) must be "taken out of himself" as it were, through his own hobbies and the hobbyhorses of others. The nervous "tracks" on which "his little gentlemen" traveled during conception have been damaged. But a visit from Tristram to the great "nerve doctors"—the Cheynes, Cullens, and Adairs—would have proved futile: he might as well have sent his manuscript, which is as good a case history of a "male hysteric" as has ever been compiled. Yet Tristram himself might have been shocked to have been tendered this diagnosis. What Sydenham and his medical followers opined about male hysteria and gender at the end of the seventeenth century took decades to filter down to the ordinary person in any sophisticated way. Popular culture was indeed permeated with notions of hysteria, as I have been suggesting throughout this chapter, but Sydenham's views required decades to filter through to other doctors, let alone the lay public. A generation after Laurence Sterne's death in 1768, Edward Jenner, the Gloucestershire doctor and medical researcher into smallpox, was astonished to find himself a member of this filtered class. "In a female," Jenner wrote, "I should call it Hysterical—but in myself I know not what to call it, but by the old sweeping term nervous."[292] The difference was extraordinarily significant for him.

One of hysteria's other paradoxes was that it was alleged both to afflict males and to safeguard them *against* it. This was a curious double take seemingly reserved for hysteria, although traces of the incongruity are also found in the theory of gout and consumption at the time. The dou-

ble bind rendered men safe and vulnerable at the same time. How are
these theoretical "doubles" explained? Under what framing? If run
through the gamut of possibilities, it is seen that gender and patriarchy,
power and marginalization alone can explain the double status of hysteria. The nerves have merely been the convenient pawns of a grander
landlord. For the professional medical world of the eighteenth century
was still preponderantly—as it would be in the nineteenth century and
much of our own—a male-centered universe.[293] William Hogarth's male
doctors, "consulting" as they often do in his prints, could not see to what
degree they were monolithically set against the few females who appeared in them and were an indirect cause of the very hysterical suffering they claimed they sought to relieve. It is hardly surprising then that
the theory of *male* hysteria between Sydenham and the Victorians revealed what it genuinely was by describing its Other, its Counter, its
Double: *female* hysteria.

Hordes of male doctors, exclusively generating medical theory, now—
for the first time—institutionalized female hysteria by claiming that men
could be afflicted by it but in actuality rarely were. Whether in Scotland
or the West Country, in France or Germany, the results of these gender
debates were more or less identical, often derived from one another.[294]
The task then was to demonstrate precisely *why* women were more
prone. But as the uterine debility hypothesis had been overthrown, the
most persuasive mode was to argue from so-called incontrovertible universals: women's innate propensity to nervousness; their domestic situation in a private world conducive to hysterical excess; their insatiable
sexual voracity granted from time immemorial—these as God-given, inevitable, unchangeable conditions. But all the while it was acknowledged
that men were also prone, and proving theoretical consistency by occasionally diagnosing male hysterias and documenting them in the published literature.

Today, we understand the complexity of Enlightenment hysteria only
if we are willing to view its paradoxes, its double binds, within large social and cultural contexts, and only if we are capable of conceding that
medical theory then was consistent and internally logical so long as doctors were not asked to be held accountable for the cultural conditions
in which hysteria flourished. The state of laboratory verifiability and
clinical observation of patients in a condition such as hysteria was still
small compared to other maladies. A hundred years later, in Freud's
Vienna, there would still be debate about the objectivity of the clinician's
gaze. What counted for more than objective gaze in the world of Whytt,
Cullen, and Jenner was a view of "woman" that naturally—almost pre-
ternaturally—seemed to lend itself to the hysteria diagnosis.

XIV

It was not accidental then that treatises on madness began to appear in numbers at the historical moment that resistance set in to the monolithic theories of "the nerve doctors," especially their hysteria diagnosis. This overlap is a complex phenomenon involving theory and practice, as well as social conditions in Western European societies that were becoming more repressive of their poor classes after approximately the mid-eighteenth century. Given the degree to which nerves had earlier been held to account for everything pathological in body and mind—the gamut from affections and passions to the wildest imagination—some doctors began to doubt whether this could be so. I refer, of course, to the well-known treatises by the Batties and Monros, the Perfects and Pargeters in the second half of the eighteenth century, who in varying degrees felt ambivalent about nervous diagnosis in relation to perceived lunacy and derangement; in brief, the company discussed by the late Richard Hunter and Ida Macalpine.[295]

Their collective position permits us to understand how the rival theory of madness developed in relation to the hysteria diagnosis, as well as to comprehend to what degree the hysteria diagnosis had become a barometer of social conditions lorded over by notions of gender—surely a mental zone embracing more than a medical category. The spaces of confinement—madhouses public and private, the clinic, the hospital, prisons of one type or another, attics and closets—are as revealing here as the theory of madness itself. The line between so-called hysterics, female and male, and other types of lunatics was not finely drawn. Incarceration could be ordered for one type as easily as another. There were no specially ordained "hysteria hospitals" (although there were dedicated wards by late century such as the one in Edinburgh). Treatment and therapy for incarcerated hysterics were usually identical to that for other derangements. Furthermore, if the late eighteenth-century madhouse had not yet become the nineteenth-century nervous clinic, there were nevertheless structural similarities in both their methods of diagnosis and applied therapies. But there was one other difference between the diagnoses of madness and hysteria. Unlike the broad base of Enlightenment nervous conditions, madness was not then (in the age of William Battie and A. Monro) a stigma-free organic illness. It was closer to our polluted view of those afflicted with AIDS.[296]

Stigma was nothing new. It had attached to diagnoses of derangement for centuries. What differentiated it now, in the medical realm of the late eighteenth century, was its new gender lines, often drawn with rank and social class as firmly in mind as any gender base. As Baglivi had pronounced at the turn of the century: "Women are more subject than Men to Diseases arising from the Passions of the Mind."[297] He and other physicians continued to stress that madness especially afflicted "poor women." Not so hysteria, a female condition said to afflict as many of the rich as the poor and perhaps more.[298] Nor was madness gendered along the lines it would later be in the nineteenth century, in the decadent world of such subsequent "nerve doctors" as Charcot and Weir Mitchell, nor believed to imitate other diseases (Whytt's "Proteus and the chameleon"). Thus hysteria and madness drifted sharply apart in this dimension: the former deemed by medical professionals to be stigma-free, the latter tarnished by it. But in most other considerations the margins between madness and hysteria were irreparably blurred, and there was as much disagreement as agreement about which of the two diseases was more chronic and lingering. Nor was there much lucidity about, or significant differentiation of, somatic pain in relation to the two conditions. The patients' pain was often thought to be identical in both conditions, affirmed in either state to have been explicitly lodged in an organic site. So in these often contradictory conceptualizations of the late eighteenth century we are actually not far from the radical positivism of late nineteenth-century science and medicine.

One other contrast between lunacy and hysteria cannot be omitted before making the central point about their difference. This is the lunacy that did not announce its pathology through the explicitly acceptable language of organic nervous obstruction but which was said to be something else: *hysteria masquerading as lunacy.* Hysteria could present both ways—this was one of the features of its protean ability to imitate. And it may have been one reason the proprietors of Bedlam could open its doors to the public "to view the lunatics for a penny," without considering that they were inflicting pain upon patients. This "lunacy that was something else" leads us, moreover, to interrogate the rise of madness in the clear light of the hysteria diagnosis. Fortunately, the point is not so simple as a somatic (bodily) versus psychogenic (mental) hysteria.[299]

A broad gaze over the eighteenth century buttressd by a cursory bibliographical column makes the point loud and plain. When Thomas Tryon, the neo-Pythagorean guru of health and diet, commented on lunacy in his 1703 *Discourse of the Causes of Madness,* he was persuaded that madness was still supernaturally induced through possession of devils and spirits, and he harbored no sense of a medicalized, let alone secularized, condition or category. Only one generation later Charles Perry, a licensed physician who traveled widely in the Orient and compiled massive treatises on the Levant, published a treatise *On the Causes and*

Nature of Madness (1723) claiming that lunacy was a mechanical defect in the nervous constitution, a position echoed for years to come in other works of "mechanical medicine," as in Giovanni Battista Morgagni's *Seats and Causes of Diseases* . . . (English version 1769). A few years later Andrew Wilson tried to refine the classification of all these conditions, but shortly thereafter William Rowley, another English physician who specialized in "female diseases," jumbled the categories together again in *A treatise on female, nervous, hysterical, hypochondriacal, bilious, convulsive disease; apoplexy & palsy with thoughts on madness & suicide, etc.*[300] Rowley's classifications were weak, to say the least. Had he been a student at Edinburgh and listened to the lectures of Cullen and the other professors stressing the importance of classification in medicine, he would not have written as he did, but Rowley was a practitioner, not a theorist, and the intricacies of the female constitution and its maladies were beyond him.[301] Not a year went by, it seems, without the appearance of some medical treatise aiming to distinguish among these conditions. Over these decades writing continued about the dangers of religious melancholy leading to madness and hysteria, as in John Langhorne's *Letters on Religious Retirement, Melancholy, and Enthusiasm* (London, 1762) or in the real-life cases of poets such as Christopher Smart, William Cowper, and (some would later say) William Blake.

Wordsworth performed something of a poetic amalgam of these traditions linking religion and hysteria, especially in the strange medical case of Susan Gale, the lonely mother whose intense passion he describes in "The Idiot Boy." Susan's "solitary imagination" lies at the base of her undiagnosed medical condition, just as the medicalized imagination did for so many hysterics examined by Wordsworth's contemporary physicians. Alan Bewell discussed the figure of Susan and "maternal passion" and claimed that the theory of hysteria plays a central role in the poetry of this great Romantic poet. "As a major figure in Wordsworth's mythology of origins," he wrote, "the lonely witch/hysteric provided him with a figural and empirical means for imagining in palpable terms the genesis of language and culture."[302] These are large claims, but substantiated, I think, by the sweeping role the theory of hysteria played in the European Enlightenment.

But why, one asks, was there a need for a madness diagnosis in the first place if hysteria had been so broad and protean a category since the time of Sydenham that it could embrace most "mad" symptoms? This is the question that must be put if we are to make entry to the world of the nineteenth century, the milieu expounded in chapter 3, by Roy Porter. To restate the matter, where did hysteria and its rival, madness, stand in relation to gender and the mind/body dilemma (considered separately and in tandem) if there was need for a new condition called *madness* in the eighteenth century?

There is no simple answer to this all-important question, in itself bound to provoke debate. On one hand, it may be argued that madness was not new in the eighteenth century, and yet even a cursory glance at its discursive representations from 1600 forward shows a sudden outburst of writing in this century. More crucially on the question about gender and the mind/body split, there is no clear-cut division in the late eighteenth century, as I have been stressing, between madness and the hysteria diagnosis. On the other hand—and the adversative is as weighty—the doctors and even their patients clearly have something in mind when they point to the condition of the one or the other. And many readers today will be struck by the fact that Battie's important discussion of madness never refers to hysteria or ever uses the word. No one can read these treatises on madness—by Battie, Monro, and their cohorts—and come away believing one has read a treatise on hysteria. At the same time, and equally paradoxically, the patients' symptoms often presented identically and were described in the same language for both conditions. These are the inconsistencies that must be faced if we are to move into the world of nineteenth-century "nervousness."

When the artist Joseph Farington recorded that his friend, Hone, had "been in a very nervous Hysterical state, the effect of anxiety of mind,"[303] did he mean hysteria or madness? Across the channel, when French physician Pierre Pomme, who interested himself in few diseases more than nervous ones, published his treatise on "Hysterical Affections in Both Sexes,"[304] did he mean hysteria or insanity or both? Pomme's boundaries are not drawn. Likewise for other medical writers of varying ranks and abilities. William Falconer's work on hysteria and madness was geared to strengthen the psychogenic bases of derangement by showing how fierce is "the Influence of the Passions upon Disorders of the Body."[305] So too John Haygarth's treatise *Of the Imagination, as a Cause and as a Cure of Disorders of the Body,* written only a few years later.[306] But at the same time Benjamin Faulkner, who owned and operated a private madhouse in Little Chelsea in London, complained that both hysteria *and* madness had "given birth to endless conjecture and perpetual error."[307] He was doubtless right, and John Haslam, for two decades an official at Bethlehem, who wrote from long experience in the prison-houses of madness, found himself writing treatises on insanity without invoking hysteria.[308] Paradoxically, it is as if the two conditions were identical, yet oceans apart. The lists could be extended many times. Yet the matter is not lists but definition, categories, classification, and—from the patient's point of view—appropriate therapies for each condition. What then was madness if it was taxonomically bred in the heyday of the hysteria diagnosis? From what need was it sprung? And what had the thousand-year-old hysteria ultimately become if it required the birth of a new malady—madness—to assuage its philosophical and practical defects? Foucault provided no answers in his classic works on madness, and the fault may not be his. Or is it that the late eighteenth-century doctors generating this welter of theory really believed they had discovered some intrinsic difference now lost to time? Can the crux be the massive amount—perhaps too massive—of extant evidence? Anyone can study these early treatises on madness—from Battie to Haslam; in France, from Pomme to Pinel—and explicate them page by page. It is more difficult to pronounce authoritatively on the *silences* of these discourses, such as the categorical lacuna discovered when William Battie's paradigmatic *Treatise on Madness* defines madness by refraining from glancing at the concept of hysteria. I am therefore suggesting that we need to study these works, both on hysteria and madness, for their silences as well as their revelations.

In conclusion, there is plenty of evidence to suggest that the Enlightenment nerve doctors conceptualized hysteria as light years away from lunacy, the latter normally conceptualized as a "diseased passion of the mind" often occurring without pathological nervous involvement and without a lingering and chronic madness. Lunacy, madness, insanity: the three are interchangeable terms in their conceptualization—but not so *hysteria*. Here then is the categorical imperative once again.[309] For them, hysteria was not a malingering malefactor, but a curable condition of the body's nervous apparatus thrown into convulsion. Hysteria was thus not essentially the inflammation of the reproductive organs unduly excited, as it would again be in the nineteenth century with its retaliative clitoridectomies and antimasturbation techniques, but the nerves laboring under some extraordinary local distress, lesion, or fever.

Still, approximately by the turn of the nineteenth century hysteria was thought to be the more baffling of the two diseases—hysteria and madness—if also the less chronic condition, and now apparently losing ground to a more treatable "insanity." As Whytt had emphasized in Edinburgh a generation earlier with characteristic humility and wisdom, the body's nervous organization, following the laws of sympathy and sensibility, regulates all mind/body traffic. Even so, Whytt had to claim (following Sydenham who had seen so profoundly into the mysteries of hysteria) that hysteria is entirely *un*predictable whereas insanity was not.[310]

But the discourses on madness, committed as they were to medical materialism, also built mystery into the essence of secularized modern man.[311] Down through the eighteenth century the Enlightenment nerve doctors had constructed their theoretical edifices on the dualistic model they inherited from a post-Cartesian legacy; as well, they wrote in an intellectual milieu desperate to construct an infallible "science of man"— one as predictable for his or her frail states as strong states. Nevertheless, in generating their versions of hysteria, and then later of madness, they carved out space for man's mystery, enigma, anomaly. The endeavor demonstrated a philosophical tolerance that would serve the nineteenth century well. It also helped to legitimate anomalous, irrational, and enigmatic creatures of both genders as the victims of a medical condition still requiring medical research and authentic classification.

By the turn of the nineteenth century the male nerve doctors had palpably defeminized and dehumanized their female lunatics, often recording their case histories as if these mad patients were "unisex": conflating female and male discourse into a new version. Pinel, for all his well-deserved reforms in Paris, was the odd man out. "Ur-Enlightenment" and humanitarian figure that he was, he also displayed the most unusual versions of compassion and sympathy for his patients. But even Pinel could not resolve the definitional disputes on the boundaries of the two conditions, hysteria and madness, nor did he try.[312] In the flow of theory, female lunacy was said to imitate male, a position as old as genesis itself, and just as female voices were recorded in the terms and tropes of the male, no different from the protean imitations hysteria had performed.

As hysteria had *imitated* virtually every other disease, according to Sydenham and Whytt, now, at the end of the eighteenth century, the case histories of women's derangement resembled those of men. It was an odd form of representation, no less baffling than all philosophical mimesis.[313] But women not only lost their sexual identity, they even lost the voice—the expressive voice—presiding over their collective discourse. The reason and control of the "mad doctors" burned feminine unreason out of the medical annals of the late eighteenth century, so much did the doctors fear it. Instead, they replaced it with a logic and language of their own: a male grammar and syntax that prevailed up to the time of Josef Breuer and Freud. Our contemporary American feminists have enlightened us here—as Mary Jacobus and Juliet Mitchell have so convincingly written—when cautioning that "women's writing can never be anything *other than hysterical.*"[314] We can almost reconstruct the position from the social vantage of the last two centuries by gleaning how inevitable it was that women would eventually retrieve the pathetic voices they had lost. No wonder that in our own time hysteria's "his-story" (history) has been transformed into "her-story": the retrieval of a grammar and syntax long suppressed as much as any set of diagnoses and therapies.

To return to the world of Enlightenment hysteria as it approached the turn of the century, not until William Cullen, near century's end, did the womb reappear, and then just momentarily, only to be discredited once again. Cullen's bizarre implication of the womb clung firmly to a somatic etiology, and in this sense it may be said to have had a temporary retarding effect. He not only invoked the hysterical womb but linked it to nervous conditions and the class he called "neuroses," claiming in *First Lines of the Practice of Physic* (1777), as had Sydenham and others before him, that hysteria was the most "protean of all diseases." "The many and various symptoms," he wrote, "which have been supposed to belong to a disease under this appellation, render it extremely difficult to give a general character or definition of it." But Cullen's explanation retains some of the mystery of hysteria in ways that had been lost on his less enlightened colleagues in Edinburgh and elsewhere. He gazed deeply into women; he understood their anatomies as well as *neuroses* (a word he virtually coined and made his own).[315] He somehow gathered that the constant redefinition of hysteria's cause from the Renaissance to his own time was ultimately consistent with the socioeconomic developments he witnessed around him: in rank, class, and economic means. His version of hysteria was as sociological as Sydenham's, and it captured the age-old counterpoint of endorsing and rejecting the womb etiology that had been in vogue from the time of Hippocrates.

Au fond there *is* something unique to women and implicitly powerful, if destructively so, in the idea of the raging womb compared to the much tamer and vaguer notion that women have "inherently weak" nervous systems merely because of inferior "inner spaces."[316] But even at that time, in the 1770s and 1780s, Cullen's strong paradigm about hysteria and neurosis took shape within the contexts of a developing rival theory of madness. Another chapter would be necessary to chart with clarity and precision its overlaps with hysteria. Yet rank and class never lurked very far behind these considerations of the role of gender in hysteria and madness. Now, in a European world that would soon be plunged into the night of chaos and political anarchy, both medicine and culture conspired to rob the middle nouveau riche of its newest and most fashionable garb: nervous affliction. If the poor could be hysterical, as they were in Edinburgh, what was left for the "mad rich in London and Paris"? The pattern appeared to be global and local at once—as paradoxical in this sense as the gender-bound nature of the actual hysteria. Throughout Europe, nerves signified one thing preeminently: rank and class. What differed from place to place, locale to locale, were the forms of social control and patriarchal expression of the nerves. To these disparities, the medicine of the time was almost entirely oblivious and insensitive, and nothing proved it more than the prolific treatises on hysteria and madness. Meanwhile, the doctors churned out their vast collective annals of hysteria diagnoses, one of the largest in the medico-historical literature.

XV

In conclusion, I have been suggesting that the history of hysteria is essentially a social history. Even in the periods privileged here—the Renaissance and the Enlightenment—class structures were clearly falling apart in England by the 1760s (one thinks of the Middlesex riots, which were little more than the mass hysteria of the mob). Under this new class stress, gender and sex were further constrained, and slowly, very gradually, the onset of what would become, when full-grown and full-blown, Victorian prudery set in.[317] But mass hysteria also needs to be considered within its sociopolitical contexts. For example, a case can be made that the onania crusades—the antimasturbation campaigns—of the eighteenth century manifested themselves in social forms that amounted to mass hysteria. The drive to blot out all masturbation as the road to insanity was in part a grass-roots movement; it was also abundantly discussed in the popular writings of Samuel Auguste Tissot, the prolific Swiss doctor who made "anti-masturbation" the centerpiece of his voluminous works, a chapter in social history that has now been retrieved by Roy Porter. The remarkable aspect of this sweeping manifestation of mass hysteria is the degree to which everyone then was persuaded of the evils of masturbation: hardly a voice in the long eighteenth century dared to cry out in favor of masturbation. A phenomenon merely "in the air" of a former culture (the Renaissance or the Enlightenment) may be difficult to retrieve, but it is not so when thousands of words have been expended on it, as was the case regarding onania. Regency and Victorian repression of sexuality, and other nineteenth-century versions on the Continent, are unthinkable without the social upheaval created by the antimasturbation crusades extending over many decades in the eighteenth century. The process created a new bourgeois repression of sexuality in late eighteenth-century England, and property, the law, consumer consumption, and finances all combined to make woman's lot worse than it had been in the Renaissance—not worse in any absolute sense but worse in relation to desire and expectation. But the role of shame and shaming in hysteria must also be considered. Those extraordinary nerve doctors from Willis to Cheyne, Whytt to Cullen, who found a clear organic substrate, safeguarded their patients against the charges that brought shame: the notion that they were poorhouse malingerers who had feigned these symptoms to improve their sad economic condition. By contrast, early eighteenth-century nerve doctors tended to indict cultural volatility as the culprit in hysteria and hypochondriasis. Luminous literati and salon sophisticates were victims of vertiginous life-styles said to enervate the nerves and sap their tonic strength. These nerves had not been originally defective at birth; they became so through high living under the new urban and suburban stress. By the late eighteenth century the poor had filtered up, and now they too were being victimized in this new recension of the disease. The effect of economic shoring, of aping the rich without the resources to do so, clearly had its nervous consequences. Long before Robert Carter wrote about workhouse hysterics from a psychogenic point of view that cast them in a bad light,[318] others in late eighteenth century had developed a similar angle of explanation. In Scotland the hinge was social rank, as the poorer the woman, the more hysterical—and pathetic—her case was adjudged to be.

Ironically, what Cullen and his cohorts saw in Scotland and England, Mesmer did not see in France. Veith credited Mesmer as a hero within the history of hysteria for reasons that misinterpret his works and inflate his hypnotism. She hails Mesmer as of towering importance to the cracking of the hysteria code, on the grounds that his demonstration of the capacity of hypnosis to control the body through tapping unconscious mental networks ultimately bore fruit in psychogenic theories of Charcot's France and Freud's Vienna.[319]

Yet Mesmer never contended that the origins of his patient's hysterias were psychological, nor did he tout his own capacity to work cures through mental suggestion. He is not the harbinger of an internal millennium of the psyche, but of a poised nervous system vulnerable at every turn. *Pace* Veith, but this is as flawed an interpretation of Mesmer as is the notion that his contemporary, Emanuel Swedenborg, the ardent post-Newtonian mystic, was more mystic than scientist, which no reading of his works can substantiate. Mesmer was as staunch in his Newtonianism as the British iatromechanists, forever maintaining that animal magnetism was a physically grounded, etherial fluid coursing through the cosmos, possessed of the capacity, when properly funneled through the afflicted, to relieve illness-causing obstructions.[320]

When Louis XVI's investigating commission denied the reality of such a material substance, concluding that Mesmer actually performed his cures by the use of raw "imagination," such undercutting of his claims to a material substratum punctured his credentials and ruined his aspirations. Hysteria in the French Revolution is, of course, an immensely difficult subject because it blends so cunningly into other radically misogynistic behaviors, including the cataloging of egregious acts committed by women from the beginning of French history. It may be that such extreme antifeminism was itself a display of the mass hysteria on which I have commented at different points in this chapter, and that as the 1790s evolved, retrogression rather than progress occurred in this patriarchal society.[321]

Even so, the long-term student of hysteria before, and beyond, Freud wants, of course, to compare this Mesmerian agenda with Freud's. A century later, it was the failure of hypnotism that initiated Freud's passage from an organic to a psychogenic etiology of hysteria. But there is no evidence that Mesmer, any more than Swedenborg, regarded his theories of nervous disorders and their therapies as grounded in anything other than Newtonian matter theory. So too the notorious Marquis de Sade, although under rather different ideological conditions and in different genres. The Sade whose women are told by their hedonistic instructors that "they are their anatomy"; the Sade whose first principle and holy gospel is not a latter-day Cartesian mind/body relation but a physics of pleasure and pain;[322] this Sade also possesses a notion of hysteria that is much more organic than psychogenic.

The powerful idiom of the nerves receded very slowly in the nineteenth century, as did the organic basis of disease. This is one reason that, in England, Regency and even Victorian treatises on hysteria often resemble, or seem to be variations on the theme of, Enlightenment hysteria: an old malady with a familiar ring. The nineteenth-century neurasthenic patient—as Roy Porter and Elaine Showalter demonstrate in chapters 3 and 4—remains forever on the verge of nervous collapse, weakened by nervous debility, with atonic nerves, spirits, and fibers that require strengthening above all. Restore the eighteenth-century capitalizations and syntax, and one has not moved very far from the world of Mandeville and Monro, Cheyne and Cullen, Willis and Whytt. This will not change until the psychogenic theory and etiology of hysteria overtake the organic in the late nineteenth century. And even then, the riddle of "the elusive disease" will continue to be, as it has been in our century, hysteria's inescapable organic resonances.

It is not my place in this chapter to poach in the groves of Charcot. But viewing Charcot in reverse anachronism—for example, from the perspectives of Sydenham and Mesmer—helps to expound what will be at high stake in the world of hysteria anatomized by Roy Porter and Elaine Showalter. Like Sydenham and Mesmer—even Swedenborg and Blake, to select more extreme examples—Charcot has been more misunderstood than understood in relation to hysteria. A spiritual brother of Sydenham, Charcot wanted hysteria to be the most *universal* of all diseases—but with this difference. Sydenham had *observed* it to be the most universal and protean, independent of his own ideological gain, but he had not wished it so; Charcot willed it because it legitimated his own scientificity, and no sense is made of his theory of hysteria without viewing it within the visual perspectives of the age and the broad contexts of his own life, as his biographers and best students have now shown.[323]

The leap between Sydenham and Charcot is also maximal in other ways. The positivists among Charcot's circle rejected the old Aristotelian view of pain as an emotion. Current medical knowledge, since the late eighteenth century, had identified pain with organic lesions in, and constrictions of, the nervous system. Women who complained of chronic pain that could not be located in the nervous system ran the risk of finding themselves classified as hypochondriacs suffering from imaginary illnesses. What had presented itself to the Greeks as a fiery animal, an overheated, labile, voracious, and raging uterus, was now, in Charcot's world, diagnosed as a sexually diseased and morally debauched female imagination. The progress of the hysteria diagnosis from 1750 to 1850 had now been completed, and novelist Samuel Richardson's lighthearted precept about "every woman being a rake at heart"—put forward by Mrs. Sinclair's female debauches in *Clarissa Harlowe*—had come round full circle in Charcot: from the Greeks to the Victorians. Woman's generative organs had given her this capability, in the ancient world as well as the Victorian. Nowhere would this diseased female imagination—perceived to be cunning and artful as well as deceitful— present itself more grotesquely than in the hysterical females seen by Briquet, photographed by Charcot, and fictively imagined by novelists such as Dickens in *Little Dorrit* in the figure of Flora, the diminutive child-wife forever in a hysterical swoon.[324]

Perhaps this is why—but in part only—the early nineteenth-century novel is so heavily permeated with tyrannical husbands and child-wives on the verge of madness, only to be locked up in dingy attics by their husbands where they hallucinate, like Charlotte Perkins Gilman, imprisoned by her doctors and her yellow wallpaper. All point to a conception of hysteria whose most revelatory dimensions remain its basis in gender and social class power and control.

The complex story of the medical, scientific, ideological, political, and patriarchal way the nineteenth century crafted *hysteria before Freud* as an exclusive province of upper-class male physicians remains to be told.

NOTES

1. This raises the philosophical question about medical categories as distinct from others; some discussion of the subject is found in Lester King, *The Philosophy of Medicine: The Early Eighteenth Century* (Cambridge, Mass.: Harvard University Press, 1978), 49–50, in the context of Greek philosophy and medicine. Throughout this chapter the question of medical categories never lies far from my imagination. What can a "medical malady" or "medical condition" be if it can embrace almost every type of symptom?

2. This fact should not cause students such as those of us who contribute to this book to become positivists and think we can know *everything* about hysteria as a philosophical, medical, and representational category; for hysteria and representation see below in this section and in section XIV; for the dangers of such belief see Edward Davenport, "The Devils of Positivism," in *Literature and Science: Theory and Practice,* ed. Stuart Peterfreund (Boston: Northeastern University Press, 1990), 17–31. The "is" and "as is" of hysteria is a double-headed hydra.

3. The generalization must be qualified: For the intimate connection between hysteria and psychoanalysis, pre- and post-Lacanian, see Alan Krohn, "Hysteria: The Elusive Neurosis," in *Psychological Issues* (New York: International Universities Press, 1978); Monique David-Ménard, *Hysteria from Freud to Lacan: Body and Language in Psychoanalysis* (Ithaca, N.Y.: Cornell University Press, 1989); and the important bibliographical detective work of Mark Micale, "On the 'Disappearance' of Hysteria: A Study in the Clinical Deconstruction of a Diagnosis," unpublished paper delivered to the Institute of Neurology, Queen Square, London (1988), and "Hysteria and Its Historiography: A Review of Past and Present Writings," *History of Science* 27 (1989): 223–260, 317–351.

4. Discussions of the strange *disappearance* of hysteria include: Mark Micale's works (n. 3); Krohn, "Hysteria"; and, from a literary point of view, the fiction of Marguerite Duras (see sections II and III). For conversion syndrome, see M. I. Weintraub, *Hysterical Conversion Reactions: A Clinical Guide to Diagnosis and Treatment* (Lancaster: MTP Press, 1983); David-Ménard, *Hysteria from Freud to Lacan.*

5. Female sexuality is not, of course, synonymous with feminism or any other political women's movement; what I designate by the threat of female sexuality in history is eloquently discussed in Caroline Bynum, ed., *Gender and Religion: On the Complexity of Symbols* (Boston: Beacon Press, 1986); Elaine Showalter, *The Female Malady: Women, Madness and English Culture, 1830–1980* (London: Virago, 1987); Susan Rubin Suleiman, ed., *The Female Body in Western Culture: Contemporary Perspectives* (Cambridge, Mass.: Harvard University Press, 1985).

6. Such vigilance paid to the linguistic aspects of scientific and medical discourse has been at the top of my own agenda for two decades; see G. S. Rousseau, *Enlightenment Borders: Scientific—Medical: Pre- and Postmodern Discourses* (Manchester: Manchester University Press, 1991). I use the term "emplot" (i.e., emplotted, emplotment, emplotments) to denote the way cultural practices and material conditions are encoded in a discourse, and throughout this chapter I particularly want to understand how various medical theories of hysteria assume a particular vision of culture and then emplot that vision into a text. Questions of further representation, genre, and rhetoric are another matter.

7. For the claim and its limits, see G. S. Rousseau, "Medicine and the Muses: An Approach to Literature and Medicine," in *Medicine and Literature,* ed. Marie Roberts and Roy Porter (London: Routledge, 1993), 23–57. For numbness and headache among hysterical types, see Oliver Sacks, *Migraine: The Evolution of a Common Disorder* (Berkeley, Los Angeles, London: University of California Press, 1985), 196–207. See also section IX for Willis's model of hysteria in relation to migraine.

8. See sections III and IX for detailed discussion of Sydenham's theories and therapies.

9. See Krohn, "Hysteria," 343.

10. Even the most theoretical and philosophically advanced of medical theorists has avoided this matter of category, and Micale's various bibliographical studies (n. 3) do not address the issue.

11. I take this to be a main point of David Morris's chapter on hysteria in his fine study of *The Languages of Pain* (Berkeley, Los Angeles, Oxford: University of California Press, 1992).

12. William Shakespeare, *Hamlet, The Riverside Shakespeare,* ed. G. B. Evans (Boston: Houghton Mifflin Co., 1974), I.ii. 82. The standard work is by R. Klibansky et al., *Saturn and Melancholy* (London: Nelson, 1964). For the relation of eros and ecstasy see Arthur Evans, *The God of Ecstasy* (New York: St. Martin's Press, 1988), and M. Screech, *Ecstasy and the Praise of Folly* (London: Duckworth, 1980). For Lacan biographically and in relation to hysteria, see: Stuart Schneiderman, *Jacques Lacan: The Death of an Intellectual Hero* (Cambridge, Mass.: Harvard University Press, 1983); Elizabeth Roudinesco, *Jacques Lacan and Co.: A History of Psychoanalysis in France* (New York: Alfred A. Knopf, 1987); Catherine Clement, *The Life and Legend of Jacques Lacan,* trans. Arthur Goldhammer (New York: Columbia University Press, 1983).

13. This remains one of the main points, collectively speaking, of the ten authors writing in G. S. Rousseau, ed., *The Languages of Psyche: Mind and Body in*

Enlightenment Thought (Berkeley, Los Angeles, Oxford: University of California Press, 1990).

14. See Julia Kristeva, *Desire in Language: A Semiotic Approach to Literature and Art* (New York: Columbia University Press, 1980), and idem, *Black Sun: Depression and Melancholia* (New York: Columbia University Press, 1989). The trope of hysteria and melancholy is pervasive in her writing, as her best commentators have recognized: see, for example, J. Fletcher and A. Benjamin, eds., *Abjection, Melancholia and Love: The Work of Julia Kristeva* (London: Routledge, 1989).

15. Michel Foucault, *The History of Sexuality, Vol. 1, An Introduction* (London: Penguin, 1978), 104.

16. "Numbing" was not a term commonly used in any language in the period preeminently discussed in this chapter, although for a contemporary use in a medical context see M. Liger, M.D., "A Treatise on the Gout: From the French of M. Charles Luis Liger," *Critical Review* (April 1760): 283–288. Nevertheless, I continue to invoke it fully aware of its somewhat anachronistic usage and based on its common appearance in twentieth-century parlance and printed writing, especially in the works of such "nervous writers" as Virginia Woolf, Simon de Beauvoir, Marguerite Duras, and Samuel Beckett. In English, the word had acquired several usages by 1800, especially in physiological and medical contexts, but was not regularly used in the vocabulary of the nerves. For the standard definitions in English ca. 1750, see Samuel Johnson, *A Dictionary of the English Language*, 2 vols. (London, 1755).

17. The extended quarrel of the ancients and moderns, which is seminal for any understanding of the period covered by this chapter, taught its contestants as much, and we do well to learn from the intellectual ravages of three centuries; see R. F. Jones, *Ancients and Moderns* (St. Louis: Washington University Press, 1936), and Joseph Levine, *Humanism and History: Origins of Modern English Historiography* (Ithaca, N.Y.: Cornell University Press, 1987).

18. See George Lincoln Burr, "The Literature of Witchcraft," *Papers of the American Historical Association* 4 (1890): 37–66; Henry Charles Lea, "Materials toward a History of Witchcraft" (Philadelphia, 1939; reprint, New York and London: T. Yoseloff, 1957); Russell Hope Robbins, *The Encyclopedia of Witchcraft and Demonology* (New York: Crown, 1959); and the several books by William Monter, the acknowledged expert on European witchcraft.

19. The literature is reviewed in J. Dall'Ava Santucci, *Des sorcières aux mandarines: Histoire des femmes médecins* (Paris: Calmann-Levy, 1989).

20. It is found in and has its own curious provenance, having been quoted by many writers in the last century, and by some who figure in this chapter, having often been cited by Marguerite Duras and, most recently, by David Morris; see Marguerite Duras, *Writing on the Body* (Urbana and Chicago: University of Illinois Press, 1987), and David Morris, *The Culture of Pain* (Berkeley, Los Angeles, Oxford: University of California Press, 1991), chap. 5. Curiously, Monter does not discuss the account in his many books on witchcraft.

21. Jules Michelet, *Satanism and Witchcraft: A Study in Medieval Superstition* (New York: Citadel Press, 1939), 23, 39, 41, 79, 327–329.

22. See Kristeva, *Desire in Language*, and David-Ménard, *Hysteria from Freud to Lacan*, who extends Kristeva's *jouissance* to the whole field of knowledge but without relating it to hysteria in the way I attempt here.

23. T. F. Graham, *Medieval Minds: Mental Health in the Middle Ages* (London: Allen & Unwin, 1967); T. K. Oesterreich, *Possession: Demoniacal and Other* (New York: Richard R. Smith, 1930); Robbins, *The Encyclopedia of Witchcraft and Demonology*; John Demos, *Entertaining Satan: Witchcraft and the Culture of Early New England* (New York: Oxford University Press, 1982).

24. For mass hysteria see Bryan Wilson, *Magic and the Millennium: A Sociological Study of Religious Movements of Protest among Tribal and Third-World Peoples* (London: Heinemann, 1973); Michael J. Colligan et al., eds., *Mass Psychogenic Illness: A Social Psychological Analysis* (Hillsdale, N.J.: L. Erlbaum Assoc., 1982). As late as 1989, several hundred musical performers became violently ill in the Santa Monica Civic Auditorium in California. A team of UCLA psychiatrists investigated the case and published their findings in the *American Journal of Psychiatry*, reporting that this was a classic case of "group psychogenic illness." See J. Scott, "1989 Santa Monica Illness That Struck 247 called Mass Hysteria," *Los Angeles Times*, September 4, 1991 (B1, 3). The Los Angeles riots of April 1992, may in time receive a similar diagnosis.

25. An early work making this point is Albertus Krantz's *De passionibus mulierum* (1544); see also Kate Campbell Hurd-Mead, *A History of Women in Medicine, from the Earliest Times to the Beginning of the Nineteenth Century* (Haddam, Conn.: Haddam Press, 1938); Michael MacDonald, "Women and Madness in Tudor and Stuart England," *Social Research* 53, no. 2 (1986): 261–281; Caroline Walker Bynum, *Holy Feast and Holy Fast: The Religious Significance of Food to Medieval Women* (Berkeley, Los Angeles, London: University of California Press, 1987); Alexander Walker, *Woman Physiologically Considered, as to Mind, Morals, Marriage, Matrimonial Slavery, Infidelity and Divorce* (Hartford, Conn., 1851); D. P. Walker, *Spiritual and Demonic Magic from Ficino to Campanella* (London: Warburg Institute, 1958); idem, *Unclean Spirits: Possession and Exorcism in France and England in the Late Sixteenth and Early Seventeenth Centuries* (London: Scholar Press, 1981); Keith Thomas, *Religion and the Decline of Magic* (Harmondsworth, Middlesex: Penguin, 1973); Brian Easlea, *Witch Hunting, Magic and the New Philosophy* (Brighton, Sussex: Harvester, 1980), esp. chap. 4.

26. For further evidence see Graham, *Medieval Minds*; B. L. Gordon, *Medieval and Renaissance Medicine* (London: Peter Owen, 1959); Richard Neugebauer, "Treatment of the Mentally Ill in Medieval and Early Modern England: A Reappraisal," *Journal of the History of the Behavioral Sciences* 14 (1978): 158–169; Beryl Rowland, *Medieval Woman's Guide to Health* (Kent, Ohio: Kent State University Press, 1981); Mary Frances Wack, *Lovesickness in the Middle Ages: The Viaticum and Its Commentaries* (Philadelphia: University of Pennsylvania Press, 1990), the most useful of these works for hysteria, especially for her commentary on Bona Fortuna's fourteenth-century *Treatise on the Viaticum*; see Wack, *Lovesickness in the Middle Ages*, 131, 174–179, 290–291.

27. Wack, *Lovesickness in the Middle Ages*, 175. The classic work is, of course,

Jacques Ferrand's 1623 *Treatise on Lovesickness*, ed. Donald A. Beecher and Massimo Ciavolella (Syracuse, N.Y.: Syracuse University Press, 1989).

28. Examples are found in S. Anglo, *The Damned Art: Essays in the Literature of Witchcraft* (London: Routledge & Kegan Paul, 1985). Comparison of these images with modern ones of the hypnotic prove useful; see Leon Chertok and Isabelle Stengers, *Le coeur et la raison: L'hypnose en question de Lavoisier a Lacan* (Paris: Editions Payot, 1989).

29. Oesterreich's *Possession: Demoniacal and Other* is still useful, but also see A. Rodewyk, *Die dämonische Besessenheit in der Sicht des Rituale Romanum* (Aschaffenburg: Paul Pattloch Verlag, 1963).

30. See these works by Marguerite Duras: *The Lover* (New York: Grove Press, 1976); *The Malady of Death* (New York: Grove Press, 1986); and *Writing on the Body*.

31. This example assumes upper-class hysterics; hysteria in relation to poverty and poor nerves is discussed in sections IX and XIV.

32. The point has been eloquently made by Morris in *The Languages of Pain*, chap. 5. The locales also provide surfeits of pleasure; this point about pleasure must be stressed.

33. Easlea, *Witch Hunting*, esp. chap. 4; Demos, *Entertaining Satan*.

34. P. Janet, *L'état mental des hystériques*, 2d ed. (Paris: F. Alcan, 1911), 708.

35. See Alice Jardine, *Gynesis: Configurations of Woman and Modernity* (Ithaca, N.Y.: Cornell University Press, 1985); R. Satow, "Where Has All the Hysteria Gone?" *Psychoanalytic Review* 66 (1979–80): 463–477; Patricia Fedikew, "Marguerite Duras: Feminine Field of Hysteria," *Enclitic* 6 (1982): 78–86. This form of analysis has been developed with regard to Kristeva and Lacan in David-Ménard, *Hysteria from Freud to Lacan*, and in William Holsz, *Sexual Subversions* (London: Allen & Unwin, 1989).

36. Such numbness, however, does not figure into recent medical analyses: see Gilbert H. Glaser, "Epilepsy, Hysteria and 'Possession,'" *Journal of Nervous and Mental Disease* 166, no. 4 (1978): 268–274; S. B. Guze, "The Diagnosis of Hysteria: What Are We Trying to Do?" *American Journal of Psychiatry* 124 (1967): 491–498. For comparison between the nineteenth century and earlier periods and the broad cultural factors involved, see J. Goldstein, "The Hysteria Diagnosis and the Politics of Anticlericalism in Late Nineteenth Century France," *Journal of Modern History* 54 (1982): 209–239, and idem, *Console and Classify: The French Psychiatric Profession in the Nineteenth Century* (Cambridge: Cambridge University Press, 1991).

37. See William B. Ober, "Margery Kempe: Hysteria and Mysticism Reconciled," in *Bottoms Up! A Pathologist's Essays on Medicine and the Humanities* (Carbondale, Ill.: Southern Illinois University Press, 1987), 203–220; C. M. Bache, "A Reappraisal of Teresa of Avila's Supposed Hysteria," *Journal of Religion and Health* 24 (1985): 300–315.

38. Not surprisingly, there is no male equivalent containing an ideology even remotely similar to the one found in the feminist agenda. What indeed *do* contemporary feminists say about *male* hysteria? For a start, see Micale above.

39. For the philosophical problem of representation, at least since the advent

of the Cartesian revolution in thought, see Dalia Judovitz, *Subjectivity and Representation in Descartes: The Origins of Modernity*, Cambridge Studies in French, ed. Malcolm Bowie (Cambridge: Cambridge University Press, 1988); and, for more recent times, James L. Larson, *Reason and Experience: The Representation of Natural Order in the World of Carl von Linné* (Berkeley, Los Angeles, London: University of California Press, 1971), and Richard Rorty, *Contingency, Irony, and Solidarity* (Cambridge: Cambridge University Press, 1989); idem, *Philosophy and the Mirror of Nature* (Princeton, N.J.: Princeton University Press, 1980).

40. Sources for Sydenham are provided in n. 41 and in Sections V–VII.

41. For Sydenham, see especially Kenneth Dewhurst, *Dr. Thomas Sydenham (1624–1689): His Life and Original Writings* (Berkeley and Los Angeles: University of California Press, 1966). Lady Mary Wortley Montagu, the brilliant aristocrat, world traveler, and friend of poet Alexander Pope, was deeply impressed by Sydenham's ability to describe the real condition of hysteria: "I have seen so much of hysterical complaints, tho' Heaven be praised I never felt them, I know it is an obstinate and very uneasy distemper, tho' never fatal unless when Quacks undertake to cure it. I have even observed that those who are troubled with it commonly live to old age. Lady Stair is one instance; I remember her screaming and crying when Miss Primrose, my selfe, and other girls were dancing 2 rooms distant. Lady Fanny has but a slight touch of this distemper: read Dr. Sydenham; you will find the analyse of that and many other diseases, with a candor I never found in any other author. I confess I never had faith in any other physician, living or dead. Mr. Locke places him in the same rank with Sir Isaac Newton, and the Italians call him the English Hippocrates. I own I am charmed with his taking off the reproach which you men so saucily throw on our sex, as if we alone were subject to vapours. He clearly proves that your wise honourable spleen is the same disorder and arises from the same cause; but you vile usurpers do not only engross learning, power, and authority to yourselves, but will be our superiors even in constitution of mind, and fancy you are incapable of the woman's weakness of fear and tenderness" (*The Complete Letters of Lady Mary Wortley Montagu*, ed. Robert Halsband [Oxford: Clarendon Press, 1965], 3:171). Dr. Thomas Trotter, the influential early nineteenth-century English physician, thought that Sydenham and Cheyne had been the two *most influential physicians* of the last hundred years barring none; see Ida Macalpine and Richard Hunter, *George III and the Mad Business* (New York: Pantheon Books, 1969), 290.

42. For the word "nervous" set into its cultural context and a history of this development, see G. S. Rousseau, "The Language of the Nerves: A Chapter in Social and Linguistic History," in *Language, Self, and Society: A Social History of Language*, 2d ed., ed. Peter Burke and Roy Porter (Oxford: Polity Press, 1991), 213–275.

43. Good surveys of this science and Sydenham's role in it are found in Michael Hunter, *Science and Society in Restoration England* (New York and Cambridge: Cambridge University Press, 1981); idem, *The Royal Society and Its Fellows, 1660–1700: The Morphology of an Early Scientific Institution* (Chalfont St. Giles, Bucks: British Society for the History of Science, 1982).

44. Sydenham's notion of imitation (*imitatio*) was the traditional Aristotelian

one described in the *Poetics*; for textual examples see Thomas Sydenham, "Processes Integri: Chap. 1: On the Affection Called Hysteria in Women; and Hypochondriasis in Men," in *The Works of Thomas Sydenham, M.D.*, trans. R. G. Latham, 2 vols. (London: Sydenham Society, 1848–1850), 1: 281–286, and idem, *The Whole Works of That Excellent Practical Physician* (London, 1705).

45. A synchronic view of hysteria evaluates all its theories at once by comparative and dialectical means; a diachronic view allows them to evolve chronologically, decade by decade. The difficulty with the latter is that narrators generating the diachronic story pretend in one decade (e.g., the 1730s) that they do not know its influence on the next (e.g., the 1740s), which they of course do, and this entails a myth about diachronic method they themselves never believe. The linguistic theorists of the period covered in this chapter were often searching for synchronic structures in the development of languages.

46. See sections IX and XIV.

47. Ibid. See n. 174 below.

48. The hysteria of Duras's women continues to be narrated by others as well. For example, in Jim Harrison's 1990 short story "The Woman Lit by Fireflies," the protagonist suffers from the same agonies; see *The New Yorker*, July 23, 1990, pp. 26–55.

49. This point remains the thrust of Krohn's work in "Hysteria" (n. 3), in which the author lays equal emphasis on psychosomatic medicine and psychoanalysis. For the psychosomatic connection in the English Enlightenment, see John Midriff's marvelously satirical and humorous *Observations on the Spleen and Vapours: Containing Remarkable Cases of Persons of both Sexes, and all Ranks, from the aspiring Directors to the Humble Bubbler, who have been miserably afflicted with these Melancholy Disorders since the Fall of the South-sea, and other publick Stocks; with the proper Method for their Recovery, according to the new and uncommon Circumstances of each Case* (London, 1720), and W. F. Brown, "Descartes, Dualism and Psychosomatic Medicine," in *The Anatomy of Madness*, ed. W. F. Bynum, Roy Porter, and Michael Shepherd (London: Tavistock Publications, 1985), 2: 40–62.

50. For the background see A. E. Taylor, *A Commentary on Plato's Timaeus* (Oxford: Clarendon Press, 1928), 638–640; G. E. R. Lloyd, *Science, Folklore, and Ideology* (Cambridge: Cambridge University Press, 1983).

51. Plato's view, as I have suggested, was that of the womb as living animal; see D. F. Krell, "Female Parts in *Timaeus*," *Arion* 2 (1975): 400–421. For phallocratic discourse and the role of women, see Eva C. Keuls, *The Reign of the Phallus: Sexual Politics in Ancient Greece* (New York: Harper & Row, 1985). For the Renaissance modification of this view, see Krant, *De passionibus mulierum* (1544); Edward Shorter, *A History of Women's Bodies* (Harmondsworth: Penguin, 1983); idem, *Women in the Middle Ages and the Renaissance: Literary and Historical Perspective* (Syracuse: Syracuse University Press, 1986); Mary Beth Rose, *Women in the Middle Ages and the Renaissance: Literary and Historical Perspective* (Syracuse: Syracuse University Press, 1986); I. MacLean, *The Renaissance Notion of Woman* (Cambridge: Cambridge University Press, 1980); Joan Kelly-Gadol, "Did Women Have a Renaissance?" in *Becoming Visible: Women in European History,* ed. Renate Bridenthal and Claudia Koonz (Boston: Houghton Mifflin Co., 1967).

52. Nowhere is this better seen than in the historiography of hysteria provided by Micale in his various works; see n. 3.

53. See especially the contemporary testimonies in J. De Valmont, *Dissertation sur les Maléfices et les Sorciers selon les principes de la théologie et de la physique, où l'on examine en particulier l'état de la fille de Tourcoing* (Tourcoing, 1752); A. Galopin, *Les hystériques des couvents, des églises, des temples, des théâtres, des synagogues, et de l'amour* (Paris, 1886); Klibansky et al., *Saturn and Melancholy* (n. 12); Catherine-Laurence Maire, *Les convulsionnaires de Saint-Médard: Miracles, convulsions et prophéties Paris au XVIIIe siècle*, Collection Archives (Paris: Gallimard Julliard, 1985).

54. Krohn, "Hysteria," all the more evident because hysteria is so "real" and afflicts patients suffering "real" symptoms.

55. Looking ahead, this will be one of Sydenham's main points about hysteria in relation to all other medical conditions, despite the neglect of it by medical historians; see, for example, Dewhurst, *Dr. Thomas Sydenham*; Jeffrey M. N. Boss, "The Seventeenth-Century Transformation of the Hysteric Affection, and Sydenham's Baconian Medicine," *Psychological Medicine* 9 (1979): 221–234.

56. Reflection through power and marginalization had been one of Foucault's main points about hysteria in *Madness and Civilization: A History of Insanity in the Age of Reason* (New York: Pantheon Books, 1965); see also David Armstrong, *Political Anatomy of the Body* (Cambridge: Cambridge University Press, 1983).

57. For these debates see the valuable work of Ian Hacking, Nancy Cartwright, Mary Hesse (her late works; she experienced a conversion from her earlier more internalist position), Larry Laudan, Ernan McMullin, Arthur Fine, and Ronald Giere.

58. Valuable information is found in Colligan, *Mass Psychogenic Illness* (n. 24), and Wilson, *Magic and the Millennium*.

59. As emphasized by Krell, "Female Parts in *Timaeus*"; see also Shorter, *History of Women's Bodies*.

60. Ibid.

61. See the discussion of Shakespeare and Rabelais in section VI.

62. Elaine Pagels, *Adam, Eve and the Serpent* (New York: Vintage Books, 1989); MacLean, *Renaissance Notion of Woman*; Carroll Camden, *The Elizabethan Woman* (New York: Elsevier Press, 1952).

63. For the psychophysiological implications of this turning point as they affect hysteria, see Richard B. Carter, *Descartes' Medical Philosophy: The Organic Solution to the Mind-Body Problem* (Baltimore: Johns Hopkins University Press, 1983); Brown, "Descartes, Dualism and Psychosomatic Medicine."

64. For Sydenham's relation to Cartesianism see Dewhurst, *Dr. Thomas Sydenham*.

65. As he traveled through the Levant in the 1590s, William Richard searched for Oriental equivalents; see his *History of Turkey* (London, 1603).

66. See Susan Sontag, *Illness as Metaphor* (New York: Random House, 1979). The defect for gout will soon be remedied in a book in preparation by G. S.

Rousseau and Roy Porter, *Gout: The Patrician Malady* (Princeton, N.J.: Princeton University Press, 1994).

67. A point discussed by Henry Siegerist, *Civilization and Disease* (Ithaca, N.Y.: Cornell University Press, 1944); Frederick F. Cartwright, *Disease and History* (London: Hart-Davis, 1972); Leon Edel, "Disease and the Novel," *TLS*, 30 May 1986: 591.

68. Susan Sontag, *AIDS and Its Metaphors* (New York: Farrar, Straus and Giroux, 1989).

69. Juliet Mitchell, *Woman: The Longest Revolution* (London, 1984), 288–290.

70. For some of the socioeconomic causes see Dall'Ava Santucci, *Des sorcieres aux mandarines*; Bridget Hill, *Women and Work in Eighteenth-Century England* (New York: Oxford University Press); Rita Goldberg, *Sex and Enlightenment: Women in Richardson and Diderot* (Cambridge: Cambridge University Press, 1984).

71. Rose, *Women in the Middle Ages and the Renaissance*; Pagels, *Adam, Eve and the Serpent*; less astute is Camden, *Elizabethan Woman*.

72. Not even the tradition of the "good surgeon" in the Renaissance and Enlightenment changes this situation; in this sense Jonathan Swift's Lemuel Gulliver, the "good surgeon" of Swift's exotic travels, comes at the end of a tradition rather than the beginning of a new one.

73. See n. 34 for Janet.

74. See Stephen Wilson, *Saints and Their Cults* (Cambridge: Cambridge University Press, 1989); H. R. Lemay, "Human Sexuality in Twelfth- through Fifteenth-Century Scientific Writings," in *Sexual Practices and the Medieval Church*, ed. Vern Bullough and James Brundage (Buffalo: Prometheus Books, 1982), 187–205. Here philology is also instructive: the word "hysteria" did not enter Anglo-Saxon, Middle English, or the Romance languages until the sixteenth century, but "melancholia" (as black bile) was already being used by the medical doctors in the thirteenth, often as a synonym of *"chlorosis."* The appearance of *"furor uterinus"* begins in the thirteenth century, but "nymphomania" (the word) had not yet been invented; its first use, as a condition, is found as late as 1775 in M. D. T. Bienville, *Nymphomania; or A Dissertation concerning the Furor Uterinus* (London, 1775); see G. S. Rousseau, "The Invention of Nymphomania," in *Perilous Enlightenment* (Manchester: Manchester University Press, 1991), 44–64. No work brings these traditions—verbal and visual, philological and scientific—so well together as Klibansky et al., *Saturn and Melancholy*.

75. A brief account is found in Wack, *Lovesickness in the Middle Ages* (n. 26). The classic source for melancholy as *both* male and female remains Robert Burton's *Anatomy of Melancholy* (1621). See also T. S. Soufas, *Melancholy and the Secular Mind in Spanish Golden Age Literature* (Columbia: University of Missouri Press, 1990), who considers melancholy the key to the transition between medieval and Renaissance mentalities but who is rather silent on its genderization in the Renaissance. In *Melancholy and Society* (Cambridge: Harvard University Press, 1992), Wolf Lepenies expands on the intersection of melancholy and secularism in its utopian and political dimensions.

76. Soufas, *Melancholy and the Secular Mind*, 131.

77. Ibid.

78. It is surely anachronistic to imagine that the objection was then made, or could have been made, among the midwives and their patients in the name of lesbianism: that was never a concern; if there was concern, it was on grounds that the midwives (the *obstetrices*) as well as patients were becoming sexually aroused and carnally sacrificed; see B. Ehrenreich, *Witches, Midwives, and Nurses* (Old Westbury, N.Y.: Feminist Press, 1973); Jacques Gelis, *La sage-femme ou le médecin: Une nouvelle conception de la vie* (Paris: Fayard, 1988).

79. For the early genderization and pathologization of the soul see Joseph Schumacher, *Die seelischen Volkskrankheiten im deutschen Mittelalter* (Berlin: Neue Deutsche Forschungen, 1937); R. B. Onians, *The Origins of European Thought about the Body, the Mind, the Soul, the World, Time, and Fate* (Cambridge: Cambridge University Press, 1951); and an early work, Johann Ambrosius Hillig, *Anatomie der Seelen* (Leipzig, 1737). For hysteria and possession, see Oesterreich, *Possession: Demoniacal and Other*; Glaser, "Epilepsy, Hysteria and 'Possession'" (n. 36); and a modern philosophical approach, J. D. Bernal, *The World, the Flesh and the Devil: An Inquiry into the Future of the Three Enemies of the Rational Soul* (London: Cape, 1970). The milieu of these early hysterics was a culture of ecstasy marked by a gap between first- and third-person discourse. The first-person narratives (confessions of hysterics) were almost never written; they include the diaries of mad women and other convulsionaries, neither of whom had any public authority.

80. Ferrand's *Treatise of Lovesickness* has been astutely discussed by Foucault and now magnificently edited (n. 27); for Platterus (Platter) and his works as they relate to the traditions of hysteria see Stanley W. Jackson, *Melancholia and Depression* (New Haven, Conn.: Yale University Press, 1987), and Platterus, *Beloved Son: The Journal of Felix Platter, a Medical Student in Montpellier in the Sixteenth Century* (London: Frederick Muller, 1961). Ferrand makes the important observation that males, whom he viewed generically as *homo publicus,* suffered many *other* disappointments than love, but that even among amorous males there is no greater loss or cause for unhappiness and despair.

81. Ideas adumbrated by the influential Binswangers in Freud's Vienna. See the writings of Freud's contemporary, Austrian psychiatrist Otto Ludwig Binswanger, esp. *Die hysterie (Vienna,* 1904), a work of almost one thousand pages, and the important book of his son Ludwig, *Melancholie und Manie* (Pfullingen, 1960), a study of anger in relation to hysteria. The elder Binswanger wrote studies of hysteria, neurasthenia, epilepsy, and madness. From the early modern period (ca. 1500 forward), anger was associated with possession and demonism; later, in the seventeenth century, with war and attention; yet the modern social history of anger awaits its student.

82. See A. Luyendijk, "Of Masks and Mills: The Enlightened Doctor and His Frightened Patient," in *The Languages of Psyche,* ed. Rousseau (n. 13), 186–231; the classic eighteenth-century statement is by John Bond, *An Essay on the Incubus, or Night-Mare* (London: Wilson & Durham, 1753); a theoretical approach to the spectatorial nighttime world that glances at the early period is found in Terry Castle, "Phantasmagoria," *Critical Inquiry* 15 (1988): 26–61.

83. For the opposite view, that it was pure possession, see Graham, *Medieval Minds*, 99–101.

84. Veith, *Hysteria*, 59–66, and chap. 6, "The Non-conformists."

85. Ibid., 61.

86. Ibid., 110.

87. Bodin, the author of *De la démonomanie des sorciers* (Paris: Jacques du Pays, 1581) and other works on magic, reasoned that "madwomen are never burned . . . and Hippocrates whom you [Weyer] should know, teaches you on his part that those women who have their menses, are not subject to melancholy, madness, epilepsy" (quoted in Veith, *Hysteria*, 111). For Weyer see Graham, *Medieval Minds*; J. J. Cobben, *Jan Wier, Devils, Witches and Magic* (Philadelphia: Dorrance, 1976); Carl Binz, *Doctor Johann Weyer: Ein rheinischer Arzt, der 1. Bekaempfer des Hexenwahns: Ein Beitrag zur Geschichte der Aufklaerung und der Heilkunde* (Weisbaden: Dr. Martin Saendig, 1969).

88. See also Baldinus Ronsseus, *De humanae vitae primordiis hystericis affectibus* (Leiden, 1594), for a similar point.

89. For one approach to Weyer's life see Cobben, *Jan Wier, Devils, Witches and Magic*. See also the apparatus in Johannes Weyer, *Witches, Devils, and Doctors in the Renaissance: Johannes Weyer's De Praestigiis Daemonum*, ed. George Mora, M.D. (Binghamton, N.Y.: University Center at Binghamton, 1990; originally published 1583).

90. Timothy Bright, *A Treatise of Melancholie. Containing the Causes thereof, & reasons of the strange effects it worketh in our minds and bodies: with the physicke cure, and spirituall consolation for such as haue thereto adioyned an afflicted conscience. The difference betwixt it, and melancholie with diuerse philosophicall discourses touching actions, and affections of soule, spirit, and body: the particulars whereof are to be seene before the booke* (London, 1586; reprint, Amsterdam and New York: Da Capo Press, 1969). For Bright see also Jackson, *Melancholia and Depression*.

91. The text has now been edited with useful commentary by Michael MacDonald in *Witchcraft and Hysteria in Elizabethan London: Edward Jorden and the Mary Glover Case—Tavistock Classic Reprints in the History of Psychiatry* (London: Routledge, 1990).

92. During the period 1550–1650 the nomenclature was variable, some authors preferring one term over another, and it is almost impossible to differentiate among these terms in the medical literature. All three are used in John Sadler, *The Sicke Womans Private Looking-Glasse, wherein Methodically are handled al uterine affects, or diseases arising from the wombe; enabling Women to informe the Physician about the cause of their griefe* (London: Anne Griffin, 1636), 130.

93. For the cultural milieu of the devil see Walker, *Spiritual and Demonic Magic* (n. 25); Brian Vickers, *Scientific and Occult Mentalities in the Renaissance* (Cambridge: Cambridge University Press, 1984); Wayne Shumaker, *The Occult Sciences in the Renaissance* (Berkeley, Los Angeles, London: University of California Press, 1972); A. Macfarlane, *Witchcraft in Tudor and Stuart England* (London: Routledge & Kegan Paul, 1970); and for the connection with erotic life and sexuality, Ioan P. Culianu, *Eros and Magic in the Renaissance* (Chicago: University of Chicago Press, 1989).

94. Edward Jorden, *A Brief Discourse of a Disease Called the Suffocation of the Mother* (London: John Windet, 1603), B3 2.

95. See A. E. Taylor (n. 50) for the Platonic sources.

96. The politics of Jorden's *"furor uterinus"* is discussed in D. H. Bart Scully et al., "The Politics of Hysteria: The Case of the Wandering Womb," in *Gender and Disordered Behavior: Sex Differences in Psychopathology*, ed. E. S. Gomberg and V. Franks (New York: Brunner/Mazel, 1979), 354–380. For models of the uterus in the previous few centuries, especially the seven-cell uterus, see Robert Reisert, *Der seibenkammerige uterus* (Hanover: Würzburger medizinshistorische Forschungen, 1986).

97. Along the line of Scully's "politics of hysteria," one wonders why the female could not masturbate to provide the much-needed moisture. Was male sperm alone capable of providing the moisture, or was masturbation too delicate a topic to address? For the politics and ideology of masturbation in history see Jean Paul and Roger Kempf Aron, *Le pénis et la démoralisation de l' Occident* (Paris: Bernard Grasset, 1978).

98. Jorden, *Suffocation of the Mother*, G2 2.

99. Nor will the genderization cease with the innovative Jorden. Throughout the seventeenth century, the "mother" will become increasingly associated with nature; see James Winn, *"When Beauty Fires the Blood": Love and Arts in the Age of Dryden* (Ann Arbor: University of Michigan Press, 1992). Likewise, its metaphors attach to anatomy, then consistently said to be the "mother of science"; see A. J. Luyendijk, "Anatomy, Mother of Art and Science: Controversies between English and Dutch Scientists, 1690–1725," a talk delivered at the Wellcome Institute Symposium on the History of Medicine, 1988. By the eighteenth century, anatomical preoccupation with the "suffocation of the mother" will have moved anatomically and gynecologically from the womb to "the mother's imagination," now said by doctors to be the most important aspect of fetal marking during the act of reproduction; see G. S. Rousseau, "Pineapples, Pregnancy, Pica, and *Peregrine Pickle*," in *Tobias Smollett: Bicentennial Essays Presented to Lewis M. Knapp*, ed. G. S. Rousseau and P. G. Boucé (New York: Oxford University Press, 1971), 79–110. And by the early nineteenth, the "mother" becomes the key to the mystery of androgyny; see D. L. Hoeveler, *Romantic Androgyny: The Woman Within* (University Park: Pennsylvania State University Press, 1990). While a study of the medicalization of the imagination in the Renaissance and Enlightenment is badly needed, a study of the transformations of the image of "the mother," construed literally and metaphorically, visually and iconographically also remains a desideratum.

100. The jungle of rhetoric is so dense in these treatises, especially in Jorden's, that it is worthwhile to construe these works as medical romances designed to sway a particular male audience in a predictable direction. Within these dense tropics of discourse (to borrow a phrase again from Hayden White's *Tropics of Discourse* [Baltimore: Johns Hopkins University Press, 1982]), one trope alone stands out over and over again: analogy. Analogy, common in the medical literature of the time, is everywhere present in this construction of hysteria, as in this important passage by Jorden about the "affections of the mind": "the per-

turbations of the minde are oftentimes to blame for this [i.e., hysteria] and many other diseases. For feeling we are not masters of our owne affections, wee are like battered Cities without walles, or shippes tossed in the Sea, exposed to all manner of assaults and daungers, even to the overthrow of our owne bodies" (Jorden, *Suffocation of the Mother*, G2 2).

101. See Veith, *Hysteria*, 122–123.

102. C. E. McMahon, "The Role of Imagination in the Disease Process in Pre-Cartesian History," *Psychological Medicine* 6 (1976): 179–184.

103. Veith, *Hysteria*, 122.

104. Ibid., 123.

105. Jorden, *Suffocation of the Mother*, B3 3.

106. Ibid., B3.

107. Ibid., 25.

108. Ibid., G3 3.

109. Ibid.

110. Ibid., A3.

111. Ibid.

112. Ibid., A4. Epilepsies and convulsions were considered important signs throughout the seventeenth century; see Jean Chastelain, *Traité des convulsions* (Lyon, 1691).

113. Joubert was an esteemed physician and contemporary of Rabelais; see his *Erreurs populaires et propos vulgaires touchant la médecine et le régime de santé* (Bordeaux, 1579). Bakhtin was fascinated by him for his literary contributions to the "Hippocratic novel" and to the semiotics of laughter: "The famous physician Laurent Joubert, published in 1560 a special work under the characteristic title: *Traité du Ris, contenant son essence, ses causes et ses mervelheus effeis, curieusement recherchès, raisonnés et observés par M. Laur. Joubert.* In 1579 Joubert published another treatise in Bordeaux, *La cause morale du Ris, de l'excellent et tres renommé Démocrite, expliquée et temoignée par ce devin Hippocrate en ses épîtres* (The moral cause of laughter of the eminent and very famous Democritus explained and witnessed by the divine Hippocrates in his epistles). This work was actually a French version of the last part of the "Hippocratic novel" (Mikhail Bakhtin, *Rabelais and His World* [Cambridge, Mass.: MIT Press, 1968], 68).

114. Georges Lote, *La vie et l'oeuvre de François Rabelais* (Paris: Droz, 1938), 163: "Medicine became the science of the sixteenth century; it exercised a great influence and inspired confidence which it no longer retained in the seventeenth century."

115. See R. Antonioli, *Rabelais et la médecine* (Geneva: Dros, 1976); Lucien Febvre, *The Problem of Unbelief in the Sixteenth Century: The Religion of Rabelais* (Cambridge, Mass.: Harvard University Press, 1982); Graham, *Medieval Minds*; and Bakhtin, *Rabelais and His World*, esp. 316–317, 355–363; Bakhtin, always sensitive to the Hippocratic tradition for its glorious narrative legacy, raises the fascinating possibility of a "grotesque hysteria": "These two areas [the bowels and the phallus] play the leading role in the grotesque image, and it is precisely for this reason that they are predominantly subject to positive exaggeration, to

hyperbolization; they can even detach themselves from the body and lead an independent life, for they hide the rest of the body, as something secondary" (317)—so too the grotesque image of the "wandering womb" and the suggestion of its "independent life."

116. Samuel Putnam, ed., *The Portable Rabelais* (New York: Viking Press, 1946), 477–479, especially the passage in *Pantagruel* beginning "I call it an 'animal,' in accordance with the doctrine of the Academics . . ."

117. Joseph Lieutaud, *Historia anatomico-medica*, 2 vols. (Paris, 1767).

118. See L. J. Rather, "Thomas Fienus (1567–1631): Dialectical Investigation of the Imagination as Cause and Cure of Bodily Disease," *Bulletin of the History of Medicine* 41 (1967): 349–367.

119. Useful here is K. E. Williams, "Hysteria in Seventeenth Century Primary Sources," *History of Psychiatry* 1 (1990): 383–402.

120. Supplemental to the works on women in the Renaissance mentioned in nn. 51 and 62 are Barbara and Henri van der Zee, *1688: Revolution in the Family* (London: Penguin Books, 1988); Bonnie S. Anderson, *A History of Their Own: Women in Europe from Prehistory to the Present* (New York: Harper & Row, 1988); K. M. Rogers, *The Troublesome Helpmate: A History of Misogyny in Literature* (Seattle: University of Washington Press, 1966).

121. The diligent historian wants to know, of course, what *does* remain, and the reply is little. What is clear is that voices are being silenced: those of hysterics trying to find their own first-person voices and identities when all those insistent on generating third-person discourse did not want to hear them. For the dire psychological consequences of such silencing within a patriarchal Western culture in which female sexuality has been the source of terrific male terror, see Wolfgang Lederer, *Gynophobia ou la peur des femmes* (Paris: Nizet, 1967), translated as *The Fear of Women* (New York: Grune & Stratton, 1968); Jardine, *Gynesis* (n. 35); E. Fischer-Homberger, *Krankheit, Frau und andere Arbeite zur Medizingeschichte der Frau* (Bern, Stuttgart, Vienna: Hans Huber, 1979).

122. MacDonald, "Women and Madness in Tudor and Stuart England" (n. 25).

123. For the ritual of the *danse macabre* in relation to malingerers see chap. 5 (Sander Gilman), and Harold Speert, *Iconographia Gyniatrica: A Pictorial History of Gynecology and Obstetrics* (New York: Macmillan, 1973).

124. G. Greer, *The Female Eunuch* (London: MacGibbon & Kee, 1970), 47–53.

125. See esp. Galopin, *Les hystériques des couvents* (n. 53), but also Thomas, *Religion and the Decline of Magic* (n. 25); I. M. Lewis, *Ecstatic Religion* (Harmondsworth: Penguin, 1971); Michel Feher et al., eds., *Fragments for a History of the Human Body* (New York: Zone, 1989), vol. 1; Bynum, *Gender and Religion* (n. 5).

126. Although the ideological view of women continued to alter during the seventeenth century, the belief that their hysteria was primarily the result of a rampaging *menarche* continued to be strong, and doctors did what they could to assuage the effects of the paroxysm and genital upheaval. The menses provided doctors and patients alike with a paradoxical situation: on the one hand, they

could not be suppressed; on the other, once rampaging, they wreaked vast physiological damage. Pharmacologically, juleps and apozems were administered with hops to induce the menses, on the theory that hops produced nocturnal dreams and would calm the hysterically ill when under the spell of a fever to sleep. This preparation continued to be used into the eighteenth century; see Johann Delaeus, *Upon the Cure of the Gout by Milk Diet: & An Essay upon Diet by William Stephens* (London: Smith & Bruce, 1732).

127. It may also be that homophobia (in our modern sense a problematic word that has come to be a metonymy denoting fear of the excessively *male*) has a place in this history and its linguistic configurations. See Katherine Cummings, *Telling Tales: The Hysteric's Seduction in Fiction and Theory* (Stanford, Calif.: Stanford University Press, 1991). In "Freud and Fliess: Homophobia and Seduction," in *Seduction and Theory: Readings of Gender, Representation, and Rhetoric,* ed. Dianne Hunter (Urbana: University of Illinois Press, 1989), 86–109, S. N. Garner studies the language of Freud's hysterical women in the light of their fear of same-sex relations. Furthermore, one wonders if there is any connection between the so-called demise of hysteria in our century and the monumental growth of homophobia.

128. J. W. Hebel, ed., *The Works of Michael Drayton* (Oxford: Shakespeare Head, Blackwell, 1961), "Poly-Olbion," p. 128, Song VII, lines 19–28.

129. Marie E. Addyman, "The Character of Hysteria in Shakespeare's England," doctoral dissertation, University of York, York, England, 1988. Janet Adelman appears to agree but embroiders the idea from a psychoanalytic perspective in *Suffocating Mothers: Fantasies of Maternal Origin in Shakespeare's Plays Hamlet to The Tempest* (London: Routledge, 1990).

130. Adelman, *Suffering Mothers,* 3. For further background, see F. D. Hoeniger, *Medicine and Shakespeare in the English Renaissance* (Newark: University of Delaware Press, 1992).

131. Hoeniger, *Medicine and Shakespeare,* 2.

132. Ibid., 137.

133. The point seems to be buttressed by Micale's studies on the history of male hysteria; see n. 3.

134. The belief of G. S. Rousseau, "Literature and Medicine: The State of the Field," *Isis* 72 (1981): 406–424, and Peter B. Medawar, *The Hope of Progress: A Scientist Looks at Problems in Philosophy, Literature and Science* (Garden City, N.Y.: Anchor Books, 1973).

135. Devon Hodges, *Renaissance Fictions of Anatomy* (Amherst: University of Massachusetts Press, 1985); B. G. Lyons, *Voices of Melancholy: Studies of Literary Treatments of Melancholy in Renaissance England* (London: Routledge & Kegan Paul, 1971), who is particularly useful in describing Burton's rhetorical strategies and devices of persuasion in the "Perturbations of the Minde"; see esp. pp. 132–134.

136. This transformation of knowledge is discussed by Joscelyn Godwin, *Athanasius Kircher: A Renaissance Man and the Quest for Lost Knowledge* (London: Thames & Hudson, 1979); Michel Foucault, *The Archaeology of Knowledge* (New

York: Pantheon Books, 1972); C. C. Camden, "The Golden Age and the Renaissance," *Literary Views* (1988): 1–14; in the contexts of the body in F. Bottomley, *Attitudes to the Body in Western Christendom* (London, 1979); in the carnivalization of knowledge in Bakhtin, *Rabelais and His World.*

137. Compare the nineteenth-century medicalization of homosexuality. Work on positivism for periods before 1800 seems to be virtually nonexistent. One wonders whether the principle was also operative in the late nineteenth century when the winds of positivism were blowing so strongly.

138. One obvious place to start with is Thomas Laqueur's *Making Sex: Body and Gender from the Greeks to Freud* (Cambridge, Mass.: Harvard University Press, 1990).

139. Ibid., 98–132; P. Hoffmann, *La femme dans la pensée des Lumières* (Paris: Ophrys, 1977); R. Thompson, *Unfit for Modest Ears* (London: Macmillan, 1979).

140. Laqueur, *Making Sex* (n. 138), 70–98; idem, "Orgasm, Generation and the Politics of Reproductive Biology," *Representations* 14 (1986): 1–14; idem, "Amor Veneris, vel Dulcedo Apperatur," in *Fragments for a History of the Human Body,* ed. Feher (see n. 125), 3: 90–131.

141. (London: Anne Griffin, 1636). The astrological, herbal, and Hebrew signs on the frontispiece are worth considering in the light of Sadler's approach to hysteria. Chap. 13, "Of the generation of monsters," considers the "Divine" or "Naturall" Generation of Monsters in relation to the health of the mother's womb and the state of her imagination, which "workes on the child after conception" (139). The period produced other works similar to Sadler's, many of which refer to the "mother's fits" as a common expression representing the "green-sickness," now endemic among pubescent virgins. But Robert Pierce, *Bath memoirs: or, Observations in Three and Forty Years Practice, at the Bath, what Cures have been there wrought* (Bristol: Hammond, 1697), 34–37, cautioned that "Women's Diseases could affect women at all times in their lives: they are subject to when they are young, or when more adult; when marry'd or when unmarry'd; when Childless, or when they have had Children." Pierce claims that "the Hysterick Passion, or Fits of the Mother," often arose out of the green sickness, i.e., the condition of pubescent teenage girls. Thus Mrs. Elizabeth Eyles, from the Devizes, in the County of Wilts, age 16, being very far gone in the "green-sickness," developed "Mother-fits withal."

142. The quotations from Harvey in this paragraph are found in William Harvey, "On Parturition," in his *Works* (London: Sydenham Society, 1847), 528–529, 542–543; idem, *Exercitationes de generatione animalium* (London, 1651), 542. See also R. Brain, "The Concept of Hysteria in the Time of Harvey," *Proceedings of the Royal Society of Medicine* 56 (1963): 317–324. Along similar lines Jane Sharp warned that retention of seed (putrefied menstruum) was harmful, and hence advised lusty maids to marry; see her *Midwife's Book, or the Whole Art of Midwifery Discovered Directing Childbearing Women How to Behave Themselves in Their Conception, Breeding, Bearing and Nursing Children* (London, 1671), 52.

143. In his *Nymphomania* (n. 74), Bienville writes as if the term had been perennially used, predating the Elizabethan world of Jorden and Bright.

144. Such had been the alleged politics in paradise: see J. G. Turner, *One Flesh: Paradisal Marriage and Sexual Relations in the Age of Milton* (Oxford: Oxford University Press, 1987). Tradition had it that hysteria was nonexistent among the pre-Adamites, the sect of men and women who ran about the primordial garden naked and in a state of perfect nature; for the neo-Adamite sects of the Renaissance and Enlightenment, see Michael Mullett, *Radical Religious Movements in Early Modern Europe* (Boston: Routledge, 1980).

145. See Peter Brown, *The Body and Society: Men, Women, and Sexual Renunciation in Early Christianity* (New York: Columbia University Press, 1990); Lemay, "Human Sexuality in Twelfth- through Fifteenth-Century Scientific Writings" (n. 74); for a more esoteric version of the debates, Maire, *Les convulsionnaires de Saint-Médard* (n. 53).

146. Sharp, *Midwife's Book*, 52. It was not uncommon in the period for male quacks to assume female pseudonyms, especially one as common as "Jane Sharp." Sharp claimed that his book was based on "vast knowledge" and that he wrote primarily for women in simple language they could understand.

147. See William Harvey, *Exercitationes de generatione animalium* (n. 142), 543. For comparison in the sexual domain, see the views of Nicolas Venette, *The Mysteries of Conjugal Love Revealed*, 3d ed. (London, 1712), and Roy Porter, "Love, Sex and Medicine: Nicolas Venette and his *Tableau de l'Amour Conjugal*," in *Erotica and the Enlightenment*, ed. P. Wagner (Frankfurt: Peter Lang, 1990), 90–122.

148. Harvey, *Exercitationes*, 542. See also Laqueur, "Orgasm, Generation and the Politics of Reproductive Biology" (n. 140).

149. See L. Jordanova, *Sexual Visions, Images of Gender in Science and Medicine Between the Eighteenth and the Twentieth Centuries* (Madison: University of Wisconsin Press, 1989); MacLean, *Renaissance Notion of Woman* (n. 51); for the social construction of womanhood and gender in history, L. Schiebinger, *The Mind Has No Sex? Women and the Origins of Modern Science* (Cambridge, Mass.: Harvard University Press, 1989).

150. The point was made in the eighteenth century especially; see Henry Burdon, *The Fountain of Health: or a View of Nature* (London, 1734); James MacKenzie, *The History of Health and the Art of Preserving It*, 2d ed. (Edinburgh, 1759); for the history of the notion, Roy Porter and Dorothy Porter, *In Sickness and in Health: The British Experience, 1650–1850* (London: Fourth Estate, 1988), chap. 10.

151. These are ideological matters *au fond* and could not be politely put until this century; see Pagels, *Adam, Eve and the Serpent* (n. 62). The sermonists of the seventeenth and eighteenth centuries often alluded to it but in the language of ellision; for both realms, physiological and religious, see P. Zacchia, *De affectionibus hypochondriacis libri tres. Nunc in Latinum sermonem translati ab Alphonso Khonn* (Augsburg, 1671).

152. See Hill, *Women and Work*, who accepts Lawrence Stone's marriage statistics in *The Family, Sex and Marriage in England: 1500–1800* (London: Weidenfeld & Nicholson, 1977) as reliable.

153. Also suggested by contemporary social commentators such as Peter Annet in *Social Bliss considered in marriage and divorce: cohabiting unmarried, and public whoring. Containing things necessary to be known by all that seek mutual felicity, and are ripe for the enjoyment of it* (London, 1749). Examples of the prescription of sexual intercourse are found in Adalheid Giedke, *Die Liebeskrankheit in der Geschichte der Medizin*, University of Düsseldorf, Ph.D. thesis, 1983.

154. For anger in relation to melancholy in early modern history, see L. Binswanger, *Melancholie und Manie* (n. 81).

155. For the sexes see J. H. Hagstrum, *Sex and Sensibility: Ideal and Erotic Love from Milton to Mozart* (Chicago: University of Chicago Press, 1980); Turner, *One Flesh* (n. 144); for sex, gender, with a glance at hysteria in Milton see Annabelle Patterson, "No meer amatorius novel?" in *Politics, Poetics, and Hermeneutics in Milton's Prose*, ed. D. Loewenstein and J. G. Turner (Cambridge: Cambridge University Press, 1990), 85–101, esp. 101, n. 18.

156. The most important of the many works on this topic is Richard Baxter's *The Cure of Melancholy and over much Sorrow by Faith and Physick* (London, 1682); see also Baxter's *Reliquiae Baxterianae*, part iii, sec. 184 (London, 1696).

157. As was apparent in the development of the Theophrastan character in the late seventeenth century, as well as in the arrangement of the genders; see first its history and relation to the traditions of hysteria in Chester Noyes Greenough, *A Bibliography of the Theophrastan Character in English with Several Portrait Characters* (Cambridge, Mass.: Harvard University Press, 1947), and two important studies: Benjamin Boyce, *The Theophrastan Character in England to 1642* (Cambridge, Mass.: Harvard University Press, 1947); J. W. Smeed, *The Theophrastan "Character": The History of a Literary Genre* (Oxford: Oxford University Press, 1985).

158. See H. M. Weber, *The Restoration Rake-Hero: Transformations in Sexual Understanding in Seventeenth Century England* (Madison: University of Wisconsin Press, 1986), and Turner, *One Flesh* (n. 144). For the broader philosophical issues involved in the construction of sexuality, see A. I. Davidson, "Sex and the Emergence of Sexuality," *Critical Inquiry* 11 (1987): 16–48.

159. Stone, *Family, Sex and Marriage in England: 1500–1700* (n. 152), and R. Trumbach, *The Rise of the Egalitarian Family* (New York: New York University Press, 1978).

160. See R. Trumbach, "Sodomy Transformed: Aristocratic Libertinage, Public Reputation and the Gender Revolution of the Eighteenth Century," in *Love Letters between a Certain Late Nobleman and the Famous Mr. Wilson*, ed. M. S. Kimmel (New York: Harrington Park Press, 1990), 106.

161. See Hill's hypothesis about female mobility in relation to the rise of prostitution in *Women and Work*.

162. For the transformation of these gender relations in the period see R. Trumbach, "The Birth of the Queen: Sodomy and the Emergence of Gender Equality in Modern Culture, 1660–1750," in *Hidden from History: Reclaiming the Gay and Lesbian Past*, ed. M. Duberman, M. Vicinus, and G. Chauncey, Jr. (New York: NAL Books, 1989), 45–60, whose thesis deserves consideration.

163. See Sydenham (n. 44), 282–283.

164. For medical theory before Sydenham (i.e., in the period 1600–1680), advocating the position that the patient may be afflicted with the one or the other, see G. S. Rousseau, "Towards a Semiotics of the Nerve: The Social History of Language in a New Key," in *The Social History of Language II,* ed. Peter Burke and Roy Porter (Oxford: Polity Press, 1991), 76–81 (Appendix); some discussion of the subject is also found in P. E. A. Roy, "De l'hypochondrie," *Archives de Neurologie* 20 (1905): 166–183.

165. The hypochondrium was, anatomically speaking, located within the intercostal cavity, yet little differentiation was made at this time, from what I can gather, between male and female intercostal cavities; perhaps it was one more aspect of Thomas Laqueur's "one sex" theory; see Laqueur, *Making Sex* (n. 138). In *Sex and Reason* (Cambridge: Harvard University Press, 1991), Richard Posner sees deeply into the biological and legal dimensions of these differences but practices a flawed method by virtue of ignoring local sociohistorical practices, as in the now remote Restoration ethos of sexuality.

166. See Dewhurst, *Dr. Thomas Sydenham* (n. 41), and Boss, "Seventeenth-Century Transformation of the Hysteric Affection" (n. 55).

167. For "psyche-ologia" as a neologism, and for its linguistic ramifications in both medicine and rhetoric at this time, see G. S. Rousseau, "Psychology," in *The Ferment of Knowledge: Studies in the Historiography of Science,* ed. G. S. Rousseau and Roy Porter (Cambridge: Cambridge University Press, 1980), 167–172.

168. See his important treatise on the gout, originally published in 1683 as a *Treatise on Gout and Dropsy* and reprinted in 1705. Some of Sydenham's ideas on gout also appeared in *Of the Four Constitutions* (an undated manuscript in the Bodleian Library, Oxford [MS Locke, c. 19, ff. 170–176]) and in his *Theologia Rationalis* (which exists in four manuscript versions).

169. For Sydenham's medical practice see Dewhurst, *Dr. Thomas Sydenham* (n. 41); J. F. Payne, *A Biography of Dr. Thomas Sydenham* (London: Longman's, 1900); L. M. F. Picard, *Thomas Sydenham* (Dijon, 1889).

170. Locke served as Sydenham's assistant and amanuensis, later as his co-practitioner and collaborator. Discussion of the Locke-Sydenham relation is found in Dewhurst, *Dr. Thomas Sydenham* (n. 41), 39–41, 55–56, 73–76, 164–169, and H. Isler, *Thomas Willis, 1621–1685, Doctor and Scientist* (New York: Hafner, 1968).

171. No evidence indicates whether or not Sydenham read Lepois on hysteria, and Sydenham's most authoritative biographer (Dewhurst) is silent on the matter; Boerhaave comments on the importance of Lepois's theories of hysteria in his 1714 preface to Lepois's select observations (*Selectiorum observationum . . .*). For Lepois and hysteria, see Jackson, *Melancholia and Depression* (n. 80).

172. For Lepois see Veith, *Hysteria,* 129; the translation provided here is Veith's.

173. Ibid., 129.

174. Sydenham's published medical works are few; for a list see Dewhurst, *Dr. Thomas Sydenham* (n. 41), 190; there are even fewer that survive in manuscript

(ibid., 190). Comments on his significance within the history of medicine are found in C. D. Martin, "A Treatise on the Gout," *Critical Review* (March, 1759): 281–282, as well as in the 1753 edition of some of his works published by John Swan. A study of his style in the *Epistolary Dissertation* in relation to the language of the time would repay the effort and might shed further light on his theory of hysteria.

175. Veith, *Hysteria*, 140. Sydenham pronounced here clearly and succinctly, as in everything else he wrote. His main points are that hysteria has been misunderstood in its most fundamental principles (i.e., as the most transformative of all conditions); in its affliction among the genders and social rank; and, after affliction, in its physical and mental manifestations.

176. It is worth emphasizing, at the cost of belaboring the obvious, that *all* seventeenth- and eighteenth-century physicians claimed to treat patients for the "hysterical passion," or the many other names by which it was known. There was nothing unusual about this at all. The only difference was the degree to which the particular physician specialized in these cases. Doctors like Willis and Sydenham, and later on Cheyne and Adair, were known as "nerve doctors," or specialists in hysterical passions, and patients with these complaints accordingly flocked to them.

177. Lepois did not emphasize the animal spirits but wrote of "a collection of liquid accumulated in the hind part of the head and here collected with the effect that it swells and distends the beginnings of the nerves"; see Henri Cesbron, *These pour le doctorat en medecine: Histoire critique de l'hystériae* (Paris: Asselin et Houzeau, Libraires de la Faculté de Medecine, 1909), who quotes and translates this passage in French; Veith, *Hysteria*, 129. The liquid existed without regard to gender, and this is precisely why Lepois could justify a view that women are not naturally predisposed to hysteria any more than men. But Lepois's view was not known in England, his works were never translated into English, and I have found no evidence in the writings of English-speaking doctors that they were aware of Lepois's theory.

178. For Willis's primary medical works, brain theory, beliefs about the interface of brain and nervous system, and view of hysteria in the light of these basic theories, see G. S. Rousseau, "Nerves, Spirits and Fibres: Toward the Origins of Sensibility," in *Studies in the Eighteenth Century*, ed. R. F. Brissenden (Canberra: Australian National University Press, 1975), 137–157; for Willis and hysteria exclusively see Boss, "Transformation of the Hysteric Affection" (n. 55).

179. The best treatment of Willis's medical theory is R. Frank, "Thomas Willis and His Circle: Brain and Mind in Seventeenth-Century Medicine," in *Languages of Psyche*, ed. G. S. Rousseau (n. 13), esp. pp. 131–141. Frank comments on Willis's important clinical observation that "postmortems showed the wombs of hysterical women to be perfectly normal" (p. 134). Willis's *Affectionum . . . hystericae* (1672) has never been translated into English, despite its status as one of the most important neurological works of the early modern period. But Willis's salient point about the etiology of hysteria was the blood-brain connection: essentially, that any "derangements within the blood" were conveyed

to the brain and the nerves, and hence the neural trajectory of the condition rather than any other transmission. The mid-twentieth-century historian of physiology, Professor John Fulton of Yale University, viewed Willis as a hybrid English Freud cum physiologist, noting that Willis's *Cerebre anatome* (1664) was one of the "six cornerstones of modern neurology," together with books by Hitzig, Ferrier, and Sherrington, and that in the sphere of the relation of the cerebellum and involuntary action, so important to any scientific or secular theory of hysteria, "there was little further advance after Willis until 1809"; see J. Fulton, *Physiology of the Nervous System,* 2d ed. (London: Macmillan, 1943), 463.

180. Willis himself had coined such words as "neuro-logia" and "psychelogia" but never used the term psychological malady or hysteria or any other condition; see Rousseau, *Ferment of Knowledge* (n. 167), 146–148.

181. T. Laqueur, *Making Sex* (n. 138).

182. The emotions were undergoing a paradigmatic shift at this time; see G. Rosen, "Emotion and Sensibility in Ages of Anxiety: A Comparative Historical Review," *American Journal of Psychiatry* 124 (1967): 771–783; L. J. Rather, "Old and New Views of the Emotions and Bodily Changes," *Clio Medica* 1 (1965): 1–25; for a summary of their changes in the moral and philosophical realms, F. Hutcheson, *An Essay on the Nature and Conduct of the Passions* (London: J. Knapton, 1730).

183. Latham, *Works of Thomas Sydenham* (n. 44), vol. 2, 85. For a contrasting condition to the sedentary life, see the effects of "the glass delusion"; Gill Speak, "An Odd Kind of Melancholy: Reflections on the Glass Delusion of Europe (1440–1680)," *History of Psychiatry* 1 (1990): 191–206. For these violent mood swings and outbursts of unexpected behavior see John Ball, *The Modern Practice of Physic,* 2 vols. (London, 1760), 2: 229.

184. See G. S. Rousseau, "Science and the Discovery of the Imagination in Enlightened England," *Eighteenth-Century Studies* III (1969): 108–135.

185. By the mid-eighteenth century the "nervous system" had become entrenched, in medical theory as well as diagnosis, and in anatomy and physiology as well; see D. Smith, *A Dissertation upon the Nervous System to show its influence upon the Soul* (London, 1768); A Monro, *Experiments on the nervous system, with opium and mealline [sic] substances; made chiefly with the view of determining the nature and effects of animal electricity* (Edinburgh: A. Neill & Co. for Bell & Bradfute, 1793). For its development, see E. T. Carlson and M. Simpson, "Models of the Nervous System in Eighteenth-Century Psychiatry," *Bulletin of the History of Medicine* 43 (1969): 101–115. C. Lawrence has studied the cultural ramifications in "The Nervous System and Society in the Scottish Enlightenment," in *Natural Order: Historical Studies of Scientific Enlightenment,* ed. Barry Barnes and Steven Shapin (Beverly Hills, Calif.: Sage Publications, 1979), 19–40; for the early nineteenth-century view, see C. Bell, *The Nervous System of the Human Body* (London, 1824, reprinted 1830).

186. Today, viewed from our feminist and pro-abortion ideologies, the idea would be ridiculed as preposterous despite the strong vestiges of it that remain everywhere in the civilized world, but viewed from the perspective of the sci-

ences of man, which relied so heavily on anatomy and physiology for their underpinnings, it was easy to make a case for it. No one should think these two
last subjects—anatomy and physiology—were free of the politics and ideologies
that intervene in all science.

187. See n. 182.

188. See G. S. Rousseau, "Cultural History in a New Key: Towards a Semiotics of the Nerve," in *Interpretation and Cultural History*, ed. J. H. Pittock and
A. Wear (London: Macmillan, 1991), 25–81.

189. The passage appears in Latham, *Works of Thomas Sydenham* (n. 44), vol.
2, 85.

190. Beliefs about hysteria were still drawn almost exclusively from *Western*
models, and despite the expansionism and discoveries of the last century, geographical insulation still served to produce disease according to climatic and
national characteristics; see W. Falconer, *Remarks on the Influence of Climate, Situation, etc. . . . on the disposition and temper . . . of mankind* (London: C. Dilly, 1781).

191. Latham, *Works of Thomas Sydenham* (n. 44), vol. 2, 85.

192. As early as 1943, Henry Siegerist wrote about disease within history
from a broad perspective, and claimed that there had always been an intimate
connection between disease and art (i.e., literature, painting, poetry, drama,
etc.), a view that seems not to have had much influence on Veith. Had Siegerist
gazed further back than to Charcot in his discussion of hysteria, he would have
seen how true his intuition was for the seventeenth and eighteenth centuries;
see H. Siegerist, *Civilization and Disease* (n. 67), 184–185, 191–194.

193. For the nervous constitution by 1900, see J. Goldstein, *Console and Classify* (n. 36), and J. Oppenheim, *"Shattered Nerves": Doctors, Patients, and Depression
in Victorian England* (Oxford: Oxford University Press, 1991).

194. Latham, *Works of Thomas Sydenham* (n. 44), vol. 2, 85.

195. Ibid.

196. Ibid., vol. 2, 54.

197. Ibid.

198. Highmore espoused his theory of hysteria in three works primarily: *Ex-
cercitationes duae, quarum prior de passione hysterica, altera de affectione hypochondriaca*
(Amsterdam: C. Commelin, 1660); *Hysteria* (Oxford: A. Lichfield and R. Davis,
1660); *De hysterica et hypochondriaca passione: Responsio epistolaris ad Doctorem Willis*
(London, 1670).

199. Quoted in Richard Hunter and Ida Macalpine, *Three Hundred Years of
Psychiatry, 1535–1860* (London: Oxford University Press, 1963). See also Boss,
Seventeenth-Century Transformation of the Hysteric Affection (n. 55); Isler, *Thomas
Willis* (n. 170).

200. T. Willis, *An Essay on the Pathology of the Brain* (London, 1684), 71.

201. Beliefs about the effeminacy of men antedate the Restoration, of
course, but the idea acquired altogether different currency then. For some of
the reasons see Trumbach, "The Birth of the Queen" (n. 162); J. Turner, "The
School of Men: Libertine Texts in the Subculture of Restoration London" (a talk
given at UCLA, 1989); for a remarkably detailed case history of male effeminacy

of the playwright Richard Cumberland in the eighteenth century, see K. C. Balderston, ed., *Thraliana: The Diary of Mrs. Thrale 1776–1809*, 2 vols. (Oxford: Clarendon Press, 1942; rev. ed. 1951), 2: 436–440.

202. The term *category* as I have been using it in this chapter should not suggest philosophical so much as medical category. Disease was then understood almost entirely within the terms of categories and classifications, as the wide taxonomic tendencies of the era had doctors compiling and classifying every disease in terms of its major symptoms, anatomic presentations, organic involvements, and so forth. See D. Knight, *Ordering the World: A History of Classifying the World* (London: Macmillan, 1980).

203. Baglivi held a chair of medical theory in the Collegio della Sapienza in Rome, having been elected to it by Pope Clement XI. His book *De praxi medicina* (1699; English trans. 1723) was written with a knowledge of Sydenham's theories. He believed that hysteria was a mental disease caused by passions of the troubled mind; in this sense, he is less accurate and intuitive than Sydenham but nevertheless important. For Italian hysteria and hypochondria see Oscar Giacchi, *L'isterismo e l'ipochondria avvero il malo nervosa . . . Giudizii fisioclinici-sociali* (Milan, 1875).

204. See B. Mandeville, *A Treatise of the Hypochondriack and Hysterick Passions* (London, 1711; reprinted 1715; 3d ed. 1730).

205. Willis's anatomical "explosions" are discussed by R. G. Frank, "Thomas Willis and His Circle: Brain and Mind in Seventeenth-Century Medicine," in *The Languages of Psyche*, ed. Rousseau (n. 13), 107–147; Sacks, *Migraine* (n. 7), 26–27; for Willis's rhetoric and language see D. Davie, *Science and Literature 1700–1740* (London: Sheed & Ward, 1964).

206. For these shifts in knowledge at large see Thomas S. Kuhn, *The Structure of the Scientific Revolution* (Chicago: University of Chicago Press, 1970; rev. ed.); Rom Harré, "Philosophy and Ideas: Knowledge," in *Ferment of Knowledge*, ed. Rousseau and Porter (n. 167), 11–55.

207. Even Veith's survey in *Hysteria* makes this fact abundantly clear.

208. The evidence for entrenchment is provided in the remaining portion of this chapter and remains a central theme of this essay, as it does in J. Wright, "Hysteria and Mechanical Man," *Journal History of Ideas* 41 (1980): 233–247, and for numbers of medical historians such as A. Luyendijk.

209. For some of the evidence of the opposite view see P. Hoffmann, *La femme dans la pensée des Lumières* (Paris: Ophrys, 1977); Hill, *Women and Work*.

210. So much has now been written about this relatively small group that one hardly knows where to direct the curious reader; a good place is J. Todd, *Sign of Angellica: Women, Writing, and Fiction, 1660–1800* (London: Virago, 1988), and for one case history, written in depth, R. Perry, *The Celebrated Mary Astell: An Early English Feminist* (Chicago: University of Chicago Press, 1986).

211. A thorough linguistic study of these words ("spleen," "vapors," "hysterics") reconstructed in their local contexts would reveal shades of difference, but there are an equal number of examples of overlap and interchangeability; see also section XIII. For the witch trials, see K. Thomas, *Religion and the Decline*

of Magic (Harmondsworth, Middlesex: Penguin, 1973); for the famous 1736 case of the witch of Endor, B. Stock, *The Holy and the Demonic* (Princeton, N.J.: Princeton University Press, 1983).

212. John Purcell, *A Treatise of Vapours, or, Hysterick Fits* (London: J. Johnson, 1707), 91.

213. Radcliffe had a large and established practice of wealthy aristocratic clients, many of whom suffered from hysteria, but he wrote little; his famed repertoire of remedies continued to be published during and after his lifetime and was edited by apothecary Edward Strother; see J. Radcliffe, *Pharmacopoeia Radcliffeana* (London, 1716).

214. A good discussion of the scene is found in John Sena, "Belinda's Hysteria: The Medical Context of *The Rape of the Lock,*" *Eighteenth-Century Life* 5, no. 4 (1979): 29–42.

215. J. Butt, ed., *The Twickenham Edition of the Works of Alexander Pope* (New Haven, Conn.: Yale University Press), 234.

216. For the post-Popean iconography of Belinda as hysteric see C. Tracy, *The Rape Observ'd* (Toronto: University of Toronto Press, 1974), 81, especially D. Guernier's illustration of Belinda swooning.

217. An interesting pharmaceutical study could be written compiling these remedies in the eighteenth century. For example, the *Gentlemen's Magazine* regularly printed "receipts" for female hysteria and "male lovesickness"; see the June 1733 issue, p. 321, prescribing the tying of a woman's head in a noose next to a cricket allegedly stung by the noise! Domestic *vade mecums* such as W. Buchan, *Domestic Medicine* (London, 1776), and standard pharmacopeias such as J. Quincy, *The Dispensatory of the Royal College of Physicians* (London, 1721, many editions), also prescribed. Hysteria was a virtual industry for apothecaries for the entire period, especially in cordials to prevent miscarrying.

218. For the all-important iatromechanism of the period at large see T. M. Brown, "From Mechanism to Vitalism in Eighteenth-Century English Physiology," *Journal of the History of Biology* 7 (1974): 179–216; Rousseau, "Nerves, Spirits and Fibres" (n. 178); G. Bowles, "Physical, Human and Divine Attraction in the Life and Thought of George Cheyne," *Annals of Science* 41 (1974): 473–488; H. Metzger, *Attraction Universelle et Religion Naturelle chez quelques Commentateurs Anglais de Newton* (Paris: Nizet, 1938); more recently for iatromechanism in the work of Dr. Cheyne, see G. S. Rousseau, "Medicine and Millenarianism: 'Immortal Doctor Cheyne,'" in *Hermeticism and the Renaissance: Intellectual History and the Occult in Early Modern Europe,* ed. Ingrid Merkel and Allen Debus (Washington, D.C.: Folger Shakespeare Library, 1988), 192–230, and for the roles of rhetoric and language in Cheyne's writings, see Rousseau, "Language of the Nerves," in *Social History of Language,* ed. Burke and Porter (n. 42). I consider Cheyne's *Essay of the True Nature and Due Method of Treating the Gout* (London: G. Strahan, 1722) among his most important works for laying out his theory of iatromechanism and post-Newtonian application.

219. The Dutch were important in the development of a *mechanical* theory of hysteria, the great and influential Dr. Boerhaave himself having identified

hysteria as the most baffling of all female maladies. Boerhaave's writings set hysteria on a firm mechanical basis on the continent; for his theory of hysteria and its adoption by his followers, especially Anton de Haen in Holland, Gerard van Swieten in Austria, and Robert Whytt in Scotland, see A. M. Luyendijk, "Het hysterie-begrip in de 18de eeuw," in *Ongeregeld zenuwleven*, ed. L. de Goei (Utrecht: NcGv, 1989), 30–41, a volume rich in the bibliography of hysteria and dealing exclusively with the modern history of female uterine maladies. Luyendijk is right to claim that throughout the eighteenth century every aspect of "the sick woman" was sexually charged and sexually liminal; see A. M. Luyendijk, "De Zieke Vrouw in de Achttiende Eeuw," *Natuurkundige Voordrachten* 66 (1988): 129–136.

220. See Rousseau on Cheyne ("Medicine and Millinarianism," n. 218). By 1750 hysteria had become "nationalized" (i.e., Dutch hysteria, Scottish hysteria, etc.) and a study of its nationalistic idiosyncrasies would make for fascinating reading.

221. It undid his psychologizing and cultural determination, neglected his primary point about hysteria as a disease of imitation (see n. 44), and replaced it with a radical anatomizing and mechanizing of the nervous system capable of accounting for rises and falls of hysteria in both genders. Indeed, after Sydenham the theory of imitation virtually went under, finding no place in Cheyne's system, where the word never appears. It may be more than coincidental that Sydenhamian hysteria as a *disease of imitation* declines concomitantly with the larger aesthetic and philosophical theory of imitation in the same period; see F. Boyd, *Mimesis: The Decline of a Doctrine* (Cambridge, Mass.: Harvard University Press, 1973).

222. For Robinson see *A New System of the Spleen* (London, 1729), quoted in Richard Hunter and Ida Macalpine, *Three Hundred Years of Psychiatry* (n. 199); Klibansky et al., *Saturn and Melancholy* (n. 12); Jackson, *Melancholia and Depression* (n. 80), 291–294; T. H. Jobe, "Medical Theories of Melancholia in the Seventeenth and Early Eighteenth Centuries," *Clio Medica* 19 (1976): 217–231.

223. G. Cheyne, *The English Malady: or, a Treatise of Nervous Diseases of All Kinds* (London: Strahan & Leake, 1733), 184; see also O. Doughty, "The English Malady of the Eighteenth Century," *Review of English Studies* 2 (1926): 257–269; E. Fischer-Homberger, "On the Medical History of the Doctrine of the Imagination," *Psychological Medicine* 4 (1979): 619–628, which discusses the medicalization of the imagination in relation to the hysteric affection, and, most important, R. Porter, "The Rage of Party: A Glorious Revolution in English Psychiatry," *Medical History* 27 (1983): 35–50.

224. Cheyne, *English Malady*, 14. Samuel Richardson, the novelist and printer, had printed the book for his friend and claimed that Cheyne chose the title ("English") because he held the squalor and polluted air responsible for London's being "the greatest, most capacious, close and populous City of the Globe"—and also called it the "*English* malady" because hysteria was so called in derision by continental writers (*English Malady*, 55; C. F. Mullett, ed., *The Letters*

of Doctor George Cheyne to Samuel Richardson 1733–1743 [Columbia: University of Missouri Press, 1943, 15]).

225. R. James, *A Medicinal Dictionary; Including Physics, Surgery, Anatomy, Chemistry, and Botany, in All Their Branches. Together with a History of Drugs . . .* (London: T. Osborne, 1743–1745), article entitled "hysteria."

226. Curiously, no systematic study has been undertaken despite the large amount of recent feminist scholarship in the field of eighteenth-century studies; it awaits its avid student, for whom the sheer amount of material between 1700 and 1800 will make for a field day of scholarship. Some material for the nineteenth century is found in Y. Ripa, *La ronde des folles: Femme folie et enfermement au XIXe siecle* (Paris: Aubier, 1986). Müller, who became a leading anthropologist in Germany, wrote his medical thesis at the University of Paris in 1813 on "le spasme et l'affection vaporeuse"; as late as the 1840s some French doctors still considered "spleen" a valid category of the hysteria-hypochondria syndrome; see D. Montallegry, *Hypochondrie-spleen ou névroses trisplanchniques. Observations relative à ces maladies et leur traitement radical* (Paris, 1841).

227. For Swift and hysteria see Christopher Fox, ed., *Psychology and Literature in the Eighteenth Century* (New York: AMS Press, 1988), 236–237.

228. M. DePorte, *Nightmares and Hobbyhorses: Swift, Sterne, and Augustan Ideas of Madness* (San Marino, Calif.: Huntington Library Press, 1974), 125 ff.

229. For evidence of the linguistic confusion in the primary medical literature, see W. Stukeley, *Of the Spleen* (London, 1723); J. Midriff, *Observations on the Spleen and Vapours; Containing Remarkable Cases of Persons of both Sexes, and all Ranks, from the aspiring Directors to the Humble Bubbler, who have been miserably afflicted with these Melancholy Disorders since the Fall of the South-sea, and other publick Stocks; with the proper Method for their Recovery, according to the new and uncommon Circumstances of each Case* (London, 1720); J. Raulin, *Traité des affections vaporeuses du sexe* (Paris, 1758). There is also a wide literature of spleen and vapors, as in Matthew Green, *The Spleen, and Other Poems . . . with a Prefatory Essay by John Aikin, M.D.* (London: Cadell, 1796). For comparison of this early eighteenth-century outbreak of spleen with outbursts in America at the end of the nineteenth century, see T. Lutz, *American Nervousness, 1903: An Anecdotal History* (Ithaca, N.Y.: Cornell University Press, 1991), a study of the "neurasthenia plague" of 1903 that gave rise to hundreds of cures and potions. Midriff wondered if certain types of "spleen" appeared in particular types of wars and not others.

230. See Purcell, *Treatise of Vapours* (n. 212); some discussion of these matters is found in O. Temkin, *The Falling Sickness* (Baltimore: Johns Hopkins University Press, 1974).

231. For the extensiveness of this Newtonianism in medical theory, see N. Robinson, M.D., *A new theory of physick and diseases, founded on the principles of the Newtonian philosophy* (London, 1725), with much emphasis on hysteria; in theology and cosmic thought, J. Craig, *Theologia . . . Mathematica* (London, 1699); more generally, I. Prigogine, *Order Out of Chaos: Man's New Dialogue with Nature* (New York: Bantam Books, 1984). James Thomson the poet and author of *The Seasons,*

the most widely read English poem of the eighteenth century, also reflects this pervasiveness; see A. D. McKillop, *The Background of Thomson's Seasons* (Minneapolis: University of Minnesota Press, 1942). For Newtonianism and the popular imagination, M. H. Nicolson, *Newton Demands the Muse* (Princeton, N.J.: Princeton University Press, 1946).

232. Roy Porter has chronicled aspects of this development in *Mind-Forged Manacles: A History of Madness in England from the Restoration to the Regency* (London: Penguin, 1987); see also for madness in this period and its relation to current scientific movements: V. Skultans, *English Madness: Ideas on Insanity 1580–1890* (London: Routledge, 1979); M. Foucault, *Madness and Civilization: A History of Insanity in the Age of Reason* (New York: Pantheon Books, 1965), 120–132. Dr. Charles Perry, a mechanist and contemporary of Cheyne, Robinson, and Purcell, makes perceptive points about madness in relation to hysteria in his treatise *On the Causes and Nature of Madness* (London, 1723).

233. For the humanitarianism of madness, see D. Weiner, "Mind and Body in the Clinic: Philippe Pinel, Alexander Crichton, Dominique Esquirol, and the Birth of Psychiatry," in Rousseau, *Languages of Psyche* (n. 13), 332–340.

234. See Rousseau, "Medicine and Millenarianism" (n. 218).

235. G. Cheyne, quoted in L. Feder, *Madness in Literature* (Princeton, N.J.: Princeton University Press, 1980), 170. Cheyne's prose abounds with weird syntax, ungrammatical constructions, and neologisms; "fantastical" rather than the simpler word *strange* is just the sort of word found in his vocabulary.

236. *The English Malady* (1733), 353.

237. Ibid., 354.

238. Sir Richard Blackmore, *A Treatise of the Spleen and Vapours* (London, 1725), 320. In a rather similar prose, William Buchan in his *Domestic Medicine* (Edinburgh, 1769), 561, discussing "hysteric and hypochondriacal affections," noted that these nervous disorders were "diseases which nobody chuses to own." It is important to insist on the yoking of hysteria and hypochondria *ever since Sydenham undercut (except in name) hysteria as a gendered disease.* Blackmore argued from the perspective of one who had lived through the revolution in nomenclature as well as gender: "Most Physicians have looked upon Hysteric Affections as a distinct Disease from Hypochondriacal, and therefore have treated some of them under different Heads; but though in Conformity to that Custom I do the same, yet . . . I take them to be the same Malady." Blackmore admitted that women suffered worse, "the Reason of which is, a more volatile, dissipable [sic], and weak Constitution of the Spirits, and a more soft, tender, and delicate Texture of the Nerves." Yet, he insisted, "this proves no Difference in their Nature and essential Properties, but only a higher or lower Degree of the Symptoms common to both." This more "delicate Texture of the Nerves" was the fulcrum on which the theory of nervous diseases, including hysteria, was to be pegged for the next century and remains a crucial development in the history of medicine in the Enlightenment. For some of its cultural resonances, see Rousseau, "Cultural History in a New Key," in *Interpretation and Cultural History*, ed. Pittock and Wear (n. 188), 25–81.

239. Blackmore, *Treatise of the Spleen and Vapours* (n. 238), 319. It is important to reiterate Sydenham's consistent use of this nomenclature for males, which fell under his gender collapse of the disease and which was generally adopted by his students and followers into the time of Blackmore and Robinson: men were always "hypochondriacal," while women remained "hysterical," and no amount of anatomical similitude between the genders could account for the linguist disparity; for some discussion, see E. Fischer-Homberger, "Hypochondriasis of the Eighteenth Century—Neurosis of the Present Century," *Bulletin of the History of Medicine* 46 (1972): 391–401.

240. Nicholas Robinson, *A new system of the spleen, vapours, and hypochondriack melancholy; wherein all the decays of the nerves, and lownesses of the spirits are mechanically accounted for. To which is subjoined, a discourse upon the nature, cause, and cure of melancholy, madness, and lunacy* (London, 1729), 144.

241. Ibid., 345. More generally for this "physiological psychology" see DePorte, *Nightmares and Hobbyhorses* (n. 228); Rather, "Old and New Views of the Emotions and Bodily Changes" (n. 182); Jobe, "Melancholia in the Seventeenth and Eighteenth Centuries" (n. 222).

242. Looking ahead, these factors will coalesce later on in the century, in the world of Adair, Heberden, Cullen—Cheyne's followers. For the medical profession in the eighteenth century in relation to the development of other professions, see Geoffrey S. Holmes, *The Professions and Social Change in England 1680–1730* (Oxford: Oxford University Press, 1981), and idem, *Augustan England: Professions, State and Society, 1680–1730* (London: Allen & Unwin, 1982).

243. For the role of quacks in this milieu see R. Porter, *Health for Sale: Quackery in England 1650–1850* (Manchester: Manchester University Press, 1989), and "Female Quacks in the Consumer Society," *The History of Nursing Society Journal* 3 (1990): 1–25.

244. Veith, *Hysteria*, 155.

245. I.e., the essentially anti-vitalistic principle that all is brain and body, nothing mind. Twentieth-century science has spelled the death knell of scientific vitalism despite its many vestiges in the biological and neurological realms. For the anti-vitalistic strains and what I am calling the triumph of the neurophysiological approach of contemporary twentieth-century science, see J. D. Spillane, *The Doctrine of the Nerves: Chapters in the History of Neurology* (Oxford, New York: Oxford University Press, 1981); W. Riese, *A History of Neurology* (New York: MD Publications, 1959); for the linguistic implications, M. Jeannerod, *The Brain Machine: The Development of Neurophysiological Thought* (Cambridge, Mass.: Harvard University Press, 1985); H. A. Whitaker, *On the Representation of Language in the Human Brain: Problems in the Neurology of Language* (Los Angeles: UCLA Working Papers in Linguistics, 1969).

246. Cheyne, *English Malady*, 271 ff.

247. For nymphomania, see n. 74.

248. The animal spirits continued to prove troublesome for experimenters and theorists until the middle of the eighteenth century; for this complicated chapter in the history of science and medicine, see E. Clarke, "The Doctrine of

214 G. S. ROUSSEAU

the Hollow Nerve in the Seventeenth and Eighteenth Centuries," in *Medicine, Science, and Culture: Historical Essays in Honor of Owsei Temkin*, ed. L. G. Stevenson and Robert P. Multhauf (Baltimore: Johns Hopkins University Press, 1968), 123–141; for its linguistic representations and diverse metaphorical uses, Rousseau, "Discovery of the Imagination" (n. 184); the interchanges between the rhetorical and empirical (or scientific) domains here would make a fascinating study that has not been undertaken on a broad canvas.

249. See Laqueur, *Making Sex* (n. 138); Feher, *History of the Human Body* (n. 125).

250. Cheyne, *English Malady*, ii (preface).

251. For nightmares and hysteria, see A. M. Luyendijk-Elshout, "Mechanism contra vitalisme: De school van Herman Boerhaave en de beginselen van het leven," *T. Gesch. Geneesk. Natuurw. Wisk. Techn.* 5 (1982): 16–26; idem, "Of Masks and Mills" (n. 82); and, more generally, Castle, "Phantasmagoria" (n. 82).

252. Two generations after Pope, Hannah Webster Foster (1759–1840) thought that the nerves of the coquette distinguished her from other types; see *The coquette; or, The history of Eliza Wharton. Reproduced from the original edition of 1797* (New York: Columbia University Press, 1939), as did David Garrick in his play of the same name, but a century earlier there was no such notion in Philippe Quinault's *La mère coquette* (written as Sydenham was composing his essay on hysteria) or in the *State Poems* on court coquettes written during Swift's period.

253. S. Greenblatt, *Renaissance Self-fashioning: From More to Shakespeare* (Chicago: University of Chicago Press, 1980), whose use of self-fashioning must be credited.

254. P. M. Spacks, *The Female Imagination* (London: Methuen, 1976); idem., *Imagining a Self: Autobiography and Novel in Eighteenth-Century England* (London: Routledge, 1976); K. O. Lyons, *The Invention of the Self* (Carbondale: Southern Illinois University Press, 1978); J. Mullan, *Sentiment and Sociability* (Oxford: Oxford University Press, 1988); and literary criticism dealing with the literature of sensibility.

255. G. S. Rousseau, "Nerves, Spirits and Fibres" (n. 178); for the scientific dimension in mid-eighteenth century, see Haller's physiological revolution; for the popular cults, see an anonymous "Descant on Sensibility," *London Magazine* (May 1776); for the literary dimension, Hagstrum, *Sex and Sensibility* (n. 155); and L. I. Bredvold, *The Natural History of Sensibility* (Detroit: Wayne State University Press, 1962).

256. I tried to document this point about the semiology of disease then in "'Sowing the Wind and Reaping the Whirlwind': Aspects of Change in Eighteenth-Century Medicine," in *Studies in Change and Revolution: Aspects of English Intellectual History 1640–1800*, ed. Paul J. Korshin (London: Scholar Press, 1972), 129–159.

257. The new code is not evident in John Playford's seventeenth-century treatises, but begins to be apparent in the drama (Wycherly's *Love in a Wood*) and in treatises by dancing masters written after ca. 1740.

258. This complex and largely nonverbal code remains to be deciphered; it

is something as yet not understood about the Augustan "self-fashioning" (to invoke Greenblatt's fine term) of the nerves.

259. The new role of consumption of every type cannot be minimized in this period: see N. J. McKendrick et al., *The Birth of Consumer Society: The Commercialization of Eighteenth-Century England* (London: Europa Publications Limited, 1982); J. Brewer, *The Sinews of Power: War, Money, and the English State, 1688–1783* (Cambridge, Mass.: Harvard University Press, 1990); for the reaction, M. Caldwell, *The Last Crusade: The War on Consumption* (New York: Atheneum Publishers, 1988); for the medical diagnosis and its economic implications see such contemporary medical works as C. Bennet, *Treatise of Consumptions* (London, 1720); for drink and its relation to nervous sensibility, compare T. Trotter, *An Essay, Medical, Philosophical and Chemical on Drunkenness* (London: Longmans, 1804).

260. I tried to explain the chain of reasons from medical and philosophical, to social and popular, in "Nerves, Spirits and Fibres" (n. 178) and "Cultural History in a New Key" (n. 188), but much work remains to be done—I have barely scratched the surface of the Enlightenment cults of sensibility.

261. See M. Foucault, *Madness and Civilization: A History of Insanity in the Age of Reason* (New York: Pantheon Books, 1965), 132. My own thought has been influenced as much on the semiotic domain by Tzvetan Todorov in *The Conquest of America: The Question of the Other Translated from the French by Richard Howard* (New York: Harper & Row, 1985).

262. Richard Sennett, *The Fall of Public Man* (New York: Alfred A. Knopf, 1979).

263. It could not have elevated sensibility and the conditions (hysteria) that depended on it, *without* a prior theory of the "sciences of man." There are fine studies of this subject, but they usually omit the medical dimension entirely; for the best, see Sergio Moravia, *Filosofia e scienze umane nell'eta dei lumi* (Florence: Sansoni, 1982). The point needs to be related to the development of the science of man; Moravia saw much but did not make the important connections; he saw narrowly only the new science of man but not its implication for self-fashioning.

264. Even Peter Gay had made this seminal point about Haller in the opening pages of *The Enlightenment: An Interpretation*, 2 vols. (New York: Alfred A. Knopf, 1966–69), 1:30, in "The Spirit of the Age" and "The Recovery of Nerve," as did Henry Steele Commager in *The Empire of Reason* (New York: Anchor Doubleday, 1977), 8–10, in the famous paean to Haller who "took all knowledge for his province" (p. 8) and who "in the breadth and depth of his knowledge was perhaps unique" (p. 10). However, Haller's shrewd *fusion* of a medical *and* literary language of sexual sensibility (*sensibilität*) has been less well understood by historians forever bent on merely assessing his contribution to the history of European science, the Swiss Enlightenment, or the intellectual development of Göttingen.

265. Elsewhere I have tried to make the argument that the medical and scientific revolutions of the Enlightenment have still not been integrated into the culture at large, nor into the developing medical profession; Goldstein's *Console*

and Classify (n. 36) is an exemplary book for this type of work carried out for the next century. For the legacy of the "nervous revolution" in medicine in the next century see also Oppenheim, *"Shattered Nerves"* (n. 193).

266. See Rousseau, *Languages of Psyche* (n. 13).

267. Mechanical philosophy had been applied to every other domain, including painting, diet, health, government, so why not to manners? For a list of applications, see Rousseau, "Language of the Nerves" (n. 42), 60–61; for an example in music, R. Browne, *Medicina musica: Or a Mechanical Essay on the Effects of Singing, Musick, and Dancing, on Human Bodies* (London, 1729). As late as 1757, manners are still being described in mechanical metaphors; see J. Brown, *An Estimate of the Manners and Principles of the Times* (London: L. Davis & C. Reymers, 1757).

268. William Heberden, *Medical Commentaries* (London: T. Payne, 1802), 227.

269. Ibid., 235. Heberden did insist, however, that "their force will be very different, according to the patient's choosing to indulge and give way to them."

270. The role of medical schools was also great in this; see section X.

271. See F. J. McLynn, *Crime and Punishment in Eighteenth-Century England* (London: Routledge, 1989).

272. For the evidence see Wright, "Hysteria and Mechanical Man" (n. 208). Servants often aped these affectations of spleen and vapors to other servants, but rarely would they do so with their mistresses, who usually saw through the pretense. In Gay's *The Beggar's Opera*, Lucy explains her unacceptable behavior to the rivalrous Polly in terms of the vapors, but without recalling (if she ever knew it) that "Affectation" had been one of the handmaidens in Pope's "Cave of Spleen" in *The Rape of the Lock*.

273. For his life and works, see Rousseau, "Cultural History in a New Key" (n. 188); Philip Gosse, *Dr. Viper: The Querulous Life of Philip Thicknesse* (London: Cassell, 1952); A. Brunschwig, *Enlightenment and Romanticism in Eighteenth-Century Prussia* (Chicago: University of Chicago Press, 1974). For Whytt, see R. K. French, *Robert Whytt, the Soul, and Medicine* (London: Wellcome Institute for the History of Medicine, 1969).

274. James Makittrick Adair, *Essays on Fashionable Diseases* (N.P., 1786), 4–7.

275. The phrase is usually quoted from *An Epistle to Dr. Arbuthnot*, line 132; see also Marjorie Hope Nicolson and G. S. Rousseau, *This Long Disease My Life: Alexander Pope and the Sciences* (Princeton, N.J.: Princeton University Press, 1968). But Pope had used it earlier in a letter to Aaron Hill, March 14, 1731 (*Correspondence*, III. 182), commenting on his chronic infirmities, which he thought had predisposed his "manly temperament" to certain "softer activities."

276. For Pinel and hysteria see D. Weiner, "Mind and Body in the Clinic," in Rousseau, *The Languages of Psyche* (n. 13), 391–395.

277. For a list of many of these medical dissertations see G. S. Rousseau, "Discourses of the Nerve," in *Literature and Science as Modes of Expression*, ed. F. Amrine (Dordrecht: Kluwer Academic Publishers, 1989), 56–60.

278. M. Micale, "A Review Essay of Male Hysteria," *Medical History* (1988).

279. For some examples see Boss, "Transformation of the Hysteric Affection" (n. 55).

280. Biographical material is found in Thomas Guidott, *The Lives and Characters of the Physicians of Bath* (London, 1676–77; reprint of 1724–25 is edition referred to here) and *Some Particulars of the Author's [i.e., Guidott] Life* in Guidott's ed. of Edward Jorden's *Discourse of Natural Bathes and Mineral Waters* (London, 1669, 3d ed.). Guidott dedicated his books to Maplet and in 1694 saw through the press Maplet's treatise on the effects of bathing.

281. Guidott, *Lives and Characters of Physicians of Bath*, 128–142. Subsequent passages are found on these pages.

282. Throughout my reading I wondered if Guidott had read Sydenham on hysteria, but have been unable to make a case for or against. The larger point, however, is that one would not have to read a particular text to know, and even espouse, the fundamental aspects of the paradigm.

283. Elsewhere I shall demonstrate that it was this paradigm that informed, in part, theoretical explanations of all-male friendship (on grounds that sensitivity gravitated to like sensitivity), and that became the substratum of later discussions about effeminacy and sodomy.

284. For example, *Gideon's Fleece; or the Sieur de Frisk. An Heroic Poem . . . by Philo-Musus, a Friend to the Muses* (London, 1684).

285. Philippe Hecquet, *Le naturalisme des convulsions dans les maladies de l'épidémie convulsionnaire* (Soleure, 1733); Hillel Schwartz, *The French Prophets: The History of a Millenarian Group in Eighteenth-Century England* (Berkeley, Los Angeles, London: University of California Press, 1980); idem, *Knaves, Fools, Madmen, and that Subtile Effluvium: A Study of the Opposition to the French Prophets in England, 1706–1710* (Gainesville: University Presses of Florida, 1978).

286. Edith Sitwell, *The English Eccentrics* (Boston: Houghton Mifflin Co., 1933).

287. Hugh Farmer, *An Essay on the Demoniacs of the New Testament* (London: G. Robinson, 1775). For Farmer's interest in miracles, demons, spirits, and hysterics, as well as his medical case history and life, see Michael Dodson, *Memoirs of the Life and Writings of the Late Reverend and Learned Hugh Farmer* (London: Longman & Rees, 1804). This work differs from physician Richard Mead's *Treatise concerning the Influence of the Sun and the Moon upon Human Bodies, and the Diseases Thereby Produced* (London, 1748). In Mead, male hysteria is explained according to *external* phenomena (for example moon, waves, tides) acting through Hartleyan vibrations and magnetism upon the human Nerves and then the imagination. In this sense Mead, like Farmer, different though their professions were, should both be considered kindred in the mindset of counter-nerve. For counter-nerve see Rousseau, "Cultural History in a New Key" (n. 188), 70–75, and Richard Kuhn, *The Demon of Noontide: Ennui in Western Literature* (Princeton, N.J.: Princeton University Press, 1976).

288. Loneliness was an element of their alienation as securely as any other

factors, as has been noticed by John Sitter in his *Literary Loneliness in Mid-Eighteenth-Century England* (Ithaca and London: Cornell University Press, 1982).

289. For a very limited study in one hospital during the 1780s see G. B. Risse, "Hysteria at the Edinburgh Infirmary: The Construction and Treatment of a Disease, 1770–1800," *Medical History* 32 (1988): 1–22. Risse has suggested that the organic diagnosis rather than any remotely psychogenic etiology enhanced the bedside discourse shared between these Edinburgh professors and their pupils. Men were not taken in at Edinburgh, but they were in Paris and Vienna. Highborn and low, female and male: all were treated and eventually admitted without regard to gender.

290. *The Adventures of Tom Jones, a Foundling* (1749), Bk. XVI. Smollett, a physician-novelist who knew medical theory more intimately than Fielding, portrays many more hysterics, male as well as female, especially in his "psychiatric novel" *The Adventures of Sir Launcelot Greaves* (1762). Karl Miller believes that Greaves's "weakness of the nerves," the malady his quack doctor assigns, is a foreshadowing of modern, almost Beckettian, "nervousness," and "the more nervous people there are, the more we may need spitting images, a comedy of hurt." See his provocative chapter entitled "Andante Capriccioso," in his *Authors* (Oxford: Clarendon Press, 1989).

291. Bienville, *Nymphomania* (n. 74). Works had been written before 1775 on the behavior or activity we would now, anachronistically, call nymphomania, but Bienville was the first to write an entire treatise using the word and concept.

292. G. Miller, ed., *Letters of Edward Jenner* (Baltimore: Johns Hopkins University Press, 1983).

293. This fact surfaces repeatedly in the study of female maladies in Barbara Duden, *The Woman beneath the Skin: A Doctor's Patients in Eighteenth-Century Germany* (Cambridge, Mass.: Harvard University Press, 1991).

294. Those who think "hordes" is excessive to describe the proliferation of hysteria theory should consult the bibliographical evidence; see J. Sena, *A Bibliography of Melancholy* (London: Nether Press, 1970) and Rousseau, "Cultural History in a New Key" (n. 188), 76–81, which are themselves but the tip of the iceberg.

295. Richard Hunter and Ida Macalpine Hunter, *Three Hundred Years of Psychiatry* (n. 41); William Battie, *A Treatise on Madness* (London: Dawsons, 1962); William Perfect, *Cases of Insanity . . . Hypochondriacal Affection . . .* (London, 1781); William Pargeter, *Observations on Maniacal Disorders* (Reading, 1792; reprint, London: Routledge, 1989).

296. The classic works remain Klaus Doerner's *Madmen and the Bourgeoisie* (Oxford: Basil Blackworth, 1981; originally published in German in 1969), which appeared before Foucault's insightful *Birth of the Clinic: An Archaeology of Medical Perception* (New York: Vintage Books, 1973).

297. Cited above at the end of Section X.

298. For some of the evidence related to rank and class in Edinburgh see Risse, "Hysteria at the Edinburgh Infirmary" (n. 289).

299. And yet this opposition remains one of the most persistent contrasts in

the history of hysteria in the early modern period surveyed in this chapter; as I worked my way through the massive amounts of material available from over two centuries (1600–1800), I was struck to what massive degree the body-mind model kept reifying itself in the discourses of hysteria.

300. See Andrew Wilson, *Medical Researches: Being an inquiry into the nature and origin of hysterics in the female constitution, and into the distinction between that disease and hypochondriac or nervous disorders* (London: C. Nourse, 1776), and William Rowley, *A treatise on female, nervous, hysterical, hypochondriacial, bilious, convulsive disease; apoplexy & palsy with thoughts on madness & suicide, etc.* (London: C. Nourse, 1788).

301. The point about Cullen and taxonomy in medical theory has been well made by C. Lawrence, "Nervous System and Society" (n. 185). See also John Thomson, *An Account of the Life, Lectures and Writings of William Cullen,* 2 vols. (Edinburgh: William Blackwood & Sons, 1859).

302. See Alan Bewell, *Wordsworth and the Enlightenment: Nature, Man, and Society in the Experimental Poetry* (New Haven, Conn.: Yale University Press, 1989), 175.

303. K. Cave, ed., *The Diary of Joseph Farington,* 16 vols. (New Haven, Conn.: Yale University Press, 1982–   ), 10:3705.

304. *Traité des Affections Vaporeuses de deux sexes, ou Maladies Nerveuses vulgairement appelés de nerfs* (Paris: Imprimerie Royale, 1782).

305. W. Falconer, *A Dissertation on the Influence of the Passions upon Disorders of the Body* (London: C. Dilly, 1788).

306. London: Rivington, 1800.

307. Bath: R. Crutwell, 1800.

308. John Haslam, *Observations on Insanity* (London: Rivington, 1798), reissued in 1809 as *Observations on Madness & Melancholy: Including practical remarks on those diseases; together with cases: and an account of the morbid appearances of dissection*; idem, *Illustrations of Madness* (London: Routledge, 1810).

309. See n. 1 above. For madness from Renaissance to Enlightenment more generally, see *Anatomy of Madness,* ed. Bynum, Porter, and Shepherd.

310. See section XIII and n. 273.

311. It is not accidental, for example, that Battie's *Treatise on Madness* (1757) appeared only a few years after the appearance of Julien Offray de La Mettrie's seminal announcement of materialism; see his *Man a machine. Wherein the several systems of philosophers, in respect to the soul of man, are examined . . . Translated from the French of Mons, de La Mettrie* (London: G. Smith, 1750) and E. Callot, *La philosophie de la vie au XVIIIe siècle, étudiee chez Fontenelle, Montesquieu, Maupertuis, La Mettrie, Diderot, d'Holbach, Linné* (Paris: M. Rivière, 1965). Also, as a parallel here are the nonmedical writings of women of the period, who also retain mystery as an essence of the then modern secularized woman.

312. Pinel's versions of hysteria have not been studied in any detail, but see nn. 233 and 276.

313. The imitative aspect extends, of course, beyond the theory of hysteria. For different approaches to it, see Mark Johnson, *The Body in the Mind: The Bodily*

Basis of Meaning, Imagination, and Reason (Chicago: University of Chicago Press, 1987) and Barbara Stafford, *Body Criticism: Imaging the Unseen in Enlightenment Art and Medicine* (Cambridge, Mass.: MIT Press, 1991).

314. Italics mine; see Mary Jacobus, *Reading Woman: Essays in Feminist Criticism* (New York: Columbia University Press, 1986), 201; and Mary Jacobus, Evelyn Fox Keller, and Sally Shuttleworth, eds., *Body/Politics: Women in the Discourses of Science* (London: Routledge, 1990).

315. See n. 300 and for Cullen and neurosis, J. M. Lopez Piñero, *Historical Origins of the Concept of Neurosis* (Cambridge: Cambridge University Press, 1983). Echoes of Robert James's, *Medicinal Dictionary* (2 vols. [London, 1745]) article on "Hysteria" are found in Cullen's works.

316. A recent social critic has noted that the main reason twentieth-century homosexuals build up their muscles in gyms is their misogynist contempt of weak "inner spaces"—a materialist hypothesis at least.

317. There are fundamental ways in which the history of hysteria resembles that of gender and sex itself, and it is wrong to believe that hysteria resides in a class entirely apart from these. For the social construction of all of these see Peter Wright and Andrew Treacher Wright, eds., *The Problem of Medical Knowledge: Examining the Social Construction of Medicine* (Edinburgh: Edinburgh University Press, 1982); Cynthia Eagle Russett, *Sexual Science: The Victorian Construction of Womanhood* (Cambridge, Mass.: Harvard University Press, 1989); Celia Kitzinger, *The Social Construction of Lesbianism* (London: Sage Publications, 1987); David F. Greenberg, *The Construction of Homosexuality* (Chicago: University of Chicago Press, 1989); Thomas Laqueur, "Onanism, Sociability, and Imagination: Medicine and Fiction in the Eighteenth and Early Nineteenth Century," a talk delivered at the University of California, Berkeley, 1991.

318. R. B. Carter, *On the Pathology and Treatment of Hysteria* (London: John Churchill, 1853).

319. Veith, *Hysteria,* 221–228. For this view in another key see L. Chertok and R. de Sausurre Chertok, *The Therapeutic Revolution: From Mesmer to Freud* (New York: Brunner Mazel, 1979), but for sounder approaches to the Mesmeric phenomenon see V. Buranelli, *The Wizard from Vienna: Franz Mesmer and the Origins of Hypnotism* (London: Routledge, 1976); R. Darnton, *Mesmerism and the End of the Enlightenment in France* (Cambridge, Mass.: Harvard University Press, 1968).

320. For Mesmer's Newtonianism see R. Cooter, "The History of Mesmerism in England," in *Mesmer und die Geschichte des Mesmerismus,* ed. H. Schott (Stuttgart: Franz Steiner, 1985), 152–162.

321. Some have seen the evidence of these misogynistic outbursts in the debates about female reproductivity; see Pierre Darmon, *The Myth of Procreation in the Baroque Period* (London: Routledge, 1982); *Damning the Innocent: A History of Persecution in Pre-Revolutionary France* (New York: Viking Press, 1986).

322. I owe the phrase to David Morris; see D. Morris, "The Marquis of Sade and the Discourses of Pain: Literature and Medicine at the Revolution," in *The Languages of Psyche,* ed. Rousseau (n. 13), 291–331.

323. Roy Porter provides the scholarship, but see also G. Didi-Huberman, *Invention de l'Hysterie: Charcot et l'Iconographie Photographique* (Paris: Macula, 1982).

324. F. Kaplan, *Dickens and Mesmerism: The Hidden Springs of Fiction* (Princeton, N.J.: Princeton University Press, 1975).

PART II

Thematic

THREE

The Body and the Mind, The Doctor and the Patient

Negotiating Hysteria

Roy Porter

DISEASES

A central aim of medical history must surely be to chart the history of disease, for without that, we will never fully gain a sense of people's health, sufferings, morbidity profiles, life expectations, and expectations out of life.[1] Some historians go so far as to claim that pathogens have perhaps been the most potent agents of sociopolitical change at large.[2] And without proper understanding of microbes and toxins, it has been contended, the history of hysteria will be misread. For according to Mary Matossian, what contemporaries and scholars alike have identified as eruptions of mass hysteria—the late medieval witch craze, religious revivals, *la grande peur*—ought properly to be read as the symptoms of ergotism.[3]

Yet, as is shown by scholarly scepticism toward such claims, identifying past diseases presents daunting challenges. With all our semiotic skills and modern clinical expertise, are we able to decode the medical texts, eyewitness accounts, and mortality records of bygone centuries and alien cultures, and trace the natural histories of diseases?[4] Was the "ague" of early modern England truly malaria, or "quinsey" a streptococcal infection? On the basis of Thucydides' description of the so-called "great plague" of Athens, scholars have come up with dozens of disease labels (though such is the debris of discarded identifications, that only fools should rush in).[5]

The hazards of retrospective diagnosis teach a salutary scepticism. After all, as epidemiologists know, microorganisms themselves mutate, following unpredictable evolutionary biogeographies. Perhaps the Athenian plague, or the decimating "great sweat" of early-Tudor England, that mysterious disorder, were due to pathogens that came and went. And, in any case, our forebears may have reacted to this or that infection in ways foreign to modern symptomatologies—to the despair of the historical epidemiologist but the delight of the shameless relativist. The former expects disease to obey laws, regularly producing predictable effects; the latter may, by contrast, luxuriate in the heterogeneity of subjective experiences of affliction.[6] Medical historians must soldier on, using what evidence they can: skeletal remains, artifacts (paintings, photographs), and written testimony, though words may be false friends: what early moderns called "cholera" was certainly not the "Asiatic" cholera that swept Europe and North America in the nineteenth century, although its identity still baffles inquiry.[7]

So what of hysteria? Are historians to think of hysteria as a true disease, whose rise and fall can, in principle, be plotted down the centuries, so long as we exercise vigilance against anachronistic translation of archaic concepts? Or is it a veritable joker in the taxonomic pack, a promiscuous diagnostic fly-by-night, never faithfully wedded to an authentic malady—or worse, a wholly spurious entity, a fancy-free disease name, like Prester John, independent of any corresponding disease-thing, a cover-up for medical ignorance? Or, worse still, may hysteria truly have been the doctors' Waterloo: a real disorder, but, as Alan Krohn hints, one so "elusive" as to have slipped our nosological nets?[8]

For reasons clear to every reader of this book, "hysteria" inevitably induces doubts. Yet why shouldn't a history of hysteria be written? Not one expecting (in the manner of Professor Matossian) to unearth a microtoxin as *vera causa*, nor even one tracing progress from medical confusion to medical clarification. But a history of hysteria experiences, that is, of people labeled as hysterical, or identifying themselves as suffering from the condition, and embodying it in their behavior; one taking into account all the intricate negotiations, denials, and contestations bound to mediate such multifarious sickness presentations.[9]

Such a history could be written while judgment is suspended about hysteria's ontology. Scholars, after all, habitually trace the incidence of various fevers—low, spotted, and remitting—while remaining in the dark as to their etiology; "war fever" or "gold fever" are also discussed without obligation to specify the root cause of these drives. The embossing of hysteria—perhaps unlike spotted fever—with cultural meanings does not discredit such a project, but makes it all the more inviting.

We should expect not a single, unbroken narrative but scatters of occurrences: histories of hysterias, in fact. Yet the chronological epicenter is bound to be the nineteenth century. As Helen King has shown in chapter 1, antiquity and medieval Europe had no need of the hysteria concept.[10] And—so runs G. S. Rousseau's discussion in the previous chapter—though from Renaissance to Enlightenment physicians developed the hysteria diagnosis, it remained largely subordinate to discourses about melancholy and the nerves.

It was during the nineteenth century that hysteria moved center-stage. It became the explicit theme of scores of medical texts.[11] Its investigation and treatment made the fame and fortunes of towering medical figures—Charcot, Breuer, Janet, and Freud. Hysteria came to be seen as the open sesame to impenetrable riddles of existence: religious ecstasy, sexual deviation, and, above all, that mystery of mysteries, woman.

Moreover, people began to suffer from hysteria, or (what amounts to the same thing) to be said to suffer from hysteria, in substantial numbers. In novels[12] and newspapers, police reports and social surveys, the predicaments of mass society, crowd behavior, street life, and social pathology were endlessly anatomized in the idiom of hysteria.[13] And—often in compound forms, such as hystero-epilepsy—hysteria became traded as a common currency between the sick, their families, their medical attendants, and the culture at large: witness the repeated illness episodes undergone in the 1830s by Ada Lovelace, Byron's daughter (needless to say, the word carried deeply divergent nuances for Ada, her mother, her husband, and her flock of medical attendants).[14]

Hysteria's clientele broadened. One senses that, in the eighteenth century, the term still circulated in rather confined, indeed, refined, circles. That changed. As may be seen from Charcot's practice, hysteria became, at least by the *belle epoque,* established as a disorder of males as well as females,[15] of sensitive and silly alike: perhaps none was wholly immune. In his discussion in chapter 5, Sander Gilman documents the extension of "hysterical" to certain ethnic types, notably Semites.[16]

Furthermore, as Edward Shorter has emphasized, a multitude of nineteenth-century records—police, hospital, and Poor Law—testify that the terminology of hysteria shed most of its class exclusiveness. Shop girls, seamstresses, servants, street walkers, engine drivers, navvies, wives, mothers, and husbands too, were now eligible for depiction as hysterical alongside their betters, and not merely (as in Restoration comedy) as mimicry à la mode.[17] The coming of mass society evidently democratized the disorder.

Institutional evidence attests this. In the mid-nineteenth century, Robert Carter alluded to hysteria epidemics in workhouses as though such outbreaks were common.[18] Victorian asylum records show patients sectioned with hysteria written into their diagnosis or figuring in their case notes.[19] Establishments—hydros, spas, retreats, sanatoria, nursing homes—started catering to private patients suffering from hysteriform conditions.[20] Shorter has explored the procedures that filtered invalids of a certain class or income into superior institutions (with greater freedom and privileges), under choicer diagnostic verbiage. Considerable linguistic tact was requisite. Too psychiatric a diagnosis could suggest psychosis, or downright lunacy, with connotations unacceptable for the family. An overly physicalist term might come too near the bone by suggesting a tubercular condition or syphilis and its sequelae. Dexterity with diagnostic euphemisms was at a premium: this became the age of "neurasthenia."[21]

Finally, and to us, most famously, there was the string of clients climbing the stairs at Berggasse 19. If some were "hysterics" largely by virtue of being so designated by others, Freud's patients, it seems, mainly volunteered. Freud strenuously contested his patients' "denials," but none of them, not even Dora, seems to have denied that he or she was hysterical.[22]

One could thus trace the hysteria wave (or one might say craze, epidemic, or simply spread). Its cresting at that time seems perfectly amenable to explanation, without need to resort to crass reductionism (vulgar labeling or social control theory, or the medical dominance model). Cultures, groups, and individuals respond in different ways to life's pains and pressures; idioms of suffering and sickness can be more or less expressive; direct or indirect; emotional, verbal, or physical; articulated through inner feelings or outward gesture. Varied repertoires clearly register the tensions, prohibitions, and opportunities afforded by the culture (or subculture) at large, reacting to expectations of approval and disapproval, legitimation and shame, to prospects of primary penalty and secondary gain.[23]

Some societies legitimize psychological presentations of suffering, while others sanction somatic expression. Affluent New Yorkers are today allowed, even expected, to act out trauma psychologically. Mao's China, by contrast, apparently condemned such performances as lapses into inadmissible subjectivism and political deviancy. Hence "feeling bad" in the Republic had to be couched in terms of a physical debility or malfunction that escaped censure and solicited sympathy and relief.[24]

In this respect, the sickness culture of nineteenth-century Europe and North America seems to have borne some resemblance to modern China. In a fiercely competitive economic world, high performance was expected, with few safety nets for failures. There were intense pressures toward inculcating self-control, self-discipline, and outward conformity (bourgeois respectability). Personal responsibility, probity, and piety were, furthermore, internalized through strict moral training, imparted via hallowed socialization agencies like the family, neighborhood, school, and chapel. Guilt, shame, and disapproval were always nigh. In such stringent force fields, feelings of distress or resentment, anxiety or anger, were inevitable but difficult to manage; they were commonly "repressed" or rerouted into one of the rare forms of expression that were legitimate: the presentation of physical illness. Being sick afforded respite and release to those who needed temporarily or permanently to opt out.[25] And the system was skewed so that some took the strain more than others. Women were disproportionately burdened, being more isolated and incurring intenser expectations of moral and sexual rectitude; ladies often had time for reflection without outlets for their talents.[26]

Such concatenations of circumstances—high pressures, few safety valves—seem almost tailor-made for hysteria, viewed (as, of course, many nineteenth-century physicians themselves viewed it) as a disorder whereby nonspecific distress was given somatic contours.

Symptom choice involves complex learning and imitative processes. Picking up hysteria was aided by the fact that nineteenth-century public life put on view an abundance of physical peculiarities: gait disorders, paralyses, limps, palsies, and other comparable handicaps. Such conditions were the effects of birth defects and inherited diseases, of syphilis, lead and mercurial poisons at the workplace, of overdosing with unsafe drugs, industrial accidents, and high levels of alcoholism with consequent *delirium tremens*. The visibility of real biomedical neurological disorders enticed and authenticated those seeking a sickness stylistics for expressing inner pains.

Shorter has further argued, as have many feminist scholars, that a certain rhyme and reason may be discerned in the symptom selection.[27] The gastric disorders men widely "adopted" were compatible with continuing an active life, and hence with a certain model of masculinity. Being a hysterical woman, by contrast, meant exhibiting a battery of incapacitating symptoms emblematic of helplessness, enfeeblement, and (with lower limb paralyses) immobilization, acting out thereby, through sickness pantomime, the sufferer's actual social condition. Hysteria was thus mock escape by self-mutilation (a male analogue finally emerged in the First World War with shell shock).

We need detailed a history "from below" of rank-and-file nineteenth-century hysterics, and not just of such "immortals" as Blanche Wittmann, Léonie B., and Anna O. It would enhance our grasp of the elective affinities between disease and culture, confirming the adage that every society gets the disorders it deserves. Alongside epidemiology, medical history needs to study the history of illness, that is, of sufferers' conditions, regardless of science's judgment upon their authenticity. Aside from metaphysical questions (is hysteria a real disease?), it is clear that our great grandparents suffered from hysteria, no less than Elizabethans underwent the "sweat" or we succumb to "depression," "stress," or low-back pain; it is the job of historians to explain how and why.[28]

This grass-roots history of hysterics, this social history of symptoms, should be high on the agenda. But it is not what the remainder of this chapter tackles. Instead, I shall explore the medical profession's attempts to resolve the hysteria mystery, a disorder enigmatic because it hovered elusively between the organic and the psychological, or (transvaluating that ambivalence) because it muddled the medical and the moral, or (put yet another way) because it was ever discrediting its own credentials (were sufferers sick or shamming?). In this, I have in mind several larger goals. I want to explore the opportunities hysteria offered, and the puzzles it posed, for the medical profession: was it to be their finest hour or their Waterloo? I shall probe how differential readings of hysteria suited diverse sectors of a profession increasingly specialized and divided. Not least, I wish to gauge hysteria's symbolic replay (parody even) of the interactions between doctors and patients, suggesting how, in psychoanalysis, it launched a wildly new and deeply aberrant script of doctor-patient interplay.

HYSTERIA/MYSTERIA

Nineteenth-century doctors habitually represented hysteria as a challenge, a tough nut to crack. Chameleonlike in its manifestations, and often aggravated by their ministrations, it did not fight by the Queensbury Rules.

Medicine's flounderings suggest that hysteria proved something "other," the one that got away. Consensus never crystallized as to its nature and cause. In recent years, it has waltzed in and out of the *Diagnostic and Statistical Manual,* the English-speaking world's authoritative psychiatric handbook. Disgruntled doctors have often proposed conceptual slum clearance and a fresh terminological start: Josef Babinski wanted to rename it "psychasthenia" or "pithiatism," Janet suggested "psychasthenia," and certain contemporary physicians prefer "Briquet's syndrome,"[29] all in the, surely vain, hope that old confusions were but word deep. As the shrewd reassessments of Alec Roy, Harold Merskey, Alan

Krohn, and others have made clear, medicine today remains deeply divided as to whether hysteria is a skeleton in the cupboard or a ghost in the machine; a phantom like "the spleen," or a bona fide disorder. And if authentic, is it organic or mental? A disease that has largely died out or been cured, or one camouflaging itself in colors ever new?[30]

Such battles long since spilled over time's border into the terrain of history. A cast of heroes and villains from the past has been recruited to play key roles. Indeed, as Helen King established earlier in this volume, when Renaissance doctors first needed to develop the hysteria concept, high priority was given to manufacturing a pedigree going all the way back to Hippocrates.[31] Physicians have also turned to the past to exercise their skills in retrospective diagnosis: preferred readings of hysteria will, it is assumed, be vindicated if they lead to the identification of former outbreaks. After all (so argued nineteenth-century biomedics), what is medical science if not an engine for discovering nature's universal laws, operating uniformly through time and space, in the past, present, and future? Thus Charcot declared in ringing tones that "L'Hystérie a toujours existé, en tous lieux et en tous temps."[32] In *Les Demoniaques dans l'art* (1887), jointly written with his colleague Antoine Richer, he contended that what benighted ages had mistaken for mystics and demoniacs were archetypically hysterics. By thus exposing the hysteria so long hidden from history, Charcot strengthened his claim to be, in the there-and-then as well as the here-and-now, the all-conquering "Napoleon of the neuroses." Further medical demystification of religious enthusiasm by D.-M. Bourneville and other intimates of the *charcoterie* helped mobilize the radical, anticlerical medical politics of the Third Republic.[33]

Psychiatrists such as Gregory Zilboorg subsequently developed these retrospective diagnoses of early modern demoniacs as sick people possessed, not by the devil, but by disease, as people fit, not for the flames, but for the couch. In propagating such views, analysts from Freud to present psychohistorians have presented themselves as pioneers of therapeutic methods and historical readings both enlightened and scientific.[34]

HISTORIOGRAPHY

And historians of hysteria have characteristically followed in their footsteps: it was no accident that the first substantial chronicles of hysteria were written by Charcotian protégés.[35] Such works have assumed that the annals of medical history, down the centuries and across the cultures, point to outcrops of a disorder now identifiable as hysteria, and that the medical mission of understanding, classifying, and treating it can be recounted as a progression from superstition to science, ignorance to expertise, prejudice to psychoanalysis. The standard English-language history, Ilza Veith's *Hysteria: The History of a Disease* (1965), is wholly cast within this mold.[36]

As her title indicates, Veith's premise is that hysteria is an objective disease, the same the whole world over. It had been known to doctors—East and West—at least from 1800 B.C., Veith contended, though it was the Greeks who had given it its name. Medieval Christendom's gestalt switch, treating psychosomatic symptoms as the stigmata of Satan, had entailed a gigantic regression.[37] Fortunately, far-sighted Renaissance physicians such as Johannes Weyer had recaptured hysteria from the theologians, seeing it as a disease, not a sin.

Even so, true understanding (and treatment) continued to be hamstrung by a fallacious medical materialism misconstruing hysteria as organic—standardly, an abnormality of the womb, or, in later centuries, of the nervous system and brain stem. Veith particularly deplored the "increasingly sterile and repetitive neurological basis that had emanated from Great Britain for nearly two hundred years," sparked, above all, by George Cheyne's "nervous" theory, whose "affectation and absurdities are such that it scarcely merits elaborate discussion"—even the Scottish iatromechanist's "references to his own distress," Veith uncharitably grumbled, "seem inconsequential."[38] Not least, she argued, somatic hypotheses had been marred by misogyny. Overall, such ideas were precisely the obstacles that, in Freud's view, had "so long stood in the way of [hysteria] being recognized as a psychical disorder."[39]

Fortunately, according to Veith, a counterinterpretation had emerged, albeit by fits and starts. Brave spirits such as Paracelsus, Edward Jorden, Thomas Sydenham, Franz Anton Mesmer, Philippe Pinel, Ernst von Feuchtersleben, and Robert Carter began to develop "an amazing amount of anticipation" of the insight—finally triumphant with Freud—that hysteria was psychogenic, the monster child of emotional trauma aggravated by bourgeois sexual repression, especially of females.[40] Thanks principally to Freud, this libidinal straitjacket had finally been flung off, leading to the disorder's demise in the present century: Veith's narration concluded with Freud.

It says something for the vitality of medical history that, twenty-five years later, Veith's recension appears hopelessly outdated. For one thing, hers was heroes-and-villains history, being particularly free with bouquets for those who "anticipated" Freud's psychosexual theory. Among these,

the mid-Victorian practitioner Robert Carter received her most ful-
some floral tributes, for having effected "a greater stride forward" than
"all the advances made since the beginning of its history."[41] This rosy
interpretation of Carter grates, however, upon a modern generation
primed on antipsychiatry and feminism. After all, it was precisely his
judgment that hysteria was psychogenic that enabled Carter to indict
hysterical women as not sick but swindlers, sunk in "moral obliquity,"
cynically exploiting the sick role to manipulate their families and getting
perverse sexual kicks out of the repeated vaginal examinations they demanded. Carter, however, saw through their tricks and advocated sub-
jecting them to ordeal by psychiatric exposure.[42] With Dora's case in
mind, we might wryly agree with Veith that Carter did indeed "antici-
pate" Freud, but such a compliment would, of course, be backhanded,
underlining that Freud too could be a misogynistic victim blamer and
therapeutic bully. Faced with the deviousness of hysterics, Freud con-
fided to Wilhelm Fliess his sympathy for the "harsh therapy of the
witches' judges."[43]

More generally, Veith's "history of a disease"—indeed, of a "mental
disease"[44]—conceived as a joust between benighted (somatic) theorists,
who "retarded" comprehension, and their forward-looking psychological rivals, suffers from the stock shortcomings of wise-after-the-event
Whiggism.[45] Past theorists are graded by the yardstick of Freud, whose
theory is taken as the last word. With hindsight derived from the psychodynamic revolution, Veith organizes her history of hysteria around
an essential tension between (wrong) somatogenic and (valid) psychogenic claims.

A radically different reading is offered by Thomas Szasz. For Szasz,
hysteria is not a real disease, whose nature has been progressively
cracked, but a myth forged by psychiatry for its own greater glory.
Freud did not discover its secret; he manufactured its mythology.[46]
Drawing upon varied intellectual traditions—logical positivism, Talcot
Parsons's theory of the sick role, ethnomethodology, and the sociology
of medical dominance—Szasz has made prominent, in his *The Myth of
Mental Illness*,[47] psychoanalysis's "conversion" of hysteria into a primary
psychogenic "mental illness" marked by somatic conversion, the translation, as William R. D. Fairbairn put it, of a "personal problem" into a
"bodily state."[48] "I was inclined," reflected Freud, "to look for a *psychical*
origin for all symptoms in cases of hysteria."[49]

Exposing this as a strategy integral to a self-serving "manufacture of
madness," Szasz counters with a corrosive philosophical critique. By thus
privileging the psyche, Freud was in effect breathing new life into the

obsolete Cartesian dualism, resurrecting the old ghost in the machine, or rather, in the guise of the Unconscious, inventing the ghost in a ghost.[50] For Szasz, on the other hand, the expectation of finding the etiology of hysteria in body or mind, above all in some mental underworld, must be a lost cause, a dead end, a linguistic error, and an exercise in bad faith. For the "unconscious" is not a place or an organ but, at most, a metaphor; Freud stands arraigned of rather naively pictorializing the psyche in hydraulic and electrical terms, of reifying the fictive substance behind the substantive.[51]

Properly speaking, contends Szasz, hysteria is not a disease with origins to be excavated, but a behavior with meanings to be decoded. Social existence is a rule-governed game-playing ritual. The hysteric bends the rules and exploits their loopholes. Not illness but idiom (gestural more than verbal), hysteria pertains not to a Cartesian ontology but to a semiotics, being communication by *complaints*. Since the hysteric is engaged in social performances that follow certain expectations so as to defy others, the pertinent questions are not about the origins, but the conventions, of hysteria.[52]

Sidestepping mind/body dualisms, Szasz thus recasts hysteria as social performance, presenting problems of conduct, communication, and context. Freud believed mind/body dichotomies were real, though typically mystified, and attempted to crack them. Szasz dismisses these as *questions mal posées,* deriving (like Freud's "discovery" of the unconscious) from linguistic reification or bad faith, and he aims to reformulate them.

If idiosyncratic, Szasz's analysis is also a child of its time. Modern linguistic philosophy, behaviorism, and poststructuralism all depreciate the etiological quest: origins, authors, and intentions are discounted, systems, conventions, and meanings forefronted. Szasz does not, of course, expect that his paradigm-switch will magically switch off all the uncontrollable sobbing, fits, tantrums, and paralyses. But it offers alternative readings of such acts, while undermining expectations that tracking hysteria will lead to the source of the Nile, that is, the solution of the riddle of mind and body.[53]

Szasz's resolution of hysteria is bracing, but it is achieved at the cost of reducing its past to pantomime: his adoption of the language of game-playing turns everyone, sufferers and medics alike, into manipulative egoists. Illness is just a counter in a contest. So why embrace this dismissive, belittling view? It is because Szasz is at bottom an old-school medical materialist: disease is really disease only if it is organic.[54] Were hysteria—were *any* so-called mental illness—somatically based, it would have a real history (afflicting people, being investigated by physicians). Lacking organic "papers," its past, rather like those of transubstantiation or of perpetual-motion engines, is a blot, a disgrace, a fiction, a tale of knaves and fools worthy of some philosophe's pen. Thus, for equal but opposite reasons, Veith and Szasz both short-circuit hysteria's history. Veith (oddly like Charcot) feels obliged to trace it from the pharoahs to Freud; Szasz thinks the history of hysteria *begins* with Freud's psychodynamic empire building. Believing *hysteria* psychogenic, Veith recounts her "history of a disease" as the road to Freud. Believing *disease* must be somatic, Szasz paints hysteria's history as the pageant of a dream. Both approaches trivialize the intricate texture of hysteria down the ages, the true understanding of which must respect, not explain away, the enigmas of multifaceted, evanescent pain in a culture within which mind/body relations have been supercharged and devilishly problematic.

Yet Veith's and Szasz's polarized readings are, in their own way, highly exemplary, for they both highlight mind/body disputes in hysteria's etiology. Down the centuries, physicians long lamented how hysteria remained sphinxlike, *because* mind/body relations themselves proved a conundrum. Veith's desire to divide her protagonists into ("retarding") materialist and ("progressive") psychological camps is, however, misguided, for it freezes the rhetoric of the Freudian era and anachronistically backprojects it. Yet Szasz's mythic history, subserving his own debunking and liberating polemic, also cuts corners, above all by seemingly denying any significant developments before Freud. Many recent historians, especially Mark Micale,[55] have, by contrast, insisted on the enormous intricacy and indeterminacy of the story of hysteria. Above all, as will be explored below, it would be simplistic to imply that early theories were exclusively either somatogenic or psychogenic; most commonly they were attempts to dissect and plot the puzzling entente between the passions of the mind and the constitution of the body. Our story is thus not a matter of either/or but of both/and. And it is, above all, a history in which the very notions of mind and body, and the boundaries and bridges between them, were constantly being challenged and reconstituted.

Hence this chapter will focus on medical theorizings of mind/body pathologies. It will thus engage the metaphysics of hysteria, examining the theoretical underpinnings that made possible a succession of puzzles, problems, and solutions. The story of hysteria (I will argue) makes scant sense if restricted to internal, technical skirmishings over nerves and neurons, passions and pathogens. Far more was at stake, not least because, as Szasz has insisted, hysteria became an exemplary disease, the disorder that single-handedly launched psychoanalysis.

Small wonder this wider history is requisite, for the biomedical doctrines of body and brain, psyche and soma, have never been neutral post-mortem findings, hermetically sealed from the symbolic meanings accreting around sickness in daily experience, meanings of utmost significance for doctrines of human nature, gender relations, moral autonomy, legal responsibility, and the dignity of man.[56] Medicine's authority, its prized scientificity, may have rested upon its vaunted monopoly of expertise over the human organism, but its public appeal has equally hung upon its ability to attune its terms and tones to the popular ear. The historian of hysteria must, in short, bear in mind the wider determinants: changing ideas of man, morality and culture, and the politics of medicine in society.

MIND AND BODY: MEDICAL
MATERIALISM AND HEGEMONIC IDEALISM

I wish to explore a further dichotomy—Charcot's historical metaphysics juxtaposed against Freud's—to show its exemplary status for understanding the mind/body politics of hysteria.

To secure their credentials, many nineteenth-century medics proclaimed a powerful metahistory: Auguste Comte's scheme of the rise of thought, from the theological, via the metaphysical, up to the scientific plane.[57] As embraced by positivists, par excellence those in Charcot's circle, such a progressive schema implied that sickness had, at the dawn of civilization, been misattributed to otherworldly agencies (spirit possession, necromancy, etc.), subsequently being mystified into formulaic verbiage (humors, animal spirits, complexions) dissembling as explanations. Growing out of such mumbo jumbo, physicians had finally learned to ground their art in the nuts-and-bolts real-world of anatomy, physiology, and neurology.[58] Through abandoning myths for measurement, words for things, metaphysics for metabolism, medicine had at long last grasped the laws of nature, which would prove the prelude to effective therapeutics. According to Charcot (as will further be explored below), hysteria would be solved by pursuing the science of the body.

Freud, however, though Charcot's sometime student, cuts across the grain of this explanatory strategy—indeed, presents a case of ontogeny reversing phylogeny. The young Freud had been inducted into the Germanic school of neurophysiology, whose creed (paralleling the positivist) espoused the triple alliance of scientific method, medical materialism, and intellectual progress: explanations of the living had to be somatically grounded or they weren't science. Though initially endorsing this neurological idiom, Freud, in his own theorizings of neuroses and hysteria, eventually adopted a thoroughgoing psychodynamic stance, eventually formulating a battery of mentalist neologisms—the unconscious, ego, id, super ego, death wish, and so on—which logical positivists have ever since derided as throwbacks to Comte's "metaphysical" stage.[59] In tandem, Freud's therapeutics moved from drugs (e.g., cocaine), through hands-on, pressure-point hypnosis, to the purely psychical (free speech associations).[60] Freud, some would say, was a kind of mental recidivist.

In thus privileging the mind as *primum mobile,* Freud challenged biomedicine's bottom line—and regarded himself as victimized for his pains, while energetically milking his self-image as a persecuted heretic.[61] Yet, by so doing, he has won a standing ovation from twentieth-century high culture, predisposed to believe that explanations of human behavior predicated upon the workings of the *mind,* however dark and devious, must be more profound, humane, insightful, true, and titillating even, than any formulated in biochemical or genetic categories.[62] As we have seen, Veith herself assumed that once Freud finally discovered hysteria to be *psychogenic,* the curtain could be brought down to rapturous applause. Psychoanalysis's "discovery of the unconscious,"[63] unlocking the secrets of human desires, both normal and pathological, remains one of the foundation myths of modernity.

In addressing the rival paradigms of fin de siècle hysteria, we thus find a cross fire—the one scientific, ratifying positivist laws of the organism; the other convinced that meaningful explanations of action must derive from an ontology of the psyche. This is an instructive dichotomy (biologism/mentalism), reproducing in a nutshell two clashing configurations of Western thought.

On the one hand, psychoanalysis's mentalism is underpinned by the pervasive and prestigious Idealism, philosophized by Platonism and the Cartesian *cogito,* long underwritten by Christian theology, and, in secular garb, still the informal metaphysical foundations of the humanities in C. P. Snow's "two cultures" dichotomy. Such hierarchical, dualistic models programmatically set mind over matter, thinking over being, nurture over nature, head over hand, as higher over lower, the mental being ontologically superior to the corporeal. Macrocosmically, brute matter was subordinate to the Divine Mind or Idea, acting through immaterial agencies; likewise, microcosmically, the achievement of *mens sana in corpore sano* required that mind, will, or spirit must command base flesh— and, as Theodor Adorno, Norbert Elias, Foucault, and others have argued, the civilizing process, that celebrated march of mind demanded by capitalism, long entailed the intensification of body-disciplining techniques.[64] Within this view, sickness is regarded (like crime, vice, or sin) as the aftermath of reason losing control, either because the metabolism itself has been highjacked (for instance, in the delirium of fever), or when civil war erupts within the mind itself, leading to the "mind forg'd manacles" of mental illness.[65]

Freud torpedoed theology, wrestled with philosophy, but loved science. His views of the drives and the unconscious naturally could not countenance the Christian-Platonic divine-right monarchy of Pure Reason: it is, after all, the mission of psychoanalysis to debunk such illusions (purity indeed!) as projections, sublimations, and mystifications.[66] Nor could he accept at face value the doctrinaire distinctions between freedom and necessity, virtue and appetite, love and libido, and so on postulated by philosophical Idealism. These—like so many other values—were not eternal verities, gifts from the gods, but problematic, sublimated, even morbid, constructs ("defences"). Nevertheless, the thrust of Freudian psychodynamics—his point of departure from Wilhelm Brücke, Charcot, and Fliess, and then from some of his own *epigoni* such as Wilhelm Reich—lay in denying the sufficiency of biology or heredity to explain complexities of behavior, healthy or morbid. In the case of complexes, the body becomes the battleground for struggles masterminded elsewhere.[67]

Freud was deeply torn. Clinical experience led to his giving sovereignty to the psyche. Yet herein lay a profound irony, for he was also, as Peter Gay has aptly emphasized, a child of the old Enlightenment itch to smash Idealism, unveiling it as the secret agent of false consciousness, repression, and priestcraft.[68] He was, moreover, heir, by training and temper, to the crusading medical materialism and biophysics of his youthful heroes—Hermann Helmholtz, Theodor Meynert, and his mentor, Brücke, not to mention Charcot himself. For such luminaries, as for the Freud of the abandoned 1895 Project, doing science meant translating behavior into biology, consciousness into neurology, random experience into objective laws. And in pursuing such positivist approaches, nineteenth-century bioscientists were, as Lain Entralgo has stressed, further endorsing the disposition, from the Greeks onward, in what was significantly titled "physick," to enshrine the body as the ultimate "reality principle."[69]

The body provides sufficient explanation of its own behavior. Diseases are in and of the organism. They are caused by some fluid imbalance, physical lesion, internal dislocation, "seed" (or foreign body), excess, deficiency, or blockage; material therapeutics—drugs and surgery—will relieve or cure. Abandon such home truths, such professional articles of faith, and the autonomy and jurisdiction of biomedical science and clinical practice melt like May mist. Once it were admitted that sickness could not be sufficiently explained in and through the body—unless it could be said, at some level, "in the beginning, was the body"—medicine would forfeit its title as a master discipline, grounded upon prized clinicoscientific expertise. Unless sickness is translatable into the lingo of lesions and laws, why should not anyone—priests, philosophers, charlatans, sufferers—treat it as well as a doctor? Herein lies the explanation of why scientific medicine committed itself, from the Renaissance, to evermore minute anatomical and physiological investigations, even though the therapeutic payoffs long remained unconvincing.

Yet this strategy for ratifying professional credentials through a science of the body naturally ran the risk of counterproductivity. For, in a culture-at-large in which Idealism was hegemonic, medicine thereby exposed itself to the charge that its incomparable organic expertise was purchased at the price of higher dignity: a liability perfectly summed up in Coleridge's damnation of the doctors for their debasing somatism: "They are *shallow* animals," judged the ardent Platonist, "having always employed their minds about Body and Gut, they imagine that in the whole system of things there is nothing but Gut and Body."[70]

The program widely, if tacitly, adopted by medicine since the scientific revolution of locating disease explanations within the body seemed unexceptionable when addressing conspicuous conditions—tumors or dropsy, for instance—involving physical abnormalities. It has proved more problematic, however, where pain flares seemingly independently of manifest external lesions: even today medicine is embarrassed when faced with common complaints such as nervous exhaustion, stress, or addiction. And medicine's claims encounter special strain in cases where disturbances are sporadic and seemingly irrational. It is in these borderland areas, the fields of so-called functional and nervous disorders where sickness experience wants secure somatic anchorage, that medical credit is least convincing. If suffering lacks lesions and localizations, why should it be medicine's province at all? After all, leading critics from within the profession, notably Thomas Szasz, have invoked medicine's cherished criteria (logical positivism and methodological materialism) to contend that, since physick's kingdom is the body, and medicine is thus definitionally organic (else it is a chimera), the very idea of primary mental illness should be struck off the register as a category error, a misleading metaphor—or, worse, a pious fraud, smacking of professional bad faith.[71] Medicine has jurisdiction over the somatic, but who authorized its writ to run one step beyond? As G. S. Rousseau's essay has shown, physicians long ago hoisted their flag over hysteria; but the terra incognita has ever proved remarkably resistant to assured colonization.

Thus ours has been a civilization in which, in an ideological shadow play of the sociopolitical order, hegemonic Idealism has traditionally enthroned mind over what theology denigrated as the "flesh," forever too, too solid and sullied.[72] At the same time, medicine, by embracing (proto)-positivist notions of science and professional territorial imperatives, has espoused a praxis affording it control over the organic. Superficially it might seem that these two drives—enshrining spirit, yet making matter the foundation stone of science—are radically incommensurable. Yet doctors live in the world and medicine needs to be credit-worthy; or, in other words, accommodations have ever been reached, or ensure that cultural idealism and medical materialism work in broad harmony, rather than on a collision course.[73]

Medicine, philosophy, and theology developed thought-packages designed to demarcate the domains and specify the pathways of mind and matter. Thus, so ran long-standing prescriptions, the rules of health required that mind must be in the saddle, enacting the precepts of philosophers and preachers. Whenever the reign of reason is challenged, when brute flesh mutinies, the resultant state is sickness, and then the mentor makes way for the doctor. In any case, and giving the lie to Coleridge's slur, physicians themselves, time out of mind, have prescribed liberal doses of willpower as the recipe for "whole person" well-being: be healthy-minded, think positive, exercise self-control. As Michael Clark has brilliantly shown, late Victorian doctors characterized the sound, responsible person as one who tempered the will and disciplined the body, channeling the energies, like a true Aristotelian, into healthy public activity. By contrast, the hypochondriac or degenerate was trapped in morbid introspection, prisoner, in Henry Maudsley's graphic phrase, of the "tyranny of organization."[74]

So cultural Idealism and medical materialism, though perhaps worlds apart, have rarely been daggers drawn. Each assigned roles to the other within its own play. Even medical materialists such as Julien de La Mettrie recognized that, taken to extremes, to reduce man to nothing but *l'homme machine* would be self-disconfirming, while no less an idealist than Bishop George Berkeley did not hesitate to tout tar-water as a panacea.[75] Thus cultural Platonism and medical materialism are best regarded as uncomfortable matrimonial partners, who have engaged in partial cooperation to frame images of the constitution of man, the dance of soma and psyche, the triangle of sanity, salubrity, and sickness, and, not least, of the politics of the moral/physical interface.[76]

For doctors have to operate in the public domain, jostling with rivals in expertise and authority, and their services ultimately have to please paying patients. So medicine cannot afford to bury itself in sprains and pains but must engage with wider issues—religious, ethical, social, and cultural. The public wants from doctors explanations no less than medications; society looks to the profession for exhortation and excuses. Medicine is called upon to supply stories about the nature of man and the order of things. Moreover, because medicine has never enjoyed monopoly—nor has it been monolithic; it has been divided within itself—it has developed multiple strategies for securing its place in the sun.

It would, in fine, be myopic to treat medicine as a limited technical enterprise. This is especially so when we are faced with interpreting the peculiarities of hysteria, a disorder that, as indicated, dramatically rose and fell between the Renaissance and the First World War, a trajectory indubitably linked to larger cultural determinants affecting patients and practitioners alike.

Hysteria presented doctors with a tease, a trial, and a break. The hysteria diagnosis, critics griped, was the most egregious medical hocuspocus, attached to symptom clusters physicians could not impute to some more regular cause. The symptoms were heterogeneous, bizarre, and unpredictable: pains in the genitals and abdomen, shooting top to toe, or rising into the thorax and producing constrictions around the throat (*globus hystericus*); breathing irregularities; twitchings, tics, and spasms; mounting anxiety and emotional outbursts, breathlessness, and floods of tears; more acute seizures, paralyses, convulsions, hemiplagias, or catalepsy—any or all of which might ring the changes in dizzying succession and often with no obvious organic source. Faced with such symptoms, what was to be done? The mystery condition (spake the cynics) was wrapped up as "hysteria." Such, according to the mid-seventeenth-century neurologist Thomas Willis, was the physicians' fig leaf worn to hide their cognitive shame:

> [W]hen at any time a sickness happens in a Woman's Body, of an unusual manner, or more occult original, so that its causes lie hid, and a Curatory indication is altogether uncertain, . . . we declare it to be something hysterical . . . which oftentimes is only the subterfuge of ignorance.[77]

Evidently, things did not improve. A full century later, William Buchan still felt obliged to dub hysteria the "reproach of medicine," since the "physician . . . is at a loss to account for the symptom."[78] Was hysteria then just a will-o'-the-wisp, a fabulous beast or phantom? Or was it an authentic malady, whose essence lay in having no essence, being prodigiously protean, the masquerading malady, mimicking all others?[79] And if hysteria were such a desperado, was it truly not a disease at all, but some kind of Frankenstein's monster, a brain-child of the medical imagination finally turned upon its own creators?

In the light of these grander issues—the problems of medicine's continued attempt to confirm its place within the wider culture, the mind/body ambivalence of hysteria, the brevity of hysteria's heyday, and the construal of hysteria as an anomalous monster disease—it can hardly be illuminating to write, as did Veith, about the "history of a disease" in the same manner that one might sensibly survey smallpox and its medical eradication. It would be doubly misleading to imply that medical advances successively laid bare the true roles played in the etiology of hysteria by mind and body; for, as just suggested, mind and body are not themselves cast-iron categories, but best seen as representations negotiated between culture, medicine, and society.[80] Hence, in the remainder of this chapter, I shall explore some different meanings successively assumed by hysteria, in a world in which medicine was battling to extend its sway.

My account will emphasize the initiatives of medicine. Not because I believe that doctors had unique special insight into the condition,[81] or, contrariwise, that hysteria was cynically manufactured by a malign medical mafia. I do so, rather, believing that, like invisible ink when heat is applied, hysteria was a condition chiefly rendered visible by the medical presence. Without the calling of medical witnesses to witch trials, early modern physicians would rarely have pronounced upon these bizarre behaviors. Without the leisured sufferer whose purse spelled good times for private practice, Enlightenment physicians would not have had a tale to tell of nervousness. Without confinement in the Salpêtrière hospital in the proximity of epileptics, and, above all, without the electric atmosphere of Charcot's clinic, Blanche Wittmann and other stars of hysteria would have wasted their swoonings on the desert air.[82] Robert Carter, who was cynical about those "actresses," reflected that nature knew no such being as a solitary hysteric: hysteria was a public complaint presupposing an audience—mass hysteria definitionally so.[83] Was hysteria, then, purely iatrogenic, or, at least, as Eliot Slater would put it, "a disorder of the doctor-patient relationship"?[84] Maybe, though it would be more judicious to say that the nineteenth century was hysteria's golden age precisely because it was then that the moral presence of the doctor became normative as never before in regulating intimate lives.

CONTINUITIES: TOWARD
NINETEENTH-CENTURY NERVOUSNESS

As Rousseau showed in the previous chapter, Enlightenment sensibilities were confronted with actions and sufferings not easily compatible with vaunted paradigms of conduct or classifications of disease. The appearance of such alienation and irrationality has commonly been blamed, by modern countercultural critics, upon the dualistic doctrine of man proclaimed by the new philosophy, above all the Cartesian severed head and divided self, derived from the absolute rule of the *cogito* in the age of reason.[85] It is possible to take a view more sympathetic to eighteenth-century structures of feeling. The new availability of a plurality of models of living (Christian, civic humanist, individualist, scientific, and so forth) perhaps afforded welcome psychological Lebensraum to those—for instance, members of the newly emergent intelligentsia—who did not fit easily into rigid prescriptions. Dualistic models and multiple prototypes allowed a certain indeterminacy, or psychological *je ne sais quoi*, to be built into the makeup of modern man, allowing the accommodation of eccentricity and difference.[86]

Such margins of tolerance were sorely needed. For, as the Enlightenment era relaxed religious requirements, it was also applying intenser personal strains. Its exhausting commitment to the life of intelligence, its demand for politeness, and its relentless pressures for self-awareness and -realization, spelled more stressful standards of behavior, and hence highlighted their obverse: abnormality. In the rarefied atmospheres of sophisticated courtliness and brilliant urbanity, the body was required to be disciplined and drilled, yet also displayed. Inner sensibilities had to find expression at the tea table or in the salon through refined, subtle, and often veiled codes of etiquette, revealing but concealing through actions compelled to speak louder than words. The lingua franca for negotiating such repression-expression tensions lay in nervousness, a body language ultra flexible, nuanced, and ambivalent, yet brittle and fitful.

For life lived through the idioms of nervous sensibility carried high risks. Want of *nerve* betrayed effeminacy; want of *nerves*, by contrast, exposed plebeian dullness; yet volatile excitability could be too much of a good thing, a lapse of tact, culminating in hysterical crises. A golden mean—poised decorum spiced with idiosyncratic difference—was the goal. Achievement of this hazardous role adjustment, this accommodation between the hypervisible narcissistic individual and a society demanding Chesterfieldian conformism, was perhaps facilitated by precisely that divided Cartesian self so often berated by modern critics. Such a dualism—the man-behind-the-mask playing out the ontology of the ghost in the machine—allowed a certain distance, a disowning, a usable tension between self and body. Diderot, Sterne, Casanova, and Rousseau all demonstrated, through their lives and writings, the rich potential for dramatic self-expression afforded to the "new person" by the novel polysemic idioms of impulse, feeling, imagination, nerves, and, ultimately, hysteria.[87]

Enlightenment thinkers professed bafflement at the Sphinxian riddles of psyche/soma affinities. "The action of the mind on the body, and of the body on the mind," noted a leading authority on madness, "after all that has been written, is as little understood, as it is universally felt."[88] This ontological equivocation, this suspension of judgment, surely enhanced that respect with which the post-Sydenham hysteric was treated in a private practice milieu in which, as Nicholas Jewson has stressed, some rough-and-ready parity governed patient/practitioner relationships.[89] Thus, that great clinician, William Heberden, a man utterly *au fait* with the symptoms, saw hysteria as a condition all too readily provoked by the "slightest affection of the sense or fancy, beginning with some uneasiness of the stomach or bowels." "Hypochondriac men and hysteric women" suffered acidities, wind, and choking, leading to "giddiness, confusion, stupidity, inattention, forgetfulness, and irresolution," all proof that the "animal functions are no longer under proper command."[90] But, a man of his time, he was loath to dogmatize as to the root cause. For,

> our great ignorance of the connexion and sympathies of body and mind, and also of the animal powers, which are exerted in a manner not to be explained by the common laws of inanimate matter, makes a great difficulty in the history of all distempers, and particularly of this. For hypochondriac and hysteric complaints seem to belong wholly to these unknown parts of the human composition.[91]

Like most contemporary clinicians, Heberden was prepared to live with the mystery visitor. "I would by no means be understood, by any thing which I have said, to represent the sufferings of hypochondriac and hysteric patients as imaginary; for I doubt not their arising from as real a cause as any other distemper."[92]

In other words, the historical sociology of Enlightenment hysteria is defined by the clinical encounter between the sensitive patient and the sympathetic physician. The ambience was elitist, and it was, in principle at least, unisex. Ridiculing uterine theories of hysteria as anatomical moonshine, Richard Blackmore had concluded that "the Symptoms that disturb the Operations of the Mind and Imagination in Hysterick Women"—and by these symptoms he meant "Fluctuations of Judgment, and swift Turns in forming and reversing of Opinions and Resolutions, Inconstancy, Timidity, Absence of Mind, want of self-determining power, Inattention, Incogitancy, Diffidence, Suspicion, and an Aptness to take well-meant Things amiss"—these, he insisted, "are the same with those in Hypochondriacal Men."[93] How could an age nailing its colors to the mast of universal reason, a culture whose moral vocabulary turned upon sense and sensibility, define hysteria as the malaise of the mucous membrane?

This clinical rapport forged in the century after Sydenham between fashionable doctor and his moneyed patients did not cease in 1800: far from it. Nineteenth-century medicine presents a Frithian panorama of well-to-do, time-to-kill, twitchy types of both sexes being diagnosed as hysterical, or perhaps by one of its increasingly used euphemistic aliases, such as "neurasthenic,"[94] and being treated, by general practitioners and specialist nerve doctors alike, with a cornucopia of drugs and tonics, moral and behavioral support, indulgence, rest, regimen, and what-you-will—in ways that surely would have won the imprimatur of Samuel Tissot, Théodore Tronchin, or Heberden.[95] Such continuity may show that Victorian medicine failed in its quest for the promised specific for hysteria. But it would be more to the point to emphasize that, from Giorgio Baglivi to George Beard, the canny clinician knew that the hysteric's prime needs were for attention, escape, protection, rest, recuperation, reinforcement—physical, moral, and mental alike. The least plausible indictment against either Mandeville or Weir Mitchell is that they tried to force hysteria onto some Procrustean bed. For them, the protean language of nerves permitted the sufferer to bespeak his or her own hysteria diagnosis as a nonstigmatizing cloak of disorder. It was Mitchell who was wont to speak of "mysteria."[96]

In the nineteenth century, the rest home, clinic, and sanatorium supplemented the spa-resort to provide new recuperative sites for the familiar nervous complaints of the rich. Their therapeutic rationale, however, was old wine in new bottles. Nerve doctors continued to emphasize the force field of the physical, emotional, and intellectual in precipitating hysteria (or, later, neuropathy, neurasthenia, etc.); they defined hysteria, formally at least, as gender nonspecific, independent of gynecological etiology. There was life still in the old Enlightenment idiom of the nerves. Above all, by cushioning neurasthenic patients within a somatizing diagnostics of nervous collapse, nervous debility, gastric weakness, dyspepsia, atonicity, spinal inflammation, migraine, and so forth, fashionable doctors could forestall suspicions that their respectable patients were either half mad or malingering sociopaths.[97]

Not least, "nerves" precluded moral blame, by hinting at a pathology not even primarily personal, but social, a *Zeitgeist* disease. Eighteenth-

century nerve doctors tended to indict cultural volatility: salon sophisticates were victims of exquisitely vertiginous life-styles that sapped the
nerves. By contrast, in later recensions of the diseases of civilization,
High Victorian therapists on both sides of the Atlantic pointed accusing
fingers at the pitiless competition of market society. As Francis Gosling
has shown, George Beard and Weir Mitchell argued that career strains
in the business rat race devitalized young achievers; brain-fagged by
stress and tension in the cockpit of commerce, they ended up nervous
wrecks, their psychological capital overtaxed. Cerebral circuits suffered
overload, mental machinery blew fuses, batteries ran down, brains were
bankrupted: such metaphors, borrowed from physics and engineering,
were reminders that disorders were physical, offering convincing explanations why go-getting all-American Yale graduates like Clifford Beers
should suffer nervous breakdowns no less than their delicate and devoted sisters.[98]

Such decorous somatizing also permitted physicians to exhibit dazzl-
ing therapeutic machineries, targeted at bodily recuperation: baths and
douches, passive "exercise," massage, custom-built diets programmed to
make weight, fat, and blood; regimes of walking, games, and gym; occupational therapy, water treatments, electrical stimuli, relaxation, routine,
and so forth. This paraphernalia of remedial technologies obviously
spelled good business for residential clinical directors. Strategically, such
routines were said to benefit patients by deflecting them from morbid
self-awareness, training attention more beneficially elsewhere.

For nineteenth-century physicians began to voice fears of morbid introspection, that hysterical spiral arising from patients dwelling upon
their disorders.[99] Precepts for healthy living widely canvassed—by sages
such as John Stuart Mill and Thomas Carlyle no less than medical gu-
rus—deplored egoistic preoccupation as the road to ruin, to suicide
even, and advised consciousness-obliterating, outgoing activity.[100] For
the hysteric was typically regarded as the narcissist or introvert. From
her Freudian viewpoint, Veith has blamed Weir Mitchell for not encouraging his rest-cure convalescents to talk their psychosexual problems through, implying that this silence may have been due to prudery.
One suspects, in truth, the doctor's reticence reflects neither puritanism
nor shallowness, but savvy: a conviction that some matters were better
left latent, lest they inflame morbid tendencies.[101]

"Only when bodily functions are deranged," warned the mid-Victorian British physician Bevan Lewis, do "we become . . . conscious of the
existence of our organs."[102] In his caution about consciousness, Lewis
was of a mind with the leaders of British practice—Charles Mercier,

David Skae, Henry Maudsley, and Thomas Clouston—who saw hysteria as the penalty for excessive introspection, especially when accompanied by a- or anti-social dispositions and, worse still, by auto-erotism.[103] It was, consequentially, dangerous to discuss such dispositions freely with patients, lest this encourage further morbid egoism and attention-seeking, and all the attendant train of self-absorption, daydreaming, reverie, and solitary and sedentary habits. Prompted to dwell upon herself, Maudsley feared, the hysteric would most likely sink into solipsistic moral insanity or imbecility;[104] for, as the patient progressively abandoned her power of will—"a characteristic symptom of hysteria in all its protean forms"—she would fall into "moral perversion," losing

> more and more of her energy and self-control, becoming capriciously fanciful about her health, imagining or feigning strange diseases, and keeping up the delusion or the imposture with a pertinacity that might seem incredible, getting more and more impatient of the advice and interference of others, and indifferent to the interests and duties of her position.[105]

For their own sakes, therefore, patients must be taken "out of themselves"—through therapeutic hobbies, exercise, and sociability. Thus Sir William Bradshaw, the society physician in Virginia Woolf's *Mrs. Dalloway*, notoriously instructs the shell-shocked war victim Septimus Smith to pull himself together and cultivate a sense of proportion. Through the caricature of this pompous ass, Woolf expressed her contempt for such London physicians as Sir George Savage and Maurice Craig, who treated her own nervous collapses with the moral anodyne of the rest cure. Yet Woolf herself was no less scathing, in a terribly English way, about the asininities of sex-on-the-brain Germanic psychiatrists. There is no sign that she favored having Freudian "mind doctors" open Freudian windows onto her psyche.[106]

In short, powerful currents through the nineteenth century and beyond continued to class hysteria as a disease of nervous organization. Doctors fixed upon physical symptoms, and treated them with physical means, steering clear of too much skirmishing with, or stirring up, the mind. If blinkered and complacent, such approaches were not necessarily obtuse. The contrasting protocols of Charcot's Tuesday Clinic[107] and the Freudian couch arguably hysterized hysteria, as one might douse a fire with gasoline. Yet if continuities with the Enlightenment may be seen, there are gear shifts too; above all, perhaps, a certain waning of medical sympathy for the nervous hysteric in the generations after 1800, thanks to a sterner Evangelical prizing of self-reliance.[108] If the Enlightenment indulged a certain fascination for idiosyncracy, Victorian mores took their stand against the egoistic sociopath. To these sociopaths we turn.

CHANGE: WOMEN, BODY, AND SCIENTIFIC MEDICINE

Concentrating on continuities with the past risks skewing nineteenth-century outlooks on hysteria. It was, all agree, hysteria's *belle epoque,* thanks above all to the startling emergence and convergence of mutually reinforcing conditions: a profound accentuation of the "woman question," coterminous with an evidently not unrelated expansion in organized medicine.

As Elaine Showalter fully explores in chapter 4, the question of feminine nature became a burning issue. Romanticism rang the changes on the paradoxes: wife and whore, *femme fragile* and *femme fatale,* weak but wanton—woman, it seemed, was an appallingly irresistible cocktail of innocence and morbid sexuality.[109] Bram Dijkstra, among others, has traced the sensationalization of that mythology toward the turn of the century.[110] In the shadow of such stereotypes, women experienced profound conflicts over rival ideals and expectations.[111] To hook a husband, a woman had to be childlike and dependent, yet also a tower of strength as the household manager of that great moral engine, the family, and robust enough to survive innumerable pregnancies. Wives had to be pure, yet pleasing, or risk being supplanted by the "other woman." Hence they had to develop their talents, yet intellectual aspirations were censured as unnatural, imperiling their manifest biological destiny as willing wombs. And if, stupefied by such pressures, paradoxes, and prohibitions, women showed signs of bewilderment or bridling, what did this prove but that they were spoiled, difficult, and capricious, further proof of the necessity for male and medical control? When proto-feminist protest mounted, it gave further evidence to those who saw hysteria as the root of all female activism. History, anatomy, destiny, evolution—all were conscripted to clamp women in their place.[112]

And so, of course, as fine feminist scholarship has shown, was medicine.[113] Yet the medical profession itself was in the toils of traumatic transformation. Space limits here preclude any adequate exploration of the upheavals in the internal organization and public facade of medicine during the nineteenth century, but a few developments must be mentioned, playing as they did key parts in reshaping hysteria.

Amid the throng of professional groups competing for recognition and rewards, medicine contributed noisily to the clangor, frantically asserting its own unique vocation. Doctors sought tighter professional organization and public privileges. Teaching and research assumed greater institutionalization in university and laboratory. And, thanks to such developments, medical discourse became increasingly directed to professional peers. With new ladders of advancement, and the expansion of research schools and scientific circles, professional *esprit de corps* grew commensurably, entailing a certain displacement of the patient, who was increasingly downgraded to an object of "the medical gaze." All such changes had, as we shall see, profound implications for the hysteric.[114]

Overpopulated, insecure, but ambitious, medicine fractured into a proliferation of subdisciplines, with new specialties multiplying and vying for funds and fame. As Ornella Moscucci has demonstrated, obstetrics and gynecology pioneered identities of their own, staking out the new terrain of women's medicine. Neurology took shape as a specialty; Russell Maulitz has traced the rise of pathology. Public health came of age, and alliances between the social sciences and the emergent specialties of organic chemistry and bacteriology helped to forge modern epidemiology. Psychiatry blossomed, colonizing its own locations, above all, the asylum and the university polyclinic.[115]

And all such heightened division of labor led to different schools, national groups, and subspecialisms vaunting their own cognitive claims: in some cases, basic science, in others, clinical experience or laboratory experimentation, keyed to the microscope. L. S. Jacyna has stressed the espousal by professional medics of ideologies of scientific naturalism, centered on the laws of life.[116]

Nineteenth-century medicine reoriented itself beyond the sickbed into the clinic: the vast, investigative teaching hospital, equipped with advanced patho-anatomical facilities and a never-failing supply of experimental subjects. At the same time, with the emergence of the industrial state, medicine also found itself enjoying greater interaction with sociopolitical institutions. Examining vast disease populations in their new public capacity, physicians had to confront fresh questions: latency, disposition, contagion, diathesis, constitution, and inheritance.[117]

In short, scientific medicine flexed its muscles and spread its wings. It was courted by the public; it craved official authorization. Hence, doctors made bold to become scientific policymakers for the new age. The questions they addressed—matters of hygiene, efficiency, sanity, race, sexuality, morality, criminal liability, and so forth—were inevitably morally charged; many physicians claimed medicine as the very cornerstone of public morals. And so physicians shouldered an ever greater regulatory role, acting as brokers and adjudicators for state, judiciary, and the family. Turning technical expertise into social and moral directives, medicine spoke out upon social order and social pathology, progress, and degeneration. As will now be seen, new medical specialties claimed jurisdiction over hysteria, and made it yield moral messages to slake, or stoke, Victorian anxieties.[118]

PROBLEM WOMEN: GYNECOLOGY AND HYSTERIA

As Thomas Laqueur has contended, research in the late eighteenth and early nineteenth centuries into human sexuality did not resolve the mystery of woman, but deepened it. The more that was discovered, however tentatively and tardily, about menstruation and conception, the more medical science confirmed the truth that hegemonic male culture was independently affirming: women were *different*.[119] Traditional Greek-derived biomedical teachings had represented the female reproductive apparatus as an inferior, imperfect inversion of the male. But during the eighteenth century and beyond, medicine and culture were abandoning that view and combining to reconstruct women as radically *other*.[120] And not merely other, but bizarre.

It had become acknowledged that, contradicting medical teachings going back to Hippocrates, female orgasm was unnecessary for conception. Investigations into ovulation also appeared to show that menstruation in women, unlike other mammals, occurred independently of libidinal excitation. In short, the relationship between erotic stimulus on the one hand, and conception on the other, became utterly (and uniquely) problematic. Female sexuality thus seemed, from the viewpoint of research into generation, a mystery, apparently biologically superfluous, and perhaps even pathological.[121]

Pontificating upon the riddles of female sexuality became the stock-in-trade of emergent gynecology. Elbowing aside "ignorant midwives" and the much-mocked *accoucheurs,* specialist surgeon-gynecologists made their bid to pass themselves off as more than mere operators: being rather experts, qualified to hold forth on the overpowering role of reproduction in determining female life patterns, in a set of scientific discourses in which womb became a synecdoche for woman.[122] Nineteenth-century medicine, claimed Foucault, forged a new hysterization of women's bodies. This was precisely the achievement of gynecology, largely backed by the equally junior disciplines of sexology and psychological medicine, against the backdrop, just sketched, of the establishment of specialized, scientific medicine.[123]

In a context of patriarchal values ultra-suspicious of female sexuality,[124] gynecologists set about designating the physiology and pathology of this perplexing being. Once the chasm between arousal and conception had been established, female libido—so volatile, capricious, even rampaging—was revealed as inherently dysfunctional, dangerous even. So why the peculiar sensitivities of clitoris and vagina, all too susceptible to physiological and emotional disturbance? Was not even the uterus itself troublesome beyond the demands of childbearing? Were not women enslaved by their generative organs? And if so, what was to be done? Confronted with streams of female patients—many tortured with internal pain, others dejected, still others "delinquent"—these were the problems upon which the growing corps of women's disease specialists built their platform.

The answers offered by emergent gynecology portrayed women's health as desperately womb-dependent. Since the very *raison d'être* of the female lay in procreation,[125] properly directed thereto, erotic arousal had a certain value, within the walled garden of matrimony. Yet what of the risk of arousal among adolescent girls, spinsters, and widows? Abstinence was socially expected, yet continence had its quandaries, leading to chlorosis, wasting conditions, and emotional waywardness.[126] Frustration fueled fantasies and could lead to masturbation, an activity imperiling health—physical, moral, and mental.[127] In short, the female reproductive system was so precariously poised that almost any irregularity, whether excitation or repression, was sure to provoke hysteriform disorders.

Hysteria had ever been regarded as the charade of disease.[128] Now doctors feared it as eros in disguise. Its swoonings, jerks, convulsions, and panting blatantly simulated sexuality, affording surrogate outlets and relief, while the sufferer escaped the stigma of lubricity. Not least, in the throes of a fit, the hysteric was bound to be touched, pampered, and subjected to medical examination and treatment, all of which nineteenth-century doctors regarded as erotically gratifying.[129]

Gynecology and psychophysiology thus joined forces to make female sexuality problematic, highlighting the role of the sexual organs in provoking hysterical conditions widely believed to precipitate moral insanity. "Convulsions . . . in early life," judged the top late Victorian psychiatrist, Henry Maudsley, were indices of the "insane temperament," even in subjects not yet actually insane.[130] Such precocious, displaced eroticism could trigger long-term disturbances.

Early in the century, psychiatrists had pinpointed the links between menstrual abnormalities and hysteria. John Haslam, apothecary at Bethlem Hospital, observed that in "females who become insane, the disease is often connected with the peculiarities of their sex."[131] In a similar vein, the influential psychiatric spokesman, George Man Burrows, drew attention to "various sanguiferous discharges, whether periodical, occasional, or accidental," all of which "greatly influence the functions of the mind."[132] Herein, argued Burrows, lay the key to female troubles, for "every body of the least experience must be sensible of the influence of menstruation on the operations of the mind"—it was, he judged, no less than the "moral and physical barometer of the female constitution."[133] Burrows tendered a physiological explanation based upon "the due equilibrium of the vascular and nervous systems":

> If the balance be disturbed, so likewise will be the uterine action and periodical discharge; though it does not follow that the mind always sympathises with its irregularities so as to disturb the cerebral functions. Yet the functions of the brain are so intimately connected with the uterine system, that the interruption of any one process which the latter has to perform in the human economy may implicate the former.[134]

Ripeness for childbearing was the mark of the healthy woman. Hence, Burrows emphasized, were menstruation interrupted, "the seeds of various disorders are sown; and especially where any predisposition obtains, the hazard of insanity is imminent."[135]

Equally, he judged, local genital and uterine irritations would generate "those phantasies called longings, which are decided perversions or aberrations of the judgment, though perhaps the simplest modifications of intellectual derangement."[136] What was the explanation?

> These anomalous feelings have been referred to uterine irritation from mere gravitation, and so they may be; but they first induce a greater determination of blood to the uterus and its contents, and then to the brain, through the reciprocal connexion and action existing between the two organs.[137]

It was two-way traffic. Amenorrhea was sometimes "a cause of insanity,"[138] but, reciprocally, "cerebral disturbance" could itself cause "menstrual obstruction,"[139] further exacerbating mental disorder, for "terror, the sudden application of cold, etc., have occasioned the instant cessation of the menses, upon which severe cerebral affections, or instant insanity, has supervened."[140]

In line with the times, Burrows also blamed menopause for severe female disturbance. Once again, he emphasized, the primary change was physiological:

> The whole economy of the constitution at that epoch again undergoes a revolution. . . . There is neither so much vital nor mental energy to resist

the effects of the various adverse circumstances which it is the lot of most to meet with in the interval between puberty and the critical period.[141]

Yet, in the opinion of the less-than-gallant Burrows, sociopsychological forces were also at work:

> The age of pleasing in all females is then past, though in many the desire to please is not the less lively. The exterior alone loses its attractions, but vanity preserves its pretensions. It is now especially that jealousy exerts its empire, and becomes very often a cause of delirium. Many, too, at this epoch imbibe very enthusiastic religious notions; but more have recourse to the stimulus of strong cordials to allay the uneasy and nervous sensations peculiar to this time of life, and thus produce a degree of excitation equally dangerous to the equanimity of the moral feelings and mental faculties.[142]

Double jeopardy surrounded the menopausal crisis.

Overall, Burrows judged hysteria intrinsic to the female sexual constitution: "Nervous susceptible women between puberty and thirty years of age, and clearly the single more so than the married, are most frequently visited by hysteria."[143] Its root, he emphasized, was organic: "Such constitutions have always a greater aptitude to strong mental emotions, which, on repetition, will superinduce mental derangement, or perhaps epilepsy."[144]

Unlike Enlightenment physicians, though prefiguring later Victorian opinion, Burrows feared hysteria, because it was always liable to flare into a dangerous, even incurable, condition. "Delirium is a common symptom of hysteria," he warned, "and this symptom is prolonged sometimes beyond the removal of the spasm of paroxysm."[145] Thus, in the event of a repetition of hysterical fits, "the brain at length retained the morbid action, and insanity is developed." Indeed, because "hysteria is of that class of maladies which, wherever it is manifested, betrays a maniacal diathesis," it followed that "habitual hysteria clearly approximates to insanity."[146]

This prognosis (uterine disturbances lead to hysterical conditions that precipitate insanity proper) became standard to nineteenth-century medicine. "The reproductive organs . . . when unduly, unseasonably, or exorbitantly excited," argued Alfred Beaumont Maddock, are not only "necessarily subject to the usual advent of those physical diseases which are the inheritance of frail humanity, but are also closely interwoven with erratic and disordered intellectual, as well as moral, manifestations."[147] Such female disorders were, Maddock judged, the direct result of "the peculiar destiny that [woman] is intended by nature to fulfil, as the future mother of the human race."[148] Others concurred. "Mental derangement frequently occurs in young females from Amenorrhoea," argued John Millar, "especially in those who have any strong hereditary predisposition to insanity."[149]

This "Hysteric's Progress," arcing almost literally from womb to tomb, was evoked most vividly by that gloomy giant of late Victorian psychiatry, Henry Maudsley. Maudsley traced the slippery slope from hysteria to "hysterical insanity," a "special variety" of the complaint connoting

> an attack of acute maniacal excitement, with great restlessness, rapid and disconnected but not entirely incoherent conversation, sometimes tending to the erotic or obscene, evidently without abolition of consciousness; [and also] laughing, singing, or rhyming, and perverseness of conduct, which is still more or less coherent and seemingly wilful.[150]

Such disturbances "may occur in connection with, or instead of, the usual hysterical convulsions," although, Maudsley warned, "the ordinary hysterical symptoms may pass by degrees into chronic insanity."[151] Gynecological and psychiatric causes were virtually inseparable: "Outbursts of temper become almost outbreaks of mania, particularly at the menstrual periods. An erotic tinge may be observable in her manner of behaviour; and occasionally there are quasi-ecstatic or cataleptic states."[152]

Such conditions, emphasized the highly materialist Maudsley, were "the effect of some condition of the reproductive organs on the brain." Their cerebral fibers warped, sufferers would not hesitate to exploit their self-dramatizing potential, Maudsley admonished, pointing to the "extreme moral perversion shown by such hysterical young women of a nervous temperament as imagine that their limbs are paralysed and lie in bed or on a couch day after day."[153] There was, however, a moral sting in the tail of Maudsley's materialism. Like most of his cloth, he judged that the optimum treatment for young ladies in this "extremely perverted moral state" was moral, requiring that "the patient be removed in time from the anxious but hurtful sympathies and attentions of her family, and placed under good moral control." If, instead, "it be allowed to go on unchecked, it will end in dementia, and it is especially apt to do so when there is a marked hereditary predisposition."[154] Not surprisingly, Maudsley linked hysterical insanity to nymphomania, both following from "the irritation of the ovaries or uterus."[155]

Such anxiety-making, misogynistic views—singling out women and blaming the uterus—were no peculiarity of the English. The eminent German psychiatrist Wilhelm Griesinger identified hysteria as symptomatic of local disorders of the uterus, ovaries, and vagina.[156] Like his

English counterparts, Griesinger espoused a doctrinaire medical materialism in which bio-reality was definitionally somatic, and phenomena apparently without bodily correlates were to be presumed imaginary. Female hysteria, he disclosed in his *Mental Pathology and Therapeutics* (1845), was thus either the product of genital disease or a work of art. Authentic hysteria was somatic, involving the "morbid action of . . . the brain,"[157] generally provoked by vaginally seated erotic stimulus, itself in turn sparked by menstrual pain and irregularities, constrictions and stoppages, and exacerbated by habitual masturbation. But hysteria was often faked—a characteristic foible of a sex whose entire demeanor was pockmarked by dishonesty, deceitfulness, and emotional waywardness. Griesinger's "reversion to a somatic explanation for hysterical disturbances," judged Veith, "must be looked upon as a regression from the psychiatric concepts of Pinel and Feuchtersleben," above all because he had a "blind spot" for women's sexual frustration.[158]

Thus the new sciences of gynecology and psychological medicine provided twin pillars supporting the rehabilitation of uterine theories of hysteria that became so prominent throughout the nineteenth century. These led in turn, with growing frequency, as Jeffrey Masson has amply documented, to surgical interventions, including the practice of hysterectomy and ovariectomy and the occasional resort to clitoridectomy or cauterization by figures such as Baker Brown and Alfred Hegar, touted as radical solutions to *mental* disorders no less than to local infections. It was not unknown, Ornella Moscucci has shown, for English surgeons to recommend genital operations for preventive psychiatric purposes.[159] Against the backdrop of the "woman problem," aggressive medicalization thus reinstated, in new guise, the uterine pathology theory, both regendering and re-eroticizing the condition.

NEUROLOGY AND HYSTERIA

Enlightenment scientific medicine classed as "nervous" those protean behavioral disorders, floating free of determinate lesions, which it termed the vapors and spleen, hysteria, hypochondria, and melancholy. Assimilating hysteria by this verbal sleight of hand to one of the major organic systems proved strategically adroit, allowing the incorporation of the anomalous within prestigious, systematizing, and bodily anchored disease schemata.

Neurological models proved equally fruitful in the nineteenth century, in context of the special diagnostic and bureaucratic needs of the public hospital and the mammoth mental asylum.[160] Institutional medicine had the burden of processing—and the benefit of studying—an infinitely wider range of morbid conditions than ever before encountered close up and en masse: chronic, progressive, and degenerative disorders, above all. Hospital medicine, on the Paris model, took advantage of the unique availability of poor patients for observation, experiment, and postmortem investigation. Diagnostic acumen, therapeutic nihilism, and patho-anatomical expertise combined to lay bare a host of degenerative disorders.[161] The asylum likewise provided unparalleled opportunities for long-term surveillance (and subsequent autopsy) of epilepsy, dementia, general paresis, speech and gait defects; of what would eventually be identified as multiple sclerosis; of Parkinson's disease, Huntingdon's chorea, cerebral palsy, and a host of other hitherto little-tracked sensorimotor disturbances. Such conditions, many feared, were spreading; they certainly afflicted a hard core of patients in nineteenth-century public institutions, workhouses, and infirmaries, and the "back wards" and chronic and incurable wings of Europe's and North America's mushrooming lunatic asylums.

Though typically defying not just cure but even anatomical localization, such conditions at least squared with a popular and plausible comprehensive sickness scenario, whose parameters were nature and history: degeneration.[162] Disorders otherwise baffling to science were increasingly normalized by being termed constitutional, hereditary, and degenerative. In the absence of tangible lesions, even postmortem, the individual's pedigree, the family history, became, as it were, a display of lesions dredged up from the past: the generational deterioration, for instance, from alcoholic great grandparents, through a nymphomaniacal prostitute of a grandmother, to a hysterical mother, and finally perhaps to an epileptic child. Such genealogical declensions apparently laid the disease affinities bare.

It is against this wider degenerationist backdrop, and in context of the drive to translate intractable disorders into neurology through deploying the patho-anatomical methods pioneered in the clinic, that the career of Jean-Martin Charcot assumes such monumental importance in framing yet another paradigm of hysteria. Historians have rightly drawn attention to the great professor's exercise of Svengalian authority over his female patients.[163] Yet something far more complex was going on. The hysteria that Charcot studied—or, better perhaps, that he and his patients co-produced—was a palimpsest of a performance, many layered with meanings. It bespeaks the utter docility of the body, under the charismatic authority of mind (above all, the robot behavior of the hypnotized). It marks deflected, oblique protest—a resistance that, incapable of verbalization, was converted into somatic signals of violence and burlesque.[164] It may also be read as duplicitous seduction: were not the patients, or their diseases, duping the scientistic, voyeuristic doctors, thereby ironically confirming—had Charcot only known!—fin de siècle medicine's conviction of the pathognomy of the feminine, and insensibly ratifying male phobias about woman as the femme fatale?

These are just some of the facets of gender politics in Charcotian hysteria, further dissected in chapter 4 by Elaine Showalter. Against such a background, a different aspect also deserves emphasis: Charcot's burning desire to make hysteria reputable, distinguished even, within the somatizing enterprise of scientific medicine. As Trillat and Micale have emphasized, despite his location at the Salpêtrière, Charcot never was, nor aspired to be, a psychiatrist or alienist in the great tradition of Pinel and Esquirol.[165] He was an ardent neurologist, committed to the techniques of pathological anatomy, proud to hold a Clinical Chair of the Nervous System. He aimed to reduce neurological chaos, hysteria included, to order. He was faced with fiendishly complex symptom clusters. Such conditions as "epilepsy, hysteria, even the most inveterate cases, chorea, and many other morbid states . . . come to us like so many Sphynx," he confessed, defying "the most penetrating anatomical investigations." For precisely that reason, he observed, sceptics urged that hysteria "should be banished to the category of the unknown."[166] Not so! His ambition, initially at least, was to pin down nervous phenomena to organic lesions, and thereby to bring regular system to general paralysis, neuralgias, seizures, epileptiform fits, spastic symptoms, tabes dorsalis, and, not least, hysteria.[167]

And in attempting this Herculean labor, far from focusing exclusively upon a troupe of star hysterics, Charcot aimed to show that hysteria partook of the characteristics of neurological disorders as a whole, dispersed among the community at large. He thus took pride in his demonstrations that hysteria visited males as well as females, parents and children alike, a galaxy of ethnic groups, and, above all, the whole social spectrum.[168] With hysteria, the more it was universal, the surer the grounding for its "scientificity."

Addressing thus the range of its manifestations, Charcot's project was committed to massive clinical scrutiny of hysterical pathology—motor and sensory symptoms, bizarre visual abnormalities, tics, migraine, epileptiform seizures, somnambulism, hallucinations, word blindness, alexia, aphasia, mutism, contractures, hyperaesthesias, and numerous other deficits—devising critical experiments (e.g., upon eyesight and hearing peculiarities), refining comparison and measurement, and compiling lavish and multigenerational patient histories.[169] The contented positivist could leave no variable unturned.

Charcot had some measure of success in mapping hysteria onto the body. He was delighted to discover, for instance, hysterogenic points, zones of hypersensitivity which, when fingered, provoked an attack, analogous perhaps to the pressing of an electric light switch. Such a discovery confirmed his conviction of the reality of "latent hysteria."[170] Yet his early faith that scientific investigation into hysteria would systematically reveal demonstrable neurological substrates increasingly proved a forlorn—or, at least, a premature—hope.

By consequence, Charcot found he needed to satisfy himself with an epiphenomenalist account of the regularities and laws of hysteria, derived from its manifestations. Characteristically, he couched his praise for his predecessor, Pierre Briquet, in just these terms; Briquet's achievement lay in having shown that "hysteria is governed, in the same way as other morbid conditions, by rule and laws, which attentive and sufficiently numerous observations always permit us to establish."[171] Building thereupon, Charcot thus claimed to have established the series or stages of manifestations, from *petite hystérie* through *hystérie ordinaire* up to the *grande attaque d'hystéro-epileptique*. In this way clinical observations permitted the uncovering, he claimed, of the natural histories of extended families of related deficits: hemilateral anesthesias, pharyngeal anesthesias, *grandes paroxysmes*, palpitations, chorea, Saint Vitus dance, tertiary neurosyphilitic infections, and temporal lobe epilepsy. If Sydenham had seen hysteria as the *exception* to the natural history of diseases, the positivist Charcot, by contrast, believed he could incorporate it within such a taxonomy. "These diseases," he insisted, "do not form, in pathology, a class apart, governed by other physiological laws than the common ones."[172]

It is this passion to illuminate hysteria's hidden disposition, its diatheses and frequencies, that explains Charcot's lasting passion for hypnosis and his brief encounter with metalloscopy. Hypnosis served Charcot as a kind of litmus test. It became an article of faith with him that the capacity to be hypnotized was a crucial experimental demonstration of underlying, organic, hysterical pathology. Hypnosis was the dowser's twig, pointing to the reservoir of the pathological; hence his eagerness to discredit Hippolyte Bernheim's view that hypnotic states were normal and potentially universal. For Charcot, hypnotizability was the giveaway of the pathological.[173]

For similar reasons, as Anne Harrington has demonstrated, Charcot's circle became fascinated by Victor Jean-Marie Burq's metalloscopic experiments. Burq claimed that distinct metals, each possessed of its own *force neurique,* had the power, when brought close to a subject, to modify behavior. Indeed, the bio-magnetist Burq even appeared to have the capacity, through deploying rods of diverse alloys, to transfer hypnotic and hysteric conditions from organ to organ, and from individual to individual, depending upon their "metallic personality." Burq's neo-Mesmeric use of rods offered further confirmation to the credulous Charcot (in a manner echoing Mesmer himself) that hysteria and its kindred nervous conditions derived from authentic, if ill-understood, organic substrates, being subject to the universal physical laws governing the atomic structures of different metals. Manipulation of mood by the manipulation of metals showed the very laws of cause and effect at work, no less clearly than using magnets to make iron filings dance. In drawing upon Burq, the *charcoterie* (group of disciples of Charcot) thus further hitched its wagon to the rising star of late-nineteenth-century physics, with its prestigious doctrines of ethers and quasi-occult energy sources.[174]

How then do we appraise Charcot's characterization of hysteria? It was clearly in part the product of the interprofessional rivalries of medicoscientific specialisms discussed earlier. In championing physiological methods to plot hysteria onto the body, Charcot was planting patho-anatomy's flag on a condition contested by alienists and clinicians, gynecologists and obstetricians. Charcot never approached hysterical patients from the standpoints of psychiatry or psychology. His investigative techniques remained largely indifferent to the probing of their consciousness.[175] Why?

Institutional ensconcement in the "living pathological museum" of the Salpêtrière[176] and staunch Third Republic positivism confirmed in Charcot a concept of science which gave priority to establishing the laws of life, grounded in the totality of the living organism. Hence he set consciousness to one side as essentially secondary. Of course, he had no doubt that hysteria attacks were commonly sparked by mental and emotional trauma, albeit, naturally, in individuals already endowed with a hysterical constitutional diathesis. And, equally, he had to put his patients' minds to the test in critical experiments, to winkle out malingerers and self-publicists: his pneumograph machine, for example, gave graphic proof that, unlike a genuine cataleptic, a bogus cataleptic will register fatigue. Hindsight reveals the deep pathos in Charcot's boast that the "province of the physician" is "to dissipate chicanery."[177]

But overall, Charcot—unlike certain of his protégés such as Janet[178]— showed scant professional interest in what were then being called the psychology or psychodynamics of the patients he used for experimental and pedagogical purposes. This was partly the result of circumstances. It is likely, after all, that Charcot's main face-to-face contact with such patients lay in clinical demonstrations, his assistants and students having been delegated to subject them to prior personal examination. Charcot was thereby probably the unwitting victim of *both* doctor *and* patient compliance, yes-people all in his Napoleonic empire. In any case, his Tuesday Clinic subjects were but working-class Parisian girls. Would a Charcot consider it scientifically fruitful to interrogate such riffraff personally? (For the sake of his illusions, it was perhaps just as well that he didn't.) One wonders whether Charcot used identical, that is, neurological, approaches on his private patients: it was certainly his contention that, in hysteria, "everything follows definite rules—always the same, whether the case is met with in private or hospital practice." [179] Charcot the public figure, the institutional man, and champion of the discipline of neuropathology, was wholly wedded to the positive scientific pursuit of hysteria as a pathology of the constitution. We know all too little of how far the public Charcot also had a double, one prepared to elaborate on the more psychological perspectives implied by his notorious aside, "*C'est toujours la chose génitale*"—a remark reestablishing precisely that link between hysteria and lubricity which he habitually denied. [180]

Charcot played the scientist, an epiphenomenalist insistent that hysteria was a function of the body. Science's point of entry lay not in psychology but in physiological stigmata, reinforced by degenerationist neuropathy ("contracture diathesis" or "latent hysteria"). "Neuropathic heredity," he believed, "figures conspicuously in the etiology of hysteria," [181] for "hysteria is often hereditary." [182] Hysteria, of course, had its emotional correlates (attention seeking, coquettishness, lying), but these were chiefly by-products, symptomatic of more basic psychophysiological defects embedded in bodies over the generations. [183]

HYSTERIA, PSYCHIATRY, AND THE CLINICAL ENCOUNTER

Nineteenth-century transformations in medicine and society produced their reconceptualizations of hysteria. Gynecology and psychological medicine interacted to represent hysteria as a woman's disease, stemming from the reproductive system and generating an emotional pathology. By contrast, the patho-anatomical gaze of hospital medicine imagined a hysteria that was unisex and indexed by multiple behavioral irregularities that were deemed ultimately neuro-physiological. In this highly schematic account, a third and final initiative remains to be discussed: the development of a psychological theory of hysteria.

The intellectual roots of this approach lie in lunatic asylum reform around the turn of the nineteenth century. Leading asylum superintendents, particularly Chiarugi, Pinel, Johann Reil, and the Tukes (William and Samuel), repudiated traditional organic nosologies and medical therapeutics as misconceived and inefficacious, urging instead techniques of moral management and moral therapy. Within their theories, insanity was redefined as springing from consciousness—the intellect and the passions—thus necessitating treatment on psychological principles, by appeals to reason, humanity, and the feelings (fear and esteem, pleasure and pain, etc.). Herein lay the founding of psychiatry. Being chiefly concerned with desperate asylum cases, such authors naturally had rather little to say about hysteria per se. But their vision of an authentic secular psychopathology later proved a source of inspiration and authority.[184]

Psychological theories of hysteria were developed by doctors active in bourgeois private practice. This should come as no surprise. Such practices necessitated protracted and intimate contact with patients, women above all, who—whatever their actual medical histories—were utterly *au fait* with the power possessed by sickness and invalidism to secure respite or leverage within the politics of the family. The culture of sensibility, particularly among those on whose hands time hung heavily, encouraged hypersensitivity to malaise. Bourgeois sufferers were both introspective and vocal in their complaints, rationalizations, and demands. Little wonder that the affinity between hysterical symptoms and the outpourings of consciousness might be thought to stare physicians in the face.

I have argued earlier that doctors typically refused this association. Theirs was a mental set which, by professional article of faith, and almost by way of reflex, equated sickness with the somatic. Many chose, as suggested above, for their patients' peace of mind, surreptitiously to translate complaints into somatic ailments (nervous stomach, and so forth), believing this recourse optimal, for all concerned, for negotiating tricky conditions. A few, however, broke out of this convention, perhaps this pious fraud. Why this happened in the particular case is generally impossible to decipher. The consequences were, however, quite radical: translating hysteria into a malady of the mind drastically changed the rules of the game. It typically reduced hysteria from a disease into a deceit; exculpation turned to indictment; and a darker psychopathology emerged of the pretend hysteric, almost without exception female. Hysteria as the disease-mimicking disease made way for the hysteric as the woman (or the woman's *unconscious*) pretending to be ill.

These moves appear most starkly in the writings of Robert Carter, a man praised by Veith for his "clear insight into the psychopathology of hysteria" and his "advanced" discovery of sexual etiology.[185] Carter was a young general practitioner in the leafy London suburb of Leytonstone when he published his *On the Pathology and Treatment of Hysteria* in 1853.[186] In it, he reviewed all available somatic theories of the condition—Cullen's and Pinel's view that it was a morbid condition of the uterine nerves; Cheyne's and Caleb Parry's indictment of the stomach; Highmore's claim that it was consequent upon lung and heart congestion; the notion, associated with Whytt, Tissot, Boerhaave, and Boissier de Sauvages, that it was a disease of the nervous system; Willis's theory, revived by Etienne Georget, that it was a morbid condition of the brain; Gerard Van Swieten's "morbid condition of the spinal cord," and so forth. All without exception he judged as lacking authenticated foundation; for "the disease itself is too shifting and variable to depend upon any definite change in any individual organ."[187] Above all, attempts to ground hysteria in "irritation of the uterus and ovaria [were] . . . utterly untenable"—indeed, merely circular.[188] Hysteria, in short, was not somatic at all, but psychological: "The emotional doctrine affords an easy and complete solution of the difficulty." Indeed, its etiology lay specifically in "the sexual feelings," these being "both more universal and more constantly concealed than any others."[189]

What was the mechanism of the psychological theory of hysteria? Drawing upon the writings of W. B. Carpenter, Thomas Laycock, and other British psychophysiologists, he explained that, within the regular self-adjusting system of the metabolism, strong emotions (fear, joy, etc.) should properly find healthy outlet in physical release such as tears, laughter, flight, and so on. Obviously, central among the emotions were the sexual passions. Ideally these found natural fulfillment in erotic activity, ultimately in orgasm. Discharging such desires rarely posed problems for males.[190]

In modern civilization, however, the double standard commonly denied such relief to women—a result of high moral expectations and the "habitual restraint" imposed upon ladies by respectability. Denied the "safety valve"[191] of such direct, physiological outlets, women were forced to bottle up their amatory longings and suffer what Carter called repression. Intense personal crises (e.g., a broken engagement) could easily cause that dam to burst, however, whereupon indirect tension release was unintentionally gained in hysteria—expressed in outbreaks of un-

controllable sobbing, shaking, fits, temper, and the like. Such hysteria—
"a disease starting with a convulsive paroxysm"[192]—Carter called "primary"; it was, in a sense, a spontaneous compensatory mechanism designed to make the best of a bad situation. Some salutary tension-
discharge was at least achieved, and eventually the sobbing or tantrum
would play itself out and calm would be restored. Primary hysteria of
this kind did not require the physician's services.

Hysteria did not stop there, however. For unfortunately, "the suggested or spontaneous remembrance of the emotions"[193] attending the
primary fit could easily provoke further attacks, which Carter dubbed
"secondary hysteria." Sufferers, relatives, and doctors alike could help
forestall such secondary attacks by providing appropriate distractions.
Such prevention was prudent, for patients quickly habituated themselves to secondary hysteria, finding it provided them with compensatory pleasures—not least, attention.

Worse, such indirect gratifications readily deteriorated into "tertiary
hysteria," which Carter defined as a condition "designedly excited by the
patient herself through the instrumentality of voluntary recollection,
and with perfect knowledge of her own power to produce them."[194] In
short, tertiary hysteria—Carter's prime concern—was an ego-trip, mo-
bilized by the patient's will, for tyrannizing others. The tertiary hysteric,
in Carter's view, had thus sunk to appalling depths of moral depravity,
contriving to manipulate all around her, so as to gratify her whims and
domineering spirit, and enable her to bask in the "fuss and parade of
illness."[195] Because this exercise of will was wholly camouflaged in somatic expressions, it naturally compelled sympathy (the patient, after all,
appeared dramatically sick), without risking suspicions of shamming.
The greater the sympathy it won, the more tyrannical it became. Hysterics grew expert in their art. Thus, to create an effect, Carter noted,
"hair will often be so fastened as to fall at the slightest touch," and other
histrionic effects would testify to the "ingenuity of the performer."[196]

Such a minx, manipulating a "self-produced disease" in which the patient herself had full "power over the paroxysm,"[197] could be overcome
only by a battle royal engaged by the physician, willing to enter into a
war of wills. Defeating the "tricks" of such a monster of "selfishness and
deceptivity," possessed of a "mendacity that verges on the sublime,"[198]
was not, however, an easy matter; for the symptoms of physical illness
(including in the extreme case the tacit threat of fasting unto death)
were powerful weapons to have in one's armory. Carter knew medical
means were utterly irrelevant (no Mesmeric magnets for him). Psychological warfare was needed to defeat "the ends which she proposes to

herself for attainment."[199] First, the hysteric had to be separated from her parents and friends and incarcerated in the physician's home. Once there, under no circumstances should the doctor "minister to the hysterical desire."[200] Every bid of the patient to use hysterical tantrums to command attention had to be steadfastly ignored and thus proven futile: no notice was to be taken of convulsions, self-starving, or acts of self-mutilation; above all, the hysteric's cravings for surrogate sexual gratification, especially through demands for vaginal examinations with a speculum, had to be resisted.[201] Normal, sociable behavior was, by contrast, to be encouraged and rewarded.

No holds were barred. The hysteric was mistress of duplicity, and, in response, the physician would often find it necessary to "completely deceive her."[202] His most difficult task was to find tactful ways of communicating to the hysteric that her wiles had been rumbled and the game was up. Diplomatically done, this would afford her the opportunity to surrender with honor, and put herself "completely in the power of her interlocutor,"[203] whereupon she might make a clean breast of things, preparatory to being reincorporated, as the prodigal daughter, into normal, bourgeois life (that life whose constraints and double standards, Carter himself had initially acknowledged, were responsible for hysteria in the first place).

Several aspects of Carter's account of how to tame a hysterical shrew and bring her to "humiliation and shame" are worth noting.[204] For one thing, his psychological reading of hysteria drew heavily upon the idiom and premises of early nineteenth-century psychiatry; Carter explicitly valued "moral management" and "moral therapy."[205] He proposed turning his own abode into a hysterics' asylum, in whose gothic isolation the battle for the mind could be waged. One might gloss this by noting that as a young general practitioner, Carter was in no position to contemplate the laborious investigation of the laws of hysteria as undertaken by Professor Charcot at the Salpêtrière. Economics forced Carter—as to some degree Freud after him—to be concerned with cure rather than scientific exploration, and to have an eye to fees.

Drawing upon contemporary asylum psychiatry, Carter forged a conceptual triangle of elective affinities, profoundly pregnant for the future, linking (1) psychological explanation with (2) female nature and (3) a sexual etiology ("sexual emotions are those most concerned in the production of the disease").[206] In other words, in its grave forms, hysteria was a matter of *mental* acts (frauds), perpetrated by *women*, in order to achieve surrogate *sexual* gratification. By contrast, however, to earlier uterine theories, Carter's hypothesis did not lay blame at the door of female anatomy: rather what Hack Tuke later called a "paralysis of the will" was at fault. Although Carter noted that "if the state of society permitted free expression"[207] of female sexual desires, hysteria might dissolve away, he produced not a critical sociology of hysteria but a moralizing indictment of self-indulgent women. In this, his idiom explicitly echoed the witch-hunt, as when he remarked that the hysteric who made a hash of faking disease thereby "betrays the cloven foot."[208]

The social histories of Victorian medicine on the one hand, and of women on the other, leave it surely no accident that the prototypical psychogenic theory of hysteria was misogynistic and victim blaming. For the *raison d'être* of psychologizing hysteria was precisely to deny its authenticity as a malady, exposing it as fraud involving a terrible "degree of perversion of the moral sense."[209] In the history of hysteria, sexual etiologies, genderedness, and victim blaming have ever gone together.

CONCLUSION

This chapter has been highly selective. In concentrating upon the viewpoint of doctors, it has had little to say about how sufferers represented hysteria to themselves, nor indeed about why people "somatize."[210] It has had nothing to say about intriguing subsets of hysteria—mass hysteria, the hysterical personality—in which mind/body issues also significantly underpin the controversies. It has neither examined the intricacies of Freud's formulations over a period of some twenty years, nor surveyed Freud's contemporaries such as Janet and Babinski.[211] It would, however, seem that the dissolution of the hysteria diagnosis in the wake of Freud may be seen, in part at least, in terms of those shifts in modern ontology mentioned earlier in the discussion of Szasz's contribution. Monique David-Ménard, for instance, has suggested that the Lacanian translation of the location of the psyche from the Freudian mental underground to the domain of language has in effect rendered utterly obsolete most of the mind/body issues so fiercely disputed by the eighteenth- and nineteenth-century doctors discussed in this chapter. Not surprisingly. The psychoanalytical enterprise, unlike the Victorian family or the World War I trench, unlike the nerve sanatorium or the gynecological operating table, is entirely a theater of words.[212]

And this is the point. In the case of hysteria, disease formulations, I have been arguing, go with circumstances: doctors, patients, physical milieux, intellectual and cultural landscapes. My concern has been to argue that hysteria could be fashioned as a disorder, precisely because the culture-at-large sustained tense and ambiguous relations between representations of mind and body, which were, in turn, reproduced in the hierarchical yet interactive ontologies of morality and medicine, and, yet again, reflected by the sociological interplay of clinical encounters. In hysteria, as with other disorders, different fields of force break in distinctive ways, and medicine plays double games. Sometimes its mission is reductionist, resolving hysteria now into the womb, now into mere willfulness. In other circumstances, medicine seeks to render hysteria real, protecting its mysteries. In hysteria, mind and body may be seen as sublimated representations of doctors and patients.

NOTES

1. See H. O. Lancaster, *Expectations of Life: A Study of the Demography, Statistics and History of World Mortality* (New York: Springer Verlag, 1990); James C. Riley, *Sickness, Recovery and Death: A History and Forecast of Ill Health* (London: Macmillan, 1989); Alex Mercer, *Disease, Mortality and Population in Transition: Epidemiological-demographic Change in England since the Eighteenth Century as Part of a Global Phenomenon* (London: Leicester University Press, a division of Pinter Publishers, 1990); Roderick Floud, Kenneth Wachter, and Annabel Gregory, *Height, Health, and History: Nutritional Status in the United Kingdom, 1750–1980* (Cambridge: Cambridge University Press, 1990); Mark Nathan Cohen, *Health and the Rise of Civilization* (New Haven, Conn.: Yale University Press, 1989).

2. W. H. McNeill, *Plagues and Peoples* (Oxford: Basil Blackwell, 1976); A. Crosby, *Ecological Imperialism* (Cambridge: Cambridge University Press, 1986).

3. Mary Kilbourne Matossian, *Poisons of the Past: Molds, Epidemics, and History* (New Haven, Conn.: Yale University Press, 1989). It is claimed that some of Freud's "hysterical" patients in reality suffered from organic disorders that Freud, in his zeal for psychodynamic explanations, omitted to investigate. See E. M. Thornton, *Hypnotism, Hysteria and Epilepsy: An Hysterical Synthesis* (London: Heinemann, 1976); Lindsay C. Hurst, "What Was Wrong with Anna O," *Journal of the Royal Society of Medicine* 75 (1982): 129–131; and the discussion in Mark Micale, "Hysteria and Its Historiography: A Review of Past and Present Writings," *History of Science* 27 (1989): 223–261, esp. p. 45.

4. The issues of shifting medical terminology are well discussed in J. H. Dirckx, *The Language of Medicine: Its Evolution, Structure, and Dynamics* (New York: Praeger Publishers, 1983); see also Roy Porter, "The Doctor and the Word," *Medical Sociology News* 9 (1983): 21–28.

5. James Longrigg, "Plague of Athens," *History of Science* 18 (1980): 209–225.

6. Such matters lead, of course, to questions as to the meaning of the term *disease* itself; see W. Riesse, *The Conception of Disease: Its History, Its Versions and Its Nature* (New York: Philosophical Library, 1953); G. Risse, "Health and Disease: History of the Concepts," in W. T. Reich, ed., *Encyclopedia of Bioethics*, 2

vols. (New York: Free Press, 1978), 579–585; O. Temkin, "Health and Disease," *Dictionary of the History of Ideas* 2 (1973): 395–407.

7. On cholera, see Margaret Pelling, *Cholera, Fever and English Medicine 1825–1865* (Oxford: Oxford University Press, 1978).

8. See Alan Krohn, *Hysteria: The Elusive Neurosis*, appearing in *Psychological Issues*, nos. 45/46 (New York: International Universities Press, 1978). These problems are intelligently addressed for a comparably elusive condition, asthma, in J. Gabbay, "Asthma Attacked? Tactics for the Reconstruction of a Disease Concept," in *The Problem of Medical Knowledge*, ed. P. Wright and A. Treacher (Edinburgh: Edinburgh University Press, 1982), 23–48. Modern psychiatrists are themselves unsure of the current validity of the hysteria diagnosis. See, for example, several of the contributions in Alec Roy, ed., *Hysteria* (Chichester: John Wiley & Sons, 1982), especially Henri Ey, "Hysteria: History and Analysis of the Concept," 3–19; René Major, "The Revolution of Hysteria," *International Journal of Psycho-Analysis* 15 (1974): 385–392; D. W. Abse, *Hysteria and Related Mental Disorders* (Bristol: Wright, 1987); E. M. R. Critchley and H. E. Cantor, "Charcot's Hysteria Renaissant," *British Medical Journal* 289 (22–29 December 1984): 1785–1788; Harold Merskey, "Hysteria: The History of an Idea," *Canadian Journal of Psychiatry* 28 (1983): 428–433; idem, "The Importance of Hysteria," *British Journal of Psychiatry* 149 (1986): 23–28.

For invaluable reflections on the relations between modern thinking, historiographical trends, and the history of hysteria, see Micale, "Hysteria and Its Historiography" (part 1), 223–261; idem, "Hysteria and Its Historiography" (part 2), 319–350; idem, "Hysteria and Its Historiography: The Future Perspective," *History of Psychiatry* 1 (1990): 33–124.

9. I believe Elaine Showalter's chap. 4 embodies these goals.

10. Though it developed ideas of diseases of the womb, and diseases of love: see Danielle Jacquart and Claude Thomasset, *Sexuality and Medicine in the Middle Ages* (Cambridge: Polity Press, 1989).

11. From the high serious—for instance, F. C. Skey, *Hysteria* (London: Longman, 1867)—to the highly stigmatizing: Robert Thornton, *The Hysterical Woman: Trials, Tears, Tricks, and Tantrums* (Chicago: Donohue & Hennebury, 1893).

12. For the representations of hysteria and other exemplary diseases in art and the media, see Elaine Showalter's and Sander Gilman's chapters. See also S. Sontag, *Illness as Metaphor* (New York: Farrar, Straus & Giroux, 1978); idem, *AIDS and Its Metaphors* (London: Allen Lane, 1988); Sander Gilman, *Difference and Pathology* (Ithaca and London: Cornell University Press, 1985); idem, *Disease and Representation: Images of Illness from Madness to Aids* (Ithaca, N.Y.: Cornell University Press, 1988); idem, *Seeking the Insane: A Cultural History of Madness and Art in the Western World* (New York: Wiley, 1982).

13. Ian Dowbiggin, "The Professional, Sociopolitical, and Cultural Dimensions of Psychiatric Theory in France, 1840–1900," Ph.D. dissertation, University of Rochester, 1986; idem, "French Psychiatric Attitudes toward the Dangers

Posed by the Insane ca. 1870," in *Research in Law, Deviance, and Social Control*, ed. Andrew Scull and Steven Spitzer, vol. 9 (Greenwich, Conn.: JAI Press, 1988), 87–111; Jan Goldstein, "The Hysteria Diagnosis and the Politics of Anticlericalism in Late Nineteenth Century France," *Journal of Modern History* 54 (1982): 209–239; J. Guillais, *Crimes of Passion* (Cambridge: Polity Press, 1989); Ruth Harris, "Melodrama, Hysteria and Feminine Crimes of Passion in the Fin-de-Siècle," *History Workshop* 25 (1988): 31–63; Robert Nye, *The Origins of Crowd Psychology: Gustave LeBon and the Crisis of Mass Democracy in the Third Republic* (London: Sage, 1975); Daniel Pick, *Faces of Degeneration: Aspects of a European Disorder c. 1848–1918* (Cambridge and New York: Cambridge University Press, 1989); Yannick Ripa, *Women and Madness: The Incarceration of Women in Nineteenth Century France* (Cambridge: Polity Press, 1990); S. Moscovici, *L'Age des foules: Un Traité historique de Psychologie des masses* (Paris: Fayard, 1981).

14. On Ada Byron, see D. Stein, *Ada: A Life and Legacy* (Cambridge, Mass.: MIT Press, 1985); for a parallel case, see Roger Cooter, "Dichotomy and Denial: Mesmerism, Medicine and Harriet Martineau," in *Science and Sensibility: Gender and Scientific Enquiry, 1780–1945*, ed. Marina Benjamin (Oxford: Basil Blackwell, 1991), 144–173; generally on patients' accounts of their own conditions, see Dorothy Porter and Roy Porter, *Patient's Progress: Doctors and Doctoring in Eighteenth-Century England* (Cambridge: Polity Press, 1989); idem, *In Sickness and in Health: The British Experience 1650–1850* (London: Fourth Estate, 1988).

15. Mark Micale, "Charcot and the Idea of Hysteria in the Male: A Study of Gender, Mental Science, and Medical Diagnostics in Late Nineteenth Century France," *Medical History* 34 (1990): 363–411.

16. Also discussed in Mark Micale, "Diagnostic Discriminations: Jean-Martin Charcot and the Nineteenth Century Idea of Masculine Hysterical Neurosis," Ph.D. thesis, Yale University, 1987.

17. Edward Shorter, "Paralysis: The Rise and Fall of a 'Hysterical' Symptom," *Journal of Social History* 19 (1986): 549–582; and, more fully, his *From Paralysis to Fatigue: A History of Psychosomatic Illness in the Modern Era* (New York: Free Press, 1992).

18. Robert B. Carter, *On the Pathology and Treatment of Hysteria* (London: John Churchill, 1853).

19. Edward Shorter, "Private Clinics in Central Europe, 1850–1933," *Social History of Medicine* 3, 2 (1990): 159–196; idem, "Women and Jews in a Private Nervous Clinic in Late Nineteenth Century Vienna," *Medical History* 33 (1989): 149–183; Anne Digby, *Madness, Morality and Medicine: A Study of the York Retreat, 1796–1914* (Cambridge: Cambridge University Press, 1985), 217, 287; Charlotte Mackenzie, "A Family Asylum: A History of the Private Madhouse at Ticehurst in Sussex, 1792–1917," Ph.D. dissertation, University of London, 1987; Trevor Turner, "A Diagnostic Analysis of the Casebooks of Ticehurst Asylum 1845–1890," M.D., University of London, 1990.

20. Suzanne Poirier, "The Weir-Mitchell Rest Cure: Doctors and Patients," *Women's Studies* 10 (1983): 15–40; R. D. Walter, *S. Weir Mitchell, MD, Neurologist: A Medical Biography* (Springfield, Ill.: Thomas, 1970); Janet Browne, "Spas and

Sensibilities: Darwin at Malvern," in *The Medical History of Waters and Spas*, ed. Roy Porter (London: Wellcome Institute, *Medical History Supplement* 10, 1990), 102–113; Susan E. Cayleff, *Wash and Be Healed: The Water-Cure Movement and Women's Health* (Philadelphia: Temple University Press, 1987).

21. Edward Shorter, "Mania, Hysteria and Gender in Lower Austria, 1891–1905," *History of Psychiatry* 1 (1990): 3–31; Francis Gosling, *Before Freud: Neurasthenia and the American Medical Community, 1870–1910* (Urbana: University of Illinois Press, 1987).

22. William J. McGrath, *Freud's Discovery of Psychoanalysis: The Politics of Hysteria* (Ithaca, N.Y.: Cornell University Press, 1986); John Forrester, *The Seductions of Psychoanalysis: Freud, Lacan and Derrida* (Cambridge: Cambridge University Press, 1990); C. Bernheimer and Clare Kahane, eds., *In Dora's Case: Freud, Hysteria and Feminism* (New York: Columbia University Press, 1985).

23. D. Mechanic, "The Concept of Illness Behaviour," *Journal of Chronic Disease* 15 (1962): 189–194.

24. For excellent cross-cultural comparative accounts, see A. Kleinman, *Patients and Healers in the Context of Culture: An Exploration of the Borderline between Anthropology, Medicine, and Psychiatry* (Berkeley, Los Angeles, London: University of California Press, 1980); idem, *Social Origins of Distress and Disease: Depression, Neurasthenia, and Pain in Modern China* (New Haven, Conn.: Yale University Press, 1986); idem and B. Good, eds., *Culture and Depression: Studies in the Anthropology and Cross-Cultural Psychiatry of Affect and Disorder* (Berkeley, Los Angeles, London: University of California Press, 1985).

25. For some accounts of these pressures Victorian ideals exerted, see Walter Houghton, Jr., *The Victorian Frame of Mind* (New Haven, Conn.: Yale University Press, 1957); Eric Sigsworth, ed., *In Search of Victorian Values* (Manchester: Manchester University Press, 1988); Martin Wiener, *Reconstructing the Criminal: Culture, Law and Policy in England, 1830–1914* (Cambridge: Cambridge University Press, 1991). For further instances see H. Martineau, *Life in the Sick-Room: Essays by an Invalid*, 2d ed. (London: Moxon, 1854); idem, *Autobiography*, 2 vols. (London: Virago, 1983; 1st ed., 1877).

26. Among the mass of excellent recent feminist scholarship, see, for instance, Joan Jacobs Brumberg, *Fasting Girls: The Emergence of Anorexia Nervosa as a Modern Disease* (Cambridge, Mass.: Harvard University Press, 1989); Lynne Nead, *Myths of Sexuality: Representations of Women in Victorian Britain* (Oxford: Basil Blackwell, 1988); Cynthia Eagle Russett, *Sexual Science: The Victorian Construction of Womanhood* (Cambridge, Mass.: Harvard University Press, 1989).

27. Shorter, "Paralysis"; Elaine Showalter, *The Female Malady: Women, Madness and English Culture, 1830–1980* (London: Virago, 1987); and see op. cit. (ref. 17). Against feminists who claim that hysteria is an effective form of rebellion, Showalter effectively counterargues for the self-victimization thesis. See also Ann Dally, *Why Women Fail* (London: Wildwood House, 1979); idem, *The Morbid Streak* (London: Wildwood House, 1978). For shellshock see Martin Stone, "Shellshock," in *Anatomy of Madness*, ed. W. F. Bynum, Roy Porter, and Michael Shepherd, vol. 2 (London: Routledge, 1985), 242–271; Edward M. Brown, "Be-

tween Cowardice and Insanity: Shell Shock and the Legitimation of the Neuroses in Great Britain," *Science, Technology and the Military* 12 (1988): 323–345.

28. Gilman, *Disease and Representation*, valuably indicates the sociocultural factors behind so many representations of illness.

29. On Briquet's syndrome see Maurice Dongier, "Briquet and Briquet's Syndrome Viewed from France," *Canadian Journal of Psychiatry* 28 (October 1983): 422–427. See also J. Babinski and J. Froment, *Hysteria or Pithiatism and Reflex Nervous Disorders in the Neurology of War* (London: University of London Press, 1918).

30. Harold Merskey, "Hysteria: The History of an Idea," *Canadian Journal of Psychiatry* 28 (1983): 428–433; idem, "Importance of Hysteria."

31. And see also Helen King, "From Parthenos to Gyne: The Dynamics of Category" (Ph.D., University of London, 1985), and James Palis, E. Rossopoulos, and L.-C. Triarkou, "The Hippocratic Concept of Hysteria: A Translation of the Original Texts," *Integrative Psychiatry* 3 (1985): 226–228. Compare A. Rousselle, *Porneia: On Desire and the Body in Antiquity* (Oxford: Basil Blackwell, 1988).

32. (Hysteria has always existed, in all places and in all times.) Quoted in E. Trillat, *Histoire de l'Hystérie* (Paris: Seghers, 1986), 272.

33. J.-M. Charcot and P. Richer, *Les Démoniaques dans l'art* (Paris: Delahaye and Lecrosnier, 1887); J. Carroy-Thirard, "Possession, Extase, Hystérie au XIX siècle," *Psychanalyse à l'Université* (1980), 499–515; idem, *Le Mal de Morzine: De la Possession a l'hystérie* (Paris: Soin, 1981); see also J. Devlin, *The Superstitious Mind: French Peasants and the Supernatural in the Nineteenth Century* (London: Oxford University Press, 1987); Jan Goldstein, *Console and Classify: The French Psychiatric Profession in the Nineteenth Century* (Cambridge: Cambridge University Press, 1987); idem, "The Hysteria Diagnosis and the Politics of Anticlericalism in Late Nineteenth Century France," *Journal of Modern History* 54 (1982): 209–239; Catherine-Laurence Maire, *Les Posedées de Morzine 1857–1873* (Lyons: Presses Universitaires de Lyons, 1981); G. H. Glaser, "Epilepsy, Hysteria and 'Possession'; A Historical Essay," *Journal of Nervous and Mental Disease* 166 (1978): 268–274; on the underlying medical politics, see Jack D. Ellis, *The Physician-Legislators of France: Medicine and Politics in the Early Third Republic, 1870–1914* (Cambridge: Cambridge University Press, 1990); Bernard Brais, "The Making of a Famous Nineteenth Century Neurologist: Jean-Martin Charcot (1825–1893)," M. Phil. thesis, University College, London, 1990.

34. The foundational text for this reading is G. Zilboorg, *The Medical Man and the Witch During the Renaissance* (Baltimore: Johns Hopkins University Press, 1935); and more generally, idem, *A History of Medical Psychology* (New York: Norton, 1947). The self-validating aspects of this ploy have been explored by T. Szasz, *The Myth of Mental Illness* (New York: Paladin, 1961).

35. See the discussion in Micale, "Hysteria and Its Historiography," 226.

36. I. Veith, *Hysteria: The History of a Disease* (Chicago: University of Chicago Press, 1965). Veith's book is assessed in Harold Merskey, "Hysteria: The History of a Disease: Ilza Veith," *British Journal of Psychiatry* 147 (1985): 576–579, and

in Micale, "Hysteria and Its Historiography," 223–261. Elaine Showalter offers in chap. 4 a more sympathetic appraisal of Veith and her work, in context of the ideological constraints shaping her stance, all abundantly clear from Veith's autobiography, *Can You Hear the Clapping of One Hand?* (Berkeley, Los Angeles, London: University of California Press, 1988). The following pages should be read alongside Elaine Showalter's more personal assessment of Veith below, which sympathetically and convincingly reconstructs Veith's study from a biographical viewpoint. The aim of my discussion is rather different: it is to show the inbuilt historiographical biases resulting from uncritically accepted Freudian perspectives.

37. This characterization of the Middle Ages is revealed as complete caricature in Helen King's essay in chap. 1, and in Jacquart and Thomasset's *Sexuality and Medicine in the Middle Ages*, 173ff.

38. Veith, *Hysteria*, 156, 157, 183.

39. J. Breuer and S. Freud, *Studies on Hysteria*, in *The Standard Edition of the Complete Works of Sigmund Freud*, ed. J. Strachey et al., vol. 3 (London: Hogarth Press, 1959), 86.

40. Veith, *Hysteria*, viii.

41. Ibid., 199.

42. Carter, *Pathology and Treatment of Hysteria*; A. Kane and E. Carlson, "A Different Drummer: Robert B. Carter on Nineteenth Century Hysteria," *Bulletin of the New York Academy of Medicine* 58 (1982): 519–534.

43. For a sample see Bernheimer and Kahane, *In Dora's Case;* J. Gallop, *The Daughter's Seduction: Feminism and Psychoanalysis* (Ithaca, N.Y.: Cornell University Press, 1982); Dianne Hunter, "Hysteria, Psychoanalysis, and Feminism: The Case of Anna O.," *Feminist Studies* 9 (1983): 464–488; Showalter, *Female Malady*; J. M. Masson, *The Assault on Truth: Freud's Suppression of the Seduction Theory* (London: Faber, 1984; Harmondsworth, Middlesex: Penguin, 1985); idem, *A Dark Science: Women, Sexuality and Psychiatry in the Nineteenth Century* (New York: Farrar, Straus & Giroux, 1986); M. Rosenbaum and M. Muroff, eds., *Anna O: Fourteen Contemporary Reinterpretations* (New York: Free Press, 1984). For Freud and the witch-hunters, see J. M. Masson, ed., *The Complete Letters of Sigmund Freud to Wilhelm Fliess, 1887–1904* (Cambridge, Mass.: Harvard University Press, 1986), 225.

44. Veith, *Hysteria*, vii.

45. Veith doles out dozens of accolades and brickbats. See, for instance, the judgment on Paré, that his "return to the ancient views on hysteria, though seemingly a regression, was actually a scientific advance": Veith, *Hysteria*, 116; or the view that Jorden showed "extraordinary perceptiveness" because he recognized the role of mental passions (123); likewise the "surprisingly contemporary overtones" of Burton's "blunt assertion of the evils of enforced sexual abstinence" (127).

46. Szasz, *Myth of Mental Illness*. If Szasz's point is well taken, the shortcoming of his view, however, is that he has nothing to say about pre-Freudian accounts of hysteria.

47. Ibid.; also relevant are idem, *The Manufacture of Madness* (New York: Dell Publishing Co., 1970).

48. Szasz, *Myth of Mental Illness,* 100.

49. Ibid., 65.

50. E. Gellner, *The Psychoanalytic Movement* (London: Paladin, 1985); A. C. Macintyre, *The Unconscious* (London: Routledge, 1958).

51. For such psychological pictorialization, see Graham Richards, *On Psychological Language* (London: Routledge, 1989).

52. Szasz, *Myth of Mental Illness,* 19. For instance, the hysteric behaves in a womanly way (being ultra weak) to avoid fulfilling womanly functions (e.g., having sex, having babies, keeping house).

53. Ibid.

54. The rigidity, arbitrariness, and ahistoricity of Szasz's view of disease are well analyzed in Peter Sedgwick, *Psychopolitics* (London: Pluto Press; New York: Harper & Row, 1982).

55. Micale, "Hysteria and Its Historiography," (part 1), 223–261; (part 2), 319–350.

56. Points well made in Ludmilla Jordanova, *Sexual Visions: Images of Gender in Science and Medicine between the Eighteenth and Twentieth Centuries* (Hemel Hempstead: Harvester Wheatsheaf, 1989).

57. See Ian Hacking, *The Taming of Chance* (Cambridge: Cambridge University Press, 1990); G. Canguilhem, *On the Normal and the Pathological* (Dordrecht: D. Reidel, 1978).

58. J. Goldstein, "The Hysteria Diagnosis and the Politics of Anticlericalism in Late Nineteenth Century France," *Journal of Modern History* 54 (1982): 209–239.

59. For classic complaints about the ascientificity of Freud, see K. R. Popper, *The Open Society and Its Enemies* (Princeton, N.J.: Princeton University Press, 1971); H. J. Eysenck, *The Decline and Fall of the Freudian Empire* (Harmondsworth: Viking, 1985); E. Gellner, *The Psychoanalytic Movement* (London: Paladin, 1985).

60. Excellent and contrasting discussions are offered in F. Sulloway, *Freud: Biologist of the Mind* (New York: Basic Books, 1979); William J. McGrath, *Freud's Discovery of Psychoanalysis: The Politics of Hysteria* (Ithaca, N.Y.: Cornell University Press, 1986); Isabel F. Knight, "Freud's *Project*: A Theory for *Studies on Hysteria,*" *Journal of the History of the Behavioral Sciences* 20 (1984): 340–358; B. B. Rubinstein, "Freud's Early Theories of Hysteria," in *Physics, Philosophy and Psychoanalysis: Essays in Honor of Adolf Grünbaum,* ed. R. S. Cohen and L. Laudan (Dordrecht: D. Reidel, 1983), 169–190.

61. Hannah Decker, *Freud in Germany: Revolution and Reaction in Science, 1883–1907* (New York: University Press International, 1977).

62. See S. Marcus, *Freud and the Culture of Psychoanalysis* (Boston: Allen & Unwin, 1984).

63. H. T. Ellenberger, *The Discovery of the Unconscious* (London: Allen Lane, 1970); L. L. Whyte, *The Unconscious Before Freud* (New York: Doubleday, 1962).

64. See M. Foucault, *Discipline and Punish* (Harmondsworth: Penguin, 1979); Theodor T. Adorno and Max Horkheimer, *Dialectic of Enlightenment* (New York: Herder & Herder, 1972); N. Elias, *The Civilizing Process* (Oxford: Basil Blackwell, 1983); and discussion in Dorinda Outram, *The Body and the French Revolution: Sex, Class and Political Culture* (New Haven and London: Yale University Press, 1989), and Roy Porter, "Body Politics: Approaches to the Cultural History of the Body," in *New Perspectives on Historical Writings*, ed. P. Burke (Cambridge: Polity Press, 1991).

65. For histories of mind/body doctrines, see J. Yolton, *Thinking Matter: Materialism in Eighteenth Century Britain* (Minneapolis: University of Minnesota Press, 1983); G. S. Rousseau and Roy Porter, "Introduction: Toward a Natural History of Mind and Body," in *The Languages of Psyche: Mind and Body in Enlightenment Thought*, ed. G. S. Rousseau (Berkeley, Los Angeles, Oxford: University of California Press, 1990), 3–44; B. S. Turner, *The Body and Society: Explorations in Social Theory* (Oxford and New York: Basil Blackwell, 1984). Critiques of mind/body dualism are offered in F. Barker, *The Tremulous Private Body* (London: Methuen, 1984); M. Berman, *The Re-enchantment of the World* (Ithaca, N.Y.: Cornell University Press, 1981). For the Blakean quotation, see Roy Porter, *Mind Forg'd Manacles: A History of Madness from the Restoration to the Regency* (London: Athlone, 1987).

66. There is a hostile account of Freud's hostility to religion in N. Isbister, *Freud: An Introduction to His Life and Work* (Cambridge: Polity Press, 1985); see also Norman O. Brown, *Life and Against Death: The Psychoanalytical Meaning of History* (London: Routledge & Kegan Paul, 1957).

67. Hence orthodox Freudianism's dismissal of Wilhelm Fliess's or Wilhelm Reich's biologism.

68. Peter Gay, *Freud: A Life for Our Time* (London: Dent, 1988). The non-believer in psychoanalysis might observe that Freud substituted the psychoanalytic priesthood for the Christian.

69. P. Lain Entralgo, *Mind and Body* (London: Harvill, 1955); for a good account of medicine's metaphysics, see Lester S. King, *The Philosophy of Medicine: The Early Eighteenth Century* (Cambridge, Mass.: Harvard University Press, 1978). On the Project see Isabel Knight, "Freud's *Project*: A Theory for *Studies on Hysteria*," *Journal of the History of the Behavioral Sciences* 20 (1984): 340–358.

70. E. L. Griggs, ed., *Collected Letters of Samuel Taylor Coleridge* 1 (Oxford: Clarendon Press, 1956), 256: Coleridge to Charles Lloyd, Sr., 14 November 1796; for discussion see Roy Porter, "Barely Touching: A Social Perspective on Mind and Body," in *Languages of Psyche*, ed. Rousseau, 45–80.

71. Szasz, *Myth of Mental Illness*, 8off.

72. F. Bottomley, *Attitudes to the Body in Western Christendom* (London: Lepus Books, 1979); Peter Brown, *The Body and Society: Men, Women and Sexual Renunciation in Early Christianity* (New York: Columbia University Press, 1988).

73. Of course, there is also a long history of attempts, from both sides, to deny the other, e.g., Berkeleyan immaterialism or the kind of dogmatic medical materialism developed from the time of La Mettrie, trying to prove that consciousness is either a complete delusion or at most epiphenomenal. See Roy

Porter, "Medicine in the Enlightenment," in *Inventing Human Science*, ed. C. Fox and R. Porter (Berkeley, Los Angeles, Oxford: University of California Press, 1994). The point is, as I go on to show, that such arguments have largely remained marginal rather than mainstream.

74. M. Clark, "'Morbid Introspection,' Unsoundness of Mind, and British Psychological Medicine, c. 1830–1900," in *Anatomy of Madness*, ed. W. F. Bynum, Roy Porter, and Michael Shepherd, Vol. III (London: Routledge, 1988), 71–101; idem, "The Rejection of Psychological Approaches to Mental Disorder in Late Nineteenth Century British Psychiatry," in *Madhouses, Mad-Doctors and Madmen*, ed. A. Scull (London: Athlone, 1981), 271–312; W. F. Bynum, "The Nervous Patient in Eighteenth and Nineteenth Century Britain: The Psychiatric Origins of British Neurology," in *Anatomy of Madness*, ed. Bynum, Porter, and Shepherd, Vol. I (London: Tavistock, 1985), 89–102; more generally see B. Haley, *The Healthy Body and Victorian Culture* (Cambridge, Mass.: Harvard University Press, 1978); Martin Wiener, *Reconstructing the Criminal: Culture, Law and Policy in England, 1830–1914* (Cambridge: Cambridge University Press, 1991), 168f.; Charles E. Rosenberg, "Body and Mind in Nineteenth-Century Medicine: Some Clinical Origins of the Neurosis Controversy," *Bulletin of the History of Medicine* 63 (1989): 185–197.

75. M. H. Nicolson and G. S. Rousseau, "Bishop Berkeley and Tar Water," in *The Augustan Milieu: Essays Presented to Louis A. Landa*, ed. H. K. Miller (Oxford: Clarendon Press, 1970), 102–137; Marina Benjamin, "Medicine, Morality and the Politics of Berkeley's Tar-Water," in *The Medical Enlightenment of the Eighteenth Century*, ed. Andrew Cunningham and Roger French (Cambridge: Cambridge University Press, 1990), 165–193.

76. The very complex interplay of mind and body in medical therapeutics is splendidly brought out in Rosenberg, "Body and Mind in Nineteenth-Century Medicine," 185–197.

77. Thomas Willis, *Essay of the Pathology of the Brain* (1684), 69, quoted by Veith, *Hysteria*, 134.

78. W. Buchan, *Domestic Medicine, or a Treatise on the Prevention and Cure of Diseases by Regimen and Simple Medicines* (Edinburgh: Bayou, Auld, & Smellie, 1769), 561.

79. The discussion in "Bourgeois Hysteria and the Carnivalesque," by Peter Stallybrass and Allon White, in *The Politics and Poetics of Transgression* (London: Methuen, 1986), 171–190, is highly relevant. They argue that civilization's need to repress the carnivalesque produced a return of the repressed in hysteria. Thus hysteria was a mockery of official mind/body relations.

80. See Rousseau and Porter, "Introduction," in *Languages of Psyche*, ed. Rousseau, 3–44.

81. Feminist historians have plausibly argued that late nineteenth-century female hysterics, such as "Anna O" or Charlotte Perkins Gilman, possessed better insight into their condition than the doctors who treated them. See above, n. 43; and Mary A. Hill, *Charlotte Perkins Gilman: The Making of a Radical Feminist, 1860–1896* (Philadelphia: Temple University Press, 1980).

82. For hysteria in the limelight see Ruth Harris, "Melodrama, Hysteria and

Feminine Crimes of Passion in the Fin-de-Siècle," *History Workshop* 25 (Spring, 1988), 31–63; idem, "Murder under Hypnosis in the Case of Gabrielle Bompard: Psychiatry in the Courtroom in Belle Epoque France," in *Anatomy of Madness*, ed. Bynum, Porter, and Shepherd, Vol. II, 197–241; J. Guillais, *Crimes of Passion* (Cambridge: Polity Press, 1989); G. Didi-Huberman, *Invention de l'Hystérie: Charcot et l'Iconographie Photographique* (Paris: Macula, 1982).

83. Carter, *Pathology and Treatment of Hysteria*, 159f. On mass hysteria see Moscovici, *Age des Foules*; Robert Nye, *Crime, Madness and Politics in Modern France* (Princeton, N.J.: Princeton University Press, 1984).

84. Eliot Slater, "What Is Hysteria?" in *Hysteria*, ed. A. Roy (Chichester: John Wiley, 1982), 37–40, esp. p. 40.

85. Berman, *Re-enchantment of the World*, and classically Theodor T. Adorno and Max Horkheimer, *Dialectic of Enlightenment* (New York: Herder & Herder, 1972). For a more balanced view of Descartes's impact, see T. Brown, "Descartes, Dualism and Psychosomatic Medicine," in *Anatomy of Madness*, ed. Bynum, Porter, and Shepherd, 2:40–62; R. B. Carter, *Descartes's Medical Philosophy* (Baltimore: Johns Hopkins University Press, 1983).

86. Here see John Mullan, "Hypochondria and Hysteria: Sensibility and the Physicians," *The Eighteenth Century: Theory and Interpretation* 25 (1984): 141–174; H. Mayer, *Outsiders: A Study in Life and Letters* (Cambridge, Mass.: MIT Press, 1984).

87. P. M. Spacks, *The Female Imagination* (New York: Knopf, 1975); idem, *Imagining a Self: Autobiography and Novel in Eighteenth Century England* (Cambridge, Mass.: Harvard University Press, 1976); K. O. Lyons, *The Invention of the Self* (Carbondale: Southern Illinois University Press; London: Feffer & Simons, 1978); Janet Todd, *Sensibility: An Introduction* (London: Methuen, 1986); and, for nerves, see especially G. S. Rousseau, "The Language of the Nerves: A Chapter in Social and Linguistic History," in *Language, Self and Society: The Social History of Language*, ed. P. Burke and R. Porter (Cambridge: Polity Press, 1991), 213–275; and Roy Porter, "'Expressing Yourself Ill': The Language of Sickness in Georgian England," in *Language, Self and Society*, ed. Burke and Porter, 276–299.

88. B. Faulkner, *Observations on the General and Improper Treatment of Insanity* (London: H. Reynell, 1789), p. 1; Faulkner added that it had "given birth to endless conjecture, and perpetual error." See also W. Falconer, *A Dissertation on the Influence of the Passions Upon Disorders of the Body* (London: C. Dilly, 1788); J. Haygarth, *Of the Imagination, as a Cause and as a Cure of Disorders of the Body* (Bath: Cadell & Davies, 1800).

89. Nicholas Jewson, "The Disappearance of the Sick Man from Medical Cosmology 1770–1870," *Sociology* 10 (1976): 225–244; idem, "Medical Knowledge and the Patronage System in Eighteenth Century England," *Sociology* 8 (1974): 369–385; D. Porter and R. Porter, *Patient's Progress*.

90. William Heberden, *Medical Commentaries* (London: T. Payne, 1802), 227.

91. Ibid., 225.

92. Ibid., 235. Heberden did insist, however, that "their force will be very different, according to the patient's choosing to indulge and give way to them."

93. Sir Richard Blackmore, *A Treatise of the Spleen and Vapours; or, Hypochon-*

driacal and Hysterical Affections (London: Pemberton, 1725), quoted in Richard Hunter and Ida Macalpine, *Three Hundred Years of Psychiatry: 1535–1860* (London: Oxford University Press, 1963), 320.

94. Barbara Sicherman, "The Uses of a Diagnosis: Doctors, Patients and Neurasthenia," *Journal of the History of Medicine and Allied Sciences* 32 (1977): 33–54.

95. See W. F. Bynum, "Rationales for Therapy in British Psychiatry: 1780–1835," *Medical History* 18 (1974): 317–334; idem, "The Nervous Patient in Eighteenth and Nineteenth Century England: The Psychiatric Origins of British Neurology," in *Anatomy of Madness*, ed. Bynum, Porter, and Shepherd, 1:89–102; Bonnie Ellen Blustein, "'A Hollow Square of Psychological Science': American Neurologists and Psychiatrists in Conflict," in *Madhouses, Mad-doctors and Madmen*, ed. A. Scull (London: Athlone, 1981), 241–270; M. Clark, "'Morbid Introspection,' Unsoundness of Mind, and British Psychological Medicine, c. 1830–1900," in *Anatomy of Madness*, ed. Bynum, Porter, and Shepherd 3:71–101; M. Clark, "The Rejection of Psychological Approaches to Mental Disorder in Late Nineteenth Century British Psychiatry" in *Madhouses, Mad-Doctors and Madmen*, ed. Scull, 271–312. For Tissot see Antoinette Emch-Dériaz, *Towards a Social Conception of Health in the Second Half of the Eighteenth Century: Tissot (1728–1797) and the New Preoccupation with Health and Well-Being* (Ann Arbor, Mich.: University Microfilms International, 1984).

96. Quoted in Andrew Scull, *Mental Disorder/Social Disorder* (Berkeley, Los Angeles, London: University of California Press, 1989), 275.

97. Gosling, *Before Freud*. Of course, it was women who disproportionately underwent the rest-cure hysteria treatments meted out in these clinics. Some, such as Charlotte Perkins Gilman, who was treated by Silas Weir Mitchell, and Virginia Woolf, rebelled against what they considered to be demeaning and counterproductive therapeutics. Elsewhere in this book, Elaine Showalter explains the powerful social, cultural, and medical forces that particularly exposed women to such treatments. See Hill, *Charlotte Perkins Gilman*; Suzanne Poirier, "The Weir-Mitchell Rest Cure: Doctors and Patients," *Women's Studies* 10 (1983): 15–40; R. D. Walter, *S. Weir Mitchell, MD, Neurologist: A Medical Biography* (Springfield, Ill.: Thomas, 1970).

98. Gosling, *Before Freud*; A. Rabinbach, "The Body without Fatigue: A Nineteenth Century Utopia," in *Political Symbolism in Modern Europe: Essays in Honor of George L. Mosse*, ed. S. Drescher, D. Sabean, and A. Sharlin (London: Transaction Books, 1982), 42–62; Shorter, "Paralysis," 549–582; idem, "Mania, Hysteria, and Gender in Lower Austria," 3–32; Clifford Beers, *A Mind That Found Itself* (Pittsburgh: University of Pittsburgh Press, 1981; 1908); Norman Dain, *Clifford W. Beers: Advocate for the Insane* (Pittsburgh: University of Pittsburgh Press, 1980); George Beard, *A Practical Treatise on Nervous Exhaustion (Neurasthenia)* (1880); idem, *American Nervousness: Its Causes and Consequences* (New York: Putnam, 1881); Charles Rosenberg, "The Place of George M. Beard in Nineteenth Century Psychiatry," *Bulletin of the History of Medicine* 36 (1962): 245–259; S. Weir Mitchell, *Doctor and Patient* (Philadelphia: Lippincott, 1888); idem, *Lectures on the Diseases of the Nervous System, Especially in Women* (Philadel-

phia: Lea, 1881); idem, *Doctor and Patient* (Philadelphia: Lippincott, 1888); idem, *Fat and Blood: An Essay on the Treatment of Certain Forms of Neurasthenia and Hysteria* (Philadelphia: Lippincott, 1877); Kenneth Levin, "S. Weir Mitchell: Investigations and Insights into Neurasthenia and Hysteria," *Transactions and Studies of the College of Physicians of Philadelphia* 38 (1971): 168–173.

99. A particular worry of Maudsley's: Trevor Turner, "Henry Maudsley: Psychiatrist, Philosopher and Entrepreneur," in *Anatomy of Madness*, ed. Bynum, Porter, and Shepherd, 3:151–189.

100. For Mill and Carlyle, see Barbara T. Gates, *Victorian Suicide: Mad Crimes and Sad Histories* (Princeton, N.J.: Princeton University Press, 1988), and B. Haley, *The Healthy Body in Victorian Culture* (Cambridge, Mass.: Harvard University Press, 1978); John M. Robson and Jack Stillinger, eds., *Autobiography and Literary Essays by John Stuart Mill* (Toronto: University of Toronto Press, 1981): *Collected Works of John Stuart Mill*, vol. 1. It has often been noted that hysteria cases were never prominent in England. Was this because well-bred young people were trained against introspection and in habits of healthy-minded out-goingness? For some support for this view, see M. Jeanne Peterson, *Family, Love and Work in the Lives of Victorian Gentlewomen* (Bloomington: Indiana University Press, 1989).

101. Veith, *Hysteria*, 212–220. Veith proceeds on the Freudian assumption that such women were suffering from sexual frustration. But why should we assume this? For one thing, it might be argued, per contra, that such patients were pleased to go on rest cure because it offered an *escape* from sexual demands. For another, as Peter Gay has contended, our vision of the frustrated, sex-starved Victorian women may be mythical. See Carl H. Degler, "What Ought to Be and What Was: Women's Sexuality in the Nineteenth Century," *The American Historical Review* 79 (1974): 1467–1490; P. Gay, *The Bourgeois Experience, Victoria to Freud*: vol. 1, *The Education of the Senses*; vol. 2, *The Tender Passion* (New York: Oxford University Press, 1984 and 1986).

102. Bevan Lewis, *A Textbook of Mental Diseases* (London: Griffin, 1889), 143.

103. M. Clark, "'Morbid Introspection,' Unsoundness of Mind, and British Psychological Medicine, c. 1830–1900," in *Anatomy of Madness*, ed. Bynum, Porter, and Shepherd, 3:71–101; A. N. Gilbert, "Masturbation and Insanity: Henry Maudsley and the Ideology of Sexual Repression," *Albion* 12 (1980): 268–282. For an exemplary source, see D. Hack Tuke, *Illustrations of the Influence of the Mind upon the Body in Health and Disease, Designed to Elucidate the Action of the Imagination* (London: Churchill, 1872).

104. Henry Maudsley, *Body and Mind* (London: Macmillan & Co., 1873), 79–80.

105. Ibid.

106. On Woolf see Roger Poole, *The Unknown Virginia Woolf* (Brighton: Harvester Press, 1982); Stephen Trombley, *"All That Summer She Was Mad": Virginia Woolf* (London: Junction Books, 1981); Elaine Showalter, *The Female Malady* (New York: Pantheon, 1986); Elizabeth Abel, *Virginia Woolf and the Fictions of Psychoanalysis* (Chicago: University of Chicago Press, 1990).

107. Jean-Martin Charcot, *Charcot the Clinician: The Tuesday Lessons: Excerpts*

from Nine Case Presentations on General Neurology Delivered at the Salpêtrière Hospital in 1887–88, translation and commentary by Christopher G. Goetz (New York: Raven Press, 1987).

108. Well emphasized in Martin Wiener, *Reconstructing the Criminal: Culture, Law and Policy in England, 1830–1914* (Cambridge: Cambridge University Press, 1991), 40f.

109. M. Praz, *The Romantic Agony* (Oxford: Oxford University Press, 1933); M. Poovey, *Uneven Developments: The Ideological Work of Gender in Mid-Victorian England* (London: Virago, 1989).

110. Bram Dijkstra, *Idols of Perversity: Fantasies of Feminine Evil in Fin de Siècle Culture* (Oxford: Oxford University Press, 1986).

111. Peterson's *Family, Love and Work in the Lives of Victorian Gentlewomen* has warned us not to equate advice for women with actual women's lives, reminding us that many women escaped, or coped perfectly happily with these pressures.

112. For women as defined by Victorian science and society see Cynthia Eagle Russett, *Sexual Science: The Victorian Construction of Womanhood* (Cambridge, Mass.: Harvard University Press, 1989).

113. See most recently Ornella Moscucci, *The Science of Woman: Gynaecology and Gender in England, 1800–1929* (Cambridge: Cambridge University Press, 1990); Londa Schiebinger, *The Mind Has No Sex? Women in the Origins of Modern Science* (Cambridge, Mass.: Harvard University Press, 1989); Lynne Nead, *Myths of Sexuality: Representations of Women in Victorian Britain* (Oxford: Basil Blackwell, 1988); Thomas Laqueur, *Making Sex: Body and Gender from the Greeks to Freud* (Cambridge, Mass.: Harvard University Press, 1990).

114. There is a disappointing lack of studies of the wider social significance of the nineteenth-century revolution in medicine. See however M. Jeanne Peterson, *The Medical Profession in Mid-Victorian London* (Berkeley, Los Angeles, London: University of California Press, 1978); A. J. Youngson, *The Scientific Revolution in Victorian Medicine* (London: Croom Helm, 1979). This situation will be rectified by the forthcoming work by W. F. Bynum, *Basic Science and Clinical Medicine in Nineteenth Century Society* (Cambridge: Cambridge University Press, 1994). Michel Foucault, *The Birth of the Clinic,* trans. A. M. Sheridan Smith (London: Tavistock, 1973), is highly suggestive.

115. For the development of these professional specialties see, for instance, E. Lesky, *The Vienna Medical School of the Nineteenth Century* (Baltimore: Johns Hopkins University Press, 1976); R. Maulitz, *Morbid Appearances: The Anatomy of Pathology in the Early Nineteenth Century* (Cambridge: Cambridge University Press, 1987); L. S. Jacyna, "Somatic Theories of Mind and the Interests of Medicine in Britain, 1850–1879," *Medical History* 26 (1982): 233–258; E. Clarke and L. S. Jacyna, *Nineteenth Century Origins of Neuroscientific Concepts* (Berkeley, Los Angeles, London: University of California Press, 1987); A. Scull, *Social Order/ Mental Disorder: Anglo-American Psychiatry in Historical Perspective* (London: Routledge, 1989), esp. "From Madness to Mental Illness: Medical Men as Moral Entrepreneurs," 118–161; Constance M. McGovern, *Masters of Madness: Social Origins of the American Psychiatric Profession* (Hanover and London: University

Press of New England, 1985); Moscucci, *Science of Woman*; B. Latour, *The Pasteurization of France* (Cambridge, Mass.: Harvard University Press, 1988).

116. Jacyna, "Somatic Theories of Mind"; illuminating is L. Fleck, *Genesis and Development of a Scientific Fact* (Chicago: University of Chicago Press, 1979).

117. Foucault, *Birth of the Clinic*, trans. S. Smith; D. Armstrong, *The Political Anatomy of the Body* (Cambridge: Cambridge University Press, 1983); Canguilhem, *On the Normal and the Pathological*.

118. Ian Dowbiggin, "Degeneration and Hereditarianism in French Mental Medicine 1840–1890: Psychiatric Theory as Ideological Adaptation," in *Anatomy of Madness*, ed. Bynum, Porter, and Shepherd, 1:188–232; Nye, *Crime, Madness and Politics in Modern France*.

119. Elaine Showalter and English Showalter, "Victorian Women and Menstruation," *Victorian Studies* 14 (1970): 83–89; Thomas W. Laqueur, "Orgasm, Generation, and the Politics of Reproductive Biology," in *The Making of the Modern Body*, ed. C. Gallagher and T. Laqueur (Berkeley, Los Angeles, London: University of California Press, 1987), 1–41; E. Gasking, *Investigations into Generation, 1651–1828* (London: Hutchinson, 1967); F. J. Cole, *Early Theories of Sexual Generation* (Oxford: Clarendon Press, 1930).

120. On women and difference see Ludmilla Jordanova, *Sexual Visions: Images of Gender in Science and Medicine Between the Eighteenth and Twentieth Centuries* (Hemel Hempstead: Harvester Wheatsheaf, 1989); S. Gilman, *Difference and Pathology* (Ithaca and London: Cornell University Press, 1985).

121. On this pathologizing of female sexuality, see G. J. Barker-Benfield, *The Horrors of the Half-Known Life: Male Attitudes towards Women and Sexuality in Nineteenth Century America* (New York: Harper, 1976); C. Smith-Rosenberg, "The Hysterical Woman: Sex Roles and Role Conflict in Nineteenth Century America," *Social Research* 39 (1972): 652–678; C. Smith-Rosenberg and C. Rosenberg, "The Female Animal: Medical and Biological Views of Woman and Her Role in Nineteenth Century America," in *Women and Health in America: Historical Readings*, ed. J. W. Leavitt (Madison: University of Wisconsin Press, 1984), 12–27; Lorna Duffin, "The Conspicuous Consumptive: Woman as an Invalid," in Delamont and L. Duffin, eds., *The Nineteenth Century Woman: Her Cultural and Physical World*, ed. S. Delamont and L. Duffin (London: Croom Helm, 1978), 26–56.

122. The best account of the rise of British gynecology in the nineteenth century is Moscucci, *Science of Woman*.

123. Michel Foucault, *Histoire de la sexualité*, vol. 1, *La volonté de savoir* (Paris: Gallimard, 1976) (trans. Robert Hurley, *The History of Sexuality: Introduction* [London: Allen Lane, 1978]).

124. Nancy F. Cott, "Passionlessness: An Interpretation of Victorian Sexual Ideology," in *Women and Health in America: Historical Readings*, ed. J. W. Leavitt (Madison: University of Wisconsin Press, 1984), 57–69.

125. Discussions of views such as this can be found in Smith-Rosenberg and Rosenberg, "Female Animal," in *Women and Health in America*, ed. Leavitt, 12–27.

126. On chlorosis see K. Figlio, "Chlorosis and Chronic Disease in Nineteenth-

Century Britain: The Social Constitution of Somatic Illness in a Capitalist Society," *Social History* 3 (1978): 167–197; I. S. L. Loudon, "Chlorosis, Anaemia and Anorexia Nervosa," *British Medical Journal* (1978), I, 974–977; Joan J. Brumberg, "Chlorotic Girls 1870–1920: A Historical Perspective on Female Adolescence," in *Women and Health in America*, ed. Leavitt, 186–195.

127. On masturbation see E. H. Hare, "Masturbatory Insanity: The History of an Idea," *Journal of Mental Science* 108 (1962): 1–25; R. H. MacDonald, "The Frightful Consequences of Onanism," *Journal of the History of Ideas* 28 (1967): 423–441; J. Stengers and A. Van Neck, *Histoire d'une Grande Peur: La Masturbation* (Brussels: University of Brussels Press, 1984).

128. Hysteria was the mimic disorder. Charcot spoke of "neuromimesis," "this property possessed by functional diseases of resembling organic ones"; he discussed the problem of "simulation" as a kind of "art for its own sake" (l'art pour l'art) done "with the idea of making a sensation, to excite pity." J.-M. Charcot, *Clinical Lectures on Diseases of the Nervous System*, trans. T. Savill (London: New Sydenham Society, 1889), 14. This has been reprinted in the Tavistock Classics in the History of Psychiatry series (London: Routledge, 1990), with a fine introduction by Ruth Harris.

129. See the strictures of Carter: Carter, *Pathology and Treatment of Hysteria* (London: John Churchill, 1853), 69.

130. Maudsley, *Body and Mind*, 62–64.

131. John Haslam, *Considerations on the Moral Management of Insane Persons* (London: R. Hunter, 1817), 4–5. Haslam stressed that this was a matter of exclusive medical judgment, for "of such circumstances those who are not of the medical profession would be unable to judge."

132. George Man Burrows, *Commentaries on Insanity* (London: Underwood, 1828), 146–148.

133. Ibid. See Vern Bullough and Martha Voght, "Women, Menstruation and Nineteenth Century Medicine," in *Women and Health in America: Historical Readings*, ed. Leavitt, 28–38; J. Delaney, M. J. Lupton, and E. Toth, *The Curse: A Cultural History of Menstruation* (New York: Dutton, 1976). For comparable views to those of Burrows, see Thomas Laycock, *An Essay on Hysteria* (Philadelphia: Haswell, 1840); idem, *A Treatise on the Nervous Diseases of Women: Comprising an Inquiry into the Nature, Causes and Treatment of Spinal and Hysterical Disorders* (London: Longman, 1840); idem, *Mind and Brain, or the Correlations of Consciousness and Organization*, 2 vols. (Edinburgh: Sutherland & Knox, 1860); Alex Leff, "Thomas Laycock and the Cerebral Reflex," *History of Psychiatry* 2 (1991): 385–408. All such writers bear out Michael Clark's point, that Victorian psychiatrists looked to organic causation: M. J. Clark, "The Rejection of Psychological Approaches to Mental Disorder in Late Nineteenth Century British Psychiatry," in *Madhouses, Mad-Doctors and Madmen*, ed. Scull, 271–312.

134. Burrows, *Commentaries on Insanity*, 146.

135. Ibid.

136. Ibid.

137. Ibid., 147.

138. Ibid.

139. Ibid.

140. Ibid.

141. Ibid., 148.

142. Ibid.

143. Ibid., 191.

144. Ibid.

145. Ibid.

146. Ibid. Nevertheless, Burrows admitted that "occasional hysteria, however, in young and susceptible females whose nervous systems are always highly irritable, may certainly occur without any such suspicion."

147. Alfred Maddock, *On Mental and Nervous Disorders* (London: Simpkin, Marshall & Co., 1854), 177.

148. Ibid.

149. John Millar, *Hints on Insanity* (London: Henry Renshaw, 1861), 32.

150. Maudsley, *Body and Mind*, 79.

151. Ibid.

152. Ibid.; A. N. Gilbert, "Masturbation and Insanity: Henry Maudsley and the Ideology of Sexual Repression," *Albion* 12 (1980): 268–282; Trevor Turner, "Henry Maudsley: Psychiatrist, Philosopher and Entrepreneur," in *Anatomy of Madness*, ed. Bynum, Porter, and Shepherd, 3:151–189.

153. Henry Maudsley, *The Pathology of Mind* (New York: Appleton, 1886), 464.

154. Maudsley, *Body and Mind*, 79–80.

155. Ibid. On earlier views of nymphomania see G. S. Rousseau, "Nymphomania, Bienville and the Rise of Erotic Sensibility," in *Sexuality in Eighteenth-Century Britain*, ed. P.-G. Boucé (Manchester: Manchester University Press, 1982), 95–120. For fears of sexually active women, see Elizabeth Lunbeck, "'A New Generation of Women': Progressive Psychiatrists and the Hypersexual Female," *Feminist Studies* 13 (1987): 514–543.

156. Veith, *Hysteria*, 197.

157. W. Griesinger, *Mental Pathology and Therapeutics*, trans. C. Lockhard Robertson and James Rutherford (London: New Sydenham Society, 1867). For similar views expressed by other German neurologists, see F. Schiller, *A Moebius Strip: Fin-de-siècle Neuropsychiatry and Paul Moebius* (Berkeley, Los Angeles, London: University of California Press, 1982).

158. Griesinger, *Mental Pathology and Therapeutics*, trans. Robertson and Rutherford, 1; Veith, *Hysteria*, 197.

159. Jeffrey M. Masson, *Against Therapy* (London: Fontana, 1990); idem, *A Dark Science: Women, Sexuality and Psychiatry in the Nineteenth Century* (New York: Farrar, Straus and Giroux, 1986); Moscucci, *Science of Woman*; A. Scull and D. Favreau, "A Chance to Cut Is a Chance to Cure: Sexual Surgery for Psychosis in Three Nineteenth Century Societies," in *Research in Law, Deviance and Social Control*, vol. 8, ed. S. Spitzer and A. Scull (Greenwich, Conn.: JAI Press, 1986), 3–39; A. Scull and D. Favreau, "The Clitoridectomy Craze," *Social Research* 53

(1986): 243–260; Ann Dally, *Women under the Knife: A History of Surgery* (London: Hutchinson, 1991). See Isaac Baker Brown, *On the Curability of Certain Forms of Insanity, Epilepsy, Catalepsy and Hysteria in Females* (London: Robert Hardwick, 1866). More generally upon gynecological violence, see Roger Cooter, "Dichotomy and Denial: Mesmerism, Medicine and Harriet Martineau," in *Science and Sensibility: Gender and Scientific Enquiry, 1780–1945*, ed. Marina Benjamin (Oxford: Basil Blackwell, 1991), 144–173.

160. See broadly E. Clarke and L. S. Jacyna, *Nineteenth Century Origins of Neuroscientific Concepts* (Berkeley, Los Angeles, London: University of California Press, 1987); Anne Harrington, *Medicine, Mind and the Double Brain: A Study in Nineteenth Century Thought* (Princeton, N.J.: Princeton University Press, 1987).

161. For the new medicine of the nineteenth-century hospital, see Foucault, *Birth of the Clinic*, trans. S. Smith (London: Tavistock, 1973); E. H. Ackerknecht, *Medicine at the Paris Hospital, 1794–1848* (Baltimore: Johns Hopkins University Press, 1967); L. Granshaw and Roy Porter, eds., *The Hospital in History* (London: Routledge, 1989); C. E. Rosenberg, *The Care of Strangers: The Rise of America's Hospital System* (New York: Basic Books, 1987), esp. the discussion in the introduction.

162. For degenerationism, see Dowbiggin, "Degeneration and Hereditarianism in French Mental Medicine," in *Anatomy of Madness*, ed. Bynum, Porter, and Shepherd, 1:188–232; Nye, *Crime, Madness and Politics in Modern France*; D. Pick, *Faces of Degeneration: A European Disorder, 1848–1918* (Cambridge: Cambridge University Press, 1989); J. E. Chamberlin and S. L. Gilman, *Degeneration: The Dark Side of Progress* (New York: Columbia University Press, 1985); S. Gilman, *Difference and Pathology* (Ithaca, N.Y.: Cornell University Press, 1985).

163. Didi-Huberman, *Invention de l'Hystérie*. For Charcot see Pearce Bailey, *J.-M. Charcot, 1825–1893: His Life—His Work* (London: Pitman Medical, 1959); A. R. G. Owen, *Hysteria, Hypnosis and Healing: The Work of J. M. Charcot* (London: Dobson, 1971).

164. Stallybrass and White, "Bourgeois Hysteria and the Carnivalesque," in *Politics and Poetics of Transgression* (London: Methuen, 1986), 171–190; from the literary viewpoint, quite helpful is Martha Noel Evans, *Fits and Starts: A Genealogy of Hysteria in Modern France* (Ithaca, N.Y.: Cornell University Press, 1991).

165. Trillat, *Histoire de l'hystérie*; Micale, "Hysteria and Its Historiography" (part 2), 319–350. For the French alienist tradition see Jan Goldstein, *Console and Classify: The French Psychiatric Profession in the Nineteenth Century* (Cambridge: Cambridge University Press, 1987).

166. Charcot, *Clinical Lectures*, trans. Savill, 12. See also Charcot, *Charcot the Clinician*, translation and commentary by Goetz.

167. E. W. Massey and L. C. McHenry, "Hysteroepilepsy in the Nineteenth Century: Charcot and Gowers," *Neurology* 36 (1986): 65–67.

168. Points well made in Mark Micale, "Diagnostic Discriminations: Jean Martin Charcot and the Nineteenth Century Idea of Masculine Hysterical Neurosis," Ph.D., Yale University, 1987; idem, "Hysteria Male/Hysteria Female:

Reflections on Comparative Gender Construction in Nineteenth Century France and Britain," in *Science and Sensibility*, ed. Benjamin, 200–242; see also Charcot, *Clinical Lectures*, trans. Savill, 77.

169. Charcot, *Clinical Lectures*, trans. Savill, 131–166.

170. Ibid., 77.

171. Ibid., 13. For Briquet see Pierre Briquet, *Traité Clinique et Therapeutique de l'hystérie* (Paris: Baillière, 1859); Maurice Dongier, "Briquet and Briquet's Syndrome Viewed from France," *Canadian Journal of Psychiatry* 28 (1983): 422–427; François M. Mai, "Pierre Briquet: Nineteenth-Century Savant with Twentieth-Century Ideas," *Canadian Journal of Psychiatry* 28 (1983): 418–421; idem and Harold Merskey, "Briquet's Concept of Hysteria: An Historical Perspective," *Canadian Journal of Psychiatry* 26 (1981): 57–63; idem, "Briquet's *Treatise on Hysteria*: A Synopsis and Commentary," *Archives of General Psychiatry* 37 (1980): 1401–1405. Briquet saw hysteria as a neurosis of the brain.

172. Charcot, *Clinical Lectures*, trans. Savill, 13.

173. For Bernheim see H. Bernheim, *Suggestive Therapeutics: A Treatise on the Nature and Uses of Hypnotism* (Westport, Conn.: Associated Booksellers, 1957).

174. A Harrington, "Metals and Magnets in Medicine: Hysteria, Hypnosis and Medical Culture in Fin-de-Siècle Paris," *Psychological Medicine* 28 (1988): 21–38; idem, "Hysteria, Hypnosis, and the Lure of the Invisible: The Rise of Neo-Mesmerism in Fin-de-Siècle French Psychiatry," in *Anatomy of Madness*, ed. Bynum, Porter, and Shepherd, 3:226–246. Rather similarly Charcot discovered, in the case of one male hysteric, that when the skin of the patient's scrotum was pinched, the patient began a hysterical attack. One is not surprised. Charcot, *Clinical Lecures*, trans. Savill, 239.

175. Points well made by Micale, "Hysteria and Its Historiography" (part 2), 319–350.

176. Charcot, *Clinical Lecures*, trans. Savill, 3.

177. Ibid. Charcot raised the possibility of "contagious imitation" only to dismiss it: 7.

178. P. Janet, *The Major Symptoms of Hysteria: Fifteen Lectures Given in the Medical School of Harvard University*, 2d ed. (New York: Macmillan, 1929).

179. Charcot, *Clinical Lecures*, trans. Savill, 14.

180. For Charcot and sex, see Emily Apter, *Feminizing the Fetish: Psychoanalysis and Narrative Obsession* (Ithaca, N.Y., and London: Cornell University Press, 1991).

181. Charcot, *Clinical Lecures*, trans. Savill, 85.

182. Ibid., 99. Hereditary diathesis offered one cast-iron reason why *male* hysteria existed.

183. A point well made in Ruth Harris, "Murder under Hypnosis in the Case of Gabrielle Bompard: Psychiatry in the Courtroom in Belle Epoque France," in *Anatomy of Madness*, ed. Bynum, Porter, and Shepherd, 2:197–241.

184. See Scull, *Social Order/Mental Disorder*; Michel Foucault, *Madness and Civilization, History of Insanity in the Age of Reason*, trans. Richard Howard (New

York: Random House, 1965); A. Digby, *Madness, Morality and Medicine* (Cambridge: Cambridge University Press, 1985); M. Fears, "Therapeutic Optimism and the Treatment of the Insane," in *Health Care and Health Knowledge*, ed. R. Dingwall (London: Croom Helm, 1977), 66–81; idem, "The 'Moral Treatment' of Insanity: A Study in the Social Construction of Human Nature," Ph.D. thesis, University of Edinburgh, 1978.

185. Veith, *Hysteria*, 202, 209.

186. Carter, *Pathology and Treatment of Hysteria*. See also Kane and Carlson, "A Different Drummer: Robert B. Carter," 519–534; Elaine Showalter examines Carter's work (see chap. 4) from the viewpoint of gender.

187. Carter, *Pathology and Treatment of Hysteria*, 83.

188. Ibid.

189. Ibid.

190. See Alex Leff, "Thomas Laycock and the Cerebral Reflex," *History of Psychiatry* 2 (1991) 385–408.

191. Carter, *Pathology and Treatment of Hysteria*, 17.

192. Ibid., 2.

193. Ibid., 43.

194. Ibid.

195. Ibid., 46.

196. Ibid.

197. Ibid., 51.

198. Ibid., 56.

199. Ibid., 96.

200. Ibid., 129.

201. Ibid., 67.

202. Ibid., 106.

203. Ibid., 113.

204. Ibid., 111.

205. Ibid., 95.

206. Ibid., 35.

207. Ibid., 26.

208. Ibid., 122.

209. Ibid., 107.

210. It would be intriguing, for example, to examine Judge Schreber in this light. See Ida Macalpine and Richard Hunter, eds., *Memoirs of My Nervous Illness, by Daniel Paul Schreber* (London: William Dawson & Sons, 1955).

211. For discussion of mind and body as theorized within the intellectual framework of psychoanalysis, see Sander Gilman's essay (chap. 5) and also his *The Jewish Body* (London: Routledge, 1991). It would, of course, be desirable to extend the discussion in the present essay further than the threshold of psychoanalysis, up toward the present day, but that would be a gigantic undertaking. On hysteria within psychoanalysis itself, the items cited in the following note offer a helpful way in. On the broader developments and debates within twentieth-century psychiatry, see nn. 8 and 30 above.

212. Monique David-Ménard, *Hysteria from Freud to Lacan: Body and Language in Psychoanalysis* (Ithaca, N.Y.: Cornell University Press, 1989); John Forrester, *The Seductions of Psychoanalysis: Freud, Lacan and Derrida* (Cambridge: Cambridge University Press, 1990).

FOUR

Hysteria, Feminism, and Gender

Elaine Showalter

Hysteria has taken many strange turnings in its long career, but one of
the most surprising is the modern marriage of hysteria and feminism,
the fascination among feminist intellectuals, literary critics, and artists
with what Mary Kelly calls "the continuing romance of hysteria."[1] Feminist understanding of hysteria has been influenced by work in semiotics and discourse theory, seeing hysteria as a specifically feminine
protolanguage, communicating through the body messages that cannot
be verbalized. For some writers, hysteria has been claimed as the first
step on the road to feminism, a specifically feminine pathology that
speaks to and against patriarchy. For others, the famous women hysterics of the nineteenth century have been taken to epitomize a universal
female oppression. As the French novelist and theorist Hélène Cixous
melodramatically inquires, "What woman is not Dora?"[2]

This ardent reclaiming of hysteria in the name of feminism is a new
twist in the history of the disorder. Throughout its history, of course,
hysteria has always been constructed as a "woman's disease," a feminine
disorder, or a disturbance of femininity, but this construction has usually
been hostile. Hysteria has been linked with women in a number of un-
flattering ways. Its vast, shifting repertoire of symptoms reminded some
doctors of the lability and capriciousness they associated with female nature. "Mutability is characteristic of hysteria because it is characteristic
of women," wrote the Victorian physician Edward Tilt. "*La donna è
mobile.*"[3] Doctors have tended to favor arguments from biology that
link hysteria with femaleness: "Women are prone to hysteria because
of something fundamental in their nature, something innate, fixed or

given that obviously requires interaction with environmental forces to become manifest but is still a primary and irremediable fate for the human female."[4] "As a general rule," wrote the French physician Auguste Fabre in 1883, "all women are hysterical and . . . every woman carries with her the seeds of hysteria. Hysteria, before being an illness, is a temperament, and what constitutes the temperament of a woman is rudimentary hysteria."[5] The hysterical seizure, *grande hystérie,* was regarded as an acting out of female sexual experience, a "spasm of hyperfemininity, mimicking . . . both childbirth and the female orgasm."[6]

In the twentieth century, these views about an essential and organic female biology that produces hysteria have mutated into more psychological portraits that link hysteria with *femininity*—with a range of "feminine" personality traits. In a psychoanalytic context, women have been seen as disadvantaged in mastering oedipal tasks and thus disposed to hysterical behaviors. Thus, according to the British analyst Gregorio Kohon, "A woman at heart always remains a hysteric."[7] Paul Chodoff notes that hysterical behaviors "may present as . . . unattractive, noisy, emotional displays . . . or as the hysterical (histrionic) personality disorder—a DSM-III diagnostic label, referring to habitual and sustained patterns of behavior characteristic of some women."[8] The diagnosis becomes "a caricature of femininity" but also an exaggeration of the cognitive and personal styles that women are encouraged to develop as attractively "feminine."[9]

Until recently, stories about hysteria were told by men, and women were always the victims in these stories rather than the heroines. In the past few decades, however, the story of hysteria has been told by women historians as well as by male doctors and psychoanalysts. They have argued that hysteria is caused by women's oppressive social roles rather than by their bodies or psyches, and they have sought its sources in cultural myths of femininity and in male domination. What we might call the "herstory" of hysteria is the contribution of feminist social historians to this project, in works that concentrate on the misogyny of male physicians and the persecution of female deviants in witch-hunts.[10]

But as Mark Micale notes, "No line of evolution within the historiography of hysteria is more complicated than the feminist one."[11] The feminist romance with hysteria began in the wake of the women's liberation movement of the late 1960s and the French *événements* of May 1968, when a young generation of feminist intellectuals, writers, and critics in Europe and the United States began to look to Freudian and Lacanian psychoanalysis for a theory of femininity, sexuality, and sexual difference. They began with the Viennese women who were treated by

Freud and Breuer for hysteria, and who had in a sense given birth to the psychoanalytic method, the "talking cure." Feminist interpretations of hysteria in women offered a new perspective that decoded physical symptoms, psychotherapeutic exchanges, and literary texts as the presentations of conflict over the meaning of femininity in a particular historical context. Hysteria came to figure as what Juliet Mitchell calls "the daughter's disease," a syndrome of physical and linguistic protest against the social and symbolic laws of the Father.[12]

Many Lacanian feminist critics interpret hysteria as a women's language of the body, or pre-oedipal semiotics. Still others see bisexuality as the significance of the syndrome. Thus Jane Gallop writes, "Freud links hysteria to bisexuality; the hysteric identifies with members of both sexes, cannot choose one sexual identity. . . . If feminism is the calling into question of constraining sexual identities, then the hysteric may be a protofeminist."[13] Similarly, Claire Kahane defines "hysterical questions" as questions about bisexuality and sexual identity: "Am I a man? Am I a woman? How is sexual identity assumed? How represented?"[14]

But could hysteria also be the *son's* disease, or perhaps the disease of the powerless and silenced? Although male hysteria has been documented since the seventeenth century, feminist critics have ignored its clinical manifestations, writing as though "hysterical questions" about sexual identity are only women's questions. In order to get a fuller perspective on the issues of sexual difference and identity in the history of hysteria, however, we need to add the category of gender to the feminist analytic repertoire. The term "gender" refers to the social relations between the sexes, and the social construction of sexual roles. It stresses the relational aspects of masculinity and femininity as concepts defined in terms of each other, and it engages with other analytical categories of difference and power, such as race and class. Rather than seeking to repair the historical record by adding women's experiences and perceptions, gender theory challenges basic disciplinary paradigms and questions the fundamental assumptions of the field.[15]

When we look at hysteria through the lens of gender, new feminist questions begin to emerge. Instead of tracing the history of hysteria as a female disorder, produced by misogyny and changing views of femininity, we can begin to see the linked attitudes toward masculinity that influenced both diagnosis and the behavior of male physicians. Conversely, by applying feminist methods and insights to the symptoms, therapies, and texts of male hysteria, we can begin to understand that issues of gender and sexuality are as crucial to the history of male experience as they have been in shaping the history of women.

In particular, we need to see how hysteria in men has always been regarded as a shameful, "effeminate" disorder. In many early studies the male hysteric was assumed to be unmanly, womanish, or homosexual, as if the feminine component within masculinity were itself a symptom of disease. John Russell Reynolds wrote in *A System of Medicine* that hysterical men and boys were "either mentally or morally of feminine constitution."[16] In his case studies of male hysteria at the end of the nineteenth century, Emile Batault observed that hysterical men were thought to be "timid and fearful men. . . . Coquettish and eccentric, they prefer ribbons and scarves to hard manual labor." These expectations made it difficult for doctors to accept the hysteria diagnosis in men who seemed conventionally virile. While it might be possible to "imagine a perfumed and pomaded *femmelette* suffering from this bizarre malady," Batault noted, "that a robust working man has nerves and vapours like a woman of the world" strained credulity.[17]

The prejudices and stereotypes Batault protested at the Salpêtrière are alive and well in the twentieth century. "One gets the impression," an analyst notes, "that a male hysteric is one who behaves 'like a woman.'"[18] Wilhelm Reich described the male hysteric as characterized by "softness and over-politeness, feminine facial expression and feminine behavior."[19] The image of the hysteric in psychiatric literature is such that "the man who would most closely fit the description would be a passive homosexual."[20] Thus discussions of male hysteria, rather than transforming the discourse of hysteria as representing the worst aspects of femininity, actually reinforce the stereotype that it is the disease of weak, passive, overly emotional people, whether female or male.

Gender constructs, moreover, are not restricted to the medical profession. They also inflect the way we write the history of medicine and psychiatry. While feminist literary critics often seem narrow in their use of history, limiting their textual interpretations to a tiny group of famous doctors and patients, historians are rarely sensitive to figurative language and to the inscriptions of gender ideology in medical texts. History can show us where to look for a more accurate and complete picture of hysteria, but literary criticism can show scientists and historians how to read the texts and gender subtexts of medicine, psychiatry, and history itself. For while social historians of hysteria have been sensitive to the ways that attitudes toward women shaped and distorted the work of doctors like Robert Brudenell Carter, Charcot, or Freud, they have written as if they too were not influenced by gender constructs. Issues of sexual difference are relevant to historiography as well as medicine.

Moreover, writing about hysteria is different for women than it is for men. Because of traditional beliefs about the potential hysteria of *all* women, women scholars are more conscious of the need to find an objective, impersonal, and scientific language and discourse about the subject. How can one who is potentially hysterical, "at heart always a hysteric," transcend her nature to write about the disorder? Since feminism has often been interpreted as hysteria by male physicians and social critics, women writing about hysteria in the early part of the twentieth century may have avoided feminist interpretations of hysterical phenomena.

On the other hand, men writing about hysteria, in males or females, can masquerade their own emotions as reason, or disguise feeling and prejudice behind other terminologies and self-definitions. In his study *L'hystérique, le sexe, et le médecin,* the French psychiatrist Lucien Israël discusses the "unconscious complicity between sick men and male doctors to avoid the shameful and infamous diagnosis of hysteria." But when he talks about what he terms "successful hysterics," people who in their adult lives seemed to outgrow their adolescent hysteria, or transformed what had been hysterical symptoms into social causes, Israël mentions only women, such as Mary Baker Eddy, the founder of Christian Science, and Bertha Pappenheim, or Anna O., who became a German feminist leader. He sees their dedication as an evolutionary form of feminine hysteria itself, an obsessive desire to become the *maître* rather than submit to him, an acting out of fantasies of devotion. Thus female activism becomes merely a constructive pathology, and feminism only a healthier form of hysteria. It does not occur to Israël to label Flaubert or Sartre a successful hysteric, let alone to speculate on the way this scenario might explain the career decisions of male psychoanalysts.[21]

Language has played a major role in the history of hysteria; to pry apart the bond between hysteria and women, to free hysteria from its feminine attributes, and to liberate femininity from its bondage to hysteria, means going against the grain of language itself. To begin with, as Helen King shows in chapter 1, hysteria has always been etymologically linked with women and the feminine because of its name. We can argue that when Freud's Viennese colleague dismissed Freud's talk on male hysteria because men didn't have wombs, he was pathetically out of date; nonetheless, the word itself has become so generically linked with the feminine in popular understanding that we need to specify male hysteria the way we specify women writers, whereas to say female hysteria sounds redundant.

Because of this understanding and the stigma it has carried, throughout the centuries doctors have sought to find other names for hysteria in men. As Israël explains, "The hysteria diagnosis became for a man . . . the real injury, a sign of weakness, a castration in a word. To say to a man 'you are hysterical' became under these conditions a form of saying to him 'You are not a man.'"[22] To avoid such a confrontation, doctors sought unconsciously to mask the hysteria diagnosis under other terms; in France in the nineteenth century, for example, it was known as "neurospasme," "tarassis," "didymalgie," "encéphalie spasmodique," or "neuropathie aigue cérébro-pneumogastrique."

Furthermore, hysteria is invariably represented as feminine through the figures of medical and historical speech. Evelyn Fox Keller, Ludmilla Jordanova, Emily Martin, and Cynthia Russett, among others, have begun in recent years to analyze the gendered rhetoric and epistemology of scientific inquiry, through close reading of the figures, metaphors, and representations that have always been part of medical discourse.[23] Such images are not merely decorative or accidental, they argue, but are a fundamental part of the gendered language that science shares with other human discourses. As Jordanova notes, "the biomedical sciences deploy, and are themselves, systems of representation. If devices like personification and metaphor have been central to scientific thinking, then the notion of representation becomes a central analytical tool for historians."[24] Helen King points out that the history of hysteria depends on a series of texts, on the way language was deployed and translated within these texts, and on the narratives of female power and powerlessness that were based upon them. In order to understand the longevity and cultural force of these narratives, we need to look at terminology, metaphor, and narrative techniques as well as at statistics and theories.

In his recent study, for example, Etienne Trillat discusses the theories of male hysteria that have flourished for several centuries. But his images tell a different story. "All psychoanalytic theory was born from hysteria," he writes, "but the mother died after the birth." Even in denying the sexual etiology of hysteria, thus historiography reinscribes it through language echoing the traditional terminology for hysteria, the "suffocation of the mother" or the "mother."[25]

We could also look at the striking metaphor Breuer used in *Studies on Hysteria* when he called hysterics "the flowers of mankind, as sterile, no doubt, but as beautiful as double flowers."[26] The image is botanical, sexual, and aesthetic. In cultivated flowers, doubling comes from the replacement of the stamens by petals. Like the double flower, Breuer implies, the hysteric is the forced bud of a domestic greenhouse, the product of luxury, leisure, and cultivation. Her reproductive powers have been sacrificed to her intellect and imagination. Like the curved flowers of Art Nouveau, or the *Jüngenstihl,* she is also an aesthetic object, standing in relation to a more sober "mankind" as feminine and decorative. Finally, the hysteric is seductive and attractive, but incapable of maternity or creativity. From Breuer's point of view, as the case studies make clear, the hysteric's sterility and her intense abnormal flowering go together, as if to echo Victorian stereotypes about the incompatibility of uterine and cerebral development.

But from the woman's point of view, sterility may result from being in advance of one's time and unable to find a partner. The same metaphor is used by Olive Schreiner, herself an example of the New Woman who overcame hysterical disorders to lead an important career as a feminist and writer. Schreiner imagined that if sex and reproduction could be separated, human sexuality, especially female sexuality, might become like the cultivated rose, which "having no more need to seed turns all its sexual organs into petals, and doubles, and doubles; it becomes entirely aesthetic."²⁷ For Schreiner, the hysteric is thus a member of the sexual avant-garde.

Male homosexuals too can be read, perhaps more precisely than women, into Breuer's metaphor of the double flower. They are Schreiner's highly evolved beings who have perforce separated sexuality from reproduction, and who must pour their creativity into art. In his study of Oscar Wilde, for example, Neil Bartlett calls Wilde's green carnation the symbolic flower of the gay man: "A homosexual, like a hothouse flower, declares his superiority to the merely natural. . . . Homosexuals are sterile . . . they blossom in the form of works of art."²⁸

It is not surprising that the metaphors of hysteria should contain double sexual messages about femininity and masculinity, for throughout history, the category of feminine "hysteria" has been constructed in opposition to a category of masculine nervous disorder whose name was constantly shifting. In the Renaissance, these gendered binary oppositions were set up as hysteria/melancholy; by the seventeenth and eighteenth centuries, they had become hysteria/hypochondria; in the late nineteenth century they were transformed into hysteria/neurasthenia; during World War I, they changed yet again to hysteria/shell shock; and within Freudian psychoanalysis, they were coded as hysteria/obsessional neurosis. But whatever the changing terms, hysteria has been constructed as a perjorative term for femininity in a duality that relegated the more honorable masculine form to another category.

If we go back to medical records from the early seventeenth century, we find a differentiation between hysteria, a disorder that was believed to have its origins in displacement of the uterus and the accumulation of putrid humors; and melancholy, a prestigious disorder of upper-class and intellectual men. Vieda Skultans has pointed out that "the epidemics of melancholy which swept the fashionable circle of London from 1580 onwards curiously bypassed women."[29] She sees a connection between the misogynistic literature that flourished during the late seventeenth century and the emergence of hysteria as a significant diagnostic category. By the end of the seventeenth century, melancholy and hysteria had been joined by new fashionable diseases: the spleen, vapours, and hypochondria; and these disorders were also differentiated by gender. Spleen and vapours were seen as akin to hysteria, female maladies that came from the poisonous fumes of a disordered womb. As Roy Porter has discussed in chapter 3, late seventeenth-century accounts of the neurological aspects of hysteria that moved away from the uterine theory also advanced theories of male hysteria. In these accounts physicians were agreed that hysterical men were much rarer than hysterical women, that they behaved in womanish ways, and that their affliction should be called "hypochondriasis." According to Thomas Sydenham, for example, hypochondriacal symptoms were as similar to hysterical symptoms "as one egg is to another" and could be seen in "such male subjects as lead a sedentary or studious life, and grow pale over their books and papers."[30]

In the eighteenth century, there was a gender split in the representation of the body, with the nervous system seen as feminine, and the musculature as masculine.[31] Doctors made a firm gender distinction between forms of nervous disorder, assigning hysteria to women and hypochondria to men. According to the French physician Jean-Baptiste Louyer-Villermay, these categories also corresponded to a psychology of sex differences. Turbulent passions, ambitions, and hate, which were natural to men, predisposed them towards hypochondria, while in women the dominant emotion was that of love.[32] Concern with the feminizing label of hysteria obviously affected diagnosis; when Edward Jenner had hysterical symptoms, he noted that "in a female I should call it hysterical—but in myself I know not what to call it but by the old sweeping term nervous."

In England, most Victorian medical men "had the idea that there was a mental disease for each sex—hypochondriasis for the male and hysteria for the female."[33] By the nineteenth century, the sexual specificity of hysteria and hypochondriasis had become a medical dogma, so that "when hysteria is admitted in men, it is understood nevertheless as a female affliction."[34] Thus the Viennese doctor Ernst von Feuchtersleben in 1824 argued that if women showed signs of hypochondriasis they must be "masculine Amazonian women," while hysterical men "are for the most part effeminate men."[35] But whereas hypochondriasis had started as a dignified illness that a man might even claim with some masculine self-respect, during the nineteenth century it too gradually became established as a form of mental disorder that carried its own stigma. In the eighteenth century, the man of cultivation and intellect who suffered from a variety of afflictions was universally admired, but when it became embarrassing for men to acknowledge that they were hypochondriacs, and such people, like Jane Austen's Mr. Woodhouse, became figures of fun, a new masculine term was required to set along-side hysteria.

In 1873, this gap in the medical lexicon was filled by the term *neurasthenia*. "Undoubtedly *the* disease of the male subject in the late nineteenth century,"[36] neurasthenia was first identified in the United States and linked with the nation's nervous modernity. In *American Nervousness*, George M. Beard, who named the new disorder, defined neurasthenia as a condition of nervous exhaustion, an "impoverishment of nervous force." He believed that neurasthenia was caused by industrialized urban societies, competitive business and social environments, and the luxuries, demands, and excesses of life on the fast track. In a sense then, neurasthenia was a source of pride and a badge of national distinction and racial superiority. To be stressed was "one of the cardinal traits of evolutionary progress marking the increased supremacy of brain force over the more retarded social classes and barbarous peoples." To Beard, reports of missionaries, explorers, and anthropologists seemed to show that primitive, savage, and heathen groups were simpler and less sensitive than middle-class Americans.[37] Bushmen and Sioux Indians did not become neurasthenic like Boston bankers and New York lawyers.

Like hysteria, neurasthenia encompassed a staggering range of symptoms, from blushing, neuralgia, vertigo, headache, and tooth decay to insomnia, depression, chronic fatigue, fainting, and uterine irritability. But unlike hysteria, neurasthenia was an acceptable and even a valuable illness for men. While it affected both men and women between the ages of fifteen and forty-five, it was most frequent "among the well-to-do and the intellectual, and especially among those in the professions and in the higher walks of business life, who are in deadly earnest in the race for place and power."[38] It was definitely, in short, the neurosis of the male elite. Many nerve specialists, including Beard himself, had experienced crises of nervous exhaustion in their own careers, and they were highly sympathetic to other middle-class male intellectuals tormented by vocational indecision, overwork, sexual frustration, internalized cultural pressure to succeed, and severely repressed emotional needs. When Herbert Spencer visited the United States in 1882, he was struck by the widespread ill health of American men: "In every circle I have met men who had themselves suffered from nervous collapses, due to stress of business, or named friends who had crippled themselves by overwork."[39] But French and English men, doctors from these countries were quick to argue, could be nervous too. In Paris, Charcot noted that "the young men who graduate from the Ecole Polytechnique, who intend to become heads of factories and rack their brains over mathematical calculations, often become victims of these afflictions."[40] The male patients in Charcot's private practice, who came from the middle and upper classes, were more likely to be called "neurasthenic" than "hysterical."[41]

The social construction of neurasthenia reflected the romance of American capitalism and the identification of masculinity with money and property. Beard's metaphors repeatedly emphasized the economic and technological contexts of American nervousness. Neurasthenics were in "nervous bankruptcy," perpetually overdrawing their account, rather than "millionaires of nerve force."[42] The neurasthenic man

> is a dam with a small reservoir behind it, that often runs dry or nearly so through the torrent as the sluiceway, but speedily fills again from many mountain streams; a small furnace, holding little fuel, and that inflammable and combustible, and with strong draught, causing quick exhaustion of materials and imparting unequal, inconstant warmth; a battery with small cells and little potential force, and which with little internal resistance quickly becomes actual force, and so is an inconstant battery, requiring frequent repairing and refilling; a dayclock, which if it be not wound up every twenty-four hours, runs utterly down; evolving a force sometimes weak, sometimes strong, and an engine with small boiler-power, that is soon emptied of its steam; an electric light attached to a small dynamo and feeble storage apparatus, that often flickers and speedily weakens when the dynamo ceases to move.[43]

This epic metaphor vividly suggests the specter of the masculine engine wearing out, the depletion of sperm cells, the lack of ejaculatory force. It reflects late nineteenth-century male sexual anxieties of impotence caused by mental or physical overwork. Herbert Spencer put this idea forward quite straightforwardly in an article written for the *Westminster Review* in 1852. "Intense mental application," Spencer argued, "is accompanied by a cessation in the production of sperm-cells," while correspondingly, "undue production of sperm-cells involves cerebral inactivity," beginning with headache and proceeding to imbecility.[44]

This theory cut both ways. On the one hand, lack of desire for women could be explained by devotion to intellectual tasks; on the other hand, overindulgence in sex could lead to intellectual decline. Thus for some male intellectuals, the neurasthenia diagnosis relieved anxiety about lapses from conventional masculine sexuality by classifying them under the manly heading of overwork. Spencer himself was cited by Beard as one of the world's most distinguished neurasthenics, "doing original work on a small reserve of capital force." In 1853, after a vigorous climbing expedition in the Alps, Spencer had noticed odd symptoms—palpitations, insomnia, "cardiac enfeeblement," a "sensation in the head." Although he lived another fifty years, he treated himself as an invalid, pampering himself with rest and recreation, putting in earplugs when a conversation threatened to become too exciting, "keeping up the cerebral circulation" by wetting his head with saltwater and encasing it in flannel and a rubber nightcap. Despite what one might regard today as real social handicaps, Spencer was seen by his male friends as a great marital catch, and with shrewd pre-Freudian insight into his problem, they urged him to take a wife, recommending "gynoepathy" as a cure for his ills. Spencer however resisted, and as Gordon Haight wisely remarks, with neurasthenia "he bought safety from the perils of marriage."[45]

But the construction of neurasthenia as masculine was an illusion. In the United States, equal numbers of male and female patients were reported in the medical journals.[46] However, cases were differentiated in terms of both gender and class. In middle-class men, the disorder was attributed to overwork, sexual excess, anxiety, ambition, sedentary habits, or the use of alcohol, tobacco, or drugs. Beard estimated that one out of every ten neurasthenics was a doctor. In working-class men, sexual excess, trauma, and overwork were cited as the main causes of the disease. And in all women, childbirth and reproductive disturbances came at the top of the list, with overwork a factor for working-class women and attending college a factor for middle-class women.[47] Gosling notes that the case histories of male patients are much more interesting, detailed, and varied than those of women; "because men normally led more varied lives than most women, involving themselves in career, family, and social activities both within and outside the domestic circle, physicians made greater distinctions in the causes to which they attributed male nervousness. Physicians also questioned men in more detail about their habits and personal affairs, partially because they were more likely to suspect men of hidden vice and partially because of the delicacy of raising intimate issues with members of the opposite sex."[48]

In England, neurasthenia quickly lost its sheltering power for men and became a female malady like hysteria. Indeed, Havelock Ellis estimated that there were fourteen neurasthenic women for every neurasthenic man. Explanations for neurasthenia in women drew on some of the same sources as the explanations about men, but with a different moral emphasis. Edward Clarke in the United States and Henry Maudsley in England drew on new theories of the conservation of energy to argue that mental and physical energy were finite and competing. Women's energy, post-Darwinian scientists believed, was naturally intended for reproductive specialization. Thus women were heavily handicapped, even developmentally arrested, in intellectual competition with men. Nervous disorder would come when women defied their "nature" and sought to rival men through education and work, rather than to serve them and the race through maternity. While competition was a healthy stimulus to male ambition, it was disastrous for women, who furthermore did not have the outlet of athletics to relieve their strained nerves. The higher education of women in universities was obviously then a threat not only to their health but to their reproductive capacities. "What Nature spends in one direction, she must economise in another direction," Maudsley wrote, and thus the young woman who gave herself over to learning would find her sexual and reproductive organs atrophying, her "pelvic power" diminished or destroyed, and her fate one of sexlessness and disease.[49] The neurasthenic Girton or Vassar girl was overworking her brain and uterus into sterility.

The standard treatment for neurasthenia was the rest cure, developed by the American Dr. Silas Weir Mitchell (1829–1914) after his experience in the Civil War. First described in 1873, the rest cure involved seclusion, massage, immobility, and "excessive feeding." For six weeks the patient was isolated from her friends and family, confined to bed, and forbidden to sit up, sew, read, write, or do any intellectual work. She was expected to gain as much as fifty pounds on a rich diet that began with milk and built up to several substantial daily meals. Mitchell was well aware that the sheer boredom and sensory deprivation of the rest cure made it a punishment to the patient: "When they are bidden to stay in bed a month, and neither to read, write, nor sew, and have one nurse—who is not a relative—then rest becomes for some women a rather bitter medicine, and they are glad enough to accept the order to rise and go about when the doctor issues a mandate which has become pleasantly welcome and eagerly looked for."

The rest cure evolved from Mitchell's work with "malingering" soldiers in the Civil War, whom he had assigned to the most disagreeable jobs, so that after a few weeks in the latrines they were eager to return to the front.[50] But it also depended on his feelings on the differences between men and women and their social meaning:

> For me the grave significance of sexual difference controls the whole question, and if I say little of it in words, I cannot exclude it from my thought of them and their difficulties. The woman's desire to be on a level of competition with man and to assume his duties is, I am sure, making mischief, for it is my belief that no length of generations of change in her education and modes of activity will ever really alter her characteristics. She is physiologically other than man. I am concerned with her now as she is, only desiring to help her in my small way to be in wiser and more healthful fashion what I believe her Maker meant her to be, and to teach her how not to be that with which her physiological construction and the strong ideals of her sexual nature threaten her as no contingencies of man's career threaten in like measure or like number the feeblest of the masculine sex.[51]

A determined opponent of higher education for women, a critic of Vassar and Radcliffe and especially of "the horrible system of coeducation,"[52] Mitchell, like other Victorian physicians, believed that the female reproductive system and the brain derived their nourishment from the same source, and that women should not try to learn too much during adolescence when the menstrual function was being established. "I firmly believe," he wrote, "that as concerns the physical future of women they would do better if the brain were very very lightly tasked and the school-hours but three or four a day until they reach the age of seventeen at least."[53] He also advised mothers not to allow their pubescent daughters to take strenuous exercise. The quest for knowledge, he felt, destroyed that subtle and tender feminine charm which was the only source of masculine love: "For most men, when she seizes the apple, she drops the rose."[54]

While Mitchell was aware that hysteria in women of the middle and upper classes was largely caused by "the daily fret and wearisomeness of lives which . . . lack those distinct occupations and aims" that sustained their brothers and husbands, he did not seem to make the connection between his program of female ignorance and passivity, and women's later inability to lead healthy lives.[55] He preferred women patients who were silent and acquiescent to those with inquiring minds. "Wise women choose their doctors and trust them," he wrote in *Doctor and Patient*. "The wisest ask the fewest questions. The terrible patients are nervous women with long memories, who question much where answers are difficult, and who put together one's answers from time to time and torment themselves and the physician with the apparent inconsistencies they detect."[56] In his novel *Roland Blake,* Mitchell created such a terrible patient in the figure of Octapia Darnell, a repugnant hysteric whose sickly tentacles wound themselves about her hapless family. He preferred to use women's trust in him in effecting a cure: "If you can cause such hysteric women as these to believe that you can cure them, you enlist on your side their own troops, for as you can create symptoms, so you can also create absence of symptoms."[57]

Furthermore, the treatment assumed that the patient be "pliant and wealthy": one who did not work, or at least did not need to work. Middle-class women were thus the best candidates for the rest cure, since men and the poor were unlikely to be willing to spend six to eight weeks in idleness. Doctors thus modified the treatment for their male patients, who might simply be advised to get to bed early and to travel first-class. As the Chicago neurologist Archibald Church observed, "We cannot put [men] to bed with any expectation that they will stay there. I have tried it repeatedly and have nearly always failed. Men do not take to the recumbent position for any considerable length of time with equanimity. The fact of their being in bed constitutes an aggravation; and irritation is what we wish to exclude."[58]

Women were just as irritated by isolation and enforced idleness as men. Mitchell's patients indeed included many of the leading feminist intellectuals, activists, and writers of the period, including Jane Addams, Winifred Howells, Charlotte Perkins Gilman, and Edith Wharton. For them, feminist scholars have argued, the rest cure seemed like a regression to infancy, in which the patient was forced back into "womblike dependence" on the parental team of godlike male doctor and subservient female nurse, and reeducated to "make the will of the male her own";[59] or a disciplinary treatment that punished unconventional aspirations; or even a pseudo-pregnancy that symbolically put the deviant woman back in her biological place. Forbidden by Mitchell to write or draw, Gilman came close to a breakdown: "I would crawl into remote closets and under beds—to hide from the grinding pressure of that profound distress."[60] Casting Mitchell's advice to the winds, she went to work again, "work, in which is joy and service, without which one is a pauper and a parasite." For Gilman, hysteria was the result of passive acquiescence to the strictures of a patriarchal society, but it could be overcome by purposeful activity, in her case writing. She wrote the chilling short story "The Yellow Wallpaper" (1892), a Gothic tale of a young mother suffering from a "temporary nervous depression—a slight hysterical tendency," who goes mad during a rest cure, as a protest against Mitchell, but there is no evidence that he ever read or responded to it. Similarly,

Dr. Margaret Cleaves insisted on the importance of work for women's mental health, and the dangers of the rest cure: "The hardest cases I have had to take care of professionally," she wrote, "are those who have acquired the rest cure habit. I have a physician under care now, this time a woman, who regrets piteously that she was not given something to feed her intelligence instead of an unqualified rest cure."[61]

But even women doctors did not have the cultural authority to contest medical dogmas. Later Freud did have the authority to criticize Mitchell. In *Studies on Hysteria,* in a passage that might be seen as a medical acknowledgment of Gilman's experience, he advised combining the rest cure with analysis: "This gives me the advantage of being able . . . to avoid the very disturbing introduction of new psychical impressions during a psychotherapy, and . . . to remove the boredom of a rest-cure, in which the patients not infrequently fall into the habit of harmful daydreaming."[62] Still, the rest cure was not really discredited until World War I, when it was discarded as inappropriate and even harmful as a therapy for men.

The rest cure was one form of fin-de-siècle therapy that asserted male medical domination over the nervous woman. Treatments for hysterical women in the late nineteenth century were even more tyrannical, and doctors found reasons not to apply them to men. In England the model for this approach, based on established notions about the charismatic male physician and the manipulative sickly woman, had been pioneered by Robert Brudenell Carter and described in his book *On the Pathology and Treatment of Hysteria* (1853). Only twenty-five when he wrote his book, Carter adopted the tone of a much more mature and established man, a persona that was very much part of his whole program for asserting sexual and medical authority over the wayward hysterical girl. While Carter recognized that there were also cases of hysteria in men, he insisted that they were rare and anomalous. Not only were emotional derangements "much more common in the female than the male," but also women were forced by social pressure to conceal their feelings and desires, especially sexual ones. Moreover, the "morbid and insatiable . . . craving for sympathy" that led to sick behavior was "ten times stronger in women than in men."[63]

During a season when he served as the director of an agricultural workhouse, Carter had to contend with a number of young married women who had been separated from their husbands and children. These women had no real outlet for their feelings of loneliness and anxiety, and some had begun to have daily fits of crying and screaming. Carter found the attacks an administrative nuisance and set out to stop them. Whenever a woman had an attack, he made a large group of the others nurse her, insisting that none of them could have any food until all the symptoms of the attack had subsided. Very quickly the "hysterical" women became so unpopular with the others that the fits ceased to occur.

Carter's attitude toward middle-class hysterics was equally antagonistic, but his methods of managing them had to be more subtle. In his view, the hysterical girl is a clever, persistent, and desperate person who has entered into a sustained deception, and would "lose caste" if exposed. Therefore she is prepared for a long siege against the doctor who would make her well—that is, make her give up her symptoms. While he thoughtfully considers the efficacy of rough treatments for hysterics, such as unpleasant medicines, blows, or buckets of cold water, Carter concludes that most hysterical girls would be able to tolerate such attacks and turn them against the doctor, undermining his authority: "A young woman who is living at home will have too much courage and endurance to be beaten by the torture, and . . . a certain amount of perseverance on her part will exalt her into a martyr in the eyes of her family, and will enable her to bid defiance to professional denunciations."[64] Thus he advocated removing the patient from her family to the doctor's home, where she could be under constant surveillance.

The plan for treatment he outlines is basically a form of blackmail, threatening the hysteric that if she does not reform her ways, the doctor will expose her malingering and disgrace her in the eyes of her family and friends. In fact, by the time this threat is pronounced, the doctor has already secretly told the family his diagnosis and sworn them to secrecy, so the hysteric is operating in the midst of a conspiracy or game in which everyone is collaborating to trick her. Telling the family of the plot is necessary to effect the patient's separation from them. When she is removed from all her accustomed sources of sympathy and support, the doctor can have full power over her habits and treatment.

British attitudes toward the understanding and management of the hysterical woman followed Carter's example. In general, Victorian doctors saw hysteria as a disorder of female adolescence, caused both by the establishment of the menses and by the development of sexual feelings that could have no outlet or catharsis. Adolescence was a risky time for girls, many doctors observed, not only because the reproductive organs had so great an influence on their entire well-being but also because "the range of activity of women is so limited, and their available paths of work in life so few . . . that they have not, like men, vicarious outlets for feelings in a variety of healthy aims and pursuits."[65] While men, wrote

Charles Mercier, had the "safety-valve" of exercise, women's feelings were bottled up, so that in adolescence, "more or less decided manifestations of hysteria are the rule."[66] "All kinds of . . . barriers to the free play of her power are set up by ordinary social and ethical customs," wrote Dr. Bryan Donkin. "'Thou shalt not' meets a girl at every turn."[67] F. C. Skey, who delivered a series of lectures on hysteria to the medical students at St. Bartholomew's Hospital in 1866, noticed that his patients were primarily adolescent girls with domineering parents, girls who "exhibited more than usual force and decision of character."[68]

Despite their sympathy for the plight of Victorian girls, Victorian doctors found their hysterical patients selfish, deceitful, and manipulative. Henry Maudsley denounced the "moral perversion" of hysterical young women who "lie in bed" all day, "when all the while their only paralysis is a paralysis of the will."[69] Skey followed Carter's lead in recommending "fear and the threat of personal chastisement" for hysterical women.[70] In the title of one American medical text, hysteria was a matter of "trials, tears, tricks, and tantrums."[71]

In France, working-class hysterical women patients at the Salpêtrière were regarded with the same hostility by such doctors as Jules Falret. Falret denounced the women as "veritable actresses; they do not know a greater pleasure than to deceive . . . all those with whom they come in touch. The hysterics who exaggerate their convulsive movement . . . make an equal travesty and exaggeration of the movements of their soul, their ideas, and their acts. . . . In a word, the life of the hysteric is nothing but one perpetual falsehood; they affect the airs of piety and devotion, and let themselves be taken for saints while at the same time abandoning themselves to the most shameful actions; and at home, before their husbands and children, making the most violent scenes in which they employ the coarsest and often most obscene language and give themselves up to the most disorderly actions."[72]

Why did hysteria become such a frequent phenomenon in the late nineteenth century? Why were doctors like Carter, Mitchell, Falret, and Skey so contemptuous of their female patients and so dictatorial in their treatments? A number of theories have been advanced to explain the phenomenon of fin-de-siècle hysteria. The feminist historian Carroll Smith-Rosenberg gives an answer that is sympathetic to both hysterical women and their male physicians. She sees female hysteria as stemming from sex-role conflicts that emerged in the nineteenth century. She has argued that the American hysteric was typically the idle middle-class woman, both "product and indictment of her culture." Reared to be weak, dependent, flirtatious, and unassertive, many American girls grew up to be child-women, unable to cope with the practical and emotional demands of adult life. They defended themselves against the hardships and obligations of adulthood "by regressing towards the childish hyper-femininity of the hysteric." Faced with real responsibilities and prob-lems, these women fled from stress by choosing a sick role in which they won continued sympathy and protection from the family. Thus hysteria provided a solution to the feminine conflict between idealized sex roles and quotidian realities: "The discontinuity between the roles of courted young woman and pain-bearing, self-sacrificing wife and mother, the realities of an unhappy marriage, the loneliness and chagrin of spin-sterhood, may all have made the petulant infantilism and narcissistic self-assertion of the hysteric a necessary social alternative to women who felt unfairly deprived of their promised social role and who had few strengths with which to adapt to a more trying one."

Male physicians like Mitchell dealing with these women may some-times have been harsh and insensitive, Smith-Rosenberg concludes, but they were not necessarily more misogynistic than other men of their time. Their profession made it necessary for them to make analytic state-ments about femininity, while their gender demanded that they establish an authoritative relationship with their patients. Thus the physician too was a product of his gender and culture, "standing at the junction where the cultural definitions of femininity, the needs of the individual female patient, and masculinity met."[73] If hysterical women were victims of a culture that did not prepare them to meet the responsibilities of adult-hood, their doctors too were victims of a sex-role conflict that required them both to identify with the fathers and husbands of their patients, and to provide answers and cures for the problems of the women in a way that threatened to feminize them.

In *The History of Sexuality,* Michel Foucault suggests that hysteria was a label bestowed on female sexuality by male physicians. Rather than seeing hysteria as a solution to the double binds and dilemmas of fin-de-siècle women, Foucault describes the "hysterization of women's bodies" as one of the crucial features of psychiatric and medical power. Hys-terization was "a three-fold process whereby the feminine body was analyzed . . . as being thoroughly saturated with sexuality; whereby it was integrated into the sphere of medical practices, by means of a pa-thology intrinsic to it; whereby, finally, it was placed in organic com-munication with the social body . . . the family space . . . and the life of children; the Mother, with her negative image of 'nervous woman,' con-stituted the most visible form of this hysterization."[74]

Women's needs, roles, conflicts, feelings, and voices have little to do with the scenario of power outlined by Foucault. Instead, women are passive and apparently powerless bodies and figures who are inscribed by unnamed forces. "It is worth remembering," he insists, "that the first figure to be 'sexualized' was the 'idle' woman. She inhabited the outer edge of the 'world', in which she always had to appear as a value, and of the family, where she was assigned a new destiny charged with conjugal and parental obligations. Thus there emerged the 'nervous' woman. . . . In this figure the hysterization of woman found its anchorage point."[75] Through his use of quotation marks, Foucault casts ironic doubt on the reality of the hysterical woman's idleness or sexuality, but since his focus is on the large anonymous forces of psychiatric power, he does not supply an explanation for the hysteric's collusion or helplessness before such labeling. Nor, unlike Smith-Rosenberg, does he attempt to explain some of the motives doctors might have had for exerting such power over the definition of female hysteria, or the reasons why it became epidemic in the last decades of the century.

Neither of these influential theories can really account for the varieties and causes of hysteria in their respective contexts. To begin with, I need to emphasize once again that they exclude male hysteria from their analysis, although both are aware of its existence. Smith-Rosenberg comments in a footnote that male hysteria does not undermine her arguments about its relation to female experience for four reasons. First, "to this day hysteria is still believed to be principally a female 'disease' or behavior pattern." Second, the male hysteric is "different"—homosexual or working class. Third, "one must hypothesize that there was some degree of female identification among the men who assumed a hysterical role." Finally, she argues, male hysteria had its most typical form in shell shock.[76] These circular arguments, which Smith-Rosenberg did not reconsider when she revised her original essay for publication in the book, make it impossible for the "difference" of male hysteria to modify her concept of the "hysterical role." Male hysteria is simply a subset of female hysteria, and mimics its motives and behaviors. Applying Smith-Rosenberg's model to male hysterics, then, one would see them as childish, weak, and escapist. The alternative approach—analyzing hysterical symptoms as a response to powerlessness—does not come up.

Despite his interest in forms of discursive power, Foucault too does not consider hysteria from the point of view of the patient, although some of his references hint at the dilemma of young hysterics, both male and female, caught between domineering parents and domineering doctors. He quotes Charcot's insistence that hysterical girls and boys must be separated from their mothers and fathers and hospitalized.[77] But the idea that these power struggles might have contributed to the problems of adolescent patients is extraneous to Foucault's concerns. He is interested instead in mapping the elements by which doctors took control of the definition of sexuality.

Both Smith-Rosenberg and Foucault identify the bourgeois mother as the representative fin-de-siècle hysteric. But this picture does not correspond to the realities they each describe, nor to the clinical picture. Smith-Rosenberg acknowledges that hysteria crossed class and economic boundaries, and that it also affected working-class and farm women, immigrants and tenement dwellers. In her view these women too had failed "to develop substantial ego strengths." [78] But American doctors who treated poor women in their hospitals and dispensaries had a different view. E. H. Van Deusen, who saw many hysterical farm women at his asylum in Michigan, blamed the social isolation and intellectual deprivation of their lonely lives. [79] Similarly, most of the girls and women Falret and Charcot were treating for hysteria at the Salpêtrière came from poor families and had worked since childhood to support themselves. They were neither idle nor, for the most part, mothers. In case after case, they were the victims of poverty, sexual and financial exploitation, and ignorance. The working-class men Charcot treated in his ward, whose hysteria was usually precipitated by some kind of violent accident, seem like the brothers of the women. Foucault's highly schematic and abstract account of discursive power ignores both context and agency; it neither explains why patients manifested symptoms of distress nor explains why physicians were so eager to focus on these complaints in women and to see them as threats to the family and the state.

The "hysterisation" of women's bodies which Foucault describes can also be seen from a feminist perspective as "a reassertion of women's essentially *biological* destiny in the face of their increasingly mobile and transgressive social roles." [80] That hysteria became a hot topic in medical circles at the same time that feminism, the New Woman, and a crisis in gender were also hot topics in the United States and Europe does not seem coincidental. During an era when patriarchal culture felt itself to be under attack by its rebellious daughters, one obvious defense was to label women campaigning for access to the universities, the professions, and the vote as mentally disturbed. Whether or not women who were labeled "hysterical" were associated with the women's movement, they were often seen by doctors as resistant to or critical of marriage, and as strangely independent and assertive. These characteristics are most vividly present in the Viennese women dissected by Breuer and Freud, but English physicians like Skey and Bryan Donkin also commented on the intelligence and ambition of their hysterical patients. Any woman manifesting symptoms of hysteria aroused suspicions of a silent revolt against her domestic, class, and reproductive role. Thus nervous women received much more attention than nervous men, and were labeled as "hysterical" or "neurasthenic" in the contexts of a highly charged rhetoric about the dangers of higher education, women's suffrage, and female self-assertion in general.

In every national setting where female hysteria became a significant issue, there were parallel concerns about the ways that new opportunities for women might undermine the birthrate, the family, and the health of the nation. Intellectually competitive women, doctors warned, were sterile flowers doomed to bring forth only blossoms of hysteria and neurasthenia. In the United States, gynecologists warned against the brain-fag, headache, backache, spine-ache, and all-around sexual incompetence that New Women would produce.[81] In France, the *femme nouvelle* was blamed for the declining birthrate; new divisions of labor seemed to threaten the stability of the family and the state. As women made their first inroads into public and professional space, a fascinating alliance of artists, traditional women, and neuropsychiatrists like Charcot united in a campaign to celebrate maternity and the interiority of Woman.[82] In England the New Woman as neurotic feminist intellectual had become a recognizable type by the 1890s; "the New Woman ought to be aware that her condition is morbid, or at least hysterical," wrote one journalist.[83] She had also become a standard figure in literature, whether Thomas Hardy's Sue Bridehead in *Jude the Obscure* (1895) or George Gissing's Alma Rolfe in *The Whirlpool* (1897), whom Ian Fletcher calls "a new type of woman, the *névrose*, the modern hysteric."[84]

While hysterical girls were viewed as closet feminists and reprogrammed into traditional roles, feminist activists were denigrated as hysterics, sick and abnormal women who did not represent their sex. By the 1880s in England, it had become customary for the term "hysterical" to be linked with feminist protest in the newspapers and in the rhetoric of antisuffragists. As Lisa Tickner notes in her study of the British suffrage movement, "for half a century and more, feminism and hysteria were readily mapped on to each other as forms of irregularity, disorder, and excess, and the claim that the women's movement was made up of hysterical females was one of the principal means by which it was popularly discredited."[85] Women who found a public voice for their concerns were lampooned as "the shrieking sisterhood," a term coined by the antifeminist writer Eliza Lynn Linton, who wrote in 1883 that "one of our quarrels with the Advanced Women of our generation is the hysterical parade they make about their wants and their intentions. . . . For every hysterical advocate 'the cause' loses a rational adherent and gains a disgusted opponent."[86]

Jean-Martin Charcot's clinic at the Salpêtrière offered the best opportunity to examine the different ways that women and men were diagnosed and treated for hysteria at the turn of the century. Studies of hysteria at the Salpêtrière took their form from Charcot's charismatic style. So powerful was his influence in the 1880s that the Salpêtrière was often called the "Hôpital Charcot," and the group of disciples and admirers around him was known as the *charcoterie*.[87] They were strongly influenced by his work on male hysterics; although the Salpêtrière had traditionally been a women's hospital, under Charcot's direction a small men's ward was opened; male patients were also seen at the outpatients' clinic. Charcot took pride in his research on male subjects and regarded the study of male hysteria as one of the specialties of his clinic and of late nineteenth-century French medicine. By his death in 1893, he had published sixty-one case studies of male hysterics, and he left notes on many more. In a lecture-presentation on hysteria in men, Charcot noted that:

In some ways, this question of male hysteria is the order of the day. In France it has preoccupied physicians for the past several years. Between 1875 and 1880, there have been five dissertation defenses on male hysteria at the Faculté de Paris, and M. Klein, the author of one of these theses, done under the supervision of M. le Dr. Olivier, was able to catalog 80 cases. Since then have appeared the important publications of M. Bourneville and his students; of MM. Debove, Raymond, Dreyfus, and several others; and all these works tend to demonstrate, among other things, that cases of male hysteria can be found fairly frequently in common practice.[88]

He decried the popular belief that "the characteristic trait of hysteria is the instability and the mobility of the symptoms." Even in women, he explained, there "were hysterias of sturdy, permanent phenomena . . . which sometimes resist all medical intervention." Furthermore, men too were sometimes emotionally erratic or exhibited depression and melancholy.

Charcot's clinic was noted for the large number of female patients who, under hypnosis, produced spectacular attacks of *grande hystérie* or "hystero-epilepsy," a prolonged and elaborate convulsive seizure. The attack could be induced or relieved by pressure on certain areas of the body—what Charcot called *hysterogenic* zones—and these were especially to be found in the ovarian region. A complete seizure involved three phases: the epileptoid phase in which the patient lost consciousness and foamed at the mouth; the phase of "clownism" (Charcot was a great fan of the circus), involving eccentric physical contortions; and the phase of "attitudes passionnelles," or sexual poses. The attack ended with a back-bend called the *arc-en-cercle*.

It was crucial to Charcot's theory of hysteria that it took the same course in men and women. Thus he insisted that there were "numerous striking analogies" between male and female *grande hystérie*. Charcot's disciple Emile Batault reported with pleasure that a hysterical young man named Gui "presents the symptoms most characteristic of *grande hystérie*. The attacks are always preceded by the phenomena of testicular aura; he feels something which mounts from the inguinal region towards the esophagus; he has then a feeling of thoracic constriction which oppresses him, his temples throb violently, he has ringing in his ears and hears heavy noises like the fire of distant cannons. His head spins, he loses consciousness, and the attack begins." Because he was young and athletic, Gui's *arc-en-cercle* was also a splendid affair, which impressed Batault very mightily, as an "acrobatic performance as beautiful as it was varied."[89] Batault also found a hysterogenic zone on Gui's body located around the right testicle.

Just as it was possible to stop a hysterical attack by compressing the woman's ovaries, doctors at the Salpêtrière were convinced that it should be possible to affect the course of a man's attack by putting pressure on the testicles. But this procedure did not always have the desired effects. The doctors found that the attacks were relieved by the compression of the testicles. Others, however, obtained no effect from putting pressure on the seminal gland, and one doctor discovered, perhaps not to our surprise, that squeezing the patient's testicles made the convulsions stronger.

One of Charcot's most original contributions to the theory of male hysteria was his insistence that it should not carry the stigma of effeminacy. He emphasized the fact that hysteria often appeared among tough manual laborers; most of the cases had occurred in the aftermath of a traumatic accident, either at work or in travel. Furthermore, he stressed the working-class status, physical strength, and virile emotions of his male patients, and he mocked other doctors who had problems accepting both the class and gender of patients who clashed with their stereotypes of hysteria: "One is willing to concede that a young, effeminate man may, after indulging in excessive behavior, suffering heartache, or experiencing deep emotions, exhibit several hysterical phenomena; but that a manly artisan, solid, unemotional, a railway engineer, for example, might, following a railway accident, a collision, a derailing, become hysteric, the same way as a woman—this, it appears, surpasses the imagination."[90]

Nonetheless, there were significant sexual differences in Charcot's concept of male hysteria. In terms of language, it was often called "hystérie virile" or "hystérie traumatique" to mark its distinction from female hysteria. Although it followed the same course of behavior in men and women, Charcot believed hysteria had different causes that depended on gender. As Mark Micale observes, "Women in his writings fell ill due to their vulnerable emotional natures and inability to control their feelings, while men got sick from working, drinking, and fornicating too much. Hysterical women suffered from an excess of 'feminine' behaviors, hysterical men from an excess of 'masculine' behaviors."[91]

Moreover, although some of Charcot's male hysterics were as colorful and dramatic as the women, they did not attract as much attention from doctors, writers, artists, and journalists. The "wild man" Lap . . . sonne, for example, was covered with symbolic tattoos, such as a veiled woman he called "the night," and he earned his living eating live rabbits in fairs. But while Blanche Wittmann became the "Queen of Hysterics" performing at the Salpêtrière clinic, Lap . . . sonne is remembered only as a case study. The actual numbers of male hysterics were few; overall, male patients comprised no more than five to ten percent of the whole immense hospital population.[92] On the other hand, during the 1870s, the percentage of women patients at the Salpêtrière diagnosed as "hysterical" rose as high as twenty percent.[93]

In addition to the theoretical and statistical differences between male and female hysteria, there were differences in its representation. As Sander Gilman explains in chapter 5 in this book, the hysterical clinic of Charcot was organized primarily around the visual, the photographic, the theatrical, and the spectacular. He was famed for his probing gaze that seemed to penetrate not only to the heart of the patient but also to the souls of his assistants, interns, and associates. His student and biographer Georges Guillain described the examination sessions in which the naked patient sat like an artist's model while Charcot silently studied every detail of the body.[94] Roger Martin du Gard wrote about Charcot's "piercing, prying gaze" and his "tyrannical way of fixing you with his stare."[95] Havelock Ellis too recalled Charcot's "disdainful expression, sometimes even it seemed, a little sour."[96]

This intensely scrutinizing male gaze mingled the mesmerizing power of the hypnotist and the commanding eye of the artist with the penetrating vision of the scientist piercing the veil of nature. It was very much associated with masculinity itself. Charcot's stare was contrasted with the downcast eyes of his hysterical women patients, and with the "soft, poetic and languorous" gaze of his hysterical male patients.[97]

Through his theatrical lecture-demonstrations (Sarah Bernhardt, acting in cross-dressed parts at the same time, was often compared to the hysterical queens of Charcot's amphitheater[98]), and even more through the photographic atelier that captured images of the hysterical women for the volumes of *iconographies*, Charcot emphasized the visual manifestations of hysteria and the hysterical body as an art object. His representations of gender were allied to aesthetic conventions about the female body, whether in painting, photography, or drama. Charcot not only borrowed from art in making the female body the focus of his investigation, but through his photographic atelier also contributed to the historical emergency of a "regime of representation" in which, according to the art critic Griselda Pollock, "the hysterized body of woman . . . was made the object of pathological scrutiny and deciphered in terms of masculine gaze and speech."[99]

The fascination with the female body as art and symbol extended also to Charcot's influence on his family. His wife and daughters were artists who worked with him in the family atelier. In 1892, Madame Charcot showed her work in the Exhibition of the Arts of Woman in Paris, contributing a large carved and decorated coffer, whose dark surfaces and fantastically painted inner panels suggested both the structure of the mind her husband had studied in hysteria—"a rational facade and an irrational interior"—and the image of woman promoted by the Central Union of the Decorative Arts and the Women's Committee of which she was a member.[100] As Debora Silverman has shown, "a prominent part of the Central Union program in the 1890s was the definition of interior space as distinctively feminine and the promotion of . . . woman as the queen and artist of the interior," in response to "the challenge of the *femme nouvelle* or 'new woman,' who was perceived as threatening to subvert women's roles as decorative objects and decorative artists."[101] Through the performances of Blanche Wittmann, the "Queen of Hysterics," and other famous hysterics at the Salpêtrière, Charcot too promoted women as artists of the interior, and paradoxically returned them to the status of decorative objects.

Even Charcot's contemporaries, however, were critical of the callous way that Charcot exhibited his hysterical stars and of his exposure of their secrets. In his antimedical satire *Les Morticoles* (1894), Leon Daudet caricatured Charcot as the voyeuristic neurologist "Foutange," who sadistically interrogates a hysterical girl: "And so, in front of two hundred sniggering persons, these wretches must display their shame, their own, and their families' taints, and reveal their intimate secrets. . . . Foutange penetrates with diabolical skill to the depths of these stunted creatures."[102] Axel Munthe, a Swedish doctor practicing in Paris at the time, gave a vivid description of Charcot's Tuesday lectures, when "the huge amphitheatre was filled to the last place with a multicoloured audience drawn from tout Paris, authors, journalists, leading actors and actresses, fashionable demimondaines." The hypnotized women patients put on a spectacular show before this crowd of curiosity seekers. "Some of them smelt with delight a bottle of ammonia when told it was rose water, others would eat a piece of charcoal when presented to them as chocolate. Another would crawl on all fours on the floor, barking furiously when told she was a dog, flap her arms as if trying to fly when turned into a pigeon, lift her skirts with a shriek of terror when a glove was thrown at her feet with a suggestion of being a snake. Another would walk with a top hat in her arms rocking it to and fro and kissing it tenderly when she was told it was her baby."[103]

Feminists were indignant at Charcot's treatment of women, often comparing it to the atrocities of vivisection. Writing in the English antivivisectionist journal *Zoöphilist,* one woman condemned the "no less disgusting experiments practiced on the lunatics and hysterical patients in the Salpêtrière. The nurses drag these unfortunate women, notwithstanding their cries and resistance, before men who make them fall into catalepsy. They play on these organisms . . . on which experiment strains the nervous system and aggravates the morbid conditions, as if it were an instrument. . . . One of my friends told me that she . . . had seen a doctor of great reputation make one unhappy patient pass, without transition, from a celestial beatitude to a condition of infamous sensualment. And this before a company of literary men and men of the world."[104] In an essay in the *Revue scientifique des femmes* (1888), C. Renoz accused Charcot of a "sort of vivisection of women under the pretense of studying a disease for which he knows neither the cause nor the treatment."[105]

Furthermore, the textual case studies of the hysterical women patients lend themselves to feminist interpretation of oppression and exploitation. Augustine, who spent five years as a patient at the Salpêtrière, is a particularly dramatic example. She came to the Salpêtrière at the age of fifteen in October 1875, suffering from pains in the stomach and convulsive attacks during the night which sometimes left her paralyzed. Although she had not yet begun to menstruate, Augustine had the appearance of a sexually mature woman. One does not have to search far for the traumatic experiences that had precipitated her hysterical attacks. Beginning at puberty, she had been subjected to sexual attacks by men in the neighborhood, and at the age of thirteen, had been raped by her mother's lover, who had threatened to slash her with a razor if she did not comply. During the seizures which began immediately thereafter, she imagined that she was being bitten by wild dogs or surrounded by rats; sometimes she had hallucinations of the rapist with a knife. Treated with ether and amyl nitrate, Augustine spoke incessantly about her visions, but while the doctors recorded her words, they were not interested in the contexts of her experience. Instead she was repeatedly photographed in revealing hospital gowns demonstrating the various stages of *grande hystérie*. In 1879, her condition improved and she was taken on as a nurse in the hospital. But the respite was brief; by April 1880 she was once again having frequent attacks, to which the doctors responded with increasingly severe measures: ether, chloroform, straitjackets, and finally, confinement in a padded cell. Although she was sufficiently improved to attend a concert on the Salpêtrière grounds in June, she used the opportunity to run away, but she was caught on the boulevard outside. Her health grew worse; in addition to the attacks, she injured herself in futile efforts at freedom. The last entry about Augustine is September 9, 1880: she "escaped from the Salpêtrière, disguised as a man."[106]

One cannot help rejoicing at Augustine's escape, and her male disguise seems like a coded statement about hysteria and gender; despite Charcot's insistence on the equality of male and female hysteria, men had an easier time getting out of the Salpêtrière. Victimized by sexual predators, she endured symbolic rapes at the hands of her doctors, who endlessly recorded her menstrual periods, her vaginal secretions, her physical contortions, and her sexual fantasies, but paid no attention to her sense of betrayal by her mother and brother, as well as by the men who had abused her.

In 1928, Augustine became the pin-up girl of the French surrealists, who reproduced her photographs to celebrate the fiftieth anniversary of hysteria, which they called "the greatest poetic discovery of the end of the nineteenth century." For Louis Aragon and André Breton, Augustine was the "delicious" embodiment of the sexy "young hysterics" they so much admired.[107] In 1982, Georges Didi-Huberman made Augustine the martyred heroine of his study of Charcot, the "masterpiece" of Charcot's hysterical museum.[108] She is also becoming an exemplary figure for feminists. I wrote about her in *The Female Malady* in 1985; a group of feminist scholars, choreographers, and dancers based at Trinity College in Connecticut have produced a performance work about her called "Dr. Charcot's Hysteria Shows"; and a successful play, *Augustine: Big Hysteria,* was staged in London in 1991.[109]

But we need to be cautious about seeing Charcot as a misogynist. While he was famous for these performances with women, Charcot also took a liberal position on women's rights. The Salpêtrière journal *Progrès Médical* campaigned for women's admission to medical school, and some of Charcot's students and externs were women. The first French dissertation on hysteria by a female physician, Hélène Goldspeigel's *Contribution à l'étude de l'hystérie chez les enfants* (1888) was written under Charcot's supervision at the Salpêtrière.[110]

Indeed, one of the earliest histories of hysteria was Glafira Abricosoff's *L'hystérie aux XVIIe et XVIIIe siècles* (1897). Abricosoff had been a student of Charcot's and dedicated her book to the memory of "my illustrious master, J.-M. Charcot." As she explained in her introduction, "It is to him that I owe my medical knowledge, and it is, in a sense, out of gratitude for my dear departed master that I have wished to retrace the historical variations of a malady on which his brilliant perspicacity and his penetration have shed so much light."[111] Abricosoff's history makes no special case for women, but rather stresses the existence of male cases. Throughout her book Abricosoff drew attention to those writers such as Joseph Raulin who had observed and described male hysteria, and who had insisted that it could not be an exclusively female disorder. Her book is an example of one form of early feminist history of hysteria.

Another effort by a woman doctor to deal with hysteria was the book of Dr. Georgette Déga, who had studied at the medical faculty of Bordeaux. Déga attributed hysteria to the inadequacies of women's education. Hysteria, she wrote, was "the victory of the lower centers over the higher," and mathematics was the best discipline for hysterical women.[112] One can imagine that she believed medical training to be even better.

It is interesting to speculate on the reasons why Charcot's work on male hysteria did not have a lasting effect on medical discourse, why history has remembered Augustine and forgotten the hysterical men Charcot described. In the British medical community, there had always been resistance to the idea of male hysteria, which had been camouflaged under other terminologies, organic explanations, and forms of denial and projection. As Micale concludes, "Charcot's hysterization of the male body in the 1880s was sharply at variance with dominant medical models of masculinity, and it ran counter to reigning Victorian codes of manliness. It required from Victorian physicians the application of an ancient and denigratory label to members of their own sex. And per-

haps most disturbing, it suggested the possibility of exploring the feminine component in the male character itself." [113]

Furthermore, Charcot's death in 1893 precipitated a long period of
"dismemberment" of his work during which the concept of hysteria fell
into disrepute, and some claimed that he had been a charlatan who
coached his hysterical female patients in their performances or produced their symptoms through suggestion. [114] Men were omitted from
the record. Even Pierre Janet reinforced the belief that all the hysterics
were women when he remarked in his lectures at the Harvard Medical
School in 1920 that "by a kind of international irony, people were willing
to admit, after the innumerable studies made by French physicians, that
hysteria was frequent only among French women, which astonished nobody, on account of their bad reputation." [115]

Ironically, the work of Sigmund Freud, Charcot's most famous student, also played a major role in the suppression of male hysteria after
Charcot's death. Freud came to Paris to study at the Salpêtrière from
October 1885 to March 1886. His original plan for the research trip was
quickly changed, as he became overwhelmed by the personality, accessi-
bility, and orginality of Charcot, who became a professional role model
as well as a mentor. The ambiance of Charcot's clinic was very different
from that which Freud had been used to in Berlin. Charcot was spontaneous, generous, and open to criticism and argument, and Freud found
the democratic atmosphere both surprising and stimulating: "The Professor's work proceeded openly, surrounded by all the young men acting
as his assistants as well as by the foreign physicians. He seemed, as it
were, to be working with us, to be thinking aloud and to be expecting
to have objections raised by his pupils. Anyone who ventured might put
a word in the discussion and no comment was left unnoticed by the great
man. The informality of the prevailing terms of intercourse, and the way
in which everyone was treated on a polite footing of equality—which
came as a surprise to foreign visitors—made it easy even for the most
timid to take the liveliest share in Charcot's examples." [116]

Following Charcot's lead, Freud began by emphasizing that hysteria
could affect both sexes, a position that was acceptable to his medical colleagues. On October 15, 1886, when he read his paper "On Male Hysteria" to the Vienna Psychiatric Society, several of the doctors present
testified that male hysteria was already well known. Theodor Meynert,
who publicly expressed skepticism about Charcot's symptomatology,
later "confessed to Freud that he had himself been a classical case of
male hysteria, but had always managed to conceal the fact." [117] In 1887–
88 Freud translated Charcot's *Leçons de Mardi*, which contained most of

Charcot's case studies of men. In "Hystérie," an essay he published in a medical encyclopedia in 1888, he further condemned the "prejudice, overcome only in our own days, which links neuroses with diseases of the female sexual apparatus." Here he also noted the incidence of hysteria in both boys and girls, as well as in adult men. Although rarer in men than in women, hysteria, Freud argued, is more disruptive for men, because it takes them away from their work: "The symptoms it produces are as a rule obstinate; the illness in men, since it has the greater significance of being an occupational interruption, is of greater practical importance."[118]

In his work on hysteria, Freud took Charcot's theories to their logical extremes. Whereas Charcot had maintained that male and female hysteria had different causes, but similar effects, Freud argued that all hysteria came from traumatic origins. But the trauma did not have to be a railway accident or an injury in the workplace; it could be a disturbing sexual experience that had been forgotten and repressed. Furthermore, hysteria could be cured by having the patient recall and relive, or abreact, the originating trauma, whether by hypnosis or through the process of dream analysis and free association. The symptoms of hysteria, Freud noted, were created through a process of symbolization, and expressed emotional states.

Although he continued to acknowledge the existence of male hysteria, Freud's work on hysteria in Vienna concentrated on women. In contrast to Charcot, who examined, measured, and observed hysterics, but paid no attention to what they said, Freud and his colleague Joseph Breuer were the first to actually listen to hysterical women and to heed their complaints. In *Studies on Hysteria* (1895), he and Breuer worked out the fundamental technique of psychoanalysis. Most of their patients were middle-class Jewish women who found themselves imprisoned in traditional roles as dutiful daughters. Frustrated in their intellectual ambitions, expected to stay home and care for their brothers and father until they married, these bright and imaginative young women developed a wide range of symptoms—limps, paralyses, crippling headaches, and most significantly, aphonia, or loss of voice. By encouraging them to talk, to recount their dreams, to recall repressed memories of sexual traumas and desires, Freud and Breuer found that they could cure the women's symptoms. *Studies on Hysteria* thus seemed to lay the groundwork for a culturally aware therapy that respected women's words and lives.

In the case of Anna O., or Bertha Pappenheim, the connections between hysteria and feminism seemed particularly clear because after her analysis with Breuer in 1882, she went on to become a feminist activist. She translated Mary Wollstonecraft's *Vindication of the Rights of Woman* into German, wrote a play called *Women's Rights,* and was the co-founder and director of the Judischer Frauenbund, the League of Jewish Women. In her hysterical seizures, Anna became unable to speak her native German, and instead spoke either Yiddish, which she called "the woman's German," or a jumble of English, Italian, and French. These linguistic symptoms have been read symbolically by feminist critics as the repression of women's language or its impossibility within patriarchal discourse. Dianne Hunter analyzes Pappenheim's hysterical symptoms as a linguistic protest against the German father tongue. In Anna O.'s case, "speaking German meant integration into a cultural identity [she] wished to reject," the patriarchy in which she was an immobilized daughter.[119] Hunter concludes that Anna O.'s hysteria was a "discourse of femininity addressed to patriarchal thought," signifying both through the body and through nonverbal language the protest that could not be put into words.[120] As she began to verbalize this protest in her conversations with Breuer, and to relive some of her dreams and hallucinations, Anna's symptoms were relieved. But she was not cured until she took complete control of language and subjectivity in her own writing. She remained ill for seven years after her treatment with Breuer, visiting sanatoriums during relapses. Anna O. recovered completely only with the publication of her first book, *In the Rummage Store,* in 1890. Rather than continuing her role as the passive hysterical patient, through writing she became one who controlled her own cure.[121]

By the turn of the century, the sympathy with women's intellectual and creative frustrations and the openness to their words so marked in *Studies on Hysteria* had become codified in the interests of Freud's emerging psychoanalytic system, a system that depended very much on domination over the patient. We see this increased rigidity in his famous case history of Ida Bauer, the young Viennese girl he called "Dora." Dora was brought to Freud by her father when she was eighteen. Intelligent and ambitious, Dora was stifled by the requirements of her role as the marriageable daughter of a bourgeois family, when she longed to go to the university and to have a career rather than a husband. Dora was a Viennese version of the New Woman of the 1890s, the feminist who seeks higher education and wishes to avoid marriage. Freud never met Dora's mother, whom he regarded as a boring case of "housewives' neurosis." Although Dora felt contempt for her mother's monotonous domestic life, it was the life for which she too was destined as a woman. Her mother was "bent upon drawing her into taking a share in the work of the house." Dora could find no support for her intellectual aspirations from either parent. Although she had a governess who was "well-read and of advanced views," Dora believed that the governess was neglecting her and was really in love with her father. She arranged to have the woman dismissed. Afterward, she struggled alone with the effort to keep up her serious reading, and she attended lectures specially given for women. Her older brother, however, went off to the university, and later became a prominent Austrian politician.

Moreover, Dora was treated like a pawn or a possession by her father and denied the rights to privacy or personal freedom. He was having an affair with the wife of a friend, Herr K., who had attempted to seduce Dora when she was only fourteen, and she felt that "she had been handed over to Herr K." by her father in exchange for Herr K.'s complicity in the adultery. Professing to be anxious about her depressive state of mind, but really, Dora believed, afraid that she would betray his sexual secrets, her father then "handed her over" to Freud for psychotherapeutic treatment. He wanted Freud to persuade Dora that her perceptions were simply adolescent fantasies. He hired Freud hoping for an advocate to "bring her to reason." [122]

As Jeffrey Masson observes, Dora had good reason to be upset: "She felt conspired against. She was conspired against. She felt lied to. She was lied to. She felt used. She was used." [123] Moreover, Freud's determination to label her as a hysteric did not depend upon the severity of her symptoms. Indeed, unlike the other women treated for hysteria by Breuer and Freud, Dora's "symptoms" were few and slight. She had a nervous cough, headaches, depressions. While he acknowledged that Dora's case was no more than "petite hystérie," Freud believed that the very ordinariness of her symptoms made her an ideal subject. Since he was committed from the start to the hysteria diagnosis, Freud interpreted all of Dora's behaviors and statements in accordance with his theories about the origins of hysteria in childhood sexual trauma and repressed desires. Many of his views, such as the belief that "gastric pains occur especially often in those who masturbate" and that masturbation was related to hysteria, are now seen as Victorian sexual superstition. But Freud's interpretations of Dora's fantasies, which have as little basis as his statements about her physical symptoms, are still accepted in psychoanalysis. He told her that she was really attracted to Herr K., in love with her father, and in love with himself. He ignored the appalling circumstances of Dora's family situation, and she finally broke off the therapy.

The conclusion of *Dora* echoes the endings of many Victorian novels about women: "Years have gone by since her visit. In the meantime the girl has married . . . she had been reclaimed once more by the realities of life." In fact Dora's problems were not resolved by marriage, although Freud borrows it as a literary device to signify a happy resolution of the therapeutic plot. In the case histories of male patients, however, Susan Katz points out, these closed marriage plots are significantly absent; "the forms of Freud's case histories reflect his ideological positions toward women and men."[124] Similarly, Toril Moi reminds us, when Freud writes about Little Hans, he "never ceases to express his admiration for the intelligence of the little boy," while Dora's intelligence is represented as a form of neurotic resistance.[125]

In addition to its plot and themes, Dora's case had other literary characteristics. While Breuer, in the case of Anna O., commented on the broken language and multilingual nature of the hysteric's speech, Freud himself first drew attention in the Dora case to the fragmentary and discontinuous nature of the hysteric's narrative, and to the physician's responsibility for reorganizing it into a coherent whole. As he explained, hysterics like Dora were unable to tell an "intelligible, consistent, and unbroken" story about themselves. They repressed, distorted, and rearranged information; their volubility about one period of their lives was sure to be followed "by another period in which their communications run dry, leaving gaps unfilled and riddles unanswered." And this incapacity to give an "ordered history of their life" was not simply characteristic of hysterics, Freud claimed; it was in a sense the meaning of hysteria. If the hysteric could be brought to remember what was repressed, and to produce a coherent narrative, she would be cured.

Thus the therapist's task was to construct such a narrative for the patient. Freud was confident that no matter how elusive and enigmatic the hysteric's story, the analyst could reconstruct a logical, scientific, and complete narrative. "Once we have discovered the concealed motives," he wrote, "which have often remained unconscious, and have taken them into account, nothing that is puzzling or contrary to rule remains in hysterical connections of thought, any more than in normal ones."[126]

In doing so, moreover, he had not only to fill in the gaps in the hysteric's own story but to overcome her resistance to his narrative interpretations. In order for the therapy to work, the hysteric had to accept and believe the narrative of the analyst. In his later papers on psychoanalytic technique, Freud described the process as one of combat in which "the patient brings out of the armory of the past the weapons with which he defends himself against the progress of the treatment—weapons which we must wrest from him one by one."[127] The analyst, Freud insisted in "The Dynamics of Transference," must win "the victory whose expression is the permanent cure of the neurosis."[128] But Dora was quite uncooperative in this regard. She flatly denied Freud's narrative embellishments of her story, would not accept his version of her activities and feelings, and either contradicted him or fell into stubborn silence. Finally she walked out on Freud by refusing to continue with therapy at all.

Freud viewed this resistance as the problem of her transference; Dora, he argued, had projected onto him her feelings of erotic attraction for her father and Herr K. and was punishing him with her rejection. If Freud is a reliable narrator, what happened in his exchange with Dora was that he succeeded in penetrating the mystery of her hysterical symptoms. In his terminology, he unlocked her case and exposed her sexual secrets. Unable to face the truth, Dora ran away from her therapy and remained sick for the rest of her life. Freud was a heroic pioneer who was disappointed in his efforts to help.

But if Freud is an unreliable narrator, a very different plot emerges. In this case, Dora is a victim of Freud's unconscious erotic feelings about her that affected his need to dominate and control her. It's significant that Dora has no voice in Freud's text, that we get nothing of her direct dialog, and that her historical and Jewish identity are both suppressed. Unlike Anna O., she never became a subject, only the object of Freud's narrative. His interpretations of her problem reflect his own obsessions with masturbation, adultery, and homosexuality. He never understands her story at all; he simply tries to bully her into accepting his version of events. His vaunted penetration of her secrets is really a kind of verbal rape. Dora's departure is then a heroic gesture of self-assertion and defiance. Her unhappy subsequent life was the result of Freud's failing her and leaving her defenseless in a social environment hostile to intellectual women. His interpretation of her story is more about himself than about her.

Contemporary analysts agree that for a variety of reasons psychoanalysis could only have been developed out of work with hysterics. "I think . . . that psychoanalysis had to start from an understanding of hysteria," Juliet Mitchell writes. "It could not have developed . . . from one of the other neuroses or psychoses. Hysteria led Freud to what is universal in psychic construction and it led him there in a particular way—by the route of a prolonged and central preoccupation with the difference between the sexes. . . . The question of sexual difference—femininity and masculinity—was built into the very structure of the illness."[129] Because hysterics formed strong and explicit transferences to their doctors, they were analyzable and thus were an ideal group from which to generate a psychoanalytic theory. Kurt Eissler has hypothesized that "the discovery of psychoanalysis would have been greatly impeded, delayed, or even made impossible if in the second half of the nineteenth century the prevailing neurosis had not been hysteria."[130]

What is left unsaid in these claims, however, is that only female hysterics offered these opportunities. The gender of the hysteric was crucial in leading Freud to the theory of sexual etiology of the neuroses. Had his patients primarily been men, had he written a case study of "Dorian" rather than "Dora," the history of psychoanalysis would look very different. The gender difference depends in part on Freud's reliance on cultural myths of masculine and feminine development in shaping his interpretation of hysteria.

At the turn of the century, hysteria was still popularly and medically conjoined with female deviance. In France, despite the "dismemberment" of Charcot, the hysteric was still seen in a theatrical context as a performer: "The hysteric is an actress, a comedienne," wrote P. C. Dubois in 1904, "but we never reproach her, for she doesn't know that she is acting."[131] The most vehement negative statements associating feminism with hysteria came during the militant suffrage campaign. "One does not need to be against women suffrage," the London *Times* editorialized in 1908, "to see that some of the more violent partisans of that cause are suffering from hysteria. We use the word not with any scientific precision, but because it is the name most commonly given to a kind of enthusiasm that has degenerated into habitual nervous excitement." In a notorious article called "On Militant Hysteria," Dr. Almwroth Wright traced feminist demands to the "physiological emergencies" that constantly threatened women. Suffragist protest, especially when it involved working-class women, wrote the *Daily Chronicle*, was simply "hysterical hooliganism."[132] The representations of the militant feminist and the hysteric were conflated in the popular press, reflecting the view that nervous disorders were visible and detectable through study of the physiognomy. As Sander Gilman shows in chapter 5 in this book, the face of the hysteric had been presented as the chief sign of hysterical "difference" through the popularized images and photographs of Charcot's atelier, and through his studies of religious trance and possession in art as hysterical manifestations. Thus, the *Daily Mirror* wrote on 25 May 1914, the "hysterical ecstasy" of the suffragettes could be seen "unmistakably in the expression of the face."[133]

But with the outbreak of war and the abrupt end of the suffrage campaign, there were expectations that hysteria was dying out. "One doesn't dare any longer to speak of hysteria," wrote one doctor in 1914.[134] But

the Great War changed all this confident prediction with a great epidemic of hysteria among men. There had been scattered warnings of
hysteria among soldiers before 1914. During the Boer War, the British
surgeon C. A. Morris noted neurasthenic problems among the troops,
which he attributed to privation, exhaustion, and mental strain. There
were similar instances during the Russo-Japanese War of 1904–1905,
and in 1907, the term "war neurosis" was introduced at the Congrès
Allemand de Médicine Internationale.[135]

But World War I, in the words of Sándor Ferenczi, offered "a veritable museum of hysterical symptoms."[136] In all the European armies,
war neurosis was extensive. In England by 1916, nervous cases accounted for as much as 40 percent of the casualties in the combat zone.
By 1918 there were over twenty war hospitals for mental patients in the
United Kingdom. And by the end of the war, eighty thousand cases had
passed through army medical facilities. One-seventh of all discharges
were for nervous disorders. "It is a wonderful turn of fate," marveled
the British psychologist W. H. R. Rivers, "that just as Freud's theory of
the unconscious and the method of psycho-analysis founded upon it
should be so hotly discussed, there should have occurred events which
have produced on an enormous scale just those considerations of paralysis and contracture, phobia and obsession, which the theory was designed to explain."[137]

The psychiatric theories that developed around war neurosis reflect
the ambivalence of the medical establishment upon confronting hysterical behavior in fighting men. The first problem was in naming the disorder. When Dr. Charles S. Myers saw cases of amnesia, impaired vision,
and emotional distress among British soldiers in France, he noted "the
close relation of these cases to hysteria." But like doctors before him,
Myers did not want to use the feminizing term "hysteria," and thus he
argued that the symptoms could be traced to a physical injury to the central nervous system caused by proximity to an exploding shell. He chris-
tened the disorder "shell-shock." Later Myers would concede that the
lack of evidence of any organic relation between exploding shells and
neurotic symptoms made shell shock "a singularly ill-chosen term," but
its simplicity, alliteration, and military sound made it the label that won
out over such other alternatives as "anxiety neurosis," "war strain," and
"soldier's heart."[138] The efficacy of the term "shell shock" lay in its power
to provide a masculine-sounding substitute for the effeminate associations of hysteria, and to disguise the troubling parallels between male
war neurosis and the female nervous disorders epidemic before the
war. French doctors were also reluctant to identify war neuroses as hys-

teria, partly because of the internal struggle over the reputation of Charcot. They called war neurotics *pthiatiques,* in Babinski's term, or, more
harshly, *simulateurs.* Military authorities, indeed, regarded shell shock as
a form of cowardice or malingering, and some senior army officers
thought that patients should be court-martialed and shot.[139]
   One of the striking aspects of shell shock was the class difference in
symptoms; "shell-shocked officers tended to suffer from chronic anxiety
states while men in the ranks generally suffered from acute hysterical
disorders."[140] In the ranks, symptoms tended to be physical: paralyses,
limps, blindness, deafness, mutism. In officers, symptoms tended toward
the emotional: nightmares, insomnia, depression, anxiety attacks. Sexual
impotence was widespread in all ranks. Explanations for the differences
were class-based. Myers explained that "the force of education, tradition, and example make for greater self-control in the case of the Officer. He, moreover, is busy throughout a bombardment, issuing orders
and subject to worry over his responsibilities, whereas the men can do
nothing during the shelling but watch and wait until the order is received for an advance."[141] Some British doctors saw a one-to-one cause-
and-effect relationship between the hysterical conversion symptom and
the trauma that had caused it. According to Thomas Salmon, "A soldier
who bayonets an enemy in the face develops a hysterical tic of his facial
muscles; abdominal contractions occur in men who have bayonetted enemies in the abdomen; hysterical blindness follows particularly horrible
sights; hysterical deafness appears in men who find the cries of the
wounded unbearable, and the men detached to burial parties develop
amnesia."[142]
   There were two major ways of treating shell shock during the war,
both designed to get men functioning and back to the trenches as fast
as possible, and these treatments were differentiated according to rank.
Shell-shocked soldiers were treated with the hostility and contempt that
had been accorded hysterical women before the war. As in the nineteenth century, working-class men were linked with hysterical women
as the antagonists of doctors. "The case of a psycho-neuropath," wrote
Frederick Mott, "really consists of a mental contest, resulting in the victory of the physician."[143] Not only in England but in all European countries, shell-shocked ordinary soldiers were subjected to forms of disciplinary treatment, such as isolation, restricted diet, public shaming, and
painful electric faradization, or shocks to the afflicted parts of their
bodies. The treatments known as "quick cure," "queen square" (for the
London hospital where it was practiced), "torpedoing," "torpillage,"
"manière forte," "terrorism," or "Uberrümplung" (hustling) were in fact

semi-tortures designed to make the hysterical symptom more unpleasant to maintain than the threat of death at the front. German physicians, for example, were divided between those who looked for the organic lesions of nervous trauma and those who believed the symptoms manifested a wish to escape that was independent of any specific traumatic incident. While in the short term these methods did terrorize patients into dropping their symptoms, when they were returned to the front, more disabling and permanent conditions emerged. H. Stern estimated that out of three hundred soldiers "cured" and sent to the front, less than two percent could be maintained.[144] After the war, a special Austrian commission was appointed to investigate the treatment of war neurotics in the Vienna General Hospital under Professor Julius Warner-Jauregg, who believed all shell-shock cases to be malingerers. In his report for the commission, Freud testified that "there were cases of death during the treatment and suicides as a result of it," but Warner-Jauregg was acquitted.[145]

More advanced psychiatrists adopted psychotherapeutic techniques in the treatment of shell-shocked officers, using abreactive or cathartic methods such as hypnosis, dream analysis, and free association. Officers were given various kinds of rest cures similar to those assigned to neurasthenics. When men were the patients, however, the rest cure had to be revised. Military doctors felt that intense activity was necessary for the restoration of masculine self-esteem. As H. Crichton-Miller advised, "Rest in bed and simple encouragement is not enough. . . . Progressive daily achievement is the only way whereby manhood and self-respect can be regained."[146] The treatment of isolation and rest, G. Elliot-Smith and T. H. Pear reminded doctors, had been developed in civilian life for "well-to-do women living in the lap of luxury" and could not be good for hardy military men.[147] Although the men of the first group of neurasthenic cases treated in English military hospitals were given the Weir Mitchell rest cure, it was later reported that these patients remained ill throughout the war.[148]

In dealing with shell shock, doctors seemed to have forgotten or ignored Charcot's work with male hysterics. They lacked a neutral vocabulary for discussing the cases in the contexts of masculinity; instead, shell shock was described as the product of womanish, homosexual, or childish impulses in men. W. H. R. Rivers had argued that war neurosis was a form of regression to an earlier form of development, either to animal instincts, primitive defenses, or infantile behaviors. Hugh Crichton-Miller also observed that, especially among the ranks, war neurosis produced "a condition which is essentially childish and infantile in its

nature."[149] T. A. Ross suggested that the training of a soldier "tended
to make him regress to a childish attitude. . . . The soldier is above all
things to learn what he is told at once without argument as a child is."[150]
Wartime regression to a lower level of maturity also seemed to explain
the proliferation of superstitions, magical beliefs, rituals, and rumors
that, as Paul Fussell has shown, made the Great War a "new world of
myth."[151]

When doctors dismissed shell-shock cases as malingerers or *simulateurs,* they were often hinting at the effeminacy that had always been
part of the male hysteria diagnosis. Freudians shared this view. Karl
Abraham, among the Freudians, was one who argued that war neurotics were passive, narcissistic, and impotent men to begin with, whose
latent homosexuality was brought to the surface by the all-male environment.[152] In London, the tiny group practicing Freudian psychotherapy—David Eder, David Forsyth, and Ernest Jones—also argued for a
sexual etiology for shell shock.

Their interpretations, however, were greeted with predictable out-
rage by such anti-Freudian members of the older generation as Charles
Mercier. Reporting in *The Lancet* on a shell-shock patient, Forsyth described him as "a case of unconscious homosexuality with marked anal
eroticism." Mercier made an angry response:

> Unconscious pain, unconscious homosexuality, unconscious Oedipus com-
> plex, and other unconscious states of consciousness of the psycho-
> analysts . . . were a great mystery to me until I learnt from one of their
> victims what these expressions meant. This poor man had suffered many
> things for many months from many psycho-analysts, until at last he turned
> upon his tormentors . . . with these words: "It is true . . . that I now have
> these filthy thoughts, *but it is you that have put them into my mind."*

The following week, Mercier was seconded by Dr. Robert Armstrong-
Jones, who called for the professional outlawing of psychoanalysis. Then
came a rebuttal from Forsyth, wondering how "those who still repudiate
psycho-analysis and the sexual etiology of the neuroses can remain blind
to what must long have been recognized by every thoughtful reader of
your paper—namely, that the sexual instinct is clean and pure. It will
not do nowadays to dress it up in mid-Victorian prejudices as a repulsive
and disreputable bogie to frighten our intelligence."[153]

Some famous shell-shock patients, such as Siegfried Sassoon, Wilfred
Owen, and Robert Graves, were indeed homosexual or bisexual. For
most, however, the anguish of shell shock included more general but intense anxieties about masculinity and fears of homosexuality, even as

they refused to continue the masquerade of masculinity. What John Lynch has called "the exploitation of courage" in the Great War may be more accurately called the exploitation of manliness.[154] Soldiers were recruited and socialized through appeals to "traditional masculine virtues" and through promises of "the fulfillment of masculinity on the battlefield."[155] In combat, displays of manly stoicism and heroics were expected and encoded. As Paul Fussell notes in his glossary of the romantic vocabulary of World War I, to be "manly" meant not to complain.[156] Martin Stone points out that shell shock was thus generated by the military ethos of masculinity: "The soldier was encouraged to kill at the expense of unleashing infantile sadistic impulses that had previously been successfully repressed. He was encouraged to form close emotional bonds with other men and yet homosexuality was forbidden."[157] If the essence of manliness was not to complain, then shell shock was the body language of masculine complaint, a protest against the concept of "manliness" as well as against the war.

The impact of male hysteria in the field of psychological medicine was complex. On one hand, psychologists who had worked with shell shock challenged Freud's view that sexual factors were basic to the understanding of hysteria. Unable to revise a theory based on female hysteria in the light of male experience, these men instead argued that "shell shock had effectively 'disproved' Freud's theory of sexuality."[158] On the other hand, the Freudian establishment did not take the lessons of shell shock as a clue to expanding the theory of hysteria. Indeed, the theory only rigidified, with psychoanalysts insisting that the cause of hysteria had to be sought in infant traumas and repressed family experiences, rather than modifying their position to take immediate social factors into account.

The one or two voices who might have had something new and important to add to the conversation were prematurely stilled. W. H. R. Rivers was one of these. Rivers was a Cambridge psychologist and anthropologist who had studied in Germany, and who took an interest in the work of Freud. In his early fifties and unmarried when he became a military doctor, he found in the study of shell shock both a rich source of material for his theories of the unconscious and a personal involvement that changed the course of his career. The war, he wrote in *Instinct and the Unconscious*, had been "a vast crucible in which all our preconceived views concerning human nature have been tested."[159] In his therapeutic practice, Rivers relied on what he called "autognosis," or self-understanding, which involved the discussion of traumatic experiences; and reeducation in which "the patient is led to understand how his newly acquired knowledge of himself may be utilized . . . and how to turn energy, morbidly directed, into more healthy channels."[160] Rivers's work was tragically abbreviated by his death in 1922.

Rivers may have been particularly effective as a therapist because he shared some of the characteristics of his patients. Speech disorders, especially stammering, were the most common neurasthenic symptom among officers and played a prominent role in the case studies of his patients.[161] Rivers, the son of a speech therapist who specialized in the treatment of stutterers, had stammered all his life, although his biographer speculates that he did not stammer in German. He was also sexually repressed and almost certainly homosexual.

In his postwar writings, Rivers explored the psychoanalytic issues of fear and anxiety which had come out of his war work at Craiglockhart Hospital. Proposing "suggestion-neurosis" as a term for hysteria, he argued that military training reinforced suggestibility, especially in private soldiers. In his view, "the symptoms of hysteria are due to the substitution, in an imperfect form, of an ancient instinctive reaction in place of other forms of reaction to danger." In explaining the mutism that was a frequent feature of shell shock, Rivers made connections to "the suppression of the cry or other sound which tends to occur in response to danger." He also began to apply to female hysteria, or as he called it, "the hysteria of civilian practice," some of the ideas about gender anxiety he had developed in working with men. "We have to discover why hysteria should be so frequent in women, and so rare in men, under the ordinary conditions of civil life . . . ," Rivers wrote. "Women are always liable to dangers in connection with childbirth to which men are not exposed, while the danger element, real or imaginary, is more pronounced in them than in the male in connection with coitus."[162]

But theories about women's fears seemed less important by this time because after the war and the passage of women's suffrage in England and the United States, it was believed that female hysteria declined and even disappeared. Edward Shorter has noted that "the image of the dynamic 'New Woman' of the 1920s . . . plays an obvious role in the decline of the hysterical paralyses that once were quite common among young women: the New Woman, who rode motorcycles and smoked in public, simply did not develop a paralysis as a legitimate way of communicating her distress."[163] Other scholars have also pointed to social changes as determinants of the decline. With the gradual emancipation of women, they have argued, the social conditions that had produced hysteria were no longer operative. According to the psychoanalyst Monique David-Ménard, for example, "the repression of sexuality at the end of the nineteenth century" was the cause of hysteria; "through the spectacular side of hysteria, women expressed what was impossible to say concerning sexuality."[164] If hysteria was the result of the sexual repression of the past, it made sense that it would vanish in our more liberated age.[165]

And indeed for much of this century, female hysteria seemed to be on the wane, as feminism was on the rise. It is striking as well that Freud's female disciples were virtually silent on the question of hysteria. It is not a topic in the works of Karen Horney, Melanie Klein, Anna Freud, or other members of the postwar generation. When a woman analyst, Elizabeth Rosenberg Zetzel, finally did deal with hysteria, she did not question Freudian assumptions and shibboleths. A student of Ernest Jones and D. W. Winnicott, Zetzel trained in psychiatry at Maudsley Hospital during 1938–39 and then served for six years during the war in the Emergency Medical Service and Armed Forces. Zetzel worked with hysterical soldiers and described her experiences in her first analytic paper, "War Neurosis: A Clinical Contribution," published in 1943. The three case studies, she later observed, served "as a model or blueprint" for her major work. Zetzel is quite approving of her male patients: "They were all happily married; they all had a steady work record; they had all shown ambition, social conscience, and a good capacity for sublimation."[166]

In contrast, when she worked with female hysterics in Boston after the war, Zetzel was much more critical. Although the women she called "true good hysterics" were "notably successful in the area of work," they had "failed to achieve a mature heterosexual relationship." Zetzel echoed Freud in her indifference to the double messages in the lives of her hysterical women patients, most of whom were intellectuals and students at various Boston universities. While she noted that "all of these patients have, in addition, been able to make and keep friends," she was certain that their difficulties with men came from their unresolved oedipal conflicts and penis envy, rather than from men's discomfort with gifted ambitious women.[167] Instead of pursuing the paradoxes of their lives, and the apparent uselessness of Freudian therapy in solving them, she focused instead on their analyzability and suitability for treatment. For, she wrote,

There are many little girls
Whose complaints are little pearls
Of the classical hysterical neurotic.
And when this is true
Analysis can and should ensue,
But when this is false
'Twill be chaotic.[168]

In such contemporary psychoanalytic writing by women as deals with hysteria, Freudian dogma has made it difficult for women analysts to accept hysterical symptoms in their male patients. Monique David-Ménard studied psychoanalysis at the Ecole Freudienne in Paris. In her practice, like most women analysts, she sees more women than men patients. David-Ménard claims not to know "what masculine hysteria is. Sometimes I say to myself when I hear a male patient who is very identified with a woman, 'Perhaps that came from hysteria,' but I always end up saying, 'It's not really that.'" [169] Her book *Hysteria from Freud to Lacan* (1983) is a densely argued philosophical comparison of Freud and Lacan, rather than a feminist reading of their work.

Yet a feminist interpretation of hysteria does not come naturally to women psychoanalysts or historians simply because they are women. David-Ménard, for example, has said in an interview, "I don't define myself as a feminist whether as a philosopher or as a psychoanalyst." [170] A feminist standpoint is situated within a particular cultural and intellectual framework, which offers an interpretative vocabulary and a support network for those who put it to use. Thus we need to read and evaluate women's writings about hysteria within their own historical context and with an understanding of the impact of gender at a particular moment for professional women.

Ilza Veith's *Hysteria* (1965) is an excellent case in point. According to Mark Micale, the book "established the 'standard' historical view of the subject for an entire generation of French, British, and North American readers." [171] Ilza Veith is one of the pioneering scholars of the history of medicine in the United States. Born in Germany in 1915, she studied medicine in Geneva and Vienna before coming to the United States in 1937. While she had hoped to become a plastic surgeon, "there was no thought in the thirties that a woman could receive a residency or assistantship in surgery." [172] Instead she trained with Henry Sigerist at Johns Hopkins and in 1947 received the first doctorate in the history of medicine in the United States.

For contemporary historians sensitized by feminist scholarship, Veith may seem indifferent to or unaware of the feminist questions in hysteria. She accepts wholeheartedly the Freudian view of hysteria and uses it as the resolution of the book, crediting psychoanalysis with the conquest of hysteria; it was the intensified understanding of the cause of hysteria by leading psychiatrists during this century, she wrote, that "contributed to the near-disappearance of the illness." [173] Roy Porter in chapter 3 questions Veith's uncritical acceptance of Freud and her blindness to the misogyny of prepsychoanalytic therapists like Carter. Mark Micale, too, points out that although she "might have been expected to respond differently," Veith "maintained a studied silence on the intersexual aspects of the disorder."[174] Yet such a judgment carries its own assumptions about gender, ignores the circumstances in which the book was written, and misses the way that Veith, like many women writing about hysteria, felt pressured to avoid a feminism traditionally linked with the disorder itself.

Veith does indeed point out a number of the intersexual issues of hysteria, albeit in a restrained language. In one of the few metaphors of her book, she comments that "the scarlet thread of sexuality" runs throughout the "tangled skein" of the history of hysteria.[175] She thus presents the issue as sexuality rather than femininity, although the allusion to the scarlet letter (and to the great American heroine Scarlett O'Hara) suggests that this sexuality was in fact related to women. For much of the book, when Veith describes or quotes accounts that link hysteria with female sexuality and reproduction, she generalizes from them to discuss a more universal and ungendered "sexuality." With regard to the Greek origins of the term, for example, she notes that "the association of hysteria with the female generative system was in essence an expression of awareness of the malign effect of disordered sexual activity on emotional stability." Veith's careful neutrality extended also to her discussion of witchcraft and the witch trials. "It is evident from the forgoing that women were the chief targets in the witch hunts," she mildly observes, without speculating further on the clerical misogyny and profound male anxieties that were projected onto women during the witch trials.[176] Veith is similarly tolerant with regard to nineteenth-century medicine. She attributes Robert Brudenell Carter's hostility toward women to his "youthful impatience" with his female patients, and when she talks about the "punitive" aspects of Victorian treatment of hysterical women, calls them "misanthropic" rather than "misogynistic."[177]

In her most substantial discussion of sex roles and attitudes, however, Veith explains that the "manifestations of this disease tended to change from era to era quite as much as did the beliefs as to etiology and the methods of treatment. The symptoms, it seems, were conditioned by social expectancy, tastes, mores, and religion, and were further shaped by the state of medicine in general and the knowledge of the public about medical matters." Women created or reproduced hysterical symptoms in accordance with their age's ideas about femininity: "Throughout history, the symptoms were modified by the prevailing concept of the feminine ideal. In the nineteenth century, especially, young women and girls were expected to be delicate and vulnerable both physically and emotionally, and this image was reflected in their disposition to hysteria and the nature of its symptoms. Their delicacy was enhanced by their illness, and as a result, the incidence of overt manifestations was further increased."[178] This comes very close to contemporary feminist analyses of hysteria.

Yet to judge Veith's work by contemporary feminist standards is to misunderstand the historical nature of gender ideology. Women historians and psychoanalysts of Veith's generation, including Elizabeth Zetzel, had a very different context than our own for their thinking about sexual difference, as several recent studies have illustrated. Joan Scott shows in her overview of American women historians that the post–World War II period saw the emergence of "a new discourse . . . that emphasized the masculine qualities of historians, associating them with the preservation of national traditions and democracy." Veith, like other women historians receiving their doctorates during this period, "had the further challenge of repudiating the disabilities assumed to come with womanhood."[179] Serious historians were judicious, unemotional, objective, impersonal. Similarly, in a series of interviews with women psychoanalysts who trained during the 1920s, 1930s, and 1940s, Nancy Chodorow found a very different gender consciousness from that of the 1980s operative in their views of feminism and psychoanalysis. Gender was not a meaningful or salient category to them; few had noticed discriminatory treatment; they had not thought about the conflicts between Freudian views of femininity and their own professional careers. But rather than accusing them of bad faith, blindness, or repression, Chodorow concluded that "gender-emphasis" or the "relative downplay of gender issues" are "not only objectively determined by a structural situation" but are also "subjective features of identity and culture." The "salience of meaning of gender" was not a historical constant but rather "a highly constructed product of one's time and place."[180]

In Veith's case, her position as a woman academic in a male-dominated profession may have led her to emphasize objectivity, neutrality, and indirection rather than to have taken a forceful and explicit feminist stand. Her book appeared in the last moments of calm before the storm of the women's liberation movement; sexual politics, however, was a term still to be invented by Kate Millett, and feminist scholarship did not yet exist.

Ilza Veith's autobiographical writings cast much light on the circumstances under which she wrote *Hysteria* and make clear that she was not unaware of sexism and its effects on the female psyche. In describing herself for *Who's Who*, she wrote, "In a long and severely handicapped life I have had to live with chronic illness and pain. Thanks to my husband's endless patience and helpfulness, I have learned to accept what cannot be changed, and to change what can be altered. I have had a successful and highly satisfactory academic career in spite of endless obstacles that lie in the way of a woman scholar."

Some of the details behind this summation can be found in Veith's most recent book, *Can You Hear the Clapping of One Hand?* (1989). Here she describes the severe stroke that she suffered in 1964 while she was completing *Hysteria*. Just fifty years old, and having moved to California to take up a professorship at the University of San Francisco, Veith woke up one morning to find that her entire left side was paralyzed. She had been experiencing odd symptoms for over a month, including migraine headaches, disturbed vision, and olfactory hallucinations. Yet, despite her training as a medical historian, Veith had not consulted a doctor. Why? Because symptoms like these were frequently attributed in the medical literature to women with "hysterical personality." Veith was embarrassed to think that she herself might be a hysteric, and thus she ignored the warning signals of a serious stroke. Moreover, when she experienced paralysis of the left side—the side usually afflicted in cases of hysteria—Veith was persuaded that she was only hysterical and "deluded myself that if I admitted the hysterical nature of my hemiplagia to myself and others, it would simply go away." Patronized and subtly punished by doctors in the hospital when she refused to behave like a suitably ignorant and docile female patient, Veith learned more about sexism in medicine than has ever been revealed in her professional writing. She has never recovered the use of her left arm.

In contrast to Veith's emphasis on the ungendered nature of hysteria, contemporary feminist critics have argued that while "Freud's assertion that hysteria afflicted both men and women was a liberating gesture in the nineteenth century," the most liberating gesture for feminists today is to reclaim hysteria "as the dis-ease of women in patriarchal culture."[181] Some have argued for a continuity or even a similarity between hysteria and feminism. In the 1970s, it became an important strategy of radical feminism to redefine as terms of female power the hostile labels that had been attached to rebellious or deviant women through history. Thus early women's groups were called the Witches, the highly successful English feminist publishing company is called Virago, and a major French feminist journal was called *Sorcières*. Feminists saluted the hysterics of the past as heroines of resistance to the patriarchal order.

Dora has indeed become a paradigmatic figure for contemporary feminist criticism. Because she walked out on her psychoanalysis, she has appeared to some as a defiant figure and precursor, what Mary Jacobus calls "the first feminist critic of Freud." [182] In her manifesto on women's writing, "The Laugh of the Medusa," Hélène Cixous takes Dora's story as a revolutionary discourse of the feminine, saluting Dora as "the indomitable, the poetic body . . . the true 'mistress' of the Signifier." [183] In *The Newly-Born Woman* (1975), Cixous took the position that hysteria was the "nuclear example of women's power to protest," and that Dora belonged to the pantheon of feminist history: "Dora seemed to me to be the one who resists the system, the one who cannot stand that the family and society are founded on the body of women, on bodies despised, rejected, bodies that are humiliating once they have been used." [184] Cixous's play *Portrait de Dora* (1976) tries to restore Dora's subjectivity and to reconstitute the other buried female figure in Freud's case history, the mother. Interpretations of Freud's case history are now legion, and the book *In Dora's Case* brings some of these feminist readings together.

It's important to note, however, that the fascination with Dora and hysteria has also been controversial within feminist theory. In her debate with Cixous in *The Newly-Born Woman*, Catherine Clément was more skeptical about the ultimate power of hysteria as a form of feminine subversion. She maintained that the hysteric is unable to communicate because she is outside of reality and culture—that, in Lacanian terms, her expression remains in the Imaginary, outside the Symbolic. Thus "hysterical symptoms, which are metaphorically inscribed on the body, are ephemeral and enigmatic. They constitute a language only by analogy." Hysterics should be classed not with feminist heroines, but with deviants and marginals who actually reinforce the social structure by their preordained place on the margin. Indeed, their roles are ultimately conservative: "Every hysteric ends up inuring others to her symptoms, and the family closes round her again, whether she is curable or incurable." With regard to Dora, Clément is cool and level-headed: "You love Dora, but to me she never seemed a revolutionary character." [185] In order to affect the symbolic order, or the material world, she argues, the hysteric must somehow break through her private language and act. Thus for Clément, the "successful hysteric" is one, like Anna O./Bertha Pappenheim, who becomes a writer, social worker, and feminist leader.

Overall it seems paradoxical that Dora, a notoriously unsuccessful hysteric, should have emerged as a feminist heroine in the 1970s, singled out by women writers and intellectuals who had been able to have the education and activity Ida Bauer sought in vain. It is bizarre to find Dora put forward as a feminist ideal and saluted by successful writers like Cixous, when Dora's own aspirations were to become a woman of learning, perhaps a writer. Historically, Dora never found her own voice. While feminist artists and critics can attempt to re-imagine her story, we must recognize, with Clément, that her rebellion ultimately turned back on the self.

Dora's feminist power, paradoxically, is as a tragic literary figure. Feminist critics have taken up the concept of "hysterical narrative" to describe a story that is fragmented and incoherent, like Freud's case study; or the Lacanian concept of "hysterical discourse" to describe the metaphoric language of the body.[186] The impasse over Dora, feminism, and hysterical narrative, however, needs to be placed within the broader contexts of gender. As Toril Moi has pointed out, what Freud describes as the "incoherence" of the hysteric's story has less to do with the nature of hysteria or with the nature of woman than with the social powerlessness of women's narratives: "The *reason* why the neurotic fails to produce coherence is that she lacks the *power* to impose her own connections on her reader/listener."[187] How can Dora's story have plausibility for male ears in a culture when women's plots are so limited? When narrative conventions assign women only the place of object of desire, how can a woman become the subject of her own story?

In order to understand the gender issues in hysterical narrative, we need to have case studies of male hysterics by women analysts. Since "the dominant narrative of a male doctor treating a woman patient maintains the normative structure of men occupying positions of authority over women, the importance of the gender of the participants in the therapeutic dialogue is obscured."[188] Only in the past few years have women psychoanalysts begun to look at the problem of male hysteria and to examine issues of transference and countertransference between male patients and female therapists. Such studies require a "new narrative line that specifically addresses the relationship of boys to their mothers and the quite different meanings of power and sexuality for men and women in our culture."[189] When their case studies are published, we will be able to ask whether the body language, speech, and narrative of the hysteric is a discourse of femininity or a narrative imposed by the man who tells the story.

Other contemporary feminist theories locate in hysteria an attempt to give weight and meaning to aspects of the feminine which are despised or nonfunctional in the patriarchal social order. As Diane Herndl explains, hysteria "has come to figure as a sort of rudimentary feminism and feminism as a kind of articulate hysteria."[190] Juliet Mitchell describes hysteria as a "pre-political manifestation of feminism," an unconscious protest by women "in terms of their definitional and denigrated characteristic—emotionality. If femininity is by definition hysterical, feminism is the demand *for* the right to be hysterical."[191]

This romanticization and appropriation of the hysteric nostalgically assumes that she is a heroine of the past. "Où sont-elles passées les hystériques de jadis," asked Jacques Lacan in 1977, "ces femmes merveilleuses, les Anna O., les Emmy von N.? . . . Qu'est-ce qui remplace aujourd'hui les symptômes hystériques d'autrefois?"[192] We might answer that the despised hysterics of yesteryear have been replaced by the feminist radicals of today, by contemporary women artists and poets, and by gay activists. In the popular mind, the pejorative association of feminism with hysteria and morbidity has not died yet. In 1983, for example, a controversy erupted in the *Times Literary Supplement* over the use of "hysterical" as a critical term for the poetry of Sylvia Plath and other "man-hating" feminist poets. Defending her position, Anne Stevenson wrote, "Hysteria is the very stuff of revolutions—and not only female revolutions . . . a passionate single-minded psychological condition which, immune to humour as to reason, fails to achieve the detachment essential for self-criticism."[193]

Moreover, those revolutions connected to gender and race continue to seem more "hysterical" than others. In December 1989, when the AIDS activist group ACT-UP and the abortion rights group WHAM staged a demonstration at Saint Patrick's Cathedral in New York City, interrupting the Sunday Mass, the *New York Times* editorialized: "Arguments over AIDS, homosexuality and abortion are not going to be advanced by hysterics, threats or the disruption of religious services."[194] What had been hysterical hooliganism in the suffrage campaigns was now attributed to other groups.

Black activists and radicals have also been stigmatized as hysterics and neurotics, leading to distrust of psychotherapy in the 1960s and 1970s among African-Americans.[195] Yet, from another perspective, Freudian insights can illuminate the experience of racism and its effects on the psyche. In his autobiography *Dusk of Dawn* (1940), W. E. B. Du Bois described the gradual effects of racial segregation on the black mind:

> It is as though one, looking out from a dark cave in a side of an impending mountain, sees the world passing and speaks to it; speaks courteously and persuasively . . . [but] it gradually penetrates the minds of the prisoners that the people passing do not hear; that some thick sheet of invisible but horribly tangible plate glass is between them and the world. They get excited; they talk louder; they gesticulate. [Then some persons may become "hysterical."] They may scream and hurl themselves against the barriers. . . . They may even, here and there, break through in blood

and disfigurement, and find themselves faced by a horrified, implacable, and quite overwhelming mob of people frightened for their very own existence.[196]

Du Bois's description of the social origins of hysterical behavior in racism has relevance for other oppressed groups, particularly because it does not minimize the costs of hysteria. When unhappiness and protest go unheard for a long time, or when it is too dangerous for these negative emotions to be openly expressed, people *do* lose their sense of humor and their powers of self-criticism, whether they are feminists, people with AIDS, black activists, or East Germans, Rumanians, and Bulgarians. Anger that has social causes is converted to a language of the body; people develop disabling symptoms, or may even become violent or suicidal. "Hysteria," as Du Bois knew, is painful and disfiguring; rather than being a romantic ideal, it is a desperate behavior for women or men. It is much safer for the dominant order to allow discontented men and women to express their dissatisfaction through psychosomatic illness than to have them agitating for economic, legal, and political rights. It is thus that Dianne Hunter calls hysteria "feminism lacking a social network in the outer world."[197]

What about hysteria now? In 1986, Etienne Trillat declared, "Hysteria is dead, that's for sure. It carried its mysteries with it to the grave."[198] Phillip Slavney describes his study *Perspectives on "Hysteria"* (1990) as "perhaps the last book with *hysteria* in its title written by a psychiatrist." The terms "*hysteria, hysteric* and *hysterical*," he argues, "are on the verge of becoming anachronisms."[199]

These announcements of hysteria's death are surely premature, for they neglect the cultural and symbolic meanings of the term, which cannot be obliterated by professional fiat. To write a *history* of *hysteria* at the end of the twentieth century we need also to recognize the correspondence that has developed between the two words. While for centuries the etymological link between "hysteria" and *hystera* dictated certain assumptions about female sexuality, today the correspondence between "hysteria" and *histoire* seems much more important. Above all, the hysteric is someone who has a story, a *histoire,* and whose story is told by science. Hysteria is no longer a question of the wandering womb; it is a question of the wandering story, and of whether that story belongs to the hysteric, the doctor, the historian, or the critic. The stories of race and gender in hysteria still remain to be told, and thus this book cannot be the final narrative, but is only another installment in the long and unfinished history of hysteria in Western civilization.

NOTES

1. Hal Foster, interview with Mary Kelly, in *Interim* (New York: The New Museum of Contemporary Art, 1990), 55.

2. Hélène Cixous and Catherine Clément, *The Newly Born Woman*, trans. Betsy Wing (Minneapolis: University of Minnesota Press, 1987), 47.

3. Edward Tilt, *A Handbook of Uterine Therapeutics and of Diseases of Women*, 4th ed. (New York: William Wood, 1881), 85.

4. Paul Chodoff, "Hysteria and Women," *American Journal of Psychiatry* 139 (May 1982): 546.

5. A. Fabre, *L'hystérie viscérale—nouveaux fragments de clinique médicale* (Paris: A. Delahaye & E. Lecrosnier, 1883), 3.

6. Mark S. Micale, "Hysteria and Its Historiography: A Review of Past and Present Writings, II," *History of Science* 27 (1989): 320.

7. Gregorio Kohon, "Reflections on Dora: The Case of Hysteria," *International Journal of Psychoanalysis* 65 (1984): 73–84.

8. Chodoff, "Hysteria and Women," 545.

9. See P. Chodoff and H. Lyons, "Hysterical Personality: A Re-evaluation," *Psychoanalytic Quarterly* 34 (1965): 390–405; and Harriet A. Lerner, "The Hysterical Personality: A 'Woman's Disease,'" in *Women and Mental Health*, ed. Elizabeth Howell and Marjorie Bayes (New York: Basic Books, 1981), 196–206.

10. For an overview and critique of this work, see Mark S. Micale, "Feminist Historiography of Hysteria," in "Hysteria and Its Historiography, II," 319–331. See also Elaine Showalter, *The Female Malady* (New York: Pantheon Press, 1985).

11. Micale, "Hysteria and Its Historiography, II," 331.

12. See Juliet Mitchell, "Femininity, Narrative, and Psychoanalysis," in *Women: The Longest Revolution* (London: Virago, 1984).

13. Jane Gallop, "Nurse Freud: Class Struggle in the Family," unpublished paper, Miami University, 1983.

14. Claire Kahane, *In Dora's Case: Freud-Hysteria-Feminism*, ed. Claire Kahane and Charles Bernheimer (New York: Columbia University Press, 1985), 22.

15. See Joan W. Scott, "Gender: A Useful Category of Historical Analysis," *American Historical Review* 91 (December 1986): 1053–1075.

16. J. Russell Reynolds, "Hysteria," in *A System of Medicine*, ed. J. Russell Reynolds (London: Macmillan, 1866–1879), 2:307; quoted in Mark Micale, "Charcot and the Idea of Hysteria in the Male: A Study of Gender, Mental Science, and Medical Diagnostics in Late Nineteenth-Century France," *Medical History* 34 (October 1990).

17. Emile Batault, *Contribution à l'étude de l'hystérie chez l'homme* (Paris, 1885), 48.

18. D. M. Berger, "Hysteria: In Search of the Animus," *Comprehensive Psychiatry* 12 (1971): 277.

19. Wilhelm Reich, *Character-Analysis*, 3d ed., trans. Theodore P. Wolfe (New York: Farrar, Straus & Giroux, 1949), 189.

20. Chodoff and Lyons, "Hysterical Personality," 739.

21. Lucien Israël, *L'hystérique, le sexe, et le médecin* (Paris: Masson, 1983), 60, 197 (my translation).

22. Ibid., 60.

23. See Evelyn Fox Keller, *Reflections on Gender and Science* (New Haven, Conn.: Yale University Press, 1985); Ludmilla Jordanova, *Sexual Visions: Images of Gender in Science and Medicine between the Eighteenth and Twentieth Centuries* (Hemel Hempstead: Harvester Wheatsheaf, 1989); Emily Martin, *The Woman in the Body: A Cultural Analysis of Reproduction* (Boston: Beacon Press, 1987); and Cynthia Eagle Russett, *Sexual Science: The Victorian Construction of Womanhood* (Cambridge: Harvard University Press, 1989).

24. Jordanova, *Sexual Visions*, 5.

25. Etienne Trillat, *L'histoire de l'hystérie* (Paris: Seghers, 1986).

26. Josef Breuer and Sigmund Freud, "Studies on Hysteria," *Standard Edition of the Complete Psychological Works of Sigmund Freud*, ed. J. and A. Strachey (London: The Hogarth Press, 1955), 2:240 (hereafter cited as SE).

27. Olive Schreiner, letter to Karl Pearson, in *The Letters of Olive Schreiner*, ed. Richard Rive (Oxford: Oxford University Press, 1987), 86.

28. Neil Bartlett, *Who Was That Man?* (London: Serpent's Tail, 1989), 46.

29. Vieda Skultans, *English Madness: Ideas on Insanity, 1580–1890* (London: Routledge & Kegan Paul, 1978), 81.

30. Thomas Sydenham, *Works of Thomas Sydenham*, 1848, 2:85, quoted in Ilza Veith, *Hysteria: The History of a Disease* (Chicago: University of Chicago Press, 1965), 141.

31. Jordanova, *Sexual Visions*, 59.

32. Jean-Baptiste Louyer-Villermay, *Recherches historiques et médicales sur l'hypochondrie* (1802), quoted in Trillat, *L'histoire de l'hystérie*, 103.

33. M. Jeanne Peterson, "Dr. Acton's Enemy: Medicine, Sex, and Society in Victorian England," *Victorian Studies* 29 (Summer 1986): 578 n. 29.

34. Stephen Heath, *The Sexual Fix* (London: Macmillan Publishers, 1982), 30.

35. Ernst von Feuchtersleben, *The Principles of Medical Psychology*, trans. H. E. Lloyd, ed. B. G. Babington (London: Sydenham Society, 1847), 228.

36. John H. Smith, "Abulia: Sexuality and Diseases of the Will in the Late Nineteenth Century," *Genders* 6 (Fall 1989): 110.

37. George M. Beard, *American Nervousness: Its Causes and Consequences*, 1881; reprint (New York: Arno Press, 1972); and *Sexual Neurasthenia: Its Hygiene, Causes, Symptoms, and Treatment* (New York: Treat, 1884).

38. Beard, *Sexual Neurasthenia*, 204.

39. Spencer, quoted in Howard M. Feinstein, "The Use and Abuse of Illness in the James Family Circle," in *Ourselves, Our Past: Psychological Approaches to American History*, ed. Robert J. Brugger (Baltimore: Johns Hopkins University Press, 1981), 230.

40. Jan Goldstein, *Console and Classify: The French Psychiatric Profession in the Nineteenth Century* (New York: Cambridge University Press, 1987), 336.

41. See the case of M. Defly and the discussion in Micale, "Charcot and the Idea of Hysteria in the Male."

42. See Russett, *Sexual Science*, 116.

43. Beard, *Sexual Neurasthenia*, 59.

44. Herbert Spencer, "A Theory of Population Deduced from the General Law of Animal Fertility," *Westminster Review*, n.s. 1 (1852): 263.

45. Gordon Haight, *George Eliot: A Biography* (New York and Oxford: Oxford University Press, 1968), 118–119.

46. F. S. Gosling, *Before Freud: Neurasthenia and the American Medical Community* (Urbana: University of Illinois Press, 1987), 34.

47. Ibid., 47, 55.

48. Ibid., 47, 63.

49. See Edward Clarke, *Sex in Education* (Boston: J. R. Osgood, 1873); and Henry Maudsley, "Sex in Mind and Education," *Fortnightly Review* 15 (1874): 466–483.

50. Ernest Earnest, *S. Weir Mitchell, Novelist and Physician* (Philadelphia: University of Pennsylvania Press, 1950), 51.

51. Silas Weir Mitchell, *Doctor and Patient* (Philadelphia: J. B. Lippincott, 1888), 48.

52. S. Weir Mitchell, *Lectures on Diseases of the Nervous System Especially in Women*, 2d ed. (London: J. & A. Churchill, 1885), 15.

53. S. Weir Mitchell, *Wear and Tear: Hints for the Overworked*, 4th ed. (Philadelphia: J. B. Lippincott, 1872), 38–39.

54. Mitchell, *Doctor and Patient*, 139.

55. Mitchell, *Lectures on Diseases of the Nervous System*, 14.

56. Mitchell, *Doctor and Patient*, 48.

57. Mitchell, *Lectures on Diseases of the Nervous System*, 76.

58. Quoted in Gosling, *Before Freud*, 115.

59. See Ann D. Wood, "The Fashionable Diseases: Women's Complaints and Their Treatment in Nineteenth-Century America," in *Clio's Consciousness Raised: New Perspectives on the History of Women*, ed. Mary Hartman and Lois W. Banner (New York: Harper & Row, 1971), 9; G. Barker-Benfield, *The Horrors of the Half-Known Life* (New York: Harper Colophon, 1976), 130; and Suzanne Poirier, "The Weir Mitchell Rest Cure: Doctor and Patients," *Women's Studies* 10 (1983): 15–40.

60. Gilman, *The Living of Charlotte Perkins Gilman* (1935), reprint (New York: Arno Press, 1972), 96.

61. Margaret Cleaves, *The Autobiography of a Neurasthenic* (Boston: Gorham, 1910), 198. See also Poirier, "Weir Mitchell Rest Cure," 28–29; and Constance M. McGovern, "Doctors or Ladies? Women Physicians in Psychiatric Institutions, 1872–1900," in *Women and Health in America*, ed. Judith Walker-Leavitt (Madison: University of Wisconsin Press, 1984), 442–443.

62. Breuer and Freud, "Studies on Hysteria," *SE* 2:311.

63. Robert Brudenell Carter, *On the Pathology and Treatment of Hysteria* (London: John Churchill, 1853), 25, 53.

64. Ibid., 97–98.

65. Henry Maudsley, *The Pathology of Mind* (London: Macmillan, 1879), 450.

66. Charles Mercier, *Sanity and Insanity* (New York: Scribner & Welford, 1890), 213.

67. H. B. Donkin, "Hysteria," in *Dictionary of Psychological Medicine*, by D. H. Tuke (Philadelphia: P. Blakiston, 1982), 619–620.

68. F. C. Skey, *Hysteria*, 2d ed. (London: Longmans, Greem, Reader & Dyer, 1867), 77–84.

69. Maudsley, *Pathology of Mind*, 397–398.

70. Skey, *Hysteria*, 60.

71. Robert Thornton, *The Hysterical Woman: Trials, Tears, Tricks, and Tantrums* (Chicago: Donohue & Hennebery, 1893).

72. Jules Falret, *Etudes cliniques sur les maladies mentales et nerveuses* (Paris: Librairie Baillière et Fils, 1890), 502.

73. Smith-Rosenberg, "The Hysterical Woman: Sex Roles and Role Conflict in Nineteenth-Century America," *Social Research* 39 (1972); reprinted in Smith-Rosenberg, *Disorderly Conduct*, 197–216.

74. Michel Foucault, *The History of Sexuality*, trans. Robert Hurley (New York: Vintage, 1980), 104.

75. Ibid., 121.

76. Smith-Rosenberg, *Disorderly Conduct*, 331 n. 5.

77. Foucault, *History of Sexuality*, 112.

78. Smith-Rosenberg, *Disorderly Conduct*, 200.

79. Van Deusen, "Observations on a Form of Nervous Prostration," *American Journal of Insanity* 25 (1869): 447; cited in Smith-Rosenberg, *Disorderly Conduct*, 332 n. 14.

80. Lisa Tickner, *The Spectacle of Women* (Chicago: University of Chicago Press, 1988), 196.

81. Smith-Rosenberg, *Disorderly Conduct*, 259–260.

82. See Debora Silverman, "The 'New Woman,' Feminism, and the Decorative Arts in Fin-de-Siècle France," in *Eroticism and the Body Politic*, ed. Lynn Hunt (Baltimore: Johns Hopkins University Press, 1991), 144–163.

83. [William Barry], "The Strike of a Sex," *Quarterly Review* 179 (1894): 312.

84. Ian Fletcher, Introduction, *British Poetry and Prose* 1870–1905 (London: Oxford University Press, 1987), xvii.

85. Tickner, *Spectacle of Women*, 194.

86. Linton, *The Girl of the Period and Other Essays* (London: Macmillan, 1883).

87. See Mark S. Micale, "The Salpêtrière in the Age of Charcot: An Institutional Perspective on Medical History in the Late Nineteenth Century," *Journal of Contemporary History* 20 (October 1985): 709.

88. Charcot, "A propos de six cas d'hystérie chez l'homme," in *J. M. Charcot: L'Hystérie*, ed. E. Trillat (Toulouse: Privat, 1971), 156.

89. Batault, *Contribution à l'étude de l'hystérie chez l'homme*, 110.

90. Charcot, "A propos de six cas d'hystérie chez l'homme," 157–158.

91. Micale, "Charcot and the Idea of Hysteria in the Male," 66.

92. See Micale, "The Salpêtrière in the Age of Charcot," 703–731.

93. Goldstein, *Console and Classify*, 322.

94. Cited in Elisabeth Roudinesco, *La Bataille de cent ans: Histoire de la psychanalyse en France* (Paris: Ramsay, 1982), 1:35.

95. Quoted in Ruth Harris, *Murders and Madness: Medicine, Law, and Society in the "Fin de Siècle"* (Oxford: Clarendon Press, 1989), 162.

96. Quoted in Fielding H. Garrison, *Introduction to the History of Medicine* (Philadelphia: Saunders, 1924), 640.

97. Batault, *Contribution à l'étude de l'hystérie chez l'homme.*

98. See Roudinesco, *La Bataille de cent ans,* 1:76.

99. Griselda Pollock, *Vision & Difference: Femininity, Feminism, and the Histories of Art* (London: Routledge & Kegan Paul, 1988), 189–190.

100. On the art of the Charcot family, see Debora Silverman, *Art Nouveau in Fin-de-Siècle France* (Berkeley, Los Angeles, Oxford: University of California Press, 1989), 192–193, 196.

101. Silverman, "'New Woman,' Feminism, and the Decorative Arts in Fin-de-Siècle France," 147–148.

102. See Toby Gelfand, "Medical Nemesis, Paris 1894: Leon Daudet's 'Les Morticoles,'" *Bulletin of the History of Medicine* 60 (1986): 155–176.

103. Axel Munthe, *The Story of San Michele* (London: John Murray, 1930), 296.

104. *Zoöphilist* 7 (November 1887): 110; quoted in Mary Ann Elston, "Women and Anti-Vivisection in Victorian England, 1870–1900," in *Vivisection in Historical Perspective*, ed. Nicolaas A. Ruphe (London: Routledge & Kegan Paul, 1987), 281.

105. Goldstein, *Console and Classify*, 375.

106. See the accounts of Augustine, also called "Louise" and "X . . ." in D. M. Bourneville, *Iconographie photographique de la Salpêtrière*, Vol. II (1878): 124–167; and Vol. III (1879–80): 187–199. I am grateful to the staff of the Library of the College of Physicians of Philadelphia for assistance with these materials.

107. Louis Aragon and André Breton, "Le cinquantenaire de l'hystérie," *La Révolution surréaliste*, no. 11 (1928): 20.

108. See Georges Didi-Huberman, *Invention de l'Hystérie: Charcot et l'Iconographie Photographique de la Salpêtrière* (Paris: Macula, 1982).

109. The critic Dianne Hunter is active in this group. See also Showalter, *Female Malady*, chap. 6; and Coral Houtman, *Augustine*, unpublished television play, London, 1989.

110. At least one woman, however, attacked his hostility toward women doctors. See the comments of C. R., "Charcot dévoilé," in Goldstein, *Console and Classify*, 375.

111. *L'hystérie aux XVIIe et XVIIIe siècles* (Paris: Steinhel, 1897).

112. Georgette Déga, *Essai sur la cure préventive de l'hystérie féminine par l'éducation* (Felix Alcan, 1898), 29. See also Jacqueline Carroy, "Le noviciat de l'hystérie selon Georgette Déga," *Psychanalyse Universitaire* 12 (1987): 141–152.

113. Mark Micale, "Hysteria Male/Hysteria Female: Reflections in Comparative Gender Construction in Nineteenth-Century France and Britain," in *Science*

and Sensibility: Essays in the History of Gender, Science, and Medicine in Nineteenth-Century Britain, ed. Marina Benjamin (New Brunswick, N.J.: Rutgers University Press, forthcoming).

114. See Trillat, *Histoire de l'hystérie,* 199–204.

115. Pierre Janet, *The Major Symptoms of Hysteria* (New York: Macmillan, 1920), 10–11.

116. Freud, "Paris Report," *SE* 3:10.

117. Cited by Ernest Jones, *The Life and Work of Sigmund Freud,* edited and abridged by Lionel Trilling and Steven Marcus (New York: Basic Books, 1961), 207n.

118. Freud, "Hystérie," *SE* 1:41, 52.

119. See Dianne Hunter, "Hysteria, Psychoanalysis, and Feminism: The Case of Anna O," *Feminist Studies* 9 (1983): 467–468.

120. A significant contribution to this work was made by Hunter in her essay "Hysteria, Psychoanalysis, and Feminism."

121. See Diane Price Herndl, "The Writing Cure: Charlotte Perkins Gilman, Anna O, and 'Hysterical' Writing," *NWSA Journal* 1 (1988): 64–68.

122. Sigmund Freud, *Dora: An Analysis of a Case of Hysteria* (New York: Collins, 1964). See also *In Dora's Case: Freud—Hysteria—Feminism,* ed. Charles Bernheimer and Claire Kahane (New York: Columbia University Press, 1985).

123. Jeffrey Masson, *Against Therapy* (London: Fontana, 1990), 101.

124. See Susan Katz, "Speaking Out against the 'Talking Cure': Unmarried Women in Freud's Early Case Studies," *Women's Studies* 13 (1987): 297–324.

125. Toril Moi, "Representations of Patriarchy: Sexuality and Epistemology in Freud's Dora," in *In Dora's Case,* ed. Kahane and Bernheimer, 196.

126. Breuer and Freud, "Studies on Hysteria," *SE,* 2:254.

127. Freud, "Remembering, Repeating, and Working Through," *SE* 12:151.

128. Freud, "The Dynamics of Transference," *SE* 12:108.

129. *The British School of Psychoanalysis,* ed. Gregorio Kohon (London: Free Association Books, 1986), 386.

130. Kurt Eissler, "The Effect of the Structure of the Ego in Psychoanalytic Technique," *J. of American Psychoanalytic Association,* Vol. I (1953): 114.

131. Dubois, *Les psychonévroses et leur traitement moral* (Paris: Masson, 1904), 14.

132. Tickner, *Spectacle of Women,* 203.

133. Ibid., 316 n. 198.

134. P. Guriaud, *Hystérie et folie hystérique* (AMP 1914), in Trillat, *L'histoire de l'hystérie,* 241.

135. Claude Barrois, *Les névroses traumatiques* (Paris: Bardas, 1988), 20–21.

136. "Deux types de névroses de guerre," *Oeuvres complètes* (Paris: Payot, 1970), 2:238–252.

137. On W. H. R. Rivers, see the biography by Richard Sloboden, *W. H. R. Rivers* (New York: Columbia University Press, 1978); and Showalter, *Female Malady,* chap. 7.

138. See Charles S. Myers, *Shell-Shock in France* (Cambridge: Cambridge University Press, 1940), 25, 37, 66.

139. Myers, *Shell-Shock in France*, 83; and W. McDougall, *An Outline of Abnormal Psychology* (London: Methuen, 1926), 2.

140. Martin Stone, "Shellshock and the Psychologists," in *The Anatomy of Madness*, ed. W. F. Bynum, Roy Porter, and Michael Shepherd (London: Tavistock, 1985), 261.

141. Myers, *Shell-Shock in France*, 40.

142. Quoted in Eric Leed, *No Man's Land: Combat and Identity in World War I* (Cambridge: Cambridge University Press, 1979), 179.

143. Frederick W. Mott, *War Neuroses and Shell Shock* (London: Hodder & Stoughton, 1919), 171.

144. H. Stern, "Evolution du problème des psychoneuroses de guerre," *Annales médico-psychologiques* (1947) 2:249–270.

145. Jones, *Life and Work of Sigmund Freud*, 494–495.

146. Quoted in Thomas Salmon, *The Care and Treatment of Mental Diseases and War Neuroses ("Shell Shock") in the British Army* (New York: War Work Committee of the National Committee for Mental Hygiene, 1917), 40.

147. G. Elliot-Smith and T. H. Pear, *Shellshock and Its Lessons*, 4th ed. (London: Longman, Green, 1919), 32–33.

148. R. D. Gillespie, *The Psychological Effects of War on Citizen and Soldier* (New York: Norton, 1942), 21; quoted in Stone, "Shellshock and the Psychologists," 21.

149. Crichton-Miller, quoted in Salmon, *Care and Treatment*, 40.

150. Thomas A. Ross, *Lectures on War Neurosis* (Baltimore: Williams, 1941), 78.

151. Paul Fussell, *The Great War and Modern Memory* (New York: Oxford University Press, 1975), 22–29.

152. Karl Abraham, in *Psycho-analysis and the War Neuroses*, ed. Sándor Ferenczi (London: International Psycho-analytical Press, 1921), 24.

153. See *The Lancet*, 25 December 1915; 15 January 1916; 22 January 1916; and 19 February 1916.

154. P. S. Lynch, "The Exploitation of Courage," M.Phil. thesis, University of London, 1977.

155. Stone, "Shellshock and the Psychologists," 261, 263.

156. Fussell, *The Great War and Modern Memory*, 273–274.

157. Stone, "Shellshock and the Psychologists," 262.

158. Stone, "Shellshock and the Psychologists," 245.

159. W. H. R. Rivers, *Instinct and the Unconscious* (Cambridge: Cambridge University Press, 1922), 252.

160. Rivers, "Psycho-Therapeutics," in *Encyclopedia of Religion and Ethics*, ed. James Hastings, 13 vols. (Edinburgh: T. & T. Clark, 1918), 10: 440.

161. See, for example, the case study of a claustrophobic officer who stammered in Rivers, *Instinct and the Unconscious*.

162. Rivers, *Instinct and the Unconscious*, 133, 135, 136.

163. Edward Shorter, "Mania, Hysteria, and Gender in Lower Austria,

1891–1905," *History of Psychiatry* 1 (1990): 4. See also Shorter, "Paralysis: The Rise and Fall of a 'Hysterical Symptom,'" *Journal of Social History* 19 (1986): 549–582.

164. Interview with Monique David-Ménard in *Women Analyze Women,* ed. Elaine Hoffman Baruch and Lucienne J. Serrano (New York: New York University Press, 1988), 54–55.

165. David-Ménard in *Women Analyze Women,* ed. Baruch and Serrano, 54.

166. Elizabeth Zetzel, *The Capacity for Emotional Growth* (New York: International Universities Press, 1970), 14.

167. Ibid. 236–238.

168. Ibid., 245.

169. Baruch and Serrano, *Women Analyze Women,* 55.

170. Ibid., 49.

171. Micale, "Hysteria and Its Historiography, I," 227.

172. Ilza Veith, *Can You Hear the Clapping of One Hand? Learning to Live with a Stroke* (Berkeley, Los Angeles, Oxford: University of California Press, 1989), 94.

173. Ibid., 274.

174. Micale, "Hysteria and Its Historiography, II," 319.

175. Veith, *Hysteria,* viii.

176. See, for example, Carol F. Karlson, *The Devil in the Shape of a Woman: Witchcraft in Colonial New England* (New York: Vintage Books, 1989).

177. Veith, *Hysteria,* 208, 210.

178. Ibid., 209.

179. Joan W. Scott, "American Women Historians, 1884–1984," in *Gender and the Politics of History* (New York: Columbia University Press, 1988), 186.

180. Nancy J. Chodorow, *Feminism and Psychoanalytic Theory* (New Haven, Conn.: Yale University Press, 1989), 215, 219.

181. Kahane, *In Dora's Case,* 31.

182. Mary Jacobus, *Reading Woman: Essays in Feminist Criticism* (New York: Columbia University Press, 1986), 200.

183. Hélène Cixous, "The Laugh of the Medusa," in *New French Feminisms,* ed. Elaine Marks and Isabelle de Courtivron (Amherst: University of Massachusetts Press, 1980), 257.

184. Cixous and Clément, *Newly-Born Woman,* 154.

185. Ibid., 5, 9, 15, 157.

186. On hysterical narrative see Madelon Sprengnether, "Enforcing Oedipus: Freud and Dora," in *In Dora's Case,* ed. Kahane and Bernheimer, 267–271.

187. Toril Moi, *Feminist Theory and Simone de Beauvoir* (London: Basil Blackwell Publisher, 1990), 82.

188. Lisa K. Gornick, "Developing a New Narrative: The Woman Therapist and the Male Patient," in *Psychoanalysis and Women: Contemporary Reappraisals,* ed. Judith L. Alpert (Hillsdale, N.J.: Analytic Press, 1986), 257–286.

189. Gornick, "Developing a New Narrative," 258.

190. Herndl, "Writing Cure," 53–54.

191. Mitchell, *Women: The Longest Revolution: Essays in Feminism, Literature and Psychoanalysis* (London: Virago, 1984), 117.

192. Quoted in Elisabeth Roudinesco, *Histoire de la psychanalyse en France,* I: 82–83.

193. Anne Stevenson, "The Hysterical Women's Movement," *Times Literary Supplement* (9 September 1983), 961. There are interesting correspondences between Sylvia Plath's most famous poem, "Daddy," and the case of Anna O., although this textual connection is not at all the kind of hysterical parallel Stevenson had in mind.

194. "The Storming of St. Pat's," *New York Times* (12 December 1989), Sec. A, 24.

195. Lena Williams, "Psychotherapy Gaining Favor among Blacks," *New York Times,* (22 November 1989), Sec. I, 1.

196. Quoted in Arnold Rampersad, "Psychology and Afro-American Biography," *The Yale Review* (1989): 7.

197. Hunter, "Hysteria, Psychoanalysis, and Feminism," 485.

198. Trillat, *L'histoire de l'hystérie,* 274.

199. Phillip R. Slavney, *Perspectives on "Hysteria"* (Baltimore: Johns Hopkins University Press, 1990), 190.

FIVE

The Image of the Hysteric

Sander L. Gilman

THE FUNCTION OF THE "REAL" IMAGE OF THE HYSTERIC IN DEFINING THE NATURE OF HYSTERIA

In the history of hysteria one image haunts the eye. It is an 1887 painting by André Brouillet of Jean-Martin Charcot presenting his pet hysteric, "Blanche" (Blanche Wittman), to the members of his neurological service at the Salpêtrière.[1] This portrait, clearly standing within the great tradition of Rembrandt's anatomies and echoing the 1876 portrait, *Pinel Freeing the Insane,* by Tony Robert-Fleury, which hung in the main lecture hall at the Salpêtrière, has one rather anomalous moment. (Brouillet [1824–1908] was after all a student of Gérôme, whose history paintings always hide a mystery.) All of Charcot's staff are men, with the exception of the one nurse, who is about to catch the somnambulistic patient. Only these two women are placed in such a manner so as to see the rear of the hall; all of the male figures have their backs (or sides) to the rear. And on the rear wall is an enlarged drawing by Charcot's colleague Paul Richer of the *arc-en-cercle* stage of "grand" hysteria. Charcot described this stage in an 1877 lecture: "The patient suddenly falls to the ground, with a shrill cry; loss of consciousness is complete. The tetanic rigidity of all her members, which generally inaugurates the scene, is carried to a high degree; the body is forcibly bent backwards, the abdomen is prominent, greatly distended, and very resisting."[2] In Broulliet's engraving, Richer literally sits at Charcot's right hand, sketching the patient who is replicating his own drawing.[3] Only the women see (and "know," that is, act upon) the image of the hysteric. Their image of the hysteric, both as patient and as health-care practitioner is con-

André Brouillet's image of Jean-Martin Charcot presenting his "pet" hysteric, "Blanche" (Blanche Wittman), to the members of his neurological service at the Salpêtrière (1887). (Bethesda, Md.: National Library of Medicine.)

sciously formed by the visual image of the hysteric as created by a male physician.

The late nineteenth century understood such a pattern as the very model for knowing the world. Oscar Wilde suggested that we learn about nature from the work of art. "External nature," according to Wilde, "imitates Art. The only effects that she can show us are effects that we have already seen through poetry, or in paintings."[4] And, we might add, in photographs.[5] This is precisely what Blanche Wittman did at the Salpêtrière, as she learned from the representations of the hysteric how to appear as a hysteric.[6]

This image does not stand alone but is representative of a series of representations of the hysteric during the latter half of the nineteenth century. In the Jacques-Joseph Moreau de Tours 1890 image, *Hysterics of the Charité on the Service of Dr. Luys,* a wider range of representa-

Tony Robert-Fleury's *Pinel Freeing the Insane* (1876), which hung in the main lecture hall at the Salpêtrière. (Paris: The Library of the Salpêtrière.)

Jacques-Joseph Moreau de Tours, *Hysterics of the Charité on the Service of Dr. Luys* (1890). (Bethesda, Md.: National Library of Medicine.) Photo courtesy Yale Medical Library.

tions of the hysteric is present.[7] Dr. J.-B. Luys (1848–1897), the author of an early photographic medical atlas,[8] stands to the rear of the room, with his white mutton-chop whiskers, as his female patients perform. (Moreau de Tour had himself been an intern under J.-É.-D. Esquirol, the creator of the first modern psychiatric atlas, at Charenton.[9]) Luys had described and photographed the hysterics of the Salpêtrière for his 1887 study of the effects of hypnotism as therapy.[10] All of the patients in Moreau de Tours's image are seemingly oblivious to what immediately captures the eye of the viewer. On the rear wall of this ward, a permanent fixture of the room inhabited by the patients, is a chart recording the different phases of hypnosis, the stages that the patient is expected to pass through as she performs for her male audience. It is part of the world of the patient, a means through which to learn how to structure one's hysteria so as to make one an exemplary patient. Indeed, this is paralleled within the images that are so central to Jules Luys's own work, by the photographs of his pet patients, especially "Esther," taken by his brother Georges, which illustrate his 1887 study of the emotions of the hysteric.[11]

These patients are seen. There is no attempt to mask their identity. In the case studies of the period (even as early as Pinel) there is the use of initials or masked names. But in the visual images that Esquirol brings there is the assumption that the face (its structure or its expression) is so important that it does not need to be masked. But there is also the understanding, given the artistic license of the engraving and the lithograph, that there would be sufficient difference between the image of the patient and the final representation as to mask the patient's identity. (This is not always the case, as one can see in Georges-François-Marie Gabriel's admittedly unpublished image of Eugéne Hugo, the brother of the author.[12]) The exception to this seems to prove the rule. In the *Nouvelle iconographie de la Salpêtrière,* Charcot's house organ, there are rarely images of patients that are intentionally masked, usually naked women, such as the image of a young anorexic female reproduced in the fifth volume.[13] (The *Nouvelle iconographie de la Salpêtrière* is not the only journal of its type. The *Revue photographique des Hôpitaux des Paris* flourished in the 1870s.)

The importance of the image of the hysteric represented as learning from the medical images that surround her can be gleaned from the following anecdote. In an account of Charcot's experiments with hypnotism in the *British Medical Journal* of 5 October 1878, Arthur Gamgee, Professor of Physiology at Owens College, Manchester, observed:

> One of the patients was suspected of stealing some photographs from the hospital, but she indignantly denied the charge. One morning [Mr.]

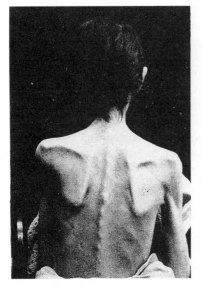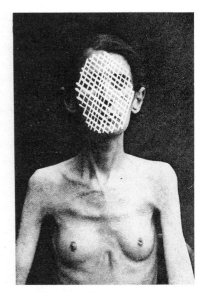

The masked image of the hysteric. From Louis Battaille, "Deux Cas d'Anorexie Hystérique," *Nouvelles Iconographie de la Salpêtrière* 5 (1892), plate opposite p. 277. Photo courtesy Wellcome Institute Library, London.

Richer, after having made some experiments upon other subjects, found the suspected thief with her hand in the drawer containing the photographs, having already concealed some of them in her pocket. [Mr.] Richer approached her. She did not move; she was fixed—she was transformed into a statue, so to speak. The blows on the gong made in the adjoining ward had rendered her cataleptic at the very moment when, away from the observation of all, she committed the theft.[14]

It is Paul Richer, the creator of the archetypal image, the ornament of the lecture room in which rounds were held, who captures the "cataleptic" woman, a figure so mired in her internalization of his idea of the hysteric that she literally freezes as an incidental occurrence to the "experiment" taking place just beyond her ken.[15] This is not the world of Charcot in the role of Pinel "freeing the insane," whose image graced the public lecture hall in which the so-called Tuesday lectures took place. For here the "insane" patient is captured rather than freed by the intervention, no matter how incidental, by the physician. But why is this woman stealing photographs?[16] And whose photographs are they?

The photographs are those of the exemplary patient taken by Albert Londe, the head of the photographic service at the Salpêtrière, indeed

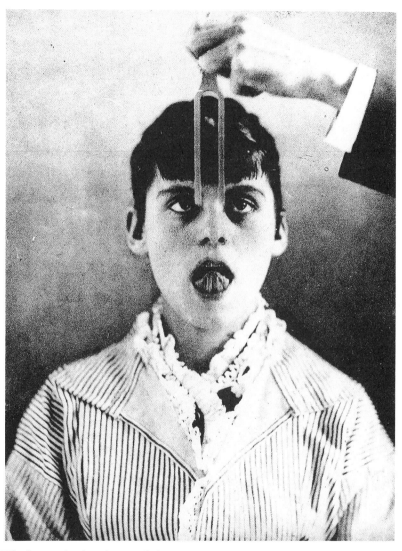

The hypnotized patient and the tuning fork. From Paul Richer, "Gonflement du cou chez un hystérique," *Nouvelles Iconographie de la Salpêtrière* 2
(1889), plate 34. Photo courtesy Wellcome Institute Library, London.

the first professional photographer to have a full-time appointment in any hospital in Europe. His job was to document the progress and manifestation of the patient's disease, to capture the stages and processes as they represented themselves on the visible surface of the patient, on the patient's physiognomy, posture, actions, as a means of cataloging the disease process. This Linnaean means of describing illnesses through their visible signs and symptoms (to use Jean-Martin Charcot's term, taken from the witch-hunting manuals of the Inquisition, the *stigmata* of the illness, from the *stigmata diaboli* that marked the body of the witch) dominated nineteenth-century European, but especially French, psychiatry. To describe was to understand, to describe in the most accurate manner meant to avoid the ambiguity of words, and to rely on the immediate, real image of the sufferer.

But the malleability of the symptoms in hysteria troubled the fin-de-siècle scientist. As Charcot noted, "Symptoms . . . have their destiny: *Habent sua fata.*" Symptoms, "after having enjoyed a certain degree of favour, doubtless on account of the theoretical considerations connected with [them, have] gone somewhat out of fashion . . ." But this is to be understood from the standpoint only of the physician-nosologist; from the standpoint of the patient, the symptoms are real, even if the patients are duplicitous: "You will meet with [simulation] at every step in the history of hysteria, and one finds himself sometimes admiring the amazing craft, sagacity, and perseverance which women, under the influence of this great neurosis, will put in play for the purposes of deception— especially when the physician is to be the victim. . . . It is incontestable that, in a multitude of cases, they have taken pleasure in distorting, by exaggerations, the principal circumstances of their disorder, in order to make them appear extraordinary and wonderful."[17] This deception is, for Charcot and his time, an absolute sign of the hysteric, and it can only be read correctly by a good diagnostician.

For hysteria must be "seen" to have observable symptoms, such as the changes of the skin or the wasting of the body, to be understood as a real disease: "Hysteria is a real disease, as real as small-pox or cancer, and . . . it has a physical basis, probably of a chemical nature, although this is yet very imperfectly understood."[18] As an early review of the first major journal from the Salpêtrière devoted to the visual representation of the insane noted, the camera was as necessary for the study of hysteria as the microscope was for histology.[19] This fantasy of realism captured the belief of the nineteenth century, both the doctor's and the patient's. For the doctor, the image is the patient, as it is for the patient. This search for an ontological representation of illness parallels the undertaking of the exemplary fin-de-siècle scientist, Louis Pasteur, whose germ theory of contagious disease relied on the visibility of the germ for its power.[20] As Georges Canguilhem notes: "After all, a germ can be seen, even if this requires the complicated mediation of a microscope, stains and cultures, while we would never be able to see a miasma or an influence."[21] To see the patient means to develop the technique for seeing, a technique that is "scientific"; the patient, in turn, as the object of the medical gaze becomes part of the process of the creation of an ontological representation of the disease, a representation that is labeled hysteria. This does not deny the underlying pathology of the hysteric; it reflects only the meaning attributed to the symptoms created to represent the pathology as a disease.

One can speculate on whether the official nosology of American (and increasingly, world) clinical psychiatry, the DSM-IIIR (soon to be DSM-IV), in its restructuring of hysterical neurosis into conversion disorder, dissociative disorder, histrionic personality disorder, and brief reactive psychosis, did more than relabel an existing disease or whether these new labels are the self-conscious description of the manifestation of the hysteric in the 1980s.[22] But at least the compilers of DSM-IIIR saw their undertaking as the description of the disease, rather than as the search for its etiology. This does not mean, however, that the physician and the patient place any less reliance on the meaning of these definitions in order to shape our contemporary sense of the patient. How many patients today learn to have "conversion disorders" or "factitious disorders with psychological symptoms" from the medicalized world in which they—the sufferers from the dis-ease of hysteria—must function?

For the patient knows how to be a patient, as we see mirrored so well in André Brouillet's image of Charcot, only from the representation of the way the physician wishes to see (and therefore to know) the patient as the vessel of a disease, not any disease, but the disease of images and imagining, hysteria. It is this shared sense of the importance of the image, for the doctor as well as for the patient, which is reflected in the image of the hysteric.

TOWARD A THEORY OF "REALISTIC REPRESENTATION" IN NINETEENTH-CENTURY THOUGHT

In my work on Hugh W. Diamond's mid-nineteenth-century introduction of photography into the treatment of the mentally ill, I was struck by the fact that Diamond believed he could cure at least some of his patients by exposing them to photographs of themselves. The "realism"

Hugh W. Diamond, a portrait of a case of "religious melancholy."
(London: Royal Society of Medicine.)

of the photograph was assumed to have a therapeutic function because
of its mode of representation. Such a view underlined the importance of
all images for the alienists of the nineteenth century. Thus there was a
constant striving for verisimilitude, not only for nosological purposes
(that is, in order to categorize the illness) but also for therapeutic reasons. Seeing one's own difference provided the "healthy" aspect of the
mind with the juxtaposition between the "normal" and the "abnormal."
The desire to see the absolute border between these states encouraged
the nineteenth-century scientist to seek out and "see" the difference. As
Friedrich Nietzsche put it (paraphrasing Claude Bernard): "It is the

value of all morbid states that they show us under a magnifying glass certain states that are normal—but not easily visible when normal."[23] Disease itself is seen as a means of "seeing" the normal. And normality is an unself-conscious state like that of observers, who are never aware of that role until they self-consciously begin to think of themselves as observers through their training as "scientists" and, therefore, become aware of the meaning attached to the act of seeing.

But it was only with the introduction of the photograph that the power of such contrast—for the patient—was clearly articulated. Diamond stated in his 1856 paper "On the Application of Photography to the Physiognomic and Mental Phenomena of Insanity," read before the Royal Society, that "there is another point of view in which the value of portraits of the insane is peculiarly marked—viz. in the effect which they produce upon the patients themselves—I have had many opportunities of witnessing this effect—In very many cases they are examined with much pleasure and interest, but more particularly in those which mark the progress and cure of a severe attack of Mental Aberration."[24]

Diamond's course of treatment was straightforward. He presented his patients with images of themselves that seemed to startle them into an awareness of their madness, because of the radically realistic image of them as demented. Through this confrontation with a "realistic" image of their insane physiognomy, they began to realize their own altered perception of reality. In his talk, he presented the case of "A. D., aged 20," whose "delusions consisted in the supposed possession of great wealth and of an exalted station as a queen."[25] He photographed her. Her reaction to the images she saw reflected the "startle" effect inherent in the newness of the medium of photography: "Her subsequent amusement in seeing the portraits [of herself in various stages of her illness] and her frequent conversation about them was the first decided step in her gradual improvement, and about four months ago she was discharged perfectly cured, and laughed heartily at her former imaginations."[26] If we can extend Diamond's argument, we can suppose that the nineteenth-century alienist saw the patient-observer as sharing the implication of the photographic image, the startle effect that accompanied the introduction of this new medium of representation.

In further work on the use of photography as a means of psychotherapy, I discovered that other alienists of the period, such as Sir William Charles Hood, the director of the Bethlem Asylum, undertook similar applications of photography. I initially extrapolated certain broader generalities about the reaction to the photograph by the first generation to see photographs after their invention in 1839. (This first period occurred a full decade later in Great Britain than in the rest of Europe because both Daguerre's and Fox Talbot's methods of fixing images were under patent during the 1840s only in Great Britain. In the rest of Europe, the daguerreotype at least was in the public domain by the early 1840s.) I believed that the earliest photographs were such a radical mode of representing the reality of the self as different that they had some type of psychological shock effect. That is, they so disoriented patients as to where the already distorted line between what is real or unreal lay, that patients were forced to reexamine their own psychological confusions. I was convinced, however, that it was the perception of the self, the image of the self as the mad person, which caused the "startle" effect.[27] And that was the radical difference of the photograph, as perceived by those in this first generation to see photographs.

George S. Layne, in an essay in 1981, contradicted this finding, while still supporting my sense of the radical break with existing models of perception.[28] He uncovered the fact that the brothers William and Frederick Langenheim provided lantern slides for the "moral" treatment of the patients in the Philadelphia Hospital for the Insane a year before (1851) Diamond exposed his patients to their own images in the Surrey County Lunatic Asylum. But the Langenheim images were not of the patients, but rather were general images such as landscapes and street scenes, yet they had shock value in treating the patients. So it seemed to be not the image of the self but the radical newness of the medium that caused the "startle" effect.

One of the reasons that the "startle" effect was so pronounced as to be useful in therapy in the public asylums was that the working-class inmates of the asylums did not share the bourgeois and upper-class tradition of seeing and understanding visual objects which had developed out of the "realistic" philosophy of Enlightenment art. Even prints and engravings, understood as aesthetic objects, had been, for the most part, out of the financial reach of the proletariat. Theirs was a world with limited access to images—the absence of cheap illustrated newspapers (soon to appear in Great Britain in the middle-class form of the *Graphic* and the *Illustrated London News*) meant that their world of images was the crude broadside with its lithographed (or indeed woodcut) image. But the middle and upper classes had a tradition of seeing and speaking about art, at least in terms of the reproduction of the work of art as engravings (such as the Broulliet and Moreau de Tours images). For them, even if the "startle" effect occurred (or perhaps because it occurred), the objects recorded were understood in terms of a historical continuity of perceiving aesthetic images. And, indeed, the entire history of early photography is full of references to the continuity of the photograph with earlier modes of representation. A letter from Elizabeth Barrett Browning as late as 1843 reflects both the "startle" effect and the language in which it was articulated:

> My dearest Miss Mitford, do you know anything about that wonderful invention of the day, called the Daguerreotype?—that is, have you seen any portraits produced by means of it? Think of a man sitting down in the sun and leaving his facsimile in all its full completion of outline and shadow, steadfast on a plate, at the end of a minute and a half! The Mesmeric disembodiment of spirits strikes one as a degree less marvellous. And several of these wonderful portraits . . . like engravings—only exquisite and delicate beyond the work of the engraver—have I seen lately—longing to have such a memorial of every Being dear to me in the world. It is not merely the likeness which is precious in such cases—but the association, and the sense of nearness involved in the thing . . . the fact of the very shadow of the person lying there fixed for ever! It is the very sanctification of portraits I think—and it is not at all monstrous in me to say what my brothers cry out against so vehemently . . . that I would rather have such a memorial of one I dearly loved, than the noblest Artist's work ever produced.[29]

Such photographic images were perceived as a clear continuation of other, older means of the reproduction of images. Elizabeth Barrett Browning's vocabulary is initially taken from that of one of the fine arts, engraving. She is startled by the perceived realism of the image, but she places it within the Victorian model of progress in the reproduction of visual images. The photograph seems to her to be "exquisite and delicate beyond the work of the engraver." And yet her perception of this new medium is such that it draws on the science of the day, mesmerism, with its own "startle" effect, as its initial analogy. And, indeed, the "art" of engraving is the most highly mechanical of all the fine arts of the period. These associations, first between the various modes of creating and reproducing images, and then between the aesthetic and the scientific, dominate the discourse of the first generation to view photographs.

Alexander von Humboldt, in a letter dated 7 January 1839 to the Duchess Friederike von Anhalt-Dessau, stresses this admixture: "Objects that express themselves in inimitable fidelity, light fixed by the art of chemistry to leave enduring traces within a few minutes and to circumscribe clearly even the most delicate parts of contours—to see all of this magic (admittedly without color) . . . certainly speaks incontrovertibly for reason and the power of imagination."[30] The mix of the language of science and the language of art is clear here with Humboldt's perception of the photograph as the product of a science rooted in the imagination, but producing aesthetic objects (which he sees as flawed in part because of their colorlessness). Edgar Allan Poe, in one of his 1840 essays on the daguerreotype, makes many of the same verbal associations.[31] Thus the articulation of the "startle" effect in the middle and upper classes points to a confusion in the vocabulary in which this effect was to be addressed: Is it a continuation of the older forms of representation (and therefore to be considered "art") or is it a new and different mode of representation (and therefore to be considered "science")? What all were agreed upon in that first generation was that the images were "real." It was that "realism," prefigured by the aesthetic theory of the Enlightenment, which framed the perception of the photograph and which provided the vocabulary in which the "startle" effect was articulated. The presence of the "startle" effect would seem to be a universal among those individuals exposed to the first photographs. It is no surprise that the first photographer-physicians, such as Hugh Diamond, who incorporated the "image" within their mode of treatment, were also constrained to see (and to know) the photograph in terms of its "startle" effect.

It is with the general understanding of the function of the photograph that the aesthetic tradition of representing the mentally ill begins to be submerged and there evolves a sense of collaboration—already implicit in the meaning given to the realism of the photograph by doctor and patient alike—about the educative function of images. But it is in the different function of images of the patient and images of the physician that the application of this problem in the history of seeing is to be found. For with the craze for the carte-de-visite, which began in the 1850s, all gentlemen and gentlewomen had to have their pictures taken. Indeed, as I have argued elsewhere, the very absence of photographs of those who understood themselves to be part of the world of society is an interpretable fact.[32] How very different for those whose images are taken from them, the mentally ill, the criminal, the maimed. For their images do not grace the storefronts of the photographers; their images become ersatz representations of the nosology that they represent. These "real" images, these images that startle, are images of the disease and not of the patient. And again it is the movement from the aesthetic to the real, from the artistic to the therapeutic, from the image of the patient to the definition of the patient's reality that lies at the center of this world of images. The image is the essence of the patient, it gives the patient form. The patient, or at least the presentation of the patient, quickly becomes the creation of the physician's sense of the correctness of the patient's disease. With the hysteric, the very nature of the illness provides for the patient a demand for the forming touch of the authority, for the control implicit in the worldview that generates "real" images. For hysteria is the classic disease of the imagination—not of the uterus—as Charcot (and then Freud[33]) understood. But the shaping of the imagination through the "realism" of the photograph lies behind the pilferage described in Gamgee's account of the Salpêtrière incident. For can we imagine that the patient in the Salpêtrière is stealing back her identity, her sense of self, in removing the image of the hysteric from the grasp of the physicians?

MEDICAL AND AESTHETIC MODELS FOR THE REPRESENTATION OF THE HYSTERIC

The image of the hysteric does not simply arise out of Jean-Martin Charcot's personal interest in the visual representation of the hysteric at the Salpêtrière.[34] Charcot does not invent the act of "seeing" hysteria. His own interests in capturing the visual aspect of his patients combined with his own perception of his hysterical patients to record the image of his patients as early as his first years at the Salpêtrière, the 1860s. Charcot comes to his task of understanding his patient with a long personal need to see and represent the patient. But his view is not unique, it is part of a long-standing European tradition of representing the insane, into which the image of the hysteric must be fitted. Indeed, it is a tradition which is as much popular as it is scientific. For Moreau de Tours's image provides us with another context for the structuring of the hysteric—the world of the hypnotizable patient, the image of the mesmerizable female. For hysteria, from the eighteenth century, is a disease of the imagination, not a disease of the womb.

The image of the patients of the Viennese physician Franz Anton Mesmer and his students during the 1780s provides one of the keys to the representation of the hysteric at the end of the 1800s.[35] After his arrival in Paris in the winter of 1778, the representation of Mesmer becomes part of the tradition of representing the insane. In a contemporary cartoon reflecting a mesmerist session, it is not merely that the quack physician is indicated by his ass's ears. More important is that the patients gathered about the mesmerist's "tub" are represented in the traditional pose of the melancholic (with head on hand on knee) and the lovesick (swooning in the chair). The latter becomes identified retrospectively with the *arc-en-cercle* position of the hysteric (in some of the historical writing of the mid-twentieth century), because of the associa-

Le Magnétisme dévoilé

The image of the mesmerist. (Paris: Bibliothèque nationale: Cabinet of Prints.)

tion of the hysteric with the sexual (in many different ways), while the melancholic vanishes from any consideration as a forerunner of the image of the hysteric. The visual representation of the mesmerist and the patient are all means of limiting the scope of the diseased to the identifiable individual.

The suppression of the political radicalism associated with one of the most influential groups under Nicolas Bergasse after the French Revolution meant that there was a general tendency to see the mesmeric patient as an asocial being who only shammed illness out of a sense of social uselessness. Likewise, the mesmerist was understood, not as a force for change, but as a quack. The cartoons of the patient and the physician from the 1780s had already carried that message. In one such image a mesmeric healer, wearing an ass head, begins to mesmerize a young, female sufferer.[36] Her position echoes the association of disease and sex-

The "ass-mesmerists." (Paris: Bibliothèque nationale: Cabinet of Prints.)

uality in the *arc-en-cercle* position of the grand hysteric, as she begins to lie back in her chair as her moral seduction begins. Mirrored in the background is the representation of the sexual exploitation of the female patient by the mesmerist, warned against in the secret appendix to the Report of the Royal Commission on Mesmerism. Here the physician is as hypersexual as the patient.

In another image the conceit of the ass-mesmerists is repeated.[37] They are being driven out of the scene by the shining truth of the report of the Royal Commission held by Benjamin Franklin. What is central to this image is that the mesmerists are represented as a compound sign. They are both madmen and devils. They are viewed as a parody of the images of the demonic evil spirits released from the mad as healed by Christ (and his saints) in the traditional iconography of madness. Here the split-hoofed image of the devil as well as the broomsticks associated with flying witches are employed. But this image of the healer is also that of the insane, for the split-hoofed figure is brandishing a scourge, which is one of the traditional icons of the insane. The figure of the *arc-en-cercle* in the representation of the patient is here reversed. The blindfolded, naked patient is seen in the closed mesmeric tub, not arched but collapsing inward. This can be seen as antithetical to another image of the mes-

merist healing process, the circle of "magnetized" hands, in which a
seemingly unconscious female is represented in the left foreground;
balancing the portrait of Mesmer, the healer, in the right foreground.[38]
The imagery of this representation is tied to an understanding of the
"meaning" of mesmerism and the mesmerist treatment in the course
of the nineteenth century. The disrepute of the mesmerist, labeled as
insane or demonically possessed, and thus in need of the sort of control represented by Franklin, Antoine-Laurent Lavoisier, and the Royal
Commission, is carried over into the disrepute associated with the very
naming of the treatment. The image of the physician, as well as the patient, is drawn into question in these associations. Such images remain
associated with the idea of the hysteric through the visual representation
of the patient.

The mesmerism patient is understood at the close of the nineteenth
century to be one of the precursors of the fin-de-siècle hysteric. The
image of the physician, as in the portraits of Charcot and Luys, must be
quite different from that of the mesmerist; it must be separated from
the image of the quack. Rather this image must be associated with the
heroic image of the alienist, the image of Pinel as a force of social change
(like Franklin). Merely changing the label of the mode of treatment
from mesmerism to hypnotism or electrolization was not sufficient. The
very relationship between the hysteric and the physician must be merged
into the highest level of institutionalized medical representation—that
of the image of science in the science of creating images.

The image of the hysteric in the medical literature of the nineteenth
century is an essential image of deviance. It is an image that is taken—at
least in its most radical form—out of another context. The central image
of the hysteric, the essential *attitudes passionnelles* in Charcot's vocabulary
of images, is a sign of quite a different disease—tetanus. The *arc-en-cercle*
stage of Richer's image of grand hysteria (and its retrospective reading
of the image of the swooning mesmerist patient) was consciously mod-
eled on an image taken from the literature on the representation of
anatomy and pathology for artists, rather than from a purely medical
source.[39] Taken from the second edition of Sir Charles Bell's *Essays on
the Anatomy and Philosophy of Expression* (1824), this image is rooted in a
specific understanding of the nature of medical semiotics. Bell notes:

> I throw in this sketch to remind the painter that in *convulsion*, although
> there may appear to him an accidental and deranged action of the muscu-
> lar frame, there is no such thing in nature. It is a disease he is representing,
> which has definable symptoms, and it will ever present itself with the same
> characters.[40]

The range of the positions of the hysteric. Given best in Paul Richer, *Études cliniques sur le grande hystérie ou hystéro-épilepsie* (Paris: Delahaye & Lecrosnier, 1881), plate 5. (Bethesda, Md.: National Library of Medicine.)

The opisthotonic position. From Sir Charles Bell's *Essays on the Anatomy and Philosophy of Expression* (London: John Murray, 1824), p. 101. (Bethesda, Md.: National Library of Medicine.)

Bell's observation may well hold true for tetanus, but the opisthotonic position chosen by him to represent the unalterability of the relationship between sign and causation is adapted by Charcot and later by Freud and given specific meaning in regard to the representation of the illness of the nerves and mind in the hysteric. One must note that Charcot is not the first "modern" scientist to call upon tetanus as his ontological representation for "seeing" the body. John Brown (1735–1788), in evolving the concept of the irritability of the muscles from the work of Albrecht von Haller, argues that health and disease are not at all different states since the forces that produce each have the same action.[41] His example is a comparison of the normal contractions of the muscles and the pathological appearance of the opisthotonus in tetanus. The opisthotonus is one of the most striking manifestations of any disease. But it is also an almost infallible sign for the physician, since its outcome is almost surely negative. In a world in which the power of the physician lay, not in the ability to cure, but in the ability to foretell the course of a disease, the meaning of this sign for doctor and patient alike was clear. Thus Brown, Bell, and Charcot all call upon the image of the opisthotonus as a sign of the visual interpretability of disease and, therefore, the power of the physician's insight over the disease. At the end of the nineteenth century there was still a clear need to provide differential diagnosis between tetanus and hysteria for the practitioner. Among other signs, tetanus was described as presenting "persistent rigidity with tendency to opisthotonos . . ." while hysteria presented "opisthotonos persistent, and intense rigidity between convulsions."[42] In seeing the patient, little distinction was made between organic and functional deficits.

Charcot in seeing the hysteric evolves his own system of representing the disease. He sees the hysteric as suffering from a weakness of the nerves and the disease as being caused by a trauma (such as an accident or violence). Thus the hysteric patient was predisposed to the disease— at least once he or she was exposed to some traumatic event. It is clear that Charcot evolved this view through his treatment of the patients at the Salpêtrière—epileptic and hysterical female patients who were as different from him (and his class) as was possible.[43] The counterargument to this view was evolved by John Hughlings Jackson, whose initial interest was sparked by his wife's epilepsy. This view was one of universal susceptibility. Seeing the disease as a pattern of the dissolution of the higher functions of the nervous system through the presence of a lesion, Jackson understands the symptoms of the hysteric as signs of the lower (and therefore earlier) functions of the nervous system. This evolutionary model sees the symptoms of the hysteric as signs of the structure of the more primitive psychic organization. Both views—the view that calls upon trauma and biological predeterminism as well as the view that calls upon the model of the nervous system being layered to represent the evolutionary history of the mind—come to be absorbed in the fin-de-siècle debates about hysteria.[44]

As early as 1888, Sigmund Freud calls up the figure of the opisthotonus in the context of attacks of hystero-epilepsy.[45] He continues this argument as late as 1908 when he understands coition to be a form of "minor epilepsy." For "a hysterical attack is the reflex mechanism of the act of coition—a mechanism which is ready to hand in everybody, including women, and which we see coming into manifest operation when an unrestrained surrender is made to sexual activity."[46] Thus Freud explains the opisthotonus as the antithesis of the embrace—the internalized enactment of coitus. But this is an image that does not vanish, but is rather consistently transmuted.

Freud uses the image of the opisthotonus as the antithetical image to coitus within his initial reworking of Charcot's nosological criteria. Seeing the reality of the opisthotonus as the key to the somatic nature of hysteria meant understanding the concept of trauma as existing in real experience rather than in fantasy. Sándor Ferenczi, in his clinical diary of 1932, can call upon "a case in which in relaxation ('trance') opisthotonic positions did appear: when contact could be established with the patient, she reported that the position was a reaction to a feeling of painful excitation in the genital passage, which the patient described as painful hunger: in this position, psychic unpleasure and defense against ardent desire are simultaneously represented."[47] Ferenczi traces this reaction formation back to the actual seduction of the female child by her father. All of these references—and Charcot's own vocabulary of images, especially the opisthotonus—stem from a vocabulary of images which clearly (at least in the medical literature of the nineteenth century) defined the line between the healthy and the diseased. The opisthotonus is a sign of the presence of a disease—whether a form of hysteroepilepsy or a signifier of pathological sexuality or a real seduction.

There is a one-to-one relationship between the sign and the meaning. Given Freud's own complicated formulas for the generation of symbolic meaning, already documented in detail in his 1900 *Interpretation of Dreams*, it is striking that in returning to the subject matter of the hysteric, which he and Josef Breuer had begun to explain in 1895 as the result of the suppression of real traumatic events—that is, precisely the sort of seduction of children by adults in authority (parents) to which Ferenczi, quite opposed by Freud, returns some three decades later—he reverts to a pattern of explanation that relies on the meaning of the visual image.

The association between images of the tetanal opisthotonus is in no way limited to the neurological literature coming out of the Salpêtrière or out of the Viennese schools of psychoanalysis. During World War I, Arthur F. Hurst reflected on the relationship between the hysterical etiology of "war contractures" ("battle fatigue" or posttraumatic neurosis) as opposed to those contractures which have their origin in a localized infection.[48] For Hurst the question of the differential diagnosis of hysterical contracture (here localized in contrast to the full-body opisthotonus) as opposed to localized tetanus is questionable. It is clear that in time of war the duration of the cure—a "single sitting by persuasion and reeducation" in the first case or "months of treatment" in the latter—would place emphasis on seeing the majority of such cases as quickly healable. The assumption in Hurst's presentation is that the confusion between real (i.e., somatic) and hysterical contractures advocated by continental neurologists such as Josef Babinski and Jules Froment marks a faulty distinction between a biological and a psychological illness.[49] Such an argument would be parallel to Freud's attempt to collapse the distinction between real epilepsy and hysterical epilepsy. The images of the case of tetanus as opposed to the hysteric are, however, quite illuminating. For the half-body portrait of the soldier with his wound prominently displayed relates the image of the contracted arm to the entire individual; the hysterical arm stands alone. Here the role of the representation of the arm comes to play a central role. The case described, that of "Sergt. M" who "was wounded in the right forearm on April 10, 1917," is "recognized as hysterical . . . as the deformity was identical with that shown in a photograph of a so-called reflex contracture in Babinski and Froment's book." It is the representation of the hysteric which defines the disease and which defines both the treatment of the disease and the patient's response: "On the day of admission the hand was continuously manipulated, the patient being persuaded at the same time that it would rapidly relax. In ten minutes complete relaxation was obtained and the deformity disappeared." The relationship between seeing correctly and the patient's response is here made absolute. As Elaine Showalter notes, the transition from the image of the female pet patient of nineteenth-century clinical psychiatry to the image of the male sufferer from traumatic neurosis (shell shock) meant a drastic realignment of the presuppositions of gender.[50] Hurst sees the male hysteric as ill but as quickly curable, a factor that sets the soldier apart from the long tradition of more or less professional (i.e., long-term) female patients at the Salpêtrière. What he teaches his hysterics is to see themselves as "men"—to confront their illness and return to service.

Jean-Martin Charcot (and his colleague Paul Richer) provide the reader (and viewer) of these late nineteenth-century images of the hysteric with a set of antecedent images from sources other than the unspoken one of the mesmerist.[51] In their study of the representation of the insane—specifically the hysteric in the art of the West—they create their own history and conclude it with a clinical chapter outlining their "universal" nosological categories of hysteria, which they see as "valid for all countries, all times, all races."[52] Charcot and Richer begin by outlining the representation of possession in religious art from the early middle ages through the seventeenth century. They offer sixty-seven illustrations, often in line form, to provide visual proof of the continuity between the images of the Catholic mystic and the modern hysteric. Beginning with the fifth-century representation of possession in the Romanesque mosaics of Ravenna to images of Saint Catherine of Sienna, Charcot and Richer begin to build their case for the parallel (and therefore the universality) of their visual categories of hysteria.

The assumption is that there is an explicit continuity between Catholic religious experience, as represented by the practitioners, and the neurological pathologies of nineteenth-century France.[53] Thus the aesthetic representation of ecstasy becomes a clinical sign of psychopathology. Their movement is however not merely on the level of the equation of

The image of the possessed as the hysteric. From J.-M. Charcot and Paul Richer, *Les Démoniaques dans l'art* (Paris: Adrien Delahaye et Emile Lecrosnier, 1887), p. 4. Photo courtesy Wellcome Institute Library, London.

the religious-aesthetic and the clinical. For they cite one image (and text) from the general realm of medicine, and that is Sir Charles Bell's image of opisthotonus. The passage they quote is identical to the one cited above. Their argument is that the image of opisthotonus is parallel to a number of the images of possession that they offer, specifically the early seventeenth-century image of Saint Nilus by Domenicho Zampieri called Domenichino (1581–1641). Like their discussion of a sketch for the child in Raphael's *Transfiguration,* there is a stated assumption that the reality of the symptoms of hysteria are exactly parallel to the immutable reality of the symptoms of tetanus. In their final chapter, on the contemporary representation of the hysteric, Charcot and Richer draw on the images of the stages of the "hysterical convulsion" which Charcot had established in the 1880s. The parodies of religious experiences, from the position of prayer to the position of crucifixion find their visual representations in this chapter,[54] as does the classic *arc-en-cercle* position of the opisthotonus taken from Bell.[55]

What is most striking from the viewpoint of the history of the representation of the hysteric is that there is a continuity to the overall reception of the image of the hysteric which transcends the school of the

One of the topoi used to depict the history of the hysteric is this sketch for the child in Raphael's *Transfiguration*. From J.-M. Charcot and Paul Richer, *Les Démoniaques dans l'art* (Paris: Adrien Delahaye et Emile Lecrosnier, 1887), p. 29. Photo courtesy Wellcome Institute Library, London.

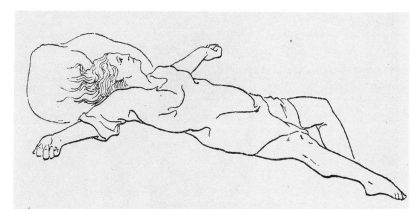

The self-crucified hysteric. From J.-M. Charcot and Paul Richer, *Les Dé-moniaques dans l'art* (Paris: Adrien Delahaye et Emile Lecrosnier, 1887), p. 100, lower image. Photo courtesy Wellcome Institute Library, London.

Salpêtrière. Thus if we return to the British images taken from Arthur F. Hurst's study of hysterical contractures, we can see that Charcot and Richer, in citing images from Louis Basile Carré de Montgeron's account of the Jansenist miracles,[56] had already set the stage for the representation of the nonfunctional limb as a primary sign of hysteria. The link between the female and the victim of shell shock is made through the representation of the body part that makes them unable to be mobile in a society that demands mobility as a sign of group identity. The meaning ascribed to mobility from the eighteenth century to the twentieth century is quite different (the middle-class woman becomes a full member of the new religious sect when she is healed; the soldier returns to his fighting unit when he is healed). But central to the image of cure is the image of mobility. The visibly nonfunctional limb, with the alteration in gait or in posture, marks the hysteric as diseased. The images taken from the history of religion have already provided a model for the representation of the affected area as the target for healing. The analogy between the mentally ill and the enthusiastic and/or rigorous fundamentalism of religious schismatics such as the Jansenists had already been made by Philippe Pinel in the wake of the French Revolution. Citing a range of British sources in a French Catholic context, Pinel was forced to see the hypermoralism of the Jansenists as setting them apart from French society. He labeled them the pathological equivalents of the Methodists.[57] Charcot's citation of Jansenism as the central visual clue to the history of hysteria ties the image of the hysteric, not merely

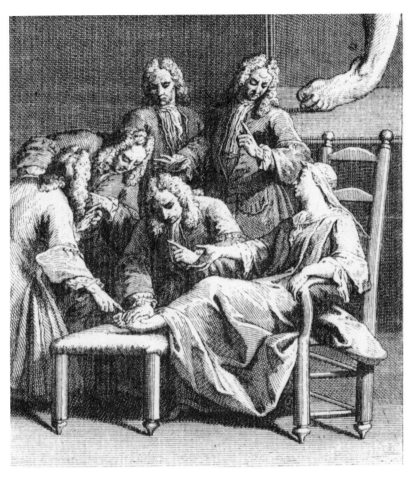

The religious cure of the "hysteric." From Louis Basile Carré de Montgeron, *La verité des miracles operés par l'intercession de M. de Pâris et autres
appellans demontrée contre M. L'archevêque de Sens,* 3 vols. (Cologne: Chez les
libraires de la Campagie, 1745–47), as reproduced in J.-M. Charcot and
Paul Richer, *Les Démoniaques dans l'art* (Paris: Adrien Delahaye et Emile
Lecrosnier, 1887), p. 81. Photo courtesy Wellcome Institute Library,
London.

to "religion" but to the religion of spiritual excess, to religions such as Methodism and, in a specific manner that will be discussed below, to the mystical religion of the Eastern Jews.[58]

The religious rigidity and the enthusiasm of the Jansenists came to stand for the perversion of the spirit which was as pathological as the diseases of the hysteric. Paul Regnard brings a series of the *attitudes passionnelles* in his photographs of Augustine from the second volume of the *Iconographie de la Salpêtrière*.[59] These images mimic the positions of the Jansenists, but they are without doubt images of pathology. The parallels make both sets of images pathognomonic.[60] As with the images of the Jansenists, the images of the hysterics are closely associated with visual hallucinations, with the seeing of what is not there as a sign of the falsification of the imagination. William Hammond, in his 1876 history of hysteria, continued this "liberal" discourse of the Salpêtrière which associated disease and religion. He noted that "in these undeveloped forms of both diseases, as noticed among the Jansenist convulsionnaires, the affected individuals appeared as if struck by the sight of some object before unseen, and the contemplation of which filled them with the most ravishing joy."[61] Here the pathologization of seeing is the mirror image of the clinical gaze of Charcot, who sees the disease, the disease of the fantasy, the disease of religion.

Thus Charcot and Richer undertake what many scientists of the nineteenth and twentieth centuries do—to write the history of their own discovery in order to show its universality across time (if not across cultures). But this history of the representation of hysteria, drawing on the power of the new secularized religion of science in displacing its antecedent Christianity, becomes the model through which the hysteric is visually categorized. This tradition does not stop with Richer and Charcot. Students of Charcot's provide some of the later material. Henry Meige (after 1901 the editor of the *Nouvelle Iconographie de la Salpêtrière*) and Jean Heitz both contribute essays to the *Nouvelle Iconographie de la Salpêtrière* on the artistic image of the hysteric well into the twentieth century.[62] Within the German tradition, the physician-historian-art critic Eugen Holländer incorporates many of these images in writing his history of the image of the impaired in classical art.[63] Holländer quotes liberally from the same visual sources as Charcot and Richer—citing Raphael and the various images of religious possession. Jean Rousselot continues this image in his study of medicine in art into the post–World War II era.[64] His work begins with the representation of the Greeks, such as the Bacchic scene of "dying Bacchante," now in the Uffizi. He comments in his caption: "In point of fact, a depiction of hysteria. At

The representation of religious ecstasy as pathological sign. From Paul Regnard, *Les maladies épidémiques de l'esprit: sorcellerie magnétisme, morphinisme, délire des grandeurs* (Paris: E. Plon, Nourrit et Cie., 1887), p. 95. The image is an engraving of a photograph taken from the *Iconographie de la Salpêtrière*. (Bethesda, Md.: National Library of Medicine.)

the far right, a hysterical woman, her body bent in the shape of an arc."
All of these works assume a continuity of the meaning of the image of
the hysteric from the ancient Greeks to their contemporaries. And all
of them stress the continuity between the ancient representation of religious experience (rather than images of pathology) and modern experiences of disease (rather than religion). This asymmetry provides a
powerful subtext for the association between images of religion and
those labeled in the popular mind as being associated with categories
constructed as or labeled as religious ones—such as the Catholic (or at
least the Catholic cleric) and, in an equally complex manner, the Jew.

The "warfare between theology and science," to paraphrase the title
of A. D. White's classic nineteenth-century study,[65] which is played out
within the secularized Christian discourse of late nineteenth-century
psychopathology, is nowhere more clearly evident than in Paul Regnard's 1887 monograph (with 120 images) on the visual relationship
between magnetism, morphinism, and madness, which begins with the
visual equation between the witch and the mad.[66] Regnard, a physician
and the professor of physiology at the National School of Agronomy,
was the coeditor (with Désire-Magloire Bourneville of the Bicêtre) of the
original, three-volume edition of the *Iconographie photographique de la Salpêtrière*[67] as well as a well-received medical atlas.[68] His study of 1887,
which is dedicated to "cher maitre," Charcot, assumes the interrelationship of all forms of mass hysteria. His first example is the witch. He provides a series of plates from Abraham Palingh's study of witchcraft to
document the visual representation of the witch as the "grand hysteric."[69] In this context Regnard brings in other images of demonic
possession from the Renaissance to the seventeenth century (p. 41), including—as one of the images that becomes standard to the repertoire
of visual proof—the figure of the boy from Raphael's *Transfiguration*
(p. 59).

It is assumed that these pathological positions are indicative of the
association with other forms of possession, such as hysteria. To make
this absolutely clear in the reader's eye, he reproduces, in the form of
drawings which thus resemble the format of the earlier images he has
reproduced, a series of photographic images from the *Iconographie photographique de la Salpêtrière*. Of these the image of the gaze, the hallucination as experienced by the observer rather than the hysteric, stands as
the icon of pathology (p. 87). Regnard makes similar visual claims in associating the image of the hysteric with that of the sleepwalker, the drug
addict, and the person suffering from monomania. Images are produced that draw on the visual association of abnormal states—there is

The image of the witch. From Abraham Palingh, 't Afgeruckt Mom-
Aansight der Tooverye: Daar in het bedrogh der gewaande Toverye, naakt
ontdeckt, en emt gezone Redenen en exemplen dezer Eeuwe aangewezen wort
(Amsterdam: Andries van Damme, 1725), p. 50, as used in Paul
Regnard, Les maladies épidémiques de l'esprit: sorcellerie magnétisme, morphinisme, délire des grandeurs (Paris: E. Plon, Nourrit et Cie., 1887),
p. 19. (Bethesda, Md.: National Library of Medicine.)

The representation of a visual hallucination, the centrality of the eye and the gaze. From Paul Regnard, *Les maladies épidémiques de l'esprit: sorcellerie magnétisme, morphinisme, délire des grandeurs* (Paris: E. Plon, Nourrit et Cie., 1887), p. 87. (Bethesda, Md.: National Library of Medicine.)

always the assumption that there is a normal image of the productive, healthy human, and the deviant is marked by external signs, such as position, clothing, handwriting, and so on. These signs represent the symptoms of mental disorder, and all are interrelated because the signs are interrelated. But more than this is shown by moving from the witch (and the torture and cruelty inflicted on the witch [p. 33] to the miracles associated [as in Charcot] with healing the hysteric, to use his term [pp. 133, 135]. Religion and its hypocrisy, its antithetical relationship to the act of modern medical healing, are cited, and the cures of the church are ascribed to the nature of the disease entity—to hysteria. The cure of the disease of hysteria is the mass hysteria of religion. The model for this is the antiquated one of homeopathic medicine—like curing like. It is clear that Regnard, like Charcot and Richer, is looking for a more modern approach to therapy—to electrization or to the newly relabeled science of hypnotism—for their cure, not to religion. For the church, representing the institutionalization of religion in contemporary society, is the root cause of the hysteria, not its cure.

The other central model cited by Charcot and Richer in their scientific work is the model of the epileptic.[70] Stemming from Charcot's initial observations on his patients in the Salpêtrière showing the symptoms of "hystero-epilepsy" (his own composite category, which Freud borrowed), the visual image of the difference of the hysteric stems to no little degree from the tradition of representing the epileptic.[71] The image of the epileptic is in many ways parallel to that of the hysteric. Thus the "simulation" of the hysteric is paralleled by the "contradictions and exaggerations of sentiment [which] are salient characteristics of epileptics," according to Cesare Lombroso. He continues: "Epilepsy has a disastrous effect on the character. It destroys the moral sense, causes irritability, alters the sensations through constant hallucinations and delusions, deadens the natural feelings or leads them into morbid channels."[72] This need to see the pathological character of the epileptic as parallel to his or her disease is replicated in the visual image of the epileptic. While many of the visual images of the epileptic in the medical literature of the nineteenth century deal with the problems of localizing the brain lesion,[73] there is also a tradition of representing the symptoms of epilepsy through representing the patient. Charles Féré, in the *Nouvelle Iconographie de la Salpêtrière*, represents hysteria as literally written on the skin of the hysteric.[74] The parallel image is to be found in the representation of hysterical ulceration.[75] If one examines L. Pierce Clark's argument from 1898 that there are "tetanoid seizures in epilepsy," one can see the argument coming full circle to the organic model

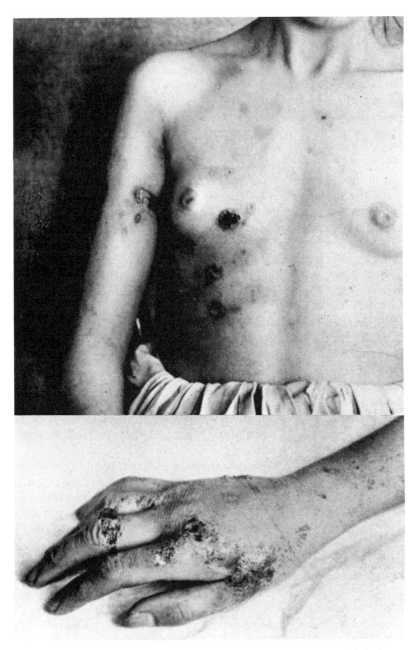

The sensitive skin of the epileptic becomes a *tabula rasa* upon which the disease can be inscribed. From Charles Féré, "Note sur un cas de méla-nodermie récurrente chez un épileptique apathique," *Nouvelle iconographie de la Salpêtrière*, 10 N.F. (1897): 332–339. (Bethesda, Md.: National Library of Medicine.)

of tetanus.[76] Indeed, the fascination with the marking of the signs and symptoms of disease on the body permeates the image of the epileptic in ways other than the search for the Jacksonian brain "lesion" that must necessarily cause the seizures.[77] Thus there are images of the malformed hands of an epileptic woman or of the corporeal asymmetry of the epileptic female.[78]

The image of the epileptic is also found within the tradition of representing the physiognomy of the insane. Thus William Alexander provides the reader with a photograph of each of the patients whose cases he reports in his 1889 study in order to present their physiognomy.[79] It is the visual appearance of the epileptic that provides the clue to his or her special, hidden flaw. The lesion must, in some overt way, write itself on the body. Some essays, such as on the baldness[80] or the altered appearance of the hair[81] of an epileptic man as a sign of his illness, are more than reminiscent of the extraordinary images of the "plinca polonica" or "Judenkratze," the fantasy skin disease attributed by Western dermatologists to the Jews of the East. In some of the recent historical literature on the history of epilepsy, much of the same tradition cited by Charcot and Richer reappear—now in the context of documenting the ongoing history of epilepsy. Thus images of religious ecstasy and possession from the early Middle Ages appear as precursors of the image of the epileptic.[82]

All of these images relate to the idea of the hysteric as continuous over time and across cultures. This is the basic assumption of the definition of a positivistic disease entity at the close of the nineteenth century. Disease is real only if it is universal. And it is universal only if it can be seen and the act of seeing reproduced. This latter axiom is rarely stated (except by the head of the Salpêtrière's photographic service, Albert Londe), but it is assumed. Thus the image of the impaired patient is the touchstone for the reality of the disease.

CREATING A COMPOSITE IMAGE OF THE HYSTERIC

It is vital to understand that the creation of a history of the image of the hysteric is not the same thing as Charcot and Richer's attempt to place the diagnostic criteria applied to hysteria in the distant past (while ignoring the more recent past). What can be undertaken in a limited way (because of the extraordinary range of visual sources) is to sketch the visual aspects associated with the idea of hysteria at the turn of the century as a means of delineating the scope of the image. Thus this section will be devoted to a catalog of those visual qualities ascribed to the hys-

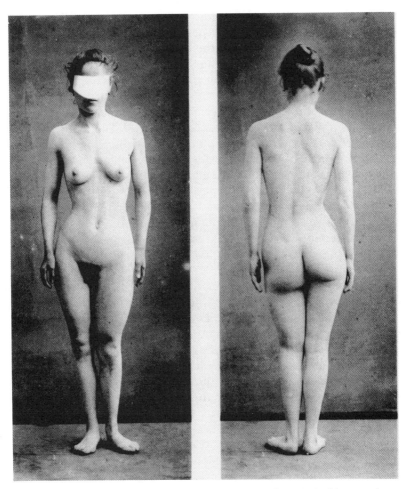

On the image of asymmetry of the epileptic, see plate XLI: "Asymetrie du corps chez une epileptique," in F. Raymond and Pierre Janet, "Malformations des mains en 'pinces de humard,'" *Nouvelle iconographie de la Salpêtrière* 10 (1897): 369–373 (an extract from their book *Nécroses et idées fixes* [Paris: F. Alcan, 1898]). Photo courtesy Wellcome Institute Library, London.

teric. We shall seek to sketch the boundaries of the representation of the visual nature of the hysteric in fin-de-siècle medical literature.

It is central to any understanding of this composite image that the desire of all of these studies, no matter what their national context, is to place themselves within the myth of the realism of the act of represen-

The face of the epileptic. From William Alexander, *The Treatment of Epilepsy* (Edinburgh and London: Young J. Pentland, 1889), p. 107. Photo courtesy Wellcome Institute Library, London.

tation and the highly specialized role that the physician (as interpreter) plays in reproducing and "reading" the image of the patient. And this reading has a clear relationship with the means of reproducing and disseminating the image of the hysteric. The startle effect has now blended into an idea of a realism that indicates a control by the scientist and the scientist alone over the new medium. (As anyone could make and possess photographs after the mid-1890s, it became more and more important for the scientific photograph to be the object of scientific interpretation. This attitude permitted many interpreters of the photograph seamlessly to become the interpreters of the new hermeticism of the X ray when it was introduced in 1895.) The reading of the photograph had also blended in with the aesthetic (or, perhaps better, artistic) tradition into which the "new" science of representation had placed the image of the hysteric. Charcot and Richer, in a paper they first published in the *Journal of Nervous and Mental Disease* in 1883, stated the case best. In noting the "immobile" physiognomy of a hysterical patient whose facial muscles had been electrically stimulated, they

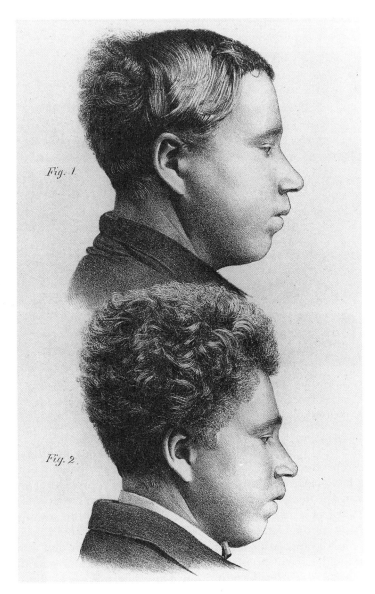

Images of the alteration of the hair in the mentally ill are already evoked in Darwin's study of the nature of expression. Here the image of the altered appearance of the hair evokes older images of the diseases of the Eastern Jews. From Dr. Räuber, "Ein Fall von periodisch wiederkehrender Haarveränderung bei einem Epileptiker," [*Virchows*] *Archiv für pathologische Anatomie und Physiologie* 97 (1884): 50–83, plate no. 2. (Bethesda, Md.: National Library of Medicine.)

observe: "The physiognomy retained immobile, in a state of catalepsy. The same is true of the attitude and the gesture that accompanied it. The subject of this transformed into a sort of expressive statue, a motionless model, representing with striking accuracy most varied expressions, which artists, without doubt, might avail themselves of to a very great extent. The immobility of the attitudes thus provoked is eminently favorable to photographic reproduction."[83] They then reproduce a series of these photographs. This argument is similar to that critique by Walter Benjamin in his essay from the mid-1920s on the reproducibility of images in the age of technology.[84] For it is important to understand that observing is not sufficient. Charcot (and Richer) turn the object observed (the hysteric) into the work of art and then are able to commodify this work of art through the reproduction of her image within the scientific text. This is not quite like the cinematic examples that Benjamin brings. It is much more similar to the extensive photographic reproductions of "great works of art" which dominated the middle-class market for art during the 1880s and 1890s. Benjamin's discussion of the "exchange of glances" between the observed and the observer creates a critical context for the learning experience of the hysteric. For it seems that the exchange of glances in this system of representation is one between an aware hysteric and an unaware physician. But the Salpêtrière gave birth to other means of seeing difference and also of recording it.

In many of these images the confusion between acquired pathognomonic signs and inherent ones is manifest. There evolves in the fin-de-siècle discussion of the physiognomy the assumption that there is an absolute relationship between the form of the skull and the shape of the face.[85] And given the emphasis on craniometric measurements as a means of speaking about the nature of the mind/psyche it is clear that the relationship between the structure of the face and the mind, already present in the physiognomy of Johann Caspar Lavater (and his predecessors) becomes an easy one. Francis Warner summarizes many of the discussions of his contemporaries, such as Charles Darwin, in *The Expression of Emotions in Men and Animals* (1872).[86] Warner stresses the "results of cerebral action upon muscles" rather than the "shape of the brain case" in seeking to find the source for the asymmetry on the face of the hysteric. She describes, however, the existence of faces that "express intellectuality" and others that express "vulgarity." The latter are an example of the "coincident defective or coarse development of the brain-case and face." The former are the result of "the nerve-muscular condition of the face" and are "more directly indicative of the intellectuality of the brain; hence we should study a face as the index of the brain, when it is seen in action as well as when at rest." This view can be seen as representative of the medical literature of physiognomy at the turn of the century. The stress on the asymmetry of the face, an asymmetry caused by the forces of the mind, rather than the marked "vulgarity" of the mental defective, can be traced back to Philippe Pinel and his representation of the "manic" and the "idiot" at the very beginning of the century. The concept of asymmetry (indeed all faces become asymmetrical with the passage of time) can introduce the importance of an aesthetics of the face of the hysteric.

James Shaw stresses the "swelling of the upper lip" in cases of "chronic hysterical insanity" as well as a "facial expression [that] often indicates the presence of migraine."[87] The face of the hysteric, specifically the hemiplegia that marks the face of the hysteric at the Salpêtrière, is an overt sign of difference. It is a distortion of the normal face—the baseline for the "beauty" of the individual.[88] Anthropological literature of the eighteenth and nineteenth centuries had debated the meaning of the varieties of beauty, especially female beauty, throughout the world.[89] The consensus was that there was a "great chain of beauty" running from the beautiful down to the ugly races which was paralleled within each race by a normative—that is, healthy—appearance as opposed to a sick appearance. This pathology of appearance underlies the representation of the asymmetrical, unaesthetic face of the hysteric. In a paper by Hurst (1918) on battle fatigue, the face of the hysteric marks the individual who can be quickly cured and sent back into battle.[90]

But if the face is marked, it is the eyes that provide the real clue. The stigmata that mark the face are most apparent in the representation of the eyes. For both the "look" of the hysteric and the gaze of the physician mark the hysteric. Building upon the nosology of hysterical blindness developed by Charcot as well as the Philadelphia ophthalmologist George Edmund de Schweinitz, Walter Baer Weidler traces the qualities of the eyes from the "contractures, spasms and palsies" of the "eyelids and extra-ocular muscles" (i.e., the representation of the appearance of the eye) to the manifestation of hysterical blindness (amblyopia or amaurosis, partial or complete loss of vision).[91] In the work of L. Lattes and A. Sacerdote from the 1920s, similar changes in the quality of the face are described in the case of a hysterical pseudo-hemorrhage of the eye.[92] It is the quality of the gaze in the photographs of the patients that is striking. The physical anomalies represented also provide the signs for the meaning read into the physiognomy. The drooping lids or the black eye add a quality of the abnormal, of the pathological, to the gaze of the patient, marking him or her as diseased.

A sculpture of a case of hemiplegia from the teaching collection
of the Salpêtrière. (Paris: The Salpêtrière.)

The disease that is sought is not in the eye. It is in the central nervous
system, in the neural network that controls the eye. It is in the brain,
the source of all hysteria, that the source of hysteria is to be found. The
image of the brain becomes the image of the internal error of the hysteric. Jules Luys, in a paper of 1881, stresses this in both his text and in
the accompanying images of localization.[93] E. Siemerling and J. Grasset
see "cerebral-spinal degeneracy" as the source of hysteria.[94] In the work
of the Hamburg physician Paul Steffens the localization of the lesion
is represented in the post-mortem image of the brain.[95] All of these
searches evoke the specter of the brain mythology that dominated much
of the localization studies at the end of the century. The search after

The eyes and the sight of the hysteric. From Walter Baer Weidler, "Some Ocular Manifestations of Hysteria," *International Clinics*, 22d ser. 2 (1912): 249–261. Plate (fig. 5) opposite p. 252. Photo courtesy Wellcome Institute Library, London.

the source of the anomalous appearance of the hysteric was quite parallel to the search after the origins of other neurological disorders. A. Alzheimer represented such a search in his 1911 paper on cerebral plaques, using photographs of dyed brain specimens as his visual proof of their existence.[96]

All of these images were seen as having parallel value. Each of them demanded (according to their interpreter) a trained eye to see and represent the source of the error. The interrelationship between the scientific drawing and the photograph, both understood as veridical in localizing the source of the pathology, stressed the gaze of the scientist, in seeing the nature of the brain through the interpretation of the symptoms.

For the hysteric, the symptoms are often written on the body. The

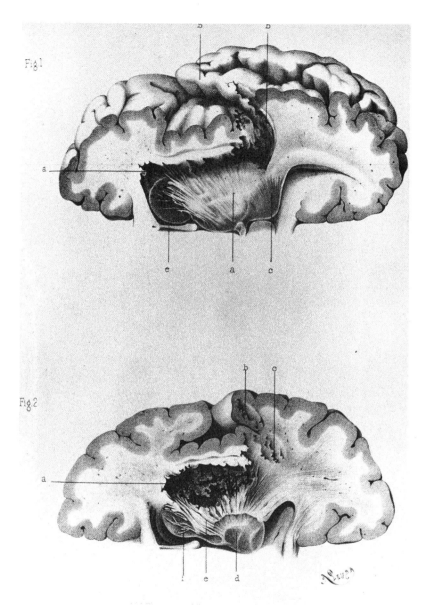

The brain of the hysteric. From Jules Luys, "Recherches nouvelles sur les hémiplégies émotives," *L'Encephale: Journal des Maladies Mentales et Nerveuses* 1 (1881): 378–398, plate 7. (Bethesda, Md.: National Library of Medicine.)

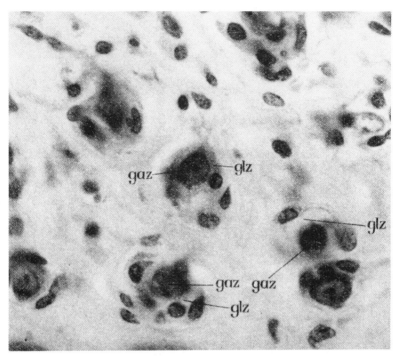

The brain structure of the hysteric. From C. von Hößlin and A. Alz-
heimer, "Ein Beitrag zur Klinik und pathologischen Anatomie der
Westphal-Strümpellschen Pseudosklerose," *Zeitschrift für die gesamte
Neurologie und Psychiatrie* 8 (1911): 203. Photo courtesy Wellcome
Institute Library, London.

function of the skin as the map of the body is one of the oldest topoi of
medicine. Reading the skin meant reading into the nature of the patient,
his or her actions, and his or her resultant diseases. The nineteenth-
century literature on masturbatory disease is full of such images,[97] as is,
not surprisingly, the literature on hysteria. The ability of the hysterics
to record written images on their skin, the hypersensitivity to touch, became one of the most fascinating symptoms for the fin-de-siècle physician. In the "modern" *Revue de l'hypnotisme* a striking image of such "skin
writing" appears.[98] In Saint Petersburg the fin-de-siècle image of the
hysteric was brought into the context of the stigmata, not Charcot's, but
the stigmata of Christ.[99] The discussion of the patient presented in this
"difficult case of hysteria" centered on the suggestibility of young Roman Catholic girls. The search after unique or strange manifestations

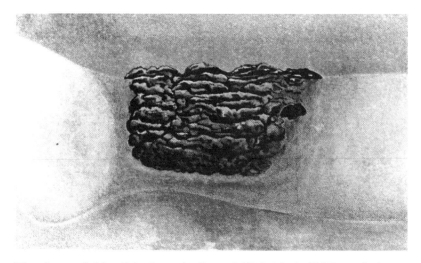

The ulcerated skin of the hysteric. From S. Weir Mitchell, "Hysterical Rapid Respiration, With Cases; Peculiar Form of Rupial Skin Disease in an Hysterical Woman," *Transactions of the College of Physicians of Philadelphia* 14 (1892): 233. (Bethesda, Md.: National Library of Medicine.)

of hysteria led S. Weir Mitchell, whose rest cure had been generally accepted as the treatment of choice by the end of the century, to examine a case of a hysterical ulcer in a twenty-four-year-old woman.[100] The differential diagnosis to this ulcer was to the ulceration of syphilis, which was "verified by the microscope." S. Róna continued the work that Moriz Kaposi had begun in Vienna, looking at specific forms of the manifestation of skin eruptions which could be labeled hysteric.[101] Thomas D. Savill, in London, undertook a similar study of the skin of his child patients and saw their hysteria inscribed thereupon.[102] In 1900 Dr. Bettmann from the Heidelberg Clinic of Wilhelm Erb described a further case of "atypical" skin inflammation in the hysteric; in 1901, a case of hysterical gangrene was described in Buffalo; in 1919, a similar case in Pisa. By 1930 a major survey of the nature of hysterical skin diseases was produced by Roberto Casazza in Pavia.[103] All of these studies (and more) are extensively illustrated. All of them relate, on one level or another, to the general assumption (countered by Jean-Martin Charcot in his theory of hysteria) that syphilis or the predisposition to syphilis played a major role in the risk for hysteria.

Many of these studies of the skin (such as that of Weir Mitchell) relate the appearance of the skin to the state of the genitalia, either in

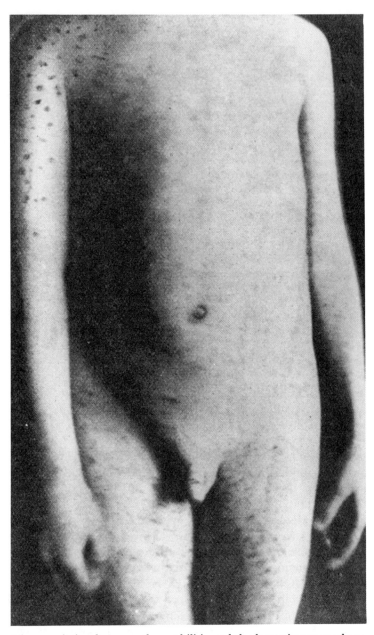

The association between the syphilitic and the hysteric was made as much on dermatologic evidence (as seen on the skin) as on psychological evidence. From Thomas D. Savill, "A Clinical Lecture on Hysterical Skin Symptoms and Eruptions," *The Lancet* (January 30, 1904): 273–278, p. 276. (Bethesda, Md.: National Library of Medicine.)

terms of gynecological examinations that are part of the case study or in terms of a discussion of the appearance of the skin in the genital regions. Charcot associated hysteria with the area of the ovaries, those areas of heightened sensitivity in the hysteric, a touch upon which could actually create hysterical episodes. This fascination with the compression of the ovaries as therapy as well as etiology is linked in the medical discourse of the period with the fascination about hysterical ischuria, the retention of urine and feces. The number of charts of the genital regions are legion, yet the number of detailed (and illustrated) studies of the form and structure of the genitalia are few. De Sinéty, a histologist at the College de France, published a series of unillustrated case studies of the genitalia of female hysterics in the mid-1870s, supporting Charcot's thesis of the centrality of sexual stimulation for the creation of the hysterical episode.[104] With the introduction of X-ray analysis there was even an attempt to represent the pelvic structure of the hysterical female, as a means of representing the disease.[105] The X ray was but a technical innovation. For the fantasies about internalized hysteria had existed prior to Charcot.[106] In 1847 Eliogoro Guitti had presented an illustrated study of the hysterical gut.[107]

The representation of the extremities, especially the hand and the foot, reflect not only the importance laid upon the hand and foot as signs of religious possession (stigmata, paralysis) but also the physical signs associated with epilepsy. Paul Sollier presents a case of contracture of the hand in a male hysteric in the fourth volume of the *Nouvelle Iconographie de la Salpêtrière*.[108] Some of the studies, such as those of Hurst, concentrate on the problem of hysterical contractures, such as Charcot's "glove anaesthesia" in the hysterical traumatic paralysis of the hand; others on the appearance of the hand, its coloration (usually blue, according to Gilles de la Tourette[109]) and marked swelling.[110] The legs are similarly examined—for the contractures of "hysterical paraplegia" (and their cure).[111] The images taken from Charcot's schematic representation of areas of anesthesia reappear over and over again to illustrate cases of the diminished ability to feel (and often to move) the limbs.[112]

The visual representation of posture and paralysis is used as a mode of visual proof of Charcot's nosological categories.[113] In an essay from the very first issue of the *Nouvelle Iconographie de la Salpêtrière* in 1888, by Georges Gilles de la Tourette, we are not only made to see the hemiplegic patient but also his gait, through a schematic representation.[114] In this case, described by Henri Lamarque and Emile Bitot, there is a comment on the plate that they had intended to use a photograph but an accident at the last moment ruined the plate and they were forced to

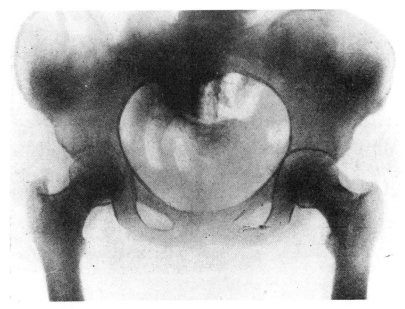

The X ray permitted the physician to see within the hysteric. From Jose M.
Jorge, "Coxalgia histérica," *Revista de la Asociacion Medica Argentina* 32
(1920): 18–29, plate opposite p. 80. (Bethesda, Md.: National Library of
Medicine.)

use a photolithograph. The form of the representation becomes central
to its message. For the photograph remains more real than any other
mode of representing the hysteric. Thus in an essay by Byrom Bramwell—one of the leading Scottish specialists on nervous diseases such as
hysteria and, one can add, one of the leading believers in a set pathognomonic representation of disease—the photograph remains the central
proof for the differential diagnosis between "hysteria" and its contractures and other forms of organic disease.[115] But this photograph has
been quite evidently cut to remove the presence of the physician or
nurse whose hands remain supporting the patient. A similar undertaking can be seen in the photograph contracture represented in the essay
by A. Steindler in Iowa City, except here the patient is given a staff on
which to rest.[116]

The realism of the photograph concentrates the gaze of the physician-
reader on the representation of the disease in the image of the patient.
Peter Davidson follows this lead with his presentation of a case of hystero-catalepsy from Liverpool.[117] The number and range of Davidson's

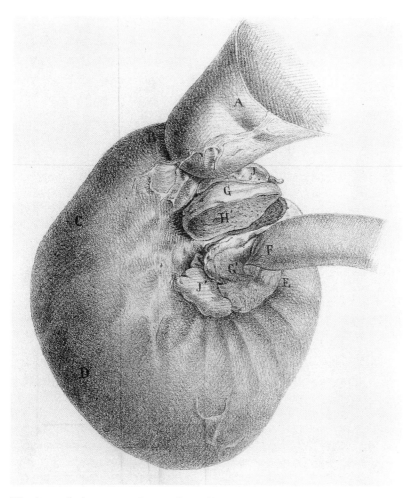

The hysterical gut as an internal manifestation of the disease. Eliogoro Guitti, "Osservazioni Cliniche," *Giornale per Servire ai Progressi della Patologia e della Terapeutica*, 2d ser. 22 (1847): 229–258, plate following p. 258. (Bethesda, Md.: National Library of Medicine.)

cases (running from rheumatoid arthritis to hystero-catalepsy) would have enabled the author to illustrate any (or indeed all) of his cases. He chose to illustrate the case of hystero-catalepsy. As late as in 1930, in an essay by Prince P. Barker, at the Veterans' Hospital in Tuskegee, Alabama, the image of the hysteric black comes to represent the image of the hysteric whose limbs are frozen.[118] Using Charcot's categories ex-

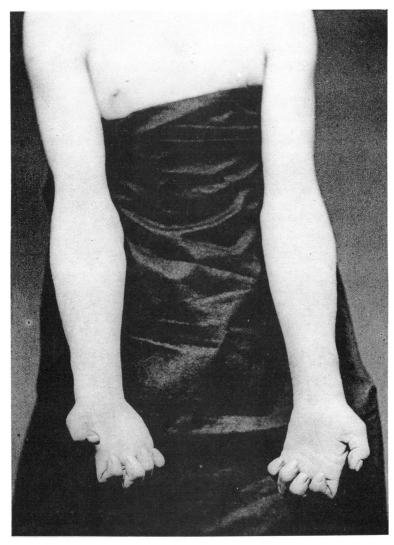

The hand of the male hysteric. From Paul Sollier, "Contracture Volontaire chez un Hystérique," *Nouvelles Iconographie de la Salpêtrière* 4
(1891): 100–106, plate opposite p. 106. Photo courtesy Wellcome Institute Library, London.

The posture of the schematic "patient." From Henri Lamarque and Emile Bitot, "Sur un cas d'hystérotraumatisme chez l'homme," *Bulletins de la Société d'Anatomie et de Physiologie Normales et Pathologiques de Bordeaux* 9 (1888): 242–257, plate with figures 6 and 8. (Bethesda, Md.: National Library of Medicine.)

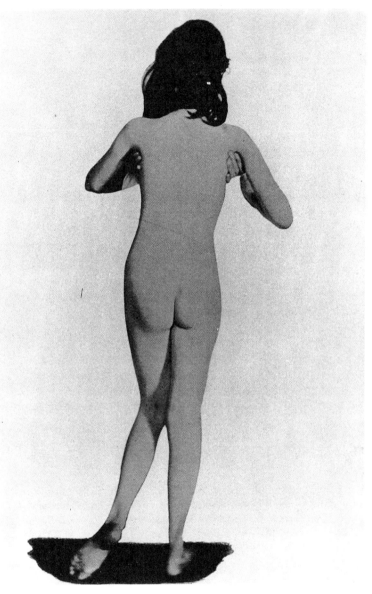

A "doctored" photograph of the hysteric. From Byrom Bramwell, "Clinical Lecture on a Case of Hysterical Contracture," *Edinburgh Medical Journal,* ns 1 (1897): 128–138, plate 5. (Bethesda, Md.: National Library of Medicine.)

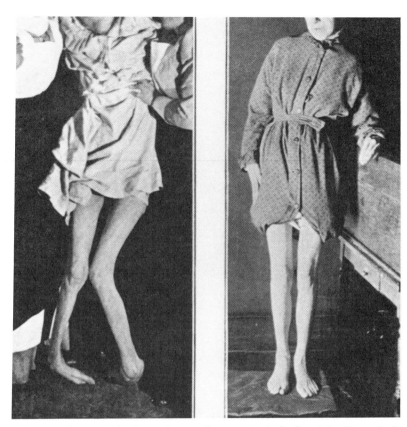

Above and verso: The hysteric posed. From A. Steindler, "On Hysterical
Contractures," *International Clinics*, 4th ser. 45 (1935): 221–229, fig. 2,
opposite p. 222. Photos courtesy Wellcome Institute Library, London.

pressly, Barker shows three images. First, an image of the "normal," that
is, pathological, posture of the patient; second, an image that in its
blurred state is to represent the range of motion in the patient; and
finally, an image of the body restored through "etherization and suggestion." Here the impact of the cinema on the idea of realism is evident.
Whereas in the work of Lamarque and Bitot such an image would be
understood as ruined, here it reveals a further aspect of the realism associated with the act of photographing.

One last form of realistic representation of the hysteric should be
discussed. For throughout the vast literature of hysteria (and other
forms of mental illness) in the nineteenth century there are uncountable

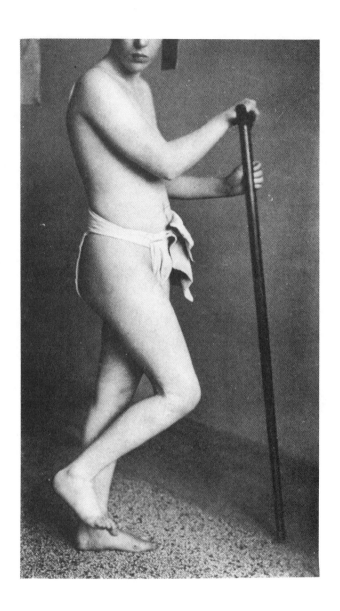

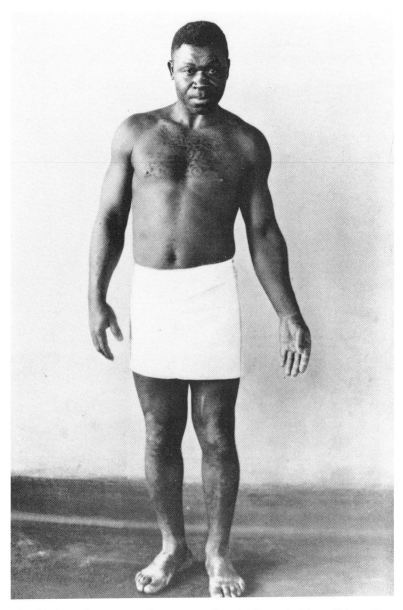

The illusion of movement in representing the hysteric. From Prince P. Barker, "The Diagnosis and Treatment of Hysterical Paralysis," *United States Veteran's Bureau Medical Bulletin* 6 (1930): 663–670, 3 plates following p. 670. (Bethesda, Md.: National Library of Medicine.)

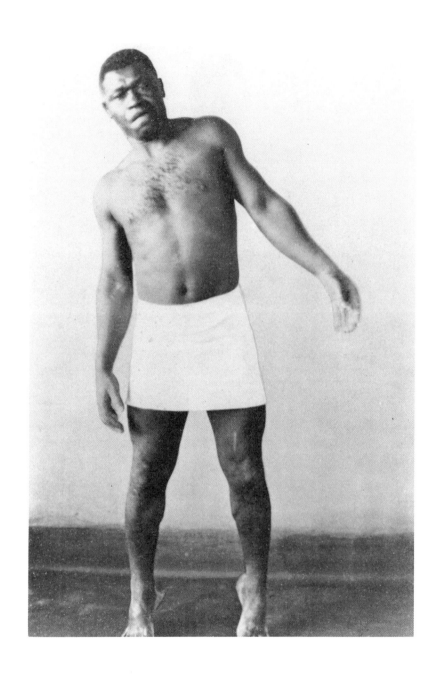

charts, graphs, and statistical tables. It is virtually unimportant what source one uses. From the medical periodicals in France[119] to those in Japan[120] or Germany,[121] one consistent image of the hysteric is that of the scientific reduction of the sufferer and the disease to schematic representations. The cry of these images is that they are the real, transcendent image of the hysteric. Like Galton's composite photographs (which will be discussed below), they give the observer an image of the totality of the disease. This fantasy of reducing the complexity of hysteria to statistics or charts rests on a notion of nineteenth-century science that everything is reducible to nonverbal form (read: mathematical), and that is precisely the claim of the photograph. For once, it is said, you eliminate narrative, you remove the subjective aspect from the evaluation of the disease and you have a real representation of the patient. Thus the use of charts and statistics in representing the hysteric is another visual means of creating an image of the disease, as sure as the images of the skin, or brain, or cellular structure of the hysteric.

HYSTERIA, RACE, AND GENDER

Sigmund Freud's reading of the ancient Greek myth of the wandering womb, which, when lodged in the throat, created the *globus hystericus*, can serve us as a detailed example of the problems attendant to "seeing" the hysteric. It is well known that Freud, in the autobiographical account he wrote of the occasion some forty years after the event, recalled the bad reception that his initial paper on male hysteria had when he presented it before the Viennese Society of Physicians on 15 October 1886.[122] Returning from his work with Jean-Martin Charcot in Paris and desiring to present his newly acquired insights about male hysteria to his home audience in Vienna, Freud presented his paper. His powerful recollection was that his hearers thought that what he "said was incredible. . . . One of them, an old surgeon, actually broke out with the exclamation: 'But, my dear sir, how can you talk such nonsense? *Hysteron* [sic] means the uterus. So how can a man be hysterical?'"[123] Freud's angry memory was aimed at the narrow-minded claim of the Viennese establishment, that it, and it alone, had command of Greek. It was the young, French-trained Freud who knew that the concept of hysteria was tied to universals (which, at that point, he understood as trauma) and was not merely a reflex of the biological uniqueness of a subgroup. It was hysteria (the hallmark of the new science) that Freud wished to rescue from the crabbed claws of a Viennese medical establishment that could not even get its Greek correct, for *hystera* is the correct form of the Greek noun

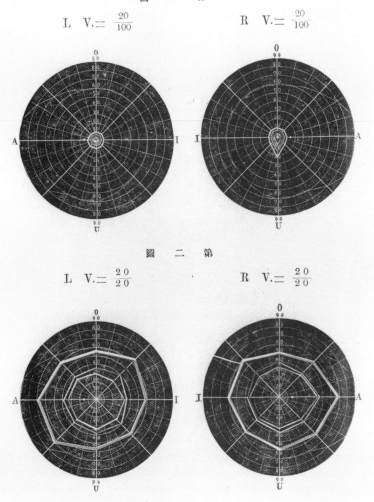

The chart as the representation of the male hysteric in Japan, as in the image of psychic forces in H. Nishi, "[Male Hysteria Cured by Suggestion]," *Chugai Iji Shinpo* 405 (1897): 5–9; 406 (1897): 11–16, image on p. 9. (Bethesda, Md.: National Library of Medicine.)

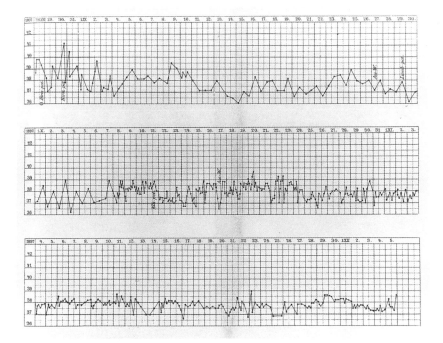

The chart as the representation of the hysteric in Germany, as in the evaluation of operations on the hearing of the hysteric in K. Rudolphy, "Ohroperationen bei Hysterischen," *Zeitschrift für Ohrenheilkunde und für die Krankheiten der
Luftwege* 44 (1903): 209–221, plate 17, opposite p. 220. (Bethesda, Md.:
National Library of Medicine.)

for uterus. Thus the young Jew (and Freud understood himself from
his exposure to the virulent "scientific" anti-Semitism of the Viennese
University as a Jew) showed his command over not only the language
of science (represented by Charcot's discourse on hysteria) but also the
language of culture (Greek). (The significance of this factor will be
shown in the course of this analysis.) Freud's understanding, like the understanding of his time, was that hysteria did not manifest itself as a disease of the womb but of the imagination. This did not absolve the female
from being the group most at risk, however, for the idea of a pathological human imagination structurally replaced the image of the floating
womb as the central etiology of hysteria. What was removed from the

category of hysteria as Freud brought it back to Vienna was its insistence on another group, the Jews, which replaced the woman as essentially at risk.

The idea of the hysteric was a central one for the imaginative world of Sigmund Freud as it was close to his self-definition. For at the close of the nineteenth century the idea of seeing the hysteric was closely bound to the idea of seeing the Jew—and very specifically the male Jew.[124] For if the visual representation of the hysteric within the world of images of the nineteenth century was the image of the female, its subtext was that feminized males, such as Jews, were also hysterics, and they too could be "seen." The face of the Jew was as much a sign of the pathological as was the face of the hysteric. But even more so, the face of the Jew became the face of the hysteric. Let us quote from one of the defenders of the Jews against the charge of being tainted by hysteria. Maurice Fishberg's *The Jews: A Study of Race and Environment* (1911) states the case boldly: "The Jews, as is well known to every physician, are notorious sufferers of the functional disorders of the nervous system. Their nervous organization is constantly under strain, and the least injury will disturb its smooth workings."[125] The origin of this predisposition is neither consanguineous marriage ("the modern view . . . [is that they] are not at all detrimental to the health of the offspring") nor the occupations of the Jew ("hysteria [is] . . . met with in the poorer classes of Jews . . . as well as in the richer classes").[126] It is the result of the urban concentration of the Jews and "the repeated persecutions and abuses to which the Jews were subjected during the two thousand years of the Diaspora."[127] These influences, found at the turn of the century primarily among Eastern Jews, according to Fishberg show the predisposition of these specific groups of Jews to illnesses such as hysteria: "Organic as well as functional derangements of the nervous system are transmitted hereditarily from one generation to another."[128] It is not *all* Jews who are hysterics, but Eastern Jews, and primarily Eastern male Jews, according to Fishberg: "The Jewish population of [Warsaw] alone is almost exclusively the inexhaustible source for the supply of specimens of hysterical humanity, particularly the hysteria in the male, for all the clinics of Europe."[129] Here Fishberg, an American Jew, misquotes the French psychiatrist Fulgence Raymond, who had stated that Jews of Warsaw formed a major sector of the mentally ill of that city.[130] It was Fishberg's misquote of Raymond that became the standard view in German psychiatry.[131] It appeared within Freud's circle when Isidor Sadger noted at the 11 November 1908 meeting of the Vienna Psychoanalytic Society: "In certain races (Russian and Polish Jews), almost every man is hysterical."[132] It is the male Jew from the East, from the provinces, who is most at risk for hysteria.

This view had been espoused by Charcot, who diagnosed on 19 February 1889 the case of a Hungarian Jew named Klein, "a true child of Ahasverus," as a case of male hysteria. Klein had a hysterical contracture of the hand and an extended numbness of the right arm and leg. It was Klein's limping that Charcot stressed. Klein "wandered sick and limping on foot to Paris" where he arrived on 11 December 1888. He appeared at the Salpêtrière the next day, "his feet so bloody that he could not leave his bed for many days." Klein "limped at the very beginning of his illness." Charcot reminded his listeners that the patient "is a Jew and that he has already revealed his pathological drives by his wanderings." His "travel-mania" could be seen in the fact that "as soon as he was on his feet again, he wanted to go to Brazil."[133] Klein also suffered from the standard numbness ascribed to the hysteric on half of his body. Wandering and limping mark the hysterical Jew as diseased, and diseased because of incestuous intermarriage.

H. Strauss of Berlin, in one of the most cited studies of the pathology of the Jews, provides a bar chart representing the risk of the Jews for hysteria.[134] It shows that male Jews suffer twice as often from hysteria as do male non-Jews. While it is clear that women still are the predominant sufferers from the disease, it shows a clear "feminization" of the male Jew in the context of the occurrence of hysteria. Freud's teacher, the liberal-Jewish neurologist Moriz Benedikt, also links the "American" quality of life with the appearance of hysteria, a disease that he understood as "a uniquely feminine nervous disease"—in men.[135] The struggle for life in the city causes the madness of the male Jew: "Mental anxiety and worry are the most frequent causes of mental breakdown. They are all excitable and live excitable lives, being constantly under the high pressure of business in town."[136] The reason for this inability to cope with the stresses of modern life lies in "hereditary influences," that is, their being Jews.[137]

And that is written on their faces, as on the faces of women. William Thackeray, in *Codlingsby*, his parody of Disraeli's novels, has his eponymous protagonist revel in the aestheticized sight of the "ringlets glossy, and curly, and jetty—eyes black as night—midsummer night—when it lightens; haughty noses bending like beaks of eagles—eager quivering nostrils—lips curved like the bow of Love" of the Jews.[138] "Every man or maiden," looks Jewish, but also looks feminine; "every babe or matron in that English Jewry bore in his countenance one or more of these

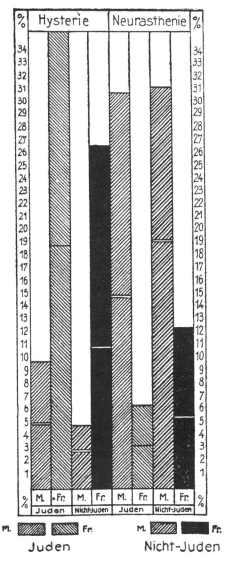

The Jewish hysteric, as represented by a chart from H. Strauss, "Erkrankungen durch Alkohol und Syphilis bei den Juden," *Zeitschrift für Demographie und Statistik der Juden,* 4 N.F. (1927): 33–39; chart on p. 35. (Bethesda, Md.: National Library of Medicine.)

The idealized "Jewish face," in a drawing by the famed fin-de-siècle
Viennese Jewish artist Ephraim Moses Lilien, is that of the female. In
Maurice Fishberg, *The Jews: A Study of Race and Environment* (London:
Walter Scott Publishing Co., 1911), p. 95. Photo courtesy Wellcome
Institute Library, London.

characteristics of his peerless Arab race." Codlingsby muses: "How beautiful they are!" when the jarring voice of Rafael Mendoza breaks his revery: "D'you vant to look at a nishe coat?" But the accent is not a true sign of the Jew's difference: "All traces of the accent with which he first addressed Lord Codlingsby had vanished, it was disguise: half the Hebrew's life is a disguise. He shields himself in craft, since the Norman boors persecuted him." The association between the falsity of the language of the Jews (which is not merely accented but duplicitous) is balanced by the "true" sight of the Jews—a factor that Thackeray parodies. What remains is that the "sight" of the Jew—the registration of the external signs of Jewishness—is a truer indicator of the nature of the Jew (or at least the perception of the Jew's nature in Thackeray's relativistic manner of representing the Jew) than is the mutable sign of the Jews' language, a language that is corrupted by as well as corrupting the world in which the Jew in the Diaspora lives.

Francis Galton actually tries to capture this "Jewish physiognomy" in his composite (i.e., multiple exposure) photographs of "boys in the Jews' Free School, Bell Lane." Galton provides types generated by multiple exposures. There he sees the "cold, scanning gaze" of the Jew as the sign of their difference, of their potential pathology.[139] It is in the Jews' gaze that the pathology can be found. This view is at least as old as Robert Burton's *Anatomy of Melancholy,* where Burton writes of the "goggle eyes" of the Jews, as well as "their voice, pace, gesture, [and] looks" as a sign of "their conditions and infirmities."[140] But it is not merely that Jews "look Jewish" but that this marks them as inferior: "Who has not heard people characterize such and such a man or woman they see in the streets as Jewish without in the least knowing anything about them? The street arab who calls out 'Jew' as some child hurries on to school is unconsciously giving the best and most disinterested proof that there is a reality in the Jewish expression."[141] The gaze of the non-Jew seeing the Jew is immediately translated into action.

The complexity of the Jewish response to this view can be measured in Joseph Jacob's discussion of Galton's finding of the absolute Jewishness of the gaze:

> Cover up every part of composite A but the eyes, and yet I fancy any one familiar with Jews would say: "Those are Jewish eyes." I am less able to analyze this effect than in the case of the nose. . . . I fail to see any of the cold calculation which Mr. Galton noticed in the boys at the school, at any rate in the composites A, B, and C. There is something more like the dreamer and thinker than the merchant in A. In fact, on my showing this to an eminent painter of my acquaintance, he exclaimed, "I imagine that

Francis Galton's "composite" and "component" images of the Jew (here
the Jewish male stands as representative for the Jew). Frontispiece to
Joseph Jacobs, *Studies in Jewish Statistics* (London: D. Nutt, 1891). Photo
courtesy Wellcome Institute Library, London.

is how Spinoza looked when a lad," a piece of artistic insight which is remarkably confirmed by the portraits of the philosopher, though the artist
had never seen one. The cold, somewhat hard look in composite D, however, is more confirmatory of Mr. Galton's impression. It is noteworthy
that this is seen in a composite of young fellows between seventeen and
twenty, who have had to fight a hard battle of life even by that early age.

For the Jewish social scientist such as Jacobs the inexplicable nature of
the Jewish gaze exists (even more than the "nostrility" that characterizes
the Jewish nose) to mark the Jew. His rationale is quite different than
that of Galton—he seeks a social reason for the "hard and calculating"
glance seen by Galton, but claims to see it nevertheless. This view reappears within the medical literature in the work of Jewish physicians, such
as Moses Julius Gutmann, who writes of the structure of the Jewish face,
of its typical form, as being the result of a combination of features that
produce "the melancholy, pained expression" (the nebbish face) that is
associated with the Jew. For Gutmann, and others, it is the result of the
"psychological history of the Jew." [142]

Sigmund Freud's own fascination for Galton's "family" photographs must also be stressed. For Freud the composite photograph is virtually the representation of the dream in his *Interpretation of Dreams* (1990). It is an obsessive metaphor, which recurs throughout the course of his work.[143] The centrality of this metaphor is a residue of Freud's earlier acceptance of Charcot's reliance on the act of seeing as the privileged form of diagnosis. It is not seeing the unique but rather the universal. And yet hidden within those claims for universality are the images of race which Galton produces parallel to his other composites, in which the eyes of the Jew (read: Sigmund Freud) and his gaze are pathologized. The clinical gaze of the Jewish physician now becomes the object of the gaze of study. The image of the eyes, found in the calculating glance of the hysteric and the epileptic, reappears in the context of race.

In Henry Meige's dissertation of 1893 on the wandering Jew in the clinical setting of the Salpêtrière, the image of the Jew and the gaze of the Jew become one.[144] Meige undertakes to place the appearance of Eastern European (male) Jews in the Salpêtrière as a sign of the inherent instability of the Eastern European Jew. He sketches the background to the legend of the wandering Jew and provides (like his supervisor, Charcot) a set of visual "images of Ahasverus." He then provides a series of case studies of Eastern (male) Jews, two of which he illustrates. The first plate is of "Moser C. called Moses," a forty-five- or forty-six-year-old Polish Jew from Warsaw who had already wandered through the clinics in Vienna and elsewhere; the second plate is of "Gottlieb M.," a forty-two-year-old Jew from Vilnius, who likewise had been treated at many of the psychiatric clinics in Western Europe. Given the extraordinary movement of millions of Eastern Jews through Western Europe, beginning in the early 1880s, toward England and America, the appearance of these few cases of what comes to be called "Munchausen syndrome" should not surprise. Without any goal, these Jews "wandered" only in the sense that they were driven West, and that some should seek the solace of the clinic where they would at least be treated as individuals, even if sick individuals, should not make us wonder. What is striking is that Meige provides images and analyses that stress the pathognomonic physiognomy of the Jew—especially his eyes. The images gaze at us, informing us of their inherent hysterical pathology. The Jew is the hysteric; the Jew is the feminized Other; the Jew is seen as different, as diseased. This is the image of the hysteric with which the Jewish scientist was confronted. His "startle" effect was to see himself as the Other, as the diseased, but most important as the feminized Other, the altered form of his circumcised genitalia reflecting the form of that of the woman.

The "wandering Jew" as the model for the psychopathology of the Eastern Jew. From Henry Meige, *Étude sur certains néuropathes voyageurs: Le juif-errant a la Salpêtrière* (Paris: L. Battaille et cie., 1893), p. 17. (Bethesda, Md.: National Library of Medicine.)

No wonder that Jewish scientists such as Jacobs, Fishberg, and Freud—in very different ways—sought to find the hysteric outside of their own self-image. For that image was immutable within the biology of race. Fishberg quotes the accepted wisdom (in order to refute it for himself and project it onto the Eastern Jew) when he cites Richard An-

The image of "Moser C. called Moses," one of the modern "wandering Jews," gazes at the reader. From Henry Meige, *Étude sur certains néuropathes voyageurs: Le juif-errant a la Salpêtrière* (Paris: L. Battaille et cie., 1893), p. 25. (Bethesda, Md.: National Library of Medicine.)

dree: "No other race but the Jews can be traced with such certainty backward for thousands of years, and no other race displays such a constancy of form, none resisted to such an extent the effects of time, as the Jews. Even when he adopts the language, dress, habits, and customs of the people among whom he lives, he still remains everywhere the same. All he adopts is but a cloak, under which the eternal Hebrew survives; he is the same in his facial features, in the structure of his body, his temperament, his character." [145] And this constancy of character, with its de-

The physiognomy and the gaze of "Gottlieb M.," a forty-two-year-old
Jew from Vilna, "proves" the psychopathology of the Jew. From Henry
Meige, *Étude sur certains néuropathes voyageurs: Le juif-errant a la Salpêtrière*
(Paris: L. Battaille et cie., 1893), p. 29. (Bethesda, Md.: National Library
of Medicine.)

viant sexual nature, leads to the disease that marks the Jew, that leads
to hysteria. Because the etiology of the Jew's hysteria, like the hysteria of the woman, was to be sought in "sexual excess."[146] Specifically in
the "incestuous" inbreeding of this endogenous group: "Being very neurotic, consanguineous marriages among Jews cannot but be detrimental

to the progeny." [147] Jews (especially male Jews) are sexually different; they are hysterical and they look it.

The clinical gaze of the Jewish physician now becomes the object of the gaze of study. The image of the eyes attributed to the Jew reappears in the context of the science of race. It is this biological definition of all aspects of the Jew that helps form the fin-de-siècle idea of the Jew. The scientific gaze should be neutral. The scientific gaze should be beyond or above all of the vagaries of individual difference. [148] As George Herbert Mead put it: "Knowledge is never a mere contact of our organisms with other objects. It always takes on a universal character. If we know a thing, explain it, we always put it into a texture of uniformities. There must be some reason for it, some law expressed in it. That is the fundamental assumption of science." [149]

But race is but one of the categories of the visualization of the hysteric that played a role in shaping the image of the hysteric in the course of the nineteenth century. For the construction of seeing the hysteric took many different forms in providing a composite image of the hysteric, an image in bits and snatches, an image that revealed the "truth" about the hysteric's difference to him- or herself. The nosology of the "categories" of difference are really quite analogous to Charcot's construction of the visual pattern of the actions of the hysteric. One can argue that Freud's intellectual as well as analytic development in the 1890s was a movement away from the meaning of visual signs (a skill that he ascribes to Charcot in his obituary of 1893) and to the interpretation of verbal signs, from the crudity of seeing to the subtlety of hearing. [150] Charcot understands the realism of the image to transcend the crudity of the spoken word. In a letter to Freud on 23 November 1891 he commented concerning the transcription of his famed Tuesday lectures that "the stenographer is not a photographer." [151] The assumption of the inherent validity of the gaze and its mechanical reproduction forms the image of the hysteric. The central argument that can be brought is that this vocabulary of seeing remains embedded in Freud's act of understanding the hysteric, who must be seen to be understood. This is not present in the earliest papers on hysteria written directly under Charcot's influence, such as Freud's differential diagnosis of organic and hysterical paralysis written in 1886. [152] For Freud the rejection of Charcot's mode of seeing the hysteric is also a rejection of the special relationship that the Jew has with the disease. The theme of the specific, inherited risk of the Jew for hysteria (and other forms of mental illness) was reflected in the work of Charcot which Freud translated. [153] But even more so this general claim about the hereditary risk of the Jew was linked to a diagnostic system rooted in belief in external appearance as the source of knowledge about the pathological. For the seeing of the Jew as different was a topos of the world in which Freud lived. Satirical caricatures were to be found throughout the German-speaking world, which stressed the Jew's physical difference, and in the work of Charcot (and his contemporaries) these representations took on pathological significance.

Indeed, Freud's purchase of a lithograph of Brouillet's painting of Charcot in August of 1889 can well be understood as a compensation of Freud's rejection of Charcot's mode of seeing and representing the hysteric. Indeed, it must also be understood as a compensation for his abandonment of his identification with the anti-Semitic Jean-Martin Charcot[154]—for whom Jews, as the essential "moderns," were at special risk as hysterics—and his new alliance with the provincial Jew Hippolyte Bernheim.[155] Such a movement parallels the abandonment of ideas of trauma—still for Charcot the cause of hysteria (in women as well as in Jews)—and its replacement with the etiology of hysteria in the psyche. As Freud states:

> For [the physician] will be able to convince himself of the correctness of the assertions of the school of Nancy [Bernheim] at any time on his patients, whereas he is scarcely likely to find himself in a position to confirm from his own observation the phenomena described by Charcot as "major hypnotism," which seem only to occur in a few sufferers from *grande hysterie*.[156]

It is the scientific "observation," the gaze of the Jew rather than the gaze directed at the Jew, which marks the distinction between Charcot and Bernheim. Freud's conversion to Bernheim's mode of seeing the "usual" rather than seeing the "unique" also marks the beginning of his rejection of reducing the origin of hysteria to the single, traumatic event.

This returns us to the problem of defining the visual precursors for Charcot and for Freud. We must trace the image of the epileptic and the meaning of trauma—two clearly linked images in Freud's vocabulary of the hysteric—to see how Freud's reading of the hysteric is linked through these images of trauma to the central image of difference, the Eastern European Jews as hysterics (or perhaps more accurately, provincial Jews as parvenus, out of their minds because they are out of their natural place). It is the discourse on the relationship between trauma and hysteria that provides the key to Freud's—and many of his contemporaries'—ambivalence concerning models for therapy.

Trauma is not a neutral concept. There has been a general acceptance of the historical model of the "railway spine," hysterical trauma resulting from railway accidents, as a means of understanding the traumatic nature of hysteria at the turn of the century.[157] Indeed, in much of the early work on hysteria these images haunt the literature. The hysteric is the sufferer from traumatic neurosis similar to that caused by experiencing a train accident, as outlined by Herbert Page in his classic work, *Injuries of the Spine and Spinal Cord* (1883), and accepted *in toto* by Charcot in his work on the neurosis of fright or shock. Both men and women are therefore equally at risk for such forms of psychopathology. Hysteria is thus merely the direct (brain or spinal cord lesion) or indirect (shock) result of trauma. And here the confusion between the models of hysteria evolved by Charcot and Hughlings Jackson must be stressed. For the traumatic event causes hysteria only in those who are predisposed to being hysteric (Charcot), but the lesion caused by trauma also releases those subterranean aspects of our earlier evolution held in check by the highest order of neurological organization (Hughlings Jackson). The Jew is predisposed to hysteria both because of hereditary and consanguinity (incestuous inbreeding) and, as we shall see, by the trauma of civilization as represented by the Jews' predisposition to the somatic diseases linked to hysteria, such as syphilis.

The fin-de-siècle image of trauma is one with modern civilization, with the train. As Sir Clifford Allbutt, Professor of Medicine at Cambridge University, stated in an essay in the *Contemporary Review* of 1895:

> To turn now . . . to nervous disability, to hysteria . . . to the frightfulness, the melancholy, the unrest due to living at a high pressure, the world of the railway, the pelting of telegrams, the strife of business . . . surely, at any rate, these maladies or the causes of these maladies are more rife than they were in the days of our fathers? To this question . . . there is, I know, but one opinion on the subject in society, in the newspapers, in the books of philosophers, even in the journals and treatises of the medical profession.[158]

And thus the railroad, railway accidents, and the speed of modern life all collaborate to create the hysteric. But nineteenth-century "railway" medicine faced a dilemma that later faced Sigmund Freud. Trauma—such as involvement in a railway crash—is the cause of hysteria, but why do not all individuals who are involved in railway crashes become hysteric? This question was answered in part by the neurologist C. E. Brown-Séquard, who, as early as 1860, had argued that there were hereditary transmissions of acquired injuries, as in the case of "animals born of parents having been rendered epileptic by an injury to the spinal cord." [159] This view quickly becomes a standard one in the literature on "railway spine." [160]

The image of the hysteric being at risk because of his or her inheritance limited the field from which the hysteric could be drawn. Thus the physician could, under most circumstances, see him- or herself as a separate category, as distanced from the hysteric as from the child of alcoholics or criminals. But not the Jewish physician. For the Jewish physician is at risk no matter which theory of hysteria one accepted. [161] Some views using the model of biological determinism had it that the Jew was at risk simply from inheritance; some views sought after a sociological explanation. But both views, no matter what the etiology, saw a resultant inability of the Jew to deal with the complexities of the modern world, as represented by the Rousseauean city. The trauma of "modern life" was closely linked to the image of the city. For nineteenth-century medicine (whether psychiatry or public health), cities are places of disease and the Jews are the quintessential city dwellers, the Americans of Europe. Richard Krafft-Ebing believed that civilization regularly brings forth degenerate forms of sexuality because of the "more stringent demands which circumstances make upon the nervous system," circumstances that manifest themselves in the "psychopathological or neuropathological conditions of the nation involved." [162] For him (and for most clinical psychiatrists at the turn of the century) the Jew is the ultimate "city person" whose sensibilities are dulled, whose sexuality is pathological, whose materialistic, money-grubbing goals are "American," whose life is without a center. It is also the city that triggers the weakness hidden within the corrupted individual. It is its turbulence, its excitement, what August Forel in *The Sexual Question* (1905) calls its "Americanism," that leads to illnesses such as hysteria:

> Americanism.—By this term I designate an unhealthy feature of sexual life, common among the educated classes of the United States, and apparently originating in the greed for dollars, which is more prevalent in North America than anywhere else. I refer to the unnatural life which Americans lead, and more especially to its sexual aspect. [163]

This is an image seen by physicians of the period as "Jewish" in its dimensions. Jews manifest an "abnormally intensified sensuality and sexual excitement that lead to sexual errors that are of etiological significance." [164] Jewish scientists, when they address this question directly, seek for a developmental rather than a hereditary reason for this evident higher rate of hysteria. They seek out the two-thousand-year Diaspora as the origin of trauma. [165] But this does not free them. Given the views of Brown-Séquard, there is really little escape no matter what the cause. The Jew becomes the hysteric and the hysteria is measured by the sexual abnormality of the Jew.

Thus when we turn to Freud's case studies, either in the collaborative *Studies in Hysteria* of 1895 or in his later and much more complex studies, such as his study of Dora (1905 [1901]), we face the question of Freud's (and Breuer's) representation of the Jew—of his "seeing" (or, perhaps better, "hearing") the Jew. In an earlier study I argued that the image of Anna O. in Breuer's case-study contribution to the *Studies in Hysteria* masked the "Jewishness" of Bertha Pappenheim.[166] In Freud's own contributions (such as the case of Katherina or Miss Lucy R.) there is the attempt to universalize the image of the hysteric through the citation— not of cases of male hysteria—but those of non-Jewish hysterics. But the common qualities ascribed to the hysteric and the Eastern, male Jew remain central to the representation of this nosological category for Freud.

This can be seen in a close reading of what has become the exemplary "case of hysteria" for our contemporary reading of the history of hysteria, Freud's case of Dora.[167] Seen by contemporary feminist critics, such as Hélène Cixous, as "the core example of the protesting force of women,"[168] it is also the classic example of the transmutation of images of gender and race (masculinity and "Jewishness") into the raceless image of the feminine. Freud used the case of Dora to argue not only for the necessary publication of case studies, but also for the needed masking of the analysand. The disguising of the identity of Dora is complete. There is no sign in the case study of the "racial" identity of Ida Bauer, the Eastern European Jewish daughter of Philip Bauer, whose syphilis was treated by Freud some six years before the beginning of Dora's analysis. Charcot (and Freud) had attempted to distance the diseases of syphilis and hysteria, and yet a relationship between the two patterns of illness remained. This omission, such as Josef Breuer's omission of his patient's "racial" identity in his narrative of Anna O.'s case, while including it in his case notes, masks a salient aspect of the case. We can best quote Freud in this regard, when he returns to the 1895 case of Katherina in 1924 and observes concerning his replacement of the relationship with the patient's father with the word "uncle": "Distortions like the one which I introduced in the present instance should be altogether avoided in reporting a case history."[169]

Perhaps as important for our reading of the suppressed aspects of the case of Dora (Ida Bauer) is the fact that her beloved brother Otto Bauer was one of the founders of the Austrian Socialist Party. His attitude toward his Jewish identity is of importance. For Austro-Marxism advocated cultural-national autonomy for all people within the diverse Hapsburg Empire—except for the Jews. These Marxists saw assimilation as inevitable and positive, and they tied assimilation to a distinct distaste for Yiddish (and subsequently Hebrew) as linguistic signs of a negative separatism (a sign that took on positive meaning when ascribed to Czech or Hungarian as "national" languages). While Otto Bauer was an "Eastern Jew" himself, as he was born of Bohemian ancestry in Vienna, he was ambivalent about the idea of race. "Race" was an acceptable label for the other national groups, since it was associated by them with positive ideas of autonomy, but for the Jews (especially Eastern Jews) it was always a sign of the pathological.[170] Bertha Pappenheim, Breuer's Anna O., stated it quite baldly in an essay published at the turn of the century. Raised in an orthodox Jewish home, for her the German-language schools developed in the Eastern reaches of the Hapsburg Empire were "a stronghold, often conquered in battle, in the fight against the malaise from which Galician Jewry suffers as from a hereditary disease."[171] It is the cure of this hereditary disease that Freud undertakes in treating Dora (and thus treating an aspect of his own identity). This is, indeed, the hidden meaning of the development of the idea of transference and countertransference which is nascent in the case of Dora and why Freud's own understanding of this process is blocked in this case.

The centerpiece of Freud's study of Ida Bauer is, according to Freud's argument, the attempt to explain the origin of a case of hysteria through the analysis of the Oedipal triangle as perceived by a patient whose object of attraction is of the same sex. The complex relationships are between her father (Philip), her mother (Käthe), and Dora; the father's lover (Frau K.) and her husband (Herr K.), the attempted seducer of Dora, who has traditionally been the focus of the interpretation of the study. Much time and effort has been expended to understand Freud's complex misreading of this case. What is clear is that there are a number of misreadings by Freud in the text. Jacques Lacan pointed out one of the central ones: that the *globus hystericus* manifested by Dora is interpreted by Freud as the symbolic representation of orality within a specific context in the case study. The lover's seduction of the impotent father is described in Freud's analysis as an act of fellatio rather than being understood as cunnilingus.[172] This displacement is, however, not merely the shift of Freud's focus from the genitalia of the female to those of the male. Rather it is a double displacement—for the act of fellatio is also the emblematic act of male homosexual contact. What such a displacement means can be found if the "scientific" context of the meaning of the act of fellatio in the medical debates of the nineteenth century are followed. Through such a contextualization we can outline Freud's understanding of the transmission of a "disease" (the collapse of language as represented by the symptom of the *globus hystericus* in Ida Bauer) as necessarily associated with the act of sucking a male's penis. Let us begin with this misreading as a sign of Freud's representation of the idea of race in the guise of the representation of the feminine, as it replaces the male's genitalia as the object of attraction—and, therefore, sight—with the woman's. For Freud the act of seeing one's genitalia is one which is especially "feminine": "The pride taken by women in the appearance of their genitals is quite a special feature of their vanity; and the disorders of the genitals which they think calculated to inspire feelings of repugnance or even disgust have an incredible power of humiliating them, of lowering their self-esteem, and of making them irritable, sensitive, and distrustful." [173] The special quality of seeing the female's genitalia, genitalia normally understood by Freud as presence in the fantasy of their absence, points toward the other genitalia, the male genitalia, seen by the male, which when "disordered" points toward pathological nature of the male. But what is this disorder? In the case study it is, on one level, the origin of Ida Bauer's understanding about the diseased nature of her genitalia, the syphilitic infection of her father. One of the most interesting qualities ascribed to the father from the very beginning of the case study is the fact that he was syphilitic. The relationship between the physical trauma of syphilis and the image of the syphilitic is central to understanding the image of the hysteric which Freud evolves in his study. In the case of Dora's father, his "gravest illness . . . took the form of a confusional attack, followed by symptoms of paralysis and slight mental disturbance." [174] Freud diagnoses this as a case of "diffuse vascular affection; and since the patient admitted having had a specific infection before his marriage, I prescribed an energetic course of antiluetic treatment." [175] Four years later the father brings his daughter to Freud for treatment. Freud argues in a footnote for the retention of the relationship between the etiology of hysteria in the offspring and the syphilitic infection of the father. "Syphilis in the male parent is a very relevant factor in the etiology of the neuropathic constitution of children." [176] Here is the trauma—this case of hysteria is a form of hereditosyphilis transmitted by the father. Freud's emphasis on this line of inheritance is not solely because Ida Bauer's father had evidently (according to the account in the case study) infected her mother (and therefore his daughter), but because the general laws of the inheritance of disease which were accepted during this period argued that the son inherits the diseases of the mother (and therefore her father) while the daughter in-

herits the diseases of the father (and therefore his mother).[177] Freud
later uncovers another sign of this biological predisposition in the fact
that "she had masturbated in childhood."[178] This is the link that brings
together the trauma (the syphilitic infection of the father), the mode
of transmission (sexual intercourse with a circumcised penis), the Jewishness of the father as represented in his pathological sexuality, and
the hysterical neurosis of the daughter. The merging of various forms
of illness, from syphilis to hysteria, is through the model of inherited
characteristics. The "real" disease is the degeneracy of the parent, and
its manifestation in specific illness can vary from individual to individual.[179] Thus syphilis and hysteria are truly forms of the same pattern
of illness.

One reading of the case would be to say that hypersexual Jewish males
pass on their Jewish disease to their daughters in the form of hysteria.
But this discourse is present in Freud's text only if we contextualize the
meaning of syphilis within the context of Freud's self-definition as a Jew
and that of his patient, Ida Bauer.

Freud creates very early on a differential diagnosis between tabes dorsalis (a label for one of the late manifestations of syphilis) and hysteria,
at least when it appears in a woman who is infected with syphilis. He
undertakes this in an extended footnote at the very beginning of the
study in which he documents the central diagnostic thesis of this case
study: that it is the ordered narrative of the patient about her illness
which is disrupted in the hysteric. In other words, the hysteric lies: "The
patient's inability to give an ordered history of their life insofar as it
coincides with the history of their illness is not merely characteristic of
the neurosis. It also possesses great theoretical significance."[180] The relationship between the sexual etiology of the hysteric and the hysteric's
discourse represents the underlying shift from an image of race to one
of gender (for as we shall see, the discourse of the Jew is a primary
marker of difference). The counterexample is brought in Freud's notes,
a case study of a patient who "had been for years . . . treated without
success for hysteria (pains and defective gait)." She narrates her "story
. . . perfectly clearly and connectedly in spite of the remarkable events
it dealt with." Freud concludes this "could not be . . . [a case] of hysteria,
and immediately instituted a careful physical examination. This led to
the diagnosis of a fairly advanced stage of tabes, which later was treated
with Hg injections (Ol. cinereum) by Professor Lang with markedly beneficial results."[181] Here the image of the "defective gait," which is one
of the hallmarks of the "hysteric" in the nineteenth century (and the history created for this image at the Salpêtrière), recurs, only to be revealed

as the final stages of syphilis. The irony is that it is Joseph Babinski whose neurological work at the Salpêtrière provided the clue for such an analysis of the impaired plantar reflex[182] and Charcot himself, in his work on intermittent claudication, who provided the racial context for such impairment.[183] (And, indeed, there is a link of intermittent claudication to the image of the hysteric.)[184] In this case of Dora, it is revealed only at the very close of the case that one of Dora's primary symptoms was that "she had not been able to walk properly and dragged her right foot. . . . Even now her foot sometimes dragged."[185] Freud sees this "disorder, the dragging of one leg," as having a "secret and possibly sexual meaning of the clinical picture."[186] Freud interprets this as a sign of the "false step" that Dora had imaged herself to have taken during the attempted seduction by Herr K. at the lake. Later Felix Deutsch, who treated Ida Bauer after she broke off her analysis with Freud, observed with surprise that the "dragging of her foot, which Freud had observed when the patient was a girl, should have persisted twenty-five years."[187] This remained a central sign for her affliction, a sign that is not solely the association between the accident she had as a child and the bed rest that accompanied it. For the incapacity of gait is also a racial sign in Ida Bauer's Vienna and is associated with the "impairment" of the Jew. For it is the Jew, in a long Austrian tradition as old as the eighteenth century, who is at greatest risk in having both impaired gait[188] and syphilis. It is this image in the case of Dora that links the impairment of the syphilitic and the hidden image of the Jew.

The association of the syphilitic infection of the father and the neurosis of the daughter is linked by Freud in his analysis of the physical symptom of leukorrhea, or genital catarrh, an increased "disgust[ing] . . . secretion of the mucous membrane of the vagina."[189] Dora associates this with her lesbian "disgust" toward Herr K.'s attempted heterosexual seduction (in Freud's reading) and the feeling of his "erect member against her body."[190] Freud's conclusion is that for Ida Bauer "all men were like her father. But she thought her father suffered from venereal disease—for had he not handed it on to her and to her mother? She might therefore have imagined to herself that all men suffered from venereal disease, and naturally her conception of venereal disease was modelled upon her one experience of it—a personal one at that. To suffer from venereal disease, therefore, meant for her to be afflicted with a disgusting discharge."[191] Freud thus interprets one of two dreams narrated to him by Dora in terms of the connection among the "disgusting catarrh," the wetness of bed-wetting and masturbation, and her mother's compulsive cleanliness. "The two groups of ideas met in

Charcot's diagnostic category of intermittent claudication was used as a marker for racial difference. From P. Olivier and A. Halipré, "Claudication intermittente chez un homme hystérique atteint de pouls lent permanen," *La Normandie Médicale* 11 (1896): 23. (Bethesda, Md.: National Library of Medicine.)

this one thought: 'Mother got both things from father: the sexual wetness and the dirtying discharge.'"[192] In the recurrent dream the connection (right word) is made through the symbolic representation of
the "drops," the jewels that her mother wishes to rescue from the fire
that threatens the family.[193] Freud interprets the "drops"—the jewelry
[Schmuck]—as a switch-word, while "jewelry" [Schmuck] was taken as an
equivalent to "clean" and thus as a rather forced contrary of "dirtied."[194]
Freud stresses that the "jewels" become a "jewelcase" in the dream and
that this term (Schmuckkasten) is "a term commonly used to describe
female genitals that are immaculate and intact."[195]

One can add another layer of misreading. As I have shown, there is
a subtext in the hidden language of the Jews. In Viennese urban dialect,
borrowed from Yiddish, Schmock has another meaning. Schmock even in
German urban ideolect had come to be the standard slang term for the
male genitals. The hidden meaning of the language of the Jews is identical to the lying of the hysteric, the central symptom of hysteria, according to Freud. This transference can be seen in Freud's early description
of the discourse of two Eastern male Jews in a letter to his friend Emil
Fluss on the return trip from Freiburg to Vienna in 1872:

> Now this Jew talked the same way as I had heard thousands of others talk
> before, even in Freiburg. His face seemed familiar—he was typical. So was
> the boy with whom he discussed religion. He was cut from the cloth from
> which fate makes swindlers when the time is ripe: cunning, mendacious,
> kept by his adoring relatives in the belief that he is a great talent, but un-
> principled and without character. I have enough of this rabble.[196]

The misreading of the text is a repression of the discourse of the male
Eastern Jew—the parvenu marked by his language and discourse as different and diseased. Hidden within the female genitalia (the Schmuckkasten) is the image of the male Jew as represented by his genitalia (the
Schmock). The replacement of the "Jewish" penis—identifiable as circumcised and, as we shall see, as diseased, by the "German" vagina stands
at the center of Freud's revision of the identity of Ida Bauer.

In my study Jewish Self-Hatred, I have extensively shown that an ancient Western tradition labels the language of the Jew as corrupt and
corrupting, as the sign of the inherent difference of the Jew.[197] This
tradition sees the Jew as inherently unable to have command of any
"Western"—that is, cultural—language (indeed, even the "holy language," Hebrew). The Jew is not only "not of our blood," as Monsignor
Joseph Frings of Cologne expressed it in 1942, but also "does not speak
our language."[198] For the acculturated Eastern Jew in Vienna, mauscheln,

the speaking of German with a Yiddish accent, intonation, or vocabulary, is the sign of this difference. And this is the language of Freud's mother, Amalia Freud née Nathanson, the invisible woman in all of his autobiographical accounts. As Freud's son Martin noted, she was a Galician Jew from Brody who remained a typical Polish Jew, "impatient, self-willed, sharp-witted and highly intelligent." She retained the language, manner, and beliefs of Galicia:

> [She was] absolutely different from Jews who had lived in the West for some generations. . . . These Galician Jews had little grace and no manners; and their women were certainly not what we should call "ladies." They were highly emotional and easily carried away by their feelings. . . . They were not easy to live with, and grandmother, a true representative of her race, was no exception. She had great vitality and much impatience.[199]

It is in the image of the mother that the qualities ascribed to the hysteric, to Ida Bauer, can be found. In suppressing the shift of language, Freud also suppresses the "hidden" reference to the "Jewish" penis. The hidden discourse of the Jew, hidden within the high German culture discourse, is ignored.

This "misreading" of the female for the male organ is in truth a "misseeing" of the genitalia as Freud traces the origin of Ida Bauer's knowledge of the act of fellatio, the "seeing" as well as sucking of the male member. Freud understands this "so-called sexual perversion" as being "very widely diffused among the whole population, as everyone knows except medical writers upon the subject. Or, I should rather say, they know it too; only they take care to forget it at the moment when they take up their pens to write about it. So it is not to be wondered at that this hysterical girl of nineteen, who had heard of the occurrence of such a method of sexual intercourse (sucking at the male organ), should have developed an unconscious phantasy of this sort and should have given it expression by an irritation in her throat and by coughing."[200] Freud reports that Dora's governess, to whom she was evidently as attracted as she was to Frau K., "used to read every sort of book on sexual life and similar objects, and talked to the girl about them, at the same time asking her quite frankly not to mention their conversations to her parents, as one could never tell what line they might take about them."[201] But it is clear according to Ida Bauer's account that she did not only "hear" about such sexual activity but learned about it in quite another way. Later in the case study, after Freud had begun to explain the homosexual attraction which Dora felt for Frau K., this narrative shifts.

After Dora's father writes to Herr K. to demand an explanation of his actions toward his daughter, Herr K. "spoke of her with disparagement, and produced as his trump card the reflection that no girl who read such books and was interested in such things could have any title to a man's respect. Frau K. had betrayed her and had calumniated her; for it had only been with her that she had read Mantegazza and discussed forbidden topics."[202] It is the book, a foreign book, that "infects" her, and makes her "sick," that is, "hysteric." Like her governess, Frau K. had used her to get access to her father. This "error" in Freud's image of the etiology of hysteria is a displacement of the image of the infected and the infecting onto the world of high culture—not "German" high culture (*Bildung*), of course, but the medical culture of the sexologist.

Paolo Mantegazza (1831–1901) was one of the standard ethnological sources for the late nineteenth century for the nature of human sexuality. His three-volume study of the physiology of love, the hygiene of love, and the anthropology of love was the standard popular introduction to the acceptable social discourse on sexuality in late nineteenth-century Europe.[203] His importance for Freud should not be underestimated. One of a group of physician-anthropologists (such as Cesare Lombroso), Mantegazza had pioneered the introduction of the study (and enjoyment) of *Erthroxylon coca* and its derivative, cocaine, in the late 1850s. Following the publication of Darwin's *Descent of Man*, Mantegazza became one of Darwin's most avid correspondents (and sources), supplying Darwin with a series of "anthropological" photographs that Darwin used for his later work.

Mantegazza's work, like that of Charcot, emphasized the "seeing" of difference, a view that is epitomized in Mantegazza's basic study of physiognomy and expression of 1885. But for late nineteenth-century science the controversial centerpiece of Mantegazza's work is his trilogy on love and sex: *Fisiologia dell' amore* (1872), *Igiene dell' amore* (1877), and *Gli amori degli uomini* (1885).[204] Cited widely by sexologists from Cesare Lombroso, Richard Krafft-Ebing, Havelock Ellis, and Iwan Bloch to Magnus Hirschfeld, Mantegazza remained one of the accessible, "popular" sources for scientific knowledge (and misinformation) for the educated public at the turn of the century. It is clear that Ida Bauer could have read (and probably did read) either Mantegazza or similar texts, whether under the tutelage of her companion or on her own initiative. What is of interest is how Freud reads this contradiction in her account: Did she read them, or only hear about their content? What is inherently dangerous about Mantegazza from the standpoint of Freud's refusal to relate to the accusation that Ida Bauer had read him? If we turn to the trilogy, it is clear (and Madelon Spregnether agrees[205]) that the text that best fits the pejorative description of Herr K. is the final text in this series, on the anthropology of sexuality.[206] There one finds an extended discussion of "the perversions of love," including "mutual onanism," "lesbianism and tribadism," as well as "histories" of these practices. (However, there are similar discussions in the seventh chapter of Mantegazza's study on the "hygiene of love," which details the "errors of the sexual drive.")

Now this is clearly what Freud should have understood—given his reading—as of importance to Ida Bauer, but what in this volume would have been of importance to Sigmund Freud? If we turn to the chapter after the one on "perversions," we come to a detailed discussion of the "mutilation of the genitals," which recounts the history of these practices among "savage tribes" including the Jews. Indeed, it is only in Mantegazza's discussion of the Jews that the text turns from a titillating account of "unnatural practices" into an Enlightenment polemic against the perverse practices of that people out of their correct "space" and "time"—the Jews:

> Circumcision is a shame and an infamy; and I, who am not in the least anti-Semitic, who indeed have much esteem for the Israelites, I who demand of no living soul a profession of religious faith, insisting only upon the brotherhood of soap and water and of honesty, I shout and shall continue to shout at the Hebrews, until my last breath: Cease mutilating yourselves: cease imprinting upon your flesh an odious brand to distinguish you from other men; until you do this, you cannot pretend to be our equal. As it is, you, of your own accord, with the branding iron, from the first days of your lives, proceed to proclaim yourselves a race apart, one that cannot, and does not care to, mix with ours.

It is circumcision that sets the (male) Jew apart. In his dissertation of 1897 Armand-Louis-Joseph Béraud notes that the Jews needed to circumcise their young males because of their inherently unhygienic nature, but also because the "climate in which they dwelt" otherwise encouraged the transmission of syphilis.[207] The Jew in the Diaspora is out of time (having forgotten to vanish like the other ancient peoples); is out of correct space (where circumcision had validity). His Jewishness (as well as his disease) is inscribed on his penis.

But what does circumcision mean for a Viennese Jewish scientist at the end of the 1800s? The debates within and without the Jewish communities concerning the nature and implication of circumcision surfaced again in Germany during the 1840s. German Jews had become acculturated into German middle-class values and had come to question the absolute requirement of circumcision as a sign of their Jewish identity. Led by the radical reform rabbi Samuel Holdheim in Germany and responding to a Christian tradition that denigrated circumcision, the debate was carried out as much in the scientific press as in the religious one.[208] There were four "traditional" views of the "meaning" of circumcision since the rise of Christianity. Following the writings of Paul, the first saw circumcision as inherently symbolic and, therefore, no longer valid after the rise of Christianity (this view was espoused by Eusebius and Origen); the second saw circumcision as a form of medical prophylaxis (as in the writing of Philo but also in the work of the central German commentator of the eighteenth century, Johann David Michaelis); the third saw it as a sign of a political identity (as in the work of the early eighteenth-century theologian Johann Spencer); the fourth saw it as a remnant of the early Jewish idol or phallus worship (as in the work of the antiquarian Georg Friedrich Daumer—this view reappears quite often in the literature on Jewish ritual murder).

In the medical literature of the time, two of these views dominated. They were the views that bracketed the images of "health" and "disease." These views saw circumcision either as the source of disease or as a prophylaxis against disease—and in both cases syphilis and masturbation, the two "diseases" that dominate the case of Dora, play a major role. Mantegazza notes that "the hygienic value of circumcision has been exaggerated by the historians of Judaism. It is true enough that the circumcised are a little less disposed to masturbation and to venereal infection; but every day, we do have Jewish masturbators and Jewish syphilitics. Circumcision is a mark of racial distinction; . . . it is a sanguinary protest against universal brotherhood; and if it be true that Christ was circumcised, it is likewise true that he protested on the cross against any symbol which would tend to part men asunder." The opposing view of circumcision in the scientific literature of the time saw circumcision as a mode of prevention that precluded the transmission of sexually transmitted diseases because of the increased capacity for "cleanliness."[209] It is classified as an aspect of "hygiene," the favorite word to critique or support the practice. (This view is closely associated with the therapeutic use of circumcision throughout the nineteenth century as a means of "curing" the diseases caused by masturbation, with, of course a similar split in the idea of efficacy: circumcision was either a cure for masturbation, as it eliminated the stimulation of the prepuce and deadened the sensitivity of the penis, or it was the source of Jewish male hypersexuality.)

A detailed medical literature links the very act of circumcision with the transmission of syphilis, so that the prophylaxis becomes the source of infection. The literature that discusses the transmission of syphilis to newly circumcised infants through the ritual of *metsitsah,* the sucking on the penis by the *mohel,* the ritual circumciser, in order to staunch the bleeding, is extensive and detailed.[210]

The *metsitsah* was understood by the scientific community of the nineteenth century as a "pathological" one, as it was labeled as the source of the transmission of disease from the adult male to the male child. In the establishment of the Viennese Jewish community during the course of the early nineteenth century the debate on the abolition of circumcision was heard as loudly as anywhere else in Central Europe. Isaac Noah Mannheimer, the rabbi of the Seitenstettengasse synagogue and the de facto "chief rabbi" of Vienna (although this title did not officially exist), while a follower of Reformed Judaism, opposed the more radical "reforms" of theologians such as Samuel Holdheim. He strongly advocated the retention of Hebrew as the language of prayer (even though he had preached in Danish during his tenure in Copenhagen) and opposed mixed marriages and the abolition of circumcision. (The link among these three central issues in the self-definition of Viennese Jewry at midcentury should be stressed.) While no compromise was found on the first two issues (Hebrew was maintained as the language of the liturgy and mixed marriages were not authorized), a striking compromise was found in the third case. Together with Rabbi Lazar Horowitz, the spiritual leader of the orthodox community in Vienna, they abolished the practice of the *metsitsah.*[211] Although Horowitz was a follower of the ultraorthodox Pressburg Rabbi Moses Sofer, the abolition of the *metsitsah* became a marker between the practices of Viennese Jewry (which did not permit it for "hygienic" reasons) and the tradition of Eastern Jewry, such as the Jews of Pressburg and Freiburg (where Freud was circumcised).

Here is the link between the emphasis on fellatio in Freud's reading of the case of Dora and the syphilis that haunts the image of the (male) Jew in the case. It is the male sucking the penis of a male in the act of circumcision. Especially in the Viennese debates concerning the retention or abolition of circumcision, this "act" played a special role. For Freud the act of fellatio would be a sign not only of "perversion" but also of the transmission of disease; it would also be a sign that incorporated his own relationship between his racial identity with his coreligionists and, indeed, with other male authority figures. Thus the act of the female sucking on the penis of the male, a "pathological" act as it represents the spread of disease (hysteria) to the daughter, is a sublimation of the act of the male sucking on the penis of the male and spreading another disease, syphilis. It also represents, in the period during which Freud was writing and rewriting the case of Dora, Freud's own articulation of the end of his "homosexual" (i.e., homoerotic) relationship with Wilhelm Fliess, whose theories about the relationship between the nose and the penis are echoed in this case study as well as elsewhere in the fin-de-siècle work of Freud.[212]

But reading Mantegazza, we can go one step farther in our analysis of Freud's understanding of the meaning of sexually transmitted disease and its relationship to hysteria. For Mantegazza introduces his discussion of the exclusivity of the Jews with the following discussion:

> It is altogether likely that the most important reason that has led men of various ages and of varying civilizations to adopt the custom of cutting off the prepuce has been that it was felt to be necessary to imprint upon the human body a clear and indelible sign that would serve to distinguish one people from another and, by putting a seal of consecration upon nationality, would tend to impede the mixture of races. A woman, before accepting the embraces of a man, must first make sure, with her eyes and with her hands, as to whether he was of the circumcised or the uncircumcised; nor would she be able to find any excuse for mingling her own blood-stream with that of the foreigner. It had, however, not occurred to the legislator that this same indelible characteristic would inspire in the woman a curiosity to see and to handle men of a different sort.

The seduction of the Jewish woman by the Other—whether the non-Jew or the lesbian—is the result of the "seeing" of the difference in the form of the genitalia. The need to "see" and "touch" the Other is the fault of the circumcised (male) Jew, whose very physical form tempts the female to explore the Other. Here we have another form of the displacement of the act of touching (sexual contact) with the permitted (indeed, necessary) act of seeing, but given a pathological interpretation. The rejection of mixed marriage and conversion by even "godless" Jews such as Sigmund Freud at this time is a sign of the need to understand the separateness of the Jew as having a positive valence. The labeling of converts as "sick" becomes a widely used fin-de-siècle trope.[213]

Ida Bauer's act of seeing her father is the act of seeing the (male) Jew. Central to the definition of the Jew—here to be understood always as the "male" Jew—is the image of the male Jew's circumcised penis as impaired, damaged, or incomplete and therefore threatening. The literature on syphilis—which certainly played a role in Freud's understanding of her father's illness as well as that of the daughter—contains a substantial discussion of the special relationship of Jews to the transmission and meaning of syphilis. For it is not only in the act of circumcision that this association is made—it is in the general risk of the Jews as the carriers of syphilis and the generalized fear that such disease would undermine the strength of the body politic. Central to the case of Ida Bauer is a subtext about the nature of Jews, about the transmission of syphilis, and about the act of circumcision.[214] Both are associated with the image of the hysteric. It is Jewishness that is the central category of racial difference for the German reader and writer of the turn of the century.[215]

For the Jew in European science and popular thought was closely related to the spread and incidence of syphilis. Such views had two readings. The first model saw the Jews as the carriers of sexually transmitted diseases who transmitted them to the rest of the world. And their location is the city—Vienna. Here the link between the idea of the Jew as city dweller, as the disease that lurks within the confinement of the urban environment, becomes manifest. The source of the hysteria of the city is the diseased sexuality of the Jew. This view is to be found in Adolf Hitler's discussion of syphilis in turn-of-the-century Vienna in *Mein Kampf* (1925). There he (like his Viennese compatriot Bertha Pappenheim[216]) links it to the Jew, the prostitute, and the power of money:

> Particularly with regard to syphilis, the attitude of the nation and the state can only be designated as total capitulation. . . . The invention of a remedy of questionable character and its commercial exploitation can no longer help much against this plague. . . . The cause lies, primarily, in our prostitution of love. . . . This Jewification of our spiritual life and mammonization of our mating instinct will sooner or later destroy our entire offspring.[217]

Hitler's views also linked Jews with prostitutes and the spread of infection. Jews were the archpimps—Jews ran the brothels—but Jews also infected their prostitutes and caused the weakening of the German national fiber.[218] But also, Jews are associated with the false promise of a medical cure separate from the social cures that Hitler wishes to see imposed—isolation and separation of the syphilitic and his or her Jewish source from the body politic. Hitler's reference is to the belief that especially the specialty of dermatology and syphilology was dominated by Jews, who used their medical status to sell quack cures.

The second model that associated Jews and syphilis seemed to postulate exactly the opposite—that Jews had a statistically lower rate of syphilitic infection—because they had become immune to it through centuries of exposure. In the medical literature of the period, reaching across all of European medicine, it was assumed that Jews had a notably lower rate of infection. In a study of the incidence of tertiary lues in the Crimea undertaken between 1904 and 1929, the Jews had the lowest consistent rate of infection.[219] In an eighteen-year longitudinal study H. Budel demonstrated the extraordinarily low rate of tertiary lues among Jews in Estonia during the prewar period.[220] All these studies assumed that biological difference as well as the social difference of the Jews were at the root of their seeming immunity.

Jewish scientists also had to explain the statistical fact of their immunity to syphilis. In a study of the rate of tertiary lues, the final stage of the syphilitic infection, undertaken during World War I, the Jewish physician Max Sichel responded to the general view of the relative lower incidence of infection among Jews as resulting from the sexual difference of the Jews.[221] He responds—out of necessity—with a social argument. The Jews, according to Sichel, show lower incidence not only because of their early marriage and the patriarchal structure of the Jewish family, but also because of their much lower rate of alcoholism. They were, therefore, according to the implicit argument, more rarely exposed to the infection of prostitutes, whose attractiveness was always associated with the greater loss of sexual control in the male attributed to inebriety. The relationship between these two "social" diseases is made into a cause for the higher incidence among other Europeans. The Jews, because they are less likely to drink heavily, are less likely to be exposed to both the debilitating effects of alcohol (which increase the risk for tertiary lues) as well as the occasion for infection. In 1927 H. Strauss looked at the incidences of syphilitic infection in his hospital in Berlin in order not only to demonstrate whether the Jews had a lower incidence but also to see (as in the infamous Tuskegee experiments among blacks in the United States) whether they had "milder" forms of the disease because of their life-style or background.[222] He found that Jews had indeed a much lower incidence of syphilis (while having an extraordinarily higher rate of hysteria) than the non-Jewish control. He proposes that the disease may well have a different course in Jews than in non-Jews. The marker for such a view of the heightened susceptibility or resistance to syphilis is the basic sign of difference of the Jews, the circumcised phallus.

The need to "see" and "label" the Jew at a time when Jews were becoming more and more assimilated and therefore "invisible" in Germany made the association with socially stigmatizing diseases that bore specific visible "signs and symptoms" especially appropriate. Mantegazza's view links the act of "seeing" the Jew sexually with the defamed practice of circumcision. In the German empire of the late nineteenth century all of the arguments placed the Jew in a special relationship to syphilis and, therefore, in a very special relationship to the healthy body politic that needed to make the Jew visible. (The central medical paradigm for the establishment of the healthy state was the public health model that evolved specifically to combat the evils of sexually transmitted disease through social control.) Western Jews had been completely acculturated by the end of the nineteenth century and thus bore no external signs of difference (unique clothing, group language, group-specific hair and/or beard style). They had to bear the stigma of this special relationship to their diseased nature literally on the skin, where it could be seen. Not only on the penis where (because of social practice) it could be "seen" only in the sexual act. And then, because of the gradual abandonment of circumcision, be "seen" not to exist at all!

Just as the hysteric is constructed out of the perceived ability to categorize and classify categories of difference visually, the syphilitic Jew has his illness written on his skin. The skin of the hysteric, like the physiognomy of the hysteric, reflects the essence of the disease. Thus the skin becomes a veritable canvas onto which the illness of the hysteric is mapped. Seeing the hysteric means reading the signs and symptoms (the *stigmata diaboli*) of the disease and representing the disease in a manner that captures its essence. It is the reduction of the ambiguous and fleeting signs of the constructed illness of the hysteric (constructed by the very nature of the definition of the disease in the nineteenth century). If the idea of the hysteric is tied to the idea of the feminization of the healthy Aryan male, or his "Jewification" (to use one of Hitler's favorite terms), then the representation of the disease must be in terms of models of illness that are convertible into the images of the feminized male. But these images of feminization are also tied to other, salient, fin-de-siècle images of race. For Jews bear the salient stigma of the black skin of the syphilitic, the syphilitic *rupia*.

The Jews are black, according to nineteenth-century racial science, because they are "a mongrel race which always retains this mongrel character." That is Houston Stewart Chamberlain arguing against the "pure" nature of the Jewish race.[223] Jews had "hybridized" with blacks in Alexandrian exile. They are, in an ironic review of Chamberlain's work by Nathan Birnbaum, the Viennese-Jewish activist who coined the word *Zionist*, a "bastard" race the origin of which was caused by their incestuousness, their sexual selectivity.[224] But the Jews were also seen as black. Adam Gurowski, a Polish noble, "took every light-colored mulatto for a Jew" when he first arrived in the United States in the 1850s.[225] Jews are black because they are different, because their sexuality is different, because their sexual pathology is written upon their skin. Gurowski's

"German-Jewish" contemporary, Karl Marx, associates leprosy, Jews, and syphilis in his description of his archrival Ferdinand Lassalle (in 1861): "Lazarus the leper, is the prototype of the Jews and of Lazarus-Lassalle. But in our Lazarus, the leprosy lies in the brain. His illness was originally a badly cured case of syphilis."[226] The pathognomonic sign of the Jew is written on the skin; it is evident for all to see.

The pathological image of the Jew was part of the general cultural vocabulary of Germany. Hitler used this image over and over in *Mein Kampf* in describing the Jew's role in German culture: "If you cut even cautiously into such an abscess, you found, like a maggot in a rotting body, often dazzled by the sudden light—a kike! . . . This was pestilence, spiritual pestilence, worse than the Black Death of olden times, and the people were being infected by it."

"Plague" (*Seuche*) and pestilence (*Pestilenz*)—a disease from without, which, like syphilis, rots the body—was the model used to see the role of the Jew. The syphilitic weakening of the racially pure Germans by the Jews was likened by Hitler to the corruption of the blood of the race through another form of "mammonization," interracial marriage:

> Here we have before us the results of procreation based partly on purely social compulsion and partly on financial grounds. This one leads to a general weakening, the other to a poisoning of the blood, since every department store Jewess is considered fit to augment the offspring of His Highness—and indeed the offspring look it. In both cases complete degeneration is the consequence.

If the Germans (Aryans) are a "pure" race—and that is for turn-of-the-century science a positive quality—then the Jews cannot be a "pure" race. Their status as a mixed race became exemplified in the icon of the *Mischling* during the 1930s. The Jewishness of the *Mischling*, to use the term from racial science that is parallel to "bastard" (the offspring of a "Black" and a "White" "race"), "looks" and sounds degenerate. They can have "Jewish-Negroid" [*jüdisch-negroid*] features.[227] And this is often associated with their facile use of language, "the use of innumerable foreign words and newly created words to enrich the German language in sharp contrast to the necessary simplicity of the language of Germanic students."[228] The Jew's language reflects only the corruption of the Jew and his or her discourse. It is the sign of the "pathological early development" of the *Mischling*, who, as an adult, is unable to fulfill the promise of the member of a pure race. The weakness, but also the degenerate facility, of the *Mischling* is analogous to the image of the offspring of the syphilitic. And thus we come full circle. For the Jew is contaminated by hysteria, whether it is the result of the trauma of infection or of heredity. And this weakness of the race is hidden within the corrupted (and corrupting) individual. Thus Hitler's image of the *Mischling* is on the offspring of a "Jewish" mother and an "Aryan" father—hidden within the name and Germanic lineage of the child is the true corruption of the race, the maternal lineage of the Jew. And as Jews claimed their lineage through the mother (rather than through the father as in German law) the *Mischling* becomes the exemplary hidden Jew just waiting to corrupt the body politic.

The image of the *Mischling*, the person impaired because of his or her heritage, brings us back full circle to the world of Ida Bauer. For here we have all of these themes of Jewish disposition and racial diagnosis summarized. The images that haunt Freud's representation of Ida Bauer—her language, the sexual acts of her imagination, their source, the relationship between pathology and infection—are all "racially" marked (at least notionally) in turn-of-the-century medical culture. For Freud, abandoning the act of seeing, an act made canonical in the work of his anti-Semitic mentor Charcot, is an abandonment of the associations of sight within this discourse of sexual difference. The case of Dora is an example of the power over language, of Freud's control over the language of his text, which reveals him not to be an Eastern Jew. Like his critique of the bad Greek of his critics when he held his first talk on male hysteria in Vienna, Freud is the master of the discourse of science and culture. Freud is a scientist who uses language as a scientist. In introducing the question of the nature of Ida Bauer's attraction to Frau K. he remarks: "I must now turn to consider a further complication, to which I should certainly give no space if I were a man of letters engaged upon the creation of a mental state like this for a short story, instead of being a medical man engaged upon its dissection." The act of writing the story is the sign of his special control of a "neutral" language, one that, as we have shown, is hardly neutral when it comes to placing Freud, the Eastern male Jew, at its center of risk. The meaning of the act of seeing for the Jewish physician shows the inherent truth of Robert Reininger's claim that "Unser Weltbild ist immer zugleich ein Wertbild,"[229] that we construct our understanding of the world from our internalized system of values.

NOTES

1. Howard W. Telson, "Une leçon du Docteur Charcot à la Salpêtrière," *Journal of the History of Medicine* 35 (1980): 58. To contextualize this image see the discussion by Anne Harrington, *Medicine, Mind, and the Double Brain: A Study in*

Nineteenth-Century Thought (Princeton, N.J.: Princeton University Press, 1987), 166–170. On the historiography of hysteria see Mark S. Micale, "Hysteria and Its Historiography," *History of Science* 27 (1989): 223–261, 319–351. See also the work on the early history of hysteria by Ilza Veith, *Hysteria: The History of a Disease* (Chicago and London: University of Chicago Press, 1965); H. Merskey, "Hysteria: The History of an Idea," *Canadian Journal of Psychiatry* 28 (1983): 428–433 as well as his "The Importance of Hysteria," *British Journal of Psychiatry* 149 (1986): 23–28; Annemarie Leibbrand and Werner Leibbrand, "Die 'koperni-kanische Wendung' des Hysteriebegriffes bei Paracelsus," *Paracelsus Werk und Wirkung. Festgabe für Kurt Goldammer zum 60. Geburtstag*, ed. Sepp Domandl (Vienna: Verband der Wissenschaftlichen Gesellschaften Österreichs, 1975); Helmut-Johannes Lorentz, "Si mulier obticuerit: Ein Hysterierezept des Pseudo-Apuleius," *Sudhoffs Archiv* 38 (1954): 20–28; Umberto de Martini, "L'isterismo: De Ippocrate a Charcot," *Pagine di storia della medicina* 12.6 (1968): 42–49; John Mullan, "Hypochondria and Hysteria: Sensibility and the Physicians," *Eighteenth Century* 25 (1983): 141–173; John R. Wright, "Hysteria and Mechanical Man," *Journal of the History of Ideas* 41 (1980): 233–247; Phillip R. Slavney, *Perspectives on "Hysteria"* (Baltimore: Johns Hopkins University Press, 1990).

2. J.-M. Charcot, *Lectures on the Disease of the Nervous System delivered at La Salpêtrière*, trans. George Sigerson (London: New Sydenham Society, 1877), 271.

3. Among the figures are Charcot beside the patient (Blanche Wittman?), Joseph Babinski in back of her, then right to left from the back of the picture are Prof. V. Cornil, unknown, Prof. M. Debove, Prof. Mathias-Duval, Al. Londe (the head of the photographic service), Prof. Joffroy (with his head in his hand); second row from the right are Dr. Guinon, Dr. Ribot (in the foreground), Dr. Jules Clarétie, Dr. Naquet, Dr. D.-M. Bourneville, Prof. E. Brissaud, Prof. Pierre-Marie, Dr. Georges Gilles de la Tourette, Dr. Ferré, and Dr. Paul Richer (with a pencil in his hand).

4. Oscar Wilde, "The Decay of Lying," in *The Soul of Man under Socialism and Other Essays*, ed. Philip Reiff (New York: Harper and Row, 1970), 72.

5. I am aware that various names were used for the various processes developed and that "photography" was but one of them. I shall use all of these terms (or at least "photograph" and "Daguerreotype") interchangeably as I am more interested in the reaction to the object than the means by which the object was produced. On the naming of the "photograph" see Wolfgang Baier, *Quellendarstellungen zur Geschichte der Fotografie* (Leipzig: Fotokinoverlag, 1965), 119–120. On the centrality of the photograph in the history of medical representation in the late nineteenth century see Renata Taureck, *Die Bedeutung der Photographie für die medizinische Abbildung im 19. Jahrhundert* (Cologne: Arbeiten der Forschungsstelle des Instituts für Geschichte der Medizin, 1980).

6. On the problem of the relationship between the shift in the symptomatic structure of hysteria and the nature of the perception of this disease entity see Annemarie Leibbrand and Werner Leibbrand, "Gestaltwandel medizinischer Begriffe am Beispiel der Hysterie und der Perversion," *Medizinische Klinik* 69 (1974): 761–765; Robert Satow, "Where Has All the Hysteria Gone?" *Psycho-*

analytic Review 66 (1979–80): 463–480 and the exchange of letters under the title "Why No Cases of Hysterical Psychosis?" in the *American Journal of Psychiatry* 143 (1986): 1070–1071. My thesis is at variance with the view of Carol Smith-Rosenberg, "The Hysterical Woman: Sex Roles in Nineteenth-Century America," *Social Research* 39 (1972): 652–678 as I believe that the role of medical science in shaping the "idea" of the hysteric is certainly of equal importance to the representation of the assigned social roles of the patient. See also Edward Shorter, "Paralysis: The Rise and Fall of a 'Hysterical' Symptom," *Journal of Social History* 19 (1986): 549–582; S. Mouchly Small, "Concept of Hysteria: History and Reevaluation," *New York State Journal of Medicine* 69 (1969): 1866–1872.

7. This plate is reproduced in Etienne Trillat, *Histoire de l'hystérie* (Paris: Seghers, 1986). The picture is to be found in the Musée de Reims, collection Roger-Viollet.

8. J.-B. Luys, *Iconographie photographiques des centres nerveux* (Paris: Baillière, 1873).

9. See Sander L. Gilman, *Seeing the Insane* (New York: John Wiley & Sons, 1982), for the broader context of the image of the hysteric.

10. J.-B. Luys, *Les émotion chez sujet en état d'hypnotisme* (Paris: Baillière, 1887). The photographic images of his patients at the Salpêtrière are reproduced in the exhibition catalogue by Jacqueline Sonolet, ed., *J. M. Charcot et l'hysterie au xixe siècle* (Chapelle de la Salpêtrière, 2–18 juin 1982), 33 (plate 74).

11. Luys, *Les émotions chez les sujets.*

12. Gilman, *Seeing the Insane*, 83.

13. Louis Bataille, "Deux Cas d'Anorexie Hystérique," *Nouvelle Iconographie de la Salpêtrière* 5 (1892): 276–278 (plate opposite p. 277).

14. Arthur Gamgee, "An Account of a Demonstration on the Phenomena of Hystero-epilepsy," *British Medical Journal* 2 (1878): 544–548. Cited by E. M. Thornton, *Hypnotism, Hysteria and Epilepsy: An Historical Synthesis* (London: William Heinemann, 1976), 144.

15. A lithographed plate based on a photograph representing the type of patient described is to be found in the image from Paul Regnard, *Les maladies épidémiques de l'esprit: Sorcellerie magnétisme, morphinisme, délire des grandeurs* (Paris: E. Plon, Nourrit et Cie., 1887), 359. Other such evocations of hysterical symptoms using the tuning fork are represented by the disembodied hand of the physician and the face of the patient. See Paul Richer, "Gonflement du cou chez un hystérique," *Nouvelle Iconographie de la Salpêtrière* 2 (1889): 17–20 (plate 34). See also the photograph of a similar patient taken from the *Iconographie de la Salpêtrière*, reproduced in the exhibition catalogue by Sonolet, *J. M. Charcot et l'hysterie au xixe siècle*, 36.

16. In this context see Esther Fischer-Homburger, *Krankheit Frau und andere Arbeiten zur Medizingeschichte der Frau* (Bern: Hans Huber, 1979); Wendy Mitchinson, "Hysteria and Insanity in Women: A Nineteenth-Century Canadian Perspective," *Journal of Canadian Studies* 21 (1980): 87–104; Regina Schaps, *Hysterie und Weiblichkeit: Wissenschaft über die Frau* (Frankfurt/Main and New York: Campus Verlag, 1982).

17. Charcot, *Lectures on the Disease of the Nervous System,* pp. 230 and 264.

18. Purves Stewart, "Two Lectures on the Diagnosis of Hysteria," *The Practitioner* 72 (1903): 457.

19. See the review of the first volume of the *Iconographie photographique de la Salpêtrière* in *Progrès médical* 7 (1879): 331. On the general background of these concepts see Léon Chertok, "Hysteria, Hypnosis, Psychopathology," *Journal of Nervous and Mental Disease* 161 (1975): 367–378; Maurice Dongier, "Briquet and Briquet's Syndrome Viewed from France," *Canadian Journal of Psychiatry* 28 (1983): 422–427; François M. Mai, "Pierre Briquet: Nineteenth Century Savant with Twentieth Century Ideas," *Canadian Journal of Psychiatry* 28 (1983): 418–421; Jean-Jacques Goblot, "Extase, hystérie, possession: Les théories d'Alexandre Bertrand," *Romantisme* 24 (1979): 53–59; E. Gordon, "The Development of Hysteria as a Psychiatric Concept," *Comprehensive Psychiatry* 25 (1984): 532–537; Leston L. Havens, "Charcot and Hysteria," *Journal of Nervous and Mental Disease* 141 (1965): 505–516.

20. On the problem of the metaphor of the "germ theory" and its role in the evolution of the depiction of the hysteric see K. Codell Carter, "Germ Theory, Hysteria, and Freud's Early Work in Psychopathology," *Medical History* 24 (1980): 259–274.

21. Georges Canguilhem, *The Normal and the Pathological,* trans. Carolyn R. Fawcett (New York: Zone, 1989), 40.

22. See the development of the redefinition of hysteria from the 1952 DSM discussions of "psychoneurotic disorders" (*Diagnostic and Statistical Manual: Mental Disorders* [Washington, D.C.: American Psychiatric Association, 1952], 31–35) to the discussion of the representation of the hysteric in DSM-III-R (*Diagnostic and Statistical Manual of Mental Disorders,* 3d ed. revised [Washington, D.C.: American Psychiatric Association, 1987], 205–207, 257–259, 269–277, 318–320, 348–349).

23. Friedrich Nietzsche, *The Will to Power,* trans. Walter Kaufmann and R. J. Hollingdale (New York: Vintage, 1968), 33.

24. Sander L. Gilman, ed., *The Face of Madness: Hugh W. Diamond and the Origin of Psychiatric Photography* (New York: Brunner/Mazel, 1976), 21.

25. Gilman, *Face of Madness,* 23.

26. Ibid., 10.

27. I am discounting at present the recent work on the physiology of stress and anxiety which may, however, provide a future basis for an understanding of the psychological "startle effect" of innovative art. The incorporation of new experiences and their articulation in terms of existing models of perception may be our means of dealing with such stress. See Jeffrey A. Gray, *The Neurophysiology of Anxiety: An Inquiry into the Functions of the Septo-Hippocampal System* (New York: Clarendon Press, 1982).

28. George S. Layne, "Kirkbride-Langenheim Collection: Early Use of Photography in Psychiatric Treatment in Philadelphia," *The Pennsylvania Magazine of History and Biography* 55 (1981): 182–202.

29. Betty Miller, ed., *Elizabeth Barrett to Miss Mitford: The Unpublished Letters*

of Elizabeth Barrett Browning to Mary Russell Mitford (New Haven, Conn.: Yale University Press, 1954), 208–209.

30. Cited by Hermann Glaser, ed., *The German Mind of the Nineteenth Century* (New York: Continuum, 1981), 16.

31. Edgar Allan Poe, "The Daguerreotype," reprinted in *Classic Essays on Photography,* ed. Alan Trachtenberg (New Haven, Conn.: Leete's Island Books, 1980), 37–38.

32. Sander L. Gilman, "Heine's Photographs," *Hebrew University Studies in Literature and Art* 13 (1985): 293–350.

33. On the background for Freud and hysteria see K. Codell Carter, "Infantile Hysteria and Infantile Sexuality in Late Nineteenth-Century German-Language Medical Literature," *Medical History* 27 (1983): 186–196; Isabel F. Knight, "Freud's 'Project': A Theory for Studies on Hysteria," *Journal of the History of the Behavioral Sciences* 20 (1984): 340–358; Russell Meares et al., "Whose Hysteria: Briquet's, Janet's, or Freud's," *Australian and New Zealand Journal of Psychiatry* 19 (1985): 256–263; Jean G. Schimek, "Fact and Fantasy in the Seduction Theory: A Historical Review," *Journal of the American Psychoanalytic Association* 35 (1987): 937–965; Ernest S. Wolf, "Artistic Aspects of Freud's 'The Aetiology of Hysteria,'" *Psychoanalytic Studies of the Child* 26 (1971): 535–554; Monique David-Ménard, *Hysteria from Freud to Lacan,* trans. Catherine Porter (Ithaca, N.Y.: Cornell University Press, 1989).

34. George Didi-Huberman, *Invention de l'hystérie: Charcot et l'iconographie photographique de la Salpêtrière* (Paris: Macula, 1982).

35. This general discussion is rooted in the work (and images) in Robert Darnton, *Mesmerism and the End of the Enlightenment in France* (Cambridge, Mass.: Harvard University Press, 1968). All his images are from the Bibliothéque nationale cabinet of prints, E.R.L. Paris.

36. Darnton, *Mesmerism and the End of the Enlightenment,* 53.

37. Ibid., 63.

38. Reproduced in Trillat, *Histoire de l'hystérie.* From the Bibliothéque nationale cabinet of prints, E.R.L. Paris.

39. As in Paul Richer's reproduction of an engraving of "la phase d'immobilté ou tétanisme," in his *Études cliniques sur la grande hystérie ou hystéro-épilepsie* (Paris: Delahaye & Lecrosnier, 1881). Plate reproduced in Didi-Huberman, *Invention de l'hystérie,* 121.

40. Sir Charles Bell's *Essays on the Anatomy and Philosophy of Expression* (London: John Murray, 1824), 101. Plate is on the same page. On Bell's image see Klaus Knecht, *Charles Bell, The Anatomy of Expression (1806)* (Cologne: Arbeiten der Forschungstelle des Instituts für Geschichte der Medizin, 1978), 121.

41. On the background of the history of hysteria in the context see Urs Boschung, "Albrecht von Haller als Arzt: Zur Geschichte des Elixir acidum Halleri," *Gesnerus* 34 (1977): 267–293; Jeffrey M. N. Boss, "The Seventeenth-Century Transformation of the Hysteric Affection and Sydenham's Baconian Medicine," *Psychological Medicine* 9 (1979): 221–234; Walter Russell Barow Brain, "The Con-

cept of Hysteria in the Time of William Harvey," *Proceedings of the Royal Society of Medicine* 56 (1963): 317–324.

42. F. de Havilland Hall, *Differential Diagnosis: A Manual of the Comparative Semeiology of the More Important Diseases* (Philadelphia: D. G. Brinton, 1887), 134–135.

43. See the discussion of the hospital and its patients in Jean-Martin Charcot, *Hospice de la Salpêtrière* (Paris: Aux bureau du progrès médical, 1892–1893).

44. On Jackson see Oswei Temkin, *The Falling Sickness: A History of Epilepsy from the Greeks to the Beginnings of Modern Neurology* (Baltimore: Johns Hopkins University Press, 1972), 305–316, 347–350.

45. Sigmund Freud, *Standard Edition of the Complete Psychological Works of Sigmund Freud,* ed. and trans. J. Strachey, A. Freud, A Strachey, and A. Tyson, 24 vols. (London: Hogarth, 1955–1974), 1:58. (Hereafter cited as *SE.*) On the background see Henri Ellenberger, *The Discovery of the Unconscious: The History and Evolution of Dynamic Psychiatry* (New York: Basic Books, 1970).

46. Freud, *SE,* 9:234.

47. *The Clinical Diary of Sándor Ferenczi,* ed. Judith Dupont (Cambridge: Harvard University Press, 1985), 63.

48. Arthur F. Hurst, "War Contractures—Localized Tetanus, A Reflex Disorder, or Hysteria?" *Seale Hayne Neurological Studies* 1 (1918): 43–52. Hurst's collected papers on hysteria appeared as *The Croonian Lectures on the Psychology of the Special Senses and Their Functional Disorders* (London: Henry Frowde/Hodder & Stoughton, 1920) with 29 plates, some taken from Charcot.

49. Joseph Babinski and Jules Froment, *Hystérie-pithiatisme et troubles nerveux d'ordre réflexe en neurologie de guerre* (Paris: Masson et Cie., 1917).

50. Elaine Showalter, *The Female Malady: Women, Madness, and English Culture, 1830–1980* (New York: Pantheon Books, 1985), 189–194.

51. *Les Démoniaques dans l'art* (Paris: Adrien Delahaye et Émile Lecrosnier, 1887). The later, expanded version of this study, *Les difformes et les malades dans l'art* (Paris: Lecrosnier et Babé, 1889), attempts to parallel all visual images of "difference." See also Louis Langlet, *Une possession au XVIe siècle: Étude medicale de la vie et de l'hystérie de Nicol Obry, Dite Nicole de Vervins 1566* (Reims: Matot-Braine, 1910), and Henri Ey, "Introduction a l'étude actuelle de l'hystérie," *Revue du practicien* 14 (1964): 1417–1431.

52. A detailed account of the stages of hysteria that are documented in the historical study can be found in J.-M. Charcot, "Leçon d'ouverture," *Progrès médical* 10 (1882): here, 336. The most detailed visual representation of the stages is to be found in Richer, *Études cliniques sur la grande hystérie.*

53. Compare Jan Goldstein, *Console and Classify: The French Psychiatric Profession in the Nineteenth Century* (Cambridge: Cambridge University Press, 1987), esp. her chapter "Hysteria, Anticlerical Politics, and the View beyond the Asylum," 322–377.

54. The plates are found on p. 99 lower and p. 100 lower.

55. The plate is found on p. 94 upper.

56. Louis Basile Carré de Montgeron, *La verité des miracles operés par l'interces-*

sion de M. de Pâris et autres appellans demontrée contre M. L'archevêque de Sens., 3 vols. (Cologne: Chez les libraires de la Campagnie, 1745–47).

The Montgeron plates reproduced by Regnard (see n. 15) are on the following unnumbered pages:

Regnard, vol. 1	*Montgeron, vol. 1*
113	Frontispiece
120, 123	Prior to p. 1 of the "II Demonstration"
127, 129	Prior to p. 1 of the "III Demonstration"
133, 134	Prior to p. 1 of the "IV Demonstration"
141, 143	Prior to p. 1 of the "VII Demonstration"
149, 151	Prior to p. 1 of the "VIII Demonstration"

Regnard, vol. 2	*Montgeron, vol. 2*
169, 176	Prior to p. 1 of the "Miracle operé sur Marie Jeanne Fourcroy"
161, 163	Prior to p. 1 of "pieces justificatives sur . . . Catherine Bigot"
172	Prior to p. 1 of "Relation du miracle sur l'auteur"

See also the essay by Georges Gilles de la Tourette, "Le Sein Hystérique," *Nouvelle Iconographie de la Salpêtrière* 8 (1895): 107–121, for the further use of images from this source.

57. See the second edition of Philippe Pinel, *Traité médico-philosophique sur l'aliénation mentale, ou la manie* (Paris: Brosson, 1809), 268. See also Theodore Zeldin, "The Conflict of Moralities: Confession, Sin and Pleasure in the Nineteenth Century," in *Conflicts in French Society: Anticlericalism, Education, and Morals in the Nineteenth Century,* ed. Theodore Zeldin (London: Allen & Unwin, 1970), 22–30.

58. This association of forms of "extravagant" and "visible" religions may well be a reaction to the charge lodged against the school of Charcot that it was "Jewish" as it advocated the laicization of the nursing staff at the major psychiatric hospitals in Paris. See Goldstein, *Console and Classify,* 364.

59. Regnard, *Les maladies épidémiques de l'esprit,* 95.

60. Désire-Magloire Bourneville and Paul Regnard, *Iconographie photographique de la Salpêtrière (service de M. Charcot)* (Paris: Progrès médical, 1877–80), 3 vols., vol. 2. Plates are reproduced in Didi-Huberman, *Invention de l'hystérie,* 139–145.

61. The idea of tracing a linear history of hysteria through examining the history of religion is not solely a "French" tradition. William A. Hammond documents the development of hysteria from the religious manifestation in the middle ages (saints as well as witches) through the "fasting girls" of the late nineteenth century and the rise of a medicalized hysteria in his *Spiritualism and Other Causes and Conditions of Nervous Derangement* (New York: G. P. Putnam's Sons, 1876), here p. 122. This is clearly part of what seems to be a "French" tradition—at least as manifested in Charcot and his influence on the Salpêtrière, since Hammond's visual sources are primarily from the Salpêtrière.

62. Jean Heitz, "Un possédée de Rubens," *Nouvelle iconographie de la Salpê-trière* 14 (1901): 274–276; Henry Meige, "Documents complémentares sur les possédés dans l'art," *Nouvelle iconographie de la Salpêtrière* 16 (1903): 319–320, 411–412.

63. Eugen Holländer, *Die Medizin in der klassischen Malerei* (Stuttgart: Enke, 1923).

64. Jean Rousselot, ed., *Medicine in Art: A Cultural History* (New York: McGraw-Hill, 1967).

65. Andrew Dickson White, *A History of the Warfare of Science with Theology in Christendom* (New York: D. Appleton, 1896).

66. Regnard, *Maladies épidémiques de l'esprit.*

67. Bourneville and Regnard, *Iconographie photographique de la Salpêtrière.*

68. Paul Regnard and M. H. Johnson, *Planches murales d'anatomie et de physiologie* (Paris: Delagrave, 1885).

69. Abraham Palingh, *'t Afgeruckt Mom-Aansight der Tooverye: Daar in het bedrogh der gewaande Toverye, naakt ontdeckt, en emt gezone Redenen en exemplen dezer Eeuwe aangewezen wort* (Amsterdam: Andries van Damme, 1725). The plates from Regnard are to be found in the original as follows: Regnard p. 19 = Palingh p. 50; 16 = 250; 17 = 268; 21 = 270; 18 (both) = 284 (both); 20 = 298. (Original in the Cornell University Witchcraft collection, BF/1565/P16/1725.)

70. On the general history of epilepsy see Temkin, *Falling Sickness.*

71. On the history of "hystero-epilepsy" see Thornton, *Hypnotism, Hysteria, and Epilepsy,* and U. H. Peters, "Hysteroepilepsie: Die Kombination von epileptischen und hysterischen Anfällen," *Fortschritte der Neurologie, Psychiatrie, und ihrer Grenzgebiete* 46 (1978): 430–439.

72. Cesare Lombroso, *Criminal Man* (New York: G. P. Putnam's Sons, 1911), 62. See the plate accompanying summary of Lombroso's views on p. 62.

73. As in M. Gonzalez Echeverria, *On Epilepsy: Anatomo-Pathological and Clinical Notes* (New York: William Wood, 1870) in which all of the images are cystological.

74. Charles Féré, "Note sur un cas de mélanodermie récurrente chez un épileptique apathique," *Nouvelle iconographie de la Salpêtrière* 10 N.F. (1897): 332–339.

75. I. Valobra, "Contribution a l'étude des gangrènes cutanées spontanées chez les sujets hystériques," *Nouvelle iconographie de la Salpêtrière* 21 (1908): 481–505 (plate opposite p. 484).

76. L. Pierce Clark, "Tetanoid Seizures in Epilepsy," *American Journal of Insanity* 55 (1898–99): 583–593 (plate opposite 589).

77. See the image of the brain in a case of "Jacksonian" epilepsy in Byrom Bramwell, *Studies in Clinical Medicine: A Record of Some of the More Interesting Cases Observed, and of Some of the Remarks Made, at the Author's Out-patient Clinic in the Edinburgh Royal Infirmary* (Edinburgh/London: Young J. Pentland, 1880): plate opposite p. 322. Such images even appear in the work generated at the Salpêtrière, as S.-F. Danillo, "Encéphalite parenchymateuse limitée de la substance grise, avec épilepsie partielle (Jacksonienne) comme syndrome clinique," *Archives de neurologie* 6 (1883): 217–236 with cytological images.

78. On the misshapen hands (as a sign of inherited capacity for epilepsy) see F. Raymond and Pierre Janet, "Malformations des mains en 'pinces de humard,'" *Nouvelle iconographie de la Salpêtrière* 10 (1897): 369–373 (an extract from their book *Nécroses et idées fixes* [Paris: F. Alcan, 1898]); and in the same essay (plate 41) the plate "Asymetrie du corps chez une epileptique."

79. William Alexander, *The Treatment of Epilepsy* (Edinburgh and London: Young J. Pentland, 1889), 107.

80. On baldness see Charles Féré, "La pelade post-épileptique," *Nouvelle iconographie de la Salpêtrière* 8 (1895): 214–217 (plate opposite p. 216).

81. Dr. Räuber, "Ein Fall von periodisch wiederkehrender Haarveränderung bei einem Epileptiker," [*Virchows*] *Archiv für pathologische Anatomie und Physiologie* 97 (1884): 50–83 (plate no. 2).

82. See for example, A. Maberly, "Epilepsy: A Brief Historical Overview," *Alberta Medical Bulletin* 29 (1964): 65–72; the "Antrittsvorlesung" of the professor for pediatrics at the University of Kiel, H. Doose, "Aus der Geschichte der Epilepsie," *Münchener medizinische Wochenschrift* 107 (1965): 189–196; anon., "Ancient Ailment," *MD* 19 (1975): 151–160; F. L. Glötzner, "Die Behandlung der Epilepsien in Vergangenheit und Gegenwart," *Medizinische Wochenschrift* 30 (1976): 123–128.

83. J.-M. Charcot and P. Richer, "Note on Certain Facts of Cerebral Automatism Observed in Hysteria during the Cataleptic Period of Hypnotism," *Journal of Nervous and Mental Disease* 10 (1883): 1–13, here p. 9 (plates opposite p. 10).

84. Walter Benjamin, *Illuminationen* (Frankfurt am Main: Suhrkamp, 1961), 148–184.

85. H. V. Eggeling, "Die Leistungsfähigkeit physiognomischer Rekonstruktionsversuche auf Grundlage des Schädels," *Archiv für Anthropologie* 12 (1913): 44–46 (with extensive plates), and Franz Stadtmüller, "Zur Beurteilund der plastischen Rekonstruktionsmethode der Physiognomie auf dem Schädel," *Zeitschrift für Morphologie und Anthropologie* 22 (1921–22): 227–272.

86. Francis Warner, "The Study of the Face as an Index of the Brain," *The British Medical Journal* 2 (1882): 314–315.

87. James Shaw, *The Physiognomy of Mental Disease and Degeneracy* (Bristol: John Wright, 1903), p. 40.

88. Gilman, *Seeing the Insane*, 204.

89. Hermann Heinrich Ploss, *Das Weib in der Natur- und Völkerkunde: Anthropologische Studien*, 2 vols. (Leipzig: T. Grieben, 1885).

90. Arthur F. Hurst, "Hysterical Left Facial Paralysis, Right Facial Spasm, Left Ptosis, Strabismus, Aphonia, Dysarthria, Paralysis of the Tongue, Paralysis of Right Arm and Both Legs, and Amblyopia following Gassing, Rapidly Cured by Persuasion and Re-education," *Seale-Hayne Neurological Studies* 1 (1918): 78–80.

91. Walter Baer Weidler, "Some Ocular Manifestations of Hysteria," *International Clinics*, 22d ser. 2 (1912): 249–261 (plate [fig. 5] opposite p. 252).

92. L. Lattes and A. Sacerdote, "Un caso di sindrome isterica oculare con

simulazione di emorragia," *Archivo di Antropologia Criminale, Psichiatira, Medicina legale e Scienze Affini* 47 (1927): 21–47.

93. Jules Luys, "Recherches nouvelles sur les hémiplégies émotives," *L'Encephale: Journal des Maladies Mentales et Nerveuses* 1 (1881): 378–398 (plate 7).

94. E. Siemerling, "Ueber einen mit Geistesstörung complicirten Fall von schwerer Hysterie, welcher durch congenitale Anomaliern des Centralnervensystem ausgezeichnet war," *Charité-Annalen* 15 (1890): 325–348 (plate p. 349), and Grasset, "Des associations hystéro-organiques: Un cas de sclérose en plaques et hystérie associées avec autopsie," *Nouveau montpellier médical,* n.s. Suppl. 1 (1892): 227–252 (plate 7).

95. Paul Steffens, "Obductionsbefund bei einem Fall von Hystero-Epilepsie," *Archiv für Psychiatrie und Nervenkrankheiten* 35 (1902): 542–546 (plate 12).

96. C. von Hößlin and A. Alzheimer, "Ein Beitrag zur Klinik und pathologischen Anatomie der Westphal-Strümpellschen Pseudosklerose," *Zeitschrift für die gesamte Neurologie und Psychiatrie* 8 (1911): 183–209 (plate, p. 203).

97. See Sander L. Gilman, *Sexuality: An Illustrated History* (New York: John Wiley & Sons, 1989), 205–210.

98. Dr. Mesnet, "Autographisme et Stigmates," *Revue de l'hypnotisme et de la psychologie physiologique* 4 (1889–90): 321–335 (plate 2).

99. Jeannot Hackel, "Über einen schweren Fall von Hysterie," *St. Petersberger Medizinische Wochenschrift* 11 (1894): 163–165.

100. S. Weir Mitchell, "Hysterical Rapid Respiration, With Cases; Peculiar Form of Rupial Skin Disease in an Hysterical Woman," *Transactions of the College of Physicians of Philadelphia* 14 (1892): 228–237 (plate, p. 233). See also Kenneth Levin, "S. Weir Mitchell: Investigation and Insights into Neurasthenia and Hysteria," *Transactions and Studies of the College of Physicians, Philadelphia* 38 (1971): 168–173.

101. S. Róna, "Über 'Herpes zoster gangrænosus hystericus—Kaposi,'" *Festschrift gewidmet Moriz Kaposi zum fünfundzwanzigjähringen Professoren Jubiläum* (Vienna and Leipzig: W. Braumüller, 1900), 209–221 (plate 12).

102. Thomas D. Savill, "A Clinical Lecture on Hysterical Skin Symptoms and Eruptions," *The Lancet* (January 30, 1904): 273–278.

103. Dr. Bettmann, "Über die Hautaffectionen, der Hysterischen und den atypischen Zoster," *Deutsche Zeitschrift für Nervenheilkunde* 18 (1900): 345–388; Grover William Wende, "Dermatitis Vesico-Bullosa et Gangrenosa Mutilans," *Transactions of the American Dermatological Association* 15 (1901): 29–50; Giuseppe Bertolini, "Due casi di gangrena cutanea in sogetto isterico," *Giornale italiano delle malattie veneree e della pelle* 60 (1919): 311–322; Roberto Casazza, "Sull'importanza di fattori psichici in dermatologia," *Bollentino della societa medico-chirurgia, Pavia* 44 (1930): 115–162.

104. Dr. De Sinéty, "Examen des organes génitaux d'une hystérique," *Archives de physiologie normale et pathologique,* 2d ser. 3 (1876): 803–807; idem, "Examen des organes génitaux d'un hystérique," *Bulletins de la société anatomique de Paris,* 4th ser. 1 (1876): 679–684; idem, "Examen anatomique des organes génitaux d'une hystérique," *Le progrès médical* 5 (1877): 113–114.

105. Jose M. Jorge, "Coxalgia histérica," *Revista de la Asociacion Medica Argentina* 32 (1920): 18–29 (plate opposite p. 80).

106. Paul Bercherie, "Le concept de folie hystérique avant Charcot," *Revue international d'histoire de la psychiatrie* 1 (1983): 47–58.

107. Eliogoro Guitti, "Osservazioni Cliniche," *Giornale per Servire ai Progressi della Patologia e della Terapeutica*, 2d ser. 22 (1847): 229–258 (plate following p. 258).

108. Paul Sollier, "Contracture volontaire chez un hystérique," *Nouvelle iconographie de la Salpêtrière* 4 (1891): 100–106 (plate opposite p. 106).

109. Georges Gilles de la Tourette and A. Dutil, "Contribution a l'étude des troubles trophiques dans l'hystérie," *Nouvelle iconographie de la Salpêtrière* 2 (1889): 251–282.

110. Arthur F. Hurst and S. H. Wilkinson, "Hysterical Anæsthesia, With Special Reference to the Hysterical Element in the Symptoms Arising from Injuries to the Peripheral Nerves," *Seale-Hayne Neurological Studies* 1 (1918–19): 171–184 (plate 38); Walter Riese, "Zwei Fälle von hysterischen Oedem," *Archiv für Psychiatrie und Nervenkrankheiten* 56 (1916): 228–234 (plates 3–4).

111. Stewart, "Two Lectures on the Diagnosis of Hysteria," 457–471, 657–665 (plate 17).

112. Vittorio Codeluppi, "Sopra un caso di grande isterismo maschile attachi d'istero epilessa cessati per suggestione," *Rivista sperimentale di freniatria e medicina legale delle alienazioni mentali* 13 (1887–88): 414–424. See also M. Carrieu, "Syndrome Vaso-Moteur dans l'Hystérie," *Montpelier médicale*, ser. 2A 1 (1892): 544–553, 566–572, 583–589; Luigi Abbamondi, "Su di un caso d'isterismo mashile," *Annali di medicina navale* 1 (1895): 185–204; D. Ferrier, "Hémiplégie et mutisme hystériques," *Congres français de médicine* 3 (1896–97): 370–375; Motta Rezende, "Reflexes na histeria," *Arquivas brasileros de medicina* 16 (1926): 53–74.

113. Henri Lamarque and Émile Bitot, "Sur un cas d'hystérotraumatisme chez l'homme," *Bulletins de la société d'anatomie et de physiologie normales et pathologiques de bordeaux* 9 (1888): 242–257 (plate with figs. 6 and 8).

114. Georges Gilles de la Tourette, "L'Attitude et la marche dans l'hemiplégie hystérique," *Nouvelle iconographie de la Salpêtrière* 1 (1888): 1–12 (plates opposite p. 8 and p. 11).

115. Byrom Bramwell, "Clinical Lecture on a Case of Hysterical Contracture," *Edinburgh Medical Journal*, n.s. 1 (1897): 128–138 (plate V).

116. A. Steindler, "On Hysterical Contractures," *International Clinics*, 4th ser. 45 (1935): 221–229 (fig. 2, opposite p. 222).

117. Peter Davidson, "Unusual Cases at the Infirmary for Children," *Liverpool Medico-Chirurgical Journal* 35 (1915): 297–308 (plate 4).

118. Prince P. Barker, "The Diagnosis and Treatment of Hysterical Paralysis," *United States Veteran's Bureau Medical Bulletin* 6 (1930): 663–670 (three plates following p. 670).

119. See, for example, the visual representation of the unconscious in the essay by L. Laurent, "De l'état mental des hystériques," *Archives clinique de Bordeaux* 1 (1892): 416–433 (plate opposite p. 430).

120. As in the image of psychic forces in H. Nishi, "Male Hysteria Cured by Suggestion" (in Japanese), *Chugai Iji Shinpo* 405 (1897): 5–9; 406 (1897): 11–16 (image on p. 9).

121. See the evaluation of operations on the hearing of the hysteric in K. Rudolphy, "Ohroperationen bei Hysterischen," *Zeitschrift für Ohrenheilkunde und für die Krankheiten der Luftwege* 44 (1903): 209–221 (plate 17, opposite p. 220).

122. This is the "myth" that Frank Sulloway (*Freud: Biologist of the Mind* [New York: Basic, 1979], p. 592) wishes to identify as "Myth One," the primal myth, in Freud's falsification of his own history. It is clear that this (and the other "myths") are fascinating insights into Freud's understanding of his own career and provide the material for interpretation, not censure.

123. Freud, *SE* 20:15.

124. In this context see John Marshall Townsend, "Stereotypes of Mental Illness: A Comparison with Ethnic Stereotypes," *Culture, Medicine and Psychiatry* 3 (1979): 205–229. See M. J. Gutmann, *Über den heutigen Stand der Rasse- und Krankheitsfrage der Juden* (München: Rudolph Müller & Steinicke, 1920), and Heinrich Singer, *Allgemeine und spezielle Krankheitslehre der Juden* (Leipzig: Benno Konegen, 1904). For a more modern analysis of the "myths" and "realities" of the diseases attributed to the Jews see Richard M. Goodman, *Genetic Disorders among the Jewish People* (Baltimore: Johns Hopkins University Press, 1979).

125. Maurice Fishberg, *The Jews: A Study of Race and Environment* (New York: Walter Scott, 1911), 6. Compare his statement in *The Jewish Encyclopedia*, 12 vols. (New York: Funk & Wagnalls, 1904), s.v. "Nervous Diseases," 9:225–227, here p. 225: "Some physicians of large experience among Jews have even gone so far as to state that most of them are neurasthenic and hysterical."

126. Fishberg, "Nervous Diseases," 9:225.

127. Ibid.

128. Ibid.

129. Fishberg, *The Jews*, 324–325.

130. "La population israélite fournit à elle seule presque tout le contingent des hystériques mâles," Fulgence Raymond, *L'Étude des Maladies du Système Nerveux en Russie* (Paris: O. Doin, 1889), 71.

131. As quoted, for example, in Hugo Hoppe, *Krankheiten und Sterblichkeit bei Juden und Nichtjuden* (Berlin: S. Calvary & Co., 1903), 26.

132. *Protokolle der Wiener Psychoanalytischen Vereinigung*, ed. Herman Nunberg and Ernst Federn, 4 vols. (Frankfurt am Main: Fischer, 1976–81), 2:40; translation from *Minutes of the Vienna Psychoanalytic Society*, trans. M. Nunberg, 4 vols. (New York: International Universities Press, 1962–75), 2:44.

133. J.-M. Charcot, *Leçons du mardi a la Salpêtrière*, 2 vols. (Paris: Progrès médical, 1889), 2:347–353. See the translation of the *Poliklinische Vorträge von Prof. J. M. Charcot*, trans. Sigmund Freud [vol. 1] and Max Kahane [vol. 2] (Leipzig: Deuticke, 1892–95), 2:299–304.

134. H. Strauss, "Erkrankungen durch Alkohol und Syphilis bei den Juden," *Zeitschrift für Demographie und Statistik der Juden*, 4 N.F. (1927): 33–39, chart on p. 35.

135. Moriz Benedikt, *Die Seelenkunde des Menschen als reine Erfahrungswissenschaft* (Leipzig: O. R. Reisland, 1895), 186–187, 223–226.

136. Cecil F. Beadles, "The Insane Jew," *Journal of Mental Science* 46 (1900): 736.

137. Frank G. Hyde, "Notes on the Hebrew Insane," *American Journal of Insanity* 58 (1901–1902): 470.

138. William Thackeray, *Works*, 10 vols. (New York: International Book Co., n.d.), 10:16–28, here p. 17.

139. Cited (with photograph) in Joseph Jacobs, *Studies in Jewish Statistics* (London: D. Nutt, 1891), xl.

140. Robert Burton, *The Anatomy of Melancholy*, ed. Holbrook Jackson (New York: Vintage, 1977): 211–212.

141. Redcliffe N. Salaman, M. D., "Heredity and the Jew," *Eugenics Review* 3 (1912): 190.

142. Gutmann, *Über den heutigen Stand*, 17.

143. Freud, *SE* 5:649; 4:293; 4:139; 5:494.

144. Henry Meige, *Étude sur certains néuropathes voyageurs: Le juif-errant a la Salpêtrière* (Paris: L. Battaille, 1893). On Meige and this text see Jan Goldstein, "The Wandering Jew and the Problem of Psychiatric Anti-Semitism in Fin-de-Siècle France," *Journal of Contemporary History* 20 (1985): 521–552.

145. Richard Andree, *Zur Volkskunde der Juden* (Leipzig: Velhagen & Klasing, 1881), 24–25, cited by Maurice Fishberg, "Materials for the Physical Anthropology of the Eastern European Jew," *Memoires of the American Anthropological Association* 1 (1905–1907): 6–7.

146. Beadles, "Insane Jew," 732.

147. Fishberg, *The Jews*, 349.

148. See L. Chertok, "On Objectivity in the History of Psychotherapy: The Dawn of Dynamic Psychology (Sigmund Freud, J. M. Charcot)," *Journal of Nervous and Mental Diseases* 153 (1971):71–80, as well as Charles Coulston Gillispie, *The Edge of Objectivity: An Essay in the History of Scientific Ideas* (Princeton, N.J.: Princeton University Press, 1960).

149. George Herbert Mead, *Movements of Thought in the Nineteenth Century* (Chicago: University of Chicago Press, 1936), 176.

150. Freud, *SE* 1:17.

151. Toby Gelfand, "'Mon Cher Docteur Freud': Charcot's Unpublished Correspondence to Freud, 1888–1893," *Bulletin of the History of Medicine* 62 (1988): 563–588, here p. 571.

152. Freud, *SE* 26:29–43. While this paper was published only in 1893, it was conceptualized if not written before Freud left Paris in 1886.

153. Toby Gelfand, "Charcot's Response to Freud's Rebellion," *Journal of the History of Ideas* 50 (1989): 293–307.

154. See the discussion in my *Difference and Pathology: Stereotypes of Sexuality, Race, and Madness* (Ithaca, N.Y.: Cornell University Press, 1985), 150–162. See also Yves Chevalier, "Freud et l'antisemitisme—jalousie," *Amitié judéo-chretienne de France* 37 (1985): 45–50.

155. Wesley G. Morgan, "Freud's Lithograph of Charcot: A Historical Note," *Bulletin of the History of Medicine* 63 (1989): 268–272.

156. Freud, *SE* 1:98.

157. See, for example, George Frederick Drinka, *The Birth of Neurosis: Myth, Malady and the Victorians* (New York: Simon & Schuster, 1984), 108–122. See also Esther Fischer-Homburger, *Die traumatische Neurose: Vom somatischen zum sozialen Leiden* (Bern: Hans Huber, 1975).

158. Sir Clifford Allbutt, "Nervous Disease and Modern Life," *Contemporary Review* 67 (1895): 214–215.

159. C. E. Brown-Séquard, "On the Hereditary Transmission of Effects of Certain Injuries to the Nervous System," *The Lancet* (January 2, 1875): 7–8.

160. As in John Eric Erichsen, *On Concussion of the Spine, Nervous Shock, and Other Obscure Injuries to the Nervous System in their Clinical and Medico-Legal Aspects* (New York: William Wood, 1886), 2, or in Hans Schmaus, "Zur Casuistik und pathologischen Anatomie der Rückenmarkserschütterung," *Archiv für klinische Chirurgie* 42 (1891): 112–122 with plates.

161. Compare Otto Binswanger, *Hysterie* (Vienna: Deuticke, 1904), 82.

162. Richard von Krafft-Ebing, *Psychopathia Sexualis: A Medico-Forensic Study*, red. ed., trans. Harry E. Wedeck (New York: Putnam, 1965), 24.

163. August Forel, *The Sexual Question: A Scientific, Psychological, Hygienic and Sociological Study*, trans. D. F. Marshall (New York: Physicians & Surgeons Book Co., 1925), 331–332.

164. Richard von Krafft-Ebing, *Text-Book of Insanity*, trans. Charles Gilbert Chaddock (Philadelphia: F. A. Davis, 1904), 143.

165. Martin Engländer, *Die auffallend häufigen Krankheitserscheinungen der jüdischen Rasse* (Vienna: J. L. Pollak, 1902), 12.

166. Gilman, *Difference and Pathology*, 182–184.

167. The discussion of this case is documented in Charles Bernheimer and Claire Kahane, eds., *In Dora's Case: Freud—Hysteria—Feminism* (New York: Columbia University Press, 1985). See also Dianne Hunter, "Hysteria, Psychoanalysis, and Feminism: The Case of Anna O.," *Feminist Studies* 9 (1983): 465–488; Maria Ramas, "Freud's Dora, Dora's Hysteria: The Negation of a Woman's Rebellion," *Feminist Studies* 6 (1980): 472–510; Arnold A. Rogow, "A Further Footnote to Freud's 'Fragment of an Analysis of a Case of Hysteria,'" *Journal of the American Psychoanalytical Association* 26 (1978): 330–356; Hannah S. Decker, *Freud, Dora and Vienna 1900* (New York: Free Press, 1990).

168. Catherine Clément and Hélène Cixous, *La jeune née* (Paris: 10/18, 1975), 283.

169. Freud, *SE* 2:134, n. 2 (added in 1924).

170. See the discussion in Robert S. Wistrich, *The Jews of Vienna in the Age of Franz Joseph* (Oxford: Oxford University Press, 1989), 483–485.

171. Bertha Pappenheim (writing as P. Bertold), *Zur Judenfrage in Galizien* (Frankfurt am Main: Knauer, 1900), 23.

172. Jacques Lacan, "Intervention on Transference," reprinted in Bernheimer and Kahane, *In Dora's Case*, 92–105. On the working out of the impli-

cations of this theme see the essays by Neil Hertz, "Dora's Secrets, Freud's Techniques" (pp. 221–242) and Toril Moi, "Representation of Patriarchy" (pp. 181–199), reprinted in Bernheimer and Kahane, *In Dora's Case.*

173. Freud, *SE* 7:84.

174. Ibid., 7:19.

175. Ibid.

176. Ibid., 7:21.

177. See the discussion of the inheritance of disease in the seventeenth chapter of Paolo Mantegazza's study of the hygiene of love, in the German translation, *Die Hygiene der Liebe,* trans. R. Teutscher (Jena: Hermann Costenoble, [1877]), 366.

178. Freud, *SE* 7:78.

179. Mantegazza notes this quite literally, stating that diseases such as syphilis, cancer, and madness can merge one into the other through the power of the inherited characteristics; see his *Die Hygiene der Liebe,* trans. Teutscher, 369.

180. Freud, *SE* 7:16–17.

181. Ibid., n. 2.

182. Joseph Babinski, "Sur le réflexe cutané plantaire dans certains affections organiques du système nerveux central," *Comptes rendus hebdomadaires des séances de la Société de biologie* (Paris) 48 (1896): 207–208.

183. On the history of this concept see W. Erb, "Über das 'intermittirende Hinken' und andere nervöse Störungen in Folge von Gefässerkrankungen," *Deutsche Zeitschrift für Nervenheilkunde* 13 (1898): 1–77.

184. P. Olivier and A. Halipré, "Claudication intermittente chez un homme hystérique atteint de pouls lent permanent," *La Normandie Médicale* 11 (1896): 21–28 (plate on p. 23).

185. Freud, *SE* 7:101–102.

186. Ibid., 7:102.

187. Felix Deutsch, "A Footnote to Freud's 'Fragment of an Analysis of a Case of Hysteria,'" reprinted in Bernheimer and Kahane, *In Dora's Case,* 41.

188. Joseph Rohrer, *Versuch über die jüdischen Bewohnener der österreichischen Monarchie* (Vienna: n.p., 1804), 26.

189. Freud, *SE* 7:84.

190. Ibid.

191. Ibid.

192. Ibid.

193. Ibid., 7:64.

194. Ibid., 7:90.

195. Ibid., 7:91.

196. Sigmund Freud, "Some Early Unpublished Letters," trans. Ilse Scheier, *International Journal of Psychoanalysis* 50 (1969): 420.

197. See my *Jewish Self-Hatred: Anti-Semitism and the Hidden Language of the Jews* (Baltimore: Johns Hopkins University Press, 1986).

198. Cited by Saul Friedländer, *Kurt Gerstein: The Ambiguity of Good,* trans. Charles Fullman (New York: Alfred A. Knopf, 1969), 148–149.

199. Martin Freud, "Who Was Freud?" in Josef Fraenkel, ed., *The Jews of Austria: Essays on Their Life, History and Destruction* (London: Vallentine, Mitchell, 1967), 202. See also Franz Kobler, "Die Mutter Sigmund Freuds," *Bulletin des Leo Baeck Instituts* 19 (1962): 149–170.

200. Freud, *SE* 7:51.

201. Ibid., 7:36, n. 1.

202. Ibid., 7:62.

203. On Mantegazza see Giovanni Landucci, *Darwinismo a Firenze: Tra scienza e ideologia (1860–1900)* (Florence: Leo S. Olschki, 1977), 107–128.

204. The authorized German editions of Mantegazza that Freud and Ida Bauer could have read are: *Die Physiologie der Liebe,* trans. Eduard Engel (Jena: Hermann Costenoble, 1877); *Die Hygiene der Liebe,* trans. R. Teutscher (Jena: Hermann Costenoble, 1877); *Anthropologisch-kulturhistorische Studien über die Geschlechtsverhältnisse des Menschen* (Jena: Hermann Costenoble, 1891).

205. Reprinted in Bernheimer and Kahane, *In Dora's Case,* 273.

206. The relevant passages in the German edition, *Anthropologisch-kulturhistorische Studien* are on pp. 132–137. All the quotations from Mantegazza are from the English translation: Paolo Mantegazza, *The Sexual Relations of Mankind,* trans. Samuel Putnam (New York: Eugenics Publishing Co., 1938).

207. Armand-Louis-Joseph Béraud, *Étude de Pathologie Comparée: Essai sur la pathologie des sémites* (Bordeaux: Paul Cassignol, 1897), 55.

208. There is no comprehensive study of the German debates on circumcision. See J. Alkvist, "Geschichte der Circumcision," *Janus* 30 (1926): 86–104, 152–171.

209. See the discussion by Dr. Bamberger, "Die Hygiene der Beschneidung," in *Die Hygiene der Juden: Im Anschluß an die internationale Hygiene-Ausstellung,* ed. Max Grunwald (Dresden: Verlag der historischen Abtteilung der internationale Hygiene-Ausstellung, 1911), 103–112 (on the Jewish side), and W. Hammer, "Zur Beschneidungsfrage," *Zeitschrift für Bahnärzte* 1 (1916): 254 (on the non-Jewish side).

210. See for example the discussion by Em. Kohn in the *Mittheilung des Ärtzlichen Vereines in Wien* 3 (1874): 169–172 (on the Jewish side), and Dr. Klein, "Die rituelle Circumcision, eine sanitätspolizeiliche Frage," *Allgemeine Medizinische Central-Zeitung* 22 (1853): 368–369 (on the non-Jewish side).

211. Max Grunwald, *Vienna,* Jewish Communities Series (Philadelphia: Jewish Publication Society of America, 1936), 376.

212. See the letter to Sándor Ferenczi of 6 October 1910 in which Freud wrote: "Since Fliess's case, with the overcoming of which you recently saw me occupied, that need has been extinguished. A part of my homosexual cathexis has been withdrawn and made use of to enlarge my own ego. I have succeeded where the paranoiac fails." Cited in Ernst Jones, *The Life and Work of Sigmund Freud,* 3 vols. (New York: Basic Books, 1955), 2:83.

213. See the discussion in Gilman, *Jewish Self-Hatred*, 293–294.

214. Ludwik Fleck, *Entstehung und Entwicklung einer wissenschaftlichen Tatsache* (1935; Frankfurt am Main: Suhrkamp, 1980). I am indebted to Fleck's work for the basic conceptual structure presented in this essay.

215. Theodor Fritsch, *Handbuch der Judenfrage* (Leipzig: Hammer, 1935), 408.

216. Bertha Pappenheim with Sara Rabinowitsch, *Zur Lage der jüdischen Bevölkerung in Galizien: Reise-Eindrücke und Vorschläge zur Besserung der Verhältnisse* (Frankfurt am Main: Neuer Frankfurter Verlag, 1904), 46–51.

217. Adolph Hitler, *Mein Kampf*, trans. Ralph Manheim (Boston: Houghton Mifflin Co., 1943), 247.

218. Compare Edward J. Bristow, *Prostitution and Prejudice: The Jewish Fight against White Slavery, 1870–1939* (Oxford: Clarendon, 1982).

219. N. Balaban and A. Molotschek, "Progressive Paralyse bei den Bevölkerungen der Krim," *Allgemeine Zeitschrift für Psychiatrie* 94 (1931): 373–383.

220. H. Budul, "Beitrag zur vergleichenden Rassenpsychiatrie," *Monatsschrift für Psychiatrie und Neurologie* 37 (1915): 199–204.

221. Max Sichel, "Die Paralyse der Juden in sexuologischer Beleuchtung," *Zeitschrift für Sexualwissenschaft* 7 (1919–20): 98–114.

222. H. Strauss, "Erkrankungen durch Alkohol und Syphilis bei den Juden," *Zeitschrift für Demographie und Statistik der Juden* 4 (1927): 33–39.

223. Houston Stewart Chamberlain, *Foundations of the Nineteenth Century*, trans. John Lees, 2 vols. (London: John Lane, 1910), 1:388–389.

224. Nathan Birnbaum, "Über Houston Stewart Chamberlain," in his *Ausgewählte Schriften zur jüdischen Frage*, vol. 2 (Czernowitz: Verlag der Buchhandlung Dr. Birnbaum & Dr. Kohut, 1910), 201.

225. Adam G. de Gurowski, *America and Europe* (New York: D. Appleton, 1857), 177.

226. Saul K. Padover, ed. and trans., *The Letters of Karl Marx* (Englewood Cliffs, N.J.: Prentice-Hall, 1979), 459.

227. W. W. Kopp, "Beobachtung an Halbjuden in Berliner Schulen," *Volk und Rasse* 10 (1935): 392.

228. M. Lerche, "Beobachtung deutsch-jüdischer Rassenkreuzung an Berliner Schulen," *Die medizinische Welt* (17 September 1927): 1222.

229. *Wertphilosophie und Ethik: Die Frage nach den Sinn des Lebens als Grundlage einer Wertordnung* (Vienna: W. Braumüller, 1939), 29.

CONTRIBUTORS

Sander L. Gilman is the Goldwin Smith Professor of Humane Studies at Cornell University and professor of the history of psychiatry at the Cornell Medical College. He is the author or editor of over thirty books, the most recent being *The Jew's Body* (1991) and *Inscribing the Other* (1991). He is the author of the basic study of the visual stereotyping of the mentally ill, *Seeing the Insane* (1982), as well as the standard study *Jewish Self-Hatred* (1986). During 1990–1991 he served as the Visiting Historical Scholar at the National Library of Medicine, Bethesda, Maryland.

Helen King is senior lecturer at St. Katharine's College, Liverpool Institute of Higher Education, and is interested in the traditions of Hippocratic medicine in the ancient world. She has written several articles about the history of gynecology and obstetrics, Hippocrates, and Greek medicine.

Roy Porter is reader in the social history of medicine at the Wellcome Institute for the History of Medicine in London and the author of various articles and books dealing with the social history of medicine. His most recent books include *In Sickness and in Health* and *Patient's Progress* (both with Dorothy Porter), and *Mind Forg'd Manacles: Madness in England from the Restoration to the Regency* (1987), which won the Leo Gershoy Prize for 1988.

G. S. Rousseau is professor of English and eighteenth-century studies at UCLA. He has written or edited books about the literature and medicine, and the literature and science, of early Modern Europe, especially during the Enlightenment. His collected essays were published in three volumes in 1991 as *Enlightenment Borders, Enlightenment Crossings,* and *Perilous Enlightenment.*

Elaine Showalter, professor of English at Princeton University, is also the current chair of the English department and the author of works dealing with feminist thought, Victorian medical history, and literary theory. Most recently, she has published *The New Feminist Criticism: Essays on Women, Literature, and Theory* (1983), *The Female Malady: Women, Madness, and English Culture, 1830–1980* (1985), and *Sexual Anarchy: Gender and Culture at the Fin de Siècle* (1991).

INDEX

Abraham, Karl, 324
Abraham, Nicolas, 95
Abricosoff, Glafira, *L'hystérie aux XVIIe et XVIIIe Siècles* (1897), 313
Abse, D. W., 8
ACT-UP, AIDS activist group, 334
Adair, Dr. James Makittrick, 124, 166–167
Adams, Francis, 7–8
Addams, Jane (1860–1935), American social worker and author, 299
Addison, Joseph, 160
Addyman, M. E., 127, 129
Adorno, Theodor, 237
Adultery, 317, 319
Aesthetics of the face of the hysteric, concept of asymmetry in, 384
Aetius of Amida, 37–39, 44, 46–47
Affectation (and hysteria), 163
African-Americans, distrust of psychotherapy in the 1960s and 1970s, 334
"Ague," the, during early modern England, 225
AIDS, x, xvi, 106, 110, 144, 175, 334–335
Alcoholism, 229
Alexander, William, image of epileptic faces from *The Treatment of Epilepsy*, 381; use of photography for the study of hysteria, 379

Alexander of Tralles, his twelve-volume *Therapeutica*, 46
Alexandria, medical school at, 35, 45, 49
ʿAlī ibn al-ʿAbbas al-Majūsī, known in Europe as Holy Abbas, 51–53; *Kamil*, 55–56; *Liber Pantegni*, 55; *Liber Regius*, 55
Ali ibn Rabbān at-Tabarī (810–861), *Firdaws al hikma* (Paradise of Wisdom), 50
Allbutt, Sir Clifford, Professor of Medicine at Cambridge University, his essay published in the *Contemporary Review* (1895), 417
Alps, the, 296
Alzheimer, A., paper on cerebral plagues, 386
American Revolution, the, 92
Amnesia, 322
Animal magnetism, 184
Animal spirits, the, 142, 145–148, 150–151, 158, 173, 236
Andree, Richard, citation by Fishberg about the Jews' susceptibility to hysteria, 412–415
Anesthesia, 10
Anna O., German feminist leader, 290, 315–316, 318, 332, 334, 419–420; *In the Rummage Store* (1890), 316; translation of Mary Wollstonecraft's *Vindica-*